THE REALITY THERAPY READER

A Survey of the Work of WILLIAM GLASSER, M.D.

THE REALITY
THERAPY READER

EDITORS   Alexander Bassin, Ph.D.

Thomas Edward Bratter, Ed.D.

Richard L. Rachin, M.P.A.

HARPER & ROW, PUBLISHERS

New York / Hagerstown / San Francisco / London

FIRST EDITION

Designed by Sidney Feinberg

Library of Congress Cataloging in Publication Data

Main entry under title:
The Reality therapy reader.

Selected articles "written by Dr. Glasser himself . . . by the three editors, and by many other therapists.

Includes index.

1. Reality therapy—Addresses, essays, lectures.   2. Glasser, William, 1925–
—Addresses, essays, lectures.   I. Glasser, William, 1925–   II. Bassin, Alexander, 1912–   III. Bratter, Thomas Edward.   IV. Rachin, Richard L.
RC489.R37R4   1976   616.8′914   74–1789
ISBN 0–06–010238–1

---

76 77 78 79 10 9 8 7 6 5 4 3 2 1

Contents

Contents

PART TWO Theory

Contents

Foreword

Since its inception in 1962, the concept of Reality Therapy has spread widely. As it has spread, both through my writings and the writings of others, a small body of literature has grown. This book is an attempt to gather what the editors and I believe to be the best articles on the subject. As I looked through the proofs before publication, it seemed to me that there were some articles of historical interest and others that essentially repeated themselves. This is evidently a necessary feature of this kind of collection, but if you take all that is here as current and factual you will be misled. My ideas have been upgraded, changed, and added to over the past fifteen years and this will continue to happen. No psychological practice can remain static, any more than anyone who uses the practice can ever learn all that is to be known about it. Things move, times change, and what seemed so evident five years ago is no longer that way. Therefore, I caution you that if you read this book with the idea of using *everything* it contains, don't.

The material here will not stand by itself—it is designed to supplement my books, and all of my books, starting with *Reality Therapy,* are a necessary prelude to what is printed here. Even then, if you intend to practice Reality Therapy, the technique cannot be learned from books. It must be learned from someone who is experienced and trained to teach, demonstrate, and role-play it, and to check you as you do the same. What this book *will* do is give you a historical and supplemental knowledge of the ideas, a knowledge sufficient for comparison and discussion at an intellectual level; nowhere does it provide by itself what you need to actually practice Reality Therapy.

The Institute for Reality Therapy, which conducts ongoing training programs, welcomes your comments and questions. We can be reached by writing:

WILLIAM GLASSER, M.D., *President*
Institute for Reality Therapy
11633 San Vicente Blvd. #104
Los Angeles, California 90049

Glasser the Man

Glasser the Man: Introduction

If anything is common to the feeling of many who have questioned the teachings of conventional psychotherapy, it would appear to be its dubious effectiveness and irrelevance. Almost entirely unadmitted, let alone discussed, it remained for a once unknown psychiatric resident to question openly the fundamental beliefs of Freudian-oriented teachings. As William Glasser described it in *Reality Therapy,* "Toward the end of my psychiatric training, I found myself in the uncomfortable position of doubting much that I had been taught. My teachers implied that there was a great deal more to be learned in the field, but only a few questioned the basic tenets of conventional psychiatry. One of these few was my last teacher, Dr. G. L. Harrington. When I hesitatingly expressed my own concern, he reached across the desk, shook my hand and said, 'Join the club.'"

Marshall Berges in "A Realistic Approach" gives a short sketch of Dr. Glasser and of his family. He then reports a number of questions, with answers by Glasser, which indicate many of his most recent feelings and the ideas he is exploring.

Arthur LeBlanc focuses his attention on the school, where Glasser's interest and concern was to turn later in *Schools Without Failure.* He distinguishes between two teaching concepts, *docere* (Latin: to teach) in which the student is viewed as an empty receptacle into which the "all-knowing" teacher pours knowledge, and *educare* (Latin: to draw out), where the teacher is seen as one who motivates learning. In schools where failure predominates, *docere* holds sway, there is little relationship between life and what

takes place in school, and little emotional and intellectual involvement occurs between teacher and student. LeBlanc attributes delinquency and withdrawal to the stultifying atmosphere of the
docere school. Children need two basic skills, he argues: (1) to
hear accurately, and (2) to speak relevantly. Without these communicative skills, the child cannot meet his basic needs, which
Glasser has described, for everyone, as love and self-worth. He
discusses Glasser's views of rigid, stereotyped, irrelevant schooling—its absurdity and cost both to the individual and society—
and what can be done to change it.

Sue Reilly portrays a very human and only infrequently seen
side of Bill Glasser. Although much the iconoclast since 1957,
when his personal battle with the conventional psychiatric wisdom
began, a portrait of someone deeply involved and almost reli-
giously committed to his work is made clear. Glasser's irreverence
toward the classical catechisms cost him dearly in his early career
and Reilly recounts his journey from these early days in obscurity
to the recognition and esteem he now enjoys. The warmth and
importance of his personal life are also depicted. For those of us
who have come to know him personally, Reilly succeeds in captur-
ing the essence of much of this man and his life without which an
understanding of Reality Therapy would be incomplete.

The remaining articles in this introductory section are either
written by Glasser or are interviews with him on specific topics.

In "Youth in Rebellion—Why?" Glasser, interviewed by *News-
week,* discusses the problems of young people. He rejects the suggestion that there is a crisis in youth morality and attributes the
difficulties in which youth find themselves to their acquiring failure
identities. His view (upon which he elaborated in 1969 in *Schools
Without Failure*) of how school contributes to, catalyzes, and reinforces this development is presented. Glasser stresses the need
for prevention as opposed to remediation—a view with which
most now agree, but still seem to do little about. Ideas that he was
to formulate more extensively later in *The Identity Society* are also
touched upon.

"A Talk with William Glasser" reemphasizes Glasser's conviction that success breeds success and failure breeds failure. The

interview extends Glasser's views regarding the frustration and failure attendant upon most children involved in traditional school programs. Glasser makes clear that the schools have not failed in accomplishing the task traditionally assigned to them, i.e., teaching survival skills. However, increased security has led to societal changes over the past twenty years now placing greater emphasis upon love, respect, and fulfillment in work—aspects of living for which traditional schools do not prepare young people. People need to learn not only technical skills, but how to make productive use of their lives. Glasser suggests various means of achieving this goal.

In "The Civilized Identity Society," Glasser provides, in skeletal form, the concepts that he presents in *The Identity Society*. He discusses the replacement of a "survival society," in which behavior was directed primarily toward keeping people fed, clothed, and reasonably comfortable, by an "identity society," in which emphasis is placed upon caring, involvement, respect, and role satisfaction. Explanations can be found for the difficulties many experience today in establishing successful identities in contemporary society. Glasser views this new identity society—he believes it replaced the civilized survival society about 1950—as similar to the primitive identity society of 500,000 years ago. It represents, to his thinking, a recurrence of intelligent, human cooperation and involvement. The change from survival to identity society is discussed as attributable to affluence, which afforded Western man the opportunity to veer off from the more mundane to more pleasurable pursuits. While Glasser views Western civilization as well into this postsurvival role (as opposed to goal-oriented era), its institutions and especially the schools, have lagged behind. The consequences of this lag are evident.

The final article in this section is entitled "How to Face Failure and Find Success." Glasser responds to the query "How do you establish a success pattern?" with a prescription of use to people regardless of their circumstances. He makes clear that a failure identity is only as handicapping as a person permits it to be. People tend either to avoid tasks they find difficult or unpleasant, or are dishonest in admitting to themselves (and others) how they really feel about such matters. Glasser describes how self-defeating this kind of behavior is. Success, he states, comes only after a person is willing to be honest about what he really wants and then decides to work at it. Glasser reminds us that planning and applying oneself to what each of us decides is important is what really counts. And if one plan does not work, it is up to each of us to work out another until we are successful. That is, if one wants to find success and avoid failure.

This first section, which introduces Glasser and provides a glimpse into his work, hopefully will whet the interest of the curious, and allay some anxieties among the skeptics. Reality Therapy is not claimed to be the new panacea. It is not a magic wand that brings about miracles. It requires hard work on the part of both client and therapist, as well as patience and commitment. Reality Therapy is, however, an effective remedy for many people for whom conventional psychotherapy does not work. It is also a means to permit social institutions to function successfully. If that sounds grandiose, we can only say, try it and find out yourself. It really works! And if departing from tradition is what holds people back, we can only suggest that such conditioned cerebral reflexes make one prey, among other things, to prejudices, continued failure, lingering poor self-images, and an advanced case of atrophy of the thinking processes. As Nietzsche put it in *Human, All Too Human:*

Every tradition grows even more venerable—the more remote is its origin, the more confused that origin is. The reverence due to it increases from generation to generation. The tradition finally becomes holy and inspires awe.

A Realistic Approach

Rushing breathlessly into the airport, glancing at his watch, clutching at a fat briefcase, the man scrambles aboard a plane. Buckling on a seat belt only moments before takeoff, he whips out a lined, legal-size, yellow pad and begins writing notes.

Very little time is wasted by William Glasser, M.D. A major figure on the U.S. lecture circuit, he uses planes the way other men use offices—a space in which to do one's work. To Glasser that means writing and reading and thinking about audiences. He turns on before large audiences the way a light bulb glows at a flick of the switch.

Talking before an audience, he sounds off passionately against the psychiatric and educational establishments. Teachers and mental health workers across the nation flock to his lectures. Even his critics concede he presents his ideas clearly and effectively. A psychiatrist and educator himself, Glasser is not a crank but a clear-headed maverick who takes an unorthodox approach to nagging problems that have been around a long time—teaching and learning, behavior and discipline.

Moving from city to city on a tight schedule, he squeezes up to 20 lectures a month into an already full agenda that includes seeing patients, helping communities to set up teacher-training centers, and writing books. Two have become major sellers: *Schools Without Failure,* which takes apart teaching and recommends reforms in the educational system; and *Reality Therapy,*

From the March 3, 1974, issue of the Los Angeles *Times*. Reprinted by permission of Arthur Pine Associates, Inc.

which delivers a kick in the shins to traditional psychiatry and sets forth Glasser's own approach to mental illness.

Glasser also has a passion for physical fitness. He keeps in plane-catching shape by playing one or two fast sets of tennis nearly every day. Bouncy and muscular (5 feet 8 inches, 155 pounds), Glasser at 48 has the freshly scrubbed face of a schoolboy and, when he lectures, the hard-hitting zeal of a missionary. Lecturing on a large scale did not come easily to him; some friends suspect that he forced himself into the role, much the way a puny youngster sets out to become an athlete.

At 19, Glasser suffered from acute shyness. Introduced to a pretty brunette named Naomi Silver, he was scarcely able to speak. For the next three weeks he telephoned her home but declined to leave his name. Somehow their friendship grew, but not before the girl's mother announced desperately, "I'm sure he's a fine young man. But do you think you could persuade him to say 'hello' when he comes to the house?"

Married to Naomi during college, Glasser earned a degree in chemical engineering, then turned to psychiatry. He became the head psychiatrist at the Ventura School for Girls, where all his patients had been in trouble with the law. Glasser perceived that the girls at Ventura viewed themselves as life's losers. Having been told regularly that they were bad, they believed it. He set out to pump them up with personal responsibility and success. He gave each girl chores that she could handle, responsibility for her own behavior, a clear-cut sense that he was interested in her welfare, and handed out praise generously. It worked.

Defying conventional therapy, which may hold that a patient is the helpless victim of past traumas and thus not responsible for erratic behavior, Glasser brushes aside the cobwebs of the past and insists that a patient develop a plan of action for the future. "I'm not interested in what happened before," he tells his patients. "What are you going to do about your own life, beginning today?"

Glasser's own life is deeply bound up with his wife and three children—Joseph, 23; Alice, 20; Martin, 16. The Glassers live in a multilevel, glass and stucco house on a hill in Brentwood. Its five-sided living room has a beamed ceiling and a massive brick fireplace. The family plays bridge together, reads books together, attends theaters together. No matter how frantic his schedule, Glasser takes time to keep up a steady involvement with his family.

Q. *What is the key to handling delinquents without punishment?*

Glasser. Doing essentially what I do with my own kids, creating lots of involvement. Instead of yelling and being punitive, or threatening to lock a kid up for 50 years, you take a more reasonable approach. You say, "Look, we don't want to put a lot of restrictive rules on you. If you do something wrong and foul up, well, everybody does that sometimes. So let's figure out a way to do it right. Sit down for an hour and figure something out, and then we'll talk about it."

Q. *Are you proposing less punishment and more discipline?*

Glasser. That's right. Right now we have no discipline, but only punishment. Discipline is when you say, "Okay, you've made a mistake. Until you can figure out a better way to do things, you are restricted. Figure out a better way, follow reasonable rules and regulations and courtesies, and we'll help you."

Q. *But that isn't punitive?*

Glasser. No, because a person has the power to change the restriction by changing his behavior. But it becomes punishment if you say, "You are restricted for the next year, even if you have changed your behavior by tomorrow."

Q. *Would you extend this to men in prison?*

Glasser. Yes. There are men in prison who, if released today, could make it in the outside world if they had someone to help plan their way, to help guide them through difficult phases. All sitting in prison does is make them more bitter and rebellious when they get out.

Q. *What's the place of rules and regulations?*

Glasser. You can't live without them. The turbulent period of the '60s occurred when students tried to live without them and found it couldn't be done.

Q. *Shouldn't your concept be put to work at the grade school level?*

Glasser. That's where I'd like to see it. I've helped a school in Texas to put the idea into practice. If a kid keeps disturbing others, he's put in a special room. He stays there until he's willing to figure out a way to make it in the regular school. A counselor is willing to work with the kid any time the kid is prepared to figure out his own problem. The counselor is ready to try anything within reason, but the kid has to give something, too.

Q. *How would you sum up the lesson?*

Glasser. The child learns that he also has to make adjustments to the world. He learns that there are certain reasonable principles one must live by, and if you're unwilling to accept them, then you cannot partake of what the world offers.

Q. *What are the boundaries of permissiveness?*

Glasser. In the Texas school, if you don't want to study, you're not restricted. If you want to go to sleep, it's okay. It raises an interesting question—is the *teacher* doing something that puts you to sleep? The assumption is, it's our fault if you're asleep. But if you're disrupting the class so the teacher can't teach and the others can't learn, then you're taken to the special room. You can't interfere with others in the class any more than you can drive your car down the wrong side of the street.

Q. *What do you substitute for punishment?*

Glasser. It's a simple concept. If you have a kid who's upset, and you whack him and say, "Stop it," you make the assumption that—miraculously—the child can learn what to do. I don't make that assumption. If a kid is doing something wrong, I don't leap to the conclusion that he knows the *right* thing to do. It's up to me to say, "Stop it. Now let's begin working something out. If you don't know the right thing, I'll help you learn it. If you do know it, let's see if we can figure out how to put it into practice." I think knowing the right thing and putting it into practice are quite different. Lots of people know they shouldn't drink and drive, but they still do it.

Q. *You would avoid the extremes of permissiveness or punishment?*

Glasser. There *has* to be an in-between method. It's ridiculous to let people do anything at all, just as it is to crack down senselessly.

Did you see the recent news story about a group of students who got life imprisonment in Turkey for smuggling hashish? That isn't going to stop hashish smuggling in Turkey. It just means that next time the students will have machine guns and kill anyone who tries to stop them. Because they figure if they are going to be put in prison for life, they might as well kill.

Q. *What's the in-between method?*

Glasser. Teaching people the value of following the rules and regulations. We don't do it at home with our kids, and we don't do it in our schools, and those are the two places where people learn. As I travel around, explaining the idea to teachers, psychologists, counselors, they say, "Oh, it's so simple," and they try it, and it works. It worked at the Ventura school and it works in a lot of elementary schools. People say nothing works in high schools, but that's not true. There is nobody in the world more reasonable, in my view, than teenagers.

Q. *How do you classify the people who are locked up today?*

Glasser. When someone kills people, like that man did up at Santa Cruz, and says to the judge, "Lock me up for life, because if I get out, I'll kill again," I'm inclined to believe him. He should be locked up for life. But that's a tiny percentage of the men in prison. Most of those we lock up are stumblebums—people with a sense of failure and no hope of doing anything positive with their lives. Under close supervision, many of them could be rehabilitated.

Q. *How does a classical psychiatrist explain crime?*

Glasser. He says that people are driven by inner, usually unconscious, psychological conflicts which they cannot control and which determine their lives. The classical psychiatrist's job is to untangle the conflicts and make the person aware of them. The theory is that once untangled and made aware, a person can straighten out his life.

Q. *How does Reality Therapy differ from that?*

Glasser. My theory is that people are driven to abnormal behavior by *loneliness* and by feelings of *worthlessness*. Thus the psychiatrist's job is to interject himself into the person's life, so that the patient no longer feels lonely, and to help him plan ways to gain a sense of worth. In this way the patient is able to give up the aberrant behavior which was, in effect, an attempt to solve his loneliness.

Q. *Do you also differ with classical educators?*

Glasser. No, my approach is patterned somewhat after theirs. John Dewey advocated some ideas half a century ago, such as get involved with kids and help them to plan their lives, but Dewey was ahead of his time. What Dewey really had in mind was that if you give a child some sense that he has a measure of control over his own destiny in school, he will be more motivated and he won't have behavior problems. And that's my approach to education. I want to give kids a chance to *win.*

Q. *What does that mean?*

Glasser. Win is just a sum-up term for success. A kid behaves the way he views himself. If he sees himself as successful, as *can-do* versus *can't-do, possible* versus *impossible, responsible* versus *irresponsible,* that's the way he will behave. The more he perceives himself in this way, the more he can attack and do something about life's possibilities. Unfortunately, the schools are filled with children who look upon themselves as losers. Offer a loser a book and he'll say, "I can't read it." Ask him to do a problem in math and he'll say, "I can't do math."

Q. *What leads him to say, "I can't?"*

Glasser. A child doesn't say that unless he's had some supporting evidence transmitted to his brain and stored there. In life we establish very quickly what we can and cannot do, and sad to say, schools have served as a clearing house for that information. If you are a Mexican kid in East Los Angeles, you learn very quickly that you cannot make it in school. That has been *communicated* to you through the school system. In that environment, you have to be a really outstanding person to come out of the school system ready for college. Because you've been taught in school, "We are losers. We can't learn."

Q. *Isn't that being changed now?*

Glasser. Sure, Cesar Chavez and others are bringing on some changes. But Chavez can strike the grapes forever and he isn't going to help Mexican workers unless the kids believe they can win in school. Because if they come out of school losers, and then Chavez raises their aspirations, they become caught in a conflict and they end up locked in jail. Every kid needs a chance to develop and win.

Q. *Do our school systems have the capabilities right now to do the job?*

Glasser. Yes. No new knowledge has to be gained. The problem is that the knowledge has not been put into practice. The reasons are that it's *hard* to do, it's *new,* it's *different,* it goes against stereotypes. It's just easier to do the wrong thing because the wrong thing is traditional. Let's do the right things. Let's give this kid in the first grade a chance to say, "I can learn to read." That can only happen through a teacher who transmits to him, "You are worthwhile. I talk to you. I accept you as a human being. Now we will learn to read. If you don't learn today, I'm here to teach you tomorrow." That's what it amounts to. With that approach by teachers, the vast disturbances begin to disappear. The kids learn, and they like it. It's happening in classes now, but there aren't enough of them.

Q. *Are you saying that whether a kid reads or not depends on his view of himself?*

Glasser. That's at least 95 percent of it. There might be a few whose eyeballs don't focus. But generally when you see a kid not reading, it's because he's *working* not to read. He actually won't look at words. He turns his eyes away. Now, obviously, if you won't look at words, you cannot read. It's like stepping up to the plate to hit a ball. If you won't watch the ball, you can't hit it. That allows you to say, "I'm not good as a baseball player."

Q. *The attitude isn't limited to kids?*

Glasser. Not at all. Take a roomful of college graduates and offer them a lesson in math. Many will say, "There's no sense in teaching me math because I can't learn it. I can't even balance my checkbook." Now where did they grow convinced of that? They weren't born that way. They learned it. We spend a tremendous amount of time and money in school teaching people that they aren't worth much and that they aren't capable. It isn't very good grammar, but my objective in the schools is to *not* teach people that they are no good.

Q. *What are your other objectives?*

Glasser. The schools first have to recognize that all of the people who work in a school are valuable, but they need reinforcement. So, a principal and his staff have to get together and talk with each other and say, "We are part of a human experience in which we care about each other. We'll help each other. We care about these children. We'll help them. We have to learn to do better with them." That sounds simplistic, but it sets an atmosphere in which a child can learn. He's lucky to be in that kind of a school because he's treated as a valuable human being.

Q. *What's the most fun in your life?*

Glasser. Giving a talk to a responsive audience and getting the feeling that they are really listening. It's fun to come up with ideas, not necessarily original but expressed in ways that move people to take action. And then, after all the talking, the deepest satisfaction comes in knowing that the message is getting across. That every day more and more kids are learning that society is not a totally and unreasonably rejecting force. That you can get along with people, but you also have to give something. To me, that's the way of the world.

About Reality Therapy

As a brash young resident in psychiatry at the plush Neuropsy-chiatric Institute at UCLA, William Glasser had suggested that the long lines of the suffering could immediately be reduced by seeing people in large groups of thirty or even forty.

Freud's worshipers vehemently cut Glasser down rather than decrease the line of pathetic neurotics of the late 1950s. How dare this hybrid from engineering bring up such a practical idea: to see the "mentally ill" for $1.00 each in a large group. What would this idea do if it ever became a trend in psychiatry? Horrors, thought the bloodless surgeons who wanted to protect their economics. To hell with the length of the lines waiting for emotional relief.

Glasser's psychiatric teachers and colleagues had all gone to medical school, done their internship in some outrageous emergency room (even moonlighting to keep their new brides in an apartment worthy of a physician's wife), and then spent a three-year residency learning the mysteries of the unconscious. With all of this preparation as a prerequisite to hanging out a $40 per hour shingle, William Glasser's idea seemed outrageous. Even revolutionary! Imagine learning that priestly language of Id, Catharsis, Sublimation, etc., and ending up in a large group of neurotics who needed employment, hobbies, or simply a new neighborhood. Traditional psychiatrists turned a deaf ear; in fact, hardly one gave a reading to *Reality Therapy*. Freud's disciples had effectively solidified psychiatry into a number of spooky dogmas.

Fortunately, psychologists, social workers, rehabilitation counselors, pastoral counselors and others felt the appeal of this action-oriented form of psychotherapy. Then, when Wolpe and his followers gave their academic blessings to symptom relief, the revolution was under way. Thanks to an engineer from Cleveland, Ohio, efficiency was installed in the field of psychotherapy for Reality Therapy restored common sense to the mental health field.

Glasser recognized, however, that the need for remediation could be reduced even more drastically by taking a preventive stance. It was time to look at the major social institution, the school. If failure was an ingredient leading to poor self-esteem and subsequent behavioral immobility, then it was time for a massive assault on that agency which had primarily introduced the whole concept of failure, namely the school.

While traditional psychiatry reinforced maladaptive behaviors by voyeuristically attending to the negative aspects of personality, Glasser, in Reality Therapy, had been insisting that the therapist find the healthy, responsible side of the client. The same spirit was now applied to schools. Instead of being ultra efficient detectives in search of error or evil, teachers were asked to be masters at finding success and goodness.

Normal schools had been graduate centers for the promotion of finding what's wrong with the child. I call this an advance degree in negative eyeballs. A child arrived at school with his sweater effectively buttoned for the first time in months, only to be told that his shoes were still dirty.

In the medieval days of thirteenth-century Scholasticism, the epistemologists had argued over how one learns. Two schools of though drew swords: "docere" (Latin; to teach) depicted a virtual pouring in of knowledge. The students were viewed as an empty receptacle to be filled by the all-knowing teacher; on the other hand, "educare" (Latin; to draw out) represented those who viewed the teacher as a catalyst. The child brought the potential for actualization. The teacher's primary role was not the distribution of facts; rather, he (no 19th Amendment in thirteenth-century Europe) was architect of an intellectual environment to motivate discovery. "Docere" describes school in terms of teachers; "educare" views school in terms of children. Obviously it isn't that much of a dichotomy. In fact, as we recall outstanding school experiences, few as they are, they were inevitably a combination of "docere" and "educare."

Glasser's contention in *Schools Without Failure* is that the failure stance to life is promoted by those who major in "docere," the dumping of knowledge into empty heads. Unfortunately, the doors to the cerebral hemisphere have recently refused to open. Facts have stayed on chalkboards and/or the written page. The teacher's spoken words have bounced off children's eardrums. Without involvement between teacher and child, there was no possibility for establishing a responsible identity through the acquisition of dual feelings of love and worth. Having failed to find love and worth in school, the 1950–1960 decade saw the spread of delinquency. Now in the 1970s delinquency is giving way to withdrawal. Both delinquency and withdrawal are irresponsible means of gaining an identity; both are the result of failure. Furthermore, it is these early failures that lead to adolescent and adult failures. The old cliché appears so valid: "Success breeds success." Whether it be finances or emotions, each needs a well-greased, smooth bandwagon.

Can you, however, imagine running a school without failures, without traditional "dunces," F's, tears, pink slips and signed report cards? Where would anxiety originate if you couldn't forge your parents' signatures on a report card? With no failures, how could parents compare you with your cousins or nephews or, above all, with your older sister who did so well?

To some, *Schools Without Failure* looked like an attack on the United States Constitution, apple pie and motherhood. Unfortunately, these frightened educators still see Glasser as a threat to democracy. He *is* a threat rather to their antiquated methods, to their need to fail students, but hardly a threat to democracy.

In the U.S. today, people feel that there is too much distance from their X on the local ballot and their subsequent voice in the Senate or House. The X seems to be so meaningless that there is a grave temptation to leave critical thinking outside of the polling booth. Meanwhile, William Glasser is attempting to restore relevance. The parents of our school children have no idea that their children see school as the most irrelevant part of their day. There is no relationship between life and what goes on in school. No wonder Orwell described a 1984 devoid of voting machines.

To be relevant, the teacher must become involved with the world of his and/or her children. Old Sigmund saw Id, Ego, Superego encapsulated in so many pounds of flesh and blood, a social isolate. We have emerged from the psychoanalytic Dark Ages to realize that our friends, relatives, classmates, teachers, etc., are the primary distributors of our emotional distress because they are the ones who supply success or failure.

The teacher of today cannot be a dispenser of knowledge. If so, he or she is a professional producer of emotional distress. To dispense knowledge is to be so irrelevant as to paradoxically become a child's worst enemy, for the dispensing of knowledge is so irrelevant that delinquency and withdrawal become the only options. After all, craziness should be met with craziness if one is to be realistic.

In the land of department store computers, children do not need knowledge. Rather, they need two basic skills: (1) *to hear accurately;* and (2) *to speak relevantly*. Having these two communicative skills, a child can acquire Love and Worth (not failure). The schoolroom child will not hear accurately when the spoken word is totally irrelevant. The 1973 pupil will not hear accurately when the written word is for those of us who don't think in terms of relevance. The children of today will not even test well when the questions are written for those of us who believe in right/wrong, true/false, black/white. The children of our schools believe that "life is a series of mysteries to be lived," rather than "a series of problems to be solved."

It is around this concept "mystery" that I think Glasser built his now famous "class circle." The circle was developed to promote involvement, to lay the basis of education. Oldtime educators still think that the school bell has something to do with the foundation for education. They are about as relevant as the textbooks that they impose on teachers. The circle is not sensitivity training; it has nothing to do with the encounter movement.

Those of us who were touching in the early 60s never saw Glasser attend. He was too conservative for Esalen, NTL [National Training Laboratories], Kairos, etc. His circle, however, was perfect for schools. Children in his circle broke the silence of our school system; they actually talked. In fact, under teachers who could lean toward the "educare" philosophy, children began to learn the two central skills of the computer age: *to hear accurately* and *speak relevantly* about a complex, mysterious world.

I want to emphasize that his three forms of the circle are concerned with these two skills: *to hear accurately* and *speak relevantly*. Without these behavioral skills the vast amounts of available knowledge will lie stagnant at the computer window. The era of human brain banks is over. Rote memory is for grandiose exhibitionists. The $64,000 TV show is for those still counting College Board scores.

We are living in a new world, whether we like the way in which Alvin Toffler described it or not. The basic reality is that our children are living in the land of infinite change. Even the sacrosanct knowledge of the red schoolhouse is passé before lunch time. The supposed facts of the 6th grade have become fiction by junior high.

In the new world of *Future Shock,* new schooling is essential. Without an entirely different attitude toward education, our children have a right to the two avenues of retreat: craziness or suicide. When adults persist in clogging up a child's world with irrelevancy, he or she has a right to scream in the spirit of Sartre that "life is absurd," or, he or she has a right to leave this land of infinite choice for nothingness via suicide. Glasser is well aware that his suggestions, his educational alternatives are not the only methods but they are part of an all-out war on a bureaucratic monstrosity, which has become the milieu for practicing failure.

A drastic change is necessary.

While sociologists or economists may view outdated school systems in terms of cultural lag or financial mismanagement, I see a more fundamental existential question, specifically, the place where a child learns to die. He or she either dies—that is, leaves reality—by creating a life of total fantasy (called craziness) or dies by suicide (called death). The school's description of reality is so irrelevant that the child logically labels this experience as absurd. Since it is so absurd there is little to no attention given. Failure follows from the "docere" oriented teacher. The children pathetically cry: "But adults, I'm simply not attending to absurdity. How can you fail me for being so bright as to not attend to irrelevance. I do not reinforce irrelevant messages. I am trying to extinguish inappropriate behavior by not attending." By this stance, our students are modeling the best known principles of behavioral modification—non-attention extinguishes behavior.

In *Schools Without Failure,* Glasser describes three forms of the Class Meeting: (1) Open Ended Class Meeting, (2) Diagnostic Curriculum Class Meeting; and (3) Problem Solving Meeting. Having recently talked with Glasser's staff who are doing in-service training throughout the United States and Canada, it is apparent that there is a priority among these circles. Without establishing a sense of caring in the "Open End Meeting" it is worthless to plunge into either a diagnostic or problem solving attempt. It is in the caring stance that the child learns: (1) acceptance of his ideas; (2) freedom to offer outlandish appearing ideas; (3) good feelings about himself. Without these fundamentals, how can the child really talk about his academic weaknesses in finding his place in the curriculum?

Sidney Jourard's "self disclosure" research has verified the cliché: tell your sins to a total stranger or a good friend. Acquaintances are not to be trusted. One never can predict what an acquaintance will do with the revealed fault or weakness. This is not paranoia, but legitimate, practical worry. Most of today's school teachers are in an acquaintance role. In such a role there is little to no involvement. The "Open Ended Meeting" is designed to move the relationship out of this gray area of no meaningful communication. Children can't tell you where they are in an academic curriculum meeting unless you are beyond the acquaintance stage. Don't ask them to violate such an overabundance of behavioral research. You are just asking the impossible. Involvement is a prerequisite to any valid sharing.

Unfortunately, many Glasser devotees have applied the three Class Meetings in a naïve, programmed manner, insisting on equal time for each form of meeting. "Boys and girls, it is time for our problem solving meeting. We must get in our three circles a week."

Ridiculous!

Neither academic diagnostic evaluation nor attempts to solve the rioting on the playground can be subjects for our cerebral attention until there is a basic involvement with its concomitant skills of hearing accurately and speaking relevantly. However, the children come only after their teachers sit in their own "Open End Meeting." The school must convey an atmosphere, not merely a technique. From the principal's office to the athletic field there has to be an overall philosophy of accurate hearing and relevant speech.

There is some evidence in psychology that schizophrenia (craziness) is promoted through the "double-bind" message; that is, one's perceptions are not consistently validated. Your voice says you love me; your physical posture reveals hatred toward me. Now you do; now you don't. In fact, all in the some moment, I hear love and hate. This picture is so confusing that some people will run into the world of fantasy where he or she can at least manufacture stability. At least in the crazy world, I know where I stand; therefore, who I am.

Some schools currently use classes to set up a double-bind culture. Grades 1, 2, 5, and 7 for example promote caring, freedom, feeling of a good self. Meanwhile, Grades 3, 4, and 6 distribute facts. School is therefore a very confusing place. Who wants that much confusion? The child has to validate his or her eyeballs. This cannot be done in the current school milieu.

To prevent this double-bind atmosphere in our schools, principals must see that the entire philosophy penetrates all grades. Allowing the "docere" philosophy to persist is support of a "crazy farm." Tenure or not, it is time for change. This does not mean wholesale dismissal of teachers. Rather, it means the generation of a new milieu within the present structure.

Open meetings at the faculty and administrative levels are on-going prerequisites for any school that wants to replace failure with *accurate hearing* and *relevant speaking*. Once trust and open communication are established, the faculty can hold fruitful curriculum, diagnostic and problem solving meetings. Without trust and its subsequent feelings of self-worth, the curriculum diagnostic meetings are merely places to defend one's pet course; problem solving attempts become the place for the heavy handed to establish new forms of discipline.

Now don't give me or others the excuse that there is no time to run such meetings either with the children or the staff. Where are you going with your precious time?

One could never accuse Glasser of being anti-intellectual. This school milieu, which is so dedicated to alleviating a failure experience, has as its goal the promotion of critical thinking. Like Victor Frankl, Glasser sees the cognitive activities, the reasoning skills, as man's highest functions.

Critical thinking is not the satirical, biting criticism of the theatre reviewer. Rather, it is a weighing of data, a looking at facts and above all a practical application to real life situations. However, without a trusting atmosphere, the child cannot sufficiently take in data presented; whether the facts come from a teacher, another student or portable computer. The recently translated German phenomenologists (Binswanger, Minkowski, Strauss, etc.) have in common that paradoxical phrase—"approach the situation with an empty mind."

If the child sees school as a testing ground, a proving ground, how can he or she come with an "empty mind"? "What's the answer?" becomes the chorus. "Get ready, Mary—she's starting from the last row today." The school room then becomes the practice area for academic sprinters. After all, anticipating the starting gun distinguishes the potential Olympian. Anticipation with a head full of rote answers is the atmosphere for survival. "Get ready, Jane, she'll probably ask you about Napoleon."

The phenomenologists describe the adult fullness of head as having: (1) need for predictions; (2) assumptions; and (3) memories. All three eliminate the possibility of taking in the moment, the present, the world before the student. A child living in a school where failure predominates learns to anticipate through a head full of anticipatory predictions based on memories and assumptions. While the phenomenologist's notion, namely an empty-headed approach, may look naive, it is that naiveté that allows for the intake of data. If the head is full, it cannot see or hear, leaving the child only with eyes and ears. The children need empty heads in order to crisscross the intake of eyes and ears into the experience of wonderment, mystery and awe: Wow! Gosh! Gee whiz! are the by-products of critical thinking.

Glasser is vehemently opposed to failure and outrageously in favor of success. Schools can be the environmental force for either. Nevertheless, when high school and junior high teachers say that it is too late, they are usually correct. The failure model with all its consequences has often become too much part-and-parcel of the school world. It has masterfully promoted silence in children who sit in anticipation: predicting from assumptions and memories.

If we could only find those empty heads, wide eyes and sensitive ears that came through the doors of our nursery schools. It's so sad that our national anxiety to effectively teach our children has backfired into a multimillion-dollar failure-oriented monstrosity.

With so much to be covered each year, with so many right-and-wrong answers to be anticipated, there is no room for thinking, real, vital, meaningful "critical thinking."

SUE REILLY

Dr. Glasser Without Failure

It is almost 3 P.M. as William Glasser, the father of Reality Therapy, wheels east on San Vicente Boulevard toward the Brentwood Medical Center in West Los Angeles where he has practiced psychiatry for 17 years.

On this warm, sunny day, 48-year-old Glasser wears the expression of a man who would rather be heading elsewhere as he makes the eight-minute run from home to office. He parks his car in the allotted space and walks into the plain three-story brick building. He is neat and trim in polo shirt, creaseless slacks and polished loafers.

After a brief appearance on the ground-floor offices of his Institute for Reality Therapy, he heads down the hallway to the world's slowest elevator. Glasser doesn't seem to mind. He's in no hurry.

On the third floor, he walks a few yards down to the small suite where he counsels as many patients as his schedule allows. It's a heavy work load which calls for Glasser to make upwards of 75 speaking appearances a year, manage two institutes, make feature-length films and television programs and oversee numerous ventures on which he consults. He also writes books.

He is just back from a speaking engagement in the Midwest, and he had been looking forward to playing tennis and relaxing today. But he accepts a journalist's intrusion on his time as good business. Bill Glasser's empire thrives on exposure.

He doesn't look like a revolutionary. He is a slender, genial, bland man with dark hair and gentle, kind eyes behind dark horn-rimmed glasses. But he has been carrying on his own personal war against the entrenched educational and psychiatric establishments for years.

The fight started back in 1957 with the UCLA School of Psychiatry. At that time he was in his last year of residency at the West Los Angeles Veteran's Hospital, working under the direction of UCLA instructors. The place reminded Glasser more of a garden than a hospital, because the main occupation of every patient appeared to be tending the vegetables. No one ever seemed to get any better, and the only way to leave the place was feet first.

It was depressingly obvious to Glasser that sitting and chatting with a patient about his past was not getting the patient up and out. When he mentioned this to his immediate superior, Dr. G. L. Harrington, a man with a slight limp, old-fashioned crew cut, and a gentle manner despite his military bearing, Harrington stood up, shook his hand and said, "Welcome to the club."

The elders of UCLA were not as generously disposed. The word that Glasser was a heretic had reached the head of the department. Glasser was called in for a friendly inquisition. He was talked to on all sides, but nothing could make him say that anything he had learned at UCLA had helped anyone as far as he could see.

"I was supposed to be overseeing Bill's cases when he was in residence at the Veteran's Administration Hospital," Harrington remembers. "I was the head psychiatrist. But our conversations never seemed to stand still long enough to focus on individuals, they always veered off into techniques.

"I knew even before Bill confessed his disbelief in classical psychiatry that it wasn't going to take him long to catch on. Hell, anybody with eyes could see it wasn't working at the VA. Who's going to believe that some poor son-of-a-bitch who's been sitting around helpless for 30-some years is getting satisfactory treatment?

"Glasser just went in there and started badgering people to get well. He just kept after them and after them and after them. He reminded me of an experience I had in a group therapy session once.

"I had been conducting this group for a long time when one night a new person came in. Everybody started talking about love and commitment and all those words that don't really mean anything, when this new woman, in a hysterical voice, started screaming 'What is love? What is love? No one ever loved me. I don't even know what you're talking about.'

"Everyone was very quiet for a while and then someone said, 'Love is someone saying, get out of bed, it's time for school. Eat your vegetables. Take your vitamins. Wash your hands. Brush your teeth.'

"That person got it exactly right. Love is unrelenting concern and involvement. And for those VA patients who didn't get it as children, they were now getting it in spades from Glasser. One thing that Bill wouldn't do was adhere to all that psychiatric pussyfooting around about what you called an inmate. The main thing was never to admit he was a lunatic. He was 'emotionally disturbed.' "

Once when Glasser was on rounds, Harrington says, he stopped in at one patient's room and the man leaped up, came after Glasser and started strangling him.

Glasser, recalling the incident, says, "Remember, I'm a pragmatist, and when that guy was acting like he'd like to see me dead, I took out down the hall as fast as my legs could carry me. Later, when the patient was more calm I asked him why he did such a thing, and he said, 'I don't know, Dr. Glasser, I must have been crazy.'

"I know you're crazy," Glasser yelled back, "but why are you trying to kill *me?* I'm your doctor!"

After Glasser's UCLA rebellion, a promised teaching position failed to materialize. Moreover, Glasser's peers were not too happy with his intellectual deviancy. He now figures that if he had had to rely on referrals from his alma mater, as most beginning psychiatrists do, he would have made about $8,000 in the past 16 years. Fortunately for Glasser it didn't work out that way.

Because of the sparsely populated waiting room at his newly opened Brentwood office, Glasser was happy to accept a position with the California Youth Authority as head psychiatrist at the Ventura School for Girls. The school had been relocated on a beautiful site near the town of Ventura in the Santa Clara Valley. The new, rambling, red-brick buildings housed about 400 14- to 16-year-olds—some of Southern California's prize recalcitrants. It was the last stop before adult prison.

From his experience at the VA hospital, Glasser knew pretty well what wasn't going to work here. But he wasn't sure just what would. He decided to take a straightforward, honest approach.

"The first person they brought in to see me," says Glasser, "was a tough-looking young lady who sprawled out in a chair and looked through me with 100-year-old eyes. I asked her why she's in Ventura and she sneered, 'because I'm emooootionally disturrrrbed.' I explained that at Ventura we have prostitutes, murderers, assaulters and burglars, but no emotionally disturbed. She stared at me for a few moments then laughed. 'I guess I'm all of those things, Doc,' she said, 'but I've sure gotten a lot of mileage out of that emotionally disturbed shit.' "

Glasser found a common quality in all the girls: they saw themselves as losers, and they didn't give a damn about themselves. They had been told they were bad so often they believed it. He decided to pump some success into them.

He worked out a program in which school, residence hall and counseling sessions were all places where honest praise was liberally dispensed. He also put each girl in charge of herself, giving her the responsibility for her own behavior. Everybody knew the rules and the penalties for breaking them. Praise worked magic. And the personal responsibility took their minds off the authority figures against which they had been rebelling. "The girls started enjoying school [grades were dispensed with], and started taking pride in their own accomplishments. The change was astounding. Visitors refused to believe it was a detention camp."

Glasser says recidivism was greatly reduced and that he still hears from many of the girls who are now wives, mothers and—some—school teachers. "They seem proud that they have become people they themselves like. One of my toughest cases, a girl who was grades behind in school, went on to graduate from college and now heads a California State project for migratory workers."

During his 12 years at Ventura School, Glasser formed some conclusions about psychiatry and wrote them down in two books: *Mental Health or Mental Illness,* published in 1961, and in 1965 *Reality Therapy,* dedicated to his old mentor, Dr. G. L. Harrington. *Reality Therapy* is still considered Glasser's main work because of its solid, concise examination of conventional therapy—which Glasser thinks doesn't work—and his own Reality Therapy—which he thinks does.

Conventional therapy assumes that mental illness not only exists but that it exists in clearly definable categories such as paranoia, schizophrenia, character disorders, etc. The only way to cure such illness is to probe into a patient's past to seek the roots of his problem, because once a patient understands the original cause of his problem, he can then work to eliminate it. An understanding of the unconscious mind, transference and insight are all objectives of conventional therapy, with the patient doing most of the work and the therapist acting as a nonjudgmental, sometimes almost nonparticipating, guide.

In conventional therapy, the therapist's role is not to change the patient's behavior. The patient is a victim of past traumas and is therefore not responsible for his erratic behavior.

Reality Therapy, on the other hand, rejects the concept of mental illness. It ignores the past and along with it just about all of the baggage of classical psychiatry. The Glasser method is open and pragmatic; the starting point is the patient's present aberrant behavior with both therapist and patient striving to define future behavioral goals and to work out ways in which to attain them. The patient and therapist make a contract to the effect that certain mutually agreed-upon behavior will be carried out. If it is not, there is no recrimination or punishment, just a reevaluation of the plan and further effort toward achieving success at it. Needless to say, Freudian psychiatrists are often driven to the brink of apoplexy by the mere mention of Glasser's name.

Glasser maintains that one of the most potent tools of his kind of therapy is the psychiatrist's honest concern for his patient and the openness and tenacity with which he exhibits this concern.

"Once a young asthmatic was sent to me by a physician who thought the symptoms might have psychological roots. The young man and I began a personal, intense therapy that was going along well until one day, during a session, the boy started gagging and turning peculiar shades of blue.

"All the time I was shoving a breathing apparatus down his throat, I was continuing what had now become a monologue. When the patient could finally breathe again, he took a few gulps of air and said, 'For God's sake, Bill, don't you ever give up?' I said I never did, and for some reason his asthma disappeared shortly after that."

More or less in conjunction with the publication of *Reality Therapy,* Glasser's Brentwood office turned into the Institute for Reality Therapy. As it began to function, word got around in the people-oriented underground that Bill Glasser in Los Angeles was having success using his therapy on institutionalized girls. Inquiries began to pour in from prison wardens, judges and others connected with penal systems.

Today the institute houses a cluster of therapists who do both individual and group counseling, and who also teach the concepts of Reality Therapy to both professionals and laymen. At least 1,000 ministers, sociologists, therapists, parents, policemen, probation officers and correctional workers have taken the course in the institute's conference room.

As the word spread about Glasser's new therapy, he became popular on the lecture circuit. . . . He began getting requests from other places, including a local school district. They hoped he might be able to do something with their ever-growing collection of Wild Ones.

"I went out to the school," Glasser recalls, "and introduced myself to the administrators who immediately shut me up in a tiny room with a very mean little boy. I looked at him and he looked at me. Since we didn't have much to say to each other, I sent him back to class.

"The administrators were ecstatic. They thought I'd already

cured the little devil. I asked them if they had a lot of mean little kids like that and they said they did. I said, 'Boy, I sure don't know what to do about that, but I'll think about it.' The next day I came back and said that I thought the kids were mean like that because they felt like failures. And when you feel like a failure you are unhappy and become very disruptive.

"I said I thought the teachers ought to stop making the kids mad and ought to try to be friends with them. I also said that I thought they ought to stop failing kids because that made them feel bad too.

"Anguish was written all over the faces of these people when they realized that they had me, this madman, under contract. They finally listened to me and things got a little better."

During his assignment with the school district, Glasser was flying all over the country lecturing on Reality Therapy. Not one to sit about idly during flight, he decided to use the time to write another book based on his most recent experiences. *Schools Without Failure* sold 53,000 copies in 1969, the first year it was out.

Basically, *Schools Without Failure* says to teachers: stop boring the kids. Stop grading them. Stop making school a concentration camp. Stop depressing them. Be friendly. Be relevant. Be helpful. Let each student progress at his own speed. Praise his progress. Develop social awareness by being socially aware yourself. Learn to listen. Learn how to allow each student to experience a little success every day.

Glasser thinks learning is great, and that if it's properly presented, the kids will too. If text books are dull, use comic books, or car books, or whatever the kids can learn from. If science books are dull, do projects that make the ideas come to life. But most importantly, let the child experience the joy of learning in a warm, enthusiastic atmosphere without that old ax—grades—hanging over his head. Grading, he believes, is a system in which few children have any success, and success is what a good classroom is all about.

Just as the book *Reality Therapy* had spawned the Institute for Reality Therapy, *Schools Without Failure* brought to life the Educator Training Center. The ETC was opened in 1969, shortly after the book went on sale, in order to handle the flood of requests for more information and teaching materials. Originally there were five people in a couple of rooms answering mail and dispensing information.

The initial funding for the center came from a grant by W. Clement Stone, the insurance tycoon, who is also an ardent and generous supporter of Richard Nixon. It is Stone's opinion that Nixon made his spectacular comeback from the debacle of the '60s because of Nixon's employment of something called Positive Mental 'Attitude, a success formula for people who can't seem to get ahead or who have lost faith in themselves. Stone is himself an admirer of the therapeutic qualities of self-confidence and success, so his interest in Glasser's concepts is readily understandable.

Today the ETC is a growing beehive of offices on the fifth floor of an office building in downtown Los Angeles. It employs 25 people, including 10 who do nothing but fly around the country teaching teachers how to create schools without failure. The other 15 are still answering requests for information and materials which now include feature films, film shorts, cassettes, books, magazines and a mound of other printed materials.

An ETC official estimates that in the past four years more than 90,000 teachers have received instruction from the ETC which they have passed along to their 3.2 million students. ETC trainers, conducting school-district workshops, have been responsible for reaching upwards of 40,000 teachers, while another 45,000 have learned Glasser techniques by taking television courses accredited by colleges throughout the country. Nobody can guess how many others have had some exposure to *Schools Without Failure* by reading the book, attending educational seminars, sending for ETC materials or hearing one of Glasser's speeches.

A visitor to the center finds enthusiasm high. It's to Glasser's credit that the people here have given up easier, sometimes better-paying jobs to take on work that can be taxing, exhausting and often frustrating. In some cases, Glasser's personality and ideas have acted like a magnet. A couple of years ago, when Glasser was making extensive speaking sorties up and down the Eastern Seaboard, he kept noticing the same black face looking up at him during every one of his talks. Finally, the man approached Glasser after one of the speeches and introduced himself as Joe Peters, a psychologist and narcotics-addiction fighter from New York.

Glasser remembers: "Joe said he was grateful for my books and lectures, which he always taped, because they gave him excellent ideas to put to use in his work with addicts. It got so that every time I gave a talk east of St. Louis, I'd look for Joe."

Peters adds: "There was no doubt about it. I thought Glasser was onto something big. That personal responsibility thing was something that just hadn't been tried with my people before. Once I got them off the idea that I was their wailing wall and told them to shape up and get some responsibility, things started popping.

"But finally I realized that I had spent hundreds of my own bucks traveling around to hear this dude talk, and what I really wanted to do was to go to work for him. So, one day I picked up the phone and asked him. It was the hardest thing I've ever done in my life, because I thought he was a god. I asked for a job and he said regretfully nothing was open. But he did invite me to come have a look around the next time I was out on the West Coast.

"Next vacation I came out and I liked what I saw. A little while later Glasser called me in New York and said if I still wanted to work for him to come on back. I arrived on his doorstep one Sunday afternoon with all my belongings piled in my car. He put me up until I found a place." . . .

If Glasser is given to preoccupation and an occasional lapse in personal sensitivity, it's perhaps because he spends so much of himself publicly. No matter whether his audience is open and receptive, or, for some reason, hostile and resistant, he knows how to reach them and he works hard at it. Recently he was invited to speak at the Lynwood school district, in the midlands of the Los Angeles urban sprawl. It's an area of rising racial disturbance and disorder in the classroom, and the teachers have listened to a parade of experts suggesting solutions. Some have been received with polite attention; some with frigid reserve. Glasser, the latest expert, walks into the situation with little advance notice.

There is an air of determined good cheer and recess about the group of 200 or so instructors as it files into Lynwood High auditorium to hear this latest traveling sage. To many of these over-worked, underappreciated people, William Glasser, a *psychiatrist,* is just another outsider making a lot of money telling teachers what is wrong with their classroom techniques and with their teaching methods.

Not only are teachers suspicious of outsiders; like cops, they think only a teacher understands another teacher. But they are going to be good scouts about it. They will listen and maybe even pick up a few ideas. In any event, it's a chance to see some of the teachers from other schools in the district.

The stage is set up for that evening's performance of *Up the Down Staircase,* and the podium and water pitcher downstage seem part of the set. Glasser, amiable, a bit late, does nothing to dispel the feeling of first night. Dressed in an expensive, darkish suit set off by a pumpkin-hued tie, he walks on to polite applause. He surveys the group through his shiny black-framed glasses, and then begins. . . .

Glasser glides smoothly through his warmup into the substance of his talk. The audience's patient, professional smiles begin to fade. He knows what's going on in the classroom and he's talking about it. Glasser knows the classroom is turning into a battlefield and that all the theory and subject material learned in teachers' colleges hasn't prepared these nice people for the realities of life. He moves on to a short explanation of why kids are the way they are today. It is right out of his newest book, *The Identity Society.*

"In the old, goal-oriented society there was a great stress on getting good grades, because that led to a degree and a good job. It was a survival society and we were interested primarily in economic security. As students, we mostly kept our mouths shut and our books open. We needed those grades and we were willing to recite the names of all the states, all the presidents and all the planets to get them.

"Today's kids have been financially secure most of their lives. They aren't worried about making money because it's always been around. What they are interested in is relevance, and if they think they aren't getting it in the classroom, they rebel.

"Kids know perfectly well that they don't need to memorize lists of presidents or anything else because that's what we have reference books for. They want to learn how to reason things out, how to do things on their own. They demand to know the mechanics of government and how to really effect change. They still want to become doctors and lawyers and schoolteachers, but they want to become those things on their own terms. They are making us, as educators, examine what we are teaching them because they are going to be damn sure it's useful.

"So now we have civil rights, youth power, a new demanding student body and discipline problems no one ever dreamed of." Glasser goes on to outline new ways of dealing with behavior problems—back to the personal responsibility theme—but he re-emphasizes a relevant program of instruction.

"I know about your curriculum problems and your state testing programs and the accountability law. But I also know that unless we engage our students in something they consider educational we are simply going to lose them. They'll drop out.

"Nothing's wrong with you," Glasser reassures them. "You have been given an almost impossible task and you are weathering it with strength and intelligence. We just have to try new ways."

Somehow they have become "our" students and Glasser has established himself as a guy with his own marbles who knows a better way to play the game. The audience listens; birds with faces uplifted waiting for sustenance. Their questions at the end of Glasser's talk reflect a determination to get a better grasp on these ideas. They are dedicated teachers who like their kids and who do not want to fail themselves. There are more questions, tough and pointed, one begetting another. After the questions are answered, the teachers file out silently, thinking. Glasser watches and seems satisfied.

Although part of Glasser's talent lies in his ability to express his ideas in simple, easily understood language, his theories have caused havoc in some school districts where parents seem determined to misunderstand. Some have complaints about his two primary techniques: one, the Glasser "circle," smacks of sensitivity training (a tool of the communist conspiracy); the other, the Glasser "contract," is a confession that teachers forcibly extract from children. Glasser is patient with people who express this point of view.

The fact is that whereas sensitivity training is often a form of hostile, direct confrontation, the Glasser classroom circle is a mutual-support system where youngsters get together in a tight, secure configuration and discuss things of real importance to them, thus making the classroom a more relevant and inviting place. The contract replaces punishment. Instead of dwelling on past mistakes, teacher and student acknowledge that a particular kind of behavior is not bringing happiness and success to the student and together they decide how the youngster can become more successful and then feel better about himself. They make a solemn commitment which the teacher checks warmly and continually to make sure it's carried out. The student is thus responsible for his own behavior and is praised by his teacher for this responsibility.

In short, Glasser's approach is a nurturing one, rather than an oppressive one. It's an idea he picked up from his own parents, whom he remembers as loving, gentle and appreciative.

He was born in the eastern section of Cleveland, Ohio, the third and last child in his family. Because of the supportive atmosphere of his home, he was always a "good boy." "I don't think I've given my parents a moment's worry in 48 years," he says.

He made good grades, played cornet in the school band and was interested in sports. Although he was somewhat shy, he made friends easily. In a burst of overachieving he earned a bachelor's degree in engineering, a master's in psychology and his medical certification at Case Western Reserve University. During his college years, he married Naomi Silver.

Naomi has, in her own way, been as successful as her husband. She has strong negative feelings about women who meddle in their husbands' work, and she has concentrated on raising a family. The visitor to the Glasser home senses in the atmosphere the same nurturing flavor that Glasser describes from his own childhood.

The house itself, perched on a hillside lot in a fashionable Brentwood neighborhood, was built from the ground up under Glasser's supervision. It grew year by year, level by level, first with the downstairs area, now mostly bedrooms, and then with the upper areas, as space was needed and money became available.

In the living room, just off the main entry hall, Glasser sits at one end of a huge, curving sofa, his feet propped up on the coffee table. He is dressed in a polo shirt, plaid bermudas and tennis shoes. A great expanse of glass window frames masses of trees, hills, a canyon and incredible Pacific sunsets.

Holding down the other end of the sofa is eldest son, Joe, 22. He is visiting from Palo Alto where he is student teaching in a Glasser model school. Naomi Glasser comes in to say hello and offer tea. Seconds later, the youngest Glasser son, Martin, 15, materializes to be introduced and ask about lemon or sugar. The middle child, Alice, 18, is off at UCLA studying for a degree in public health.

They are comfortable with each other. Why is this family so strikingly out of step in an era when parents and children are having so many difficulties? Glasser smiles. "I make my living telling people how to raise happier, more responsible children. That advice has gotten us all of this," he says, an arm sweeping the sumptuous living room. "They know what side of the bread the butter's on."

Glasser believes in giving kids as much responsibility as they can handle. He feels that one of the problems of parents today is that they take too much crap. "You have to teach kids that the destructive things they do only hurt themselves. Parents have to make children responsible for their own lives and let the kids know that bad acting is not an effective way to get back at their parents for whatever it is they're mad about."

He thinks alcoholics and dope addicts should be treated as potentially responsible human beings instead of sick animals. He believes law enforcement should concentrate on criminals who threaten society rather than those engaged in crimes against themselves. Although he says that almost one-fourth of the prescriptions written in the country are for some sort of psychic disorder, he feels that the pills at least serve a temporarily useful purpose in that they relieve the acute agonies of loneliness.

"Loneliness," he says, "is the world's greatest problem. We all have a neurological need for commitment to others, but if we haven't had success in our relationships then we avoid them. Hungry people don't look at pictures of food. More than 95 percent of the problems my patients have is with other people—women in love affairs and men at work. I think Reality Therapy works toward giving people the confidence they need to begin and succeed at new relationships."

About himself he says, "I am a cheerful person who likes to help people. I always see the bright side of things and am good at solving problems. I love to daydream, but I put a lot of my daydreaming to good use. I have no use for intellectuals. Those people you can't understand or make any sense out of. I think ideas should be expressed in the plainest possible terms so that the understanding isn't flawed. I think Clarence Day who wrote *Life with Father* was a great author, and my hero is Charles Shulz, the creator of 'Peanuts.' "

He talks about an upcoming trip to Israel. Some of the speaking appearances he will make there will be gratis. "I make some sizable donations to the state of Israel, and it seems to me that by charging for my talks I would just be taking my own money back."

While he feels his Jewishness strongly in a cultural way, religion has not played a primary role in his life. "Religion," Glasser says, "is man's way of conning himself into thinking that no matter how bad things are now, they'll be better in heaven."

Glasser's choice of close friends reflects a certain down-to-earth attitude towards life. They are a diverse group including a construction engineer and an accountant. One friend describes them as "self-made men of moderate wealth who have strong family ties."

Chet Karrass, an engineer and one of the people closest to Glasser, says, "Even in the early days when the Glassers first moved to Los Angeles and they didn't have much money, they lived nicely. You never got the feeling of stress or imbalance about them. They knew what they were doing and where they were going.

"All the time the rest of us were struggling with life's problems, those two were making things look easy. Take Bill's first book. You know who he got to edit it for him? His cousin, Robert, an engineer, because he thought Robert was precise and accurate. You know how he decided where to send the book? He went to the public library and saw that Harper and Row published most of the psychology books, so that's where he sent it. . . .

"Bill is not the one-dimensional, totally work-oriented person he may be shaping up to be in your mind. He's got an incredible imagination and a flare for the dramatic.

"Because he spends so much time on planes en route to speaking engagements, he writes most of his books in the air. And when he isn't writing books, he's writing other things. He wrote a movie fantasy once for young people, and he wrote a hilarious play. . . .

"A lot of people dabble in plays, but Bill got the drama department at Occidental College to give a reading of his one Sunday, and he invited about a hundred of his friends. Everyone had a whale of a time, including Bill, who was sitting right down in the audience laughing at his own lines. . . ."

Glasser does know what failure is, however, having experienced it, as far as we know, at least once. He wrote a book on wedlock that was so bad his usually effusive editor at Harper and Row, Harold Grove, said: "I'm not married, but if I were planning to be, that book would have put an end to it."

Grove, who over the years has become personal friends with the Glassers, makes reservations for Broadway shows and at the Park Lane Hotel on Central Park South when the couple goes to New York. And they have entertained him on his visits west. Grove himself has dealt with hundreds of authors over the years, but he comments on the lucidity of Glasser's works and says he is an admirer of both the Glasser mind and the Glasser lifestyle.

A friend, reflecting on Grove's remarks, says: "You know it really is amazing what that one very quiet person has done thus far in his relatively young life. He's not as well known in psychiatric circles as, say, a Carl Rogers. But I think someday his theories will be more far reaching—be put to work in more areas—than any other psychiatrist's in history. Bill Glasser is a very uncommon common man, and I think he'll reach the zenith of his powers when he's about 75."

Youth in Rebellion—Why?

Q. *Dr. Glasser, what accounts for the alarming rise in violence, use of narcotics and other troubles in schools? Do they reflect a crisis in youth morality?*

A. I don't call it a moral crisis; rather, it's a failure crisis. These young people we are hearing so much about—the ones who run away, shoot heroin, engage in violence and sexual promiscuity— are, by and large, youngsters who are failing in important areas of their lives. They are doing what they think is best for them at a particular time by running away from reality. They are irresponsible, they believe they are failures—but I don't think it is very useful simply to call them immoral.

Q. *In what way are they failures?*

A. In the important things: classroom achievement, making friends, having fun, winning the respect of others in responsible ways. Successful children generally don't get into serious trouble. It is when a child starts thinking of himself as a failure and there- fore not worth very much that he begins to choose to act irrespon- sibly, to strike back at others, including his parents.

Q. *Is this feeling of failure more common among young people today than it once was?*

A. If the proportion of juveniles getting arrested is going up, that is a reflection of more children failing. There are indications

From *U.S. News & World Report,* April 27, 1970. Copyright © 1970, U.S. News & World Report, Inc.

that more children are using drugs than in the past and that they are using drugs at lower age levels.

The runaway boy who winds up in a commune in the big city is quite likely to be a failure. He's the withdrawal kid, running away from a reality he can't tolerate.

Similarly, a girl can escape reality by getting involved in sex. She gains confirmation of her role as a woman if she can get someone to make love to her. If she gets pregnant—well, that is still another female role in which she thinks she can be successful. So we see illegitimacy on the rise even among middle-class youngsters. The fact that it hurts the child or that the girl ultimately may have little interest in caring for the child are not considered important by her at the time.

In the same way, coming under the influence of drugs is an attempt to escape from a reality which many young people who feel failure judge too painful to endure. The fact is that they *can* feel better for a short time by using drugs, so it is useless to criticize them as being immoral—any more than you can criticize someone for taking aspirin for a headache. We have to help them to succeed, to get rid of the pain—or we will never reduce narcotic use.

Q. *When does this sense of failure take hold?*

A. Often very early in school life, especially in the central city. Better than 9 out of 10 delinquents are school failures. The average youngster senses very early, usually in the first grade, that he is worth just about whatever grade he gets from his teachers. If he gets low grades—and we hand out low grades liberally to little kids—he gives up early. This means that if he learns the right skills *and* enough of the right answers he is a "success." If he doesn't, he is a "failure" and is labeled as such.

When you are 8, 9 or 10 years old and you believe you are a failure, you may never try again in school. The rest of your school years are like being in jail.

You see, our educational system, by and large, is a process of rote learning—even more so in the central city. This gives the teacher very little emotional or intellectual involvement with the individual child. Her job is to tell him what to memorize. His job is to sit there and memorize the answers. What he is absorbing may be absolutely mysterious to him. He may see no relevance there to his own experience, needs or feelings. But he has to memorize or fail.

The bright kids, or those with solid backgrounds at home, can often survive this process. They can memorize the thousands of things that have to be memorized, even though they think it is ridiculous. They develop a kind of schizophrenic existence, balanced between the unreality of what they are forced to do in school and the real world of their everyday living.

For over 50 per cent of children, school is failure. If they are not lucky enough to have a strong feeling of intrinsic self-worth gained at home, they're going to give up—especially when they don't even understand the things they are told to memorize.

Q. *Is this situation widespread?*

A. Very definitely, yes. I have no national statistics, but in the city of Los Angeles three quarters of the children finishing sixth grade in the inner city are not up to grade level in reading or arithmetic. Many of these, I am certain, are well along the way to becoming failures who will be causing concern to their families or the community. They will drop out, flunk out or cop out.

Until we remedy the kind of education they are getting—which means changing our whole educational philosophy—we are not going to be able to do much about the social problems they are creating.

Q. *Is home upbringing responsible for failure, too?*

A. It certainly can be. But it is the school where the child becomes more and more aware as he goes along that success in life is going to depend on how well he does in school. If the school labels him a "failure," he is going to start thinking of himself as not likely to be worthwhile in other areas of life. When he reaches that conclusion, responsible behavior doesn't seem very rewarding.

Then the child may become aggressively hostile. He strikes back and says, in effect: "I'll do as I please—and to heck with everybody else!" He may wind up in a juvenile facility or in jail. Or maybe he simply becomes passively hostile to learning, to his family, to making responsible friends, and is often generally rebellious without committing a serious offense.

The other course this failing child can follow is to choose to withdraw—which we wrongly label "mental illness." He withdraws to some degree or other from the real world and checks into a world that is more or less of his own choosing. Sometimes this is expressed in milder ways—through nervousness, through depressive spells, or in physical ailments such as back pains or ulcers.

These are all ways in which people can draw back from the real world because they don't feel competent to face reality in a way where they can judge themselves successful.

Q. *Do people have to pass judgment on themselves?*

A. Absolutely—there's no option. We always judge ourselves in every situation we face. Unless we withdraw completely, we cannot help asking: "Am I succeeding? Am I accepted? Am I worthwhile?"

If you can identify yourself as successful in most important situations—and, for a kid, school is the most important—then the evaluation process is pleasant. It helps you face up to new situations. So, in a sense, the child who succeeds tends to become more and more successful. It is really true that "nothing succeeds like success."

On the other hand, students who generally judge themselves as failures become identified increasingly with failure. And failure hurts. It becomes a part of their every move, and so they decide, quite consciously, to withdraw or become antagonistic—or both. It seems to them the only course to take because they don't feel capable of dealing effectively with reality, with the world as it actually is. So they fight it or leave it. All of us have at times failed and taken these choices, but we have bailed ourselves out, and so do some kids. But there are plenty who don't and won't unless we make success more possible.

Q. *Do these dropouts really know what they are doing?*

A. They know very well what they are doing. They are not pushed into these choices by some kind of unconscious complex that is traceable back to infancy; they are simply taking what they see as the only course that will give them a measure of satisfaction or relief from the pain of failure now.

Q. *Can such youngsters ever be brought back to reality?*

A. Yes. Some will do it of their own accord. Others can be helped by therapy, but the answer is prevention—not patch-up. The older they are, the harder patch-up becomes.

When I was working with teen-agers at the California Youth Authority's Ventura School for Girls, all we did was a patch-up job. At the Ventura School we got some good results with therapy, but some were beyond our ability to help. Many girls would tell me: "My troubles started early when I was in elementary school. If you want to do anything, that is where you have to go."

Q. *What works best with young people in trouble?*

A. My approach is this: I get involved and I ask questions designed to get them to evaluate their behavior against reality. A kid may say that smoking "pot" is good for him. I don't argue. I keep asking questions, and sooner or later if we gain a relationship he is almost certain to say that actually he is not helped by marijuana.

Then I try to help him work out a plan to change his behavior and get a commitment that he has a reasonable chance of keeping. If he doesn't keep it, I don't accept excuses and I don't look for blame. In Reality Therapy, he is responsible for what he does; he has to judge his behavior and choose to do better. If he can't at first, he may feel like trying again, and this time, or eventually—we never give up—he will keep his commitment. That can give him some feeling of success, and he will undertake further commitments because he did it himself.

Q. *Is it mainly low-income youngsters who are getting into serious troubles?*

A. No. These problem children come from the lowest and the highest levels. Of course, the affluent parent can turn to private lawyers, private schools, private psychiatrists and other resources to protect his kid and try to rehabilitate him. Low-income parents have to rely on public facilities to do the job—often meaning that it isn't done at all. But there is trouble at all levels. No group can afford to be complacent.

Q. *Is affluence itself causing some of our problems with the young?*

A. To some extent, yes. So many youngsters today are raised to feel: "Whatever happens, I'm going to survive." In the past, a child soon learned he had better get along in school or he might not have a job, or food in his belly. He found a goal early in life—just to survive.

For maybe 2 billion people in the world, that pressure still exists. I read recently that peasants in one part of Asia search through cow dung for undigested grain so that they will have enough to eat for survival. But for about a billion people in the Western world, this pressure no longer exists, and all these countries are having the same trouble with kids that we're having.

Mere survival no longer makes you a success—which opens a wide range of opportunities to cause you to feel like a failure. In fact, a man who makes $50,000 to $100,000 a year today may find reasons to feel more of a failure than did the fellow who settled for any old job in the depression of the 1930s.

Some Americans would prefer that the old pressure for survival still existed, because it did make for a more orderly and disciplined society. But it doesn't exist any more—not because young people did away with it but because of the technological revolution, changes in our political thinking and the secure way we raise our kids.

Q. *Has television played a role in this change?*

A. Very much so—not only because of the affluence it portrays and promotes so incessantly but because it exposes us to high and impossible standards of performance most of us can't emulate.

For example, kids often have a miserable time playing Little League football and baseball because the coaches pressure them as if they were pros. They are failing at having fun. The adults have to get out of kids' activities and let them have fun. If they wear uniforms like the pros they see on TV, then losing becomes a tragedy.

Television, you see, pounds home an existential message which says: "Here is the way you ought to be. Don't be satisfied with the way you are. You can be happier, more successful, more adventurous, more desirable doing it this way." Furthermore, it tells you how quiet and wonderful the 1970 automobile is and how it will make you feel happy and successful. It doesn't tell you how to get that quiet and wonderful car but implies you are less than successful if you don't have one.

Adults maybe have the experience to figure this out: We know it takes planning and scraping. But all a youngster is likely to know is that he doesn't have the car and he needs it because it will make him feel more successful.

Q. *Hasn't anyone told him that he can work to earn enough to pay for it?*

A. Maybe. But our culture today makes immediate gratification so possible that we blur future goals. We take our youngsters to doctors for colds, to dentists for expensive braces, to beauty shops to fix their hair. We buy them almost anything they want. This is true not only of the affluent but of many poor families, too. Also the same laws that used to protect kids against being exploited now make it impossible for many to work. We need jobs for kids 14 and up, and we do nothing about this.

So, you see, we gratify kids when they are young, and at the same time we demand that they work for distant goals. Telling a first-grader to study hard so he can go to a good university won't mean a thing to him, really. What he needs is success—now—or he won't work in school. That is why I consider it so important that educators make basic changes to reduce the rate of failures coming out of our school systems today.

Q. *What changes are you talking about?*

A. What we must do is to set up systematic ways for teachers and children, from kindergarten on up, to become intellectually involved together. Teachers have to see their students as individuals. Children have to feel the excitement of learning—how to solve problems and discover things for themselves—not just sit there memorizing everything in sight, or finishing 63 problems in multiplication within an hour.

Too, I think we must abolish the philosophy and the machinery of "pass or fail" in our schools.

Q. *Would you give all youngsters the same rewards regardless of achievement?*

A. No, not at all. I don't mean that every child will succeed at the same level. But teachers, in effect, should be telling the child: "I will not fail you. I won't give you credit for what you don't do, but I won't mark you down as a failure."

Of course, teachers have to keep track of a child's performance against certain standards. But this can be done through written and oral tasks which, by the way, should stress thinking—not just rote answers. Then instead of issuing ABC-type report cards in elementary school, the teacher better serves the child and parents by conferences and perhaps a written commentary from time to time on what kind of work the child is doing, where he needs to strengthen himself, and so on.

Q. *Suppose a third-grade child is pretty far behind the other members of the class in reading or arithmetic. What do you do to keep him from feeling he is a failure?*

A. If his performance is way out of line with the rest of his age group in a particular subject, I'd move him into another group for that subject for a time so that he could achieve on the same level with at least some of the classmates. Don't wait until the whole year is over and then flunk him. There is no stigma in moving him immediately to a class where he can succeed. But don't wait for him to suffer months of failure before helping him.

In the upper grades, I used to recommend "superior" or "pass" marks. Now I recommend that "A" be used for superior achievement, "B" for proficiency and "C" for minimum proficiency—because no one will give up these traditional marks. Leave the grading space blank if the youngster's work did not meet at least the minimum standard of "C." If that happened, he could repeat the course as least once—maybe more—and might be given tutoring, too. If he passed the subject the next time around, there would be nothing on his record to indicate that he "failed" the first time.

There is more to the use of ABC in my philosophy of grading

than I can detail here, but in essence my objectives are to eliminate the "failure" label and to promote fair competition among able students.

Q. *Is it part of your approach that students be free to do as they please?*

A. Oh, no. Work has to be orderly and co-operative. But I don't think physical or other punishment which is really a form of reprisal is going to produce anything more than conformity and resentment. Discipline has to be aimed at helping the youngster figure out successful ways of behavior. If a child keeps interrupting, I might discuss his actions with him, encourage him to evaluate his behavior, and maybe exclude him from class for a short time until he can return with a plan for improving his behavior and make a commitment to follow that plan.

I would hold any child to that commitment. That is, I would not in any circumstance excuse him if he did not keep to it. As a teacher, I would have to let him know that I care enough about him as a person to realize that he is hurting himself by not keeping his commitment. If I accept his excuse without questions, he would know I don't really care about him.

Do you remember the play, *The Miracle Worker,* which showed the titanic struggles between Helen Keller as a little girl and her governess, Annie Sullivan, when Miss Sullivan wouldn't give in to the girl's self-excusing and rebellion? Well, Annie Sullivan cared enough about Helen Keller to accept nothing less than commitment.

Today's young people need that kind of caring insistence from their teachers—teachers who will keep working with them until commitments are fulfilled. Only then will youngsters begin to get feelings of success—not feelings of failure. They will have started to learn that they can be responsible, which is far better than just conforming.

Q. *Would you abolish memorizing tasks entirely?*

A. Yes, for all important examinations. All tests which count should be written out or done orally. All objective tests for important or final exams must be abolished. They are all right for establishing norms or as learning aids, but that's all. To say that a student understands the American Constitution because he has memorized the Preamble and a few other parts is silly unless he also knows what the Constitution means, which can't be established unless it is written or discussed.

This is what thoughtful youngsters are rebelling against. When a student begins to depend on memory rather than on thinking, it provides him with a very thin potential for identity, for discovering the world and his place in it. To me it is significant that drug use is especially notable not just among failures but among bright students who are turned off because they consider their education irrelevant—and they are too often right.

Q. *Can teachers be found to deal with children in the ways you suggest?*

A. Yes. Teachers generally teach to expectations. If expectations were to be changed and if teachers got a reasonable amount of training in a constructive approach, most certainly they would do quite well.

We get an indication of this from teachers who come to our Educator Training Center in Los Angeles. We started this center a couple of years ago with help from the Stone Foundation of Chicago to promote a more positive and relevant kind of education for young people. About 50 schools have sent teachers and administrators to study and participate in demonstration classes which make use of the same techniques that we have installed in five public schools in Los Angeles and one in Palo Alto.

Q. *What are those techniques?*

A. Mainly they are designed to involve teachers with individual children.

The major technique we use is that of the class meeting or discussion once a day or at least three times a week. The teacher gets her class in a circle for a reasonable discussion of something of interest to children—something they're studying in class, or a news event such as the moon landing, or a personal topic like making friends. It is a kind of Socratic questioning by the teacher. In a friendly and interested but nonjudgmental way, she encourages children to think and express themselves and to listen to each other.

For instance, the teacher may ask a fifth-grade class a very simple but intriguing question: "What if your grandfather dies and leaves you a nice house, all furnished, but you don't need it because you already live in a nice house? What would you do?"

The children start exploring possibilities. Sometimes they fantasize, which is all right, too. Somebody says: "I'd rent it." "Well, why rent it?" Another says: "Because I'd have more money." But the teacher pushes: "How much rent would you charge? How much would that make in a year's time? Or what if a fellow just knocked on the door and said he wanted to rent the house—would you rent it to him?" A kid will speak up: "Well, no, I'd like to check into him." "What would you check into? His bank balance? What his neighbors think of him?"

The youngsters begin to think about this as a terribly real thing that might happen to *them* in their lives. They get excited over it. The teacher is talking about things that make sense. The child who hates arithmetic thinks about the rent money and about multiplying a month's rent into a year's income. More importantly, they get the habit of pushing from one question to the next, thinking things out.

Q. *What about youngsters too shy to speak up?*

A. We've found that such kids usually stop being wall flowers after 30 discussions or so, though it might take as many as 60. Then the shy child sometimes becomes a leader in the discussion, while the youngster who led at the start might keep quiet for a while, become a little more self-evaluative and begin to speak up more thoughtfully.

Q. *What have been the results where you've tried these techniques?*

A. Some schools have had very, very marked changes in terms of youngsters becoming more social, more confident, less destructive and better in attendance. There have been at least two instances I know of personally where autistic children—kids so buried inside themselves that they didn't even utter a word—spoke up for the first time in this kind of discussion.

We have not been going long enough to get hard data on scholastic achievement, but we do have indications that the children getting this kind of instruction are reading better for their age levels than they did. And, more importantly, they seem to be more interested and feel more successful.

I am hopeful that these techniques will be tried more widely very soon. Starting next September, the six schools where these ideas are being put into practice will be open to educators from all over the country who are enrolled in four-month courses of observation and study at our center in Los Angeles. When they complete our course they will be qualified to establish "schools without failure" in their own communities.

The interesting thing is that I think all this helps the teachers in the same way it helps the children. Teachers can begin to feel: "I am successful—I can teach, I'm really gaining ground with these kids." It is not hard to teach this way. Basically, it is a matter of caring about children and about education.

Q. *Other things being equal, would it cost more money to run schools in the way you suggest?*

A. It would cost less. Much of the money we now spend on failures could be saved.

The Ventura School [for delinquent girls] which I referred to has an operational cost to the State of $20 a day per girl. That adds up to about $7,000 a year. A good school system spends perhaps $1,000 a year per child, and a poor system may spend as little as $400 a year.

We spend our money at the wrong end—to patch up the failures.

If we can prevent failure—and I believe we can—we can save this money.

It isn't even a question of spending more money but of spending time and changing just the philosophy of operation so that schools are more responsive to children. It is a matter of understanding that youngsters didn't make this society. We created it, and we must be willing to provide the kind of schools to help them live in it. So long as we don't do this, we are going to be paying heavily for the failures—the runaways, the drug addicts, the violent ones, the welfare cases—in our society.

A Talk with William Glasser

Dr. Glasser's philosophy is deceptively simple and one that he admits is nothing new: Success breeds success, failure breeds failure, and the way schools are structured today, we define success as something open to only a small number of students. In an interview at his Institute for Reality Therapy in Los Angeles, Dr. Glasser tells Learning *senior editor Louis Dolinar what this failure syndrome means:*

If you give a hundred kids in a room a hundred facts to memorize, and you grade them on a curve, only about 15 of them are going to learn enough to get a payoff. The other 85 are going to get no payoff and feel badly. Now you could say, learning the facts was worthwhile. But was it?

It wasn't for the kids who didn't learn. But if you give a hundred kids the chance to think and give them a school setting in which thinking pays off, then almost all of them are going to end up feeling good. And if they feel good, they'll want to do more.

I've often said school for most children is like playing bingo with no prizes. You're asked to do a routine task with small reward, and nobody in his right mind plays eagerly unless he believes he has a chance for a prize. The prizes the schools use are A's, but they give out only a limited number to selected players.

Now if I'm playing real bingo with 50 people, I know that every

From *Learning, The Magazine for Creative Teaching*, December, 1972, © 1972 by Education Today Co., Inc.

time I play the game I have as good a chance to win as anyone else. But in the school bingo game, most of the cards have a little green dot at the bottom. The kids play for a while without winning and finally say, "Why is there a green dot on my card?" And the teacher will say, "Oh, I forgot to tell you. If you've got a card with a green dot, you'll never win." And they don't—and they resent it but they can't leave the game.

So the kids sort themselves out. The more successful ones drift toward the front of the room. And the less successful kids—the losers—start going to the back of the room.

When they finally get settled we have the real segregation in our society—segregation between winners and losers. And that's the segregation we're trying to stamp out with our program, stamp it out in elementary school where it starts.

The people who are fighting our Schools Without Failure program believe in that kind of segregation; they want plenty of losers and they want to keep them separated from the winners.

What I'm trying to do is let every child have some chance to win, and redefine what winning and losing mean.

There are more and more people today who accept the idea that winning does not necessarily mean having the most power or the most money. Winning might be going to sleep feeling good at night because you've got a few friends and you've done something you believe in well.

Dr. Glasser feels that reducing failure in the schools is a high-priority task for our time. In his most recent book, The Identity Society, *he talks about a radical change in human motivation that has taken place in the Western countries since the Second World War. Before that, he says, people had enough to worry about just trying to survive, get a job and make enough money to be secure and, hopefully, comfortable. Until recently, it was enough that schools train people to succeed in this basic way.*

But in the last 20 years, the affluent Western countries have mastered the basic problem of survival. Once this happened, the problems of identity—the search for mutual love and respect and for fulfillment in work—which were formerly pushed into the background by the struggle for simple survival, have emerged as our new high-priority needs. Dr. Glasser describes how the schools originally set up to help us to survive and to become secure have been less able to cope with this new quest for identity:

When a kid fails in school today, he is very likely to develop a pattern for failure in life. So we have to develop schools that can say to a kid: "OK, maybe you're not going to be an expert in mathematics and maybe you won't be able to read and understand the depths of Shakespeare. But we are going to find some way that you can really learn something you believe in and feel you did it successfully."

Then he can go and get a job because he believes in himself, in his ability to succeed. He is someone who cares about the people around him, and he has experienced the strength that comes from their care for him. But if the school turns him out believing he's a failure, feeling miserable and that people don't like him, then he doesn't have much of a chance for success in anything.

But let me make it clear: The schools have not failed in the job they were traditionally assigned to do. Our schools have done a superb job of teaching everything that is needed to run the country. You're starting a new magazine, and I'm sure that if you put out a call—"We need 100 people who are good journalists"—you could select 100 topnotch people from five or six hundred applicants. The schools have not failed in that sense. They are teaching enough people to do the work for the country.

And really, that's what my Schools Without Failure program is all about: not so much to fill the country's needs for technical skills, but to fill the shortage the country has of people who both have the skills and who know what to do with their lives.

We wouldn't have nine million alcoholics and 600,000 drug addicts if people knew what to do with their lives. So schools have to take on another function, a function they never really bargained for.

My view is similar to John Dewey's, but he was ahead of his

time. He was talking about human identity and fulfilling yourself at a time when most people were struggling for the skills needed to keep themselves alive.

So when I criticize schools, I don't criticize them for the job at which they're overwhelmingly successful. All I'm saying is that they have to do that job with even more students and another harder job with everyone.

They must help people develop the sense that "I'm somebody, people care about me, and I care about other people. I've learned successfully some things that are useful and also make sense to me, and while I may not be able to use them directly right now or later, they're still good and I feel good about what I've learned."

While I have said that the schools don't teach students how to think or discuss important issues, I don't say this critically. No one ever gave schools that job. You can't say they're a failure at what they were never assigned to do.

My point is that they should now be assigned to this job. Our country ran for several hundred years on the blind faith that there would always be enough good thinkers to figure out answers to our problems and run things. No one depended upon the schools to prepare people purposefully to do this job, and mostly they seemed to be there when we needed them.

But today that blind faith has run out. Take our pollution problem as an example. If you could get to the core of what most people believe about pollution, you would hear them say, "Somebody smart is going to come along and solve it." Everybody's got this inside hope that some messiah is going to come along and solve this and other serious problems.

But I have a feeling that we have some problems now that are going to have to be solved by concerted, cooperative, thoughtful effort. Human beings have never really done much of this kind of work, and the schools have never taught students even how to begin this necessary new process.

I don't fault the schools for that—that's never been their job in the past. But I am saying that the problems are getting so complex that schools are going to have to start to teach people to think—

really think—and to cooperate thoughtfully. Our pressing problems can no longer be solved solely by charismatic leaders.

Dr. Glasser's conviction that schools must be restructured to prevent failure translates into a number of specific approaches at Glasser schools. One of the most familiar and effective is the class meeting, in which teacher and students sit in a circle of equals, discussing goals for individuals and the class, current events and other subjects that stimulate cooperative and individual thinking, not memorization.

Dr. Glasser also writes of the need for heterogeneous classes. He feels that separating children into slow and advanced classes only encourages the growth of a failure identity among those who haven't made it to the top.

Third, he calls for the abolition of grades as we know them. Anything worse than a B, says Dr. Glasser, makes a child feel like a failure. He would substitute a credit—no-credit system, in which a child either learns the assigned material and moves on to something else, or continues to work until he's mastered the subject. Honors would be available for kids who on their own initiative do extra work. In elementary schools he would prefer parent-teacher conferences for report cards but still give those parents who wanted them report cards.

But despite his emphasis on a youngster's need for success, Dr. Glasser does not suggest that such success should be bought at a price of turning out students who can't read, write, think or speak. Here he contrasts his methods with those of some open schools and indicates where he believes the line must be drawn.

One of the mistakes the free schools are making is that their child-centered curriculum too frequently lacks substance. While the kids are enjoying themselves, they're also cheating themselves and they realize it later. They need some direction, but not all direction.

I'm not saying this of all free schools, and I'm not generally condemning the free school movement. I think that it's wrong to see it as an either-or thing, that in order to be really human, we have to unstructure the whole world and let the child remake it. I call that approach the Roasting Pig syndrome—let everybody learn to roast a pig by burning down his house.

It's thrilling to see a child rediscover something; there's no doubt about that. But it can also be a waste of time if that's all he does. In other words, I believe that a curriculum should have real substance, and reading is basic. But schools don't very often offer a variety of well-written materials. Dull books are hard to read, and compared to the television the kids watch, most school texts are dull beyond belief.

You can't really count on most kids doing a lot of reading outside of school. I wish you could, but you can't. Television has become a real roadblock. Therefore, you've got to give kids in school a much wider variety of lively books and magazines to read.

The Job Corps, for example, may have been less than successful, but at least some of the Job Corps camps did teach a lot of kids to read. To do so they literally bought paperbacks by the ton. They went to publishers and said, "Give us five tons of your paperbacks," and the publishers threw in all their old titles and everything they had in their warehouses that they wanted to get rid of. The camp director would scatter these paperbacks around the camp—throw them on tables, under beds, everywhere else—and not say a thing.

And the kids started to read. The books were all over the place and were of such variety—you know, paperbacks cover almost every subject in the world—that everybody seemed to find something he wanted to read. Easy access to good material seemed to be the key.

Well, we ought to learn from that. These kids were turned-off nonreaders, and they became readers. The failure of most schools in teaching reading is that they don't give the kids enough reason to want to read.

Teachers say to me, "How can I get these kids to read?" and I say, "Have you tried motorcycle magazines? Just go around and get some back issues or use a little PTA money to get some motorcycle magazines, bring them into class and place them around. Don't advertise them—let them sit."

Teachers who have done this say, "You know, the kids started looking at them and soon they were asking me words. Kids seem to know so much about motorcycles."

And I say, "Of course. You don't and I don't, but motorcycles are relevant for them."

Everyone wants to communicate, so most kids can be motivated to learn to read and write. Dr. Glasser's most important curricular requirement is relevance, and certainly reading and writing are easily made relevant. But how is mathematics relevant to a second grader? Here is what Dr. Glasser says:

Mathematics is something that little kids naturally like to do because the chances for their success are so good. It's one of the few subjects that's obviously self-programming.

By that, I mean a kid can see whether his answers are right or wrong. When he writes a paragraph, he doesn't know whether he's got a good paragraph or a bad one. But when you ask him how much 6 times 6 is, and he puts down 36, no one can convince him that he's not right. And when he's right he feels good.

When you get into some of the new math—set theory and all those kinds of things—all too often, there aren't enough teachers who really understand these ideas well enough to teach them.

My personal feeling is that in real life you add, subtract, divide, you do a few simple fractions, some very simple decimals and some very, very simple percentages. Ninety-nine percent of the people don't use any more math than that, and I don't think schools should feel a very deep obligation to teach everyone more than that. You may expose kids to more math and that's good, but if they don't absorb much more, you shouldn't fail them. They've already learned all they need.

Of course people ask, "How about all the engineering and science that has to be done in this country, all the research that requires deep math?" Well, I believe that very few people who are doing this work have been forced into doing it by compulsory math. They're doing it voluntarily because they like it and they're gifted at it. There are a lot of people who like math, and they're going to learn it even if they have to dig it out for themselves.

There are more than enough people who get a reward from numbers and numerical concepts to do all the science and engineering that this country needs. In fact we have a surplus of those people right now with no shortage in sight.

The Civilized Identity Society

So quickly that few have recognized what is happening, a society that had lasted for 10,000 years has begun to dissolve. In its place, a new society has been growing up, one in which the mores, habits, and goals of a hundred centuries are being profoundly altered. Some might take longer than others to recognize this colossal reorientation; many will undoubtedly spend the rest of their lives resisting the new direction of humanity. But it is real.

This, of course, is not the first time that a significant new pattern of social organization has evolved. In the approximately four million years that have elapsed since man has been considered a more or less distinguishable entity, I believe there have been three other societal transfigurations of comparable magnitude.

I call the earliest human society the *primitive survival society*. It lasted three-and-a-half million years. During that long period, man's primary goal in life was survival in a rigorous, often hostile, environment. He was able to survive because he cooperated intelligently with other members of the species in defending against predatory animals, in killing other creatures for food, in rearing the helpless human young, and in helping his fellows in myriad ways to overcome individual weaknesses. When men failed to cooperate with one another, they suffered, and sometimes they died. During those several million years, the need for intelligent

From *Saturday Review,* February 19, 1972, © SR Publishing Assets Industries, Inc., 1972. Reprinted by permission.

cooperation became built into the human nervous system by the normal evolutionary process of natural selection.

From the little we now know about these primitive strivings, we can see that as early man cooperated successfully he was able to enjoy increasing periods of rest and of freedom from stress. During these off-hours, he learned to enjoy the company of his fellows, and that enjoyment motivated him to cooperate still further. Men were helping one another not just to survive but also to feel more pleasure. As pleasure occurred more and more frequently during the millenniums of man's slow acquisition of competence in overcoming surrounding dangers, the ancient need for intelligent cooperation evolved into a sister need: the need for the human individual to be involved in the affairs of other individuals. About 500,000 years ago, in pursuit of this need, man evolved what I call the *primitive identity society*.

This was undoubtedly a natural evolution of man with time on his hands. We have some evidence that primitive identity man lived peacefully in a fairly abundant, nonstressful environment. Although there was conflict in his life, it bore little resemblance to the incessant struggle endured by primitive survival man. Able to take survival at least partially for granted, primitive identity man developed other priorities. He finally found time to have a little fun—to love and be loved, to become involved, or, for those who could not, to learn the pain of loneliness. He formulated complex kinship systems, ornate rituals, ceremonies, dances, and religious beliefs. He learned how to use both his brain and his body for enjoyment and pleasure. High on the list of pleasure activities was sex.

If an unrestrained enjoyment of that activity led to the creation of large families, no matter. There was plenty of room to spread out. So few people existed that children could grow up and leave home—find a new territory and form their own nonstressful but generally complex society just as their grandparents and parents had done. These were the years in man's evolution when intelligence, applied at leisure, produced not merely cooperation, but probably music, magic, religion, art, and poetry as well.

Wars or conflicts between groups during this time were identity wars fought for personal status rather than for power. Wars were neither organized nor lengthy; people did not systematically kill or enslave each other, nor did they prey wantonly upon one another. There was no need to do so. Even the cannibals who ate the flesh of their human victims did so not to survive but to obtain for themselves the spirit—in a sense, the identity—of the persons eaten.

One lingering example of a primitive identity society is that of the Cheyenne Indians of the Great Plains in North America. The Cheyenne were typical Plains Indians. Their problem of survival was solved by an annual cooperative buffalo hunt in which thousands of animals were killed. Some aspects of the hunt itself make more sense in terms of identity than in terms of survival. For example, though the hunt's proceeds were divided evenly among the tribe's families, each young warrior strove to kill as many buffalo as he could so as to enhance his social standing in the tribe. Warfare, which occupied much of the rest of the year, was embellished with displays of bravery that did little to ensure victory; bravery became an end in itself. Thus, prestige drives overrode the more limited military requirements, making war a deadly game rather than a quest for power or property.

The Kung bushmen of the Kalahari Desert in southern Africa are a similar example of a primitive identity society that has endured into the twentieth century. Having no single source of food equal to the buffalo, they hunt continually during most of the year. About 80 per cent of their food is supplied by the women, who gather edible plants and nuts; only 20 per cent is gained by hunting. Because most of the game animals are divided equally among the members of the tribe, the hunter receives no larger share than any other male. Still, because of great social pressure, the male spends most of his time hunting. If survival were primary, if the male were not concerned with his image, he would be better off gathering.

At one time, there were a large number of primitive identity cultures. Their populations tended to be small, and put little pressure on available food resources. As leisure time for personal involvement increased, these cultures developed more and more complex ways to maintain or enhance their role or identity. Compared with the way most people live today, it was a good life.

Over the period of the past several thousand years, however, primitive identity societies ended in many parts of the world, when population increased, until man outstripped the environment's capacity to furnish him abundant food. The discovery of agriculture, an important means of survival, caused land to become valuable. To ensure access to land, men began to prey upon their fellows. Conflict became the rule, not the exception.

Enter mankind's phase three—that which I call the *civilized survival society*. Survival again became a paramount priority, but civilized men did not revert to the cooperative instincts of their forefathers. Once the idea of conquest became common, survival of the aggressive became the ruling theme of existence. Aggressive men tried to overpower, enslave, or destroy those who posed a possible danger to them, and unhesitatingly plundered the land resources of those who posed no danger at all. Because of an innate need for involvement, these conquerors probably suffered brief pangs of guilt. But these could easily be overcome or repressed by a multitude of moral excuses, all of which rationalized the claim that the stolen resources were necessary for the conqueror's survival. A few primitive identity societies lingered during this period, but they were quickly snuffed out by the power and aggression of the civilized survivors. The American Indian is a classic example. He was identity-oriented, occasionally warlike and hostile, but seldom motivated by aggression or fear. The American frontiersmen were survival-oriented, and all but eliminated the Indian in the acquisition of power and land.

The civilized survival society was a goal-oriented society. To survive in it, men relinquished their individuality and became subservient to the group. Work became necessary, and strong men, to ensure their own survival, forced or persuaded others to labor for them. The control by one man of other men was common to this society.

Concern with role was possible for some men. But even for those, the role was not freely chosen, independent of goal, as was true in the primitive identity society. It was a limited, specialized, dependent role, related to a survival or security goal. For example: A soldier fought, a politician led, a cleric prayed. Most men, however, struggled to survive. Only during frequent wars were they able to gain even the severely restricted role of the expendable soldier. Because this dangerous role was attractive to men with no identity, there was rarely a shortage of soldiers.

A few men were able to gain an independent role in the civilized survival society and to concern themselves primarily with the pleasures of involvement with like souls. It was the rare man, however, who tried to help the many who had little chance for a life beyond bare survival. These men who helped others toward involvement are recorded in history as the great humanitarians. They were always few, however frequently history mentions them, and, much as they tried, their effect was limited. Lincoln could free the American slaves, but he could do little to give their freedom meaning.

Only after a civilized survival society became strong enough so that others did not prey on it, and satisfied enough so that it did not prey on others and waste itself in conflict, could it start to concern itself with identity—with human rights and privileges. The United States, Canada, Switzerland, and Sweden are countries in which some degree of this concern has almost always been present.

Despite such limited concern for identity, civilized survival societies have been and are power hierarchies. The top is occupied by a few strong people, the bottom by large masses grubbing for existence at a bare survival level. Between the two is a wide variety of people who make up the middle classes of any civilization. Power keeps these classes in their established order. One moves up if the order gains power, down if it loses. Any upward movement within the society threatens others because there are limited places to go. If too many or too few people exist within a class, their survival is threatened; there is either not enough or too much for them to do. Conflict occurs when they try to move out or to keep others from moving in.

No matter how many classes exist, it is always the bottommost layer of the population—the slaves, serfs, minorities, peasants, or mill hands—who do the hard, disagreeable work of the society. If many of them stop working, the whole hierarchy is threatened. Any attempt to organize this class and give it power is strenuously resisted, not only by those at the top but by almost everyone above the bottom.

Many people without identity have tried to gain a little security and a dependent role within the power structure by taking on aspects of their ruler's identity. History is replete with people who followed a leader blindly, often to their own destruction. Nazi Germany is an example. After World War I, both the upward aspiring middle classes and the always desperate lower classes in Germany were sufficiently stung by defeat and the loss of prestige to chase an illusion of power that was to destroy thirty million people. As a means for survival, wars lost their original justification long ago. They have developed into senseless power struggles. Bolstered by contrived and self-perpetuating propaganda, war as an institution has taken on an identity of its own that deludes leaders and followers alike.

Because civilized survival societies have dominated the earth for the past ten thousand years, and because the written record of man's behavior is contained entirely within that period, the human species has come to be deluded by its own propaganda. There is now a common belief that life became easier for man with the advent of civilization, that the species has enjoyed more happiness during the recorded history of settled, agricultural, property-owning people. This belief prevails in spite of little evidence to support it. In fact, there is good evidence that the lives of two-thirds of the people in the world today are much less gratifying in terms of ease and human satisfaction than were the lives of men who lived during the almost half a million preceding years of the primitive identity society.

Both primitive survival man and civilized survival man were hard pressed to survive the stresses of their environment. Both worked to survive, but with one major difference. Primitive survival man struggled against the hostile environment into which nature brought him; it was not of his own making. Civilized survival man struggled against a hostile environment almost entirely of his own making. Primitive survival man suffered from lack of food, lack of shelter, lack of ability to make tools and materials to survive, but he got along with his fellow men. Civilized survival man has demonstrated an outstanding ability to utilize the resources of his environment to his own advantage, but he has rarely demonstrated an ability to get along with his fellows.

Vestiges of the ancient tendency toward cooperation are still apparent in many of man's primitive behavioral relationships today. We cooperate, for example, to avoid suffering if we are stranded by fire or flood. But the inherent neurological need for men to cooperate for the common good has been mainly suppressed; for a hundred centuries we have denied its urges. The stresses and strains to which we have been subject in the civilized survival society have forced our conscious minds to choose behavior that conflicts with the cooperative behavioral tendencies built into the human nervous system during the two primitive societies that preceded civilization. The civilized survival society taught most men to suppress awareness of the suffering and deprivation existing all around them. The hostility and antagonism of the deprived helped the more privileged to rationalize this behavior. These defensive reactions have been so much a part of our civilized history that scholars studying the consequences have often, it seems, erroneously concluded that aggression and antagonism are innate human qualities while cooperation is not. Written history backs their theory. Human history seriously challenges it.

All the institutions of our society were, and for the most part still are, organized to preserve this 10,000-year-old distortion of our evolutionary heritage. The situation is heavily weighted against either understanding of, or preparation for, the new social stress that recently has caused most young people and a surprising number of older people to spend much of their time and energy pursuing a role independent of any specific security. Moving against the accumulated inertia of centuries, these people are trying to gain a successful identity—a pleasurable belief in themselves and in their own humanity and in the companionship of others in ways not necessarily related to security. Thus, in the past twenty or so years, a new society has begun to emerge. I call it the *civilized identity society,* because it is motivated by a respect for individual integrity. It cannot be passed off as a mere "generation gap," because the conflict involves a cleavage between contrasting cultures, not age groups.

As early as 1950, the change from a civilized survival society came about for essentially the same reason that the primitive survival society gave way to the primitive identity society half a million years ago.

The need for defense against the environment had been diminished by affluence, and the affluence made it possible for more people to become politically concerned with human pleasure and the right to enjoy that pleasure. Affluence also increased access to communications, primarily to television, which directly or indirectly urge people to enjoy themselves and to live a better life. These forces combined to strengthen actual security and to decrease everyone's concern for security, thus weakening the power hierarchy. As the weakness became evident, almost all young people and many older people took advantage of the opportunity to escape the rigid goal orientation that insecurity had necessitated for everyone below the top of the power structure.

Led by the young, the half-billion people of the Western world have begun a tumultuous revolution toward a new, role-dominated society in which people concern themselves more and more with their identities and how they might express them. Of course, people still strive for goals, but increasingly these are vocational or avocational goals that their pursuers believe will reinforce the independent human role. The goals may or may not lead to economic security, but they do give people verification of themselves as human beings. Not everyone can work at a job he would enjoy identity with, such as doctor, artist, or teacher; but now anyone can pursue a recreational goal (such as bowling or bridge-playing) or a volunteer goal (such as working at a hospital or fund-raising) that reinforces his identification as a worthy person. A young doctor's view of himself in the new identity society illustrates the changed situation:

I am a doctor not because I can make money and find a very secure place for myself high in the power structure, but because I think I can practice medicine to become involved with my fellow man. I'd like to work in an inner-city hospital, in the Peace Corps, in a "free" clinic, in research, or for the Public Health Service. I expect to get paid enough to live, perhaps to be comfortable; but, to me, being a doctor is much less to gain money, prestige, and power than it is to reinforce my own role, my belief in myself as a human. As I struggle helping others, I will enjoy the satisfaction that comes when I do this well.

The dean of my medical school has confirmed that before 1950, students who answered the standard question, "Why do you want to become a doctor?" by saying, "For the human involvement it provides" (the role answer) were often rejected as candidates for a physician's training. They were suspected of being deviants or troublemakers. The student who answered that he wanted a secure profession (the goal answer) was accepted. This attitude began to shift about 1950. Since then, many medical schools have been admitting students who proclaim interest in public service; Western Reserve University Medical School is a good example.

In the new identity society few people renounce the opportunity to struggle for an independent role. In this struggle, however, many people fail; they are unable to find such a role. They do gain an identity, but the identity is that of a failure. Failures involve themselves with feelings that reinforce their unsatisfactory attempts to find successful identities. Many retreat into unreality through the use of alcohol or drugs; or they find escape in psychosomatic ailments: headaches, back pains, digestive distress, heart palpitations. Others find independence in growing beards, participating in peace marches or in voter-registration drives. Whether children succeed or fail in their search for roles they can be proud of, the denials, the attacks, the rejections they encounter in the process are bound to separate offspring from parents. But again this is the symptom of a cultural, not necessarily a generational, gap. Today, about twenty years into the new civilized identity society, most families in the Western world are culturally divided. During the next twenty to twenty-five years, as the identity society children became parents, the gap should narrow. Now, while the gap is widening, it is important to keep in mind that the young are now struggling for involvement, that is, they believe role takes precedence over goal. They do so because they have had security and freedom within their families. They believe an independent role is natural; they do not hear admonitions that the security and freedom are temporary because they are provided by the family and not by the society. They believe that the government or private enterprise should provide work where work is necessary for the good of mankind. Work for them is not necessarily sacred. If one chooses not to work, he should have that right. When one asks, "If a person doesn't work, who will support him?" they say, "His friends." They do not believe a person has a right to prey upon others who do not wish to support him, but they believe no one should be criticized if his friends decide to care for him. They also believe that not only each person but also the government has an obligation to work to improve the quality of life for all. This obligation includes limiting births, because overcrowding is the direct path back to the survival society. The new identity society is a regeneration of intelligent cooperation and involvement, reverting back hundreds of thousands of years to humanity.

How to Face Failure and Find Success

Central to William Glasser's writing are the concepts of success and failure and the idea that a pattern of failure can be changed. What application, we wondered, did these theories of success and failure have for the recent college graduate, assuming that the transitional period from college to the working world is fraught with success/failure anxieties.

So we asked Dr. Glasser: "What advice would you give a recent college graduate about establishing a success pattern for himself once he's out of school?" Here are his comments.

GLASSER: We can't succeed in life unless we answer one key question honestly: "What do I want now?" It sounds simple, but we often try to avoid asking it because we know if we answer that question honestly, we might be disappointed.

For example, suppose you graduate this June with a teaching certificate. What you really want is a job teaching, but what happens if you look diligently and still can't find such a job? As you encounter rejection after rejection, you become increasingly hesitant to continue asking that key question—because the answer hurts.

When this happens many of us try to avoid the pain by avoiding the question. We might use the strategy of saying, "First I'll

---

From *Graduate,* © *The Graduate* magazine, 1974. Reprinted by permission of Approach 13–30 Corp., Knoxville, Tennessee.

travel, then I'll teach." Or maybe we avoid the question by answering it dishonestly, saying we really don't want to teach after all. Then we usually have to reinforce the dishonest answer by saying that what we really wanted all along was to become a secretary or a salesman. But, of course, if we still want to teach, the second answer is dishonest.

GRADUATE: The important thing, then, is being honest to ourselves, to what we want to do. But it's not always easy to maintain this honesty, particularly, as you pointed out, in the face of rejection. Are some people better able to be honest to themselves than others, and if so, why?

GLASSER: It is what you believe about yourself that determines how you will answer the question. If you see yourself as a successful person, as a "can-do" person who can get something good out of life, you will usually answer the question honestly. If, however, you see yourself as a failure, if you look at yourself as second-rate—as a "can't-do" person—you will avoid the question or answer it dishonestly.

GRADUATE: But how do you get to the first point, of seeing yourself as a "can-do" person?

GLASSER: You decide what kind of person you are. In fact, you've been deciding this all your life. Only now, after graduation, it gets tougher. It was easy in school, because to see yourself as a successful person you simply had to do okay in school. And you probably did or you wouldn't be graduating now.

So now you want to succeed, you want happiness, worth, love, fulfillment—we all do—so stop right now and ask yourself what you want to do. Don't worry about being selfish either; if you succeed in what you want to do, you will probably help others—successful people almost always do.

GRADUATE: Making a decision about what you want to do next must in turn mean making a commitment to that decision—it's all well and good to say you want to do this or that but you won't get anywhere resting on your honest decision. Do you have any suggestions as to how to proceed from here?

GLASSER: Answering the question is only the beginning. Next you have to decide whether you will *work* for your choice. It's possible that you don't have a chance to get what you want, but you'll never know unless you make a plan and try.

You can try without a plan, but again, successful people tend to make a plan and channel their efforts into that plan. It's more efficient. If you don't plan but try anyway, or if you compromise, retreat or give up, you are setting the stage for a failure that may be with you for a long time.

GRADUATE: You made a similar point in *The Identity Society* when you said something about never making a plan that attempts too much—that the plan should be ambitious enough so that some change can be seen but not so grand that failure is likely. So let's say you have a reasonable plan, where do you get the strength to work for what you really want?

GLASSER: You get it partly from something that few people understand: trying. Most people believe that strength is gained from *reaching* a goal—like making a million dollars or having a loving husband or getting a great job. To some extent that's true; strength does result from reaching a goal. But perhaps even more, strength comes from making a commitment to work for what you want. And the more honest you are in what you want, the more strength you'll have. It's the *doing,* the moving toward applying yourself physically and mentally to what you want, that builds your strength.

If you depend too much on the goal, you'll lose strength rapidly if you don't achieve your goal—and to some extent even if you do. Have you ever started a big project, worked hard, succeeded and then when you finished felt a little bit disappointed? The disappointment was not the success: it was that the job was over; the goal was valuable but the task even more so. You don't really have to worry about goals if you are willing to answer the question about what you want to do honestly and then give your decision a decent try.

Try it for six months and see if you don't begin to increase a belief in yourself that you're strong and that you can do something each day that has value to you.

If you don't try, you will first begin to avoid the question, then to answer it dishonestly and maybe finally give up asking it altogether. By this time you will be full of doubts and ready to rationalize your failure by feeling nervous, sick or inadequate. The worse you feel, the more thoroughly you will lock yourself into failure and do less and less. You'll blame everyone in the world except yourself, and life will truly pass you by.

So make a plan and if the plan doesn't work, make another; don't give up. No one can stop you from trying. Others may block you, reject you, cheat you and hurt you, but they can't stop you from trying. That's totally in your control.

Theory

Something Old, Something New, Something Borrowed: Introduction

Reality Therapy, a series of theoretical principles developed by William Glasser, emphasizes the reeducation of a person who learns how to behave in a more responsible and productive way. Focusing on the present behavior of the person, the Reality Therapist helps the individual to evaluate himself more accurately, to confront reality, to fulfill his needs in a productive way without infringing on the rights of others. The essence of Reality Therapy is the acceptance of responsibility for a person's own behavior which enables the individual to achieve success and happiness.

Reality Therapy, a common-sense approach that derives from learning theory, has antecedents in the psychotherapeutic literature. What is unique, however, is the juxtaposition of these antecedents and their interrelationships. This section contains some significant articles from practitioners of different systems of psychotherapy which reinforce and illustrate the theories of Reality Therapy.

The distinguished past president of the American Psychological Association and the leading American authority in many significant behavior science areas for almost four decades, O. Hobart Mowrer prophesied in 1965 that Reality Therapy would have a profound influence in psychiatry, psychology, and social work. In addition to his impressive and impeccable professional credentials, which included teaching at Harvard and Yale, Mowrer had been in analysis for seven years. Mowrer writes, therefore, as a former analysand, as a respected practitioner, and as an academician. In the Foreword to William Glasser's *Reality Therapy: A New Approach to Psychiatry,* Mowrer cogently predicts that "this is an extraordinarily significant book. Readers will themselves discover that it is courageous, unconventional, and challenging. And future developments will, I predict, show that it is also scientifically and humanly sound." While today, a decade after it was written, Mowrer's foreword may appear clichéd, it is important to remember that Mowrer was among the first to challenge the validity of psychoanalysis.

Glasser suggests that individuals have two basic needs: "the need to love and be loved and the need to feel we are worthwhile to ourselves and others." More recently, in *The Identity Society* (1972), Glasser documents a shift in values from struggling to survive to a preoccupation with finding and appreciating one's identity—i.e., to feel good about oneself. Glasser makes a plea for involvement, for human contact which is the crucial ingredient for any type of meaningful interpersonal social, educational, or psychotherapeutic relationship. Freud, in contrast, advocated an objective, analytic, neutral, detached, aloof relationship. Indeed, alarmingly within the last few years, a number of therapists have begun to consider the frightening possibility of "the computer as counselor," which is a modernized version of the 1920 Karel Capek play, *R.U.R.* Rossum's Universal Robots was a warning against the accelerated rate at which men were being depersonalized in the factories of the machine age. In rebuttal to this simplistic reduction of a therapeutic relationship to information dissemination by a computer, William Glasser writes, "We feel pleasure when we are involved with other people and they are involved with us; we feel pain when we are uninvolved and lonely. The path to successful identity in this new society is involvement."

Glasser, in "Notes on Reality Therapy," outlines six essential differences between Reality Therapy and more conventional psychotherapy.

C. H. Patterson begins his article with the supposition "that counseling is a human relationship." Rather than describe the technique, Patterson elects to stress the humanity of the counselor who helps the client to improve his or her self-esteem, self-respect, and confidence. Once this has been accomplished, the client will make responsible decisions, which is the goal of counseling according to Patterson. The counselor not only should trust the client to make decisions but also should respect the client as an individual who has worth. "Counseling as a Relationship," an article that predates Reality Therapy, thus stresses the humanity and involvement of the psychotherapist. In addition, a leading proponent of Carl Rogers' nondirective counseling, Patterson is to be commended because he has reduced the counseling relationship to its most essential part—i.e., the giving of the counselor of him or herself which, of course, is one of William Glasser's major points.

William Schofield, who writes from a more traditional psychiatric orientation than Glasser, addresses himself to two important questions: "Is psychotherapy nothing more than a socially sanctioned substitution for the essential resources of personal acceptance and emotional support that most of us get from our friendships? Is the psychotherapist in essence only a good friend?" While the past president of the American Society for Adolescent Psychiatry answers his own questions with an absolute "very definitely not," the reader senses that this, in fact, is not his conclusion. Later in this provocative philosophical essay, Schofield suggests that "when therapy is effective it is not unusual for the patient to end up with the feeling that his therapist is in fact his friend." Schofield posits a definition of a friend that Reality Therapists would accept, describing the psychotherapist as "the person we know to whom it matters if we are victorious or defeated, the person who will be truly happy with us in our gain, sad with us in our loss. Our friend cares about us and feels with us." Schofield is in fundamental agreement with Glasser regarding this point.

Clifford H. Swensen, in fact, has surveyed the literature regarding the psychotherapist's contribution to the therapeutic success and concludes emphatically that "the successful psychotherapist is the one who genuinely cares about, and is committed to his client." The strength of Swensen's research is a comprehensive bibliography that supports his thesis and that of Glasser.

William M. Easson courageously considers the tacit prohibition of the more analytic orientation against the post-termination friendship between the psychotherapist and patient. Easson suggests that if psychotherapy has been effective to help the patient function at an optimal level, then friendship can be a natural evolution in the relationship. Easson concludes his important treatise, which breaks new ground, by stating that "a continued friendship with a former psychotherapist may strengthen the gains made by the patient in the previous psychotherapy and may lead to very rapid growth. . . . For both the patient and the psychotherapist, this friendship can give them an opportunity to grow as friends and as individuals in the years ahead but, at the same time, it allows them to look back into their earlier treatment relationship, to the psychotherapy, and to strengthen, stabilize, and rebuild what went on then. If the psychotherapist cannot allow this kind of friendship to develop where it is natural and appropriate, he limits his own personal and professional growth and he may be undermining the gains the patient made in psychotherapy."

Nathan Hurvitz has described the operational principles and dynamics of the "self-help" movement. This article strikingly shows the compatibility of Reality Therapy with peer self-help groups such as Alcoholics Anonymous, Daytop Village, Weight Watchers, and the like. Some of the most important operational principles of the groups, according to Hurvitz, are (1) peers hold each other responsible for their behavior regardless of its causes, (2) peers focus on behavior and try to help each other to become more responsible and productive, and (3) peers use a reality-based here-and-now orientation. Hurvitz, a social worker and a psychologist, who has not been identified as a Reality Therapist, independently and unintentionally illustrates the overlap between Reality Therapy and the self-help movement.

Richard Parlour, Philip Cole, and Robert Van Vorst, who had become disenchanted with the more traditional Freudian "insight" oriented psychotherapies, devised a counseling approach that is compatible with Reality Therapy. The treatment team, which consists of a psychiatrist, a sociologist, and a psychologist, attempts to help the client evaluate his behavior and then correct it. Similar to Glasser, they believe that a significant part of the counseling process is advice giving. Parlour, Cole, and Van Vorst differ with Reality Therapy when they suggest that coercion—i.e., pressure and punishment—may be an important part of the helping relationship. Glasser, in contrast, suggests that praise is required to cement involvement.

Alexander Bassin, in his article on marriage counseling, concentrates on three major components: (1) *integrity,* which has been derived from the work of O. Hobart Mowrer, relates to the concepts that honesty and subsequent acknowledgment (confession) to significant others of a person's irresponsibility is necessary to ensure a meaningful and gratifying marital relationship; (2) *responsibility* has been defined by Glasser as behavior which permits people to fulfill their basic needs without either interfering in or depriving the efforts of others to attain their needs; (3) *transparency,* Sidney Jourard contends, is verbalizing our opinions, sharing our feelings, and being honest in interpersonal relationships. While Glasser does not specifically discuss confessing to significant others as a part of Reality Therapy, it seems clear he does not disagree with this concept. Glasser, of course, advocates transparency, since honesty is an important part of establishing involvement. Glasser extends Jourard's concept by discussing the importance of the psychotherapist in being a responsible role model.

Willard Mainord, who worked in an admissions ward of a state hospital, devised a therapy which was predicated upon the basic principles of learning theory. Like Mowrer, Hurvitz, and Glasser, Mainord rejected the medical model of the etiology of disease. Rather than attributing bizarre behavior either to psychological or to emotional dysfunction, Mainord views behavior in terms of an irresponsible choice. The patient thus understands that he possesses the freedom of choice—i.e., either to behave responsibly or to behave irresponsibly. Being more behavioristic than Glasser, Mainord suggests the reward-punishment dichotomy of learning theory. Mainord agrees with Glasser, furthermore, that the optimal therapeutic modality is working in groups.

Thomas Allen describes Adlerian strategies for behavior change. Since a person's behavior is influenced by a series of expectations and self-fulfilling prophecies, Allen suggests that the goal of Adlerian psychotherapy is to alter self-defeating, asocial beliefs. Allen presents a number of case studies which illuminate ways to help people change their behavior. On the one hand, this approach differs from Reality Therapy because it emphasizes cognition rather than behavior. Yet, on the other hand, there are many similarities between Glasser and Adler: Glasser has alluded to the positive expectations for additional growth and development which the psychotherapist must maintain to effect positive behavior change. Glasser mentions that punishment (i.e., discouragement) interferes with the psychotherapeutic alliance, and he recognizes that the key to the therapeutic process is the involvement and encouragement of the psychotherapist. Many have discussed the many similarities between Adler and Glasser.

Ira Greenberg, a psychologist, and Alexander Bassin, a social worker–psychologist–criminologist, have collaborated to describe the technique and practice of psychodrama and some of the theoretical foundations for this modality of treatment. Greenberg and Bassin disclose some similarities in the life histories of the late J. L. Moreno, the founder of psychodrama, and William Glasser.

Greenberg and Bassin document the divergent theoretical and treatment approaches. The basic techniques of psychodrama, specifically role playing, constitute important components of the actual practice of Reality Therapy, particularly in its application to corrections where role playing rehearsals of plans for finding a job, improving social relationships and skills can be employed. In the educational setting Glasser has used a number of applications of psychodramatic techniques such as role playing, role reversal, soliloquy, and empty chair, which make Reality Therapy more vital. It should be noted, furthermore, that Glasser uses role playing with mental health students to teach the principles of Reality Therapy.

Glen Holland concludes this section on related theory with a succinct and pragmatic analysis of three theories of psychotherapy: Reality Therapy, Autonomous Psychotherapy, and Integrity Therapy. Holland, a clinical psychologist, compares Glasser's, Szasz's, and Mowrer's viewpoints regarding psychoanalytic psychotherapy, rules, responsibility, and ego states.

Reality Therapy is a series of theoretical concepts and principles which can trace its origins to learning theory and existential thought. Peter Koenig suggests that "Glasser's originality is marginal. His work echoes Alfred Adler, B. F. Skinner, Norman Vincent Peale, Mary Baker Eddy, Thomas Szasz, the dicta of Horatio Alger. Yet Glasser's ideas are his own in the sense that he personally discovered them. And because he has put them together on his own, his theories have force behind them." ("Glasser the Logician," *Psychology Today,* 7:9 [February, 1974], p. 67.)

At the Beginning: Foreword to *Reality Therapy*

This is an extraordinarily significant book. Readers will themselves discover that it is courageous, unconventional, and challenging. And future developments will, I predict, show that it is also scientifically and humanly sound.

For more than a decade now, it has been evident that something is seriously amiss in contemporary psychiatry and clinical psychology. Under the sway of Freudian psychoanalysis, these disciplines have not validated themselves either diagnostically or therapeutically. Their practitioners, as persons, have not manifested any exceptional grasp on the virtues and strengths they purportedly help others to acquire. And the impact of their philosophy of life and conception of man in society as a whole has been subtly subversive.

Because they were the main "losers," laymen were the first to become vocal in their discontent, distrust, and cynicism. But today there is a "shaking of the foundations" in professional circles as well. For example, a state hospital superintendent recently said to me: "Yes, we too think we have a good hospital here. At least we aren't doing the patients any harm. And that's progress. In the past, we psychiatrists have often *spread* the disease we were supposedly treating."

Late in his training as a psychiatric resident, Dr. Glasser saw the futility of classical psychoanalytic procedures and began to experiment with a very different therapeutic approach, which he eventu-

From *Reality Therapy,* by William Glasser, M.D. © 1965 by William Glasser, Inc. Reprinted by permission of Harper & Row, Publishers, Inc.

ally named Reality Therapy. Rather than a mere modification or variant of Freudian analysis, this system is in many ways absolutely antithetical. At the outset of Chapter 2, six postulates are listed as characterizing most forms of professional psychotherapy now practiced in the United States and Canada, ranging from "simple counseling through nondirective therapy to orthodox psychoanalysis." These six postulates or presuppositions are: the reality of mental illness, reconstructive exploration of the patient's past, transference, an "unconscious" which must be plumbed, interpretation rather than evaluation of behavior, and change through insight and permissiveness. The extent of Dr. Glasser's break with this total tradition is indicated by the following simple but bold statement: "Reality Therapy, in both theory and practice, challenges the validity of each of these basic beliefs." Moreover, Dr. Glasser states that the "conventional therapist is taught to remain as impersonal and objective as possible and not to become involved with the patient as a separate and important person" in a patient's life. In Reality Therapy, the helping person becomes both involved with and very real to the patient in a way which would be regarded as utterly destructive of the transference as conceived and cultivated in classical analysis.

More concretely and positively, what then *is* Reality Therapy? Chapter 1 answers this question, in concise and nontechnical language; and Chapters 3 to 6 exemplify the approach as it has been applied in various contexts. In essence, it depends upon what might be called a psychiatric version of the three R's, namely, *reality, responsibility, and right-and-wrong.*

Dr. Glasser begins at the end of this formula and asks, early in Chapter 1: "What is wrong with those who need psychiatric treatment?" The answer is that they have not been satisfying their *needs*. Here it might appear that Reality Therapy and psychoanalysis have something in common, but not so. For Freud, the needs which are presumably unfulfilled, in the so-called neurotic, are those of sex and aggression. For Glasser the basic human needs are for *relatedness* and *respect*. And how does one satisfy these needs? By doing what is realistic, responsible, right.

Granted that it is not always clear precisely *what* is right and what is wrong, Dr. Glasser nevertheless holds that the ethical issue cannot be ignored. He says:

> To be worthwhile we must maintain a satisfactory standard of be-havior. To do so we must learn to correct ourselves when we do wrong and to credit ourselves when we do right. If we do not evaluate our own behavior or, having evaluated it, if we do not act to improve our conduct where it is below our standards, we will not fulfill our needs to be worthwhile and will suffer as acutely as when we fail to love or be loved. Morals, standards, values, or right and wrong behavior are all intimately related to the fulfillment of our needs for self-worth and [are] . . . a necessary part of Reality Therapy.

Conventional psychiatry and clinical psychology assume that neurosis arises because the afflicted individual's moral standards are unrealistically high, that he has not been "bad" but *too good,* and that the therapeutic task is, specifically, to counteract and neutralize conscience, "soften" the demands of a presumably too severe superego, and thus *free* the person from inhibitions and "blocks" which stand in the way of normal gratification of his "instincts." The purview of Reality Therapy is, again, very differ-ent, namely, that human beings get into emotional binds, not be-cause their standards are too high, but because their performance has been, and is, too low. As Walter Huston Clark has neatly put it, the objective of this (radically non-Freudian) type of therapy is not to lower the aim, but to increase the accomplishment. Freud held that psychological disorders arise when there has been a "cul-tural" interference with the instinctual, *biological* needs of the individual, whereas Glasser and others are now holding that the problem is rather an incapacity or failure at the interpersonal, *social* level of human functioning.

This categorical reversal of both the theory of neurosis and the intent of psychotherapy has far-flung implications. Freudian thera-pists and theorists concede, of course, that not everyone suffers from over-development of the superego. At least certain kinds of delinquents and criminals, they admit, have too little rather than too much conscience; and in the case of the very young and inex-perienced, their problem is similarly a deficit of character rather than a presumed excess. Thus, in the psychoanalytic frame of reference, two types of "therapy" are called for, the one essentially educative, the other re-educative or "corrective" in the sense of *undoing* the effects of past efforts at socialization which have presumably been "too successful." Dr. Glasser's view of the matter is quite different. He assumes that so-called neurotic and psychotic persons also suffer (although not so severely as do delinquents and frank sociopaths) from character and conduct deficiencies; and if this be the case, then all therapy is in one direction, that is, toward greater maturity, conscientiousness, responsibility. Glasser says:

Using Reality Therapy, there is no essential difference in the treatment of various psychiatric problems. As will be explained in later chapters, the treatment of psychotic veterans is almost exactly the same as the treatment of delinquent adolescent girls. The particular manifestation of irresponsibility (the diagnosis) has little relationship to the treatment. From our standpoint, all that needs to be diagnosed, no matter with what behavior he expresses it, is whether the patient is suffering from irresponsibility or from an organic illness.

Not only does this author assume that all "psychiatric problems" are alike; he also regards their treatment as of a piece with the educational enterprise in general. Thus in Chapter 6 it turns out that Reality Therapy is congenial to and readily applicable by classroom teachers in conjunction with their regular pedagogical activities (rather than contradictory to them); and it is also apparent that here is an approach to "child rearing" and "mental hygiene" which is *for* parents rather than against them. In a recent issue of *The Saturday Evening Post,* a housewife and mother complains bitterly (but justifiably) that psychiatrists have produced a "generation of parent-hating children." It could hardly have been otherwise, for the basic premise of psychoanalytic theory is that neurosis arises from too much training of children by their parents (and other teachers), so that this condition is patently the latter's "fault." Far from helping children to become more mature and accountable, this philosophy has steered young people toward ever deeper delinquency, defiance, and rejection of parents and authority.

Thus Reality Therapy is not something which should be the exclusive preoccupation or "property" of a few highly trained (and expensive) specialists. It is the appropriate, indeed the necessary, concern of *everyone,* for its precepts and principles are the foundation of successful, satisfying social life everywhere. Although Freudian psychoanalysts have been arch-critics of our mores, morals, and values, it is doubtful that they could themselves design and direct a viable society, for the very conventions and moral standards which analysts so freely criticize are precisely what keep groups and persons from "falling apart." As Professor C. Wright Mills (the sociologist) and Dr. Richard R. Parlour (a forensic psychiatrist) have recently pointed out, ethical neutrality and anomia cannot provide the *structure* of organization and power and the context of personal identity and meaning which are as essential to individuals as they are to groups. The work of the psychologist, Dr. Perry London, and of anthropologist Jules Henry adds further weight to this opinion.

Now we come to the second of the three R's, *responsibility.* What is it? Glasser says:

Responsibility, a concept basic to Reality Therapy, is defined as the ablty to fulfill one's needs, and to do so in *a way that does not deprive others of the ability to fulfill their needs. . . .* A responsible person also does that which gives him a feeling of self-worth and a feeling that he is worthwhile to others. He is motivated to strive and perhaps endure privation to attain self-worth. When a responsible man says that he will perform a job for us, he will try to accomplish what was asked, both for us and so that he may gain a measure of self-worth for himself. An irresponsible person may or may not do what he says, depending upon how he feels, the effort he has to make, and what is in it for him. He gains neither our respect nor his own, and in time he will suffer or cause others to suffer.

In a recent article, Dr. Glasser has expressed the same general point of view by saying: "People do not act irresponsibly because they are 'ill'; they are 'ill' because they act irresponsibly." This is an emphasis which has been almost totally absent in classical psychoanalysis. For Freud and his many followers, the neurotic's problem is not irresponsibility but lack of "insight." However, many clinicians have discovered that years of analytic questing for this objective often results in less concrete change in a patient's life than a few weeks of work on the problem of personal responsibility, consistency, accountability. (This is confirmed in the writings of Dr. Steve Pratt on the concept of *social contract* and its relation to what Professor Leonard Cottrell has termed "interpersonal competence.") In other words, it's not "insight," "understanding," and "freedom" that the neurotic needs but *commitment*. In the words of an old hymn, our petition can appropriately be:

> Holy Spirit, Right Divine, Truth within my conscience reign,
> Be my King that I may be, firmly bound, forever free.

In keeping with this way of thinking about responsibility, what is to be said about honesty, truthfulness, and integrity? As long as one assumes that the neurotic is typically over-trained in moral matters and that his condition is not in any way dependent upon decisions he himself has made and actions he has taken but is rather an expression of things that have been *done to* him, then the very possibility that dishonesty enters into the picture in any very significant way is excluded, both logically and practically. But when the so-called "sick" person is himself seen as accountable for much of his malaise, dishonesty begins to figure much more prominently. In this book there is not a great deal of explicit emphasis on getting persons who are undergoing therapy to speak the truth; but the therapist himself sets an example of personal openness and integrity, and it is hard to imagine that anyone can learn to be either responsible or realistic without also being truthful. In fact, anyone who makes a practice of misinforming others (and thus being irresponsible), eventually begins to lie to himself, in the sense of rationalizing and excusing his own deviant behavior; and when this happens, he begins to be unrealistic, to "lose contact" with reality.

In light of the widespread and growing interest today in *group* therapy, it may appear to some readers of this book that Dr. Glasser is still too much wedded to individual treatment. Such an impression is misleading. Most of the work at the Ventura School for Girls which is here described involves group methods, as does the work of Dr. G. L. Harrington at the Los Angeles Veterans' Administration Hospital and that of Dr. Willard A. Mainord at the Western State Hospital, in Washington, which are also prominently featured in this book. One of the great advantages of the group approach is that it encourages the development of rectitude, responsibility, and realism so much more rapidly than do the conventional forms of individual treatment.

Now what *is* realism, reality? Although this concept is crucial to Dr. Glasser's approach, in some ways it is the most difficult of all to pin down specifically. Two statements which bear directly on this problem follow:

> In their unsuccessful effort to fulfill their needs, no matter what behavior they choose, all patients have a common characteristic: *They all deny the reality of the world around them.* Some break the law, denying the rules of society; some claim their neighbors are plotting against them, denying the improbability of such behavior. Some are afraid of crowded places, close quarters, airplanes, or elevators, yet they freely admit the irrationality of their fears. Millions drink to blot out the inadequacy they feel but that need not exist if they could learn to be different; and far too many people choose suicide rather than face the reality that they could solve their problems by more responsible behavior. Whether it is a partial denial or the total blotting out of all reality of the chronic back-ward patient in the state hospital, the denial of some or all of reality is common to all patients. Therapy will be successful when they are able to give up denying the world and to recognize that reality not only exists but that they must fulfill their needs within its framework.
>
> . . . The therapist who accepts excuses, ignores reality, or allows the patient to blame his present unhappiness on a parent or on an emotional disturbance can usually make his patient feel good temporarily at the price of evading responsibility. He is only giving the patient "psychiatric kicks," which are no different from the brief kicks he may have obtained from alcohol, pills, or sympathetic friends before consulting the psychiatrist. When they fade, as they soon must, the patient with good reason becomes disillusioned with psychiatry.

Although implied by and embedded in Reality Therapy as a whole, there is a way of thinking about the question of what is and what is not "realistic" which can and perhaps should be made more explicit. From one point of view, it can be argued that all experience is reality of a kind. Phenomenologically, there is certainly nothing *un*real about illicit or perverse sexual behavior, criminal activities, or the total life style of persons we call neurotic or even psychotic. Literally everything that happens is reality. Therefore, some special principle or dimension is needed to make the distinction between reality and irreality fully meaningful. In short-run perspective, there is something "realistic" and "good"— in the sense of pleasurable—about all perverse, criminal, or defensive behavior. Otherwise it simply would not occur. But more precisely speaking, action can be called realistic or unrealistic only when its *remote* as well as immediate consequences are taken into consideration and compared, weighed. If the evil, pain, suffering which ultimately occur as a result of a given action exceed the immediate satisfaction which it produced, that action may be termed unrealistic; whereas, if the satisfaction which ultimately occurs as a result of an action is greater than the immediate effort or sacrifice associated with it, such an action can be called realistic. In the final analysis, it is the capacity to choose wisely between these two types of behavior that we call *reason;* and it is, I think, what the Chicago columnist, Sidney Harris, had in mind when he once characterized the truly educated man as one who knows and can properly appraise the *consequences* of his actions. It is what Alfred Korzybski meant when he spoke of the human capacity for *time-binding;* and it is what I have previously denoted by the expression, *temporal integration.* It is also, I believe, what Dr. Glasser implies when he says, in one of the passages already quoted: "A responsible person . . . is motivated to *strive* and perhaps *endure privation.* . . . An irresponsible person . . . gains neither our respect nor his own, and *in time* he will suffer or cause others to suffer" (italics added).

In a paper entitled "Formations Regarding the Two Principles of Mental Functioning" which appeared in 1911, Freud made a clear distinction between what he called the pleasure principle and the reality principle; and again the distinguishing criterion was a temporal one. However, while praising the reality principle, Freud propounded a therapeutic technique which, paradoxically, glorifies pleasure and permissiveness. It was not that Freud recommended that we totally surrender to the sway of pleasure and live entirely in the present. Rather, his argument was that "conventional morality" is unrealistic in the sense of making more demands for re-

straint and "repression" than are actually necessary. Thus he
pleaded for what he termed an "intermediate course." He said:

> We [analysts] are not reformers . . .; we are merely observers; but
> we cannot avoid observing with critical eyes, and we have found it im-
> possible to give our support to conventional morality [which] demands
> more sacrifices than it is worth. We do not absolve our patients from
> listening to these criticisms . . . and if after they have become inde-
> pendent by the effects of the treatment they choose some intermediate
> course . . ., our conscience is not burdened whatever the outcome.

Thus the crucial question is: Was Freud's conception of neurosis correct or incorrect? For a generation we have assumed that his
diagnosis of the problem was essentially sound. Today we are not
particularly pleased with the results of treatment predicated on this
view; and Dr. Glasser has given us what I believe is the best
description to date of a radically different approach. Here the
assumption, as we have already seen, is that all "clinical types"
represent *under*-socialization and that therapy, to be consistent
and effective, must in all cases be directed toward getting the
individual to be *more* responsible, *more* realistic, in the sense of
being willing to make immediate sacrifices for long-term (one may
almost say lifelong) satisfactions and gains. Some persons do not
live long enough to reap the full harvest of their virtue—and this
we all recognize as a form of *tragedy*. But the reverse situation is
folly. The trouble with "Eat, drink and be merry, for tomorrow we
die" is that we usually *don't* die tomorrow but instead live on to
reap only too fully the negative consequences of shortsighted
pleasure seeking. The habitual drunkard does not have to be very
old to have lived too long, and it is no accident that he so often
either attempts or successfully commits suicide.

Thus the therapeutic problem, basically, is that of getting another person to abandon what may be called the *primitive* pleasure
principle and to adopt that long-term, enlightened, *wise* pursuit of
pleasure, satisfaction, joy, happiness which the reality principle
implies. An immediate, assured source of pleasure is never willingly given up for a larger but uncertain remote satisfaction. And
an essential aspect of therapy, as of all education, all socialization
is that of providing the immature person with some compensation,

some substitute satisfaction for the one he is being asked, in his own long-term best interests, to give up. In the ordinary socialization of children, parental love serves this function. In his description of Reality Therapy, Dr. Glasser calls it *involvement,* of which he says:

Usually the most difficult phase of therapy is the first, the gaining of the involvement that the patient so desperately needs but which he has been unsuccessful in attaining or maintaining up to the time he comes for treatment. Unless the requisite involvement exists between the necessarily responsible therapist and the irresponsible patient, there can be no therapy. The guiding principles of Reality Therapy are directed toward achieving the proper involvement, a completely honest, human relationship in which the patient, for perhaps the first time in his life, realizes that someone cares enough about him not only to accept him but to help him fulfill his needs in the real world.

. . . How does the therapist become involved with a patient so that the patient can begin to fulfill his needs? The therapist has a difficult task, for he must quickly build a firm emotional relationship with a patient who has failed to establish such relationships in the past. He is aided by recognizing that the patient is desperate for involvement and is suffering because he is not able to fulfill his needs. The patient is looking for a person with whom he can become emotionally involved, someone he can care about and who he can be convinced cares about him, someone who can convince the patient that he will stay with him until he can better fulfill his needs.

For some readers, the foregoing discussion of involvement will be reminiscent of the psychoanalytic concept of transference, but there are marked differences, both in regard to method and objective. Psychoanalytic transference is said to be best achieved when the therapist remains inexplicit and shadowy as a person, onto whom the patient can "project" his neurotic, harsh, unrealistic, anxiety-arousing expectations of all authoritative "father figures." The therapist then, at strategic points, "reveals" himself as really kind, accepting, permissive, and in this way supposedly brings about the needed modification, or "softening," of the superego. By contrast, the objective of Reality Therapy is to support and strengthen, never to weaken, the functioning of conscience; and the method of choice involves honesty, concern, personal authenticity, and confrontation of the kind Dr. Glasser describes.

But is there not an ultimate and fatal paradox here? How can one hold that a neurotic or otherwise "delinquent" person is "responsible" and at the same time take the position that such a person needs or can benefit from treatment? Does not the very concept of treatment, or help, imply a certain helplessness and *lack* or responsibility on the part of the person who is "in trouble"? Language can at this point play an insidious trick on us if we are not extremely careful. The difficulty in the case of the irresponsible (neurotic, delinquent) person is precisely that he is *not* acting responsibly; and his great need is that of learning to behave *more* responsibly and thus *better* fulfill his own long-term needs—as well as those of society as a whole. In the present volume, Dr. Glasser is not saying that patients are *responsible for* what has happened in the past; instead, he is saying that they have not been, and are not now, *living responsibly*. There's a great difference between these two statements. And therapeutic (educative) influence from whatever quarter ought to be in the direction of helping patients improve their capacity and desire to live more responsibly, prudently, wisely from now on. Thus the concept of responsibility, far from implying or stressing the evil in man is rather one which sees and builds upon his potentialities *for good;* and it is therefore decidedly optimistic and hopeful rather than cynical or pessimistic.

Enough has now been said to show that Reality Therapy is "different." Now we must ask: Is it also *better?* Clinical evidence from several sources is cited in this book which strongly suggests an affirmative answer. No one, at this point, is claiming that the evidence is definitive. But as a research psychologist I can attest that there is today much additional supporting data of a thoroughly empirical nature and that the premises of Reality Therapy are rapidly gaining credence in many quarters. Its promise for the future therefore seems to be very bright, and the present volume fills a real need for a simply written and yet clinically informed and sophisticated description of this approach and its working assumptions. The reader will enjoy the author's clear, lively style of writing and will profit from an account which, I predict, is destined to arouse much popular as well as scientific interest.

Notes on Reality Therapy

There are major differences, both in theory and practice, between Reality Therapy and what is widely accepted as conventional psychotherapy. Conventional therapy, based either strictly or loosely upon the psychoanalytic beliefs and teachings of Sigmund Freud, is taught in almost every major college and university in the United States and Canada. Whether it is practiced in an orthodox, Freudian setting in a Park Avenue psychoanalyst's office or in a loosely structured college counseling service, it embodies the following:

1. Conventional psychiatry believes firmly that *mental illness exists,* that people who suffer from it can be meaningfully classified, and that attempts should be made to treat them according to the diagnostic classification.

2. Conventional psychiatry holds that an essential part of treatment is *probing into the patient's past life*—searching for the psychological roots of his problem because once the patient clearly understands these roots he can use his understanding to change his attitude toward life. From this change in attitude he can then develop more effective patterns of living that will solve his psychological difficulties.

3. Conventional psychiatry maintains that the patient must *transfer to the therapist* attitudes he held or still holds toward

A condensation published in *Cosmopolitan* from the book *Reality Therapy,* © 1965 by William Glasser, Inc. Published by Harper & Row, Publishers, Inc.

important people in his past life, people around whom his problems started. Using this concept, called transference, the therapist relives with the patient his past difficulties and then explains to him how he is repeating the same inadequate behavior with the therapist. The patient, through the therapist's interpretations of the transference behavior, gains insight into his past. His newly attained insight allows him to give up his old attitudes and to learn to relate to people in a better way, solving his problems.

4. Conventional psychotherapy, even in superficial counseling, emphasizes that if the patient is to change he must gain *understanding and insight* into his unconscious mind. Unconscious mental conflicts are considered more important than conscious problems; making the patient aware of them through the interpretation of transference, dreams and free associations, and through educated psychiatric guessing, is necessary if therapy is to succeed.

5. Necessarily accompanying the conviction that mental illness exists, conventional psychiatry scrupulously *avoids the problem of morality,* that is, whether the patient's behavior is right or wrong. Deviant behavior is considered a product of the mental illness, and the patient should not be held morally responsible because he is considered helpless to do anything about it. Once the illness is cured through the procedures described in Points 2, 3 and 4, the patient will then be able to behave according to the rules of society.

6. *Teaching people to behave better* is *not* considered an important part of therapy in conventional psychiatry, which holds the patients will learn better behavior themselves once they understand both the historical and unconscious sources of their problems.

Using these six essential convictions as a basis for both psychiatric theory and practice, conventional psychiatry may appear in many forms from simple counseling through nondirective therapy to orthodox psychoanalysis, but in every situation almost everyone who does therapy in the United States and Canada today would concur with these six criteria. Although some people might place more emphasis upon one than another, usually they stand unchallenged.

Reality Therapy in both theory and practice challenges the validity of each of these basic beliefs. Let's examine each concept in detail and show how Reality Therapy differs from the therapy that has been so widely accepted for so many years.

One overall difference between Reality Therapy and conventional psychiatry must be emphasized. This is the difference between the involvement necessary for Reality Therapy and the involvement necessary for conventional therapy. In Reality Therapy, achieving the proper involvement is absolutely essential. The conventional therapist is taught to remain as impersonal and objective as possible and not to become involved with the patient as a separate and important person in the patient's life. Rather, he is to strive for the transference relationship briefly described under Point 3 above.

The way Reality Therapy differs from conventional therapy on each of the six points to be discussed contributes to the major difference in involvement. The six points may be considered briefly from the standpoint of involvement.

1. Because we *do not accept the concept of mental illness,* the patient cannot become involved with us as a mentally ill person who has no responsibility for his behavior.

2. Working in the present and toward the future, we *do not get involved with the patient's history* because we can neither change what happened to him nor accept the fact that he is limited by his past.

3. We relate to patients as *ourselves,* not as transference figures.

4. We *do not look for unconscious conflicts* or the reasons for them. A patient cannot become involved with us by excusing his behavior on the basis of unconscious motivations.

5. *We emphasize the morality of behavior.* We face the issue of right and wrong which we believe solidifies the involvement, in contrast to conventional psychiatrists who do not make the distinction between right and wrong, feeling it would be detrimental to attaining the transference relationship they seek.

6. *We teach patients better ways to fulfill their needs.* The

proper involvement will not be maintained unless the patient is helped to find more satisfactory patterns of behavior. Conventional therapists do not feel that teaching better behavior is a part of therapy.

In the detailed discussion to follow, it will be clear that each of the six points of difference between Reality Therapy and conventional psychiatry contributes to the difference between the way we become involved with our patients and how conventional psychiatrists relate to theirs.

From a treatment standpoint, both the theory and practice of Reality Therapy are incompatible with the prevalent, widely accepted concept of mental illness. We believe that this concept, the belief that people can and do suffer from some specific, diagnosable, treatable mental illness, analogous to a specific, diagnosable, treatable physical illness, is inaccurate and that this inaccuracy is a major roadblock to proper psychiatric treatment.

Those who believe in mental illness assume incorrectly that something definite is wrong with the patient which causes him to be the way he is. Most psychiatrists believe that the patient was all right at one time and then fell victim to a series of unhappy life experiences which now cause his deviant behavior. When these experiences are exposed and resolved through conventional psychotherapy, the mentally ill person will recover in much the same way that the physically ill person recovers from a strep throat when the penicillin kills the streptococcus. We believe this concept misleads the doctor, the patient and those concerned with him into the false belief that the doctor's job is to treat some definite condition, after which the patient will get well. This attitude was graphically illustrated by a patient whom I treated some years ago, an imposing woman who sat down, looked directly at me and stated in all sincerity, "I'm here, Doctor. Do psychiatry!"

We believe that throughout their lives people constantly strive to fulfill their needs. Any time in their lives when they are unsuccessful in doing so, they behave unrealistically. Very strong people may behave unrealistically only under extreme stress; others may do so under less adverse conditions, sometimes from an early age, indicating a lifelong inability to form a satisfying relationship with a responsible person.

Those who believe in mental illness try to remove some specific internal psychological cause (the often heard "root of the problem") which they believe is responsible for the patient's present deviant behavior. Conventional psychiatry, almost without fail, relates this cause to instances in his previous life when the patient was unable to cope with stress. We believe that there is no noxious psychological causative agent to remove. *Our job is to help the patient help himself to fulfill his needs right now.* If there is a medical analogy which applies to psychiatric problems, it is not illness but weakness. While illness can be cured by removing the causative agent, weakness can be cured only by strengthening the existing body to cope with the stress of the world, large or small as this stress may be.

By dispensing with the idea of mental illness and calling a man irresponsible, and then describing how he is irresponsible, Reality Therapy defines the situation much more precisely. Using the latter description, it is apparent that the cause of the psychiatric patient's condition is different from that of a patient with a physical illness, who is more truly the victim of forces outside himself. Regardless of past circumstances, the psychiatric patient must develop the strength to take the responsibility to fulfill his needs satisfactorily. Treatment, therefore, is not to give him understanding of past misfortunes that caused his "illness," but to help him to function in a better way right now.

Psychiatrists discovered long ago that as much as they would have liked to follow the medical parallel and cure the patient of his brain disease, they were unable to do so because no brain pathology existed. Instead of giving up the illness concept, psychiatrists seized on the discovery of unconscious conflicts as the cause of mental illness. It was the conflicts that caused patients to be the way they are, mentally ill. Patients are led on long, expensive trips back through their childhood, often discovering that mother was the cause of it all. Once the patient is helped to wrest his childhood resentments against mother from his unconscious mind, cure is theoretically in sight.

For example, an obese young woman who has a compulsive overeating problem may find out through psychotherapy that her mother wanted a more beautiful daughter. Because obesity in a young woman is never desirable, she overeats in order to avoid facing the truth that her mother would reject her even if she were slim. She can accept the mother's rejection because she is indeed fat and unattractive, perhaps so much so that her mother and others may give her sympathy, if not acceptance. In traditional therapy, being accepted as mentally ill and having learned why, the patient will attempt to throw herself upon the therapist. Learning from him that the source of the problem is past and present unresolved conflict with her mother, she continues to eat, her appetite undiminished by this knowledge. This not-uncommon situation, where the unchanging fat and miserable patient damns her mother for years in psychotherapy, has discredited psychiatry in the minds of many people. Under these too-familiar circumstances, where the mental illness is accepted and the cause is sought and discovered to be outside herself (in this case her mother's rejection), the patient is relieved of the necessary responsibility for her part in the therapy. The fat girl's only chance of being helped is to learn that she is irresponsible, not that she is mentally ill, and that her unattractiveness is important primarily to her. Her mother is only an excuse for her irresponsibility. To help this girl we must scrupulously avoid giving her excuses for the way she is, but rather help her give up excusing her inability to fulfill her needs and guide her toward the reality that she must fulfill them regardless of her mother.

Also misleading but an important part of the mental illness concept is the use of psychiatric diagnoses to label a wide variety of "mental illnesses." The purpose of diagnosis is to select proper treatment. If we diagnose that a headache is caused by a brain tumor, a logical sequence of treatment is suggested. The treatment, which often includes brain surgery, is far different from the treatment that might be given to a severe headache caused by eyestrain or alcoholic hangover. Where treatment logically and necessarily follows diagnosis, correct diagnosis is vital; in the case of so-called mental illnesses, however, treatment by any one doctor, whether psychoanalyst or Reality Therapist, is essentially the same. Psychotherapy lacks the specific and individual treatment that follows the diagnosis of scarlet fever, syphilis or malaria.

Using Reality Therapy, there is no essential difference in the treatment of various psychiatric problems. The treatment of psychotics is almost exactly the same as the treatment of delinquent adolescent girls. The particular manifestation of irresponsibility (the diagnosis) has little relationship to the treatment. From our standpoint, all that needs to be diagnosed is whether the patient is suffering from irresponsibility, no matter with what behavior he expresses it, or from an organic illness.

Necessarily closely related to eliminating the concept of mental illness is the somewhat more radical idea of dispensing with any major inquiry into the patient's past history, ordinarily considered as essential to psychiatry as the scalpel is to the surgeon. Both professional and lay people often ask us, "How can there be any therapy if the therapist does not probe deeply into the patient's past life and uncover each twist and turn?" Light must be cast on each dark corner in the patient's previous life or you cannot help him.

Without denying that the patient had an unsatisfactory past, we find that to look for what went wrong does not help him. What good comes from discovering that you are afraid to assert yourself because you had a domineering father? Both patient and therapist can be aware of this historical occurrence, they can discuss it in all of its ramifications for years, but the knowledge will not help the patient assert himself now. In fact, in our experience the more he knows why he cannot assert himself, the less inclined he will be to do so because he now understands that self-assertion is psychologically painful. Most patients will then lean on the psychiatrist, saying, "Now that I know why I can't assert myself, what will make me lose the fear?" The psychiatrist's reply is necessarily weak. "You don't have to be afraid because your father is no longer in the picture." It would be wonderful if therapy were that simple, that knowing the root of the fear would allow the patient to become unafraid. In Reality Therapy it makes little difference what relationship the patient had with his father. We want to know what is going on *now* in all aspects of his life.

A further important difference between Reality Therapy and conventional psychiatry concerns the place of morality, or to be more specific, the place of right and wrong in the process of therapy. Conventional psychiatry does not directly concern itself with the issue of right and wrong. Rather, it contends that once the patient is able to resolve his conflicts and get over his mental illness, he will be able to behave correctly. We have found that this view is unrealistic. All society is based on morality, and if the important people in the patient's life, especially his therapist, do not discuss whether his behavior is right or wrong, reality cannot be brought home to him. It is unrealistic to ask a delinquent girl why she stole a car, why she is pregnant, why she smokes marijuana, hoping that once she discovers the reasons she will be able to resolve her conflicts and change her behavior. We believe that to stop her unsatisfactory behavior she must fulfill her needs, but that to fulfill her needs she must face the real world around her which includes standards of behavior.

Admittedly, the introduction of morality into psychotherapy may draw criticism from many sources. Some people argue that a great strength of conventional psychiatry is that it does not involve itself with this age-old question. It would be easier for us if we could avoid the issue also, but we cannot. People come to therapy suffering because they behave in ways that do not fulfill their needs, and they ask if their behavior is wrong. Our job is to face this question, confront them with their total behavior, and *get them to judge* the quality of what they are doing. We have found that unless they judge their own behavior, they will not change. We do not claim that we have discovered the key to universal right or that we are experts in ethics. We do believe, however, that to the best of our ability as responsible human beings, we must help our patients arrive at some decision concerning the moral quality of their behavior. To do so, we have found that for the purpose of therapy the following definition seems to be extremely useful. (Whether our definition could stand the test of scholarly debate with the great moral philosophers of the world is questionable, but at least it has provided us with some framework upon which to focus our therapy discussions.) We believe that almost all behavior which leads to fulfilling our needs within the bounds of reality is right, or good, or moral behavior, according to the following definition: *When a man acts in such a way that he gives and receives love, and feels worthwhile to himself and others, his behavior is right or moral.*

When a person is able to fulfill his need to feel worthwhile to himself and others, there is little conflict over whether his behavior is right, but in many instances the needs are in conflict and it is much more difficult to arrive at the correct course of behavior. For example, when a chief of state gives up his position, or a potential chief of state reduces his chances for election, because of love, who is really to say that he did right or wrong? Both Edward VIII of England and, more recently, Governor Nelson Rockefeller of New York faced a problem in which there is no absolutely responsible course. In a famous historical example, Socrates chose death rather than life with diminished self-respect, even though he had the assurance of love from friends who urged his escape. A more common situation is one in which a man, discovering his son to be guilty of a crime, is torn between reporting his child or losing his own self-respect. It is possible to think of hundreds of these moral dilemmas, but it must be made clear that responsible people who are caught in a serious conflict of needs rarely consult a psychiatrist. They recognize that it is up to them to decide what to do.

A Reality Therapist treating a patient is not afraid to pose the question, "Are you doing right or wrong?" or, "Are you taking the responsible course?" In psychiatric treatment, strengthening the patient's recognition that his present behavior is wrong or irresponsible is a powerful motivation toward positive change. When we point out what the patient is doing may be wrong instead of helping him look for excuses, he finds out that therapy is not an intellectual psychiatric game of conflict, conflict, what can be the conflict? He discovers that we really care about him, an essential step toward gaining the involvement necessary for therapy. Therefore, in order to do therapy successfully, the therapist must acknowledge that standards of behavior exist, standards accepted by both individuals and society as the best means of meeting basic human needs. Patients must be confronted by the disparity between the values they recognize as the acceptable norm and the lives they lead.

For example, many delinquent girls maintain that there is nothing wrong with prostitution. Rather than argue, I ask if they would help their daughters become prostitutes. They always answer, "No," but in the next breath they protest that prostitution is the only way they can earn a living—it's all they know.

Getting a patient to acknowledge the values she really believes in is part of the art of therapy, but once acknowledged the major task is to help her live by these standards. Unfortunately, in their effort to avoid the issue of morality, many conventional therapists accept behavior that does not lead to need fulfillment in the mistaken belief that this is the best effort the patient is capable of making.

Where standards and values are not stressed, the most that therapy can accomplish is to help patients become more comfortable in their irresponsibility. Because our effort is always directed toward helping patients fulfill their needs, we insist on their striving to reach the highest possible standards.

We are looking for neither conformity nor mediocrity in the guise of normal behavior. The most responsible men, such as Lincoln or Schweitzer, are those furthest from the norm. Our job is not to lessen the pain of irresponsible actions but to increase the patient's strength so that he can bear the necessary pain of a full life as well as enjoy the rewards of a deeply responsible existence.

The final major difference between Reality Therapy and conventional therapy is our emphasis upon the therapist's role as a teacher. In conventional therapy teaching is limited to helping the patient gain insight into the causes of his behavior. From then on it is assumed that he will either learn better ways himself or from someone else; the therapist's job is limited to making clear the conscious and unconscious determinants of his problems. In Reality Therapy we do not search for the insights so vital to conventional psychiatry. Instead we take every opportunity to teach patients better ways to fulfill their needs. We spend much time painstakingly examining the patient's daily activity and suggesting better ways for him to behave. We answer the many questions that patients ask and suggest ways to solve problems and approach people. Patients who have not been able to fulfill their needs must learn both how to approach people so that they can become more involved and how to accomplish enough so that they can gain an increased feeling of self-worth.

If, analogous to conventional therapy, which stops with insight, Reality Therapy stopped when we succeeded in getting the patient to face reality, our work would be less effective. As important as confronting reality is, it is only part of therapy. The patient must learn to fulfill his needs in the real world he has learned about, and we must teach him how whenever we can. Once involvement is gained and reality is faced, therapy becomes a special kind of education, a learning to live more effectively, which is better and more quickly achieved if the therapist accepts the role of teacher.

To summarize, Reality Therapy is not another variety of the same approach but a different way to work with people. The requirements of Reality Therapy—an intense personal involvement, facing reality and rejecting irresponsible behavior, and learning better ways to behave—bear little resemblance to conventional therapy and produce markedly different results.

How Reality Therapy Works: Two Case Histories

Recently, Margaret, a patient who had been coming once a week for a year, asked to come every other week because she felt so much better able to cope with the world than she had in the past. When I agreed that she was ready to come less often, she tried to put into words what had happened that led to her doing so much better. She found it difficult saying, "I'm the same, but I'm different. I've gotten no great insights. [She had been in traditional therapy looking for these insights for two years before coming to me.] We seemed to have talked very little of what was important, but now I feel much better, and many things that I couldn't do, I am now able to do well." She asked me if I knew what had

happened. I told her that we talked about what was really important, that I had always pointed out reality, and that I had never
accepted her irrationality, promiscuity or depression as excusable
ways of coping with her world. Rather than looking for *why* she
was the way she was, I had made sure that she knew *what* she was
doing. Margaret was motivated to change and able to change *because* nothing dramatic had been dredged from her subconscious,
because her irresponsible past had been left alone, and *because* her
fits of depression and promiscuous acting-out had not been excessively discussed. The issues at center stage in usual therapy had
been side issues in Reality Therapy. Emphasized were her daily
behavior, *what* she did rather than what she felt, and whether she
could do better. Because I refused to change my approach when
she related her checkered past and erratic present, she was able to
become involved with me, sensing that for once in her life she was
with someone who seriously expected her to act better and who
was not afraid to let her know his expectation whether or not it
might upset her.

There were, of course, some emotional outbursts, threats to end
everything, to leave town, to quit her job, to run home to her
mother, or to go back to her family in New York, all really threats
to leave therapy. In response to her threats, I asked, "How will
this action help you?" I could not help her work out her problems
unless she stayed in therapy. She was testing me. Would I become
involved with her misery, or would I continue to show confidence
in her ability to do better? Through such give-and-take we became
sufficiently involved for her to begin to fulfill her needs. I told her
to move from a shabby furnished room into a nice apartment and
buy a few decent pieces of furniture. "Even if you feel bad," I
suggested, "you don't have to live so badly." When she mentioned
a possible promotion, I told her to work for it rather than to look
around constantly for excuses to quit. Eventually she did make a
menial office job into a considerably better, even desirable job.

No longer frantically scrambling for love, she is waiting for
good friendships to build, and slowly accomplishing a few things
well. No one would describe her as happy because she hasn't that
much to be happy about, but she is no longer painfully unhappy.

Her depressions came much less often, her psychosomatic gastro-intestinal complaints have stopped, and she has weeks when she feels fairly comfortable. Even though she is a divorced woman with few friends in a strange city, she is gaining the strength to live a new life, finding not happiness perhaps but periods of peace, a new experience for her. Although she said, "Nothing really happened," we both know that all of therapy is what happened. It is this "all"—the involvement, the facing of reality, the learning better ways—that was almost impossible for her to put into words, yet it is this "all" that is therapy.

Perhaps another example will help clarify what happens in therapy. Rob came to me from a university psychiatric clinic where he had been in treatment for a year because he was failing in school, feeling depressed and complaining bitterly that his home situation was miserable and that he felt lost in the world. The resident psychiatrist was leaving, and the social worker to whom the case was referred asked me if I could see him at a reduced fee; she recognized his need for a long period of therapy with one therapist, which the clinic was unable to provide.

At nineteen Rob was despondent because he was failing in his freshman year at college, he hadn't the vaguest idea where he was heading, and he felt that life was empty. Blaming his failure on his mother and stepfather, in therapy he had hoped to find out why he was the way he was, and counted upon gaining the understanding that could change his life. After a year of conventional treatment he thought of therapy as an intellectual exercise rather than an opportunity to become involved with someone whom he cared about and who cared about him. His intellectual approach had served to keep him from getting close enough to anyone to become involved.

At our first meeting, I told Rob that I would see him once a week and that we would work on his school difficulties first. This brief statement told him that his problems were not insoluble and that I was interested in working with him. The involvement started with this simple but necessary statement. An agreement to see the patient and to help him solve his problems is basic to beginning therapy. Even with a patient who is out of contact with reality, as in a mental hospital, or violently resistant to psychiatric treatment, as a delinquent adolescent often is, this much has to be stated and then carried out with force if necessary. Whether he came to therapy voluntarily or was brought there forcibly, the patient must hear expressed the idea, *"I will see you until you can become better able to fulfill your needs."*

Next we had to settle on the fee. Although Rob's mother told him that she could pay $10 a week, I questioned her ability to do so, knowing the family's financial condition. Could he pay half himself? He was working in the college library and earning more than $12 a week. Would he be willing to pay $5 toward his therapy? By agreeing, he took several further steps toward becoming involved. First, through my suggestion, he could be less dependent upon his mother which, at age nineteen, he certainly desired to be. In turn she would be less burdened by him, which she wanted but which she was afraid of because she didn't want him to leave her, either physically or emotionally. Insecure in her third marriage, she was not ready to let go of him. Sharing the cost was beneficial to both of them; my suggestion had set the stage for him to fulfill his needs independently of her.

The therapist cannot get involved with the patient unless he is different from everyone else in the patient's life. Rob's failures were symptomatic of his lack of need fulfillment; no one in the past had been successful in getting properly involved with him. But his failures were the best he had been able to do, they seemed important to him, and he wanted to tell me about them in detail. In doing so he was trying to gain my sympathy. If I had listened then to all this "psychiatric garbage," as I like to call an unhappy past, I would have necessarily assumed a superior role. A person feels inferior when he tells of his failures and misfortunes unless he is closely involved with the listener. Rob and I were not nearly close enough at this time, so I did not fall into the common psychiatric trap in which the patient, through his miserable life history, degrades himself before the therapist.

Instead I took the initiative. I asked him to tell me his plan (a favorite Reality Therapy question). Asking him for his plan tells him that he should have a plan, or at least start thinking of one, putting him in a position where, instead of unburdening his troubles, he should begin some constructive thinking about what he is doing right now and about his future. He reacted typically by asking, "What plan, what do you have in mind?" I said, "Well, here you are at college. You must have a plan, or a goal, some place you are heading for, some idea of how to get there." At least he might have an aspiration, something we could discuss. My open question does not tie him to a concrete plan; rather I was telling him that he could bare his aspirations to me. I would listen and help direct him toward fulfillment of these aspirations if in reality they were at all possible. Still he resisted. He wanted to talk about his mother, his hated stepfather, his hated little brother, and his hated previous stepfather. These subjects were easy for him, they excused his failures, but they would lead nowhere. I reassured him by saying that we could talk about his family at any time. I wanted now to talk about what he had in mind for himself, what he could do that would lead to a satisfactory future. I wanted the focus upon him, not upon others, because only he could solve his problems.

Although this unexpected shift in attitude from that of the previous therapist, who had listened to his miseries, was hard for him to comprehend, he quickly recognized that I cared very much about him and what he could do. He began to express some thoughts that he had not dared to voice in the past: what he might really do if he could overcome the obstacles he thought were in his way, particularly the failure he felt he was in college. I said, "Forget the past. Grades can be improved, courses can be retaken. But even assuming," I continued, "all your grades were A's and B's, where would you want to go?" He had said before, "I don't know, I really don't know." But this answer was not the truth. Although he did want to be an educated professional man, he had spent so much time failing, groping and feeling sorry for his condition and for others like him (in his pseudoliberal compassion for others, which really is feeling sorry for himself), so much time blaming the world and generally wallowing in his own inadequacy and misery, that he was surprised to find that he seemed almost afraid to hope. He was not involved enough with responsible people to have a plan or even to express a hope for fear that the actual expression might blow his hope away. I told him, "If you can't come up with a plan yourself, we'll start by figuring one out together. You think about it and I will too."

The stage was now set for therapy. We could talk about almost anything because any subject might lead to a plan for him. He was young, intelligent, physically in good condition, in a good college, and there were no serious restrictions to what he might become. He had rarely talked to a responsible adult, and never to one with whom he was involved, about the world in general. We found much to talk about; in addition to many general subjects, we talked about what he was doing now at school and at home. The conversation concerning his personal life was always directed toward what he was doing rather than his opinions about what was happening to him because of his mother, stepfather or his professors.

Our conversations were not dramatic. They were earnest discussions between two people, one of whom had problems to solve because he was irresponsible, the other, a responsible person interested in helping him solve these problems. As part of the discussions, I told him about my early college days, what I did, where I failed, where I succeeded, and what I learned in the process. I was not putting myself in his shoes or being condescending, I was telling him honestly what had happened to me and how I arrived where I am. He was interested and he appreciated my openness and my warmth. The involvement grew, and as it did, I began to read his papers, to discuss his homework and to talk over his tests. I also suggested that he seek out his stepfather, get to know him, try to see his point of view and appreciate his problems in trying to head a family with two jealous stepsons. Acting on my suggestion, he was able to talk to his stepfather and began to see him in a better light. They have since become very close. As his life improved, I was able to point out what he was doing to produce the changes that we both recognized.

For the first time he began searching for a specific goal. It was not surprising that he brought up medicine, although he immediately said that it would be impossible for him to become a doctor.

He could never pass the technical subjects—chemistry, physics, math or biology—nor could he afford to go to medical school even if, by some miracle, he were accepted. He thought of himself as a liberal arts student, a thinker, an appreciator of intellectual discussion, the social sciences and the fine arts. Technical subjects had specific answers, and he was afraid of situations that called for being specific. It had never occurred to him that technical subjects might be easy if one approached them reasonably and without fear; in a sense they were easier than liberal arts subjects which did not have definite answers. In high school he only took those scientific subjects required for graduation. As a college freshman he almost failed chemistry, finally dropping the course. As his plans began to form, we continued to discuss various possibilities. Agreeing that medicine was a remote goal, I nevertheless suggested that we shouldn't rule it out. He said he would like to work with people, perhaps pointing toward social work by majoring in sociology. Generally approving of this plan, I added that medical schools were searching just as much for candidates educated in the social sciences as for those trained in the physical and biological sciences. Perhaps he might satisfy the minimum requirements for medicine while majoring in sociology. This was the final plan. Knowing where he was going, he lost his fear of technical subjects and school was no longer a problem. He was graduated with better than a B average.

In the beginning of his senior year, two years after we had started therapy, Rob began to discuss his real father, now living in the East, whom he had not seen since infancy. He obtained his address through his mother and together we composed a letter. Almost immediately he received a warm and encouraging answer. Through his successful involvement with me he was able to try to become involved with his father, someone whom he felt he needed very much. For the next three months several letters passed back and forth. One day, with no warning whatsoever, he received a letter from his uncle (his father's brother) saying that his father's wife had died from an operation following heart surgery, leaving his father with two small children—Rob's half-brother and half-sister, whom he had never seen. His father, unable to cope with this responsibility, committed suicide a week after his wife died. The uncle, who had taken custody of the children, had written Rob, the only other close relative. Rob was shaken. He asked me what to do, and when I pointed out reality, he was strong enough to agree with my evaluation of the situation. Although he originally felt he should have been able to do something to avoid his father's taking his life, I was able to reassure him that there was nothing he could have done. I did, however, point out that he did have an obligation to his half-brother and half-sister. In his own immediate feelings of guilt and self-pity, it took a little while before he realized that he should do something for them. When he recognized his responsibility to them, he snapped out of his depression and went to work harder than ever. He wrote to the children and to his uncle, told them of his interest, and received encouraging letters from all of them. Even the difficult reality of his father's death gave him an opportunity to gain self-worth, rather than use the tragedy as an excuse to lapse into his former irresponsible ways.

Soon after this tragic occurrence therapy ended. Surprising to him but not to me, he was accepted by every medical school to which he applied. His stepfather is now doing better financially and his mother continues to work; enthusiastic over his achievements, they are able to help him through medical school. Although I hear from him only occasionally, this year he did call to say he was elected president of his class in medical school.

In summary, then, our basic job as therapists is to become involved with the patient and then get him to face reality. When confronted with reality by the therapist with whom he is involved, he is forced again and again to decide whether or not he wishes to take the responsible path. Reality may be painful, it may be harsh, it may be dangerous, but it changes slowly. All any man can hope to do is to struggle with it in a responsible way by doing right and enjoying the pleasure or suffering the pain that may follow.

Counseling as a Relationship

In dealing with counseling the usual approach treats counseling as a process—as a series of stages or phases, not necessarily discrete but nevertheless discernible. We thus have the total process broken down into subprocesses: the intake process; the initial interview; the evaluation process, including interviews and testing; the problem exploration stage (including, in vocational counseling, occupational exploration); the problem solving stage, including the selection of a vocational objective; and the closing stage, which in vocational counseling includes placement.

On this view, the attention, the emphasis, of the counselor is focused upon *techniques*. Now while techniques are necessary, they are—or should be—secondary. They are not the essence of the counseling process, only means to the goal. Concern with techniques as such may be detrimental rather than helpful to good counseling. It tends to lead to a situation in which the counselor uses techniques as devices by which to manipulate or influence the client toward the acceptance of his, the counselor's, goals or objectives. This is the kind of thing represented by such phrases as counseling a client into, or out of, a vocational field, or counseling a client to accept this or that goal or objective, or toward this or that decision. To call such activity counseling is a misuse of the term, if not a desecration of the very concept. Counseling is not

From *Journal of Rehabilitation,* November–December, 1959, Vol. 25, No. 6. Reprinted by permission of the author and the National Rehabilitation Association.

something you do to, or practice upon, a client. It is something you engage in *with* a client.

The word *with* suggests that, rather than being a matter of techniques, counseling is a *relationship*. This point of view has been discussed and developed by a number of writers, but mainly in the area of psychotherapy. I think it has value in all counseling areas.

In Aid of Good Relationships

It is obvious that counseling is a *human* relationship. Since we are, of course, constantly engaged in relationships with other people, it might appear that there should be no difficulty in learning to be a counselor; we would simply apply what we know about human relationships in our work with our client. To some extent this is true. Counseling and psychotherapy are often made to appear to be more complicated, more mysterious, more esoteric, than is actually the case. The emphasis upon techniques, the attempt to classify kinds of clients and kinds of problems and to match these with specific techniques, contributes to this impression. To view counseling as basically akin to other human relationships is to remove this aura of mystery and magic. This might be threatening to some professional counselors and therapists, suggesting that learning counseling or even psychotherapy is not necessarily a long, complicated process.

Granted this is the case, we must beware of oversimplification. Counseling is based upon the principles of *good* human relations. While these principles are in general known, they are not necessarily widely practiced outside of counseling and psychotherapy, nor do they necessarily come automatically and easily. It is also true that their application in counseling as compared with their application in other interpersonal or social relationships, involves somewhat different techniques, methods, and skills. Let us consider briefly what these principles of good human relations are, and how they may be manifested in the counseling relationship.

Good human relationships are those which are productive of

or conducive to good mental and social-psychological health. Since the goal of counseling or psychotherapy is the attainment of good mental health, the basic principles of good human relations and counseling are clearly the same. One might say that the providing of good human relationships keeps people healthy, while in counseling and psychotherapy we are concerned with restoring people to good mental health or improving their mental health. What is good for one purpose is likewise useful in fulfilling the other.

What now are the requirements of good mental health which can be met as individual interacts with individual, whether in general human relationships or in specific situations such as teacher-student, employer-employee, or counselor-client relationships?

Marks of Mental Health

The first and basic requirement of every individual if he is to be mentally healthy is that he have at least a modicum of self-esteem —that he accept himself, that he feel that at least in some respects he is a person of worth. The achievement and maintenance of this self-esteem is the basic drive and motivation of every person. To have it is to be, to the extent that it is present, mentally healthy. A social environment which facilitates the development and maintenance of self-esteem is a healthy environment.

How does one go about providing such an environment? What can one do to promote self-esteem in other people? We have some evidence, both from research and from experience, regarding the conditions which promote or foster self-esteem or mental health.

It is difficult, if not impossible, to accept or respect oneself if one is not accepted or respected by others. One of the first principles of human relations, therefore, is the acceptance of others. Acceptance involves recognition of another as an individual, a unique person, who is respected as a person and treated as worthy of respect. Acceptance includes the recognition of the right of another to be himself rather than conform to what you might want him to be. One accepts others by being interested in them as individuals, showing respect for their opinions or contributions or expressions of feeling, taking time to listen to what they have to say.

It is not always easy to accept others as they are, particularly when they differ greatly from ourselves. We tend either to ignore or reject those who are unusual, or attempt to change them. It is easy to be critical, derogatory in our remarks, belittling, and condemning. Our own needs for self-esteem may interfere with our accepting and respecting others. We may want to feel superior to others in order to bolster ourselves. Our own unsatisfied need for self-esteem thus prevents us from esteeming others. Thus a vicious circle develops—a situation in which the mutual respect so necessary for good human relationships and good mental health is lacking. The circle must be broken. Those who have some security, some degree of self-esteem, must manifest respect for others who in turn may develop enough self-esteem to be able then to show respect for others, and so on. It is not always easy to listen to others—to really listen—instead of thinking of what we are going to say next. But listening to another is the simplest, most basic way of showing respect for him.

Acceptance and respect form the foundation for the second basic principle of good human relations. Acceptance leads to understanding. People want and need to be understood. They need to feel that others know and appreciate what they are, who they are, and why they are as they are and behave and think as they do. But understanding is more than "knowing what makes people tick." It entails something more than glib use of psychological terminology. Understanding of another is not obtained by standing on the outside and looking at him. It comes only from imaginatively getting on the inside and looking out, seeing things as he does. It is this kind of "feeling understood" that people want—release from the feeling that they are alone, isolated, so different that no one else sees things as they do.

A third factor in good human relationships is confidence and trust. One may not agree with another's decisions or acts, but one respects the other's rights to them—within, of course, the limits imposed by rights of other people. The recognition of freedom of thought and action means that the manipulation of others either by subtle or by overt methods, for one's own goals, or even for the presumed good of those manipulated, is not consistent with good human relations.

Finally, good human relations are characterized by openness, integrity, and honesty. There is no place for deceit, trickery, or subterfuge. Such performance is inconsistent with respect, understanding, and recognition of the freedom of choice of others.

Mutual Recognition of Worth

The existence of these conditions in human relationships appears to make possible the optimal development of the individual. They foster self-esteem, self-confidence, independence, responsible decisions and behavior. These are the characteristics of good mental health. Taken together, these conditions provide an optimum environment for the development of the individual. An important characteristic of this environment is the absence of threat. We are beginning to realize that only where threat is not present can the individual develop to his fullest potential. A threatened individual is anxious, tense, afraid, inhibited, withdrawn. Threat leads to a narrowing or restricting of perception, of thinking, of activity. Learning, or modification of behavior, does not occur. A person under threat is emotionally disturbed. Only in a non-threatening environment—one that is accepting, understanding, trustworthy, dependable, consistent—can the individual be free to learn, to solve problems, to make adequate decisions and choices, to act intelligently, to express himself—in short, to be mentally healthy.

Now the counseling relationship is a good human relationship. It could not be otherwise. The goals of the individuals concerned are the same; the basic principles must also be the same. The counseling relationship is one in which the counselor accepts the client, respecting him as an individual of worth. The counselor endeavors to understand the client. The counselor recognizes the right of the client to make his own decisions, and determine his own actions. The counselor attempts to provide a nonthreatening atmosphere in which the client may explore his problem, look at things in a different light, and reach a more adequate solution.

Or does he? How many counselors actually are applying the principles of good human relations in their counseling? I have heard counselors say, "That may be all right in psychotherapy. But we can't be permissive and completely accepting. We can't allow the client to make his own decisions. We are responsible for what happens. We have to justify the expenditure of money on the client, and we must avoid wasting money on foolish decisions." But does this justify violation of the principles of good human relations, of good mental health? It should not. Any program which requires such violation should be examined and revised. No goal which is achieved at the expense of good mental health in the client can be justified. What does it profit a counselor, a client, or society, if the client gets a job but loses his independence, self-respect, or sense of personal adequacy in the process?

Forestalling Defense Reactions

The counselor who cannot trust the client and his decisions is perhaps not able to make any better decisions himself. How many of the counselor's decisions are less foolish than those of some client? May it not be that the counselor's lack of confidence in the client is itself the cause of the client's insistence upon poor or inadequate choices?

We are all aware of the reaction of individuals to challenge, to criticism, to attempts to force changes upon them—the child who becomes more demanding the more his desires are thwarted; the girl who insists on marrying the clearly inferior boy to whom her parents violently object. Some would see such conduct as willfulness or unreasoning refusal to listen to reason. Actually, it is the universal defensive reaction to threat. So in counseling, the persistence of the client in clinging to an unsuitable choice may be a reaction to the threatening aspect of the relationship.

Some counselors are afraid to show interest in the client, acceptance of him, confidence in him, because they are afraid they will be trapped by the client, imposed upon, or taken advantage of. This attitude is not conducive to a good relationship. It indicates that the counselor feels threatened by the client.

Now it is true that the counselor in an agency that expends public money on a client has a responsibility. He must be convinced that the money is being well spent. And to do this he must evaluate the plans and program of services provided for the client. But in the counseling process itself, as we commonly think of it, it is the client who makes the decisions, even the final decision regarding his vocational objective. This has been stressed for a long time even by those who are non-client-centered to some extent, and make suggestions or list alternatives. (Such counselors commonly say, "Well, the client does have the final choice, makes the final decision.")

Thus we have a dilemma. How can we resolve this?

Evaluation Is Not Counseling

The resolution, in my mind at least, consists in the fact that the counselor *avoids making decisions during the counseling process.* The counselor's evaluation is not, on this view, a part of counseling. When he is evaluating he is not counseling. When he is evaluating, he is not doing psychotherapy. When he has to evaluate to make decisions, then he is not a counselor. What this means in practice is that the decisions should be limited to (a) the early stages of the counseling process (or prior interviews), when decisions have to be made regarding eligibility, feasibility, need for services, etc., and (b) the concluding stage, when the counselor, since he has to approve the decision of the client, must make his own decision whether he can accept that decision or not.

The evaluative attitude, then, is to the greatest extent possible kept out of the counseling process. Counseling continues on the basis of the best accepted counseling principles. If after the counseling is completed the counselor cannot accept or approve the decision or choice of the client, he simply tells the client so, giving his reasons. This can be a difficult situation to handle, since it can be threatening or coercive for the client. Actually, such outcomes are far fewer than those would expect who are unable to trust the client to make his own decisions.

Another way in which some counselors violate the principles of good human relationships is in failing to be completely honest and sincere with the client. The counselor has certain objectives or goals for the client and is perhaps afraid that the client will not reach or accept them on his own. This "bag of tricks" concept of counseling is often held by nonprofessional people, by those who make referrals to counselors in schools or other agencies to have the client "straightened out." But good human relations are open, honest, and sincere; counseling must be the same.

What Counseling Really Is

An important implication of counseling as a relationship has to do with what the counselor does or gives to the client. Rather than being concerned with giving or providing services, or even the giving of advice or information, the counselor should be concerned with his psychological contribution to the relationship. Instead of giving concrete, material, or tangible goods or services, the counselor gives himself. He gives his time, interest, attention, respect, understanding, all of which are intangible, yet are the essential elements of counseling as a relationship.

The counseling relationship then is a special application of the principles of good human relations. It is specialized in several respects. *First,* it is the conscious, ordered, purposeful application of the principles in a formal, planned situation in which one person, who is in need of special assistance, is helped by another person, who is presumably not urgently in need of help for himself. Its purpose is thus not simply the fostering or maintenance of personal adjustment or adequacy in the more or less average, adjusted, or adequate person, but the assistance of those who are in trouble, who are to some extent or in some respects inadequate, who have problems which they have been unable to resolve by themselves.

Second, the counseling relationship is closer, more intense, more concentrated, than the usual social relationship. The principles of human relations are applied in their purest form, without the formalities and banalities of ordinary social intercourse. The relationship is limited to the essentials, uncontaminated by social sparrings, which are essentially either protective defenses or reassurances. Almost all ordinary human relationships seem to have some element of threat in them, or are easily perceived as threatening by the individual who feels inadequate or needs help. The counseling relationship carefully avoids or eliminates every possible element of threat.

Third, the counseling relationship is on a deeper level than ordinary social relationships. This is possible because of the lack of threat, which enables the client to look at himself closely and deeply, to expose himself to the counselor, establishing a relationship which is unlike any other. The counselor must be especially qualified if he is to handle this intimate relationship adequately, in a way which is really helpful to the client. He must have sufficient self-esteem so that he is not threatened by the client.

Giving of Self a Paying Investment

Viewing counseling as a relationship leads us to consider it from a point of view which emphasizes new aspects. Our concern is not with techniques, with what we do, but with what we are; not with what we can give in the way of goods and services, but with how much we can give ourselves; not with tangible, concrete, limited outcomes, such as good vocational choices or other decisions, placement in employment, etc., but with whether the client has maintained or improved his self-esteem, his self-respect, his independence, his status as a human being. This is the goal of all counseling, whether educational, vocational, rehabilitation, marital, or therapeutic. Other objectives are minor, or important only as they contribute to the development of a self-respecting, responsible, independent human being. Such an outcome is not achieved by techniques or the giving of material things, but only as the result of a good human relationship, the giving of oneself in the service of others.

WILLIAM SCHOFIELD

The Psychotherapist as Friend

The theses of this essay may be stated briefly. First, man has a
need for close personal relationships with at least a few other
individuals. Second, the essential nature of the relationship between friends entails selective interdependency. Third, several
major characteristics of urban life either prevent or dilute the functions of friendship. Fourth, when the channels for forming, maintaining, and using the friendship relationship are closed or con-
stricted, the deprived individual will look for approximations.
Finally, in twentieth century western culture, the professional
psychotherapist is a sanctioned substitute friend for the otherwise
friendless, frequently without full awareness of the substitution by
either partner to the contract. Each of these propositions will be
examined.

Man is a social animal. With infrequent and usually eccentric
exceptions, the human individual chooses to work and to play, to
create and to consume in close association with other individuals.
He belongs to groups with diverse and variously overlapping memberships, varying in size and function—from the nuclear family
through neighborhood, community, city, state, and nation—from
marital dyad through church, social club, charitable organization,
trade union or professional society, political party, and so on. The
individual identifies with each group and in turn finds part of his
own identity in the roles he carries out in each. Whatever the
historical roots of his gregariousness, and whether or not *homo*

From *Humanitas: Journal of the Institute of Man,* VI:2 (Fall, 1970).
Reprinted by permission of the publisher.

sapiens' ancestors ever lived in solitary families, he is definitely a social creature now. The complexity and continuity of modern society rests upon matrices of interdependency and a division of labor. It is the exceptional individual whose choice of a truly solitary existence can be sustained either by independent wealth or an unusual endowment of talent and resources for self-sufficiency.

Man's basic social interdependencies are primarily pragmatic—resting upon the division of labor and the exchange of goods and services. In earlier times, the farmer went to the cabinetmaker for his furniture, and the shoemaker to the butcher for his meat. The advent of the mail order catalogue and the middleman have not changed in any way the basic interdependencies. The farmer no longer knows personally the man who builds his wagon; the butcher no longer knows personally the farmer who raises his beef. The pragmatic personal relationships of a simpler economy fostered more than concrete interpersonal dependencies; they provided the direct knowledge of personalities out of which could evolve the shared joys of less pragmatic pursuits. The farmer, the wheelwright, and the butcher could hunt and fish and play cards together. The trust and confidence founded on practical interdependence could expand to the shared interests of companionship and mutual concern for the total welfare of each. The primary relationships of pragmatic need evolve into the no less vital secondary relationships of psychological support.

The need for companionship is a psychological acquisition rather than a biological given. But as the late Gordon Allport explained, acquired (secondary) motives become "functionally autonomous" (Allport, 1937). Primitive man needed food for his belly. He found that hunting in "packs" was a more effective means of assuring him sufficient game for his bodily needs. But the biological need led to a group experience in which the individual acquired a preference for togetherness independent of its original purpose. Shaw's Professor Higgins (in the Lerner and Lowe version [of Pygmalion] called *My Fair Lady*) finds himself frustrated after his essential victory simply because he has become "accustomed to her face."

Pragmatic interdependency in primary face-to-face relations

fosters shared activities which in turn can generate friendship. From the mutuality of interlocking functions to the mutuality of play to the mutuality of shared, personal concerns. From commerce to companionship to compassion. We learn to trust those upon whom we must depend. In the beginning we trust them to supply our concrete needs—for food and warmth and physical protection. As we grow we come to know that these primary suppliers stand ready to provide for our total personal welfare. Ideally, the nurturant love of parent for child becomes the succorant friendship of parent for individual. Not recognizing it nominally, the child's first friends are his parents. The word "friend" derives from an Anglo-Saxon verb meaning to love. The general dissolution of the continuity of the nuclear family in western culture, the loss of physical proximity of family members means that many individuals are exposed to being, at least temporarily, without access to loving friends.

The maturing individual's circle of friends widens. But in modern, urban culture that circle is typically incomplete and broken and those who might be friends are more often only acquaintances and companions. The individual is unsure of his friendships because he is rarely sure of a basic mutual interdependence of function. As no one seems truly to need him (his goods, his services, his talents) in a directly personal way, he feels equally unneeding or undeserving of the personal, emotional support of others. Without the mutuality of some meaningful, direct transactions, companionship is superficial and does not engender a felt sharing of compassion.

Typically we do not "know" the man who delivers our milk even in those fast disappearing communities where such "personal" service is still available. We cannot even identify as an acquaintance the dairy farmer who produces it! More typically we purchase our staples from quasi-automated markets in which even the middleman is essentially faceless. The average consumer does not "know" the president of the supermarket chain, the manager of the local store, or even the butcher "in residence."

The basic social interdependencies for goods and services still operate but they have been essentially depersonalized. The commerce of daily life no longer provides (demands?) the matrix of recurrent personal exchange upon which could be founded an immediate sense of interdependency and from which could flower the core of friendship—shared concerns.

In addition to functional interdependency, friendship requires a reasonable degree of stability, of continuity in the relationship. Not only our technology but the increasing mobility of our lives tends to disrupt relationships, even to discourage their formation. It is not uncommon to hear the "organization" family, dwelling in an urban apartment or even in a suburban split-level home, express a motive to avoid the formation of true friendship with neighbors in order to avoid the emotional loss anticipated in the likelihood (great) that they will be moving on in a short while.

Thus, our technology and our mobility work together to destroy the natural breeding grounds of the friendship relation. As urban dwellers we manifest a paradox of progress—whereas formerly we lived physically separated lives but as real personalities, mutually identified in a closely interdependent community or neighborhood, we now find ourselves crowded "together" in a peculiar isolation of impersonal, apparent independence.

Given the technologically derived decay of direct dependencies, the increasingly impersonal supports for modern existence, and the increasing mobility of our population it is good evidence of man's strong need for interpersonal mutuality that most of us manage to develop and maintain vital friendships. It is one evidence of normality that we overcome the structural barriers to friendship.

However, there are many for whom the barriers seem insurmountable. These are the individuals for whom mutuality is prevented because of deep-seated feelings of inferiority, inadequacy, insecurity. Living in grave doubt, or worse in strong conviction that they have nothing to offer others, they refrain from asking for the gifts of friendship. A core of self-doubt, even of self-rejection, inhibits them from making the considerable effort required to overcome the hurdles that modern social structure puts in the path of friendship. They become isolated. And their isolation, removing them from any interpersonal experience of a corrective nature, permits the incubation of their negative self-concept. To the casual observer it may appear that these persons choose their solitary existence. But a perceptive and caring person extending the hand of friendship may find it quickly grasped. It is an intricate complex of temperamental variables and even more important early life experiences that make it impossible for this type of lonely person to make "the first move."

It has been suggested that friendships evolve out of functional interdependencies. They represent a secondary but nonetheless vital order of relationship. They are the means whereby the human personality exercises his need for a sense of "togetherness," his need for a feeling of mutuality, his need to share his successes and his sorrows. Without friends with whom to share them our achievements are diminished and our torments are augmented. In this is the simplest meaning of friend—the person we know to whom it matters if we are victorious or defeated, the person who will be truly happy *with* us in our gain, sad *with* us in our loss. Our friend *cares* about us and *feels* with us.

The neurotically inhibited, isolated, withdrawn person, doubtful of his worth and fearful of rejection or nonacceptance, is driven by the need to commune, the need for a continuing relationship that will permit him to be fully himself, to stand revealed in all his fears and hopes, in all his frustrations and uncertainties—in essence to talk about himself "outside" of the formalities of customary social roles.

The more public stereotypes of the psychotherapist entail elements that make it obvious why the neurotic isolate should turn to him for help. In essence, he is understood to be an accepting, nonjudgmental "healer" who listens sympathetically and advises wisely. To this extent, he shares with others, most notably the clergy, the function of confidant and confessor. Of his additional attributes the most important is his authority—the aura of special knowledge and expertise that surround him by virtue of his socially sanctioned role as a therapist.

The professional stereotype of the therapist is a complex of identities and roles related to theories of personality, theories of psychopathology, to techniques and tactics of removing or ameliorating neurotic symptoms, and to specialized skills developed by long experience with troubled persons. For the first fifty years of the history of psychotherapy, beginning with Freud's pioneering work at the turn of the century, theories and techniques were prominent. It was generally assumed that therapists of different theoretical persuasions were seeing truly neurotic patients and were treating them by approaches and techniques which differed in accordance with their respective theories.

For the past twenty years, with the advent of audio and visual recording equipment, it has been possible to capture the interpersonal processes of the therapist's "magic room" and to submit them to close scrutiny. In addition, both therapists and patients have been surveyed with regard to the qualities of atmosphere and attitude that characterize more and less successful therapeutic endeavors. From these researches we have arrived at an increasing consensus as to the important basic elements in psychotherapy (Fiedler, 1950).

Thus we can now say with some assurance and factual backing that a relationship perceived by the client as characterized by a high degree of congruence or genuineness in the therapist, by sensitive and accurate empathy on the part of the therapist, by a high degree of regard, respect and liking for the client by the therapist, and by an absence of conditionality in this regard, will have a high probability of being an effective therapeutic relationship (Rogers, 1965).

Expert, experienced therapists appear to be essentially similar in their transactions with patients despite whatever superficial dissimilarities they claim or might be expected from their theoretical allegiances (Fiedler, 1950; Strupp, 1955, 1960). Increasingly, it is agreed that the quality of the relationship between the therapist and patient is paramount and, further, that the achievement of an effective relationship requires particular, discernable qualities on the part of the therapist. Most generally these are qualities of warmth, empathy, and genuineness. Additionally, it is found that active participation by the therapist, clearly expressing investment in and concern for the patient, achieves better results than what has been previously considered to be the proper therapeutic mien—objective, detached, cool, and impartial interpretation and reflection. Increasingly both research findings and honest sharing of clinical experiences suggests that the effective therapist is "open" and spontaneous.

The composite image of the "good therapist" drawn by our respondents is thus that of a keenly attentive, interested, benign, and concerned listener—a friend who is warm and natural, is not averse to giving direct advice, who speaks one's language, makes sense, and rarely arouses intense anger. This portrait contrasts with the stereotype of the impersonal analyst, whose stance is detached, who creates a vacuum into which negative as well as positive feelings can flow, and who maintains a neutral though benign role, more a shadowy figure than a "real" person (Strupp, 1969, p. 117).

Are there parallels between the ideal friendship and the ideal therapeutic relationship? When a troubled person unburdens himself to a close friend he has certain expectations. Perhaps foremost is his expectation, resting possibly on past experience and partly on awareness of the human wisdom that "ventilation" brings some relief, that he will feel better after sharing his distress. Also, he usually brings an attitude of trust—an expectation that his friend will respect and preserve his confidences. He assumes that his friend will be moved to give whatever help is within his power. And he expects that his friend will be understanding, concerned and sympathetic. The combination of the reduced tension following unburdening and the relationship of trust in an accepting, concerned "other" can provide a primary therapeutic experience that frees the anxious or depressed person from the prison of his psychic isolation and enables him to carry on his struggle with more hope and less desperation.

Are the basic expectations that the neurotic isolate takes to the psychotherapist markedly different? Probably not. He expects confidentiality and compassion from the therapist. He brings to treatment some confidence that he will not be criticized for his weaknesses and that the therapist will be motivated to help him. These expectations of the supplicant, meshing with the therapist's expectations (that he can be helpful in an appropriately accepting and empathic relationship) create a therapeutic meld out of which much of the positive impact of psychotherapy may flow (Goldstein, 1962).

Is psychotherapy nothing more than a socially sanctioned substitution for the essential resources of personal acceptance and emotional support that most of us get from our friendships? Is the psychotherapist in essence only a good friend? Very definitely not. The majority of the clients of psychotherapists are not socially isolated. They have family and friends with whom they have meaningful, interdependent relationships. But they have significant anxieties, phobias, confusions, and conflicts of a neurotic nature for which they require the expert counsel and reeducation afforded through the empathic, insightful interviews of an experienced therapist who has a variety of skills and specialized knowledge for assisting the emotionally maladjusted person toward a more accurate and accepting self-concept and toward more adaptive behaviors in the management of his problems. The patient-therapist relationship is never insignificant, even when treatment may involve highly objective techniques of desensitization and reconditioning. And in those instances where the patient brings a massive distrust of others as a core element of his neurosis, the evolution and nurturance of the relationship is crucial. Regardless of beginnings, regardless of needs, and regardless of techniques, when therapy is effective it is not unusual for the patient to end up with the feeling that his therapist is in fact his friend. It is a handicap of the occupation, or possibly of certain stereotyped principles of training, that the therapist is likely to be either unaware or even self-consciously rejecting of his role as friend.

How does the skilled psychotherapist come to play a role in which his essential function is that of a substitute friend? Perhaps by simple unawareness and lack of critical orientation to his work with the individual patient. Perhaps by failure to adequately appraise the patient's social resources and to determine whether the patient in fact lacks any opportunity for the therapy of friendship. Perhaps by failure to recognize when actual treatment functions have been effectively culminated and the patient is continuing by habit, by acquired dependency and through the natural reluctance (shared by the therapist) to sever what has been a satisfying relationship. Perhaps by willingness to provide what is most commonly called "supportive" therapy.

So-called supportive therapy is generally assigned low prestige among levels and types of psychotherapy, because in essence further therapeutic gains by the patient are considered unlikely, the nature of the patient's critical problem involving situational impasses or insuperable realities. It is recognized, however, that the need for a continuing relationship, for emotional support, is crucial to the patient's capacity to maintain the struggle with some degree of morale. Supportive therapy represents a real and vital function. The question is whether the highly skilled psychotherapist is the necessary supplier of this support and should accept this function uncritically, that is, without examining the possibility that more natural and less expensive resources exist in the patient's life space (Silverman, 1965).

Is it acceptable for the skilled psychotherapist to accept a role as a substitute friend? No, except in unusual circumstances of real neurotic isolation of the patient and for a closely limited time. This prohibition derives from the critical shortage of psychotherapists in the face of the large number of persons with emotional or psychological disorders who require specific treatment over and above the meliorating effects of a relationship. If the patient is friendless because his style alienates those who might be his friends, or because he is socially fearful and inhibited, or because his distorted self-perceptions of worthlessness underlie his social withdrawal, the therapist has a meaningful task of reeducation. But he must continually strive to move his patient toward normal social commerce and to the increasing growth of his sense of identity, meaning, and worth through his relationships with others. When the therapist permits himself without awareness of limitation to function as a substitute, perhaps uncritical of the ego-inflation of being told that he is the patient's "only" or "best" friend, he is delaying the patient's growth and movement toward genuine, spontaneous relationships of true mutuality and interdependence, and he is reducing by significant measure his availability to those persons who have a critical need for his specific therapeutic skills (Schofield, 1964).

Anthropology has brought us an awareness of the formative influence of culture on personality types. It has shown that personality disruptions, emotional illness, and gross maladjustment of some individuals is a universal, cross-cultural phenomenon. Also, it has outlined the cultural elements in patterns of personality disturbance. The neurosis of the primitive nomad is different from that of the urban salesman. Finally, cultures variously prescribe the role and skills of the therapist. Historical review demonstrates within given cultures that both the style (or is it the content?) of neurosis changes over time as does the accepted mode of treatment.

The patients on whom the discipline of psychotherapy was founded were largely hysterics and phobics, persons with circumscribed pseudosomatic symptoms or handicapping fears (Brody, 1970). Such cases still appear in our clinics but with decreasing frequency. Instead of those symptoms associated with repression of conflicts and associated anxiety, we are seeing increasing numbers of persons who are systematically depressed but whose pathology is that of isolation, alienation, loneliness and loss of meaning (Maddi, 1967).

In the beginning psychotherapy was a two-person relationship between healer and patient, and the role of the therapist was clearly authoritarian. With the evolution from individual to group therapy, the directing, authoritative role of the group "leader" was continued. But new forms of individual therapy have evolved, especially in the democratically toned environment of America, and in the "nondirective" approach favored by many therapists there is deliberate avoidance of an authoritative role (Rogers, 1951). We have seen parallel movement toward therapy groups of self-selected peers and more recently to leaderless groups.

It is important to recognize that PSHPG (peer self-help psychotherapy groups) achieve their goals without the application of specific behavior modification techniques, without the existential search for identity, without the exploration of human potential, without awareness training to actualize one's potential, without the analysis of the transference neurosis, without psychodrama, without clearing engrams, without creative fighting, without mind expanding drugs, without sensory awakening, without marathons, without feeling each other up, without taking off their clothes, and without sexual intercourse between therapists and clients . . . PSHPG are fellowships whose members have a common problem and who establish such relationships with each other as peers that they reveal themselves to each other. Within such relationships, and in the presence of members who acknowledge the help they received through the fellowship, the peers make it possible and desirable to accept each other's efforts to modify their own and the others' behavior and solve their own and others' problems according to the methods and goals of the fellowship. The procedures and techniques utilized within the fellowship are those long identified with learning theory (Hurvitz, 1970).

Thus both the content of neurosis and the modes of treatment appear to be shifting. The classic psychoneurosis of Freud is still with us. But increasingly therapists are being confronted by persons whose disorder appears to be less a function of conflict and repression than of a particular deprivation, the absence of meaningful personal relationships.

Twentieth-century man struggles against his fear of isolation. "We are born alone, we die alone." Between these inescapably private experiences, we are nurtured in a culture that over-emphasizes interpersonal activity and social "adjustment" and has made solitary activity of any sort a "symptom." The child is rushed to nursery school where the combination of an activity-oriented program and concern for his socialization robs him of any opportunity to develop a reflective stance and leaves him grossly deficient in his capacity to enjoy solitude. He does not learn to be of and with an unpeopled world. As an adult, the technological depersonalization of social relations robs him of ready opportunity for meaningful and lasting friendships. He cannot live with himself and yet he may be acquaintance-rich, friend-poor. Given a significant personal problem his pride, fear, and relative isolation from "significant others" makes him responsive to the cult of the expert. He may turn to the psychotherapist—frequently for not very much more than the emotional support and thoughtful counsel he might receive from a good friend.

In all the recent flowering of new group "therapies"—sensitivity groups, T-groups, basic encounter groups, marathon groups, and finally nude marathon groups—we detect a neurotic search for "contact." But the hunger is destined to go unappeased. One cannot achieve genuine spontaneity by coming together for the purpose of spontaneity. One cannot achieve meaningful intimacy in a situation of controlled intimacy. There is an inescapable paradox in any institutionalized search for friendship—the therapist can be no better than an intimate stranger, a substitute friend (Kovacs, 1965). It is good to practice disinhibition, it is good to be able to hold a stranger in one's arms, it is good to confess to a professional listener—but that is all practice and preparation. The critical and conscientious therapist will never lose sight of the substitution, will never permit it to be needlessly prolonged, and will most clearly never permit it to be the goal of treatment.

If the abuse of the psychotherapy relationship is to be avoided, if fewer demands are to be placed on therapists to be substitute friends, if fewer individuals are to turn first rather than last to experts for emotional support, we must undertake a careful appraisal of the avenues whereby even in our technologically depersonalized civilization of apparent personal independence we can help maturing personalities toward early and continuing awareness of the need to discover, nurture, and value the critically necessary mutual interdependencies of friendship. So far the psychology of friendship has been a grossly neglected area of investigation by social scientists.

It is heartening that the practice of psychotherapy and the roles of therapists are not static. The suggestively epidemic character of the neurosis of existential anomie, the current popularity of encounter groups and growth centers with the progressive displacement of individual therapy by group approaches, and the increasing recognition of the "indigenous nonprofessional" as an effective therapeutic agent point to the possibility that we may successfully overcome the forces toward personal isolation that are fostered by our technological "independence" and the cult of the expert (Grosser, et al., 1969). In these developments there is promise not only of treatment but of prophylaxis. This is particularly clear in the broadening role of the volunteer, nonprofessional mental health worker where there is growing evidence that beyond providing extension of the expertise of the psychotherapist and reducing the manpower shortage, they may be more effective therapists than the experts.

If there is a single factor of greatest importance affecting the differences of the role relationship in the two forms of therapy, it is the monetary one. In amicatherapy, the therapeutic agent's role is nonremunerative, while in psychotherapy the patient, or someone, must pay for his services . . . It is not likely, then, that the professional, who is paid to relate to the patient, can provide the same kind of ego enhancement as the layman, who has voluntarily moved toward the patient in an un-alloyed friendship role (Mitchell, 1966).

In looking at the "hippy" subcultures that are prominent on many of our college campuses and in our large cities, we are impressed initially by certain superficial and dramatic characteristics—dress, hair style, use of drugs, apparent sexual looseness, and symbols of rebellion against the establishment. The more significant wellsprings of this movement require a longer and more careful look. Then we can see the drive toward community, the search for modes of immediate sharing, the development of direct interdependence. In the commune, the "free" store, the handcrafted dress —is there not a search for the mutuality, directness, simplicity, openness and, in essence, the quality of basic friendship, of meaningful, fulfilling relationships that they may have failed to experience in the homes of their friendless parents. They are not likely to experience fewer anxieties, frustrations, and hangups than their fathers and mothers but may it not be that they will survive their trials and, indeed, grow through their trials under the natural therapy of friends?

REFERENCES

Allport, Gordon W. "The transformation of motives," *Personality: A Psychological Interpretation,* Chapter Seven. New York: Henry Holt & Co., 1937.

Brody, Benjamin. "Freud's case load," *Psychotherapy,* VII (1970), 8–12.

Fiedler, Fred. "A comparison of therapeutic relationships in psychoanalytic, nondirective and Adlerian therapy," *Journal of Consulting Psychology,* XIV (1950), 436–445.

———. "The concept of an ideal therapeutic relationship," *Journal of Consulting Psychology,* XIV (1950), 239–245.

Goldstein, Arnold P. *Therapist-Patient Expectancies in Psychotherapy.* New York: The Macmillan Company, 1962.

Grosser, Charles, William E. Henry, and James G. Kelly, eds. *Nonprofessionals in the Human Services.* San Francisco: Jossey-Bass, Inc., 1969.

Hurvitz, Nathan. "Peer self-help psychotherapy groups and their implications for psychotherapy," *Psychotherapy: Theory, Research and Practice,* VII (1970), 41–49.

Kovacs, Arthur L. "The intimate relationship. A therapeutic paradox," *Psychotherapy: Theory, Research and Practice,* II (1965), 97–104.

Maddi, Salvatore R. "The existential neurosis," *Journal of Abnormal Psychology,* 72 (1967), 311–325.

Mitchell, William A. "Amicatherapy: theoretical perspectives and an example of practice," *The Community Mental Health Journal,* II (1966), 307–314.

Rogers, Carl R. *Client-Centered Therapy: Its Current Practice, Implications, and Theory.* Boston: Houghton Mifflin Company, 1951.

————. "The therapeutic relationship: recent theory and research." Lecture given at the University of Melbourne, Melbourne, Australia, February 6, 1965.

Schofield, William. *Psychotherapy: The Purchase of Friendship.* Englewood Cliffs, N.J.: Prentice-Hall, Inc., 1964.

Silverman, Herbert. "Varieties of 'supportive' psychotherapy," *Psychotherapy,* II (1965), 31–34.

Strupp, Hans H. "An objective comparison of Rogerian and psychoanalytic techniques," *Journal of Consulting Psychology,* XIX (1955), 1–7.

————. "Psychotherapeutic techniques, professional affiliation and experience level," *Journal of Consulting Psychology,* XIX (1955), 97–102.

————. *Psychotherapists in Action: Explorations of the Therapist's Contribution to the Treatment Process.* New York: Grune & Stratton, 1960.

Strupp, Hans H., Ronald E. Fox, and Ken Lesser. *Patients View Their Psychotherapy.* Baltimore and London: The John Hopkins Press, 1969.

CLIFFORD H. SWENSEN

The Successful Therapist

From a review of the last 20 years of research on the therapist, the conclusion seems inescapable that the successful psychotherapist is the one who genuinely cares about, and is committed to his client.

The first area of research on the therapist attempted to identify the personality traits that distinguished the successful from the unsuccessful therapist (e.g. Rolt & Luborsky, 1958). The second area of research suggested that some therapists might be more successful with one kind of patient, while other therapists might be more successful with others. This was the Whitehorn and Betz (1954) research on "A" and "B" types of therapists. The third line of research (e.g. Carson & Heine, 1962) investigated the effect of the psychotherapist's personality on the course of therapy as a function of the relationship between the personality of the therapist and the personality of the client. The fourth line of research, stimulated by Carl Rogers (1958, 1963), suggests that successful therapy requires a therapist who possesses at least two of three basic personality characteristics.

1) Personality Characteristics of Successful Therapists

Before any empirical research had been done on the characteristics of the therapist, a variety of lists of the desirable characteristics

Former title "Commitment and the Personality of the Successful Therapist." From *Psychotherapy: Theory, Research and Practice*. Volume 8, #1, Spring, 1971, © 1971. Reprinted by permission of the author and the publisher.

of the therapist were published (e.g. Cottle, 1953). Typical of these lists was that contained in the American Psychological Association (1947) report on the training of clinical psychologists, which catalogued 15 characteristics the psychotherapist should possess. These characteristics were: (1) intelligence; (2) originality; (3) curiosity; (4) interest in people; (5) insight into self; (6) sensitive; (7) tolerant; (8) warm personal relationships; (9) industrious; (10) responsible; (11) tactful and cooperative; (12) integrity, self-control; (13) ethical; (14) broad cultural background; and (15) deep interest in the field.

A series of studies attempted to identify which of these or similar personality characteristics differentiated the successful therapists from the unsuccessful therapists, with success usually rated by the therapy supervisors. . . . In these studies the single characteristic that most consistently differentiated the successful from the unsuccessful therapist was "interest in people." Other characteristics that consistently differentiated the successful from the unsuccessful therapists were: "originality," "insight into self," "warm personal relationships," and "integrity, self-control."

2) The "A" and "B" Therapists of Whitehorn and Betz

Whitehorn and Betz (1954) studied 35 psychiatrists and chose the 7 most and the 7 least effective. The top 7 had 75% of their patients discharged improved whereas the bottom group only 26.9%. They labeled these two groups "A" and "B". The "A" therapists were able to gain the confidence of their patients, more frequently formulated a conception of the motivation and the "personality-oriented" goals of the patient, and were more personally involved with their patients.

In their next study Whitehorn & Betz (1957) found that the use of insulin in the treatment improved the recovery rate of patients of the "B" therapists but had little effect on the recovery rate of the patients of the "A" therapists.

In a subsequent study (1960) they compared the "A" and "B" therapists on the Strong Vocational Interest Blank. They found that whereas "A" therapists scored high on lawyer and CPA scales, and low on the scales for printers and math and physical science teachers, the "B" therapists scored the opposite. They repeated this study on a second sample of 24 psychiatrists and obtained the same results. Whitehorn and Betz then identified the items on the Strong that differentiated "A" from "B" therapists, and used these to predict success in therapy with schizophrenics. This scale worked successfully in identifying the "A" and "B" groups from their original sample and also with a second sample from another hospital. These items indicated that the "A" therapists were motivated for activities that involved interaction with other people. Betz (1963) also found that "A" therapists were much more successful with process schizophrenics but only slightly more successful with non-process schizophrenic patients.

McNair, Callahan and Lorr (1962) found that with Veteran Administration out-patients the "B" therapists had the higher percentage of improved patients. The only difference in behavior noted between the two groups was that the "B" therapists indicated more interest in their patients at the beginning of therapy.

A study that used untrained therapists (Berzins and Seidman, 1968) reported similar results, finding that the "A" therapists performed better with schizophrenics, "B's" performed better with neurotics, and each group of therapists found it easier to select helpful responses and felt more satisfied with their performance when working with the appropriate group of patients.

Two studies have attempted to ferret out the dynamics of the interaction between these two kinds of therapists and clients. Carson, Harden and Shows (1964) concluded that the crucial factor is the interaction between therapist and patient, with the "A" therapists being more active and interested in the patient who turns away from others. They conclude that the more active therapist is the more successful therapist. Kemp (1966) concluded that the "A" and "B" types are not personality types, but rather differ in their reactions to psychopathology, with both "A" and "B" therapists being more successful with the patients who make them feel the most uncomfortable. Kemp suggests that the therapist shows more interest in the patient who gives him the most difficulty.

The one consistent theme of these studies is that the therapist is successful with the patients in whom he is interested and involved. McNair, Callahan, and Lorr suggest that similarity in interest leads the therapist to be more interested in a particular patient, while Kemp suggests that the therapist becomes most interested in the patient who gives him the most trouble.

3) Relationship between Characteristics of Therapist and Patient

Although there was speculation concerning the relationship between the personalities of therapist and client, Lesser's 1961 study was the first that found progress in therapy *negatively* related to similarity between therapist's and client's self-perceptions. Carson and Heine (1962) subsequently postulated that therapeutic progress is curvilinearly related to similarity in personality, with therapeutic progress maximal if the therapist is similar enough to the client to be able to empathize with the client, but not so similar that his problems are identical to the problems of the client. Their data supported this hypothesis.

Mendelsohn and Geller (1963) found that the more similar the therapist and client were in personality the fewer the number of therapy sessions, which suggests less success. Sapolsky (1965) found a significant relationship between complementarity on Schutz' FIRO-B scale, and improvement. Sapolsky in another study (1960) hypothesized that the "attractiveness" between subject and experimenter would increase if they were compatible, and that the greater the attractiveness the more easily they would condition verbally. His results confirmed this expectation.

Swensen (1967) reviewed the research on dyadic relationships and concluded that complimentarity on two main dimensions, dominance-submission and interpersonal approach-avoidance, would lead to a more positive relationship and thus progress in therapy would be more probable. He presented evidence that was somewhat equivocal, but tended to support this hypothesis.

Bare (1967) studied 47 counselors in interaction with 208 clients and concluded that "clients feel that their counselors get to know them well when their counselors have higher abasement and lower aggression scores than their own."

To summarize, the evidence at the moment suggests that similarity between therapist and client does not clearly lead to greater progress in therapy. Differences between the therapist and the client on some personality variables do seem to tend toward improving progress in the therapy.

Another relationship that shows promise of being fruitful is that between the therapist's values and the client's values. Deane and Ansbacher (1962) report that in a mental hospital lower class patients seem to progress more when the attendants, who are apparently similar to the patients in socio-economic class and values, are given the authority to make decisions concerning the patient's treatment. Welkowitz (1967) found that therapists' scores on the Strong and a scale of values correlated highest with the scores of their own patients who improved with therapy.

A variety of other studies have investigated the interaction of client variables with therapist personality variables, but do not clearly fit into the categories discussed above. Waskow (1963) found that judgementalness in the therapist increased the discussion of feelings by the client. Cartwright and Lerner (1963) found that patients were more likely to remain in therapy if they had high need for help, or if the therapist was empathic.

Cutler (1958) found that therapists were more likely to focus unnecessarily upon or to avoid material the patient introduces that is a personal problem for the therapist. Also the therapist's responses to problem areas introduced by the client that are also a problem to the therapist are more likely to produce "ego oriented" responses from the therapist. Sonne and Goldman (1957) hypothesized that authoritarian clients were more likely to prefer eclectic therapists to non-directive therapists, while less authoritarian clients were more likely to prefer non-directive therapists. McNair, Lorr and Callahan (1963) found that the degree of interest the therapists showed in the patient was positively related to whether or not the patient remained in therapy, regardless of whether or not the patient was predicted to be a quitter or remainer.

This potpourri of studies suggests that both similarity and complementarity of therapist and client on certain value, attitudinal or personality variables may somehow be related to therapeutic success, without indicating exactly which combination is decisive. However, certain words and phrases such as "attractiveness," "counselors get to know them well," "empathy," and "degree of interest" were noted in these studies which were designed to test diverse hypotheses in diverse ways. Their repeated use suggests that the most important factor is the therapist's interest in and involvement with the patient, and that similarity or complimentarity are of importance to the extent that they are related to the therapist's interest in and involvement with the patient. Indeed, there is much research that relates the variables of similarity and complementarity in attitudes, values and personality characteristics to interpersonal attraction and involvement (e.g. Byrne, 1969).

The Therapist's Empathy, Warmth, and Congruence

A puzzled Carl Rogers (1958, 1963, 1967) trying to examine both his own experience and the reported experience of others in doing psychotherapy, tried to determine what it was that produced constructive change in clients in psychotherapy, and concluded that the source of gain in therapy derived from three characteristics in the therapist and one in the client. The three characteristics of the therapist were: (1) empathy, (2) unconditional positive regard for the client, and (3) congruence of the therapist. The required characteristic of the client was the ability, however slight, to perceive these qualities in the therapist.

In reviewing this research Truax and Carkhuff (1967) indicate that these factors in the therapist are significantly related to the progress in therapy of all kinds of clients, including hospitalized psychotics, out-patient neurotics, delinquents, and school underachievers. These factors hold regardless of the training of the therapist, setting, and whether the therapy is individual or group. Further, therapists can be trained to exhibit these qualities. . . .

More detailed research (Truax and Carkhuff, 1967) suggests that empathy and congruence are primarily determined by the therapist himself, but that warmth may be elicited to some degree by the patient. For therapy to progress two of the three conditions must be present, and the third condition must not be completely absent. The important aspect of empathy is the average amount of empathy exhibited by the therapist and the peak amount of empathy displayed by the therapist, but low points of empathy are not related to outcome. This leads Truax and Carkhuff (1967, p. 88) to suggest that ". . . a therapist would be more helpful by striving for deeper understanding, even at the risk of occasional misunderstanding; . . ." Therapy may not only help but may also harm the patient. Additional research confirmed this observation. . . .

Finally, Truax and Carkhuff compared therapists who exhibited equivalent levels of empathy, warmth and congruence, and found that even within given levels some clients improved more with some therapists than with others, thus suggesting that there is still another factor affecting therapeutic success.

To summarize this research, the three qualities of empathy: warmth, congruence, and positive regard exhibited by the therapist are significantly related to progress in therapy. Empathy and congruence are qualities of the therapist himself, while warmth may be elicited from a therapist to a greater degree by some patients than by other patients. If these qualities are present the client improves but if they are not present the client gets worse.

Concern, Commitment and the Therapist

These studies seem to me to have a common thread running through them revealed by the rather off-hand, but repeated use of such words as "care," "concern," and "commitment." This thread points clearly to the conclusion that the really crucial element in the therapist's contribution to therapeutic success is *the therapist's commitment to the client.*

Nor, in all probability, is the importance of this aspect of the interpersonal relationship confined to psychoanalytically or non-directively oriented therapy. Sapolsky's study (1960) of the effect of the interpersonal relationship on verbal conditioning suggests that this factor must also operate when behavior modification techniques are used.

Looking at the therapist from the patient's point of view produces a similar conclusion. Strupp, Fox and Lessler (1969) in summarizing the characteristics of the "good" therapist from the patient's point of view write:

The composite image of the "good therapist" drawn by our respondents is thus that of a keenly attentive, interested, benign, and concerned listener—a friend who is warm and natural, is not averse to giving direct advice, who speaks one's language, makes sense, and rarely arouses intense anger. [p. 117]

May (1969, p. 228) argued that it is a failure of "intentionality" in the patient that is the source of most problems patients have today. May points out that the root "tend" in "intentionality" means both to "stretch toward" and "to care for." For therapy to be successful, the therapist must get at, and deal with that which the patient cares for and is stretching toward. I think there is validity to May's observation, but the research suggests that "intentionality" of the therapist must also be taken into account.

This argument points toward the necessity of developing what might be termed a "psychology of commitment." Can commitment be taught therapist trainees? The Truax and Carkhuff (1967) report suggests that something like it can be taught. Is commitment something that a given person can only give to certain other kinds of persons? This suggests developing methods for determining which kinds of people are able and likely to make commitments to which other kinds of people. What are the verbal and behavioral manifestations of commitment? The identification and measurement of these manifestations might provide early prediction of the course of therapy. The Cartwright and Lerner (1963) study of the course of therapy as a function of the therapist's empathy and the client's need to change might be a paradigm for this research.

Conversely, it may be that only certain people, by virtue of genes or early experience or purity of heart, are capable of this commitment, and that identifying these people and putting them to work doing counseling, without regard to their prior academic experience, is the solution to the problem of the production of successful therapists. The work with various kinds of "lay" therapists suggests the viability of this possibility.

Beyond therapy, the effectiveness of all kinds of interpersonal relationships ties into the matter of interpersonal commitment. May (1969) related it to love, but the research of Rosenthal (1966) and Jourard (1970) demonstrated the effect of the interpersonal relationship on the outcome of experimentation, and by implication and extrapolation, the effect of interpersonal commitment on every form of human endeavor touched by the interpersonal relationship. And that includes just about everything.

REFERENCES

Bare, Carole. Relationship of counselor personality and counselor-client personality similarity to selected counseling success criteria. *Journal of Counseling Psychology,* 1967, 14, 419–425.

Berzins, J. I. & Seidman, E. Subjective reactions of A and B quasi-therapists to schizoid and neurotic communications: a replication and extension. *Journal of Consulting and Clinical Psychology,* 1968, 32, 342–347.

Betz, Barbara. Differential success rates of psychotherapists with "process" and "non-process" schizophrenics. *American Journal of Psychiatry,* 1963, 119, 1090–1091.

Byrne, D. Attitudes and attraction. In Berkowitz, L. (editor) *Advances in experimental social psychology,* Vol. 4, New York: Academic Press, 1969.

Carkhuff, R. R. Toward a comprehensive model of facilitative interpersonal processes. *Journal of Counseling Psychology,* 1967, 14, 67–72.

Carkhuff, R. R. Lay versus professional counseling. *Journal of Counseling Psychology,* 1968, 15, 117–126.

Carkhuff, R. R. & Alexik, Mae. Effect of client depths of self-exploration upon high- and low-functioning counselors. *Journal of Counseling Psychology,* 1967, 14, 350–355.

Carkhuff, R. R. & Truax, C. B. Training in counseling and psychotherapy: an evaluation of an integrated didactic and experiential approach. *Journal of Consulting Psychology,* 1965, 29, 333–336.

Carson, R. E., Harden, Judith, & Shows, W. D. A-B distinction and behavior in quasitherapeutic situations. *Journal of Counseling Psychology,* 1964, 28, 426–433.

Carson, R. C. & Heine, R. W. Similarity and success in therapeutic dyads. *Journal of Consulting Psychology,* 1962, 26, 38–43.

Cartwright, Rosalind D. & Lerner, Barbara. Empathy, need to change, and improvement with psychotherapy. *Journal of Consulting Psychology,* 1963, 27, 138–144.

Committee on training in clinical psychology, *American Psychological Association.* Recommended gradùate training program in clinical psychology. *American Psychologist,* 1947, 2, 539–558.

Cottle, W. C. Personal characteristics of counselors, a review of the literature. *The Personnel and Guidance Journal,* 1953, 31, 445–450.

Cutler, R. L. Countertransference effects in psychotherapy. *Journal of Consulting Psychology,* 1958, 22, 349–356.

Deane, W. N. & Ansbacher, H. L. Attendant-patient commonality as a psychotherapeutic factor. *Journal of Individual Psychology,* 1962, 18, 157–167.

Jourard, S. M. Project replication: experimenter-subject acquaintance and outcome in psychological research. In Spielberger, C. (ed.) *Current Topics in Community Psychology,* New York: Academic Press, 1970.

Kemp, D. E. Correlates of the Whitehorn-Betz AB scale in a quasi-therapeutic situation. *Journal of Consulting Psychology,* 1966, 30, 509–516.

Lesser, W. M. The relationship between counseling progress and empathic understanding. *Journal of Counseling Psychology,* 1961, 8, 330–336.

Luborsky L. The personality of the psychotherapist. *Menninger Quarterly,* 1952, 6, 1–6.

McNair, D. M., Lorr, M., & Callahan, D. M. Patient and therapist influence on quitting psychotherapy. *Journal of Consulting Psychology,* 1963, 27, 10–17.

McNair, D. M., Callahan, D. M. & Lorr, M. Therapist "type" and patient response to psychotherapy. *Journal of Consulting Psychology,* 1962, 26, 425–429.

May, R. *Love and will,* New York: Norton, 1969.

Mendelsohn, G. A. & Geller, M. H. Effects of counselor-client similarity on the outcome of counseling. *Journal of Counseling Psychology,* 1963, 10, 71–77.

Piaget, G. W., Berenson, G. B. & Carkhuff, R. R. Differential effects of the manipulation of therapeutic conditions by high- and moderate-functioning therapists upon high- and low-functioning clients. *Journal of Consulting Psychology,* 1967, 31, 481–486.

Rogers, C. R. The characteristics of a helping relationship. *The Personnel and Guidance Journal,* 1958, 37, 6–16.

Rogers, C. R. Psychotherapy today, or, where do we go from here? *American Journal of Psychotherapy,* 1963, 17, 5–16.

Rogers, C. R. (Ed.) *The Therapeutic Relationship and its Impact: A study of psychotherapy with schizophrenics,* The University of Wisconsin Press, 1967.

Rosenthal, R. *Experimenter effects in behavioral research,* New York: Appleton-Century-Crofts, 1966.

Rubinstein, E. A. Analysis of self and peer personality ratings of psychotherapists and comparison with patient ratings. *Journal of Consulting Psychology,* 1958, 10, 295–298.

Sapolsky, A. Effect of interpersonal relationships upon verbal conditioning. *Journal of Abnormal and Social Psychology*, 1960, 60, 241–246.

Sapolsky, A. Relationship between patient-doctor compatibility, mutual perception and outcome of treatment. *Journal of Abnormal Psychology*, 1965, 1, 70–76.

Sonne, T. R. & Goldman, L. Preferences of authoritarian and equalitarian personalities for client-centered and eclectic counseling. *Journal of Counseling Psychology*, 1957, 4, 129–135.

Strupp, H. H., *Psychotherapists in action*, New York: Grune and Stratton, 1960.

Strupp, H. H. The therapist's contribution to the treatment process: beginnings and vagaries of a research program. In Strupp, H. H. and Luborsky, L. (Eds.) *Research in Psychotherapy*, Vol. 2, Washington, D.C.: American Psychological Association, 1962, 25–40.

Strupp, H. H., Fox, R. E. & Lessler, K. *Patients view their psychotherapy*, Baltimore: Johns Hopkins Press, 1969.

Swensen, C. H. Psychotherapy as special case of dyadic interaction: some suggestions for theory and research. *Psychotherapy*, 1967, 4, 7–13.

Truax, C. B. & Carkhuff, R. R. *Toward effective counseling and psychotherapy: training and practice,* Chicago: Aldine, 1967.

Waskow, Irene. Counselor attitudes and client behavior. *Journal of Counseling Psychology*, 1963, 27, 405–412.

Welkowitz, Joan, Cohen, J. & Ortmeyer, D. Value system similarity: investigation of patient-therapists dyads. *Journal of Consulting Psychology*, 1967, 31, 48–55.

Whitehorn, J. C. & Betz, Barbara. A study of psychotherapeutic relationships between physicians and schizophrenic patients. *American Journal of Psychiatry*, 1954, 111, 321–331.

Whitehorn, J. C. & Betz, Barbara. A comparison of psychotherapeutic relationships between physicians and schizophrenic patients when insulin is combined with psychotherapy and when psychotherapy is used alone. *American Journal of Psychiatry*, 1957, 113, 901–910.

Whitehorn, J. C. & Betz, Barbara. Further studies of the doctor as a crucial variable in the outcome of treatment with schizophrenic patients. *American Journal of Psychiatry*, 1960, 117, 215–223.

After Psychotherapy

After termination of psychotherapy, what?

Although a great deal is published about psychotherapy, relatively little is written about the termination phase of treatment and almost nothing has been said about the relationship between the former therapist and the former patient after the official conclusion of the psychotherapy process. From the literature it could be assumed that the patient and the therapist have no further contact with each other after that last psychotherapy session—but we know that often this is not so. Frequently the former therapist and the former patient continue to interact with one another as colleagues, as neighbors, and as friends. When the patient and the therapist stay in the same community, this continued relationship may be either by choice or by necessity but many therapists do maintain close contact with their former patients over wide geographical distances for periods of many years. Few psychotherapists have chosen to write about these continued experiences.

Often these friendships are warm, comfortable, and mutually gratifying and the former patient and the former therapist find their lives are enriched by the ideas and the feelings they share with one another, by the things they do together, and by the way they challenge and stimulate each other productively. In some instances, however, these ongoing relationships appear to be fraught with anxiety and with guilt because both patient and therapist have learned somewhere that friendship after psychotherapy is bad,

Former title "Patient and Therapist After Termination of Psychotherapy." From *American Journal of Psychotherapy*, XXV: 4 (October, 1971).

bizarre, or even vaguely perverted—and these attitudes seem to be largely unspoken and untested and passed on more by implication than after thoughtful evaluation. Over the coffee cups in the staff lounge, we have all heard about that psychotherapist who actually went as far as to marry that patient—and we all understood that of course this was an obvious case where transference and counter-transference ran riot. But is this necessarily so? Could this have been a time when the psychotherapy with a patient was supremely successful and the patient reached such a stage of independence, self-sufficiency, and growth ability that the therapist and the patient, after termination of psychotherapy, could share a deeply enriching relationship in the most healthy, normal fashion?

The goal of psychotherapy is to help the patient use his individual capabilities to function at his optimal level in his society—in the same way as his psychotherapist, as a reasonably healthy person, is using his individuality in his own social group. Any two people, with their own strengths, sensitivities, and interests, have the potential to stimulate and to enrich one another on the basis of their separate, unique individualities. If the psychotherapy process has been successful and the former patient is living at the level of his individual capacity and he is the kind of person whom the former psychotherapist would normally welcome as a friend, it may be the most natural development of the psychotherapy process for the psychotherapist and the patient to continue their relationship as friends now, as colleagues and as competitors—on the basis of a mutually rewarding friendship. When the psychotherapist is unable to allow himself or the patient this kind of shared growth experience, his behavior may negate many of the benefits from the psychotherapy. If the psychotherapist cannot permit himself to develop a natural personal friendship with his former patient, his inability to do so may either result from unresolved countertransference feelings or may be due to the difficulties in changing and maturing from psychotherapist to friend. As we work to make our treatment procedures more efficient, we all must consider whether the present tacit prohibition against post-termination friendship is not emotionally stunting both for the former patient and for the former psychotherapist and functions more to protect the therapist from the anxiety that comes with self-evaluation and with growth.

From my observations in working with my colleagues in different professions, with trainees at various levels of professional growth, and with my own patients, it would appear that the former psychotherapist and the former patient must work through several stages in their personal growth when they decide to allow themselves to become personal friends: (a) They both must deal with the change of roles; (b) they must allow themselves to change the focus of their interaction; and (c) they have to tolerate what can be a very difficult transition stage in the relationship.

Change of Roles

During the psychotherapy treatment, both the patient and the psychotherapist have been prone to seeing the psychotherapist as the parent-authority person who gives understanding, guidance, and direction. They have both tended to view the patient as being relatively weak, handicapped, and receptive. As the patient moved toward termination, he took over the direction and the control of his own living and his own growth. The psychotherapist allowed himself to become more "spontaneous" (1) and to relate to the patient almost on the basis of friendship. But, even at the time of termination, the psychotherapist still is seen as being more knowing and more powerful while the patient still acts in a comparatively subordinate, passive fashion in the relationship. Though the psychotherapist may indeed have become more spontaneous, this freedom is merely in his reaction to the patient's life; rarely does this spontaneity during treatment mean that the psychotherapist allows the patient to intrude into the psychotherapist's own day-to-day living. Thus, at the time of termination, the interaction between these two people still is unnaturally directed in one way—toward the patient and away from the psychotherapist.

From the psychotherapy process, the psychotherapist and the patient know that the psychotherapist understands a great deal about the patient's humanity—his strengths, his weaknesses, his hopes, and his dreams. At the same time the patient does know many things about the psychotherapist as a person from all the experiences that the two of them have lived through together: but this understanding still tends to be unspoken, untested, and to some extent, denied by both at the time of termination. In a friendship, the former patient has a right to reciprocal knowledge of his former psychotherapist. The relationship now has to move openly in both directions. The psychotherapist must become a real human being and, like any human being, at times fallible, sometimes uncertain, and occasionally awkward—in his own eyes and for his former patient to see. Some psychotherapists and some patients cannot allow the therapist to be exposed in this way. Psychotherapists may prefer to remain more shadowy, aloof, and impersonal, to the patient and to themselves. They must face the fact that by keeping this emotional distance, their actions may be contradictory to what they have been trying to achieve in the psychotherapy with the patient.

It is perhaps easier to face the anxieties about the formal mechanics of status change rather than to look closely at what this change of status now makes obvious. As this friendship relationship develops, these two people begin to realize that much of the former psychotherapy relationship was a form of mutual pretense. It now becomes clear to both that they have really known a great deal more about one another than they cared to admit during the previous psychotherapy. It will become very apparent to the psychotherapist that he may not have actually told about himself in words but he has shared his individuality in depth by everything he did with his patient; both patient and psychotherapist will now understand that the patient does know a great deal about the psychotherapist's humanity because he has learned from the psychotherapist's office, his way of dress, his mannerisms, and from what he did say and perhaps even more from what he did not say. This realization means that, as this friendship develops, these two people—the former patient and the former psychotherapist—will tend to live through again those experiences that they had in the previous psychotherapy relationship but now this reliving allows them to have an even deeper emotional understanding of what happened in that earlier psychotherapy. This knowledge may be very disturbing and often frightening to the psychotherapist who sees more clearly how much he does share and expose himself in every psychotherapy session. He can now understand how vulnerable he often is during his treatment hours. He appreciates that he is rarely as powerful or as much in control as he and his patients have believed. From the understanding he gains from a post-termination friendship, he will know that he has shown and still shows his humanity during the treatment hours and that this basic humanity has been and still is the main therapeutic force of his treatment process. The psychotherapist can recognize that he allows himself to be humanly weak in the patient's eyes but this is a weakness that is accepted and tolerated—and thus the patient learns that he too can live with his weaknesses.

This new understanding will permit the psychotherapist to look at what is still happening in his psychotherapy. He cannot deny—he need not deny—the very important psychotherapy work that goes on constantly at multiple communication levels. This new knowledge, this wider understanding, can be very unsettling to the psychotherapist but also can allow him to be much more effective and much more direct in his therapeutic work. It is unlikely that he can gain this vitally important understanding in any other way than by allowing himself to become a friend with some of his former patients in a natural growth process.

Change of Focus

In the post-termination relationship, the former patient and the former psychotherapist begin to relate to each other over a much wider area of their living. Previously their interaction has been contained within the small world of the psychotherapy office. This psychotherapy sanctum was a controlled, structured setting in which the patient and the therapist dealt only with those matters that were presented by the patient or raised by the psychotherapist. During these psychotherapy appointment sessions, both the patient and the psychotherapist had some control and some selection. Both participants could in this way decide how they were going to relate to one another and what was going to be the focus of their relationship. When the psychotherapist and the patient continue as friends after the termination of psychotherapy, this evolving relationship develops against a much wider background and they must interact with one another in situations that they cannot completely control or select.

The former patient and the former psychotherapist both appreciate now just how circumscribed their psychotherapy relationship was. They realize how they existed together in an "existential vacuum" (2) during the treatment hours. They may begin to wonder whether this seemingly limited material dealt with during the treatment was indeed relative or applicable and they may question how valid or useful treatment with such a restricted focus can be. Of course this same treatment relationship is now the basis of their friendship—and thus they may question the stability of this new friendship. When the psychotherapist and the patient allow themselves to see more of one another as individuals in a wider world, they may feel that somehow they have not really known each other in the past. They cannot avoid facing this question and so they must allow themselves to evaluate and to understand what really did happen during the psychotherapy. Only in time will they come to appreciate that it was these limitations and these boundaries in the psychotherapy interaction that gave them the freedom to work on the patient's problems in depth, a freedom that would not have been possible if they had had to deal with the totality of the patient's life or with the reality of the psychotherapist's day-to-day living. They will come to understand again how the patient was able to use the strengths and the sensitivities gained by focusing on such a limited area of his life as he dealt with the wider aspects of his social and family relationships.

It will be disturbing to the former patient and the former psychotherapist to discover just how much their fantasies about one another were realistically based or to what extent these fantasies were projections of their own personal feelings. For the former patient, the psychotherapist now becomes part of a real family, in a real home, in a real social environment. To the former psychotherapist, the patient's relatives now become solid people who say actual words and who do specific things. Sometimes all this is very similar to what the patient and the psychotherapist had imagined all along but sometimes the reality is very different. Both the psychotherapist and the patient must deal with their own shock and anxiety when they learn just how much their concepts of one another have been based all along on their own inner feelings for each other. This is a necessary growth experience for both. If the psychotherapist can allow himself to review his past treatment with this new sensitivity, he will learn just how much his psychotherapy is still molded by his personality. He can understand better now how the patient—the former patient and the patients he still has—permitted and encouraged him to believe certain things. He can realize more clearly how some patients allow him to misperceive so that they can then more easily identify with his misperceptions. The change of focus that occurs in a friendship relationship between a psychotherapist and a patient not only gives them both greater opportunity for emotional growth as they relate in different areas of their living but also strengthens the basis of their relationship as they understand more clearly what this relationship had been based on up to that time.

The Transition Stage

The development of a psychotherapy relationship into a true friendship between the former psychotherapist and the former patient has a great deal in common with the process of growth that occurs as the normal adolescent moves toward adulthood in his own family (3). In the family, the young adolescent gives up the protection and the guidance of his parents and begins to decide and to control his own destiny; during the adolescent decade he changes from being a physically small, dependent member of a family group to being a physically large, independent member of a wider social community. This transition stage, in any family, is a period of much ambivalence and anxiety for the parents and for the adolescent. Even during these uneasy adolescent years, there is a specially difficult interim stage for everyone when the teenager has given up his former dependent role but has not yet become comfortable in his new adult self-sufficiency and when his parents no longer can act as controllers but have not yet become respected advisers. At this time, when the relationships in the family are vague, uncertain, and changing, anxiety is maximal and may be very hard to tolerate.

In a similar fashion, there is an interim stage in the changing relationship of the former psychotherapist and the former patient as they become friends. Both have been comfortable in the old relationship, both wish the new friendship, but neither is quite sure how this relationship should develop. It is very tempting for both to revert to their old patterns but, if they try to do this, each one is liable to become angry in his own way because they have both sensed the greater emotional rewards that can come with a meaningful friendship. Yet they do not fully understand their new roles with one another, they are still uncertain about the changing focus of their friendship and they do not really know quite what is going to happen. At this time in their relationship when things are vague and blurred, it is easier for them both to blame this anxiety on former conflicts and earlier struggles. When the psychotherapist begins to feel this inner tension, it is simpler for him to think that he is facing conflictual anxiety from unresolved countertransference feelings rather than to admit to the deeper anxieties of introspection and new understanding. The former patient may find it difficult to face directly the fact that he is no longer protected by someone powerful; it may be easier for him to blame his uneasiness on a resurgence of conflicts previously discussed in the more familiar, psychotherapy relationship.

If the psychotherapist and the patient are to continue to grow in their interaction with one another, they must face this transition anxiety openly and directly. As they change, they have now to accept the fact that they are permitting themselves to find personal pleasure in one another. They are allowing one another to give and to receive openly from each other. The psychotherapist has to acknowledge the fact that, in allowing this natural friendship to evolve, he has made a choice—a choice for this particular patient and perhaps also a choice against other patients. He must now face the very human realization that he has never been without favorites in his psychotherapy relationships and much of his treatment process has been strongly affected by his identifications and counteridentifications with his patients. This deeper self-understanding may be profoundly disturbing for the psychotherapist but, if he can use this knowledge, he can be even more effective in his treatment procedures.

Results of a Friendship Relationship

Obviously the psychotherapist cannot and should not become a personal friend to all his patients. In those situations where the personality of the former patient and the former psychotherapist make continuing friendship a natural and appropriate development, the psychotherapist can use the increasing self-understanding that he will achieve with this new kind of relationship to make his continuing psychotherapy even richer and more meaningful. He will become more sensitive to his own treatment processes and more alert to the techniques he uses. A continued friendship with a former psychotherapist may strengthen the gains made by the patient in the previous psychotherapy and may lead to very rapid emotional growth. For the former patient, the psychotherapy process may have been a preparation for the friendship and the friendship is the realization and the proof—a proof that the patient can see and a proof that encourages him to develop his relationship ability with many other people. For both the patient and the psychotherapist, this friendship can give them an opportunity to grow as friends and as individuals in the years ahead but, at the same time, it allows them to look back into their earlier treatment relationship, to the psychotherapy, and to strengthen, stabilize, and rebuild what went on then.

If the psychotherapist cannot allow this kind of friendship to develop where it is natural and appropriate, he limits his own personal and professional growth and he may be undermining the gains the patient made in psychotherapy.

Summary

Very little has been written about continued friendship between the former patient and the former psychotherapist after termination but this does occur and not infrequently. The change of roles, the wider focus, and the difficult transitional stage in this growth to friendship give rise to many anxieties but also allow much deeper understanding. Such a friendship relationship can enrich both the patient and the therapist and gives unique insights into the meaning and the effect of psychotherapy for both participants.

REFERENCES

1. Edelson, M. *The Termination of Intensive Psychotherapy.* C. C Thomas, Springfield, Ill., 1963.
2. Pattison, E. M. The Patient after Psychotherapy. *Am. J. Psychother.,* 25:194, 1970.
3. Dewald, P. A. The Termination of Psychotherapy. *Psychiat. Dig.,* 28:33, 1967.

NATHAN HURVITZ

Peer Self-Help Groups

Although there have been some studies and impressionistic reports about peer self-help psychotherapy groups (PSHPG) such as Alcoholics Anonymous (A.A.) . . . there has been no research on the common characteristics of PSHPG to determine the source of their effectiveness. This effectiveness is acknowledged by Blum & Blum (1967):

Fox, a psychoanalyst who has had a great deal of experience in treating alcoholics, states the case in favor of A.A.: "Probably the most effective treatment we have is that of Alcoholics Anonymous" (p. 161).

Blum & Blum (1967) also suggest that Synanon has helped a greater proportion of drug addicts who have participated in its program than any other type of treatment for addicts:

Since 1958, the date of incorporation of Synanon as a non-profit foundation, it has treated nearly 500 addicts and persons with severe social and psychological problems. The majority have been addicted to narcotics, dangerous drugs, and alcohol. Of 860 who have come to Synanon, 55 per cent have stayed and kept free of addiction, even though the door is open at all times (p. 158).

The growth of the A.A. movement and the establishment of many other self-help groups modeled on A.A. emphasizes its effectiveness. The widespread development of peer self-help fellowships

Former title "Peer Self-Help Psychotherapy Groups and Their Implications for Psychotherapy." From *Psychotherapy: Theory, Research and Practice,* Vol. 7, #1, Spring, 1970. Reprinted by permission of *Psychotherapy: Theory, Research and Practice* and of the author.

is indicated by Mowrer (1964) who reported that in 1961–62 a directory of PSHPG entitled *Their Brothers' Keepers,* compiled by Dr. Maurice Jackson, listed 265 groups. Some of the groups have undoubtedly expired while new ones have been formed.

Self-help groups are formed in various ways. The established movements or fellowships such as A.A., Gamblers Anonymous, Synanon, etc. regularly receive considerable publicity in the mass media, and an address or telephone number is always given which those who are interested can follow up. Although these organizations work with little or no employed staffs, inquiries are answered promptly. When PSHPG reach the size considered optimum by the particular movement, a cadre group is assigned to form a new group in a new neighborhood or community. Groups are also formed when someone invites the leaders of an established group and prospective members from his neighborhood or community to a meeting he has planned. If there is sufficient interest and proper planning, a new group is formed. One not familiar with such groups is unaware of the intense involvement and commitment PSHPG arouse in their members. All of the members have experienced the agonies of the problem they have overcome and they are missionaries on behalf of their cause. Intense feelings of hope which are aroused in prospective members are converted into activity which requires simple organizational skills. Becoming a member of a successful movement which has achieved so much for people like themselves inspires many to undertake the necessary organizational activity.

Groups which are not affiliated with established movements are also formed in various ways. Members of A.A., Gamblers Anonymous, Synanon, etc. leave these groups for various personal or ideological reasons, and form new groups. Some of these survive apart from an established movement and may become the basis for a new fellowship. Some members of an existing group who are more compatible socially may withdraw to form a group of their own. Clergymen who learn about PSHPG organize them because they know people in their own congregations or their communities who have been or who can be served in this way. High school teachers have formed groups of students who are addicts. Therapists—psychiatrists, psychologists, social workers, psychiatric nurses, psychiatric aides—establish PSHPG in which they participate for a time, or they serve as catalysts who encourage others to form such groups.

The therapist in a metropolitan area who wishes to refer clients to a self-help group can find such groups listed in the telephone book. The therapist who is not in a metropolitan area can write to the national office of the particular organization for information about groups in his area. If there is no group in existence, he and his client may be asked to take the initiative to form such a group. If the therapist undertakes to do so he must remember that he is helping establish a "self-help" group; and if he attempts to serve as a "consultant," "advisor," or in some other continuing professional position, he is in fact thwarting the formation of a self-help group. One of the strengths of these groups comes from solving their own organizational and ideological problems. (The names and addresses of selected PSHPG are presented in Appendix I.)

My method of investigating PSHPG has included participant observation (Becker & Geer, 1967), discussions with members of self-help groups and with colleagues who are knowledgeable about such fellowships, and reviewing the literature. Self-help groups whose meetings I have observed—all in the Los Angeles area—are A.A., Al-Anon, Gamblers Anonymous, TOPS (Take Off Pounds Sensibly), Recovery, Inc., Neurotics Anonymous, Seventh Step Foundation, Weight-watchers, and a local group, Psychiatric Club of America; and I have attended Saturday night Open House programs at Synanon.

Though there are basic similarities between various PSHPG, each group, fellowship or movement has its own principles and practices. For instance, there are significant differences about rejecting and punitive behavior between the "Anonymous" groups and other fellowships, some of which expel members who deviate from group rules or expectations. Neither do the PSHPG have the same philosophy or attitude about "inspirational" and "spiritual" expressions and activities. Not all the problems that unite group members are problems to the same degree. Alcoholism, drug addiction, gambling, obesity, "neurosis," etc. have different social definitions and consequences. PSHPG also have different organizational forms which determine different kinds of interaction between members. Some groups meet once a week in each other's homes; A.A. members may meet each other several times weekly at their meeting hall, or a member may attend several different group meetings each week; and Synanon members live in a voluntary community which controls all important aspects of their lives. Some groups are known only to their members or in their local communities while others are affiliated with national movements. These and other differences make strict comparisons and definitive generalizations difficult.

The analysis of PSHPG is based upon the sociological "constructed" or "ideal" type. These constructed types or models do not exist in or represent reality but are formed to represent an extreme so they can be compared with other similarly formed extreme types. The constructed type of PSHPG is the fellowship or movement which attempts to foster maximum interaction and mutual assistance between peers, which requires complete self-revelation, and which affords the members the opportunity for mobility within their fellowship or movement as they overcome their common problems or inappropriate behavior.

My observations are not equally significant or equally valid, and several are repeated under different headings with a different emphasis. They are presented under the following headings: A. Structural and Procedural Characteristics, B. Reciprocity, C. Moral Attitudes, D. Psychological System, E. Social System, F. Group Therapy, and G. Fellowship Identification.

A. Structural and Procedural Characteristics

Peers maintain administrative authority and bookkeeping responsibility for their therapy. Free will offerings are solicited, case records are not kept, and meetings which are (almost always) open and to which visitors and observers are invited are held according to a publicized schedule. Each peer may attend as many different scheduled meetings as he wishes, he may call special or emergency meetings, and he may call upon other peers as he needs them. Meetings are conducted in homes, public and private halls, meeting rooms, etc., not designed or established for psychotherapy purposes, but rented or controlled by the peers. Peers are not required to have completed a program of professional education or to be licensed or certified; however, each fellowship or movement may have a training program for those members who wish to assume leadership positions. Peers determine therapy goals and procedures—which are to help each other solve a particular problem or change specific behavior within their movement.

B. Reciprocity

A peer status exists in the fellowship and leaders are those who help others achieve their therapeutic goals. Peers are therapists because of their ability to disclose themselves, create empathy, and encourage and support others' efforts to change according to the goals set and means determined by their fellowship. Peers acknowledge to each other that they are failures, abnormal, immature, "neurotic," etc. Peers must and do reveal themselves to each other, and all have experienced the problem or behavior which defines them as peers: alcoholism, drug addiction, obesity, "neuroticism," etc. Because peers reveal themselves and have had similar life experiences, they are role models for each other, they identify with each other, and do not question each other's ability to understand, empathize, etc. Because of their attitudes toward each other, interaction reaches the "gut" level.

C. Moral Attitudes

Peers tend to regard their problems or inappropriate behavior as a health problem and describe themselves as "sick." However they profess a moral position and are judgmental since behavior that is deviant, irresponsible, self-defeating, etc. should be changed. They may make each other feel guilty or ashamed and may punish each other for inappropriate behavior. They consider religious attitudes important and utilize "spiritual" or "inspirational" motivations.

D. Psychological System

Peers are diagnostically oriented and tend to review each other's past to determine the causes of present problems but they do not foster psychological regression. They offer "insights" and "interpretations" on the basis of "unconscious processes" and genetic and developmental material. Peers seek the "underlying causes" of the present problems which they regard as "symptoms," in accord with the "medical model," but they are not concerned with "symptom substitution" or with the emergence of greater problems if these causes are not discovered. Behavior which is not in accord with the expressed principles and goals of the movement is evidence of the member's unreadiness or unwillingness to accept his place in the fellowship and accept its discipline; and such behavior also reveals his "stupidity," "immaturity," "lack of will power" or his lack of desire to change. Peers interact with many others and experience many "transference" relationships directly. Peers hold each other responsible for their behavior regardless of its causes, they deny each other's excuses which do not help the movement achieve its goals and may harm others. They have explicitly defined expectations and goals and attempt to help each other solve their problems and modify their behavior in accord with the principles of their movement. Their primary concern is with their own and the others' behavior and they support each other's efforts and effective functioning by example, encouragement, "endorsement," exhortation, ridicule, etc. to achieve day to day goals as they look to the future. In this way they function according to the learning model.

Anyone who has the problem which defines their fellowship is eligible for membership since peers do not select each other, and they have a hopeful attitude about helping anyone who joins their movement. At the same time they will not jeopardize their movement because of a peer's deviant behavior which may threaten the well-being of others or which may destroy or damage their movement, and may deny admission to such a prospective member or expel such a peer. The more serious a member's problem, the more the others want to prove the effectiveness of their movement for him. They exert more effort on his behalf, for he has a greater potential as a leader of their movement by reporting the difference between his former and present behavior in the community and to prospective members.

Peers are active in their relationships with each other, they focus on the presenting problem, and assume that by following the principles and methods of their movement they will help each member solve his specific problem and thereby cause intrapsychic changes and enhanced self-attitudes. They may ridicule and attack each other with great hostility and they may provoke aggressive and hostile feelings; however, peers regard such attacks and provocations as others' expressions of concern and care. Peers assume that the fellowship experience will be transferred into the member's everyday life—of which the fellowship is an important part. Peers attempt to find substitute satisfactions for inappropriate behavior and may regard such substitutes as effective change devices. They continually motivate and support each other's expressed desire to change by various material and non-material recognition and rewards. Ceremonials and rituals about special dates or activities are used to reinforce the purpose and value of the fellowship. Peers are always available to assist another if he appears committed to the fellowship or wants to maintain a place within it. They give each other periodic support in accord with a meeting schedule and continuing support by their availability to each other. Appropriate behavior is required by membership in the fellowship, and such behavior is ardently if not planfully encouraged. Peers may give each other advice. They involve the families of fellowship members and develop special programs for and with them. In addition to social relationships peers help each other as members of a communications grapevine through which information about jobs, rentals, bargains, etc. is shared. Peers disclose their secrets in public and have complete knowledge about each other. Their knowledge of each other's secrets is "punishment" for behavior which may be associated with present problems, and as "atonement" serves to expiate their guilt feelings. Peers do not represent "significant others"; they are significant others; and each one's acceptance of the other is not symbolic but real. Peers encourage each other to make restitution to those whom they may have harmed in some way.

E. Social System

Peers are totally involved in a fellowship and each experience is a part of therapy—which is participation in a way of life. Peers establish a community of relationships which enable and support their efforts to change. They are involved with and concerned about each other's everyday problems and help each other function more effectively in their daily lives. Because peers are organized about a common problem they are more likely to have a heterogeneous membership in terms of race, religious identification, educational or class level, age, etc. than groups formed by professionals. As members of a social movement which has novelty and positive aspects, peers make an impact upon the community and have status as members of their fellowship. They organize community groups to support their movement and publicize it in every way they can. Those who have had an unsuccessful experience in the fellowship drop away (and are not known to new members) while those who have solved their problems maintain a place in the social system of their movement and are responsible for aiding and training others.

F. Group Therapy

All peer therapy occurs in groups; individuals may form therapeutic dyads within the structure of the fellowship. Group leadership develops and shifts as different peers help others achieve the movement's purpose thereby helping each other to gain personal benefits. The peers' consideration is, "What is in the best interest of the movement?", for by achieving it each member serves himself and others best. The movement is organized around a specific problem common to all members, and since the peers have similar histories and want to overcome the same problem they are role models for each other. A member's achievements gained prior to and outside the movement (his profession, wealth, how well known he is, etc.) may affect his status in the group: he may be treated more severely if he attempts to use it manipulatively. Peers achieve status within their movement by contrasting their former and present behavior, by helping others, by serving as "sponsors," and by undertaking greater responsibility in their movement. Since peer interaction is a continuously available opportunity for self-examination, self-assessment, peer assessment and behavior change, the fellowship offers opportunities for peers to have real life meaning for each other and to change real life behavior and attitudes. Peers are aware of their interdependence and they are concerned about their own and the others' efforts to solve their problems and to change their behavior to prove the validity of the movements to which they have committed themselves. Peers are always and immediately available to each other and being called upon by another for help is a mark of esteem which is highly regarded and reinforces the value of the movement.

G. Fellowship Identification

The peers' identification is with their movement and they are not concerned about their functioning as therapists so they may introduce innovations in psychotherapy. Peer relationships have no economic aspect and peers are not vulnerable to manipulation and seduction on this basis. Where professional therapists participate in the fellowship they play an auxilliary role and are dominated by the members. The fellowship represents and accepts the community and its authority, values, etc., which the peers accept. Community attitudes to the fellowship range from hostility to active support; in general they are skeptical and resistant. Peers are members of a movement which encourages mobility within the fellowship itself; and peers become successful according to the ways and values of their movement (which are derived from the society in which the members live). A member may become dependent upon the movement which is just like being dependent upon his addiction (if this is his problem), or it becomes a substitute problem. Peers have faith in each other because of the success of their movement in aiding others with problems like their own. Peers encourage each other to acknowledge that there is a power greater than themselves—(however they may define this power)—which is a source of help to them.

Conclusions

A. Structural and Procedural Issues:

1. One important element of psychotherapy is the human relationship which is established between the therapist and client, and if the essence of a human relationship cannot be bought, charging a fee for psychotherapy is a contradiction in terms.

2. Psychotherapy should be offered without such elements of a bureaucratic structure as fees, records, scheduled appointments, privacy, special settings, professional training, etc., except those which the participants themselves decide are helpful to them and which they want to assume to achieve their goals.

B. Reciprocity Between Therapists and Clients:

1. Therapists should be those peers who others select on the basis of criteria they determine—which may or may not include special education or training or having experienced the problem or inappropriate behavior they are attempting to overcome.

C. Moral Attitudes:

1. Spiritual and inspirational concepts and methods can be used effectively in psychotherapy.

2. Moral and judgmental attitudes can be used effectively in psychotherapy.

D. Psychological System:

1. Psychotherapy does not require searching for and interpreting the unconscious and/or the developmental sources of present

behavior; and if such a search is useful it can be conducted by untrained personnel.

2. Members of PSHPG "analyze" each other, they offer "insights into" and "interpretations of" each other's behavior, thoughts and feelings. Although many believe that this activity is the cause of psychological change, it is more likely that this change occurs because each member is expected to conform with behavior which the fellowship has defined as appropriate, and his conformity is secured by various group techniques.

3. Psychotherapy which modifies behavior and attitudes without discovering "underlying causes" does not cause "symptom substitution."

4. ·Psychotherapy does not require the creation of or analysis of the "transference neurosis."

5. The therapist's "unconditional positive regard" for the client is not a necessary or sufficient condition for psychotherapeutic change.

6. Therapists can use recognition and reward for their clients' efforts and desirable behavior and attitudes, and punishment for their clients' lack of effort and undesirable behavior and attitudes in relation to their mutually defined goals to help their clients achieve these goals.

7. Psychotherapeutic goals should be explicitly stated and all therapeutic activities should be evaluated in relation to how well they help the client achieve the stated goal.

8. Public rather than private sharing of experiences considered responsible for problem behavior, public rather than private acknowledgment of damage or harm done to others, and efforts at restitution to those damaged or harmed are effective psychotherapeutic procedures (Mowrer, 1964).

9. Negative and hostile attitudes and behavior such as ridicule and forms of punishment and expulsion from the group may help a client change his behavior when he knows that others who express such attitudes and behavior toward him have fully revealed themselves to him and fully entered a therapeutic relationship with him.

10. Therapists should offer substitute satisfactions for their clients' inappropriate behavior.

11. Advice-giving can be used constructively in psychotherapy.

12. Psychotherapy should be concerned about the client in his real-life activities and in relation to all members of his family.

13. The therapist's secretiveness about himself denies the human relationship he wants to foster and thereby limits his effectiveness.

14. Therapists are effective to the degree that they "teach" new ways of behaving to their clients by their own example.

E. The Social System of Therapy:

1. Psychotherapy should encourage people to become involved with others and participate with them in common activities and endeavors.

2. The continued participation by those peers who have been helped by the fellowship supports the expectations of new members that they will receive the help they need and serves as a self-fulfilling prophecy.

3. Psychotherapy should be conceived of and practiced as social interaction (social learning) between peers instead of intra-psychic exploration between therapist and client.

4. Although members of PSHPG profess the "medical model," they function according to the learning model.

5. The development of significant others, of a new reference group which is part of a social movement whose members simultaneously enable and constrain each other to behave in ways they have agreed are desirable and appropriate for them, is a most significant factor which aids the members of PSHPG.

F. Group Therapy:

1. Group therapy should be the principal therapeutic modality.

2. Therapists should arise out of group interaction to achieve the members' defined goals.

3. Individuals with the same problems serve as most effective role models for each other.

4. The therapy group or setting should offer the client opportunities for mobility within it.

G. Therapist's Identification:

1. Psychotherapists should encourage clients with problems to join and/or form PSHPG.

2. PSHPG are most effective when they do not have enthusiastic community support and have not been infiltrated by professionals.

3. Psychotherapy as a PSHPG movement is—or has the potential to be—more effective for more people with more and different problems and for much less money than conventional psychotherapy regardless of its guiding psychological theory and the auspices through which it is offered.

4. Since an ounce of prevention is worth a pound of cure, it is the psychotherapist's responsibility to assist in creating a social order in which the therapeutic activities conducted in PSHPG are practiced in the society as a whole as the basic relationship between people.

Concluding Remarks

It is important to recognize that PSHPG achieve their goals without the application of specific behavior modification techniques, without an existential search for identity, without the exploration of human potential, without awareness training to actualize one's potential, without the analysis of the transference neurosis, without psychodrama, without clearing engrams, without creative fighting, without mind expanding drugs, without sensory awakening, without marathons, without feeling each other up, without taking off their clothes, and without sexual intercourse between therapists and clients (McCartney, 1966). PSHPG are fellowships whose members have a common problem and who establish such relationships with each other as peers that they fully reveal themselves to each other. Within such relationships, and in the presence of members who acknowledge the help they received through the fellowship, the peers make it possible and desirable to accept each other's efforts to modify their own and the others' behavior and solve their own and others' problems according to the methods and goals of the fellowship. The procedures and techniques utilized within the fellowship are those long identified with learning theory.

The results achieved by PSHPG raise doubt about the purpose and value of some psychotherapy research. Psychodynamic concepts appear to be more interesting as literary metaphors than as guides to research into what causes people to change. And the relevance of studies that count the number of times the therapist says "uh huh" or "uh uh," or how often the therapist and client blink their eyes becomes suspect. The purpose of PSHPG is to change people and these amateurs succeed in a considerable number of cases—apparently more often than professionals do. If the methods developed in PSHPG were to be refined scientifically and fed back into these groups (with their permission and cooperation), they might be even more effective than they are. These methods could then be applied in whatever professional psychotherapy activities may be needed and which would then be as helpful as PSHPG.

If I have lost my professional objectivity and display nonprofessional enthusiasm for PSHPG it is in part due to the condescending and patronizing attitude of conventional psychotherapists to this movement. It is irritating when conventional psychotherapists explain and belittle PSHPG on the basis of psychodynamic concepts whose value as a guide to treatment is questionable. For instance, Koegler & Brill (1967) interpret the effectiveness of A.A. to the "24 hour mothering" offered by A.A., to "the maternal role which A.A. performs in the life of the alcoholic," to its "mothering role," and they assert that "The psychodynamics of alcoholism have most meaning for therapy when viewed in terms of this relationship (pp. 173–4)." They quote Hayman (1966): ". . . when the alcoholic 'hits bottom' he recognizes 'that the fantasied mother is not obtainable through alcohol.' Alcoholics

Anonymous then becomes a 'substitute for mother' (p. 175)."
Koegler & Brill also claim that "in order to stay recovered and
protected from the temptation to drink the alcoholic must literally
devote his life to A.A., its frequent meetings and frequent calls (to
go to the aid of a fellow alcoholic who has 'slipped') [pp.
173–4]." They assert that A.A. has a "religious cult-like framework" and quote approvingly from Chafetz & Demone (1962)
about the "sect or cult-like aspects of A.A. (p. 174)." In addition
they snidely declare:

There is even a bible; the old testament of A.A. is the "Big Book,"
Alcoholics Anonymous (Alcoholics Anonymous, 1957). Its new testament is *The Twelve Steps and Twelve Traditions* (Alcoholics Anonymous, 1952). Its Jehovah is Bill W., for it was he who developed the
steps and traditions and wrote his own history; he is the main motivating force of A.A. (p. 174).

A similar attitude is expressed toward Synanon. Koegler & Brill
report that at Synanon House "An extremely charismatic approach
is used in which the founder, Charles Dederich, is the focus (p.
167)." They emphasize the effectiveness of charisma as a therapeutic force and bemoan the fact that the physician has lost much
of his charisma in the process of becoming more human (sic).
They also complain:

There is a general discounting of traditional authority [in Synanon and
A.A.], with an emphasis on the superior knowledge of the group and
its leader. Rehabilitation [by Synanon] takes many years and there is
some question whether successful graduates can ever break the tie with
Synanon (pp. 167–8).

But PSHPG "work." And it is likely that more people have been
and are being helped by PSHPG than have been and are being
helped by all types of professionally trained psychotherapists combined, with far less theorizing or analyzing and for much less
money. And my zealousness for PSHPG is also due to experiences
I have had at meetings of people who, whatever their principles
and practices, have developed meaningful human relationships
with others and with them have overcome disabling problems. It is
moving, thrilling and inspiring to participate in a meeting in which
PSHPG members describe the help they have received from their

fellowship. Many of these members had their problems for many years, some had been jailed, institutionalized, and some had gone to many different conventional therapists to whom they paid thousands of dollars for help they needed but did not receive while they suffered the terrible agonies of their afflictions.

The "mental health" of the American people is becoming such a great problem that all the professionally trained psychotherapists cannot offer needed assistance (Albee, 1959; Arnoff, 1968)—if indeed these are the people who can help at all (Graziano, 1969). But each PSHPG is part of a peoples' movement which has demonstrated how well it can change individuals. This movement has yet to learn that it must assume the additional role of changing the community and the society.

The characteristics of PSHPG are reported after participant observation, receiving information from informed others, and reviewing the pertinent literature. Certain conclusions were drawn from these characteristics about the sources and agents of the psychotherapeutic effectiveness of PSHPG which may have meaning for psychotherapy principles and practices. It is now necessary to study the relative therapeutic effectiveness, and the causes of this effectiveness, of PSHPG activities with more precise instruments than one clinician's impressions to determine precisely what it is about PSHPG that makes them "work"—and also makes them more effective for some people with problems or deviant behavior than conventional psychotherapy.

REFERENCES

Albee, G. W. *Mental health manpower trends,* New York: Basic Books, 1959.

Arnoff, F. N. "Reassessment of the trilogy: Need, supply, and demand," *American Psychologist,* 1968, 23, 312–316.

Bales, R. F. "The therapeutic roles of Alcoholics Anonymous as seen by a sociologist," *Quarterly Journal of Studies on Alcohol,* 1944, 5, 267–278.

Becker, H. S. & Geer, Blanche. "Participant observation and interviewing: A comparison," *Human organization,* 1957, 16, 28–32.

Blum, Eva M. & Blum, R. H. *Alcoholism, modern psychological approaches to treatment,* San Francisco: Jossey-Bass, 1967.

Casriel, D. *So fair a house: The story of Synanon,* New York: Prentice-Hall, 1963.

Chafetz, M. E. & Demone, H. W. *Alcoholism and society,* New York: Oxford University Press, 1962.

Cherkas, M. S. "Synanon foundation—A radical approach to the problem of addiction," *American Journal of Psychiatry,* 1965, 121, 1065–1068.

Eckhardt, W. "Alcoholic values and Alcoholics Anonymous," *Quarterly Journal of Studies on Alcohol,* 1967, 8, 277–287.

Endore, G. *Synanon,* New York: Doubleday, 1968.

Gellman, I. P. *The sober alcoholic: An organizational analysis of Alcoholics Anonymous,* New Haven: College and University Press, 1964.

Graziano, A. M. "Clinical innovation and the mental health power structure: A social case history," *American Psychologist,* 1969, 24, 10–18.

Hayman, M. *Alcoholism: Mechanisms and management,* Springfield, Ill.: Charles C. Thomas, 1966.

Holzinger, R. "Synanon through the eyes of a visiting psychologist." *Quarterly Journal of Studies on Alcohol,* 1965, 26, 304–309.

Koegler, R. R. & Brill, N. Q. *Treatment of psychiatric outpatients,* New York: Appleton-Century-Crofts, 1967.

Maxwell, M. A. "Alcoholics Anonymous: An interpretation," in D. J. Pittman and C. R. Snyder (eds.), *Society, culture, and drinking patterns,* New York: John Wiley & Sons, 1962, 577–585.

McCartney, J. "Overt transference," *Journal of Sex Research,* 1966, 2, 227–237.

Mowrer, O. H. *The new group therapy.* Princeton, N.J.: Van Nostrand, 1964.

Ripley, H. S. & Jackson, Joan K. "Therapeutic factors in Alcoholics Anonymous," *American Journal of Psychiatry,* 1959, 116, 44–50.

Ross, Lillian. *Vertical and horizontal,* New York: Simon and Schuster, 1963.

Stewart, D. A. "The dynamics of fellowship as illustrated in Alcoholics Anonymous," *Quarterly Journal of Studies on Alcohol,* 1955, 16, 251–262.

Thiebout, H. M. "Therapeutic mechanisms of Alcoholics Anonymous," *American Journal of Psychiatry,* 1944, 100, 468–473.

Trice, H. M. "The affiliation motive and readiness to join Alcoholics Anonymous," *Quarterly Journal of Studies on Alcohol,* 1959, 20, 313–320.

Volkman, R., & Cressey, D. R. "Differential association and the rehabilitation of drug addicts," *American Journal of Sociology,* 1963, 69, 129–142.

Yablonsky, L. *The tunnel back: Synanon,* New York: Macmillan, 1965.

APPENDIX

Names and Addresses of Selected Peer Self-help Psychotherapy Fellowships

Al-Anon Family Group Headquarters
P.O. Box 182
Madison Square Station
New York, N.Y. 10010

Alcoholics Anonymous
General Service Office
P.O. Box 459
Grand Central Station
New York, N.Y. 10017

Daytop Village, Inc.
54 W. 40 St.
New York, N.Y. 10018

Gam-Anon National Services
P.O. Box 'M'
Norwalk, California 90650

Gamblers Anonymous
National Service Office
P.O. Box 17173
Los Angeles, Calif. 90017

Neurotics Anonymous
Room 425, Colorado Bldg.
1341 G. Street, N.W.
Washington, D.C. 20005

Overeaters Anonymous
P.O. Box 3372
Beverly Hills, Calif. 90212

Parents Without Partners, Inc.
80 Fifth Avenue
New York, N.Y. 10011

Recovery, Inc.
166 S. Michigan Avenue
Chicago, Illinois 60603

Seventh Step Foundation
7 West McDowell Road
Phoenix, Arizona 95003

Schizophrenics Anonymous Inter-
    national
Box 913
Saskatoon
Saskatchewan, Canada

Synanon Foundation, Inc.
1351 Ocean Front
Santa Monica, Calif. 90401

TOPS Club, Inc.
(Take Off Pounds Sensibly)
4575 S. Fifth Street
Milwaukee, Wisconsin 53207

RICHARD R. PARLOUR
PHILIP Z. COLE
ROBERT B. VAN VORST

Tools for Behavior Rehabilitation

In our work, we have come to recognize the traditional client-oriented, one-to-one psychotherapist-patient relationship has some serious limitations. We have found that it need not be the only or even the predominant psychotherapeutic tool. Various forms of group therapy may be far superior in many situations. In most cases we use individual therapy—but in combination with a form of group therapy that we call *The Treatment Team.*

This is a somewhat different kind of therapy group than one usually thinks of when group therapy is considered. This team is made up of involved family members, but often also includes work associates and other professional people in the community, such as clergymen, physicians, lawyers, and social case workers. These persons are selected with the assistance and written permission of the client. Members of the treatment team may attend sessions with the patient or communicate with the therapist by phone or mail.

Too often significant others are treated by therapists as nuisance factors. Frequently they stop being nuisances when they are included in the treatment team. Often they are able to make invaluable contributions.

A woman in our office said her husband would not come in for conference. Instead of accepting the information, the therapist insisted on

---

Former title "Treatment Teams and Written Contracts as Tools for Behavior Rehabilitation." From *The Discoverer,* Vol. 4, No. 1, February 1967, © 1967.

telephoning the husband. The wife protested that the call would do no good. However, having been previously authorized by her in writing to consult the husband, the therapist proceeded with the phone call, and told the husband: "Your wife is in my office. She is very upset, and we need you; will you come?" The husband's answer was enthusiastically in the affirmative. Thereafter he came regularly, contributing substantially to the solution of the problem.

However, in the early stages of therapy, we spend a limited amount of time in private conference with the client, looking for and seeking to identify matters that may be hard for him to discuss in the presence of others who are close to him in his daily life.

These individual sessions also are important because they help to assess correctly the client's handling of reality. Then, when we compare the information provided by him and by the other members of the treatment team, we obtain a highly useful index of any distortions in statements made by the client or by the others. This helps us to focus our attention and efforts quickly on the most relevant and productive areas of the case. Quite often we use frank confrontations between the client and significant other members of the treatment team to get the facts of the case out in the open and available for discussion.

Relying on the treatment team, we attempt to pinpoint and define the client's incapacitating problems in terms of *specific behavioral and attitudinal faults*. With this information at hand we are then in a position to design written *Treatment Contracts* that everyone in the team, including the client, can agree to honor. As the details of these contracts are fulfilled, the client's symptoms tend to diminish rapidly. He usually starts to feel better immediately upon agreeing to take, and then taking, definite steps toward correcting his inevitably erroneous and self-defeating way of living.

Besides offering an invaluable source of pertinent information, members of the treatment team help us to supervise and aid the client in his day-to-day carrying out of the specific corrective procedures we set up. They can report back to us the client's progress or lack of progress between meetings. This supervisory role of the client's significant others also provides an additional element of motivation for the client—*coercion*. Other therapists may shun coercion, but we have found overt, explicit coercion a highly useful and not necessarily detrimental tool for really effective therapy.

Because we focus on correcting basic character and behavior disorders rather than on symptoms, and in spite of the coercion element of much of our therapy, clients are not so inclined to discontinue therapy prematurely when their symptoms are reduced but before they have really changed their life styles. Symptom-oriented treatments tend to alter symptoms without accomplishing much toward improving lives.

A married couple in their thirties came to us complaining of sexual incompatibility. "He doesn't arouse me. I'm just not interested in sex with him," the wife lamented. The husband accused her of frigidity. Instead of letting them discuss this problem at length, we reviewed the life inventory of both of them as individuals and marriage partners. We discovered that they had not gone out together for years, hadn't had any real fun together. When the therapist suggested an outing, their response was: "Oh, that's unimportant. We don't want to do that; we're interested in sex; we came here to talk about sex; we don't want to talk about outings."

The therapist discovered that this couple also couldn't agree about how to handle money—what was to be purchased and who was to handle the funds. But again both patients protested: "This isn't what we came for; we want to talk about our *sexual* problems!" Finally, the couple couldn't agree about the training and disciplining of their children.

Despite their objections, the therapy was focused on these other nonsexual areas of failure. Through our insistence, they began a program designed to solve some of these problems. They began going out together. They worked out a financial arrangement that was both practical and reasonable. They also set up some new expectations and disciplinary methods for the children.

In a short while, when these "unimportant" other matters were improved, this couple reported that their sex life was better than they had ever known it before, yet after the first interview sex had not specifically been discussed any further. In fact, it would probably have been wasteful to do so. After improving their general pattern of family life, psychotherapy for their sex problem will probably never be necessary.

In our frame of reference it is important that the therapist be prepared and willing to give good advice when requested to do so or when it is obviously needed. Often the client will plead with the therapist for advice on how to cope with a particular problem. Rather than resorting to guessing games or tossing the question back in the client's lap with a neat reflection ploy, we freely express our viewpoint, and when we feel qualified, we give him advice. As we see it, we have both a legitimate obligation and a professional responsibility to provide leadership in therapy.

The therapist frequently is called upon to exercise what might be called a "priestly" function. He is asked to recommend procedures for clients who become involved in life crises. Like the priest, the therapist cannot guarantee that these procedures will lead to a positive specific result. But neither can he play it safe by withholding advice and instruction until the moment of scientific certitude: life moves on and decisions must be made.

Even the tribal priest has traditionally been one of the best educated and disciplined members of his group. It is a major function of the psychotherapist, as well as the priest, to bridge the gap between abstract certainty and practical reality. In ancient times the tribal priest served the religious, administrative-legal, and therapeutic needs of the group. Though these functions today are fragmented and dispersed to specialists, the practicing therapist inevitably retains the priestly function to some degree. Thus clients seek certainties from their therapist. Fortunately they will usually settle for reasonable, constructive procedures and some objective sound judgment.

But we welcome and even encourage the patient's own contributions in thinking, expressing his viewpoint, and spontaneous action when these are reasonable, appropriate and responsible. Yet we reserve the right to set the patient straight when we see indications of unreasonable, inappropriate and irresponsible thinking, talking and action.

The following case history illustrates the highly active leadership role a therapist may be required to take in getting results in a situation that originally appeared almost impossibly complicated.

A 43-year-old machinist was referred by his attorney for psychiatric evaluation and possible treatment. His wife had filed a criminal complaint against him for performing sexual acts with their fourteen-year-old daughter.

The wife had also filed suit for divorce and, according to the patient, she was absolutely unreasonable whenever he tried to visit the children or "talk things out" with her. He said that the home situation had deteriorated badly; their nineteen-year-old son was in youth prison for the second time; the fourteen-year-old daughter and thirteen-year-old son were not doing at all well in school, were dirty, poorly fed and clothed.

The patient claimed that school authorities were considering some disciplinary action against his wife because of the condition of the children.

He was quite sure that he would be able to afford private psychiatric care in spite of the financial difficulties resulting from spending several weeks in jail and later fighting his wife's divorce action; he gave as his income a figure that made these claims seem reasonable. He pointed out that his special skills were in great demand. We agreed to meet together with the wife and children. But he appeared at the next appointment with only his daughter, who previously had refused any association with him following the alleged sexual acts between them.

In later meetings the younger son and the wife also came. The wife was obese, ill-groomed, passive. She appeared so overwhelmed by her difficulties as to be uninterested in possible solutions. She frequently complained about the complete mendacity and unreliability of her husband. She was fearful that the therapist had been taken in by him. She was particularly concerned because her son was playing with matches and because neither of the children kept regular hours at home. In fact they were regularly absent from the home without permission. The son had been taken to juvenile court because of his truancy. The probation officer described the home as "a filthy mess" and stated that the son appeared psychotic because he wandered aimlessly around the home, seeming to ignore the presence of the probation officer.

The entire treatment period was four and a half months. During this time, our main effort was directed toward formulating and enforcing simple rules for the home, establishing regular social and recreational activities for the family members in addition to their regular duties at school, home and on the job.

Examples of these rules: 1. there will be one family meal per day in which all family members participate, eating at the dinner table with the television off; 2. the duties of the children at home will be listed in writing and signed by all parties concerned; 3. specific assigned duties will be agreed upon as a result of family discussions, with the therapist acting as arbiter when necessary; 4. the mother will be kept informed at all times where the children are, what they are doing, and how they can be reached; 5. the mother will know the families of the children with whom her children associate and will make every effort to co-operate with them in the rearing of their respective children; 6. the mother will be in charge of the house and will enforce the rules; 7. discipline methods will be worked out in detail in family meetings and posted on the family bulletin board.

With the permission of the parents, the therapist made contact with the probation officer and school authorities, inviting them to cooperate closely with him in sharing information and suggestions about the progress of the case.

This invitation was warmly accepted, although the school and probation authorities were unaccustomed to such close cooperation with a psychotherapist. In addition, the case was discussed at the regular Case Conference Committee Meeting for this area, a monthly meeting of representatives of various social agencies for the purpose of improved coordination of efforts.

At the request of the therapist, the representative of the Council of Churches at the Case Conference Committee agreed to contact the family and encourage their participation in activities at his church. This latter feature of the treatment program worked out particularly well, even though the children were extremely reluctant at first, feeling that they could not compete with "good people."

Treatment was considered ended when the family stopped keeping appointments. However, from time to time the mother has contacted our office voluntarily to advise us that things are coming along well. The father has left town and has very little to do with the family any more. The mother looks like a different woman—bright, cheerful, and confident. The children look very well also. The mother is supporting the children by working and receiving public aid. The family has been fulfilling its needs for counseling through the pastor of their new-found church home.

As indicated in the previous example, our cases often present a complex of accusations and counter-accusations, irresponsible performances by all parties, and a seriously deteriorated situation with a very bleak prognosis when treatment begins. Treatment then calls for two courses of action: (1) *establishing communication* lines with all family members and all the community agencies involved, so that the truth can be most readily ascertained; (2) *structuring* the situation by establishing simple rules of conduct and a program of living for the family members. This structuring involves negotiation and execution of the treatment contracts as described earlier. Commonly the first order of business in our group therapy meetings is to get a report on the performance by all members on agreements made in preceding meetings.

A 37-year-old woman with two children came to our office crying, very upset, with a long, sad story about how her husband was mistreating her. We asked that on her second visit she also bring her husband with her. Oddly, at this point the patient began to complain, not about her husband, but about her mother who lived with them. Our further exploration of the various areas of relationship between the patient and her husband indicated that the marriage was reasonably sound and that perhaps mother *was* the source of trouble. We therefore insisted that both husband and mother attend the next meeting with the patient. With all three present, there appeared to be little factual basis for this woman's complaints, although there were some other problems in the relationships—matters which she had neglected to talk about in our first meeting.

Some agreements, altering the behavior of the parties toward each other with regard to those problems, were suggested and very beneficial results were obtained promptly. Subsequent weekly family conferences dealt with problems that arose in carrying out these agreements, and modifying them as therapy progressed. The patient's initial symptoms of hysteria and blaming others soon gave way to an admission of her own unfitness as a mother and wife. Once defined, these faults eventually were resolved through improved performance, guided by treatment contracts.

Again, this case illustrates several significant points in our procedure: (1) we set up a treatment team early in the case, consisting of the client and the two immediate significant others, her husband and her mother; (2) the problem was defined in terms of specific behavioral and attitudinal faults on the part of those concerned; (3) specific treatment contracts were then created. As details of the contracts were complied with, the client's symptoms diminished. She began focusing her attention on what was actually wrong in her approach to life and began *feeling better* immediately upon correcting some of her erroneous ways of living.

One of the decisions the therapist must make pertains to this question: how open should the therapist be with his clients? In the classical stance, the therapist tends to remain rather aloof and reservedly guarded when the client inquires about any problems the therapist may or may not have had. Any reports of error in behavior or mistakes in judgment are strictly one-way—from the client to the therapist, not vice versa. The therapist never "lets his hair down," never reveals to the client that he has had problems and has made occasional errors in his own life.

It is increasingly being advocated that there be *complete* openness between therapist, client, and significant others. According to this view, the therapist should set an example of full candor with the client, should freely admit his own failings, feelings, hopes, and fears. From the evidence of several clinical reports and from our own experience, we can state that results of this approach are dramatically and consistently beneficial.

We have found that the relationship between the therapist and his clients not only endures, but seems indeed to be strengthened by surprisingly large doses of mutual openness. We of course would not condone any therapist exploiting the obvious opportunity to use the treatment situation primarily for his own benefit.

The main premises of our psychotherapeutic approach—and the features that distinguish it from other approaches—may be summarized as follows:

1. It's the therapist's job to help the client find out what is wrong with his *behavior* in life. After all, it's his behavior—what he actually does or doesn't do—that has brought him to our attention.

2. Our goal in psychotherapy is the correction of *inappropriate behavior patterns* through any and all reasonable methods and techniques. No person can make another person happy with his lot in life, but one person *can* help another improve his lot through helping him adopt more responsible behavior patterns.

3. In many cases, "self understanding" and "insight" are not the *practical* objectives of therapy. Endless hours can be wasted trying to achieve self-understanding in the client, but relatively few hours usually are required to improve his performance, to the profound benefit of himself and others who may rely on him.

4. In all cases the psychotherapist should be prepared to give his client and the relevant others good, responsible advice. In general, the psychotherapist should assume active leadership in individual and group therapy sessions.

5. The therapist should freely enlist the aid of all available significant others, including immediate family, friends, community professionals (his clergyman, attorney, physician, etc., and agencies concerned). From these he can set up a *Treatment Team* of interested others who supervise, sustain and assist the client in his day-to-day activities. Communication lines between the therapist and the treatment team should be kept open at all times so the therapist can stay informed as to the client's situation and performance in keeping his agreements. Unnecessary secrecy should be eliminated between all parties as soon as possible.

6. The therapist can vastly improve his effectiveness and speed in therapy by designing and insisting on *Treatment Contracts* between the client and the concerned others. Our Treatment Contracts specifically delineate specific actions to be performed, both by the client and the others who are close to him in his family life, work, and community activities. Besides pinning down definite areas that need positive attention, these contracts serve the invaluable function of structuring therapy. It is our observation that much faster progress is made when problems and agreed-upon methods of solving them are put down in "black and white."

7. The client's greater involvement (or reinvolvement) in community life is a legitimate and highly useful goal in our psychotherapy procedure. More and more it appears evident that alienation from his fellow man is a primary factor in mental and/or emotional disorder and that restoration of community can be a powerful motivating force in establishing new behavior patterns in place of the old.

ALEXANDER BASSIN

IRT Therapy in Marriage Counseling

Marriage counselors will probably react with moans of protest to what must sound like the presentation of another new method of treatment: "IRT Therapy? Who needs it! We're having enough trouble trying to digest the thirty-six systems of psychoanalysis and psychotherapy Robert A. Harper (1959) wrote a book about."

We respond: In New York there is a subway line also called the IRT. It is neither new nor modern. On the contrary, it is distinctly old-fashioned, noisy, inelegant—no shiny chrome, fluorescent lights, air-conditioning—but it will whisk you anywhere from Flatbush through Times Square out to the far-reaches of Flushing Meadows quickly, dependably, safely.

So with IRT Therapy. It isn't new, but comes from the distilled wisdom of the socializing procedures relating to the Judeo-Christian ethic going back some two thousand years. And it isn't fancy, but it delivers a therapeutic payload with considerable more consistency than the 60 per cent or so reported by Eysenck (1952) as the apparent batting average for conventional psychotherapy. Or, as Dr. John W. Drakeford exclaims (1965, p. 143) with excitement unusual for a professor of psychology, "It works! It really works!"

IRT Therapy emerges from three concepts which engage and

Former title "IRT Therapy in Marriage Counseling: The Power of Integrity, Responsibility, Transparency." From H. L. Silverman, ed., *Marital Counseling: Psychology, Ideology, Science* (Charles C. Thomas, Springfield, Ill.). Reprinted by permission of the publisher.

separate at various points depending upon the personality, background and life style of the practitioner, but the three concepts are intrinsically related, and are found with different degrees of emphasis in the writings of O. Hobart Mowrer, William Glasser and Sidney M. Jourard.

Integrity Therapy

Mowrer is the champion of Integrity Therapy, which will be described first in this report. He is research professor of psychology at the University of Illinois and a graduate of the University of Missouri. He received his doctorate from Johns Hopkins University, has taught at Yale and Harvard, and in 1954 was president of the American Psychological Association. His name crops up with amazing frequency both in the body and footnotes of virtually every major text on psychology. In 1953, after more than seven years of psychoanalysis by three analysts, he suffered a severe depression which brought on a three-month experience in a state hospital, as a result of which his name is now joined to that of Clifford Beers and Anton T. Boisen as founders of seminal new movements in the treatment of the mentally disturbed.

Mowrer argues that psychoanalysis with its emphasis on *removing guilt* is engaging in a basically incorrect procedure. Rather than being a villain, the accepted approach in conventional analysis, guilt serves a healthy purpose in intrapsychic reactions.

One may make a crude analogy. The symptoms of guilt could be compared to a flashing "idiot light" on the automobile dashboard, signaling that something is amiss in the mechanism. Likewise, the guilt which gives rise to a depression, for example, fulfills a useful and necessary function by reminding the sufferer of his past misdeeds, and, until he discontinues concealing the shortcomings and makes useful amends, he will continue to experience discomfort and uneasiness. In other words, guilt is to be reevaluated and conceptualized not as an enemy, but as a friendly, motivating force for good. The stifling or eradication of guilt feelings, to return to our metaphor, would be similar to tearing out the wires leading to the warning light on our automobile panel.

Mowrer was interested in developing the theoretical foundation of his experience and testing his theory with troubled people. He started with small groups in his own community in Illinois, and later introduced them at the State Research Hospital at Galesburg, Illinois, using ex-mental patients as his therapeutic co-workers, along with seminary professors and ministers on sabbatical leave working under a grant from the Ely Lilly Foundation.

Mowrer agrees with Lewin that there is nothing so practical as good theory, and he has been constantly at work turning out vast quantities of extremely well-written material flowing from a highly facile pen. His first two books in this field, *The Crisis in Psychiatry and Religion* (1961) and *The New Group Therapy* (1964), have served as the cornerstone of what he has dubbed Integrity Therapy.

The distinctive features of Integrity Therapy have been delineated by Drakeford (1965, p. 14) under a series of postulates.

1. Deterministic theories which make man a victim of heredity, environment or any other force are rejected. The individual is answerable for himself and exercises his responsibility in making personal decisions.
2. Each person has a conscience or value system which gives rise to guilt when violated. This condition should not be considered a sickness or disability but a result of the individual's wrongdoing and irresponsibility.
3. When the individual responds to personal wrongdoing by concealment, as most of us do, his guilt throws up symptoms of varying degrees of severity ranging from vague discomfort to depression and then to complete immobilization.
4. The road back to normality for the individual is to engage in acts of openness with "significant others."
5. The person in trouble needs to become involved in a group which would offer a microcosm or small world exercising both a corrective and supporting function for him.
6. Openness by itself is not enough, and the individual is under obligation to undertake some activity of *restitution or penance* appropriate to his acknowledged failure in life or act of deception.

7. To remain a truly authentic person it is not enough to remain open and make restitution. It is also necessary to feel a responsibility to carry the message of Integrity to other people in trouble.

Mowrer joins the growing movement which maintains that most perceptive and interested people can play a part in helping their troubled neighbors. In this respect he agrees with the Marriage Guidance Movement of England which uses specially trained laymen and women as cotherapists and discovered, according to an evaluation by psychiatric supervisors that:

. . . In the quality of work done there has been no difference at all between the lay counselors and the professional counselors. They simply had to admit against their prejudices that properly trained lay counselors who were properly selected in the first place can do every bit as good a job as professional counselors (Mace, 1959).

Elliott's Case

The operation of Integrity Therapy in marriage counseling may be understood by referring to a specific case situation described by Elliott (1966).

A young man of 24, married about a year, joined with five others in the new therapy group I had formed. His main presenting complaints, offered in the first session, were depression and confusion about personal and professional goals. In the process of getting acquainted with the other group members and making himself and his own concerns for therapy known, he spoke of the fact that his wife's pregnancy had recently interrupted sexual relations and that he experienced this as a severe emotional deprivation. Because of his own unloving childhood family, he said he felt an especial need for emotional closeness and reassurance from his wife and found this forced sexual separation very difficult to bear.

In the flat, discouraged tone of his voice and in his defeated and depressed posture and bearing, it was tempting to see him as one who more than anything else needed some strong affirmation and loving support from the group. Members of the group initially tended to respond to him in this way, sympathetically inviting him to talk more about his feelings, which seemed mostly to be blurred and confused.

After an interval I suggested a new tack. Perhaps, I said, we ought to invite him to talk more about his living than about his feeling, about the day-by-day structure and pattern of his life, and I added that I had come to believe that troubled feelings often follow troubling behavior. He was able to respond to this invitation by disclosing that for some years he had been taking small things from stores without paying for them. He had acquired enough psychological sophistication to connect this behavior with emotional deprivation and his need for signs of love. But his attitude towards these acts, as he reported them, was less one of defensive justification than of a kind of helpless confusion. "I know it's wrong, but I don't feel guilty about it."

I suggested that maybe he had come to the stage where his feelings had become a very unreliable guide to behavior, and that while his conscience did not function clearly enough to check his stealing or to produce clear feelings of guilt about it, it apparently was making itself known in painful and indirect fashion in his symptoms of depression and distress. To find a guide for repairing his life I suggested he would have to look to some other resource than "feelings." After some further conversation about his pattern of theft, I somewhat startled him and the other members of the group by giving him an assignment. Before the next meeting, he was to have undertaken to repay the store owners or managers for these recent thefts and was to report back the following week, his successful completion of this assignment as a condition of his good standing in the group. The unexpected character of this approach from the leader caught the whole group somewhat by surprise, but they and he quickly responded to it in a positive way as a signal of seriousness and concern for the man and for his life. At the next meeting he reported that he had carried out the assignment and already had begun to show signs of recovery from his depression and of the emergence of more positive self-feelings.

The above case illustrates Mowrer's basic concepts that psychopathology stems from: (a) tangible acts of misbehavior, deeds done in violation of one's conscience, of the standards one has accepted as valid for his life; and (b) the concealment of such misbehavior from the significant others in one's life in order to avoid the pain of disapproval, punishment or rejection. When this sequence is repeated often enough, the duplicitous behavior brings about one form or another of emotional trouble. In other words, symptoms should be read as disguised and distorted conscience signals registering a genuine, though often well-concealed, moral conflict in the person's past and present life. This view of the nature of emotional troubles requires that a program of treatment or repair would tend to reverse the process. The concealment is repaired by acts of confession, by the honest disclosure of one's self to others and ultimately to the "significant others" in one's life. The step of self-revelation must be followed by an alteration of one's behavior and by undertaking tangible reconstructive steps towards the repair of injuries done to others and to one's own self-respect.

A Case of Marriage Counseling by Integrity Therapy

A marriage counselor practicing this form of treatment was confronted by the following situation:

A crack salesman of 40 appeared for a private session stating that his marriage was breaking up. He wanted to save it, but was very dubious about the prospects. His wife was a slob, a stupid, uncultured woman and had moved away from him as his own success and affluence increased. He would have left her long ago, he told the counselor, but for the children.

The marriage counselor came directly to the point: Was there another woman in the picture?

Rather offhandedly, the client nodded affirmatively but attempted to assure the counselor that this was not a factor in their marital disagreement.

The counselor engaged in an act of "modeling." He suggested that his own life experience indicated that a satisfactory marriage must be based on mutual trust and confidence. On an occasion in his own life when he had strayed from the path of marital fidelity, he also found that all sorts of symptoms had developed and were removed only after he had revealed himself to his spouse. Yes, sooner or later, the client would have to call in his wife for a confrontation and an admission would be in order. The client blanched.

In the first place, his wife would never agree to come to the counselor, and secondly, she would "die" if she learned of the other woman.

The counselor asked if his client would be ready to participate in an experiment that seemed to work in at least 90 per cent of all marital conflict cases. Would he go to his wife and say to her: "Our marriage is falling apart. I would like to save it. I visited a marriage counselor and he indicated it was probably my fault and I would have to change my behavior and attitude if our marriage is to be salvaged. Will you come with me to see him so I can tell you about some of the bad things I've been doing that are driving us to a divorce."

It is a rare spouse that can resist the offer to hear her husband be open and self-critical!

In this case the client was finally able to confess his infidelity—whereupon the wife admitted that she had suspected this situation during the past three years (over which period the husband was certain his wife was blissfully ignorant about what was going on), and she was glad that at long last it was out in the open. She then released a flood of self-critical material about the neglect of her husband, her meanness towards him, her neglect of the home and children. Within six sessions this marriage, which seemed headed straight toward a breakup, was placed on a more solid foundation than ever. Periodically, the counselor calls on the couple in his work with new clients to provide testimony about the benefits of being honest, open, authentic, transparent in their relations with one another.

Basic Concepts of Integrity Therapy

Any wrongdoing, past or present, that an individual decides to keep secret causes him to become walled off from others in various ways. He feels he is on guard all the time to keep from being exposed as a type of person he doesn't want to be. He feels anxious, ill-at-ease, uncertain, depressed, always uncomfortable because of his dread of what others would think of him if they knew the facts of his behavior. Integrity Therapy insists, however, that what the person must do is to work up enough courage to admit frankly to others the mistakes he has made—and he will frequently find that they accept him more completely than he ever thought possible—and he will then begin to feel better himself. The more he actually begins to practice honesty with others, the easier life will become, and his symptoms will slip away. He will also be surprised to notice that others become more open to him—that they also have been holding secrets of their own which they would like to get off their chests and thus feel better, too. One person dropping a curtain of secrecy encourages another to do likewise.

Listen, say the Integrity Therapists, to that "still, small voice" within us, because what it "tells" us will help keep us psychologically satisfied. Unfortunately, this "voice" can be throttled to such an extent that it grows all but silent. Then we have no internal gyroscope to guide us, and we are in trouble. All sorts of symptoms emerge with a message: "Get back on the Integrity track!"

Integrity Therapy emphasizes the need for self-revelation, confession to significant others. It also insists that confession must be followed by restitution and good works. Mowrer has explored the history of primitive Christianity and notes how frequently public confession was a required ritual of group living; and he believes the original vitality of early Christianity may well be related to this procedure which insures honesty and integrity in interpersonal relations. He notes how frequently the most effective of the self-help groups which practice open confession, Alcoholics Anonymous, Gamblers Anonymous and others, succeed where more conventional approaches fail dismally in rescuing a victim from a life of shame and despair.

The Swami Who Ate Gur

Of course, an obvious difficulty related to the practice of Integrity Therapy is the personal strain placed on the therapist. He no longer sits in detached, faceless judgment, employing his superior knowledge of psychodynamics to effect personality alterations upon his hapless patient. He must now act as a *model* of openness about his own less-than-perfect past and must demonstrate in the existential *now* that he is a person of honesty, integrity and responsibility. Dr. Santokh S. Anant, a Sikh psychologist who was a Lilly Endowment Fellow at the University of Illinois during the summer of 1965 in Mowrer's program, tells an anecdote to illustrate this requirement.

I remember a story from one of the ancient Indian books. A mother was worried about her son's habit of eating *gur* (balls made of raw brown sugar). She was very much concerned that excessive eating of gur might affect the health of her son. She took the boy to a swami who was famous for his success in healing. When she had described her problem to the swami, he asked her to return after two weeks. At the end of two weeks she again took her boy to the swami. When her turn came to see the swami, he told the boy, "Son, you should not eat gur.

It is bad for your health," and asked them to return to their home. Probably this woman was expecting more than just a brief communication to the boy. She became quite angry and asked the swami why he could not say the same thing during her earlier visit and save her the trouble of another trip. The swami told her that his words would not have had any effect at that time because he himself was in the habit of eating gur. During these two weeks, he had given up the habit and now he was in a better position to advise the boy. The moral of the story is that one should not preach what one does not practice himself. For this reason psychotherapists have to be very careful in their own personal lives. Before they can expect their patients to live responsible lives, they have to learn to do the same themselves (1966, p. 7).

The Role of Confession in Integrity Therapy

The word "confession" stirs many unfortunate connotations in the contemporary mind. One imagines a prisoner in a police backroom, lights shining in his face, and two burly detectives are questioning him in turn until, weak and exhausted, he whimpers a "confession."

Or, as the word impinges on our eardrums, we visualize the Chinese brainwashing procedures and finally the kind of ceremonial confession related to the practices of the Roman Catholic Church.

However, what the proponents of Integrity Therapy have in mind is a confession on an entirely different style which has been described by Mowrer in a paper called "How to Talk About Your Troubles" (1965).

1. *Complaining is not confessing.* Some people are under the impression that they are engaged in confessing when they are merely reciting their difficulties and problems and telling how unbearable their life has become. The complainer is discussing how he *feels* rather than what he has *done.* Complaining irritates, bores and depresses the listener and leaves the complainer as isolated and lonely as he was before beginning his dirge.

2. *Blaming other people for our problems and difficulties is not confession.* Much that passes for confession is actually a process

of justifying a current state on the grounds that other people have caused the problem. If an individual continues to blame others it is highly improbable he will ever face himself for what he is, according to Drakeford (1965, p. 93). In an Integrity Therapy group meeting, sooner or later an experienced member is likely to speak up, "Never mind about what others did to you. What did you yourself do?" One odyssey of self-discovery is reported by a group member, "I thought I really had it made. My husband had been unfaithful and I was going to make the most of it. But the group wouldn't let me do this. They insisted that I was to blame somewhere, and it wasn't long before I came to see they were right."

3. *We should confess our faults, not our virtues.* A member is wasting the group's time if he concentrates on trying to unearth his "hidden nobility." Groups develop an alertness to people whose apparent faults are virtues. The woman who says, "I suppose I'm just too sweet and kind. I just let them walk all over me," is quickly reminded that being patient and long-suffering is not a crime. As a matter of fact, Mowrer, both in the paper quoted and in his more formal writings, argues for a strategy of (a) confessing misdeeds only and (b) concealing present and future "good works." He makes repeated reference to L. C. Douglas, the author of *Magnificent Obsession* (1929) and *Dr. Hudson's Secret Journal* (1939), whose leading characters engage as a primary therapeutic measure in what Mowrer calls "charity by stealth."

4. *We confess for ourselves, not for others.* Many people are altogether ready to be very honest about *someone else.* Mowrer insists that if confession is to be effective it must be about the speaker and not someone else.

Mowrer deals with the danger of confession, with the likelihood of a story being repeated outside the group and thus compounding the basic problem. But in Integrity Therapy there is constant emphasis on *integrity,* and therefore all understand that what is heard must be kept in the strictest confidence. Yes, it is a calculated risk, but the risk decreases as the group members become increasingly open in their own lives. Most Integrity groups, as a result, have only participants, no observers. But, in the last analysis, we guess Mowrer would say that the risk of irresponsible people talking outside the group in no way compares with the real dangers of the secrecy kept bottled within the individual.

5. *Confession must denote a willingness to come under the judgment of our fellows.* Part of the expectations of our society is for a person to be reliant and strong, with no indication of weakness. Other people are inhibited by the fear that, if they become open and acknowledge their failings, the persons to whom they confess will not understand and possibly look down on them in contempt.

This precept has particular application to marriage counseling. An erring husband is fearful that confessing misdemeanors will provide his spouse with a club to hit him over the head. Thus, many well-meaning marriage counselors observe husbands and wives deceiving each other and even encourage them not to tell, to keep their duplicitous behavior a secret. The proponents of Integrity Therapy, on the other hand, suggest that most often the counselor must have confidence that honesty, responsibility and transparency in the marital bond is more important than in other relations. Therefore, it is intrinsically incorrect as a therapeutic maneuver to permit any continuation of deceit or deception.

6. *Confessions are made to "significant others" in our lives.* No one suggests that therapeutic confession is accomplished by standing on a rooftop and bellowing one's misdeeds to every passing stranger. Integrity Therapy does not advocate indiscriminate confession. The appropriate subjects for confession are individuals important and significant in our lives, "significant others," as the phrase picked up by Mowrer from Sullivan goes.

William James, more than fifty years ago, provided additional testimony about the benefit of confession:

For him who confesses, shams are over and realities have begun; he has exteriorized his rottenness. If he has not actually gotten rid of it, he at least no longer smears it over with a hypocritical show of virtue— he lives at least upon the basis of veracity (1902, p. 89).

Jung joins James with a similar fine turn of phrase: "In keeping the matter private . . . I still continue in my state of isolation. It is only with the help of confession that I am able to throw myself into the arms of humanity, freed at last from the burden of moral exile" (1933, p. 35).

Reality Therapy

Now that we have finished with the "I," we move to the "R" of IRT therapy.

Reality Therapy, the main component of which is emphasis on *responsibility,* is the brainchild of Dr. William Glasser, an extraordinarily warm, friendly, unassuming young psychiatrist who writes in a smooth, lively style remarkably free of the polysyllabic jargonese which makes the writing of his colleagues such a strain on readers in the field. He is an even better extemporaneous lecturer, his platform presentations being full of homespun anecdotes, down-to-earth illustrations liberally sprinkled with wit and humor. He is engaged in private practice in Los Angeles and acts as consultant for the Ventura School for Girls of the California Youth Authority. He is the author of *Reality Therapy: A New Approach to Psychiatry,* which contains a lengthy foreword by the same O. Hobart Mowrer who is the father of Integrity Therapy. Mowrer writes: "This is an extraordinarily significant book. Readers will themselves discover that it is courageous, unconventional, and challenging. Future developments, I predict, will show that it is also scientifically and humanly sound."

A recent review of the volume in *Social Casework* (Jacobs, 1966) is on a similar enthusiastic level. "Once in a while there comes a book with ideas that prove revolutionary. *Reality Therapy* is such a book. It is a profound and entirely new conception of mental health and psychotherapy. It will disturb those with set ideas, but those who are uncertain about final answers will welcome it."

Glasser's book contains a slashing, no-holds-barred attack on conventional psychiatry and its current psychodynamic Freudian foundation.

First of all, Glasser argues that mental illness, as a diagnosible, treatable illness which is somehow like physical illness, does not exist; it is a myth. He questions the usefulness of the elaborate nosological systems that are employed in psychiatry and suggests that this type of labeling has a deadly, nontherapeutic impact.

Glasser asks if there is really any usefulness in one of the essential postulates of conventional psychiatry—the one which holds that one must probe into the patient's past life to search for the psychological roots of his problem in order to help the patient understand these beginnings so that he can change his attitude towards life.

Glasser attacks the concept of *transference*. Conventional psychiatry maintains that the patient must relive with the therapist his past difficulties so that a forum can be provided to explain to the patient that he is repeating the same inadequate behavior. On the whole, Glasser asserts, the therapist's interpretations of transference behavior and the subsequent alleged insights are not effective in getting patients to give up old attitudes and learn new ways to relate to people and solve their problems.

What about the unconscious? What about this basic concept of psychodynamic theory? Glasser suggests that concern about unconscious mental conflicts, which are considered in conventional therapy more important than problems of the here and now, is a waste of time. He argues: "Because no one lives a life where his needs are always fulfilled, it is impossible not to find a wealth of buried conflicts which being similar to present difficulties, seem to explain the person's inability to fulfill his needs now" (p. 42).

The conventional therapist attempts to remain completely detached and uninvolved, making no moral judgments about the behavior of his patient. Glasser, on the other hand, insists on the necessity for an emphasis on the right and wrong. Clients must be confronted with their behavior so they can judge its quality by their own standards, then they must decide what to do about it.

In conventional techniques of therapy, the main task of the therapist is to assist the client in gaining *insight*. Having gained insight, it then becomes the client's responsibility on his own to learn better ways of behaving. Glasser says: "We spend much time painstakingly examining the patient's daily activity and suggesting better ways to behave" (p. 43) rather than trying to develop insight. In other words, Glasser sees the therapist as a sort of teacher involved in a special type of education with his pupil learning to live more effectively. In concluding about the differences of his own approach and that of conventional therapy, Glasser states: "Reality Therapy is not a different variety of the same approach, but a different way to work with people. The requirements of Reality Therapy—an intense personal involvement, facing reality and rejecting irresponsible behavior and learning better ways to behave—bear little resemblance to conventional therapy and produce markedly different results" (p. 43).

Theory of Reality Therapy

"I can explain all I know about psychiatry in about fifteen minutes," Glasser told a recent meeting of Chicago schoolteachers. In essence, every human being, whether a Chinese infant girl or a Swedish king, has the same two basic psychological needs: *the need to love and be loved and the need to feel that we are worthwhile to ourselves and to others.* Helping people fulfill these two needs is the goal of Reality Therapy.

The Meaning of Responsibility

The basic concept of Reality Therapy, *responsibility,* is defined by Glasser as the *ability to fulfill one's needs, and to do so in a way that does not deprive others of the ability to fulfill their needs.* A responsible person does that which gives him a feeling of self-worth, a feeling that he is worthwhile to others. He strives for self-respect and even endures privation to attain a self-image that is worthwhile. When a responsible man says he will perform a job for us, for example, he will try to accomplish what was asked both for our sake and for his own. An irresponsible person may or may not do what he says, depending upon how he feels, the effort he has to make and "what is in it" for him. Thus, he gains neither our respect nor his own, and in time he will suffer and cause others to suffer.

The Reality Therapist

The therapist within the framework of Reality Therapy suffers some of the difficulties experienced by our righteous swami described earlier. He must be a highly responsible person—tough, involved, sensitive and human. He must be willing to fulfill his own needs and must be willing to discuss some of his own struggles so that the patient can see that acting responsibly is possible, even though difficult. He is neither aloof, superior nor sacrosanct, nor would he ever imply that what he does or what he stands for or what he values are unimportant. He must have the strength and courage to become involved, to have his values tested by the client, and to withstand intense criticism by the very person he may be trying to help. He must submit to have every fault and defect of his picked apart by the patient. He must be willing to admit that, like the client, he is far from perfect, but he is a person who can act responsibly even if it takes effort.

Furthermore, the Reality Therapist must be strong and not expedient or opportunistic. He must be able to withstand the patient's request for sympathy, for sedatives, for justification of his actions, no matter how the patient pleads or threatens. He does not condone an irresponsible action and must be willing to watch the client suffer if this helps him grow towards responsibility. "Therefore, to practice Reality Therapy takes strength, not only the strength of the therapist to lead a responsible life himself, but also the added strength both to stand up steadily to patients who wish him to accede to their irresponsibility, and to continue to point out reality to them no matter how hard they struggle against it." (Glasser, 1965, p. 23).

The Technique of Reality Therapy

In various addresses, Dr. Glasser has explained the methodology of his treatment procedure. He warns, however, that, in contrast to conventional psychiatry, the theory of which is difficult to explain but the practice easy, Reality Therapy has a simple, fifteen-minute theoretical base, but a treatment procedure that is extremely difficult to follow.

1. *Involvement*. The first and most difficult phase of Reality Therapy is the gaining of the *involvement* that the client so desperately needs but which he has been unsuccessful in attaining or maintaining up to the time he presents himself for treatment. Unless the requisite involvement develops between the responsible therapist and the irresponsible client, there can be no therapy, Glasser asserts. The guiding principles are directed towards achieving the proper involvement: a completely honest, human relationship in which the client, for perhaps the first time in his life, realizes that someone cares enough for him not only to accept him but to accept him in order to fulfill his needs in the real world.

> How does a therapist become involved with a patient so that the patient can begin to fill his needs? The therapist has a difficult task, for he must quickly build a firm emotional relationship with the patient who has failed to establish such relationships in the past. He is aided by recognizing that a patient is desperate for involvement and is suffering because he is not able to fulfill his needs. The patient is looking for a person with whom he can become emotionally involved, someone he can care about and who he can be convinced cares about him, someone who can convince the patient that he will stay with him until he can better fulfill his needs (Glasser, 1965, p. 21).

Unless the client is convinced that the therapist genuinely cares about him, there can be no prospect for change. Glasser extends this thesis to all areas of human interaction, whether it be in marriage, school or work.

2. *Reveal yourself*. Glasser differs from Mowrer in terms of emphasis of confession as an essential ingredient for therapy, but he does insist that involvement cannot be obtained if the therapist maintains the aloof "stone face," the impersonal posture that is taught in conventional psychotherapy. On the contrary, the therapist must be prepared to *reveal himself* as a person, with a family, with a car, with his own ups and downs. "If a patient asks if you have any children, don't freeze over and say, 'I'm not supposed to talk about things like that.' Tell them about your kids. Take the pictures out of your wallet and show them" (Glasser, 1966).

3. *Be subjective and personal.* Glasser feels that orthodox psychiatry, in its insistence on being objective and impersonal, is laboring under an almost impossible handicap. People simply do not change in that kind of interpersonal situation. Furthermore, not only should the therapist be subjective and highly personal, he must demonstrate this attitude by constantly speaking of himself using first person pronouns. For example, in working with a student who is not handing in his term papers, the Reality Therapist does not say, "The school administration expects you to do your homework," but "I would like you to work."

4. *Emphasize behavior, not feeling.* Unlike conventional psychiatry, which is very much concerned with providing a platform for the expression of feelings, Glasser notes: No one ever explains what the therapist is supposed to do with these feelings once they've been expressed. Glasser, on the contrary, suggests that the person speak about concrete behavior and deeds rather than philosophy and abstractions. He holds that feelings are beyond our control; behavior is not. We can't tell ourselves to start feeling happy, for example, but we can tell ourselves to *do something.* Best of all, if we can do something responsible rather than irresponsible, our behavior may help us feel better. The Reality Therapist does not mind discussing this and other concepts of his craft with the client, rather than acting as though he were in possession of some great esoteric final truth that is beyond the comprehension of mere laymen.

5. *Force a value judgment!* The most important single component of Reality Therapy as a method, next to obtaining involvement, is to so direct the conversation that the client makes a value judgment about his behavior. For example, to use a situation mentioned by Glasser, if a kid curses a teacher, we ask him, "Now, did that behavior do you any good? Did it do the teacher any good?" If the student responds that it did, there is very little you can do about it. Drop the matter for discussion at a later date. But, Glasser insists, in ninety-nine out of one hundred cases, the boy will think for a moment and then respond, "Naw, I guess it didn't. Just made a big hassle and now I'm in more hot water than ever." The client must be pressed, again and again, to evaluate the re-

sponsibility of his behavior. Is it helping him meet his needs? Is it interfering with other people meeting their needs? Is it doing him or others any good? These are the inquiries the Reality Therapist throws at the client after a firm involvement has been achieved.

6. *Don't accept excuses.* Glasser means this literally. Even if a client presents the most heartrending explanation for his behavior, simply don't waste time evaluating it, he argues. Disregard excuses. In this area, Glasser borrows a motif from the work being done at Daytop with drug addicts. Here, it has been found that the acceptance of excuses tends to lead to an evasion of responsibility. It is better to be firm and demanding than indulgent and forgiving (Shelly and Bassin, 1964, 1965).

7. *Work in groups.* Glasser indicates that the most effective way of working with people, particularly delinquents and students, is in groups. In the first place, the group provides an opportunity for the member to act as a change agent, and, secondly, it is easier to accept a perception of a situation from a peer rather than an authority figure.

Along with Willard A. Mainord (1962), Dr Glasser is convinced that the treatment of individuals with all kinds of syndromes is best accomplished in a group.

8. *Never give up.* The ability to stay with a client through thick and thin, never to give up, to retain confidence in his capacity to work out a solution, is a characteristic of the Reality Therapy method. The client may be testing the sincerity and the depth of involvement of the therapist and the therapist must be sufficiently responsible in his own right to stay at the client's side no matter how difficult and unrewarding the experience may appear to be.

Reality Therapy in Marital Counseling

The precepts and procedures of Reality Therapy appear to be ideally suited for the practice of marital counseling. Here the emphasis should be, as we see it, on current behavior, evaluation of the behavior in terms of its contribution towards a satisfactory marriage, and the working out of plans to correct any deficiencies that may become apparent even after a small number of interviews. Reality Therapy then contributes to the notion that counseling can be relatively quick, effective and satisfying both to the client and counselor.

Transparency Therapy

Now for the final letter of the insignia. Transparency is the concept presented by Sidney M. Jourard, professor of psychology at the University of Florida and the author of *The Transparent Self: Self-Disclosure and Well-Being* (1964).

I became fascinated with the phenomena of self-disclosure after puzzling about the fact that patients who consulted me for therapy told more about themselves than they had ever told another living person. Many of them said, "You are the first person I have ever been completely honest with." I wondered whether there was some connection between their reluctance to be known by spouse, family and friends and their need to consult with the professional psychotherapist. My fascination with self-disclosure led me on an empirical and conceptual odyssey. . . .

A chapter in Jourard's book is of particular interest to marriage counselors. "Sex and Openness in Marriage," he calls it and he deals in a remarkably frank, uninhibited way with the problems that develop in the marital situation and what can be done to improve matters. In terms of IRT Therapy, one comment deserves repetition:

I think that pastoral counselors will be most helpful in their task of midwifing marital well-being when and if they have themselves been able to face the breadth and depth of misery and joy in their own marriages, if they are growing persons rather than starch collars wearing the mask of a minister. There is surely nothing about being a minister that precludes being a person.

How natural it is, then, to move into the work of another outstanding exponent of honesty and transparency in human relations, Carl Rogers, whose latest volume is fittingly titled *On Becoming a Person*. What emerges from that text is the same emphasis we obtain from Jourard, that we respond affirmatively to those individuals who are prepared to be open about themselves, *congruent* at all aspects of their being in interpersonal relations.

Research on Transparency

The concept of Transparency may remain a vague abstraction immersed in a mystical aura that would make it difficult to recognize and visualize. However, when one attempts to translate a concept into the hardware of research, we are compelled to add skeleton, blood and muscle to what might be little more than a flight of fancy. Jourard, while pursuing the notion that accurate portrayal of self to others is an identifying criterion of healthy personality—while neurosis is related to inability to know one's "real self" and to make it known to others—engaged in research that is helpful in concretizing the transparency concept. He followed the characterological studies of Fromm (1957), Riesman (1950) and Horney (1950) relating to the tendency common among persons in our society to misinterpret the self to others. This trend is central to the "marketing personality," the "other-directed character," and the "self-alienated" individual as they have been described by Fromm, Riesman and Horney respectively. On the other hand, much of social science is founded upon the self-disclosures of respondents; the conditions, dimensions and circumstances relating to self-disclosure bear directly upon the very validity of many purported facts in the social sciences. Jourard concluded that a systematic analysis of self-disclosure holds promise of yielding information that is relative to many diverse areas of theory and method.

Jourard discloses that he was particularly puzzled about Karen Horney's concept of the "real self." He might have noted also the intense interest aroused by public figures when a situation develops which promises even a slight disclosure of the real person rather than the elaborately programed public relations mannequin that is manufactured for mass consumption. The popularity, for example, of the television star of a few years back, Jack Paar, who constantly joked with his audience about their interest in the "real" Paar. Carl Rogers comments wryly about the tremendous response to a lecture which contained a hint that he would speak of himself as a person.

Jourard wondered how he could adopt the concept of the "real self" for purposes out of research; and out of his thinking came the idea that the kind of personal data we all put down on an application form when we are applying for a job might have the makings of a research tool. Some application forms, labeled "confidential," asked for detailed data about oneself. Jourard asked, "Who would an applicant tell these things to besides his prospective employer or teacher?"

And then he was off, itemizing classes of information about oneself which could only be known by another person by direct verbal telling. After much fiddling this way and that, as Jourard confesses, he wound up with a sixty-item questionnaire listing ten items of information in each of six categories which he called "aspects of self." He devised an answer sheet with rows corresponding to the items and columns headed by target-persons.

The questionnaire itself reveals Jourard's attempts to concretize the transparency concept. He asks: To what target-persons— mother, father, male friend, female friend or spouse have you expressed your attitudes and opinions on: (a) what I think and feel about religion; my personal religious views; (b) my personal opinions and feelings about other religious groups other than my own; (c) my views on the question of racial integration in schools, transportation, etc.; (d) my personal views on drinking; (e) my personal views on sexual morality; how I feel that I and others ought to behave in sexual matters. (I have selected the questions at random to obtain the flavor of the basic approach.)

Another portion of the questionnaire asks questions of taste and interest: (a) my favorite foods; the way I like food prepared; my food dislikes; (b) my favorite beverages and the ones I don't like; (c) My favorite reading matter; (d) the kinds of movies that I like to see best; the TV shows that are my favorites; (e) my taste in clothing; (f) what I would appreciate most for a present, etc.

The third area involves work or study. He asks: (a) what I find to be the worst pressures and strains in my work; (b) what I find to be the most boring and unendurable aspects of my work; (c) what I enjoy most and get the most satisfaction from in my present work; (d) what I feel are my shortcomings and handicaps that prevent me from working as I'd liked to; or (e) that prevent me from getting further ahead in my work.

Jourard has prepared a questionnaire along these lines dealing with the area of the person's attitudes and feelings about money, personality, body. He asks that the self-disclosure rating scale be marked on the following continuum: *zero*—have told the other person nothing about this aspect of me; *one*—have talked in general terms about this item (other person has only a general idea about this aspect of me); *two*—have talked in full and complete detail about this item to the other person (he knows me fully in this respect and could describe me accurately); and X—have lied or misrepresented myself to the other person so he has a false picture of me.

The results of Jourard's investigations are interesting but not directly related to the focus of this paper. His particular contribution, however, is in assisting people who may be wondering about what is meant by self-disclosure—what does Paul Tillich (1952) have in mind by the title of his volume *The Courage to Be*. Jourard's answer is that being transparent means making ourselves known, expressing our viewpoint, being honest in our interpersonal relationships.

Conclusion

All this might strike many marriage counselors, as I know it impinges on the sensibilities of psychologists, social workers and therapists, as the meanderings of some long-winded philosopher who has somehow popped into the middle of the twentieth century without benefiting from the accumulated wisdom that began with Freud and his disciples. But one need merely examine the professional scene with special reference to the practice of marriage counseling to suggest that the conventional approach based on so-called psychodynamic principles is not leading us toward becoming better practitioners in working with people who are behaving irresponsibly. Perhaps these suggestions coming from Glasser, Mowrer, Jourard and an ever-increasing number of professionals and laymen should be given a more respectful hearing.

In the last analysis, however, we will stick to our beliefs and practices unless we become reasonably assured that there is something better in the offing. I would humbly suggest that my own experience in marriage counseling indicates a measured echo to Dr. Drakeford's exclamation: "It works! It really works!"

REFERENCES

Anant, Santokh S.: *Psychotherapy, Morality and Belongingness.* Mimeo, 1966.

Drakeford, John W.: *Integrity Therapy: A New Direction in Psychotherapy.* Mimeo, Fort Worth, Texas. 1965.

Eysenck, Hans J.: The Effects of Psychotherapy: An Evaluation. *J. Consult. Psychol, 16:*319–324, 1952.

Fromm, Erich: *Man for Himself.* New York, Rinehart, 1957.

Glasser, William: *Reality Therapy—A New Approach to Psychiatry.* New York, Harper & Row, 1965.

Glasser, William: Unpublished address to Chicago School Teachers, Jan. 28, 1966.

Harper, Robert A.: *Psychoanalysis & Psychotherapy—36 Systems.* Englewood Cliffs, N.J.: Prentice-Hall, 1959.

Horney, Karen: *Neurosis and Human Growth.* New York, Norton, 1950.

Jacobs, Gordon L.: Review of *Reality Therapy: A New Approach to Psychiatry. Social Casework,* June 1966, p. 388.

James, William: *The Varieties of Religious Experience.* New York, Modern Lib., 1902.

Jourard, Sidney M.: *The Transparent Self.* Princeton, Van Nostrand, 1964.

London, Perry: *The Modes of Psychotherapy.* New York, Holt Rinehart, Winston, 1964.

Mace, David R.: Marriage guidance in Britain. *Southern Baptist Family Life Education,* April, June, 1959, p. 4.

Mowrer, O. Hobart: *The Crisis in Psychiatry and Religion.* Princeton, Van Nostrand, 1961.

Mowrer, O. Hobart: *The New Group Therapy.* Princeton, Van Nostrand, 1964.

Mowrer, O. Hobart: How to talk about your troubles. Unpublished paper, 1965.

Riesman, D.: *The Lonely Crowd.* New Haven, Yale, 1950.

Rogers, Carl R.: *On Becoming a Person.* Boston, Houghton, 1961.

Salzman, L., and Masserman, J.: *Modern Concepts of Psychoanalysis.* New York, Citadel, 1962.

Shelly, Joseph A., and Bassin, Alexander: Daytop Lodge: Halfway house for drug addicts, *Federal Probation,* Dec. 1964.

Shelly, Joseph A., and Bassin, Alexander: Daytop Lodge—A new treatment approach for drug addicts. *Corrective Psychiatry, II* (No. 4): 186–195, 1965.

Tillich, Paul: *The Courage to Be,* New Haven, Yale, 1952.

WILLARD A. MAINORD

A Therapy

It has been some years now since Eysenck (2) began publishing evidence that psychotherapeutic procedures customarily employed have been ineffective. The usual response has been that there is something wrong with Eysenck, inasmuch as everyone *knows* that psychotherapy works. If any proof is needed, ask therapists and some of their patients, and it is obvious that therapy works miracles in a strangely leisurely way. And if therapies have occasionally not worked, it has been a matter of unskilled therapists, unmotivated patients, and the untreatability of many diagnostic groups. With these cozy explanations always available, we have continued merrily to train more therapists to carry out the same fruitful procedures, and have taught them, in the process, that it is only the naive and/or foolish who actually expect to modify patient behavior with any marked degree of success in less than years and years of excavating, catharting, transferring, insight seeking, and Freud knows what else.

The variations on the theme are apparently endless. Thus we can find ponderous discussions of the dilutions of transference reactions that will make group therapies ineffective. We have it as a matter of principle that something called intellectual insight is useless, but that emotional insight will transform social slobs into creative geniuses. "Symptomatic" treatment is doomed to failure

Presented at Western Psychological Association annual meeting, San Francisco, April 1962.

From William Glasser, *Reality Therapy*. New York: Harper & Row, 1965, pp. 126–133.

and active therapists are frustrated sexual exhibitionists. Untherapized therapists can deal only with their own distorted projections which will lead their patients into a psychic jungle where no Dr. Livingstone presumes. And heaven help the questioning therapist who dares doubt the dogma, for he will soon learn that his destructive powers as a deviate far exceed his constructive powers as a good union man. The usual response to this realization is for the bewildered and crushed clinician to derive yet another sub-scale from the MMPI [Minnesota Multi-Phasic Personality Inventory].

In spite of all this, a few brave souls have been raising some questions. Eysenck (if you will forgive the expression) reports that what results have been rather clearly demonstrated have had a learning theory basis and has published a book expanding this heresy (3).

Milton Wexler (6) has indicated that schizophrenic patients need a therapist who will ally himself on the side of the super-ego and give up the job of destroying the forces of inhibition.

A recovered schizophrenic patient argues (1) that the psychosis is useful only because it enables the patient to have some real and, by his own standards, terrible misbehavior remain undetected.

Mowrer (4) believes that emotional difficulties may well be the consequence of repressing the super-ego which frees one to behave in ways which will reap subsequent guilt to a point of personality disintegration.

And Skinner, strange man, argues that if you wish people to behave in more acceptable ways, you might teach them to do just that. Add to all this, the author's own unsuccessful attempts at junior analysis, vigorous non-directivity, overwhelming understanding and disgustingly complete acceptance, and the background has been laid for an attempt at some other direction of patient personality modifications.

One other point of view needs to be considered now. Szasz has been arguing (5) that mental patients should not be considered as sick people. Instead, he argues that such patients have developed a style of life that results, quite simply, in problems of living. The behavior that can be observed is problem-solving behavior, but will not be modified significantly unless the deficient style of living is improved. Not all the implications of this point of view are immediately obvious, but it does suggest that teaching the patient to believe that he is sick is to encourage him to become a passive recipient of whatever treatment the physician recommends. If the patient chooses to wait until he is "cured," chronic hospital residence might be predicted.

The therapy to be described was set up on the admission wards of Western State Hospital in Fort Steilacoom, Washington. The two wards are differentially populated by, conventionally enough, the usual two sexes. Admission policies are such that all patients between the ages of 18 and 65 who are not the victim of some known neurological condition are sent to these two wards. In the past, the patient was worked up and transferred to some other ward inside two weeks, if possible. Thus, the staffs of these two wards were not involved in any but the briefest of therapeutic efforts and saw only that problems were presented but never solved. It was hoped that it would help improve staff morale if treatment programs were set up on the admission wards.

To get a program going, the medical staff was asked to submit names of all new admissions that they felt might be able to benefit from intensive, short-term group psychotherapy. Actual selection of the patients, however, has been accomplished by a weekly staff which usually consists of the administrative chief of the ward, the chief ward nurse, a social worker if by chance some social history is known—often not the case with such new patients, and by the author. A Shipley-Hartford and a MMPI are usually available. However, the selection is primarily made by a short interview in which the patient shows some ability to verbalize, to express willingness to work at getting better, and to dimly accept the idea that responsibility for progress is the patient's. About three of every four referrals reach the group. The chief reason for rejection is an apparent lack of ability to function well enough intellectually to keep up with a vigorous and often abstract group. Average group membership is somewhere between 10 and 12.

The patient learns two things the first day in the group. First, and most importantly, all administrative decisions will be made in the group with the exception of those things that require medical training to evaluate: drugs, physical complaints, etc. This means that all passes, privileges, jobs, trial visits, and discharges will be accomplished through and in the group. Second, the patient is taught that no group member is ever sick; instead, he is crazy. When the word crazy is questioned, it is pointed out that the patient does and has done many crazy things. The word "sick" is treated like a dirty word, and any group member who tries to use this concept is in for a rough time from the rest of the group. Finally, the patient is obliged to commit him- or herself to complete honesty with the group, and no reservations to this commitment are acceptable. The patient is "dishonest" if he withholds important information from the group—either about himself or about other group members.

It is emphasized from the beginning that it is not believed that it is necessary to modify the patients' assets so that no group time will be spent in recognizing or in unearthing hidden nobility. Rather, it is suggested that any improvement in emotional tone will result from the identification and improving of methods of behaving that are essentially evasive, irresponsible, and dishonest. Sooner or later, the new group member reaches the conclusion that he or she is immoral by his or her own standards, and the group agrees. This makes it possible for the patient to come up with some concrete goals which involve the improvement of behavior in the desired direction whether or not the patient feels ready to do so.

Usually some time is spent in getting rid of what we have learned to call the "I'm-too-good-for-this-world" syndrome. The group will never accept noble reasons for bad behavior, and the patient is forced to look at all the obligations and commitments which have been accepted and given and which have not been kept.

Upon entering the group, the patient is required to pay for treatment by taking on some work detail and can earn no privileges until work has become part of the daily schedule. Inasmuch as the group members are the only permanent patients on the ward, they are given the responsibility for seeing that no work is done by the nursing staff that can be legally done by the patients.

Thus they run the kitchen, the clothes room, all housekeeping details, as well as provide clerical help wherever it is then needed in the hospital. Good performance is expected, and ground privileges are withheld if work is not satisfactory.

Group members are given the responsibility of getting off drugs as soon as they can convince their respective physicians that they are capable of functioning without pills. They are also given the responsibility of learning how to get along with staff members, even though often the staff member in question may basically be in the wrong. All staff members working with these patients are asked to lean over backwards to avoid any impression that the patient needs to be babied or favored in any way.

Responsibility is thrown at the patient in every possible way. If the patient is married to an alcoholic ne'er-do-well, the group works on how the patient may be making marriage intolerable. If the patient is dominated by a smothering parent, the group digs into the "lack of guts" of the patient. If the patient is visibly and deeply depressed, the group works to find out what are the ways in which the patient has earned and deserves to feel so badly. Any attempt to place responsibility upon anyone who is not a group member is not considered to be acceptable group behavior.

Much time is spent upon the concept of freedom of choice. While the author is philosophically a complete determinist, the concept of freedom of choice seems an essential one to obtain motivated patients who will behave in ways that can be reinforced. Thus, the group will never accept the idea that "I can't help myself when I want a drink," etc. It is at such times that the "You're not sick, you're crazy" technique seems dramatically useful. Our patients can comfortably be sick; but when told they are making crazy choices merely because it is easier that way, they typically respond with vigorous efforts to prove their ability to be responsible.

Historical material is not sought for, although typically much is spontaneously offered and discussed. However, when the patient offers some reason out of the distant past for current feelings of guilt, the group denies the validity of such an explanation and insists upon examining current reasons for guilt which are assumed to be deserved. No group member can get the group to accept the idea that guilt is the result of an over-punitive super-ego.

It is always assumed that much of the patient's behavior is designed to manipulate others, and the group is constantly alert to such manipulations which are usually in evidence right on the ward and within the group. Bids for sympathy and collections of injustices are brusquely and directly counter-attacked.

Simple learning theory notions are rigidly applied. Behaviors which are sought will be reinforced positively. Those which are troublesome are reinforced negatively. Feedback within the group is a constant part of every administrative decision. Often the group is consulted about whether or not the group has evidence that the patient has earned a yes answer to a request, but there is no attempt to pretend that the group is a democratic institution. It is clearly stated that the therapist is the expert in the group and will behave as arbitrarily as he wishes. He makes his pledge to the group that he is going to make decisions for the benefit of the patient no matter what the patient thinks about it.

The therapist deliberately takes a vigorous, directive role and tells the group that they have the job of learning how to handle him. He warns that he plans to be tough enough so that if they can handle him, they will be able to handle most anybody. Silence is not tolerated; this is merely an evasion of responsibility, although interestingly enough silence has never been a problem since the first week of the group's existence. Usually, the problem is to find enough time for all the potential participants asking to be heard.

The therapist reserves the right to speak to whomever he chooses, about whatever he chooses, and will respect no confidences unless he feels that some useful purpose would be served. He may bring into the group, at any time, anything he may have learned from any source—staff members, other patients, friends or relatives. A similar arrangement is maintained—particularly with family members—so that the therapist can speak freely to whomever he encounters. Typically, interviews with relatives are conducted in the presence of the patient although there are many exceptions to this. One of the group's rules is that there is nothing that is not appropriate for the group's consideration if it is important to the patient, and the therapist, rather than the patient, will be the judge of this.

The therapist will allow—or actually encourage—hostility expressed toward him, but will always deal with it as if the patient is guiltily defensive until it is clear that the therapist was in error—at which point he must say so. However, the patient is also given the responsibility for the non-verbal messages that may be conveyed to others, and this usually resolved the issue. The therapist is not responsible for getting silent group members to participate until the patient has been inactive long enough that the accumulated silence can be dealt with as an evasion of responsibility. The therapist will take the responsibility of seeing to it that no patient successfully fillibusters either the therapist or the group.

The therapist will use whatever techniques he wishes, including humor, scolding, delivering of ultimatums or dismissal from the group. Any patient is free to argue or to question, but it had better be from evidence or logic, or this will be seen as irresponsibility. Patient rights are given little consideration; these, too, are to be earned, not bestowed.

This perhaps sounds grim and harsh, but in practice the group is more active, engages in more humor, and is more intimately involved in both the group and in therapy than any group seen by the author over an 8-year span. Patient reaction to the therapist is often initially hostile, but soon changes to an apparently relaxed yet respectful attitude. The group feels free to express itself with a bit of hostile humor; thus the therapist found in his chair a printed sign advertising his services for five cents.

The program was initiated in September 1961, and terminated September 1962—part of the time including two groups. In that time 100 discharges were given, and by September, 1963, there have been 18 returns, all but two of which have been subsequently released again. Usually, between 40 and 50 returns could have been expected. Similar results have been obtained with three other groups, but the follow-up period has not been long enough to attempt to draw any conclusions. The 100 discharges were obtained from a treatment population of 125, of whom 13 were dropped (either at their own request or at the therapist's request) and 12 were still in treatment when the program had to be terminated. It is possible, of course, that some of the discharges have been subsequently hospitalized at some other institution, but because of the geographical conditions, it is unlikely unless they moved to another state.

The average stay in the group of the discharged patients has been slightly over 2 months. As the groups meet every day for at least an hour and a half, the average graduate has been in therapy for 60 to 70 hours.

The age range of the patients has been from 17 to 59, although the typical patient is in the late twenties or early thirties. Almost all diagnostic categories have been included, and perhaps predictably, depressed patients have been the most rapid to respond. In a surprising number of cases, the prognosis has been considered to be very poor indeed, as there has been a weighting toward patients with drinking and drug problems. No diagnostic category has been missed within the functional disorders.

We felt a good deal of uneasiness in establishing this program so it was not surprising to find that many staff members were disturbed at what we were doing. It is probable that the program would have had even more opposition if it were not so obvious that the group members themselves are vigorously pushing its value. Testimonials abound, often from unexpected sources. The best indicator, however, is that the group members talk with new arrivals, and we have far more patients asking for the group than we can possibly accommodate. We are in the process of trying to find a way to establish another group because of the patient response to the program.

It may be wondered what we do about the traditional problems of transference, repressed materials, symptom substitution, etc. The answer is, consciously, nothing. All the materials are there for a more traditional therapy, but we do not look for any particular course of therapy; we merely look for improved behavior which always seems accompanied by improved emotional states. We believe that the consequences of behavior determine emotional tone; so if we can control the behavior, we also control the feeling.

Then, with Eysenck, we are arguing the so-called symptoms are the illness, and if they are given up, therapy is complete.

It should not be concluded that we believe that the apparent success of this therapeutic technique necessarily implies anything about the genesis of emotional disorder. There has never seemed any logical necessity for psychotherapy to be determined by theories of the development of psychopathy. However, the hint is there that Mowrer may have contributed a valid notion when he suggests that we have been in error in thinking of the mental patient as a victim of too rigid standards.

It seems to us that perhaps the chief reason that this approach appeals to the patient is that it gives him hope. If he is sick, he is really quite bewildered as to what he might do about his plight. If, however, he is being irresponsible, evasive, dishonest, and deceitful and if this is causing his emotional pain, it seems obvious to him what he must do; luckily it is something he believes that he can do.

The place of the learning theory procedures should not be minimized; over and over again behaviors are identified, discussed, and then either rewarded or punished. This procedure uses only a small portion of group time, but makes the group influence felt all day, every day, and helps make each entire day part of a therapeutic experience.

The group showed its real desire to deal with important problems by scheduling, on their own, a weekly meeting to take care of problems of ward performance such as dishwashing, bedmaking, etc. Their reason for doing this was that they are unwilling to waste group time discussing these things.

We, of course, are still evolving, still questioning, and still blundering. However, some tentative conclusions can be suggested: Patients with much out-patient psychotherapy are going to be extremely difficult to reach in a short period of time; they usually have been successfully taught that they are sick. Patients who have had previous experiences with EST and have felt benefitted are the most difficult of all group members to reach. Age is less important than expected, although obviously a factor. Women are much easier to treat than men, chiefly, it appears, because men are much more concerned with saving face. If a mistake is going to be made, it will probably be on the side of asking too little rather than too much of the patient; we have found over and over again that we pay the biggest price whenever we slip on the side of being too undemanding or too accepting of deviant behavior.

While it is obvious that therapist personality traits would be important in this type of therapy, the evidence seems to indicate that the approach is teachable. One psychology intern, three R.N.'s, and one nursing assistant have been taught to run the groups adequately although, of course, they are not equally effective. The author has no doubt that his absence this week will be compensated for by substitute therapists.

Finally, we would like to close this paper with a quote from our first group member to leave the hospital. She was pregnant by a man other than her husband, but she had told him what had happened, and he was going to work at having her back. The family was financially impoverished, the husband working only part time. The patient had just discarded her parents as a source of financial help. She had three children that she would have to take care of, and it was obvious that she would have to work until she delivered. She had several physical ailments, and she had emerged from a black depression engendered by precisely the situation to which she was returning. Her final message to the group was "It's wonderful to be free."

REFERENCES

1. Anonymous. A new theory of schizophrenia. *J. Abnorm. Soc. Psycho.*, September, 1958, 57 (2):226–36.

2. Eysenck, H. J. The effects of psychotherapy: an evaluation. *J. Consult. Psychol.*, 1952, 16:319–24.

3. Eysenck, H. J. *Behavior Therapy and the Neuroses.* New York: Pergamon Press, 1960.

4. Mowrer, O. H. *The Crisis in Psychiatry and Religion.* Princeton (N.J.): D. Van Nostrand Co., Inc., 1961.

5. Szasz, T. S. The uses of naming and the origin of the myth of mental illness. *Amer. Psychol.*, 1961, 16:59–65.

6. Wexler, M. The structural problem in schizophrenia: therapeutic implications. In Mowrer, O. H., *Psychotherapy, Theory, and Research.* New York: Ronald Press, 1953.

THOMAS W. ALLEN

Adlerian Interview Strategies for Behavior Change

The Adlerian view is that behavior springs *not* from what the person "actually" is but from what he *believes* himself to be; not from the stimuli which the world thrusts upon him nor from his biological substratum but from how he *construes* those events. In other words, a person's behavior rests heavily upon his *expectations,* and after the manner of "self-fulfilling prophesies," these anticipations often contain the seeds of their own confirmation.

For example, if a person concludes that the world is a hostile place and that one is consequently well-advised to "do unto others before they do it unto him," he may well behave in a manner which others perceive as exploitative or hostile. They are then likely to respond to him in kind. These responses naturally serve to confirm his basic premises about life and entitle him to greater belligerence toward the world. Or consider the person who believes that he is but a helpless pawn of all manner of forces, both internal and external, unable to make any impact of consequence on his world. Such a person quite "logically" shrinks from life and, of course, behavior of this stripe not infrequently results in one having things done to him to a rather extraordinary extent.

The principal therapeutic objective of the Adlerian is then to alter such self-defeating, asocial beliefs, to convert a vicious cycle (self-defeating convictions which lead to behavior of a variety which generates more evidence for the original conviction) to a

From *The Counseling Psychologist,* Vol. 3, No. 1 (1971). Reprinted by permission of the author.

215

more benign spiral. The interview, although perhaps overvalued in some corners as the *sine qua non* of counseling practice, remains a useful tool in this attempt.

Disappointing Dysfunctional Expectations

The counselor's initial objective may be that of modifying the client's behavior in a way which is most likely to evoke immediate responses from his environment, responses which are at odds with his troublesome expectations. For example, one young man staunchly maintained that virtually everyone he met took an instant dislike to him and was, moreover, eager to "do him dirt." The counselor noted that his client characteristically went about with a dour expression on his face that could well be supposed to provoke defensive maneuvers on the part of others. Consequently, the client was directed to smile at others even though he didn't feel like smiling. In a week of such "hypocrisy" he found that others would respond more positively to him, given this change in his behavior. This discovery occasioned both surprise and chagrin since it tended to undermine his continuous assertions that others instinctively responded to him with hostility. Other examples of this tactic are to be found in Adler's writings and in the work of a number of contemporary writers, e.g., Milton V. Erickson's (1954) discussion of hypnotherapy and Joseph Wolpe's (1969) description of "assertive training."

In other cases, the counselor may "spit in the client's soup." "Spitting in the soup" (which Adler also termed "besmirching a clean conscience") is ostensibly derived from the boarding school technique of wresting another's rations from him by "contaminating" it with spittle. It is then but another version of the central Adlerian strategy of modifying behavior by changing its *meaning* to the person who emits it.[1] In this instance, the counselor is concerned with divining what it is that the client is up to when he behaves "systematically" and with acting in a way which will spoil this self-defeating game for him. (Remember that so-called "symptoms" are not perceived as "eruptions" but as tools which to the individual seem to be the most promising devices at his disposal to deal with life. To be sure, their disadvantages are frequently well-recognized, even publicized by the client himself, but he still maintains the behaviors as long as he perceives a slim margin of advantage to be derived from them. Of course the recognition of this advantage is frequently tantamount to its forfeiture. Thus, the right hand studiously avoids learning what the left hand is about.)

"Spitting in the soup" is an attempt to reduce a problem by undermining its utility in the eyes of the client. Consider the following instance of the maneuver:

The counselor had noted that the client, the oldest child in his family, had been born when his father was 50 years of age. When the counselor observed that he must have been really "special" to his parents the young man replied that when he was born, there had even been a special Christmas card devised in his honor. The way in which he reported this fact left little doubt that he had been the "Christ Child" in his family.

At the following session, the client said, "Guess you really hit it . . . Guess I should give up trying to be special. Is that what you are telling me?"

Counselor: Well, it's just that I'm against slavery.

Client: ?!

Counselor: You have to look so carefully at what others do in order to find out what you can permit yourself to do. You're tied to their movements. If they do something or want you to do something, then of course you *can't* do it even if you'd really like to.

By this means, the behavior which the client had previously employed to be *somebody,* somebody important, flaunting a brave banner of independence, proclaiming his dignity as someone who did what he pleased, plainly lost some of its savor to him. Now despite himself, his pleasure in it was seriously impaired since his actions had been reconstrued and might well have the opposite meaning.

"Spitting in the soup" may also involve "encouraging" a client to emphasize his symptoms even more. Adler sometimes called this ploy "antisuggestion." He tells of an 11-year-old child who literally controlled her family with her refusal to go to school. Adler suggested "spitting in her soup," saying in a very friendly manner, "School is the most important thing in the world, and if I were you, I would make even a greater fuss about it (Adler, 1956, p. 398)."

Similarly Israel Goldiamond, an avowed behaviorist who is in many ways a "crypto-Adlerian," presents an excellent example of this technique:

An "autistic" child was terrorizing his parents in Goldiamond's office with self-mutilation. He dug away at his finger with a paperclip, elaborating a small lesion and smearing the blood about. Goldiamond then took a huge novelty paperclip from his desk, straightened it into a formidable weapon, and simply handed it to the boy as if to say, "Here, do a really good job." At this point the boy stopped his self-mutilation and burst into tears.

Rudolf Dreikurs was once leading a classroom discussion when a boy began pulling the hair of the girl in front of him. Dr. Dreikurs turned to the girl and said, "Do you want me to tell you why Johnny is pulling your hair? . . . Because he likes you." At that juncture, of course, you couldn't have paid Johnny enough to persuade him to pull her hair. "Show that he liked a girl. Are you kidding? No, Sir!"

In the same vein the counselor can sometimes be helpful to "rebellious" clients by pointing out that they seldom have a chance to do what *they* want since they have to be constantly concerned with driving others up the wall. Similarly the counselor may comment on how strangely but nonetheless faithfully the revengeful client is devoted to the object of his vengeance, noting how he has greatly magnified the importance of his enemy by his "dedication" which has made him "someone."

A high school student had a vendetta going with a male teacher. The student maintained that he was innocent of any wrong-doing and that the teacher was constantly trying to provoke him. The counselor asked what it was that the teacher seemed to have in mind and the student replied that the teacher obviously wanted him to get into trouble.

The counselor looked at the student with astonishment. "How can you cooperate with such a guy?" he asked. "Cooperate with him?! I don't!" the student replied vehemently. "Ah, but you do. He wants you to get into trouble, to rise to the bait and you are careful not to disappoint him. You jump happily into his trap," the counselor said. "Obviously," he continued, "the teacher has your number, has you just where he wants you: in his power." Imagine how disappointed "Teach" would be if the student didn't fall for his line.

The student's behavior changed immediately and unmistakably.

On other occasions the counselor may want to insert a new bit of behavior in the client's repertoire, knowing that it is likely to be rewarded by the environment and retained if only the client can be induced to emit it in the first place. A technique closely related to those presented above can be of considerable utility in such a situation. I call it "sweetening the pot." In employing this maneuver the counselor sets out to imbue the behavior in question with a meaning which makes it extremely difficult for the client to eschew it without experiencing considerable discomfort.

A young man was seething in his social isolation. He was estranged from his mother who frowned on any ties which he might have with any female other than herself. After long training, he could not bring himself to initiate friendships, particularly with girls, though he came in contact with a number who interested him a good deal. Inevitably he would get cold feet just at the last moment before introducing himself or asking for a date. The counselor said in as colorful a manner as possible that whenever the young man succumbed to such fears, he might as well post a victory for his mother. He could justifiably visualize a giant smile of pleasure on his mother's face.

With this image before him, the client immediately went out and secured a date.

Avoiding the Tar Baby

If the foregoing approaches might be subsumed under the rubric, "Bre'r Rabbit's ploy" (you know, "Do anything to me, Bre'r Fox, just please, oh, please, don't throw me in the briar patch"), then another important tactic in counseling might be deemed "avoiding the client's Tar Baby," after another Uncle Remus tale. The Adlerian recognizes all too well that as self-defeating and incommodious as a particular *modus vivendi* or "identity" may be, it remains, in the eyes of the client, his best bet—and accordingly, he will defend it. As dismal as his set of expectations for himself in this world may be, they at least enable him to make sense out of the "blooming, buzzing confusion" and perhaps even entitle him to certain concessions. So, he will struggle to maintain their claim to validity.

Therefore, the client is continuously at work in an attempt to fit the counselor (along with everyone else) into his schema. It is, however, crucial that the counselor elude the traps set for him and in so doing avoid confirming certain of the client's most cherished anticipations. Often the client will, like Bre'r Fox, provide the counselor with excellent opportunities to entrap himself while the client, in the mode of the fictional fox, "lays low." For example, some clients attempt to annoy the counselor in order to establish the validity of their thesis that they are unlikable people ("See, even my counselor whose job it is to like all sorts of people, dislikes me."). Other clients will try to discourage the counselor in order to validate the hopelessness of their position or the wisdom of their decision to do nothing about it. In effect the counselor's sense of discouragement is used by such clients as license to curse the darkness and to avoid the unpleasantness involved in the attempt to generate any light by their own efforts. Yet other clients set others up to make decisions for them and then having botched them, promptly put the blame on their advisors.[2]

A high school drop-out who had been subjected to a good deal of counseling and therapy without result came to a new counselor. He said quite casually at the outset, "I suppose you want to ask me a bunch of questions about me?" The counselor who, in fact, had had some diagnostic procedures in mind demurred, "No, I don't want to pry. After all, you don't know me yet. So I don't feel it's right for me to do so. Let's get to know each other first." The counselor noticed that the client was carrying several books concerned with animal behavior. So, instead of launching into a psychological discourse of one sort or another for which the client was fully prepared, he engaged him in a spirited discussion of animal behavior, a topic which occupied portions of several more sessions and led gradually into a confrontation of a number of issues in the client's life.

The client was surprised at not being "psychologized." He had been forced to come to the counselor, but had expected to make short work of him by playing "psychiatrist" (as in Berne's games) after the fashion which had been so successful with his other "shrinks." The counselor's failure to play his "assigned" or "expected" role in the game left matters up for grabs. Unable to put the counselor in the pigeonhole which he had so carefully prepared for him, the client was left open for a productive relationship by means of which he returned to school, ultimately to graduate and go on to college.

Consider also the student who is at war with parents, with teachers, with the school and with society. He may well be eager to confirm his view of others as untrustworthy, predatory, and self-serving.[3] Thus, he may attempt to lure others, including the counselor, into some indiscretion. It is crucial for the counselor to disappoint these attempts, remaining, like Caesar's wife, "above reproach." But this assignment is by no means an easy one.[4]

A young man whose unhappiness clearly resulted from the fact that he had not been trained for cooperation, for social living, turned in upon himself and reaped the misery of isolation for his reward.

He handled his feelings of worthlessness by keeping a keen eye out for the foibles and failures of others. He argued that others were invariably hostile to him, that no matter how good he was to them, he garnered only distrust and maltreatment for his pains. As a result, he was clearly justified in shunning the world and in committing desultory small thefts.

The important task for the counselor was to *document* concretely how the young man provoked others into the responses which he expected, how he systematically discounted those experiences which contradicted his dismal model of human relations, labeling them "exceptions." At the same time, the counselor had to be wary lest he be considered yet another example of human perfidy.

Similarly, with the attention-seeker, the wise counselor is careful to attend only to those behaviors which are useful in character, declining the client's invitations to reward his "mischief" by attending assiduously to it. He will generally refuse to do battle with the discouraged client who seeks to gain a sense of self-worth by demonstrating that he can overpower the counselor. He will be likewise wary of showing hurt to the client who wishes to revenge himself upon the world.[5] Neither will he be readily trapped into expressing disheartenment in regard to his attempts to help the client who has given up and seeks confirmation of his assertions that he is a "hopeless case."[6]

William Glasser (1965) provides an excellent example of this technique:

Glasser was treating a businessman who came to therapy in order to deal with the temptation which he felt to leave his family, abandon his career, and devote himself to the homosexual life. In his attempt to legitimize a homosexual resolution of his conflict, Fred (as Glasser calls him) would argue that he was basically homosexual. If indeed he had not been born that way, the traumas which earlier uncovering therapy had identified had created him in this manner. When Glasser refused to "certify" his "basic" homosexuality, Fred played one of his trump cards. He told Glasser that when he was 17 he had had sexual intercourse with his mother. But Glasser did not fall for this "tar baby." He did not cooperate by being shocked. Fred's intention seemed to be that of making an impact on the therapist in such a way as to convince him once and for all that his past was so distorted that normality was plainly out of the quesion for him, that he was entitled to succumb to the temptations of a life with fewer responsibilities.

Glasser, however, got therapy seriously underway by responding calmly, "So what? Is that what makes you queer today?" (pp. 151ff.)

The foregoing techniques are intended to interrupt the client's dismal cycle of discouragement. The aim is, on one hand, to interfere with behavior which contains the seeds of further disillusionment or, by altering its meaning to the client, to induce behavior with greater adaptive potential. On the other hand, the intent is to abort the client's self-defeating expectation-behavior-system by responding in ways contrary to his expectations or script (Berne, 1969).

The Prime Mover: Encouragement

Since the client's underlying *discouragement* remains the principal villain in the piece as far as the Adlerian counselor is concerned, he quite naturally sees the counselor's principal task to be *encouragement*. Now encouragement does not mean reassurance, e.g., the insistence that one can certainly do whatever it is that needs doing, that everything will work out just fine in the long run, that there is nothing to be feared, that "God's in His Heaven and all's right with the world." Encouragement involves rather a convincing *demonstration* that the client has resources and options which he can bring to bear on significant issues in life.

Indeed, the success of behavioral counseling and behavior modification may well lie in the fact that the "behaviorists" have concentrated on bringing powerful techniques for encouragement to bear on human difficulties. Consider, for example, Skinner's emphasis on "successive or progressive approximations." According to this strategy a person is brought along in a series of very small, easily-negotiable steps to the criterion performance. Since the steps are so readily surmounted, the person has a virtually continuous sense of success, of progress, which serves to propel him further.

Neither should one underestimate the encouraging properties of the behaviorist's own psychological "set." Typically he assumes that the client's difficulties arise from inappropriate bits of training and that these difficulties will be dissolved when the appropriate retraining has taken place. It is not the essential person which is deficient nor some malignancy at the core of his being which is culpable. It is not a deficiency in that nebulous and impalpable, yet pervasive entity, "the personality," which deserves attention, but rather a relatively circumscribed piece of behavior. Thus, the client need not conclude, "There is something wrong with me, with the person I am in the deepest recesses of my being." He can instead say to himself, "Some of the behavior which I picked up somewhere along the way has some real disadvantages. Consequently, it would be advantageous for me to replace it with some other behavior which has a more auspicious set of results."

What is more, many behavioral counselors conduct themselves in a manner which is most "encouraging" since it serves to disabuse the client of the belief that he is nothing but a victim or pawn of forces beyond his control. Far from confirming a narrow conception of man, so-called "operant conditioning" with human beings often leads the individual to affirm his potentialities, his strengths, his responsibility for himself. For the Adlerian this state of mind is a necessary ingredient of any attempt to solve personal problems. It is the very antithesis of discouragement.

The Relationship of Encouragement

Unlike Freud who saw the human relationship between client and counselor as a source of "contamination," Adler saw it as a crucial therapeutic tool. He spoke of the counselor's "material function." In his view, in the normal socialization process, the child's mother first wins the child's interest in herself. Subsequently this interest is transferred by the mother (or in Sullivan's terms, "the mothering one") to wider and wider segments of society. In cases of psychopathology, Adler maintained, this process has malfunctioned in one way or another. Consequently, the person possesses too little "social interest" to meet the various challenges and crises posed by life in a straightforward fashion and resorts to dubious maneuvers ("symptoms") to deal with them. The counselor's task then becomes that of establishing a viable connection between the client and society. In other words, the counselor must do belatedly what the client's "mothering one" accomplished so imperfectly.

The relationship is obviously an important tool in this attempt. By establishing a positive relationship with the client the counselor often quickens the client's natural but undeveloped interest in others. The relationship with the counselor may afford the client his first meaningful glimpse of the possibility of establishing cooperative relations with others and of the rewards which such arrangements can produce. In addition, the counselor's interest is a graphic suggestion to the client that he is indeed someone of significance rather than the negative entity he fears himself to be.

The validity of Adler's observation is richly testified to by the research conducted by Carl R. Rogers, his colleagues, and students (cf. Truax and Carkhuff, 1965). This impressive body of findings points to the existence of an important relationship between a good personal relationship of counselor and client and constructive change on the part of the latter.

At the same time, the data seem to support Adler's notion that the encouragement process requires something more than a good relationship. On the whole, the relationship variables (empathy, genuineness, and warmth) employed in these many studies account for less than half of the therapeutic effect noted (Truax and Carkhuff, 1965, p. 114; Allen and Whiteley, 1968, pp. 117–125). Clearly additional strategies of encouragement are required. The following case examples are intended to illustrate some of these strategies.

1. A small 8-year old boy had found the transfer to a new school unappealing and had been (unwisely) allowed to do his work at home with the aid of a tutor. As time went on, he acted more, rather than less, "fearful of school." Indeed he resisted any attempt to induce him to conform with uncontainable fury.

His "fearfulness," or at least his resistance, extended to all manner of health care. So a crisis arose when an abcess in his tooth became a substantial threat to his well-being. Under the influence of the pain which the infection generated, he agreed to go to the dentist with his counselor. But when the moment to depart for the appointment arrived, he demurred.

The counselor's attempt at encouragement was not that of minimizing the event nor of issuing assurances (a specious form of "encouragement"). Neither did he attempt to cajole him with references of being a "big boy" and to the "fact" that big boys marched right into dentists' offices without hesitation (a not-too-subtle variety of condescension).

The counselor simply expressed his understanding of how the situation must look and feel to his diminutive client. He articulated as well as he could his sense of the magnitude of the challenge the boy perceived.

There was no reply. Then the boy left the room with an air that suggested that his decision was irrevocable. But moments later he returned fully dressed and ready to go. The surgery turned out to be quite an ordeal. Nevertheless this volatile youngster who had not long before kicked a pediatrician in the shins and run from the building in the course of a routine physical examination bore it all with an unmistakable dignity.

The pride which he took in himself for having negotiated this gauntlet subsequently provided momentum for tackling other problems, such as returning to school.

2. A 16-year old girl came into counseling as a runaway, a truant, and a desultory experimenter with a wide range of chemical substances. She had in fact made a trip to the emergency room of a general hospital as the result of an infelicitous melange of pharmaceuticals which she had injected and ingested.

Mother's attempt to help was, in the main, moralistic. She was indignant over the disgrace and difficulty which such behavior brought her. But Mother's main "contribution" was her extensive and vociferous worry. She waxed eloquent with doomsday prophesies in her effort to help. Such rantings were periodically punctuated with, on one hand, "hand washings" ("I give up . . . etc.") and, on the other, wistful odes to the virtues and accomplishments which would be her daughter's if only she would but turn her back on her evil ways.

It was, then, not surprising for the counselor to find himself confronted with a cynical girl thoroughly convinced of her own lack of worth. Indeed, her conviction was that she was so worthless that a fatal error in the use of drugs would be of little moment. She was, she insisted, well-advised to grab whatever excitement and pleasure was readily at hand since a person of her stripe could not expect very much of life in the long run.

In counseling interviews she was unable to come up with anything about herself which was positive in character. At last by listening carefully the counselor discerned that other kids tended to confide in her. She admitted that others seemed to find loyalty and circumspection in her, qualities which they themselves generally lacked. Mother, of course, saw these virtues as perversity, as collusion with a host of thoroughly depraved and marginly human beasts in a conspiracy against all that which was good in life. Encouragement consisted of a series of attempts to induce recognition of these characteristics as strengths, to help her see that mother's fulminations were in fact more a function of mother's feelings and foibles than of the client's basic depravity and to provide her with a relationship in which trust could flourish. Work with mother focused on her (mother's) feelings. The counselor expressed his understanding of her feelings and acknowledged her right to them while simultaneously attempting to help her see that their unmitigated expression tended only to lead to more difficulty for *her* since they merely served to provoke her daughter. These efforts yielded some appreciable positive consequences although the situation proved to be exceedingly difficult to resolve.

3. A late adolescent was quite depressed and having difficulty attending to her school work although she possessed considerable aptitude for it. She seemed to be hopelessly obsessed with all manner of trivial things. She pictured herself as being helpless, locked in the grip of titanic forces (traumas, drives, etc.) beyond her control.

Finally, the counselor commented on how adroitly the girl had maneuvered others—particularly her parents and various professionals —by being weak and defeated. The counselor marveled, quite honestly, at her skill in manipulating others and at the social skill implicit in this manipulation.

At first, she was thunderstruck, then, defensive, but literally minutes later she was struck by the discovery of unrecognized resources and the possibilities they offered. No longer need she wheedle others by being the helpless, bedeviled child. Anyone who was able to accomplish what she had, had resources to deal with people directly. Quite radical changes in her behavior were rapidly forthcoming.

4. A 13-year old boy was in constant trouble with school authorities and with civil authorities as well. On one occasion, after a family fight, he ran away from home. But the counselor learned from him that he had sneaked back that night in order to feed and care for his pet chickens. The counselor responded to this fact and to the positive response which he generally got from animals. The counselor further arranged situations where he could interact with animals and thereby provided effective opportunities for him to begin to construe himself in more positive terms—which had appreciable, i.e., beneficial effects on his relations with other people.

5. A seventh grader made an obvious display of his failure to do his work in class and was ostentatiously slow in complying with the teacher's request. For example,

Teacher: Please put that magazine away. It's time to get some of this work done.
Bill: OOO—KAY. (Making no move to do so.)
Teacher: Well . . .
Bill: OOO—KAY
Teacher: Please don't say that.
Bill: OOO—KAY
Teacher: I'm afraid I'm going to have to keep you for detention.

But days passed and Bill did not appear to serve his sentence. Since Bill's parents cared little or nothing about school or learning, they were no source of help. Finally, for some unfathomable reason Bill appeared for detention. But instead of working, he began to read an automobile magazine. Resisting the urge to respond to his provocation, the teacher expressed interest in the magazine. Bill then began to explain some of the technical aspects of automobiles in some detail. The teacher expressed genuine admiration for his knowledge which so dwarfed hers.

There was an immediate change in his behavior—for the better. Bill became much more pleasant in his classroom and much more cooperative. What is more, he began supporting the teacher's efforts at classroom management instead of exerting his influence in the opposite direction.

It should, perhaps, be emphasized in closing that the foregoing examples and some demonstrations to the contrary, "encouragement" is not always the result of a *tour de force* or *bon mot,* but of a continuous process of some duration. Nonetheless, "encouragement" is an extremely potent tool in human relations. Correctly understood and imaginatively implemented it can have far reaching effects in a relatively short period of time.

This paper has not attempted to present an exhaustive account of "specific" techniques which Adlerians have found to be of considerable utility in counseling. Its intent has been rather to introduce the reader to a mode of approaches to the problems which counselors confront. The key notion of Individual Psychology, socio-teleoanalytic emphasis, which underscores the pivotal position of expectations in human behavior, will hopefully suggest a number of therapeutic possibilities to the counselor as he works with his own clients.

NOTES

1. Mark Twain clearly recognized the extent to which behavior could be modified by changing the meaning it has to the behaver. He illustrates the point graphically in the fence white-washing episode in *The Adventures of Tom Sawyer*. In another context, Twain wryly asserts that had God only bidden Adam and Eve to pursue Truth, it is likely that they would have eaten the snake rather than the apple.

2. Remember the definition of an expert which has been about for many years, "An expert is a guy who is called in when it is too late to share the blame."

3. Anyone who has worked with delinquents or adult offenders rapidly becomes aware of the eagerness with which they pursue evidence of malfeasance on the part of society.

4. The point is well made in a story which Dr. Bernard H. Shulman of Chicago tells:

Two strangers were rooming together at a convention.
First: Darn, I forgot my pajamas.
Second: Don't worry. Here, I have an extra pair.
First: Rats. I forgot my towel.
Second: It's O.K. You can use mine.
First: Now doesn't that beat all! I forgot my toothpaste.
Second: You are welcome to use mine.

First: I don't even have my toothbrush.

Second: Well, it doesn't seem to be a very good idea for us to use the same toothbrush.

First: See, I knew you had something against me!

5. Adler's principal biographer, Phyllis Bottome (1939), relates an incident concerning a demanding, spiteful patient who had taken to calling Adler at odd hours with trivial questions. Finally, she called at 3:00 a.m. to ask if oranges were good for her. Of course, she was simultaneously full of apologies, "I see it's very late; I'm afraid I must have disturbed you." Adler, who well knew that her chief aim was to disturb others, simply replied, "Oh, no! Why should you think that? I was expecting you to ring up and have been sitting for the last half hour close to the telephone!" This was the last time the lady resorted to the trick (Bottome, 1939, p. 93).

6. It must be recognized that the old saw, "Can't can't do anything," is in serious error. Adler observed that, in fact, many human beings conclude that they can do a good deal better in life once their incompetence has been duly certified. This conclusion is after all not without some basis. In many situations people are able to exert a substantial influence and control by means of their incompetence.

REFERENCES

Adler, A. *The individual psychology of Alfred Adler*. Edited by H. L. & R. R. Ansbacher. New York: Basic Books; 1956.

Adler, A. *Superiority and social interest*. Edited by H. L. & R. R. Ansbacher. Evanston, Illinois: Northwestern University Press, 1964.

Allen, T. W. Commentaries. In Calia, V. & Corsini, R. (Eds.) *Critical incidents in school counseling*, 1972.

Allen, T. W. & Whiteley, J. M. *Dimensions of effective counseling*. Columbus, Ohio: Charles E. Merrill, 1968.

Berne, Eric. *Games people play*. New York: Grove Press, 1969.

Bottome, P. *Private worlds*. Boston: Houghton-Mifflin, 1939.

Dreikurs, R. Psychodynamics, psychotherapy, and counseling. Chicago: Alfred Adler Institute, 1967.

Dreikurs, R., Corsini, R., Lowe, R., & Sonstegard, M. (Eds.) Adlerian family counseling: A manual for counseling centers. Eugene, Oregon: University of Oregon, 1959.

Erickson, M. H. Special techniques of brief hypnotherapy. *Journal of Clinical and Experimental Hypnosis*, 1954, 2, 109–129.

Frankl, V. Paradoxical intention. *American Journal of Psychotherapy*, 1960, 14, 520–525.

Glasser, W. *Reality therapy*. New York: Harper & Row, 1965.

Haley, J. *Strategies of psychotherapy*. New York: Grune & Stratton, 1963.

Mosak, H. H. & Shulman, B. H. *Individual psychotherapy: A syllabus*. Chicago: Alfred Adler Institute, 1963.

Pratt, S. & Tooley, J. Toward a metataxonomy of human systems actualization: the perspective of contract psychology. In A. R. Mahrer (Ed.)

New approaches to personality classification. New York: Columbia University, 1970, 349–380.

Rotter, J. *Social learning theory and clinical psychology.* Englewood Cliffs, N.J.: Prentice-Hall, 1956.

Shulman, B. H. *Essays in schizophrenia.* Baltimore: Williams & Wilkins, 1968.

Truax, C. & Carkhuff, R. *Toward effective counseling and psychotherapy.* Chicago: Aldine, 1965.

Wagner, B. R. & Paul, G. L. Reduction of incontinence in chronic mental patients: A pilot project. *Journal of Behavior Therapy and Experimental Psychiatry,* 1970, 1, 29–38.

Wolpe, J. *The practice of behavior therapy.* New York: Pergamon Press, 1969.

IRA A. GREENBERG

ALEXANDER BASSIN

Reality Therapy and Psychodrama

A comparison of Reality Therapy and Psychodrama reveals wide areas of difference in theoretical underpinnings, techniques, applications, as well as some points of similarity. It is the purpose of this study to explore and identify major differences and likeness by reference to the works of the leading spokesmen for these significant forms of treatment.

Both Reality Therapy and Psychodrama differ from conventional therapy in that they address themselves to the task of treating other than the class of patient considered suitable for psychoanalysis. The writings of both Glasser and Moreno express concern about working with prisoners, delinquents, psychotics, the failures in the struggle for existence.

Psychodrama is the product of the creativity and industry of Jacob Levi Moreno, who was born in Bucharest, Rumania, on May 20, 1892, the child of a Jewish couple who provided him with little formal religious training beyond the traditional rituals of circumcision and Bar-Mitzvah. Nevertheless, religion has been an important part of Moreno's thinking throughout his life. Much of his writing vibrates with mystical and religious overtones as well as poetic excursions in contrast to the lean, clear, jargon-free style of Glasser.

For a little over a year, Moreno worked with the research staff of the Psychiatric Clinic of Vienna University where he had some personal contact with Freud, whose psychoanalytic theories at the time were beginning to obtain some international recognition.[1]

A year or two later, while still a medical student, Moreno be-

231

came involved in a project he described as the real beginning of group psychotherapy—the organizing of weekly discussion groups among prostitutes in the Am Spittelberg district of Vienna.

Moreno received his M.D. in 1917 about a year before the end of World War I, just forty years before Glasser obtained his medical degree. In the turbulent days of the collapse of the Austro-Hungarian monarchy, Moreno worked as the superintendent of a children's hospital and started the thought processes which were to lead to the formulations of sociometry which have become a basic theme of his theoretical system. From 1919 until 1925 he practiced psychiatry, published nine books anonymously, and founded *Das Stegreiftheatre,* the Spontaneity Theatre, which is described as the laboratory for the development of psychodramatic techniques and the forerunner of modern improvisational theatre.[2]

In 1925 Moreno came to the United States and immediately set out to introduce Psychodrama to the mental health professions and the American public. Within a few years he began the Impromptu Group Theatre in Carnegie Hall, where sessions were held three times a week. He engaged in sociometric studies among the prisoners at Sing Sing and in a move reminiscent of Glasser at the Ventura School for Delinquent Girls, Moreno was engaged for a treatment project which extended from 1932 to 1938 at the New York State Training School for Girls at Hudson, New York. He founded the journal *Sociometry* and taught in succession at Teachers College, the New School for Social Research, and New York University. In 1941, St. Elizabeth's Hospital in Washington, D.C., adopted Psychodrama for the treatment of its mental patients and installed a special stage modeled after the one at Beacon, New York, which had become the center of Psychodrama activity. The forerunner of the American Society for Group Psychotherapy and Psychodrama was founded and a journal, *Group Psychotherapy,* was published. During this period Moreno is reported to have first used the term "group psychotherapy." It is interesting to note that during 1946–1948 Moreno was involved in initiating Psychodrama and role playing at the West Los Angeles VA Hospital, the very facility where Glasser served his internship and became acquainted with Dr. J. L. Harrington a decade later.

Moreno continued to write, practice, and demonstrate Psychodrama until his death in 1974. Honors and recognition were heaped on him on an international scale and the existence of Psychodrama became known to almost every literate person.

Zerka, Moreno's wife, collaborator, and currently the head of the Psychodrama movement of the world, has identified a number of techniques employed in Psychodrama (soliloquy, self-presentation, self-realization, hallucinatory double, multiple double, mirror, role reversal, warming up, etc.)[3] but an excellent description of an actual session of Psychodrama has been prepared by Alexander King, a prominent artist, author, and heroin addict who came to the Moreno Institute in Beacon for treatment.[4] He tells how a patient, Mr. Mehlmann, is prepared for a visit from his wife. He comes to the stage and Dr. Moreno asks about his thoughts concerning the impending reunion. Then they reenact what had happened at the last visit of Mrs. Mehlmann.

It was plain to see that Mr. Mehlmann was an old trouper in psychodrama, and he was gaining authority and poise with every passing moment; as a matter of fact, he proceeded to crouch down, without any self-consciousness, behind one of the chairs to simulate his actions of the month before.

"Did your wife come up from the right side of the house?" asked Dr. Moreno.

"No, she came from the left," said Mehlmann. "She couldn't open the door with her hand on account of the packages."

A young woman, who, I later learned, was a trained practitioner in psychodrama, arose from the audience and approached the stage from the left side. She made believe that she was carrying some bulky packages in her arms, and, as she stepped onto the platform, she pretended to kick open an imaginary door.

"No!" said Mehlmann. "No! No! She kicked the door with her right foot! She don't use her left foot much, she has arthritis in the knee."

Mehlmann, it turns out, was suffering from a paranoid disturbance, and the session is not outstanding, King writes, except that in the course of describing a breakfast, the patient happened to mention the word "beigel."

However, as soon as the word was out of his mouth, a pretty dark-haired woman, called Millicent, jumped out of her seat and shouted, "Wrong!"

"You don't say 'beigel,' " said Millicent. "You're supposed to say 'bagel.' " She passed the back of her hand across her forehead and chuckled to herself. "You talk like a Galician," she said, as she sat down again.[5]

These were the first words she had uttered for almost a year. King, who was notably hostile to psychiatrists and therapeutic measures, speaks in the warmest tones of his response to Psychodrama and Dr. Moreno.

The techniques, procedures, ideas that first were suggested by Moreno have now become integral parts of a host of treatment methods, particularly those related to Gestalt Therapy and the Esalen Institute—frequently, as Moreno and his followers point out—with no acknowledgment of their source.

In terms of personality, Moreno and Glasser differ fundamentally. Moreno described himself as extroverted, intuitive rather than logical, brash, ebullient, uninhibited, unquestionably meglomaniacal at times. He urged spontaneity, the warm embrace, a minimum concern with appearance and convention. In contrast, Glasser is somewhat shy, prefers to remain in the background, and is never as dramatic and flamboyant as Moreno was. He is an excellent speaker, however, and capable of keeping an audience enthralled for hours at a time. All who know him are impressed by his common-sense, logical approach to life.

The clearest expression of indebtedness to Psychodrama takes place in Glasser's increasing use of role playing as a teaching and training device. It is his current practice, after a didactic lecture, to invite members of the audience to come to the platform and simulate the behavior of a client with a problem which Glasser "treats" before audiences of a thousand. Many viewers report that this part of a Glasser workshop or lecture is invariably the most interesting and instructive portion of the session.

In work with clients, a Reality Therapist might ask that the person describe and even act out some important episode that may have triggered a series of events related to the presenting problem. And a follower of Glasser who had been trained in Psychodrama might well employ some of the other techniques mentioned by Zerka Moreno, but this would generally be considered somewhat of a departure from the main tactics of Reality Therapy.

In treating Mr. Mehlmann, Glasser would most likely adhere to his basic paradigm of first establishing a relationship, an involvement, by engaging in friendly conversation on topics of mutual interest and then, without pressing too hard, they would enter the area of the client's "crazy" ideas. Glasser would most likely ask such a person to describe how he has been spending his time. "What are you doing?" Glasser would insist that the client describe his hour-by-hour behavior. "I understand you watched 'Peyton Place' on channel 7 from 1:30 to 2:00. Then what did you do?" After the behavior has been clearly depicted Glasser would ask him to evaluate his behavior. "Is what you're doing helping you? What is it doing for relations with your wife, your children, your employer, your friends, relatives and colleagues?"

If the client is defensive about his behavior, provides all kinds of rationalizations and excuses, Glasser would avoid arguing about the judgment. "The man convinced against his will, remains unconvinced still," Glasser believes. So he drops the subject for the time being. There will be opportunities for further discussion later.

Eventually, however, Glasser believes, a change in behavior is based on the freely made choice of the person involved. When a judgment has been made that the behavior is not satisfactory, only then can we move into another essential component of the Reality Therapy approach—making a *plan*. Glasser and the client would discuss what change in behavior, what strategy would most efficiently achieve a goal. In the case of Mr. Mehlmann, he would conclude, perhaps, that the practice of accusing his spouse of infidelity and his brother-in-law of trying to poison him was simply not paying off in terms of a decent relationship with his wife and her brother. Besides, these accusations were what was keeping him locked up in this miserable hospital. So what do we do? What plan can we work out?

Perhaps the plan would be to refrain, as much as possible, from freely and indiscreetly voicing his fears and suspicions, particularly in circles where these ideas would receive a minimum of enthusiastic reception. Could the client, by "acting as if," not talk to anybody about his strange ideas except to the therapist for fifteen minutes a week? If the client agrees, Glasser would press for a clear commitment, perhaps a written *contract,* to make the agreement as specific as possible.

Gradually, as the client found that he could elect (choose) to talk or be silent about his suspicions, and the people in his environment appeared to respond better to the new Mr. Mehlmann, he would begin to surrender some of his paranoid ideas. In any case, Mr. Mehlmann's improvement would be directly related to his involvement with Dr. Glasser, his growing self-esteem, his increased capacity to plan his own life without impinging on the rights of others to find love and self-esteem.

The psychodramatist would see Glasser's process of self-evaluation followed by a plan and a commitment as comparable to Moreno's concept of *creative spontaneity,* which he defines in general terms as an effective and adequate response on the part of a client to a new situation or a novel and adequate response to an old situation. Man's survival has depended and will continue to depend on his creative spontaneity, Moreno asserts. An individual's spontaneity may be developed or increased through what Moreno calls spontaneity training obtained in the course of repeated psychodramatic experiences.[6]

Glasser says: "We teach patients better ways to fulfill their needs," which is also Moreno's purpose in inducing increased spontaneity in patients. However, where Glasser would attempt to accomplish this educational goal by involvement, warmth, and reason, Moreno would strive to reach the same destination by action and emotion, often on a stage before an audience, under the guidance of a director with the help of assistants called auxiliary egos.

There would appear to be some differences between Glasser and Moreno in relation to an examination of the patient's history as an element in treatment. Both state they firmly adhere to the principle of the "here and now." But a Psychodrama session might devote considerable time to an examination of the patient's past, his relations with his parents, friends, teachers when he was a child, for example. Glasser would prefer to concentrate on the person's current problem on this basis: "Working in the present and toward the future, we do not get involved with the patient's history because we can neither change what has happened to him nor accept the fact that he is limited by his past."[7]

A favorite concept of Moreno is *tele,* the "feeling of individuals about one another, the cement that holds groups together."[8] It is the ability of one individual to get into the skin of another, to see the world through his eyes, to experience a strong positive relationship that is reciprocated. The closest English equivalent might be "empathy"—but it is more than this, more than Freud's *transference.* It is the feeling occasioned in Psychodrama when individuals identify with the protagonist and empathize with him, and when the protagonist is similarly emotionally engaged and returns this feeling.

The Glasserian concept closest to *tele* is *involvement,* a real, warm, positive, personal relationship between client and therapist. A person meets his basic needs for love and self-worth, for identity, the feeling and belief that we are someone in distinction to others, and that someone is important and worthwhile.[9]

The final two key concepts in the Morenean system, catharsis and insight, seem to have no exact counterpart in Glasser's theory of therapy. Catharsis for Moreno is what it was for Aristotle, the experience of an emotional purgation following the arousal of pity, fear, anxiety, or other stressful responses brought about through the action on the stage. Empathy and identification or *tele* must exist before one can experience the pain of the emotion and the relief of its expulsion, which is what occurs in a well-directed Psychodrama session. All the participants become deeply involved with each other and accordingly are able to feel the pain and sorrow, the joy or anguish that the principals are undergoing.

Glasser, on the other hand, is suspicious of prolonged discussion of intense feelings. He writes: ". . . we must not be misled by emotion as people who fail fall back upon emotion to direct their behavior; people who succeed rely upon reason and logic."[10] Yet in another context he seems to see the value of emotion.

A serious failing in most school materials is that the emotion has been completely drained out of it. Emotion helps the child see the relevance of what he is studying. Most school materials have little or no respect for the children's culture, especially for its rich emotional content. Too much school material is unrealistic, unemotional, dull. Unless school materials are changed, failures will increase because children seem unable to get started without the emotional bridge to relevance. Not only is emotion necessary in the school material, but emotion itself, so important in children's lives, should also be present in class. Laughter, shouting, loud unison responses, even crying, are a part of any good learning experience and should be heard in every class. A totally quiet, orderly, unemotional class is rarely learning; quiet and order have no place in education as all-encompassing virtues. To the degree that I have seen them practiced, they do more harm than good, as they increase the gap between the school and the world.[11]

Glasser is saying that emotion is a basic requirement for effective learning to take place in the classroom, but he stops a considerable distance short of Moreno's position about its place for effective therapy with adults. The mild, pleasant catharsis that the child experiences in a "School Without Failure" cannot be mistaken for the drained and occasionally euphoric feelings experienced in the course of a Morenean catharsis. In Psychodrama the learning of insight is the final product of the interaction of spontaneity, situation, tele—and catharsis.

Insight, as Moreno explains it, is very much like the concept of the Gestalt psychologists (who are not to be confused with the Gestalt Therapy followers of the late Fritz Perls). The insight of Psychodrama occurs through the restructuring of the protagonist's perceptual field, so that it is enlarged and the new gestalt encompasses both the problem and the solution; whereas, prior to the achievement of insight the problem may have been perceived in the foreground and the solution in the background or vice versa, but the two would not be seen simultaneously. It is only when they are seen together, Moreno would say, that insight has occurred or is about to occur. Attainment of insight would be followed by the psychodramatic enactment of decisions or through the experience of their results in future projections, that is, Psychodrama sessions dealing with the future in the here and now of the staged experience. In a sense the protagonist is expected to try out, rehearse, practice his new understanding in the staging of selected episodes, problems, contingencies he may realistically expect to face in the future.

Glasser would be inclined to question the need for the concepts of insight except as an intellectual exercise and assert that for positive change to take place the failure-oriented individual must become involved with a responsible person who will teach him how to obtain love, self-esteem, a better identity.

Glasser and Moreno are in agreement that change is difficult and painful. Moreno would help the patient become better able to cope with pain by experiencing it psychodramatically, on the stage. Glasser would depend on his involvement with the patient, on his firmness, on never giving up. "Our job is not to lessen the pain of irresponsible actions, but to increase the patient's strength so that he can bear the necessary pain of a full life as well as enjoy the rewards of a deeply responsible existence."[12]

It is fair to conclude that Glasser and Moreno, Reality Therapy and Psychodrama, differ in concepts, nomenclature and technique, but that there is enough overlap in philosophy to warrant the Psychodramatist to attempt to incorporate some of Glasser's thinking on his stage, and to encourage the Reality Therapist to feel comfortable about utilizing selected action approaches of Moreno in his practice.

REFERENCES

1. Anderson, Walt, "J. L. Moreno and The Origins of Psychodrama—A Biographical Sketch," *Psychodrama—Theory and Therapy,* edited by Ira A. Greenberg, Behavioral Publications, 1974.

2. *Ibid,* p. 209.

3. Moreno, Zerka T., "A Survey of Psychodramatic Techniques," *Psychodrama—Theory and Therapy,* edited by Ira A. Greenberg, Behavioral Publications, 1974.

4. King, Alexander, *Mine Enemy Grows Older,* New York: Holt, Rinehart & Winston, 1958, pp. 144–145.

5. *Ibid,* p. 232.

6. Moreno, J.L., *Psychodrama,* Vol. I, 1964, p. XII.

7. Glasser, William, *Reality Therapy,* New York: Harper & Row, 1965, p. 21.

8. Moreno, J. L., *Psychodrama,* Vol. I, 1964, p. XI.

9. Glasser, William, *Reality Therapy: A New Approach to Psychiatry,* New York: Harper & Row, 1965, p. 12.

10. *Ibid,* pp. 13–14.

11. *Ibid,* p. 56.

12. *Ibid,* p. 59.

Three Psychotherapies

Changes in the definition of psychotherapy as a helping relation-ship—especially changes that increase the variety of persons to whom such a relationship might prove useful—would seem to call for a new attitude toward theories of psychotherapy. In the past, to understand the nature of a helping relationship, it has been cus-tomary to stress the differences between theoretical approaches.

Here we are concerning ourselves with the similarities among three specific approaches to the theory of psychotherapy, as well as their significant differences: that of Thomas Szasz (Autonomous Psychotherapy), of O. Hobart Mowrer (Integrity Therapy), and of William Glasser (Reality Therapy). This trio is particularly interesting because each of the three has emphatic differences with what might be called traditional psychotherapeutic viewpoints.

One point of view upon which all three seem agreed is that commonly used psychiatric classifications of "mental illness" are of little value in the consideration of psychotherapeutic proce-dures. All three also question the social benefit or personal utility of excusing or explaining conduct on the grounds of mental illness.

Glasser and Mowrer agree in their strong opposition to psycho-analytic therapy procedures. But Szasz, while disagreeing with cer-tain aspects of psychoanalytic theory and practice, nevertheless retains his basic identification with the psychoanalytic approach to psychotherapy.

Former title "Three Psychotherapies Compared and Evaluated." From *The Discoverer*, Vol. 3, No. 3 (May 1966).

Mowrer is outspokenly opposed to the private practice of individual psychotherapy for a fee. Neither Glasser nor Szasz seems to object either to private treatment or to the payment of a fee. Szasz, in particular, emphasizes the view that payment of a fee by the patient is a matter of considerable importance in his psychotherapeutic procedure.

Beyond these issues, the points of view expressed are more definitely individualistic. Glasser stresses re-training the person to behave in a responsible manner with respect to existing rules and regulations. Put another way, it might be said that Glasser's technique involves teaching the patient that compliance with rules and regulations has real (i.e., demonstrable, tangible) and beneficial consequences, rather than being a burden to rebel against.

Glasser points out, however, that the patient becomes concerned about rules only when he is concerned about his relationship with the person helping him. The development of a helpful relationship depends in a very basic way upon the helper's involvement with the person being helped and upon that person's reciprocal involvement with the helper. Without this mutual involvement, Glasser contends, rules and their consequences are matters of relative indifference to the persons who are expected to obey them.

It might be said that Mowrer's group therapy is applicable to those who acknowledge the validity of rules and regulations but who have nevertheless behaved in ways that constitute violations of these rules. Mowrer believes that if the person has followed and continues to follow a life of deceptive rule breaking, he will find himself in progressively greater trouble. His suggested solution is that the person should admit to others that he has cheated and then to ask to be readmitted to the game of responsible social living on the basis of his promise to do better in the future. The person is urged to relieve his guilt for misbehavior by meaningful restitutive efforts to those who may have been harmed by his duplicitous behavior.

Szasz's approach to the psychotherapeutic relationship stresses the significance of autonomous behavior regulated only by specific and explicit agreement. This type of participation is encouraged for both therapist and patient. The therapeutic contract constitutes the specific and explicit agreements involved in the helper-patient relationship. The most desirable form of psychotherapeutic contract specifies the least number of restrictions and obligations (responsibilities) to ensure the achievement of the objectives of the relationship. A principal goal of the relationship is to allow the patient maximum freedom in the choices that will determine the nature of his own life while still recognizing the rights of others.

I have mentioned some rather obvious points of agreement and disagreement among these three positions. I would now like to suggest that the apparent disagreements may relate to "what part of the elephant" each theorist is most concerned with. The implication is not that Glasser, Mowrer, and Szasz are blind in some specialized way, but rather that the attention of each is focused upon different aspects of what may be a single developmental continuum.

The continuum referred to might be called, in common sense terms, the sense of responsibility. Another term might be "the development of attitudes toward rules." Szasz has pointed to the value of Piaget's analysis of how a child's attitudes toward rules change as he becomes older. Piaget recognizes three stages of attitudes toward rules. The first stage is represented by the period during which rules are either ignored or followed only coincidentally. The second stage is one in which rules are regarded as of super-human origin and also as eternal and inviolate. The third stage is one in which rules are seen as matters of interpersonal agreement. At the latter stage, rules can be changed, but the process of change itself must be regulated by certain "meta-rules" in order to be considered legitimate. Example: anyone may express his attitude toward existing rules, but rules are actually changed only as a result of general agreement and consent.

From this point of view, the approaches to the helping relationship of Glasser, Mowrer, and Szasz can be considered as complementary rather than antagonistic to each other. They can be seen as complementary when we regard them as describing types of relationship that may be appropriate for different stages of development in attitudes toward rules.

My suggestion is that Glasser's primary concern is with those aspects of behavior that stem from the first stage of attitudes toward rules. He is concerned when the desire for immediate impulse gratification (or the need to lessen anxiety) results in behavior that violates general social prescriptions. His efforts then are directed toward creating attitudes that encourage awareness of long-range and socially defined consequences of behavior.

Glasser's approach may be seen as primarily useful when the person is functioning in a way characteristic of human beings before they have established any consistent attitude toward rules. It would appear that Glasser has found effective methods for coping with persons in this stage and for changing them. His emphasis upon the need for involvement between helper and the helped indicates his recognition that mere reward and punishment at the human level are not necessarily adequate to change the patient's attitude toward rules.

A significant and valuable relationship between the two persons involved is needed. If such a relationship exists, the person being helped will become concerned with rules and will attempt to follow them when the helper indicates that such behavior is necessary in order to assure his continued approval and support.

When the helped person is under direct observation during considerable periods of time (such as in schools, correctional institutions, and hospitals) this method is particularly effective, because violations of the rules can be noted and effectively responded to by persons who have authority to reward or punish.

Mowrer also is concerned with this problem, but he concentrates his attention upon the attitudes that develop when a person who has reached the second stage of awareness of rules nevertheless has behaved in a way which violates socially defined standards. In this stage of attitudes toward rules, rules are regarded as eternal and inviolate, but this does not necessarily mean that the person always follows the rules. Why doesn't he? This question can be answered by observation of the child at several different stages in his development from the age of two years through adolescence. At certain times it becomes evident that the child is setting himself against the requirements of others as an apparently necessary part of his own growth toward autonomy and independence. At such times he may be described as "resistant" or "nega-tivistic" because of his obvious intent to defy, regardless of the motives of others in attempting to guide him.

Mowrer's approach to dealing with this attitude and the prob-lems it creates minimizes the role of any authoritative figure in the helping relationship. Responsibility for the helping function in-stead is vested in a group of peers who have no formal authority over the person being helped. The desire for the approval and support of this peer group helps the person resolve his attitude of defiance toward authority and the demands of those in positions of authority.

The people with whom Szasz works may function at times in terms of the ego states already described. But Szasz's method of dealing with such ego states is to attempt to evoke and reinforce an adult ego reaction. Autonomous Psychotherapy describes what is essentially (in Eric Berne's terminology) an adult-to-adult rela-tionship. Szasz's communications to the patient are rather obvi-ously directed toward his most reality-oriented (rather than rule-oriented) ego state. He seems to assume that the person being helped has what Piaget describes as the third stage of attitudes toward rules—that rules may be considered, criticized, and even changed, provided that the change follows a prescribed and agreed upon set of covenants for changing rules.

The ego state with which Szasz is concerned exists in the person who considers himself a significant and responsible component of the society in which he functions. He regards himself as capable of critically evaluating how society functions, and willingly concerns himself with attempts to change by lawful means those aspects of its functioning that he evaluates as detrimental to his own interests or to those of other persons. At the same time, he holds himself responsible for his own actions and for those agreements to which he has voluntarily committed himself. The adult ego state involves foregoing the privilege of blaming others for one's own misbehav-ior or dissatisfactions.

If it were possible to interact in terms of such an adult ego state at all times and with all persons seeking help, there are many reasons why Szasz's description of the helping relationship might be preferred to either Glasser's or Mowrer's. Problems in psychotherapy arise, however, precisely because such a relationship is not always acceptable to the person being helped, regardless of how much such a situation might appeal to the helping person. Persons functioning in terms of ego states that include Piaget's first stage of attitudes toward rules apparently cannot distinguish between their own naive disregard of rules and the highly responsible attitude recommended and encouraged by the relationship which Szasz offers. Furthermore, it is reasonable to suppose that they are not then able to accept the degree of autonomy that Szasz describes as ideal, but rather need the interest and involvement of others who have definite rules in mind for their guidance as to what constitutes acceptable behavior.

This attitude reverses itself drastically when the ego state of the person being helped is of the nature assumed by Mowrer. In this state, rules are taken extremely seriously, and the principal question is whether they must be obeyed. When rules are "tested" in actual behavior, it is discovered that they can be violated, but this discovery characteristically leads to anxiety, conflict, and guilt. At such times the opinion of his peers as to which rules are necessary and desirable may be the most acceptable form of helping relationship.

My purpose in suggesting this core theme—the development of attitudes toward rules—as a common factor explaining both similarities and differences among the three viewpoints presented, involves more than a desire for conceptual neatness and simplification. There is certainly some value in avoiding needless disputation. My greater concern, however, is with the possibility for increasing psychotherapeutic effectiveness.

Glasser's Reality Therapy enables the helper to establish a useful relationship with the person functioning in terms of relatively early and undeveloped ego states. Mowrer's Integrity Therapy meets the needs of persons functioning in terms of ego states that involve resistance to conformity with rules and with authority figures. Szasz's Autonomous Psychotherapy provides an acceptable and useful relationship to persons who wish to examine the nature of their own behavior and to decide whether or not it is compatible

with their own needs and objectives. It provides the "peer" relationship considered necessary by Mowrer but in the context of a
two-person relationship and with a somewhat more permissive
orientation toward existing rules.

If we believe, as Eric Berne has suggested, that the ego state of
any person varies from time to time, that any individual may be
quite adult in his attitudes and thinking at one time and quite child-
like at another, then the need for flexibility in the definition of a
helping relationship becomes apparent. The maximally effective
helper may turn out to be one who thinks and reacts as Glasser
does to the most child-like ego states of the person he is helping,
who thinks and reacts as Mowrer does when the person being
helped feels more responsible, and who chooses Szasz's mode of
interaction whenever the attitudes of the person being helped make
such interaction possible.

Practice

The Practice of Reality Therapy: Introduction

Reality Therapy contends that people who are lonely and unhappy and failures suffer from a common malady—i.e., they refuse to accept total responsibility for their behavior. The psychotherapeutic process is designed to help people evaluate their current behavior, to accept responsibility for it, and to plan constructive behavioral change. Glasser suggests that "the requirements of Reality Therapy—an intense personal involvement, facing reality and rejecting irresponsible behavior, and learning better ways to behave—bear little resemblance to conventional therapy and produce markedly different results."

Ernest Havemann, who discusses alternatives to psychoanalysis, believes that "compared with psychoanalytical theory, Reality Therapy is the height of simplicity; indeed, Dr. Glasser says he could teach any bright young trainee all he needs to know about the theory of Reality Therapy in a day. Applying it to patients, however, is another matter. As Dr. Glasser puts it, "Psychoanalysis is difficult to learn but easy to practice. The psychoanalyst mostly listens. The Reality Therapist engages in an active, close and often exhausting dialog. He must establish a genuine friendship with patients who may resist it, feel a genuine sympathy with their sufferings, yet be tough enough never to let his sympathy divert him from getting along with the hard task of improvement."

In *The Identity Society,* William Glasser lists seven basic principles of Reality Therapy in a specific order: involvement of the therapist with the client, focusing on current behavior, evaluation of behavior, planning responsible behavior, making a commitment to change, accepting no excuses, and eliminating punishment. Glasser deliberately has devised a flexible and workable psychotherapeutic process which provides general guidelines for practitioners. What appears interesting and significant is that in their application of Reality Therapy, Alexander Bassin, Thomas Bratter, and Richard Rachin use Glasser's seven major principles and add some of their own.

Barbara Hobbie has succeeded in condensing the primary points which Glasser has made in *Reality Therapy* in a systematic manner. The author has captured Glasser's logic and renders a service to the busy practitioner who has limited time to study the entire book.

Alexander Bassin, a co-founder of Daytop Village and former director of research for the Brooklyn Supreme Court Office of Probation, adds a final important step of never giving up in "The Reality Therapy Paradigm."

Thomas Bratter has modified Reality Therapy in his work with adolescent chemical casualties and their families—"A Group Approach with Adolescent Alcoholics." He lists two important additions to Glasser's seven principles. The psychotherapist must communicate continually his expectation for improved, more productive and responsible behavior performance. High expectations produce responsible growth and development. In addition, Bratter urges that the psychotherapist become more involved with his client/patient by assuming the role of advocate in which the professional helps the individual secure needed services such as a job, college admission, and the like. In "Helping Those Who Do Not Want to Help Themselves," Bratter shares some of his gratifying and frustrating experiences as a Reality Therapist.

Richard Rachin, whose experience has been with children and adolescents in institutions and halfway houses, lists fourteen steps in "Helping People Help Themselves." Some of Rachin's innovations are therapist transparency, elimination of asking "why," offering no sympathy for continued failure or irresponsibility, praising and approving responsible behavior, avoiding labeling people.

Richard Raubolt and Thomas Bratter added two more components to Reality Therapy while working with methadone patients in a private clinic where the goal of treatment was drug abstinence. They believe that confrontation is needed to help the individual to evaluate his or her behavior. In addition, since methadone addicts have a tendency to forget, they believe it is therapeutically indicated to draw up written behavior contracts which specify dates and actual sequential steps to be taken. It is noteworthy that this private clinic, located in a residential area, was closed as financially unrewarding because more than 40 percent were successfully detoxified from methadone.

William Poppen and Robert Welch have concluded that Reality Therapy is an effective intervention to help obese adolescents lose weight in a school setting. In addition, Poppen and Welch have discovered that weight loss occurred prior to any change of the self-concept. This finding confirms Glasser's assumption that behavior influences feelings. Obviously, this challenges the more traditional psychotherapeutic orientations which contend that the concept of self must be enhanced (strengthened) before any constructive behavior can result. Another implication is that the duration of psychotherapy can be shortened dramatically, which is what many Behavior Therapists propose.

BARBARA HOBBIE

An Anti-Failure Approach

Reality Therapy is not unique. It is unconventional. Because it is antithetical to traditional psychiatric theory and practice, it could conceivably undermine the psychiatric profession by taking therapy out of the hands of medical doctors and placing it in the hands of concerned individuals who have devoted far fewer years to their profession or who have no previous psychiatric or psychological training at all. Reality Therapy stresses warm human involvement; shuns pedagogic psychiatric categories such as dementia praecox, paranoid schizophrenia, and manic-depression; avoids examination and analysis of early trauma or past history; holds patients or clients responsible for their own recovery; and, in fact, rejects the idea that there is such a thing as mental illness. What Reality Therapy seeks to do, in short, is to force people to face their own reality and reshape their behavior in order to fulfill their needs. When people do not fulfill their needs they come to regard themselves as failures.

Reality Therapy (though it had no name at the time) began in the 1950's when Dr. William Glasser, a third year medical resident, encountered "the most obnoxious child I had ever met." The boy, Aaron, shared characteristics of many people undergoing psychiatric treatment—he indulged himself in his own emotional deprivation, had trained himself in psychiatric jargon, was capable of being highly uncommunicative either through complete with-

Former title "Reality Therapy: An Anti-Failure Approach." From *Impact,* Vol. 2, No. 1, 1973. Reprinted by permission.

drawal or plunges into jibberish, talked "around" his feelings and succeeded in making his psychiatrist miserable. *And,* he failed to improve. In desperation, Glasser armed with Freud, Jung and all the other greats of psychiatry, threw down his traditional weapons and told the kid to "shut up and listen." He began to demand of Aaron that he be responsive to other people and responsible for his actions. Glasser let Aaron know that someone cared about him and that concern is not something to give, but to share.

Reality Therapy began because Glasser perceived that conventional therapies worked only for some patients part of the time, required inordinate amounts of time—sometimes years, and frequently, did no good at all. He saw countless examples of personal, professional and academic failure—delinquency, drug abuse, sexual excesses, obesity, craziness, psychosomatic illness and other problems compounded by a lack of societal remedies. Furthermore, few people could afford to avail themselves of help. Reality Therapy offered relatively fast results, and relied on the use of a broad spectrum of helping professionals, paraprofessionals, and empathetic nonprofessionals who were willing to learn to apply its principles.

1. The principles of Reality Therapy begin with involvement.

All other principles build on it and add to it. The therapist's problem is to provide enough involvement himself to help the patient develop confidence to make new, deep, lasting involvements of his own. The helping person, whether friend, family member, or professional therapist, must be honest and never promise to give more time than he plans to give. Even patients who desperately need their therapist will, upon becoming involved, accept an honest statement from the therapist that he can give only a specific amount of time. (Glasser, 1972)

There are a number of ways to get involved with a client, but talking about his problems and his feelings about them focuses upon his self-involvement and consequently gives his failure value. Glasser tells of one client, Pat, whose manifestation of her problem was obesity.

The first part of Reality Therapy with Pat was difficult for both of us as I tried to create involvement between us and she tried to understand what I was driving at. Expecting to discuss her childhood, she found it difficult to understand that I was not particularly interested in historical material. Attempting at times to talk about her dreams and unconscious mind, she found me equally uninterested. Restricting the discussion to the present seemed sterile to her because her life was the rather humdrum existence of the rich suburban housewife who had difficulty in filling her days and much more in talking about what she did . . .

After almost a year, we began to be more involved, I could point out her irresponsibilities. My regular presence and my stand for greater responsibility encouraged her to take a chance, and change. During the whole of the second year she slowly became more responsible. Although the change was not dramatic, she was less self-centered and more able to give to others, especially her husband and children, who needed her far more than she was originally able to admit to herself. She felt a keener sense of achievement and she lost fifty pounds. (Glasser, 1965)

2. A second principle of Reality Therapy is examining current behavior. People often avoid facing their present behavior by emphasizing how they feel rather than what they are doing. Although Reality Therapy does not deny that emotions are important, successful therapists learn that unless they focus on behavior they do not help the patient. For example, a delinquent girl Glasser was treating in a group situation refused to admit her own faults and blamed Glasser for her detention in an institution.

To avoid facing reality, Liz tried to be a junior therapist in the group, blandly assuming the role of the perfectly reformed girl who was eager to point out to others the futility of their ways. With my support the group turned the tables on her, forcing her to examine her own behavior despite her efforts to avoid it. We soon recognized that she always blamed everything that happened on others, maintaining the role of the unfortunate victim of circumstances. If I pointed this out to her she would say that I, too, was against her, and therapy would be stalled. To help her face reality and stop wasting time blaming me, I told her that she could leave when she made at least a C in each of her classes.

After several months during which she tried every way to avoid doing better in cosmetology, she finally started to work a little harder.

The group pressure started the change in her behavior, which in turn led her to become involved with the group and to recognize that they really cared for her, as shown by their efforts for her. (Glasser, 1965)

3. A third principle of Reality Therapy is that the patient must now examine and evaluate his behavior in a rational way and make a judgment that what he's doing isn't beneficial. *It's like an alcoholic saying, "Gee, drinking is the worst thing for me. Pass me a drink." He knows drinking is no good but he's still drinking because he has nothing else. But when he begins to get involved with another person and then you ask him to evaluate by asking "is drinking helping you?" he'll begin to say, "Well no, it would be much better if I did something else."* Drinking is like any other companion—so is depression and a host of other problems. For example, depression serves a purpose. *The purpose it serves is that you become involved with your depression and a kind of circumscribed misery that you know and are familiar with in order to avoid facing the fact that you ought to be doing something worthwhile. The depression immobilizes you. It's painful. But it's less painful than giving it up. Sometimes I make a joke when a person tells me he's terribly depressed. I say, "Well, cheer up!" And everybody laughs at that statement, yet that's the most accurate and constructive thing I can really say. Reality Therapy gives the individual a chance to examine the situation and urges him to come to a decision.*

4. Fourth, once someone makes a value judgment about his behavior, the person helping him must assist in developing realistic plans for action. Because planning requires knowledge of what options are available, a therapist who talks with many people who are making plans gains experience not available to the average person. As many problems revolve around family life, a therapist who is married and has children is usually better able to help plan than is a therapist whose life has not included marriage and children. Encouraging the person who needs the help to make the most of the plan himself is part of the therapist's skill. The therapist sometimes puts the person in touch with someone else. Glasser has sent patients to friends or associates of his who have more

experience in particular fields to help the patient work out a detailed plan.

Never make a plan that attempts too much, because it will usually fail and reinforce the already present failure. A failing person needs success, and he needs small individually successful steps to gain it. A student who has never studied should not plan to study one hour a night; at the start, fifteen minutes once or twice a week is more realistic. (Glasser, 1972)

5. Fifth, a commitment. After a reasonable plan has been made, it must be carried out. To give the person greater motivation to fulfill the plan, ask him for a commitment. The commitment may be verbal or written; it may be given to an individual or group. It can be made between husband and wife, parent and child, teacher and student, therapist and patient. Commitment intensifies and accelerates the trying of new behavior. Without comment, without warm human desire to say, "I'll do it for you as well as for me," plans are less likely to be implemented. A written contract is good because people can remember, can have evidence of their plan to change their behavior. *At Ventura, the school for delinquent girls, we sometimes had them sign a contract when they left the school stating that they would come back. The girls objected, saying, "You don't trust us." I said, "That's right, I don't." The girls, while resentful at first, came to realize that I really cared about what happened to them. When you work with kids, you must be willing to be the adult.*

6. Sixth, accept no excuses. The therapist must insist that a commitment made is worth keeping. The only commitments many failures have made are to their irresponsibilities, their emotions, and their involvement with themselves. These commitments have mired them deeply in failure. The therapist cannot help unless he and the patients are both willing to reexamine the plan continually and make a mutual decision either to renew the commitment, if the plan is valid, or to give it up, if it is not.

Excuses let people off the hook; they provide temporary relief, but they eventually lead to more failure and a failure identity. Any time we take an excuse when we are trying to help a person gain a successful identity, we do him harm. (Glasser, 1972)

7. And finally, don't punish. Not to punish is as important as not to take excuses.

Eliminating punishment is very difficult for most people who are successful to accept, because they believe that part of their success stems from their fear that punishment will follow failure. We believe punishment breaks the involvement necessary for the patient to succeed. When he does succeed, we give praise. Unlike punishment, praise solidifies the involvement. Punishment is any treatment of another person that causes him pain, physical or mental. Praise, always involving, leads to more responsible behavior. The purpose of punishment is to change someone's behavior through fear, pain or loneliness. If it were an effective means of getting people to change, we would have few failures in our society. Many incompetent and irresponsible people have been punished over and over again throughout their lives with little beneficial effect. Instead, punishment reinforces their loneliness. Confirming their belief that no one cares about them, it drives them further into self-involvement and increases their hostility or their isolation or both. (Glasser, 1972)

These seven principles have been used by Dr. Glasser and his colleagues during the past 15 years—in Ventura, the delinquent girls' school; in Watts, California, schools; in the mental ward of a V. A. Hospital, and, as a result of the Educator Training Center, by 20 to 25 thousand school personnel in schools throughout the country. Glasser feels that these principles work because they fulfill very basic current needs of people. In his latest book, *The Identity Society,* he distinguishes people of the post World War II era from those prior to the war. People today are role oriented rather than goal oriented. Many people today, including adults, but especially the young, are seeking new life styles which will enable them to be themselves and have a personal stake in the tasks they perform. The relative affluence of our post-war society makes this search possible to some extent; we don't need to be as concerned with material struggle as were people of the pre-war era. But this change to role orientation is not uniform and this is causing not only generational conflicts but society-wide conflicts. Our major institutions—the family, the schools, the penal system, the welfare system are still operating as if achievement of goals leads to success and happiness.

The school, our major socializing institution, is the most visible offender. *The school is still saying, "Learn this or you are a failure," but kids are saying, "We won't learn unless the school can relate to us as human beings."* Those who can't find personal relevance in the schools often turn against society and themselves, taking on the identity of failure. Failure is painful, so they may try to drown this pain in antisocial behaviors such as drugs, violence, inattention or total withdrawal. Of course, kids have no monopoly on failure—adults fail too, and resort to their "painkillers" in much the same way. *What we're doing with Reality Therapy, especially in the schools, is answering a need that came up. Teachers, therapists and so on have said, "We really want a little extra help; we just don't think we can do it on our own."* Realizing that these principles could be implemented with school personnel as therapists—as long as they're truly concerned and willing to learn— Glasser began to develop a Reality Therapy training program through the Educator Training Center. *It gives those people a chance to learn. There are a number of good role-oriented therapies* (Gestalt, rational therapy, transactional analysis) which differ from one another in minor aspects only. What is important is their unifying principles, and these principles say you have to get involved with people and then you have to help them understand that they do have some control over their behavior, and that they can make changes which will improve their lives. *In the schools, particularly the urban schools, we find uninvolved, unloved, already turned-off kids—products of parents who often themselves are lonely and uninvolved and are, therefore, incapable of providing their offspring with an atmosphere conducive to personal growth and responsibility.* The schools, like it or not, are often the only place some children can get involvement, can grow emotionally as well as intellectually. *There are kids who may have rooms full of playthings but are nevertheless lonely.* They may or may not be only children—usually they are children whose parents are so involved in their own activities that the kids have no chance to participate in a functioning family. They may be "latchkey" children, coming home to empty houses. *When a child comes home to an empty house, it's hard for him not to fail.* Because the children of today are role-oriented, *they are more interested in knowing not what they can do for society, but what their parents—and the school in particular—can do for them. When they fail to get involved they are soon labeled "failures."*

What can the school do for these youngsters? It can recognize their needs and restructure itself to provide the missing elements which will help them to become involved and responsible for their own lives and for the well-being of others. *The family should, of course, provide these elements which will help them to become involved and responsible for their own lives and for the well being of others but if it doesn't—and often it doesn't—then the school must do it or all of society will bear the burden of their failure.*

In training teachers to utilize Reality Therapy, Glasser stresses involvement and commitment. One simple but highly important procedure which helps teachers begin to create involvement is a daily meeting with students.

A structured, well-planned class meeting is a good starter. I'm not talking about the ordinary class discussion. I'm talking about a meeting keyed to behaving in thoughtful, socially responsible ways. I'm talking about a meeting in which logical, orderly thinking takes priority. I'm talking about a meeting which involves everyone in the room—one in which kids learn to care for and respect each other and where meaningful participation takes precedence over the teacher's "right answer."

Another technique we've found useful is cross-grade tutoring. This is consistent with Reality Therapy principles because these "learning by teaching" experiences help children become involved with each other as well as with the teachers they help. The experiences are carefully planned to be actively problem solving, sometimes for the tutor and sometimes for the tutee. Respectful involvement between students and teachers develops as they define tutor roles, achieve an understanding of task increments, practice positive feedback, stress positive attitudes toward change, and engage in evaluation and replanning.

It is not uncommon to see a whole class moving to another grade level for a session. One activity sees the older class acting as secretaries for twenty minutes, taking dictation from lower-grade students. The tutors later return with a corrected copy of the dictated material. During the last school year, after discussing it with students, the Ventura staff decided to change room assignments so upper grades alternate with lower grades. This move facilitates the tutorial program by shortening the physical distance the upper grades have to travel, and adds to children's involvement with each other across age and grade levels. (Glasser, 1971)

There are many other individual and group techniques which teachers can use; they all involve the central core of Reality Therapy—involvement—learning to achieve this is the key. Glasser believes that most people are capable of becoming involved. This "faith" in people has generally produced results which teachers thought they were incapable of producing. *Although it isn't easy to function under the tenets of Reality Therapy, it can be done. It takes training, patience, and above all, perseverance. Grownups need to reorient their way of dealing with children academically. It is much more difficult to encourage children to think rationally for themselves than to provide them with pat answers.*

Although the schools, of necessity, perform the major socializing function for children, there is no reason to assume that Reality Therapy shouldn't be tried in other settings. These principles are definitely transferable. Families, for instance, can utilize them in strengthening their interrelationships. In his books, Glasser recounts numerous cases, of varying severity, in which families (parents and children, husbands and wives) use Reality Therapy to rethink their relationships and try to break down barriers they had created during the years. Obviously, more time and effort would be required of a family whose children were addicted to drugs or had serious mental disorders or were in a situation where divorce is imminent. Reality Therapy works best when it can be used preventively or constructively but it is, as are most therapies, usually applied as a crisis intervention measure. At this stage of a situation, Reality Therapy can provide perspective and sound principles upon which to act. For example, a teenager, Judy, starts taking "downers and uppers." When her parents discover what she is doing she pressures them to help her retain her habit by threatening suicide and in general acting out. Reality Therapy would suggest that they do the following.

Judy's parents should flatly refuse to get her any drugs. Both to keep drugs from Judy and to set a good example, they should remove all the drugs from the house including tranquilizers and sleeping pills. Parents without enough incentive to stop using pills themselves have trouble helping their daughter. Finally, and a very important point, they should not discuss drugs with her on any occasion; despite what they might have learned, they know little about the realities of taking drugs. If, after discovering she cannot get drugs, she says she will stop all drug use except a little marijuana, they should make no comment. If she persists in trying to discuss drugs, her parents should say that they know nothing about them except that they are illegal. This approach will not work with an older child, but it sometimes works well with a young, unsophisticated child who has little access to drugs and who does not enjoy the effect of the drugs herself as much as the effect her use of them has on her parents.

At the same time, her parents should work hard to establish a warm, friendly relationship, to encourage her to have friends over, and to keep involved. (Glasser, 1965)

In this newly ordained role-oriented society, people will continue to fail. But those offering them support must minimize this failure—help them rework and reshape their plans to achieve success. Reality Therapy works—but only because it is applied consistently and deliberately. *There's no magic about it.*

As a final note, however, to modify the apparent optimism held out for Reality Therapy—there are some cautions and there are some real societal and cultural dilemmas which make it difficult to apply Reality Therapy.

One of these starts with the fundamental core of human development—maternal participation in a child's upbringing. Now, at a time when most children are role-oriented, striving to achieve in a very personal, meaningful way, so are their mothers—and this produces conflict. *There is no way to get around the fact that the changing role of women is going to cause additional problems for children. Women are saying, "Look, we're human beings, and we want to fulfill ourselves in ways that go beyond their traditional one of wife, mother and housekeeper. Let somebody else take care of our children." Men, too, are looking for roles beyond their traditional one of supporting a family. Kids, though, still have the same basic needs for security and belonging—they don't know anything about Women's Lib or the need for human fulfillment in their parents. Unfortunately, there are few women so capable of*

*involvement that they can fulfill themselves outside of their homes
and still do the job with their children that need to be done.*

Another nearly overwhelming problem we face is that some of
our largest "socializing" institutions are really oriented toward
punishing people rather than helping them. Our mental institutions
rely on drugs and physical suppression of patients to muffle their
"bad" behavior rather than changing it. Our prisons and reform
schools subject people to isolation, stark surroundings, inadequate
rehabilitation programs and virtually no civil rights or personal
respect. *Not that we should release all prisoners; they are definitely
a danger to society.* But we must find better ways of dealing with
people who have already failed to adjust to and be accepted by
society. Further rejection will not produce solid citizens.

A final societal dilemma is that while our media opens new
possibilities to us by expanding our knowledge and perceptions, it
also tends to reinforce our self-image of failure. *The media establishes standards of performance so polished and refined that it
makes what young people do seem inadequate by comparison.
Aspiring athletes see the pros and think "What the heck? I'll never
make it." And they give up because they can't see the years and
years of hard work and disappointment it took the pros to make it.*
Commercials seem to assure social success through the use of this
toothpaste, that deodorant, this soft-drink, and that after-shave
lotion. *Pepsi Cola helps you to make friends is the implication.
The media has much that is good, but there's a lot that is on "just
to make a buck," and too many lonely people are exploited by the
media because they are not happy with their lives. They don't have
a sense of personal worth—they identify with failure.*

Reality Therapy like other new therapies, requires a restructuring of our institutions and our minds. By applying its principles we
can begin to initiate change—to recognize the needs of human
beings who have a poor sense of identity and an attitude of failure.
But we can make it work continually only if we first get those who
influence society and its functions to "shut up and listen." We
begin and end with involvement.

REFERENCES

Glasser, William, M. D. *Mental Health or Illness?; Psychiatry for Practical Action.* New York: Harper & Row, 1961.

Glasser, William, M.D. *Reality Therapy: A New Approach to Psychiatry.* New York: Harper & Row, 1965.

Glasser, William, M.D. *Identity Society.* New York: Harper & Row, 1972.

Glasser, William, M.D. "Roles Goals and Failure." *Today's Education,* October, 1971, p. 62.

ALEXANDER BASSIN

The Reality Therapy Paradigm

paradigm (par' à-dim, -dīm), *n.* an example or model.
Webster's Dictionary

My old friend and NYU Graduate School classmate, Abe Froehlich, one of the brightest people I have ever known, once announced that he had discovered a sure-fire technique to achieve publication in almost any professional social science journal.

"The trick is always to include a diagram consisting of three to five circles with arrows connecting them in some helter-skelter fashion, the more complicated, the better. You could mark the circles A, B, C; it didn't matter very much. The less sense it all made, the more it would impress the editors."

"Abe, you're crazy," I told him.

"Actually," Abe added without the slightest sign of intimidation, "I haven't given you the complete formula. There's an additional element that makes a paper irresistible to scientific-minded editors."

"What's that?"

"Paradigm! You must use that magic word several times in the article, under the diagram, and best of all, in the title. It's like waving catnip in front of a tiger. It drives them wild. Look at Talcott Parsons."

I snorted.

1974, unpublished article.

"But if you really want to make it with the most prestigious journals include some mathematical gibberish like:

$$\frac{R + 1}{F^2 - H} + M = W.$$

The editors think you're another Einstein and they'll knock each other down to publish your stuff."

I warned Abe he would be thrown in the booby hatch with that kind of wild talk, but I did begin to read professional papers with a more jaundiced eye.

It's considerably more than a decade since Abe and I had the above conversation and his message no longer sounds as insane as when I first heard it.[1] However, I began reading a remarkable journal, *Scientific American,* whose pages manage to dissolve the obscurity of even the most obtuse theories in the physical and social sciences by the consistent use of models, examples, diagrams. I became convinced, despite Froehlich's polemics, that a *good* paradigm, a *good* diagram, could make sparkling clarity out of a phenomenon that was otherwise murky as a midnight fog. This article represents an effort to explain the process of Reality Therapy in terms that catch the limpid transparency of Dr. Glasser's prose but also to add the structure of a pattern to enable the novitiate practitioner to turn to a mnemonic schema to help him in the early stages of learning the art of Reality Therapy, just as the Volkswagen driver is assisted by a sketch of the gearshift movements on his dashboard. Soon the diagram becomes a part of the student's nervous system, and he can turn to more intricate and creative applications of the basic formulation without even thinking of the ingredients of the paradigm.

Involvement, the Elixir of Reality Therapy

Even the most casual reading of Glasser's classic, *Reality Therapy: A New Approach to Psychiatry,*[2] and his subsequent volumes makes his essential message clear: Involvement is the lubricant that makes therapy possible. The irresponsible person cannot be induced to change his behavior unless the party acting as change-agent is perceived as a friend who is honestly concerned about his welfare. In *The Identity Society,* Glasser summarizes his position:

Involvement is the foundation of therapy. All other principles build on and add to it. As soon as possible, the person being helped must begin to understand that there is more to life than being involved with his misery, symptoms, obsessive thoughts, or irresponsible behavior. He must see that another human being cares for him and is willing to discuss his life and talk about anything both consider worthwhile and interesting.[3]

In short, Reality Therapy is not a technique or a collection of tricks and underhanded strategies that force a person to change against his will. Rather, it is an existential philosophy that can be translated into clear-cut operational components to help a troubled person arrive at a solution of his problems.

Becoming involved with an individual who is a loser, who perceives himself a failure, who is suspicious, hostile, lonely, is no easy task. Learning how to become involved is both the most important and most difficult assignment in conducting Reality Therapy.

A number of common-sense principles have evolved to help one person become involved with another, and thereby begin the process of human salvation called therapy—an unfortunate medical-model word that implies a procedure wherein one person, the patient, is hurting, and another, the therapist, administers medication.

Ways to Achieve Involvement

The Reality Therapist is warm, friendly, personal, optimistic and honest.

It is obviously easier for a lonely, alienated individual with a low self-esteem to become involved with a human being who acts in a manner that communicates the cue: I care about you, I like you, I want to get to know you, I want to be your friend. He needs a solid relationship with a person who is optimistic about the future in relation to his client. And he needs someone who is

honest, who will make no false promises, who will openly prescribe the limits of their relationship.

In contrast, the traditional therapist, who has been trained to be
remote, detached, scientific, objective (in order to avoid the development of an unmanageable transference in accord with psychoanalytic theory), simply cannot make contact with the lonely
person who is hungering for a human relationship. As a matter of
fact, psychoanalysis unquestionably is helpful for success-oriented
patients who are highly articulate, intelligent, responsible, and—
rich.

The Reality Therapist reveals himself, at least a little.

It is hard to become involved with an individual who is
shrouded in mystery, who does not permit us to know very much
about him. One cannot become involved with a person who does
not permit himself to become known. The Reality Therapist appreciates that involvement is related to intimacy. He attempts to be
open and transparent. He is prepared to discuss his own failures
and successes. When he is asked, "Do you have any children?" he
responds as one human being talking to another, not with the
cliché still taught in schools based on the psychodynamic model:
"Why do you ask that question?"

The Reality Therapist perceives a question from his client as a
positive sign of involvement. A lonely individual sees an opportunity for making a friend. He is holding up a finger in the wind to
help him decide if the therapist, a mature, responsible, prestigious
person is truly interested in the client or is merely presenting a
facade. If the therapist responds in a reserved and professional
manner, the client has his answer: This man is another one of the
stonefaces who cares nothing about me. He does not want to be
my friend. To hell with him.

*The Reality Therapist uses the first-person pronouns "I" and
"me" as much as possible.*

The person with a failure identity is aching for human contact.
His awareness opens only to stimuli of a highly personal nature.
Communication between therapist and client takes place best when
the therapist is being as personal and congruent as he can. There-

fore, speaking to the client in abstract, third-person terms or with the royal "we" of a newspaper editorial fails to penetrate his deeper consciousness. Again, the client's nerve endings send a message: This man is being impersonal with me. He is not interested in becoming my friend.

The lonely, alienated person responds to such terms and words that reflect readiness on the part of the therapist to be personal and human. Therefore, the Reality Therapist defies the Anglo-Saxon dictum about personal modesty in reference to first-person pronouns.

The Reality Therapist concentrates on the here and now.

People with problems of adjustment have been taught that in order to improve they must search through the minutiae of their life history to find that critical episode which traumatized them into their current dilemma. Reality Therapy rejects the notion based on the medical model that in order to prescribe a cure an elaborate etiology is essential. On the contrary, we tend to echo the sentiment heard at meetings of Alcoholics Anonymous where a good AA member will tell a psychologically minded drunk: "Jack, don't waste time telling us about the little red sled your big brother took away from you when you were three years old. You've got more current problems than that. What did you do today? Give us a rundown on that."

In short, Reality Therapists question the parallel in treating the individual with a psychological problem as though it were a physical ailment. It is true that in medicine it is necessary to obtain the history of the individual as it relates to his illness in order to prescribe medication. But the individual who is experiencing difficulty in adjusting to his environment, who is sad, lonely, and depressed, needs human warmth and kindliness rather than medication or surgery. The analogy to the medical model does not hold for people who are experiencing problems of living. The more we permit them to talk about the origins of their problems, the more difficult human involvement becomes, the easier it is for our clients to avoid assuming responsibility for their conditions.

The Reality Therapist puts small stock in the results of psychological tests and case histories. He is not impressed by the fanciest of Rorschach protocols, or diagnostic labels. He attempts to avoid imparting a self-fulfilling prophecy about the fate of his client by believing that a psychiatric label carries the weight of a medical term. He laughs at the notion that "mental illness" is a sort of chicken pox of the mind.

The Reality Therapist concentrates on behavior rather than feelings.

A number of competing methodologies in treating psychological problems make a great hullabaloo about feelings, as though talking about them would make them nicer and sweeter. Reality Therapists have discovered that our clients, virtually without exception, feel lousy. They feel miserable because they are lonely, friendless, and have a poor self-esteem. And the more they talk about these rotten feelings the more denigrated and contemptible they feel.

We tell our clients, frankly, that we do not know how to change feelings directly. It is true that alcohol and other drugs alter moods but they do not resolve problems. We do believe, however, "If you want to feel better, act better." We repeat, over and over, that each of us has control of his behavior and is responsible for his behavior. So let's look long and hard at our behavior . . . and the feelings will take care of themselves, eventually.

This does not mean, as some critics of Reality Therapy have asserted, that we are not interested in feelings or deny feelings. Certainly, at the beginning of our contact with a client, when the involvement is thin, we will listen politely and sympathetically to talk about feelings, which we may perceive as wallowing in self-pity, but sooner or later we must drop the awful truth on our would-be friend: Too much time spent on talking about feelings is going to ruin the chances of an honorable friendship. Let's start discussing behavior. What have you been doing lately with yourself?

The Reality Therapist asks "What?" rather than "Why?"

By this statement we mean that we discipline ourselves from asking the question about stupid behavior that tends to engulf us in a quagmire of rationalizations and self-justifications. It does no good to ask a lonely, alienated individual why he is behaving in a self-destructive fashion. Invariably, he will emerge with some excuse on the anticipation that it will be considered as a good reason for irresponsible behavior. The Reality Therapist avoids this swamp by asking *"What* did you do?" rather than *"Why* did you do it?" The world is full of excuses. The therapist himself has probably engaged in stupid behavior in his lifetime and yet if anyone were to tap him on the shoulder and ask him, "Why did you do it?," he would need only a moment to muster several hundred words of excuses and explanations. There is a good psychological basis for the West Point rule that a plebe must automatically respond, whenever he is asked for an explanation for a failure, "No excuse, sir, no excuse."

The Reality Therapist insists the client evaluate his behavior.

Here is the key point of Reality Therapy. It is frequently overlooked as we become more involved with our client. We tend to respond to self-destructive behavior on the part of the human being with whom we are emotionally involved in a subjective fashion. We render our own evaluation followed by a sermon.

Unfortunately, neither sermons nor external evaluations seem to be very effective in changing human behavior. The Reality Therapist must steel himself to ask a perennial question: "Did your behavior do you any good?" And if the response is affirmative, he must have the gall to extend the circumference of the impact of negative behavior and inquire if it was also good for mother, father, brother, grandmother, kids, wife, friends, community, company, country, and church.

We may act the devil's advocate and ask good-naturedly, "You're not saying this just to make *me* happy?"

On the other hand, if the client persists in justifying negative behavior, we may suggest that he think over his judgment and let us discuss it tomorrow or the day after. Above all, we wish to transmit the message that the client is responsible for his behavior and is required to evaluate it before any further steps are to be taken. We promise that if he still persists in a good evaluation for what he has done, we will drop the subject until such time as he may wish to take it up for another analysis.

The seminal importance of the self-evaluation of behavior on the part of a client is a primary contribution of Reality Therapy methodology. This step provides a guarantee that the client will be the master of his fate in relation to changing his values and consequent behavior. It is in accord with the humanistic philosophy that every human should be in reasonable control of his destiny.

The Reality Therapist helps the client formulate a plan.

Obtaining a socially appropriate evaluation of negative behavior does not complete the therapist's responsibility. He must move with the client into the problem-solving arena. He must help the client respond to the question, "So what are we going to do about it? What is your plan?" If the client has been expelled from school, for example, and wishes to return, we discuss what strategy would be most effective. If social skills which are not currently in the repertoire of the client are needed, we explain, demonstrate, and role-play them with the client until he is proficient. If the situation requires our official intervention, we are prepared to appear as his advocate. We readily share with him our knowledge of community resources and pitfalls. We write letters on his behalf and make telephone calls.

At the same time, the Reality Therapist is cautious about the possibility that the client may overextend himself and become engaged in a plan that may result in failure. The therapist strives for a plan that is minimal and success-assured. He thinks of evolving a plan which will operate in stages of gradually increased difficulty. He wants his client to experience success after success in working out a new program of responsible behavior. We respect the notion garnered from learning theory that a modestly graduated plan that obtains the reinforcement of success is more powerful in shaping behavior than a more ambitious procedure that may result in failure.

In formulating a plan, the Reality Therapist attempts to dispose of every possible contingency. No detail is too minuscule for consideration. "Do you have an alarm clock? Do you have carfare? Do you know what bus to take? Do you have your social security card? Do you have a necktie? Who will take care of your baby? How are you going to cope with your girl friend?" These are the kinds of petty but nitty-gritty questions the Reality Therapist must be prepared to clarify for the promulgation of a good plan.

The Reality Therapist negotiates contracts and commitments.

After a plan has been formulated, we ask, "That's a great plan you've worked out, but are you going to carry it out?" If the situation warrants, the therapist may draft a statement of intentions, a schedule, a contract, and submit it to the client for his initials. "I'd hate to think that we spent all that time in a mere intellectual exercise," he may explain to his client. He certainly would shake hands with his client and announce, "It's a deal!" Reality Therapists are aware of the mountain of experimental evidence that indicates that contracts impose an obligation that a plan of action will be consummated.[4] Furthermore, a contract frequently carries the message that we consider our deliberations important and valuable and insisting on a signature is a confirmation of the client's improved identity as a responsible human being.

The Reality Therapist does not waste time listening to excuses.

Once a plan has been formulated and a contract signed, the Reality Therapist is all business, interested in results, not excuses. He tells his erring client, "I guess you must have a good excuse for not carrying out your contract, but what good will it do for me to hear it? It certainly will not help us carry it out. What I want to know is if you still feel responsible for the contract. When do you intend to carry it out? Tomorrow at 3:00 o'clock? Good! Please see me at 4:00 o'clock and let me know what happened? OK?"

The Reality Therapist moves his client into a group as soon as possible.

The group can act as a powerful agent for consensual agreement on what constitutes responsible behavior. The client who has received some exposure to Reality Therapy is encouraged to try out his newly acquired social skills and values on a group of peers and other group members. After a time he spends longer periods in the group than with his individual therapist. Finally, he starts to use the group and profit from the interaction to become more of a self-directed individual. In his contact with the Reality Therapist he is encouraged to help weaker members of the group in terms of understanding the principles he has been able to internalize as a result of his sessions with the Reality Therapist. When he presents a specific problem in an individual session, he is urged to bring it before the group and obtain the benefit of many minds trying to resolve the problem. After a time he gradually weans himself away from dependence on the therapist except for special problems and new emergencies, and uses the group to satisfy his social hunger and needs for a wider circle of involvement.

The Reality Therapist uses praise, encouragement, rewards, and touch.

The learning theorists have demonstrated the effectiveness of positive reinforcement to influence behavioral change. Reality Therapy is prepared to add to its armamentarium whatever is humane and effective from various schools of treatment. Therefore, we perceive nothing amiss in employing the social reinforcement of praise and encouragement at every reasonable opportunity. Furthermore, since we perceive the function of the Reality Therapist as being not different from that of a friend, we respond with socially approved rewards for critical accomplishments or chronological attainments. For example, we would not consider it unprofessional to send a long-time client a birthday card or small gift.

Furthermore, we are in accord with the premise that approval, regard, respect can be communicated in nonverbal terms by socially appropriate gestures such as handshakes, pats on the shoulder, and in the case of children, a friendly stroke on the top of the head. Reality Therapy does not buy the notions derived from Esalen—massage, nude bathing and muscle kneading—but we see enough of a kernel of validity in the importance of touch to suggest the application of socially conditioned gestures of regard such as handshakes to transmit the sentiment: "I like you, I care for you."

The Reality Therapist does not press too hard.

Friendship is not a mechanical relationship in which one party always pours out his troubles and the other works on solutions to the problems. A healthy involvement requires that a whole host of subjects of mutual interest are discussed. George Bernard Shaw once said that the three most important subjects for intelligent conversation are politics, sex, and religion (values). It is a peculiar quirk of bourgeoisie society, GBS continued, that precisely these subjects are *verboten* as acceptable items for conversation in polite society. The Reality Therapist, on the other hand, permits his conversations to range through a full spectrum of human interests, including politics, sex, and values. The therapist and his client come to know each other as full personalities with a wide range of interests and opinions. They may discuss movies, TV, rock and roll; they may exchange titles of favorite books and recipes; they may talk about ambitions, fantasies, plans for the future. Under these circumstances, it is possible to move into an analysis of a problem with greater enthusiasm, clarity, and wisdom than if the partners confined their conversations to problem solving only. The client begins to perceive his therapist as a well-rounded human being and a model for responsible behavior rather than a mere technician or mental health mechanic.

The Reality Therapist never, never gives up.

Social workers over the years have observed an odd phenomenon they call *separation crisis*. A very difficult client becomes deeply involved with a worker and begins to display remarkable improvements in his behavior and attitudes. The worker feels very proud about his achievements and begins to talk about discharging the client from agency care. Then, just a few days before the separation day, the client goofs up in a most horrendous fashion. He steals the sheriff's automobile and rams it into a telephone pole causing $1,600 damages. Or he becomes roaring drunk and beats up his wife. Or he attempts to commit suicide.

What is the explanation for this bizarre, self-destructive behavior? The rationale derived from Reality Therapy is along these lines: The lonely, alienated person with a failure identity cannot believe that this remarkable, responsible therapist really likes and accepts the poor schnook of a client. So, on a subliminal level he determines to test the therapist, to establish if his regard for the client is genuine. He engages in negative behavior to find out the depth of the therapist's attachment. He is confident that the therapist will wash his hands of the whole situation and the client can then return to his well-honed identity as a failure and goof-up.

It is precisely at this moment of greatest frustration that the Reality Therapist must bite his lip in disappointment and carry on. He must prove to his client that he really cares. He must show that he accepts the essential humanity of his client and will not surrender responsibility for involvement because of the episode.

"How many times does one forgive a sinner? Seven times?" a disciple asked of Jesus.

"No, not seven times, but seventy times seven," Christ replied.[5]

A story is told about Churchill's greatest speech. It appears that when the great English statesman and orator was approaching ninety, he was invited to address the graduating class of Harrow, the school he attended as a youngster. To everyone's surprise, Churchill accepted the invitation. A thousand people jammed the auditorium to hear what many expected would be Churchill's last address. He was provided a flowery introduction by the headmaster and then slowly rose to speak. He leaned on his cane as he moved to the podium. He looked over the audience and then in a voice barely over a whisper, he said, "Never . . ."

A long pause followed and an intense silence gripped the audience.

Then, in the voice of old he thundered, *"Never, never give up!"* He turned and moved back to his seat. That was his entire speech, five words. But to many, it may have been the most impressive lesson he had to impart to the students and the adults in the audience.

The procedures for obtaining involvement contain the kernel of a paradigm to specify the nature of the Reality Therapy operation. Suppose we conceptualize Reality Therapy taking place within the confines of a life-space we symbolize with the bottle form illustrated in figure 1. Whatever interaction occurs is permeated with involvement.

Figure 1. Involvement fills the life-space of Reality Therapy interaction.

In developing the model of Reality Therapy, the thought of a sailing ship captured within the bottle occurs to us. We simplify the model by the paradigm illustration of figure 2.

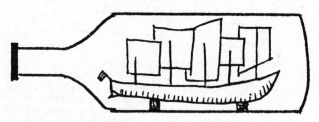

Figure 2. The beginning idea for a Reality Therapy Paradigm—a sailing ship in a bottle.

The operation of Reality Therapy is represented by five operational steps as follows:

1. WHAT? After involvement has been established, problem solving takes place by asking the question: "What are you doing? What happened? Please tell me exactly with all the details you can think of." The therapist is not satisfied with a judgment or summation; he wants the story in all its gory minutiae. In the immortal words of Sergeant Friday, he repeats, "Just the facts, mam, just the facts." He may ask the client to quote the exact verbiage employed in an argument. He may ask an assailant to throw a punch just as he did in a fistic encounter. He may ask a shoplifter

the precise technique employed to steal an item of merchandise. He may ask the homosexual exactly how he goes about cruising for partners. He may inquire of the exhibitionist what precautions he took to avoid arrest for his "compulsion."

The therapist leads his client through a series of questions such as would be applied by a good criminal defense lawyer. Where, when, and how did the episode occur? Who was there and what did each person say and do? What happened to the loot, victim, witnesses, and so on? A picture of cinemalike clarity emerges out of this line of interrogation and demonstration.

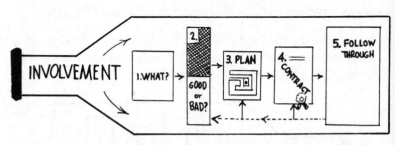

Figure 3. The Reality Therapy Paradigm: Involvement within the life-space of the therapist-client interaction permits effective problem solving to take place in stages. (1) The therapist obtains a full description of the behavior constituting the problem. (2) He requests the client to evaluate the worth of the behavior. (3) A plan is drafted to resolve the difficulty. (4) A contract is negotiated. (5) All else is follow-through, seeing that the commitment is fulfilled but without punishment or rancor.

2. GOOD OR BAD? After the episode has been described and demonstrated, the Reality Therapist pauses and raises the key question: "Did it do you any good?" He is not surprised if the client responds, "Well, it made me feel better." Nor is he astonished if the client says, "I don't know." It may be too much to expect a failure-oriented individual to blow his identity in one grand swoop. He has worked a long time to build that identity and he is not going to give it up without some struggle. The therapist may comment, "I'd like you to know that I consider this a critical question. No one can be expected to change his behavior unless he does so of his own will and desire. So, I'd like to ask you again, 'Did this behavior do you any good?' "

If the client presents a forthright response, "I think I did the right thing and I would do the same under identical circumstances," the therapist should understand that the prospect for a meaningful change in attitude and behavior is very limited. We might as well drop the project to permit time and *natural consequences* to change our client's perspective. We do not engage in argumentation or debate about the value of the client's behavior. We use only the tools of reasonable questioning and our human involvement to provide the fulcrum for a change of attitude.

By his posture and line of questions, the Reality Therapist transmits the concept that the client is responsible for his behavior and he alone can determine its value.

3. WHAT'S YOUR PLAN? After the nature of the behavior has been established and the client has evaluated it as negative and nonproductive (bad) the therapist asks: "What is your plan? What can we do to resolve this dilemma if we put our heads together? Do you have any ideas? Would you like to know what idea occurs to me?" Client and therapist engage in a sort of brainstorming session to come up with solutions to the problem. They weigh pros and cons. They call in "consultants" if necessary. They engage in role playing and rehearsal. Telephone calls are contemplated and letters are written. A clear-cut strategy is designed to cope with the difficulties. However, the Reality Therapist strives for a minimal plan which is assured of success. He is not carried away by the grandiosity of his client's proposals. "Let's resolve the problem a little at a time rather than all at once," he proposes.

4. CONTRACT. After a plan has been devised, the therapist asks, "Are you really going to carry it out? Will you do your part?" He drafts a contract and says in effect: "Just to make sure that we understand what this is all about, would you mind putting your John Hancock to this little document." The contract is specific as to time, place, and degree of effort. All loose ends are neatly tied into the package.

5. FOLLOW-UP. Everything that occurs after the initial four stages comes in the category of follow-up. The therapist arranges to meet with his client to determine how he fared with the plan.

If necessary, a new and simpler plan is formulated. New and more difficult steps in the overall plan may be delineated.

And what happens if the client fails to abide by his contract? The therapist does not waste time listening to excuses but briskly asks if he wants another schedule or a less difficult assignment. He points out that the client has the prerogative of changing the plan in accord with his own capabilities and personal interests.

Above all, no matter what happens, the therapist makes it clear he will not give up, he will stay at the client's side whatever misfortune may befall. If the client ends up in jail or in a state hospital, the therapist will remain in touch either in person or by mail.

From beginning to end, the Reality Therapist is tough-minded and gentle, serious and humorous, determined to help his client drop a failure identity and cross the barrier to success, self-worth, and human actualization.

REFERENCES

1. See Derek L. Phillips, *Abandoning Method*. San Francisco: Jossey-Bass, 1973, particularly chapter IV on "Paradigms and Falsification," and Stanislav Andreski, *Social Science as Sorcery*. New York: St. Marks Press, 1972.
2. William Glasser, *Reality Therapy: A New Approach to Psychiatry*. New York: Harper & Row, 1965.
3. William Glasser, *The Identity Society*. New York: Harper & Row, 1972, p. 19.
4. See Steve Pratt and Jay Tooley, "Human Actualization Teams: The Perspective of Contact Psychology," in *American Journal of Orthopsychiatry*, Vol. 36, 1966, pp. 881–895.
5. St. Matthew 18:21,22.

THOMAS E. BRATTER

Helping Those Who Do Not Want
to Help Themselves

Professional and Personal Biases

All psychotherapists, regardless of how much we deny, have professional and personal biases which affect the psychotherapeutic process. Before agreeing to work with an addicted individual, there are two sessions in which I interview him and then give him the opportunity to question me. If we decide to form a therapeutic alliance, it is on the basis of a fundamental agreement regarding counseling outcomes. The addicted person, at this juncture, does not need to make any commitment to become drug abstinent but should recognize that this will be one of the ultimate goals of therapy.

After working with addicted adolescents for a decade, I categorically reject the Dole and Nyswander (1965) and the Bejerot (1972) hypotheses which attribute the causes of heroin addiction to be either a biochemical or a metabiological deficiency which produces an uncontrollable desire for opiates. I reject the assumption that methadone is an essential medical cure for a metabolic disease. There has been insufficient and inconclusive scientific evidence to suggest that treatment must be restricted to medically correct a biochemical defect. In fact, Casriel and Bratter

Former title "Helping Those Who Do Not Want to Help Themselves: A Reality and Confrontation Orientation." Paper presented at Third International Symposium on Drug Abuse. Jerusalem, Israel, August 26, 1974. From *Corrective and Social Psychiatry and Journal of Behavior Technology, Methods and Therapy*, Vol. 20, no. 4 (October 1974). Reprinted by permission of the publisher.

(1974) conclude that until the metabiologic imbalance is proven "medically, to subject approximately 100,000 human beings to a potent chemical without proper controls is malpractice of the most insidious sort. . . . Psychologically, to convince addicts that there is a mystical metabolic disorder and that they must remain dependent on a potential poison rather than to strive for their autonomy is a conspiracy. Ethically, any conspiracy which places people in 'no win' situations and mitigates against their growth and development must be considered a criminal act!"

With the proliferation of therapeutic communities in the tradition of Synanon and Daytop Village, there is evidence that drug abstinence is both a realistic and attainable goal. Unmotivated addicts apparently, in addition, adjust to a drug abstinent environment when they have been incarcerated for prolonged periods. Upon their release from an institution, they elect to resume the abuse of chemicals because this has become a primary adaptive mechanism. If institutions would help inmates to learn more productive and responsible behavioral alternatives, I predict that the rate of recidivism would be diminished significantly.

It is important to recognize that I chose to be chemically abstinent. I never have smoked marihuana nor do I intend to experiment once it becomes legalized. (The government and the tobacco industry both recognize the taxation revenue potential and profit margins which will accrue so legalization for economic reasons appears inevitable.) I have seen many individuals who believed erroneously that they could use marihuana with immunity and derive pleasure, intensify their social, psychological, academic, and/or vocational inadequacies. Marihuana, as a psychotropic chemical, does not culminate with addiction to the opiates; but, I believe, cannibas will interact adversely with inadequate personalities. I imagine if there were a guarantee that I would experience only the pleasure and altered states of consciousness marihuana users claim, I might be inclined to indulge myself. Realistically, however, I know there can be no such guarantee and I am unwilling to jeopardize my freedom, my family, and my professional status. I never have placed myself in any position where I could become dependent on any mind-altering substance such as alcohol, caffeine, nicotine, etc. I feel I can be spontaneous and creative without chemicals, so I have little motivation to experiment. When addicted adolescents comment that I cannot and do not understand since I never have used drugs, I agree. I respect the awesome power of chemicals to destroy lives so I choose to remain drug abstinent. Friends have remarked that I am afraid to experiment with chemicals. They are correct. I believe it is preferable for human beings to be free of drug dependency.

The Making of a Psychotherapist

When I entered the field of the treatment of narcotic addiction, I was influenced greatly by the non-directive approach of Rogers (1961) who believed that the therapist should have a "warm regard for him (the client) as a person of unconditional self-worth—of value no matter what his condition, his behavior, or his feelings." In many situations it was difficult for me to respect the behavior of individuals with whom I tried to establish a helping relationship. I experienced contempt for addicts who had inflicted pain on themselves, their families, innocent people, and who subsequently wallowed in their own self-pity.

In order to learn more about my own feelings and the clinical dynamics of the narcotic addict, I studied a psychodynamic analytical approach. In retrospect, because I could reenact a childhood fantasy of becoming a detective, I enjoyed constructing sophisticated psychoanalytic paradigms. I came to understand my own counter transference and was fascinated to analyze patient transference. I was proud, moreover, of my therapeutic stance which allowed me to be "professional" and remain "detached," "uninvolved," "analytical," "neutral," etc. I was distressed, however, to find patients who had gained insight regarding their pathology still would continue their masochistic behavior patterns.

An incident occurred in 1964 when I was working in the Bedford-Stuyvesant area of Brooklyn which permanently altered my therapeutic orientation and approach. I encountered the first addict-pusher who confided that he financed his habit by selling narcotics to junior high students. At that time, the only contact I had with addicts was the literature which portrayed them as "dope fiends" who viciously preyed on the weak and innocent. I can recall vividly my fantasy that pushers enticed innocent youth into dark hallways, tied up their helpless victims, and then injected a poisonous white substance into their veins. In the best of the Anslinger traditions, this person would become an addict who would suffer indescribable horrors until he died of an overdose. As this young man, this "dope fiend pusher," began to relate the details of his trade, I felt my blood beginning to curdle. I lost emotional control as my mantle of detachment dissolved, and hurled invective upon invective at this "monster" who affronted my middle-class morality. When I began to reconstruct the preceding events of the day, sleep was impossible because I feared I had destroyed a person who had trusted me sufficiently to share his horrible and quite reprehensible existence. Who the hell was I to judge and condemn another person? Then I began to consider what would happen if he returned. All that week my anxiety and trepidation increased as I reckoned with the possibility that the addict would return. I devised a strategy to ask casually what the addict felt about the previous session and then offer a brief apology. When the addict appeared thirty minutes late for his appointment, I cringed in horror because I felt he was going to kill me. When I finally resolved my anxiety, I began to hear the addict's words when he acknowledged that "you are right, I am a monster. I hate myself. . . . And you know what? I haven't sold any drugs all week!"

What happened? I tried to fit the pieces of the puzzle together. I knew I had violated all of the sacred beliefs regarding the role of the therapist. I had become angry, had insulted and had rejected the client. I had lost my objectivity and detachment. But I knew that something had prompted the addict to change his behavior—i.e., to cease temporarily from selling drugs—and I had no explanation. One year later, when I visited Daytop Village, I came to understand the transformation of a pusher.

The Selection of a Professional Specialization

Ten years ago, I decided to limit my professional activities to working with the addicted and alcoholic individual. At this juncture, in my professional growth and development, I feel indebted to more than 1000 addicts who collectively have helped me in my struggle to become a more responsible, honest, spontaneous, and loving person, parent, and professional. By their constant challenging of my humanness, often I feel that these individuals have helped me more than I have helped them.

A gratifying feeling is the relative success I have attained working with a most difficult-to-reach adolescent group who has not been amenable to more traditional treatment modalities. Geist (1974) warns that the "treatment of drug-using adolescents is an arduous task, for they present innumerable problems: broken appointments, demands for availability, continual crises, frequent traveling, extreme passivity, excessive demands for the therapist to provide a panacea; all impede therapeutic progress and exasperate the therapist engaged in the comparatively more tranquil task of helping neurotically motivated adolescents. Therapy of patients from the drug culture must also struggle against a rigidly entrenched and unwitting social reinforcement of the drug ideology as a viable means of existence." I enjoy the respect of colleagues who acknowledge that they could not work with this type of individual.

There are, of course, occupational hazards. I have suffered the agony of self-doubt and of absolute failure that all psychotherapists fear by attending funerals for eight persons whose deaths were attributed to extreme narcoticism. The eight had been members of various community-based addiction treatment programs which I have directed. While they were members of my therapy group, none had been in the program for more than two months. In all candor, had they been involved longer in the group or been in my private practice, in all probability I might have decided to specialize with another group of adolescents.

A Professional versus Personal Dilemma: a "No Win" Situation for the Psychotherapist

This profession, I believe, requires a total commitment, dedication, and involvement of the psychotherapist. Consequently, my phone can ring twenty-four hours a day, seven days a week, and fifty-two weeks a year. Often, I have disrupted my personal life to respond to an emergency. I genuinely love my work and feel gratified from it. In all candor, I recognize that this permits me to fulfill many of my personal needs to become the central figure in another person's life. There can be no finer reward, I feel, than to know I have helped another human being reclaim his life from chemicals and to actualize his potential. My supervisors generally have agreed on one point: "Thomas Bratter must learn when too much involvement is no longer healthy for himself or the client/patient." I contend in rebuttal, however, that it is precisely this "responsible care and concern" which is the cornerstone of therapy.

I find myself constantly conflicted between spending too much time with adolescents and not spending enough time with my family. Carole is too understanding and permits me to attend to everyone's concerns but ours. Our two kids, Eddie (9) and Barbara (6), fortunately, have learned my confrontation style and use it with improving results. What can I say to Eddie when he observes "Daddy, all you do is to talk on the phone and help others. . . . What about me?" Or Barbara, who kissed an adolescent who was staying with us because he had no where else to go and then turned to me at dinner and said, "He's easier to kiss than you because I see him more often!" But I'm learning. Now I can say with increasing conviction, "I'm sorry I can't see you now because I choose to spend some time with my family." It still feels awkward. Someday maybe it will be easier.

One solution which I have adopted is to limit my practice to no more than ten and concurrently do some part-time teaching and consultation work.

The Treatment Process

Before establishing a therapeutic alliance, the adolescent chemical casualty continues his devour-or-be-devoured, life-or-death, fight-or-flight, destroy-or-be-destroyed struggle. He consumes a variety of drugs simultaneously which can cause decompensation or death. He duplicates his impulsive, self-annihilative behavior.

Initially treatment is a "therapeutic battle." The combatants are the active-directive and creative crisis interventions of the psychotherapist *against* the awesome self-annihilative rage and self-destructive behavior of the chemically dependent individual. The psychotherapist attempts to help the addicted adolescent control, contain, and curtail his self-annihilative behavior by adopting an authoritarian approach whereby behavioral limits not only are defined but also are enforced. The psychotherapist *imposes* himself as the central figure in the individual's life. This can be justified in survival situations. Violations of confidentiality, threats of incarceration, and aggressive crisis intervention can be explained as proof of responsible concern for the welfare of the person.

To change potential suicidal behavior requires prolonged controlled intervention which involves setting limits and implementing sanctions through which life-threatening behavior can be contained and ameliorated. Vaillant (1969) provides the justification for the constraint of the addict when he contends "to alter self-destructive behavior may require controlled intervention over time. . . . Probably, the authoritarian treatment of addiction . . . is effective not because it punishes, but because it enforces. By providing external support, such treatment meaningfully cares about the addict's needs. Perhaps the management of drug abusers should resemble the management of ignorance or immaturity." Chwast (1957) addresses the controversy regarding thought and behavioral control when he writes that he "fully appreciates the values of the . . . therapist's democratic acceptance of the right to self-determination of the client, some adaptation of this principle which emphasizes the helpful role of control and authority with antisocial clients . . . requires consideration."

The psychotherapist must be prepared to become totally involved with and committed to the addicted adolescent. Glasser (1965, pp. 21-22) suggests that:

Usually the most difficult phase of therapy is the first, the gaining of the involvement that the patient so desperately needs but which he has been unsuccessful in attaining or maintaining up to the time he comes for treatment. Unless the requisite involvement exists between the necessarily responsible therapist and the irresponsible patient, there can be no therapy. The guiding principles of Reality Therapy are directed toward achieving the proper involvement, a completely honest, human relationship in which the patient, for perhaps the first time in his life, realizes that someone cares enough about him not only to accept him but to help him fulfill his needs in the real world. . . . The ability of the therapist to get involved is the major skill of doing Reality Therapy.

This commitment, which is difficult to describe, produces awesome feelings of responsibility and pressure because the individual still continues to test limits.

The addict will ventilate his hostility and anger. By refusing to be intimidated, by continuing to confront self-destructive behavior, and by providing rational answers to angry accusations, it is possible for the psychotherapist to establish a working alliance. The explanation to angry comments inevitably remains the same. "I care enough about you that I am willing to risk your anger and rejection by stopping you from mutilating or destroying yourself. Unlike your fucked-up acquaintances who will give you either the money to cop or the poison to kill yourself, I intend to stop you. I've attended eight funerals of idiots who died of overdoses and do not wish to go to any more. When you begin to act like a responsible adult, it will be my pleasure to respond to you as such. When, however, you act like a fucked-up creep, I'll continue to treat you that way. My preference is to respect you but I am prepared to be the biggest bastard you've ever met. Make it, it's your choice!"

Once the individual adopts more responsible behavior, the psychotherapist must renegotiate the therapeutic contract. He must decrease the tightly controlling relationship which, during this phase of counseling, could become counter-productive. The individual should be given the freedom to fail and to learn from these failures. Any failure is attributed to stupidity rather than to psychological or emotional factors beyond the control of the individual. This psychotherapeutic orientation categorically rejects, as does Hurvitz (1973), the psychodynamic explanation that "people are 'inherently' or 'instinctively' aggressive and hostile, that 'unconscious' biological or instinctual forces are the causes of individual behavior and determine interpersonal relations, social interaction, and social norms. This ideology regards inappropriate behavior or emotional disorder as the 'acting out' of putative 'unconscious conflicts' associated with concepts such as the 'Oedipus complex,' 'infantile sexuality,' 'death instinct,' and others." Freudenberger (1971a) suggests that such "diagnostic categories as we have applied in the past are meaningless when we are dealing, for example, with people who have been . . . kept down by our society (who) show a lack of initiative, severe depression, or have turned to drugs." Freudenberger (1971b and 1970) elsewhere has described an alternative psychotherapeutic approach. Earlier Szasz (1960) contended that the medical model on which psychodynamic psychotherapy is based may exacerbate those problems which it purports to cure. One of the first to reject the psychodynamic model, Mowrer (1959) suggested that disturbed behavior should be considered to be a manifestation of irresponsibility rather than disease. He concluded that psychodynamic psychotherapy is "nontherapeutic."

A confrontation and Reality Therapy orientation, in contrast, assumes that the individual needs to be "habilitated" not "rehabilitated." The adolescent chemical casualty has developed what Glasser (1972) calls a "failure identity." "Lacking a success identity, many young people turn against their parents first because they know their parents care about them even though they are not involved. After their parents, they turn against society, and, in failing in school, taking drugs, and engaging in promiscuous and uncommitted sex, they turn against themselves. . . . A child with a failure identity, that is, one who lacks a concept for himself as a loved and worthwhile individual, will not work for any long-term goals." It becomes necessary for the psychotherapist to function in the capacity of an educator-consultant to help the adolescent learn more productive and responsible modes of behaviors. Counseling becomes an educational problem-solving process whereby the adolescent is assisted to select behavior which will maximize the probability of success. While describing one of the differences between Reality Therapy and psychodynamic counseling, Glasser (1965, p. 60) emphasizes the therapist's role as a teacher. "We teach patients better ways to fulfill their needs. We spend much time painstakingly examining the patient's daily activity and suggesting better ways for him to behave. We answer the many questions that patients ask and suggest ways to solve problems and approach people. Patients who have not been able to fulfill their needs must learn both how to approach people so that they can become more involved and how to accomplish enough so that they can gain an increased feeling of self-worth." An important part of this phase of psychotherapy is to help the adolescent discover meaningful and positive alternatives to drug dependency.

This psychotherapeutic philosophy assumes that Man essentially is rational. When he is confronted about the self-defeating aspects of his behavior, he will become more responsible and productive. While it is not possible to control external conditions by which Man is challenged, he can control his responses to these conditions. The addicted individual, thus, possesses the capacity to transcend his past which negates the myth that once an addict always an addict.

The Psychotherapeutic Challenge: To Maintain a Perspective

Often working with angry, addicted adolescents can be draining, discouraging, and depressing. These adolescents can provoke the psychotherapist by their grandiose demands of infantile entitlement. They expect to be rescued by the omnipotent and the therapist, who has assumed that role, realistically knows he must respond. Using a psychoanalytic orientation, in an important humanistic paper, Adler (1972) has described a similar experience and conclusion:

The art of being a good therapist consists in part of a sensitivity which can weigh how much a patient is genuinely overwhelmed and needs to be fed symbolically, and how much he can stand and examine at a specific moment. The "good mother" aspect of the therapist ultimately determines whether the patient has a corrective emotional experience similar to that of his early childhood. As many authors have described, limit-setting is an important ingredient in a group of patients whose wishes are enormous, and whose impulse control is often tenuous, and may become even more so in the heat of transference. But the vicissitudes of the therapist's helplessness and fury determine whether the limits are part of a firm, caring, facilitating operation, or a punitive, attacking, rejecting and envious assault.

The psychotherapist must recognize that the adolescent, once he develops inner controls, no longer will require limits to be set and enforced. In fact, the psychotherapist who continues to function in this role will communicate that he expects the adolescent to continue to remain self-destructive, irresponsible, and infantile.

These adolescents are adept at infuriating the therapist by making scathing personal attacks which, more times than not, wound and insult. They are adept, furthermore, at discovering the inconsistencies and hypocrisies of the therapist. Frequently, they depreciate and devalue the worth of treatment. Angry, articulate, alienated adolescents, indeed, can exasperate the therapist. Being so aroused, the psychotherapist must be careful not to agree with the adolescent that he is "helpless and hopeless" and, in addition, that therapy essentially is meaningless. The therapist can admit, like all human beings, he has been wrong. But to "give up" on an adolescent who has succeeded in hurting a professional is to condemn this person eternally.

By becoming involved with a destructive and sadistic adolescent the psychotherapist becomes vulnerable to being disappointed and insulted. He must recognize and struggle with these feelings which can prevent the psychotherapist from recognizing growth and development. A final requisite for working with these most difficult adolescents is for the psychotherapist to have unlimited stamina. Glasser (1969) suggests that these adolescents need adults "who will not excuse them when they fail their commitments, but who will work with them again and again as they commit and recommit until they finally learn to fulfill a commitment. When they learn to do so, they are no longer lonely; they gain maturity, respect, love, and a successful identity."

High Expectations for Improved Behavior: A Therapeutic Mandate

One of the most potent psychotherapeutic influences of behavior performance is the expectation of the therapist. The phenomenon has been termed the "self-fulfilling prophecy" when people become what we prophesy for them. Unfortunately many professionals have pessimistic attitudes concerning the drug dependent individual. Psychotherapists inadvertently may negatively reinforce the addicted adolescent's sense of being helpless or hopeless and of being untreatable and uneducable. I have discovered, in contrast, that when I demand improved behavioral performance, the adolescent does his damnedest to conform to these positive expectations. Dynamically, the high expectations of the psychotherapist differ from parental pressure since there is neither any possessive demand nor any reflection on the part of the therapist personally if goals are not completed. If a drop-out, for example, returns to school and receives a "C" average he is challenged as to why he did not do better. There is no rejoicing when a goal is attained; instead the adolescent might be cajoled by a derisive retort—"How about that? You finally achieved something on your own! Too bad you didn't get hit by the bolt of lightning sooner!" While this deliberately frustrates the adolescent, the implicit message is that he has the potential to achieve a more ambitious goal. A comment such as "I guess you have more ability than you previously thought" serves to motivate continued behavioral improvement. "The Pygmalion Effect" has been described by Rosenthal (1973, and 1968) regarding positive self-fulfilling educational prophecies. There needs to be more research, however, regarding the reinforcing nature of both the negative and positive self-fulfilling prophecy in psychotherapy.

The Psychotherapist as Advocate: A Neglected Dimension of the Helping Relationship

If further training, education, job placement, etc., are indicated, the psychotherapist should be prepared to function as an advocate to help the adolescent secure these services. Bratter (1973) has described this vital dimension of the therapeutic alliance when the psychotherapist protects the adolescent's interests and aggressively negotiates the most beneficial deal—even at the expense of an adversary. This relationship resembles the role of an attorney. (Interestingly, the French term for attorney is "l'avocat.") The advocate "must be prepared to assume a variety of roles to help the adolescent receive preferential treatment: negotiator, protector, intervener, broker, supporter, expeditor, representative." Often manipulation of the system and the environment are required. In extreme cases, this may require some dishonesty on the part of the psychotherapist who may "forget" and/or "minimize" the behavior/legal background of the adolescent to a prospective school or employer. This must be done selectively, after other options have failed, when the psychotherapist genuinely believes there is no way to succeed. Conceding to adolescents that dishonesty is imperative gives them a negative message. As psychotherapists, however, we must recognize that society is often pathological, racist, and corrupt and refuses to provide opportunities for self-improvement to former addicts, felons, *et al*. Any advocate, if he is to be successful, must understand this ugly reality. The advocate must be willing, once he is convinced that the adolescent has become responsible and productive, to jeopardize his professional reputation by aggressively intervening on his behalf. There are waiting lists which must be by-passed, unsympathetic bureaucrats who need to be persuaded, etc.

The Psychotherapist as Agitator?

The major concern of the psychotherapist must be to motivate and to re-educate addicted adolescents. These adolescents are helped to discover positive alternatives to chemical oblivion. If, however, they see more viable alternatives than drugs and still elect to reject them, then, perhaps, the focus should be directed toward the modification of society. In an angry and scathing attack against the status quo, Glenn and Kunnes (1973) contend: "If politics deals with power, then the therapist must always deal with politics. Therapists encourage patients either to accept the existing distributions of power in their environment or to change them, whether that power distribution be between individuals, families, communities, or countries. . . . By undergoing 'successful' therapy, a person who might have been angry and have confronted the status quo is made to feel comfortable within it. Defusing even one person's political militancy may have profound political consequences."

This is an important psychotherapeutic proposition: As psychotherapists, do we abdicate and help our clients/patients to adjust to the status quo or do we agitate and help our "people" to change the status quo?

REFERENCES

Adler, G., Helplessness in the helpers. *Journal of Medical Psychology* (1972) 45, p. 324.

Bejerot, N., *Addiction: an artificially induced drive.* Springfield: Charles C. Thomas Publisher, 1972.

Bratter, T. E., Treating alienated, unmotivated, drug abusing adolescents. *American Journal of Psychotherapy* (October, 1973), XXVII: 4, p. 594.

Casriel, D. and Bratter, T. E. Methadone Maintenance Treatment: A Questionable Procedure. *The Journal of Drug Issues* (1974), 4:4, pp. 359–375.

Chwast, J., The significance of control in the treatment of the antisocial person. *Archives of criminal psychodynamics* (1957), 2, p. 817.

Dole, P., and Nyswander, Marie A., A medical treatment for diacetylmorphine (heroin) addiction: a clinical trial with methadone hydrochloride. *Journal of the American Medical Association* (1965), 193: 8, pp. 80–84.

Freudenberger, H. J., The professional in the free clinic: new problems, new views, new goals. In Smith, David E., Bentel, David J., and Schwartz, Jerome L., (eds), *The Free Clinic; A Community Approach to Health Care and Drug Abuse.* Beloit: Stash Press, 1971a.

Freudenberger, H. J., New psychotherapy approaches with teenagers in a new world. *Psychotherapy: Theory, Research and Practice* (Spring, 1971b), 8: 1, pp. 38–44.

Freudenberger, H. J., Departure from "medical" model oriented psychotherapies. *Journal of Clinical Issues in Psychology* (March, 1970), 1, pp. 3–8.

Geist, R. A., Some observations on adolescent drug use: therapeutic implications. *Journal of the American Academy of Child Psychiatry* (Winter, 1974), 13:1, p. 67.

Glasser, W., *The identity society.* New York: Harper & Row, 1972. pp. 161–162.

Glasser, W., *Schools without failure*. New York: Harper & Row, Publishers, 1969, p. 24.

Glasser, W., *Reality therapy: a new approach to psychiatry*. New York: Harper & Row, 1965.

Glenn, M., and Kunnes, R., *Repression or revolution? Therapy in the United States today*. New York: Harper & Row, 1973. pp. 46–47.

Hurvitz, N., Psychotherapy as a means of social control. *Journal of Consulting and Clinical Psychology* (1973), 40: 2, p. 233.

Mowrer, O. H., *The crisis in psychiatry and religion*. New York: D. Van Nostrand & Co., 1959.

Rogers, C. R., A therapist's view of the good life: the fully functioning person. In Rogers, Carl R., (ed.), *On becoming a person: a therapist's view of psychotherapy*. Boston: Houghton Mifflin Company, 1961, p. 185.

Rosenthal, R., The Pygmalion effect lives. *Psychology Today* (September, 1973), 7: 4, pp. 56–62.

Rosenthal, R., and Jacobson, L., *Pygmalion in the classroom*. New York: Holt, Rinehart & Winston, Inc., 1968.

Szasz, T. E., The myth of mental illness. *American Psychologist* (1960), pp. 113–118.

Vaillant, G. E., If the drug abuser is a danger to himself, who should intervene? In Wittenborn, J. R., Brill, H., Smith, J. P., and Wittenborn, Sarah A. (eds.), *Drugs and youth: proceedings of the Rutgers symposium on drug abuse*. Springfield: Charles C. Thomas, Publishers, 1969. p. 310.

THOMAS E. BRATTER

A Group Approach with Adolescent Alcoholics

Introduction

During the last decade and a half, the most prevalent forms of adolescent behavior and fads have been "chemical cop-outs." In the late 1950's, beer and wine were the most commonly abused chemicals. In the early 1960's, marihuana replaced liquid chemicals. In the mid 1960's, the adolescent rites of initiation to adulthood were extensive experimentation with the hallucinogens, amphetamines, and barbiturates. Heroin addiction by the late 1960's malignantly afflicted significant numbers of American youth. Now, 15 years after the chemical cycle commenced, the adolescent alcoholic, almost an extinct species, appears to be proliferating. The mid 1970's, therefore, will witness the resurgence of alcoholism among our youth.

It should be noted that my professional career has been limited exclusively to working with adolescent "chemical casualties" such as the alcoholic and the narcotic addict in a group psychotherapeutic setting. During the last decade, I have spent more than 10,000 hours conducting groups. I would estimate that I have worked with more than 1,500 addicts, 500 drug abusers, and 250 alcoholics. Unfortunately, I do not have any statistics regarding the "success" rate. I say "unfortunately" because I am confident

Former title "Reality Therapy: A Group Psychotherapeutic Approach with Adolescent Alcoholics." From *Annals of the New York Academy of Sciences,* Vol. 233 (April 15, 1974), copyright © New York Academy of Sciences, 1974. Reprinted by permission of the New York Academy of Sciences.

that the successes significantly outnumber the failures. Of those with whom I have maintained contact throughout the years, I can document 300 who are chemically abstinent, are enrolled in college or graduate school, and/or are employed in progressively responsible jobs. Currently, there are approximately 100 who have been placed in therapeutic communities and some have become directors of these "self-help" programs. I must report that at least 10 are dead and approximately 50 are incarcerated in various institutions.

Initially my counseling style was essentially psychoanalytical. About a decade ago, I became a devotee of Carl Rogers' nondirective approach. More recently, I have become more behaviorally oriented and have amalgamated the principles of Reality Therapy and Confrontation. In retrospect, I believe my psychotherapeutic approach is more effective than when I began. While I would attribute this to the specific treatment intervention utilized, I cannot discount the obvious factors of my own professional growth and development with an attendant increased sophistication of the interpersonal dynamics of the adolescent chemical casualty. I would be less than candid if I did not state that often I have found my work to be discouraging, depressing, and emotionally draining. No one likes to fail and when a patient dies or is arrested, the therapist must feel a sense of failure. Fortunately, there have been more times when I have been elated, ecstatic, and excited. It is a beautiful feeling to have a youngster admitted to a college, even though he discontinued his schooling before the eleventh grade; to invite you to his wedding, or send a post card saying he is doing well and thinking of you.

The Self-Fulfilling Prophecy

Before I begin the more formalized and theoretical sections of this paper I should like to state that I believe the primary problem of the treatment of chemical casualties is that physicians and professionals remain perpetually pessimistic about any hope of recovery and/or improvement. The chemical casualty is viewed by most as "helpless and hopeless," and "untreatable and uneducable." Not surprisingly, when everyone has given up, he begins to see himself in these terms and develops the identity of a Failure.

Freudenberger (1971) emphasizes the factor of "the self-fulfilling prophecy [which] is clearly in evidence in psychotherapy with the teenager. If we [therapists] believe that a patient can be helped, often he is helped, and if we believe that he cannot be helped, then usually he turns out not to be amenable to therapy." Agreeing with Freudenberger, Curlee (1971a) states "if we are to treat alcoholics successfully, we must believe that recovery is possible—and that it is desirable."

Much of the problem seems to be contained within the definition of alcoholism. The Cooperative Commission on the Study of Alcoholism (1967), for example, has defined alcoholism "as a condition in which an individual has lost control over his alcohol intake in the sense that he is consistently unable to refrain from drinking or to stop drinking before getting intoxicated." The National Conference of Commissioners on Uniform State Laws (1971), moreover, describes a lack of self-control regarding the use of alcoholic beverages as "the inability to abstain from drinking for any significant time period, or the inability to remain sober between drinking episodes. . . . This relatively narrow definition has been the basis for the court decisions holding an alcoholic not criminally responsible for his intoxication." The American Medical Association (1968) has compounded the problem by describing alcoholism as "an illness, characterized by a preoccupation with alcohol and loss of control over its consumption such as to lead, usually to intoxication . . . and by tendency toward relapse."

These three definitions, in brief, suggest the explicit notion that the patient should not be held accountable for his behavior because there has been an insidious loss of internal control. The patient, thus, is excused for his/her behavior. Ellis (1967) proposes, in contrast, that the patient be viewed as "behaving in a self-defeating and/or needlessly antisocial manner and who will probably continue to do so in the future, and, although he is partially creating or causing (and in this sense is responsible for) his aberrant behavior, he is still not to be condemned for creating it but is to be helped to overcome it."

Fox (1972) eliminates the concept of a loss of control and elects to describe alcoholism as "a behavioral disturbance in which the excessive drinking of alcohol interferes with the physical or mental health of the individual. It is usually accompanied by a disturbance in the interpersonal relationships within the family, in the work life, and in the social environment."

Glasser (1960) describes the alcoholic as a "person who derives all his satisfactions from the consumption of large quantities of alcohol. He lives to be drunk, because when he is drunk he feels pleasure in contrast to the pain of sobriety. An alcoholic will drink almost anything in the hope of getting drunk. . . . The alcoholic gets drunk because he wants peace and contentment from the anxiety which plagues him when he is sober."

Reality Therapy: Its Psychotherapeutic Components

Reality Therapy has antecedents in the psychotherapeutic literature. What is unique, however, is their juxtaposition and interrelationships. Reality Therapy assumes that human behavior can be modified by means of psychological procedures. In its most simplistic form, Reality Therapy can be considered one of several behavioral derivatives of the reinforcement model in learning theory. Reality Therapy is, in part, an answer to Eysenck's (1952) contention that traditional psychotherapy has proven to be ineffective. Eysenck (1960), modifying his position, concluded that whatever results have been demonstrated had a learning theory as its basis. Reality Therapy stresses the cognitive, the behavioral, and emotive components in human psychology and in behavioral change.

Writing about behavior therapy, in specific, Mainord's (1967) observations can apply to Reality Therapy:

It may be wondered what we do about the traditional problems of transference, repressed materials, symptom substitution, etc. The answer is, consciously, nothing. All the materials are there for a more traditional therapy, but we do not look for any particular course of therapy; we merely look for improved behavior which always seems accompanied by improved emotional states. We believe that the consequences of behavior determine emotional tone; so that if we can control the behavior, we also control the feeling. Then, with Eysenck, we are arguing the so-called symptoms are the illness, and if they are given up, therapy is complete.

Reality Therapy can be characterized as a psychotherapeutic strategy to maximize the probability of successes while minimizing failure. *The goal of therapy, therefore, is to assist the individual to be aware of the impact of his behavior, to understand the consequences of his acts, and to become more responsible to himself, others, and to society.*

There are seven components to Reality Therapy:

1. INVOLVEMENT. Before the client will begin to examine his behavior, he must be convinced that the therapist genuinely cares for him. It is necessary for the psychotherapist to establish a climate of trust, of concern, of involvement. Strupp, Fox, and Lessler (1969) confirm Glasser's contention regarding authentic involvement when they summarize the characteristics of an effective therapist. "The composite image of the 'good therapist' drawn from our respondents is thus of a keenly attentive, interested, benign, and concerned listener—a friend who is warm and natural, is not averse to giving direct advice, who speaks one's language, makes sense, and rarely arouses intense anger." Whitehorn and Betz (1954), who studied the retrospective improvement rate of schizophrenics, discovered that successful therapists were warm and attempted to understand the patient in a personal fashion. The improvement rate was 75 percent for the empathetic therapist as compared to 27 percent for the more impersonal one. Generally, the research confirms the correlation between high levels of liking, non-possessive warmth, and empathy which have facilitated behavioral change. Rogers (1957) and Truax (1963) have focused on the combination of warmth and empathy. After reviewing twenty years of research concerning the impact of the therapist, Swensen (1971) confirmed Rogers' and Truax' hypothesis when he concluded that "the successful psychotherapist is the one who genuinely cares about, and is committed to his client. . . . The really crucial element in the therapist's contribution to therapeutic

success is *the therapist's commitment to the client.*" [Italics in original.]

Often alcoholics feel they have been rejected and misunderstood by their families and friends. They enter therapy prepared for what they consider to be an inevitable failure, and painful human encounter. Rarely does the adolescent alcoholic, when he enters therapy, have any friends. He is alienated from himself and others. The hypothesis of therapist involvement is critical when working with alcoholics who initially seem remote, resigned, and resistant. Mayer and Myerson (1971) describe their experiences in an outpatient setting with alcoholics. They believe the most important aspect of the helping relationship is the therapist's ability to establish rapport with the patient.

In order to establish a therapeutic alliance quickly, I have found it propitious, whenever appropriate, to share relevant parts of my life and discuss some of my fears, frustrations, and failures so that the adolescent alcoholic begins to recognize that others have and can share their problems. Simultaneously, the therapist becomes a human and responsible role model. Glasser (1965, p. 22) suggests new roles for the therapist which include:

The therapist must be a very responsible person—tough, interested, human, and sensitive. He must be able to fulfill his own needs and must be willing to discuss some of his own struggles so that the patient can see that acting responsibly is possible though sometimes difficult. Neither aloof, superior, nor sacrosanct, he must never imply that what he does, what he stands for, or what he values is unimportant. He must have the strength to become involved, to have his values tested by the patient, and to withstand intense criticism by the person he is trying to help. Every fault and defect may be picked apart by the patient. Willing to admit that, like the patient, he is far from perfect, the therapist must nevertheless show that a person can act responsibly even if it takes great effort.

I give the adolescent alcoholic my home phone number and encourage him to call should the occasion arise. Telephone contact can prevent intermittent drinking relapses when the patient becomes consumed by loneliness, intolerable pain, etc. In comparison to his addict counterpart who tests therapeutic limits perpetually, the alcoholic usually does not call on his own volition unless he is specifically instructed to do so.

2. CURRENT BEHAVIOR. After the therapeutic alliance, predicated on involvement, has been established, the patient begins to examine his/her current behavior rather than attitudes or emotions. Glasser (1972, p. 114) believes "people often avoid facing their present behavior by emphasizing how they feel rather than what they are doing. Although Reality Therapy does not deny that emotions are important, successful therapists learn that unless they focus on behavior they do not help the patient."

The therapeutic inquisition helps the alcoholic reconstruct the events of the day. I have found it expedient to ask questions regarding: What time did you wake up? What did you do? To whom did you speak? Did you drink? What? With whom? The patient, thus, is able to account for the entire day.

3. EVALUATION OF BEHAVIOR. During this phase of therapy the patient understands the impact of his/her self-defeating and irresponsible behavior. Eaton (1971) believes initially "the client is externally focused upon the way his present behavior appears to others . . . [subsequently] the client's focus shifts from an external observation of how he presently appears to others to an external observation of how he would appear to others if he looked or behaved the way he would like to." Perhaps, the most effective technique to enable the patient to penetrate his defenses quickly and to view realistically his irresponsible acts is confrontation. Carkhuff and Berenson (1967) have defined confrontation as an act:

initiated by the therapist, based on his core understanding of the client. It brings the client into more direct contact with himself, his strengths and resources, as well as his self-destructive behavior. The purpose of confrontation is . . . a challenge to the client to become integrated. . . . It is directed at discrepancies within the client . . . between what the client says and does . . . and between illusion and reality. . . . It implies a constructive attack upon the unhealthy. . . . The strength and intensity of a confrontation may correspond with how dominant and central the emotional pattern is to the client's life style.

In order to facilitate the patient to internalize the evaluation, Garner (1970a) advocates that the psychotherapist continually ask "What do you think or feel about what I told you [which] is intended to create the atmosphere . . . that the status quo is unacceptable, and a solution is found by continuous searching."

The dynamics of drinking are explained to the adolescent alcoholic. When he makes a decision to drink, at that time, alcohol is the most important thing. If, however, the alcoholic wants to alter his behavior, then, he must re-examine his choice. The patient learns to anticipate the intermediate and longer-range consequences of his/her behavior. When the patient not only accepts his responsibility for his behavior but also admits that he has been irresponsible, then together with the therapist they can begin the last phase of treatment.

4. PLANNING RESPONSIBLE BEHAVIOR. The alcoholic is helped to identify for himself how he believes he should behave. Garner (1970b) views this phase of treatment "as a problem-solving rather than a permissive or coercive approach." The therapist might instruct the patient specifically how to behave so as to ensure the maximum probability of success. It is possible to be responsible, the adolescent learns, if he can achieve self-discipline—i.e., he must make a thinking decision when he does not feel like it. The patient sees he can control his behavior which implies a capacity to transcend what he has done previously. He understands that he possesses elements of freedom of choice as well as the capacity to grow and develop. While the patient cannot control external conditions by which he is challenged, any person can control his responses. Learning presupposes some unlearning. Wolpe (1958) assumes "since neurotic behavior . . . originates in learning, it is only to be expected that its elimination will be a matter of unlearning." No growth can occur unless the current patterns of behavior are altered so that a temporary disequilibrium can produce a new differentiation. Marmor (1971), while attempting to compare contract psychotherapy with Behavior Therapy, contends that the "removal of an ego-dystonic symptom may . . . produce such satisfying feedback from the environment that may result in major

constructive shifts within the personality system, thus leading to modification of the original conflictual pattern. Removal of a symptom also may lead to positive change in the perception of the self, with resultant satisfying internal feedbacks, heightening of self-esteem, and a subsequent restructuring of the internal psycho-dynamic."

5. COMMITMENT. Once a plan has been determined collectively, the therapist requires a commitment from the patient to abide by it. Goals are defined in behavioral terms. The alcoholic, for example, is encouraged to take one less drink a day rather than become abstinent immediately. While this methodology embraces traditional medical detoxification procedure, Glasser (1972, p. 123) suggests that goals should be attained easily and become progressively more difficult. A person who has failed frequently needs to experience success. In contrast, failure will discourage commitment.

A treatment contract can be written which delineates specific actions to be performed. According to Parlour, Cole, and Van Vorst (1967) a treatment contract can structure therapy which resembles problem-solving. These authors have discovered that progress is quicker when the problem is defined and methods for solving it are written. One of six advantages of utilizing a written record, Thomas and Ezell (1972) have concluded, is to divide the contract into sections and make an evaluation after each step. This enables the patient to experience progress and success when solving his problems.

6. ACCEPT NO EXCUSES. The concern of the psychotherapist can be demonstrated by refusing to accept any excuses offered by the patient when goals are not attained and by maintaining high expectations of improved behavioral performance. Dynamically, the high expectations of the therapist differ from parental pressure because there is neither a possessive demand nor any reflection on the therapist personally if goals are not completed. If, however, the patient fails to attain or to maintain his commitments, the therapist can share candidly his regret.

Glasser and Iverson (no date) implore the therapist not to accept rationalizations when a commitment is not attained. Any excuse not only breaks the involvement but also communicates to the patient that the commitment was insignificant. Glasser (1969) believes that adolescents grow and develop when they have adults —i.e., teachers and therapists—who continue to insist that commitments be made and fulfilled. Glasser (1962), moreover, treats "the youngster as a potentially responsible adult rather than as an unfortunate child." Recognizing this factor of having the therapist expect the best of him, the patient continues to strive to better himself. Working toward alcoholic abstinence is a long-range goal. Other concurrent goals could be the completion of schooling, attendance in college or training, and/or finding full-time employment.

The research reinforces the fact that the patient's expectations of his/her behavioral improvement are influenced by the degree of faith and trust he has with the therapist. Orne (1968), recognizing the importance of the therapeutic alliance, has specified three elements in which the patient must believe: "(1) that his problems can be potentially relieved . . . (2) that effective means of bringing about the desired change exist . . . and (3) that the therapist [is] willing and able to provide the means by which the desired changes may take place." Frank (1968), who has studied the relationship of hope in the psychotherapeutic process, has noted positive expectations can be a catalyst which stimulates action.

7. NO PUNISHMENT. If a commitment is not consummated, additional discussion and planning are indicated. Perhaps, the contract will need to be renegotiated. Punishment, which serves to reinforce the notion of failure, is believed to be counter-therapeutic. Fox, Graham, and Gill (1972), utilizing a psychiatric model while treating outpatient alcoholics, confirm Glasser's no punishment/praise hypothesis when they assert:

Recognition must be given to the facts that, as a general rule, alcoholics have rigid, punitive super-egos and that guilt, shame, and a masochistic need for punishment are important aspects of long-term alcoholism. Hence exhortations, threats, and predictions of dire consequences are seldom effective and often prove counterproductive in the formation of a therapeutic alliance. At some level, every alcoholic realizes that alcohol is ruining his life; he need not be told this but rather helped to acknowledge it. The need is for ego support, not super-ego reinforcement.

Having already experienced the frequent pain of failure, the alcoholic responds positively to praise by the therapist. Praise stimulates and reinforces the continued growth and development of the patient.

Beyond Reality Therapy: Three Considerations

Based on ten years' experience of treating the adolescent chemical casualty and in addition to the seven components of Reality Therapy, I believe there are three important considerations:

First: My preferred choice of treatment with adolescent chemical casualties is group psychotherapy. The group can exert pressure for the individual to become more responsible. A sense of productive and positive competition exists whereby one member who has made substantial progress can challenge another: "I did it, so can you." Peers can become quasi-therapists and enforce the norms of the group. Peers focus on the presenting problem of a participant, attack and ridicule with much hostility, and then find an appropriate solution. Lieberman, Lakin, and Whitaker (1968) believe that "group feedback contributes quite directly to the therapeutic goal of helping each person to recognize and accept responsibility for the interpersonal consequences of his behavior." Often the participant can observe the self-destructive and irresponsible aspects of another's behavior, and subsequently recognize the similarity of the dynamics.

Members are encouraged to continue their associations outside the formal confines of group psychotherapy. The only stipulation is that they share with the group the significant incidents. In this sense, the formalized group becomes a "caring community" whereby each participant knows he can rely on others. This is, of course, an extension of the Alcoholics Anonymous principle of sponsorship. An experienced member of A.A., who has completed the first eleven steps, is assigned to sponsor a neophyte member. The new member is nourished back to sobriety and responsibility by the "twelfth step worker," which reinforces the growth and development of both. By helping another, he simultaneously helps himself. In the more unstructured and casual social setting, the adolescent learns more about himself and others, while simultaneously learning to relate without any dependency or abuse of chemicals. The caring community becomes an extension of the therapist and can be viewed as an additional resource. Rather than to create a prolonged dependency on me, it seems therapeutically indicated to encourage peers to depend on each other. A hierarchical order grows up in each group when the most responsible and productive members become role models and are sought out for their advice. This "earned" status has a reinforcing impact on the further amelioration of the "failure identity."

It is important to realize, furthermore, that patients find it difficult to identify with me, the therapist, because not only a significant age differential exists, but also, being a professional, I have not experienced what the alcoholic has. In fact, I have never used or abused any chemical—i.e., alcohol, nicotine, medication, etc. The perception of a group participant who has a similar experience to the one he is trying to help, therefore, has more credence than the therapist's.

Second: An effective supplement to group psychotherapy would be a concurrent referral, at the earliest opportunity, to Alcoholics Anonymous. (Either the therapist or a group member should accompany the referral to his first few A.A. meetings.) A.A. helps the patient to control his drinking. An integral part of the self-help group's meeting is devoted to assisting the alcoholic abstain from drinking. These meetings are focused on self-discipline and self-control. A.A.'s philosophy, therefore, reinforces the principles of Reality Therapy. A.A., for example, views alcoholism as an illness. Its interpretation of sickness supports the notion that the individual is powerless to control his consumption of alcohol. Anonymous (1961) writes that "we [members of A.A.] are perfectly willing to admit that we are allergic to alcohol and that it is simply common sense to stay away from the source of our allergy." The alcoholic must become abstinent if he wishes to be a responsible and productive human being. The Twelve Steps of A.A., according to Bill W. (1957), a co-founder of A.A. in 1935, suggest that the alcoholic can surmount his problem by means of self-appraisal, disclosure, and responsible behavioral change. Much of A.A.'s success originates from the premise that an alcoholic can help himself by attempting to help another who has similar life experiences.

An anonymous (1965) patient who combined both psychotherapy with A.A. dramatically reported "every gain I made in AA was reflected in my therapy, and every progress I made in therapy helped deepen and strengthened my understanding and appreciation of AA." Curlee (1971b) writes, furthermore, that "any gains he [the patient] can make in relying upon other individuals rather than upon the bottle can be used to strengthen his alliance with the therapist. Similarly, his work with his therapist may help him utilize his AA socialization more fully, especially by focusing upon harmful attitudes and behaviors that may be interfering with his relationship with other AA members."

Hurvitz, discussing peer self-help psychotherapy groups, believes that more people have been helped by this intervention than by all types of professionally trained psychotherapists combined. The basis for Hurvitz' (1970) enthusiasm is that:

Peers are active in their relationships with each other, they focus on the presenting problem and assume that by following the principles and methods of their movement they will help each member solve his specific problem and thereby cause intrapsychic changes and enhanced self-attitudes. They may ridicule and attack each other with great hostility and they may provoke aggressive and hostile feelings; however, peers regard such attacks and provocations as others' expressions of concern and care. Peers assume that the followship experience will be transferred into the member's everyday life—of which fellowship is an important part. Peers attempt to find substitute satisfactions for inappropriate behavior and may regard such substitutes as effective change devices.

A.A. fellowship encourages interpersonal dependency and comaraderie.

Third: I have found it propitious to add another dimension to the therapeutic alliance. I believe that the therapist must be prepared to become an advocate for his patient. Many times I have found it necessary to pressure aggressively for special considerations—i.e., re-admission to high school, admission to college, job placement, a suspended or reduced sentence, etc. The advocate must be prepared to assume a variety of roles to help the adolescent to receive preferential treatment: negotiator, intervener, expeditor, consultant, broker, supporter, and/or representative. At times, the advocate must assume a combative stance—even at the expense of an adversary. There are waiting lists, admissions requirements, job specifications, etc. The advocate, I believe, must maintain a loyalty to his patients and be willing to act accordingly even if it entails jeopardizing his professional relationship. It is unrealistic for the therapist to permit the patient to represent himself against impersonal, inimical, and powerful institutions. What becomes important for the patient is that he recognizes that he is worthwhile and that someone cares for him. By becoming an advocate, the therapist can serve as a role model to show the patient how he can assert himself in productive, gratifying, and responsible ways.

Conclusion: A Beginning Not an End

The more traditional methods of psychotherapy have proven to be less than effective in either the "habilitation" or "rehabilitation" of the alcoholic. The literature is replete with high rates of recidivism, of failure. Many professionals dread the possibility of working with a chemical casualty because they believe there is no "hope." I modestly hope that this presentation may cause some of you to reconsider the pessimistic prognosis and others to continue your work. To be sure, there are no guarantees of success. There are many heartaches but there are the rewards of seeing a significant number reclaim their lives from chemicals and move beyond the restricting wall of alcoholism and addiction.

My work with adolescent chemical casualties has prompted me to abandon the more traditional "professional" role of the therapist who struggles to remain objective, aloof, detached, uninvolved, neutral, benign, etc. This involvement has infuriated my supervisors who write that "he must learn when too much involvement with a client is no longer healthy." Notwithstanding that criticism, I submit that in order to facilitate meaningful behavioral and attitudinal change the therapist must be willing to become PERSONALLY INVOLVED WITH THE ALCOHOLIC. To some degree, then, the therapist, will be affected by either progress and/or regression of the patient whom he is trying to assist to help himself.

Reality Therapy, I believe, offers this promise to adolescent alcoholics because it:

1. views the alcoholic as being in control of his behavior even though he currently is irresponsible and self-destructive;
2. assists the patient to evaluate his behavior;
3. suggests the planning of responsible and productive behavior alternatives to chemical dependency, and
4. helps the patient attain these goals.

Mowrer (1972) is right: "ACT RIGHT, FEEL RIGHT!"

REFERENCES

American Medical Association, *Manual on Alcoholism*. R. J. Shearer (ed.), Chicago: American Medical Association, 1968.

Anonymous, *"This is Alcoholics Anonymous,"* New York: A.A. World Service, Inc. 1961, p. 9.

Anonymous, "My Psychiatrist, AA, and Me," *AA Grapevine*, 22:3 (August 1965), p. 39.

Bill W., *Alcoholics Anonymous Comes of Age*. New York: Harper & Brothers, 1957.

Robert R. Carkhuff & Bernard G. Berenson, *Beyond Counseling and Therapy*. New York: Holt, Rinehart and Winston, Inc., 1967, p. 171.

The Cooperative Commission on the Study of Alcoholism, *Alcohol Problems: A Report to the Nation*. London: Oxford University Press, 1967, p. 39.

Joan Curlee, "Attitudes that Facilitate or Hinder the Treatment of Alcoholism," *Psychotherapy: Theory, Research, and Practice*, 8:1 (Spring 1971a), p. 69.

Joan Curlee, "Combined Use of Alcoholics Anonymous and Outpatient Psychotherapy," *Bulletin of the Menninger Clinic*, 35:5 (September 1971b), p. 370.

Department of Health, Education and Welfare Task Force, *First Special Report to the U.S. Congress on Alcohol and Health*. Washington, D.C.: U.S. Government Printing Office, 1971, p. viii.

Martha Clayton Eaton, "Experiencing Behavioral Change," *Psychotherapy: Theory, Research and Practice*, 8:3 (Fall 1971), p. 202.

Albert Ellis, "Should Some People Be Labelled Mentally Ill?" *Journal of Consulting Psychology,* 31:5 (1967), p. 445.

Hans J. Eysenck, "Learning Theory and Behavior Therapy," in Hans J. Eysenck (ed.), *Behaviour Therapy and the Neuroses.* New York: Pergamon Press, 1960, p. 62.

Hans J. Eysenck, "The Effects of Psychotherapy: An Evaluation," *Journal of Consulting Psychology,* 16 (1952), pp. 319–324.

Richard P. Fox, Marie B. Graham, & Michael J. Gill, "A Therapeutic Revolving Door," *Archives of General Psychiatry,* 26:2 (February, 1972), p. 181.

Ruth Fox, "A Multidisciplinary Approach to the Treatment of Alcoholism," *Journal of Drug Issues,* 2:2 (Spring 1972), p. 20.

Jerome D. Frank, "The Role of Hope in Psychotherapy," *International Journal of Psychiatry,* 5:5 (May 1968), p. 383.

Herbert J. Freudenberger, "New Psychotherapy Approaches with Teenagers in a New World," *Psychotherapy: Theory, Research and Practice,* 8:1 (Spring 1971), p. 43.

Harry H. Garner, "A Review of Confrontation in Psychotherapy from Hypnosis to the Problem-Solving Technique," in Milton M. Berger (ed.) *Videotape Techniques in Psychiatric Training and Treatment.* New York: Brunner/Mazel, Inc., 1970a, p. 14.

Harry H. Garner, *Psychotherapy: Confrontation Problem-Solving Technique.* St. Louis: Warren H. Green, Inc., 1970b, p. 4.

William Glasser, *The Identity Society.* New York: Harper & Row, 1972.

William Glasser, *Schools without Failure.* New York: Harper & Row, 1969, p. 24.

William Glasser, *Reality Therapy: A New Approach to Psychiatry.* New York: Harper & Row, 1965.

William Glasser & Norman Iverson, *Reality Therapy in Large Group Counseling: A Manual of Procedure and Practice.* Los Angeles: The Reality Press (no date), p. 27.

William Glasser, "Reality Therapy: A Realistic Approach to the Young Offender," speech to the British Columbia Correctional Association. Vancouver, Canada. November 3, 1962, p. 8.

William Glasser, *Mental Health or Mental Illness? Psychiatry for Practical Action.* New York: Harper & Row, 1960, pp. 94–95.

Nathan Hurvitz, "Peer Self-Help Psychotherapy Groups and Their Implications for Psychotherapy," *Psychotherapy: Theory, Research and Practice,* 7:1 (Spring 1970), p. 48.

Morton A. Lieberman, Martin Lakin, & Dorothy Stock Whitaker, "The Group as a Unique Context for Therapy," *Psychotherapy: Theory, Research and Practice,* 5:1 (Winter 1968), p. 33.

Willard A. Mainord, "A Therapy," in Mink, Becker, Zaslaw (eds.), *Applications of Reality Therapy: A Book of Readings.* (mimeographed) 1967, p. 45.

Judd Marmor, "Dynamic Psychotherapy and Behavior Therapy: Are They Irreconcilable?" *Archives of General Psychiatry,* 24 (1971), pp. 22–23.

Joseph Mayer & David J. Myerson, "Outpatient Treatment of Alcoholics; Effects of Status, Stability and Nature of Treatment, *Quarterly Journal of Studies on Alcohol,* 32:3 (September 1971), p. 626.

O. Hobart Mowrer, "Integrity Groups: Principles and Procedures," *The Counseling Psychologist,* 3:2 (1972), p. 21.

National Conference of Commissioners on Uniform State Laws, "Uniform Alcoholism and Intoxification Treatment Act," in Department of Health, Education and Welfare Task Force (ed.), *First Special Report to the U.S. Congress on Alcohol and Health,* Washington, D.C.: U.S. Government Printing Office, 1971, p. 106.

Martin T. Orne, "On the Nature of Effective Hope," *International Journal of Psychiatry,* 5:5 (May 1968), p. 404.

Richard R. Parlour, Philip Z. Cole, Robert B. Van Vorst, "Treatment Teams and Written Contracts as Tools for Behavior Rehabilitation, *The Discoverer,* 4:1 (February 1967).

Thomas F. A. Plaut, "Some Major Issues in Developing Community Services for Persons with Drinking Problems," in the President's Commission on Law Enforcement and Administration of Justice (ed.), *Task Force Report: Drunkenness.* Washington, D.C.: U.S. Government Printing Office, 1967, p. 122.

Carl R. Rogers, "The Necessary and Sufficient Conditions of Personality Change," *Journal of Consulting Psychology,* 21 (1957), pp. 95–103.

Hans H. Strupp, R. E. Fox, and K. Lessler, *Patients View Their Psychotherapists.* Baltimore: Johns Hopkins Press, 1969, p. 117.

Clifford H. Swensen, "Commitment and the Personality of the Successful Therapist," *Psychotherapy: Theory, Research and Practice,* 8:1 (Spring 1971), p. 34.

Patience Thomas & Betty Ezell, "The Contract as a Counseling Technique," *The Personnel and Guidance Journal,* 51:1 (September, 1972).

Charles B. Truax, "Effective Ingredients in Psychotherapy: An Approach to Unravelling the Patient-Therapist Interaction," *Journal of Counseling Psychology,* 10 (1963), pp. 256–263.

John C. Whitehorn & B. Betz, "A Study of Psychotherapeutic Relationships Between Physicians and Schizophrenic Patients," *American Journal of Psychiatry,* 3, (1954), pp. 321–331.

Joseph Wolpe, *Psychotherapy by Reciprocal Inhibition.* Stanford: Stanford University Press, 1958, p. ix.

RICHARD L. RACHIN

Helping People Help Themselves

The realities of mental-health operations, said Anthony Graziano two years ago, "seldom match the idealism with which they are described in the rhetoric."

Our professional rhetoric is powerfully reinforcing when it enables us to obscure our own doubts and to disguise our own shortcomings. We seldom actually do what we say we are really doing. Sustained by their own deception, individual clinicians believe they are performing noble functions in essentially bureaucratic, unsympathetic, and doubtfully effective agencies.[1]

Graziano was not saying anything new. This same message has been delivered, with increasing volume, since the early fifties. Only recently, however, have the efficacy and ethical underpinning of classical treatment procedures been openly attacked. Today it seems almost fashionable to expose, if not castigate, psychoanalysts for defects of character and purpose—faults which they have always shared with the rest of us.

While psychotherapy, particularly of the psychoanalytic type, has never proven to be more effective or dependable than less pretentious kinds of help, orthodox practitioners tend to be as defensive as shamans in examining this incongruity. With certain notable exceptions, there is a remarkable absence of discussion

Former title "Reality Therapy: Helping People Help Themselves." From *Crime and Delinquency,* January 1974. Reprinted by permission of the National Council on Crime and Delinquency.

among psychotherapists concerning the efficacy of their treatment techniques in spite of the paucity of evidence mustered to support the belief that psychotherapy is more effective than other treatment procedures.

The influence of mental health practitioners is largely responsible for acceptance of the view that socially disapproved behavior is evidence of emotional illness. Too often the label becomes a self-fulfilling prophecy building impenetrable barriers between *them* (those labeled) and the rest of us.

People in trouble, whether they are patients in mental institutions, drug dependents, or kids who play truant, often are not in a position where they can choose to be treated or not be treated. Public agencies armed with clinical evaluations make the choice for them. The recipient of such public largesse and his family have had little to say about rejecting or terminating treatment, even when the service seems to endanger his health and well-being.[2] Explanations designed to justify these practices are patronizing and lack the evidence that would support continuing them.

Ponder Graziano's theme that American mental health practitioners seem more concerned about improving their status and enhancing their power base than they are about treating. Clinical services have not been freely available to persons needing such care—especially in correction, where both the quality and the quantity of clinical personnel have left something to be desired. Considering juvenile correction alone, the President's Crime Commission reported that, of the 21,000 persons employed during 1965 in 220 state-operated juvenile facilities, only 1,154 were treatment staff. While the accepted national standard requires one psychiatrist for every 150 juvenile inmates, the actual ratio in American institutions for children was 1:910. Forty-six psychiatrists (over half of them concentrated in five states) were then listed as the treatment backbone of juvenile correction.[3] As Donald Cressey observed, "The trap is this: We subscribe to a theory of rehabilitation that can be implemented only by highly educated, 'professionally trained' persons, and then scream that there are not enough of these persons to man our correctional agencies and institutions."[4]

Dissatisfaction with the Medical Model

The following are some of the reasons for the accelerating development of alternatives to traditional, medically based approaches to helping troubled people:

1. "The recidivism rate for offenders," writes Seymour Halleck, "remains depressingly high and the number of psychiatrists interested in treating the delinquent remains shamefully low."[5] Publicity given to crime and the problems of our criminal justice system has not led to any significant increase in the number of clinicians devoting themselves to correction.

2. Even if there were enough conventionally prepared clinicians available, it is doubtful that government would be able or willing to assume the cost of the employment. Psychiatric attention is expensive and psychiatry's patients in the correctional system have never been high on the list of public priorities.

3. Important class, cultural, and racial barriers between those treating and those being treated have hindered the development of rapport and effective treatment programs. This problem has been magnified by our dependence on institutional care and the location of most of the institutions in rural areas, where staff recruitment beyond the surrounding communities (when attempted) is usually unsuccessful. Generally, in a state with a relatively large urban population, few of the staff—but, conversely, a disproportionately large part of the inmate population—are members of city-dwelling minority groups.

4. Research has not demonstrated that people receiving conventional treatment are any better off than those not receiving treatment. While this may be disturbing to advocates of the status quo, it is well to recall Jerome Frank's words: "Comparison of the effects of psychotherapy and placebos on a group of psychiatric outpatients suggests certain symptoms may be relieved equally well by both forms of treatment and raises the possibility that one of the features accounting for some of the success of all forms of psychotherapy is their ability to arouse the patient's expectation of help."[6] We are witnessing an accelerating growth of more humane, socially accountable therapies in which people with problems de-

pend on other people with similar problems for help. The influence that human beings have on one another has long been noted, but has not been applied in practice.

Although middle-class values and standards provide no valid measure for assessing mental health or mental illness, this yardstick has been customarily employed to measure deviance and the need for correctional care, especially in juvenile courts. Fortunately, simple economics has forced a re-examination of the traditional treatment orthodoxy. We have finally come to question the concept of mental illness as behavior that deviates from an established norm and its concept of cure as intervention by professionally trained mental health practitioners.

There should be little argument about the pervasive long-term ineffectiveness of most "treatment" programs. Although poorly trained staff, crumbling and inadequate physical plants, skimpy budgets, and overcrowding contribute to their futility, it is doubtful that unlimited resources alone would make it possible to rehabilitate significantly more offenders. Many private child-care agencies with budgets and per capita costs several times those of their public counterparts have discovered this when they become involved with court-referred children—even though they have been highly selective when deciding which court-committed children they will accept. A major reason for the poor results may be that many of the ways in which most well-adjusted adults once behaved are now viewed as symptomatic of underlying pathology. Two important circumstances are usually overlooked: (1) usually behavior brought to the attention of the courts and other official agencies is disproportionately that of poor and minority group children; (2) as George Vold observed, "in a delinquency area, delinquency is the normal response of the normal individual. . . . The nondelinquent is really the 'problem case,' the nonconformist whose behavior needs to be accounted for."[7]

The imprimatur of the court clinician is usually sufficient to dispose of children whose true feelings and needs are probably better known to their peers than to anyone coming into contact with the child for the first time. As Martin Silver found, "The detection of a 'proclivity to bad behavior' is facilitated by the court's 'treatment' process." Silver goes on to quote Dick Gregory: "Being black is not needing a psychiatrist to tell you what's bugging you."

Offenders who have proved to be poor candidates for traditional treatment approaches in many cases seem responsive to peer group "here and now" therapies. As Carl Rogers expressed it, "It makes me realize what incredible potential for helping resides in the ordinary untrained person, if only he feels the freedom to use it."[8] The medical model for understanding and treating essentially psychosocial, ethical, or legal deviations makes it, as Szasz suggests, "logically absurd to expect that it will help solve problems whose very existence has been defined and established on nonmedical grounds."[9]

Nevertheless, when available in correction and more than just in name, diagnostic and treatment services essentially remain cast from the same orthodox mold. Vested interests and ignorance combine to apply a method of treatment that even Freud himself was to disavow in later life. Ironically, proposals made to improve treatment services are usually accompanied by pleas for more psychiatrists, clinical psychologists, and psychiatric social workers. The influence which mental health practitioners have had on the design and delivery of treatment services seems accounted for not by any greater success in helping people but by seemingly convincing arguments disparaging alternative approaches. Put to the test, conventional treatment practices based upon the mental health/mental illness model have been as unsuccessful with offender groups as they often have been unavailable. Operating in the penumbra of the clinician and frequently in awe of him, legislators and correctional administrators have clung tenaciously to procedures about which they understand little and feel the need to understand less. And this problem has not been restricted to correction.

The development of less costly, more effective, and readily attainable treatment alternatives can be traced to three conditions: first, a quest for involvement, understanding, and clear communication by significant numbers of people—a need which could hardly be met by the small coterie of conventional mental health practitioners; second, voluntary patients' dissatisfaction with the time and expense required for treatment; and third, a crescendo of criticism directed by practitioners and researchers at a treatment methodology that has never been validated.[10]

William Glasser shared this concern. Near the completion of his psychiatric training he began to doubt much of what he had been taught. "Only a very few questioned the basic tenets of conventional psychiatry. One of these few was my last teacher, Dr. G. L. Harrington. When I hesitatingly expressed my own concern, he reached across the desk, shook my hand and said 'join the club.' "[11]

Reality Therapy

Glasser's theories departed radically from classical procedures. He postulated that, regardless of the symptom—be it drug use, fear of heights, suspicion that others may be plotting against one, or whatever—the problem could be traced in all instances to an inability to fulfill two basic needs:

Psychiatry must be concerned with two basic psychological needs: *the need to love and be loved and the need to feel that we are worthwhile to ourselves and to others.*[12]

Glasser believed that the severity of the symptom reflected the degree to which the person was failing to meet these needs. No matter how bizarre or irrational the behavior seems to be, it always has meaning to the person: a rather ineffective but nevertheless necessary attempt to satisfy these basic needs.

Regardless of behavior, people who are not meeting their needs refuse to acknowledge the reality of the world in which they live. This becomes more apparent with each successive failure to gain relatedness and respect. Reality Therapy mobilizes its efforts toward helping a person accept reality and aims to help him meet his needs within its confines.

We fulfill our needs by being involved with other people. Involvement, of course, means a great deal more than simply being with other people. It is a reciprocal relationship of care and concern. Most people usually experience this relationship with parents, spouses, close friends, or others. When there is no involvement with at least one other human being, reality begins to be denied and the ability to meet one's needs suffers accordingly.

Glasser points out that advice given to a person who needs help is of little value. People who deny the reality of the world around them cannot be expected to respond to exhortations to do better or to behave. Involvement means having a relationship with another person who can both model and mirror reality. The Reality Therapist presumes that people who are experiencing difficulty in living are having difficulty meeting their needs within the confines of the "real world." To help someone adopt a more successful life style, the Reality Therapist must first become involved with him. Involvement is the Reality Therapist's expression of genuine care and concern. It is the key to his success in influencing behavior. Involvement does not come easily. The therapist must be patient and determined not to reject the person because of aberrance or misbehavior.

Reality Therapy and Traditional Therapy Compared

Reality Therapy rejects the classical system whereby problem-ridden people are viewed as mentally ill and their behavior is labeled according to a complex and extensive classification scheme. Instead of the terms "mental health" and "mental illness," Reality Therapy refers to behavior as "responsible" or "irresponsible." The extensive, ambiguous, and unreliable diagnostic scheme on which conventional practitioners depend is discarded. As diagnostician the Reality Therapist simply determines whether the person is meeting his needs in a manner that does not interfere with others meeting theirs. If he is, he is acting responsibly; if he isn't, he is acting irresponsibly.

Conventional procedures lead the patient back through a maze of old experiences in search of the origin of his problem, because, the analyst assumes, the patient will be unable to deal with the present until he understands how the problem began in the elusive link in the past. Reality Therapy concentrates on the present, on the "here and now" rather than the "there and then." Nothing can change the past, no matter how sad or unfortunate it may have been. The past does not influence present behavior any more than the person permits it to. The focus of the Reality Therapist, therefore, is on present behavior, about which something can be done.

Conventional therapy emphasizes the process during which the patient relives significant occurrences in his past and projects his past wishes, thoughts, and feelings onto the therapist; through interpretation of these past events the therapist helps the patient understand his present inadequate behavior. In contrast, Reality Therapy rejects the need for insight into one's past; the Reality Therapist relates to the person as he is and does not relive the past. The conventional practitioner seeks to uncover unconscious conflicts and motivations and to help the patient gain insight into these mental processes; he de-emphasizes conscious problems while helping the patient understand his unconscious through dreams, free associations, and analysis of the transference. The Reality Therapist insists that the person examine his conscious self and behavior; conceding that efforts to understand motivation or other complex mental processes may be interesting, he doubts that the results merit the time spent to obtain them: it has yet to be demonstrated, he argues, that these pursuits have anything to do with helping the person.

Conventional practice makes no ethical judgments and frees the patient of moral responsibility for his actions; it views the patient as being under the influence of a psychic illness which makes him incapable of controlling his behavior. In Reality Therapy the patient is forced to face the consequences of his behavior: Was it right or wrong? What were the results for him?

Finally, the conventionally schooled practitioner insists that his role remain inexplicit, almost ambiguous, to the patient; he does not take an active part in helping him find a more productive way to live. Although the Reality Therapist does not take over for the person, he helps him—even teaches him when necessary—to learn better ways to meet his needs.

Fourteen Steps

The Reality Therapist follows certain steps in attaining involvement and influencing responsible, realistic behavior. Responsibility, the basic concept of Reality Therapy, is defined simply as the
ability to meet one's needs without depriving others of the ability
to meet theirs. Realistic behavior occurs when one considers and
compares the immediate and remote consequences of his actions.

Step 1: *Personalizes.*—The Reality Therapist becomes emotionally involved. He carefully models responsibility and does not
practice something other than he preaches. He is a warm, tough,
interested, and sensitive human being who genuinely gives a damn
—and demonstrates it.

Step 2: *Reveals Self.*—He has frailties as well as strengths and
does not need to project an image of omniscience or omnipotence.
If he is asked personal questions he sees nothing wrong with responding.

Step 3: *Concentrates on the "Here and Now."*—He is concerned only with behavior that can be tested by reality. The only
problems or issues that can be confronted are those occurring in
the present. Permitting the person to dwell on the past is a waste of
time. He does not allow the person to use the unfavorable past as a
justification of irresponsible action in the present.

Step 4: *Emphasizes Behavior.*—Unlike attitudes or motives, behavior can be observed. The Reality Therapist is not interested in
uncovering underlying motivations or drives; rather, he concentrates on helping the person act in a manner that will help him
meet his needs responsibly. Although the person may be convinced
that new behavior will not attain responsible ends, the Reality
Therapist insists that he try.

Step 5: *Rarely Asks Why.*—He is concerned with helping the
person understand what he is doing, what he has accomplished,
what he is learning from his behavior, and whether he could do
better than he is doing now. Asking the person the reasons for his
actions implies that they make a difference. The Reality Therapist

takes a posture that irresponsible behavior is just that, regardless of the reasons. He is not interested in time-consuming and often counterproductive explanations for self-defeating behavior. Rather, he conveys to the person that more responsible behavior will be expected.

Step 6: *Helps the Person Evaluate His Behavior*.—He is persistent in guiding the person to explore his actions for signs of irresponsible, unrealistic behavior. He does not permit the person to deny the importance of difficult things he would like to do. He repeatedly asks the person what his current behavior is accomplishing and whether it is meeting his needs.

Step 7: *Helps Him Develop a Better Plan for Future Behavior*. —By questioning *what* the person is doing now and *what* he can do differently, he conveys his belief in the person's ability to behave responsibly. If the person cannot develop his own plan for future action, the Reality Therapist will help him develop one. Once the plan is worked out, a contract is drawn up and signed by the person and the Reality Therapist. It is a minimum plan for behaving differently in matters in which the person admits he has acted irresponsibly. If the contract is broken, a new one is designed and agreed upon. If a contract is honored, a new one with tasks more closely attuned to the person's ability is designed. Plans are made for the contract to be reviewed periodically.

Step 8: *Rejects Excuses*.—He does not encourage searching for reasons to justify irresponsible behavior: to do so would support a belief that the person has acceptable reasons for not doing what he had agreed was within his capabilities. Excuses do not improve a situation; they do not help a person to see the need for an honest, scrutinizing examination of his behavior. Excuses only delay improvement.

Step 9: *Offers No Tears of Sympathy*.—Sympathy does little more than convey the therapist's lack of confidence in the person's ability to act more responsibly. The Reality Therapist does not become inveigled into listening to long sad stories about a person's past. The past cannot justify present irresponsible behavior. The therapist has a relationship with the person which is based upon genuine care and concern; sympathizing with a person's misery or inability to act in a more productive and need-fulfilling manner will do nothing to improve his ability to lead a responsible life. The therapist must convey to the person that he cares enough about him that, if need be, he will try to force him to act more responsibly.

Step 10: *Praises and Approves Responsible Behavior.*—People need recognition and esteem for their positive accomplishments. However, the Reality Therapist should not become unduly excited about a person's success in grappling with problems that he previously avoided or handled poorly. But just as a person's irresponsible behavior is recognized when he is asked what he plans to do about it, so should his responsible behavior be recognized.

Step 11: *Believes People Are Capable of Changing Their Behavior.*—Positive expectations do much to enhance the chances of a person's adopting a more productive lifestyle regardless of how many times he may have failed in the past. Negative expectations, on the other hand, serve to undermine progress. It is easier to do things well when others are encouraging and optimistic.

Step 12: *Tries to Work in Groups.*—People are most responsive to the influence and pressure of their peers. It is much easier to express oneself with a group of peers than it is to relate to a therapist alone. People are also more likely to be open and honest with a peer group. Problems one often imagines are unique are quickly discovered by group members to be similar to the difficulties others also are encountering. Group involvement itself is immediate and helpful grist for observation and discussion. Learning experiences derived from interaction in treatment groups carry over to personal group encounters.

Step 13: *Does Not Give Up.*—The Reality Therapist rejects the idea that anyone is unable to learn how to live a more productive and responsible life. There are instances when a person may be unwilling to do anything about his life, but this does not mean that, given another opportunity, he will not work to change it. Failure need not be documented in a detailed case record. Case records too often become little more than repetitive and largely subjective harbingers of failure. Sometimes professionals seem more involved with records than with the people the records pretend to describe.

The Reality Therapist does not let historical material interfere with his becoming involved with people or prevent him from beginning afresh.

Step 14: *Does Not Label People.*—He does not believe that elaborate diagnostic rituals aid involvement or help the person. Behavior is simply described as responsible or irresponsible. The therapist does not classify people as sick, disturbed, or emotionally disabled.

The principles of Reality Therapy are common sense interwoven with a firm belief in the dignity of man and his ability to improve his lot. Its value is twofold: it is a means by which people can help one another, and it is a treatment technique, applicable regardless of symptomatology. It is simple to learn albeit somewhat difficult for the novice to practice. Experience, not extensive theoretical grooming, is the key to accomplishment.

Correctional clients who have proven least amenable to conventional treatment methods respond well to Reality Therapy. That its employment involves only a fraction of the time as well as the cost required by traditional (and not more effective) psychoanalytically oriented treatment modalities only further underscores its value. Until research can demonstrate its relative effectiveness and permanence, these reasons alone make its utilization well worth a try.

REFERENCES

1. Anthony M. Graziano, "Stimulus/Response: In the Mental-Health Industry, Illness Is Our Most Important Product," *Psychology Today,* January 1972, p. 17.

2. Frontal lobotomy, electric shock, and insulin therapy to relieve anxiety were far from being the most humane procedures. See Percival Bailey, "The Great Psychiatric Revolution," *American Journal of Psychiatry,* Vol. 113, 1965, pp. 387–406. Those who have complete confidence in the new wonder drugs should see Richard Elman's "All the Thorazine You Can Drink at Bellevue," *New York,* Nov. 22, 1971, pp. 40–46; also, *New York Times,* July 15, 1972, p. 7.

3. President's Commission on Law Enforcement and Administration of Justice, *Task Force Report: Corrections* (Washington, D.C.: Government Printing Office, 1967), p. 145.

4. Donald R. Cressey, remarks on "The Division of Correctional Labor," *Manpower and Training for Corrections,* Proceedings of an Arden House Conference, June 24–26, 1964, p. 56.

5. Seymour L. Halleck, "The Criminal's Problem with Psychiatry," *Morality and Mental Health,* O. Hobart Mowrer et al., eds. (Chicago: Rand McNally, 1967), p. 86.

6. Jerome D. Frank, *Persuasion and Healing* (New York: Schocken Books, 1964), p. 74.

7. Lovell Bixby and Lloyd W. McCorkle, "Discussion of Guided Group Interaction and Correctional Work," *American Sociological Review,* August 1951, p. 460.

8. Carl Rogers, *Carl Rogers on Encounter Groups* (New York: Harper & Row, 1970), p. 58.

9. Thomas S. Szasz, "The Myth of Mental Illness," *American Psychologist,* Vol. 15, 1960.

10. Eysenck quotes D. H. Malan, the Senior Hospital Medical Officer at London's Tavistock Clinic, the locus of orthodox psychoanalysis in England: "There is not the slightest indication from the published figures that psychotherapy has any value at all."

11. William Glasser, *Reality Therapy: A New Approach to Psychiatry* (New York: Harper & Row, 1965), p. xxiii.

12. *Ibid.,* p. 9.

RICHARD R. RAUBOLT
THOMAS E. BRATTER

Treating the Methadone Addict

Introduction

Methadone maintenance treatment, since the research of Dole and Nyswander (1965), has been accepted uncritically by the medical profession, the courts, and most of the concerned public as the answer to addiction. The reason is simple. Proponents have succeeded in creating a false dichotomy which treats physical dependence separate from anti-social behavior (violence, manipulation, irresponsibility, etc.).

Methadone has been termed "successful" in treating addiction since it reduces heroin usage.[1,2] Any concurrent behavioral difficulties such as excessive drinking, theft, abuse of non-narcotic drugs, or pushing are excused as failures of the rehabilitation program, not the medication. It is our contention that this treatment separation plays neatly into the hands of the manipulative, unmotivated, addiction-prone personality.

With methadone, addiction is considered a metabolic disorder requiring medication indefinitely; the symptoms (heroin craving) can be arrested but not eliminated. The addict becomes a patient. He suffers from a sickness over which he has no control and must remain under medical supervision and chemical care. He becomes dependent, passive, and weak. Expectations of success are limited to employment and a reduced criminal record. Functioning within

Former title "Treating the Methadone Addict: A Confrontation Counseling and Reality Therapy Model." From *Journal of Drug Education* Vol. 4 (1) Spring, 1974, © 1974, Baywood Publishing Co.

the established social boundaries becomes the goal with growth and development unmentioned and unexpected. Responsibility, self-reliance, maturity of feeling and action, and actualization of potential are foreign terms. The addict is considered to have a drug problem exclusively. Such feelings as self-respect and self-confidence are not emphasized in methadone maintenance treatment.

Even more disconcerting is the implicit message in substituting dependencies (methadone is highly addictive). The addict is told, in essence, that no more is required of him than his attendance. It is not surprising, then, with his psychological and social difficulties unresolved that the acting out continues. A negative self-fulfilling prophecy results. Multiple drug use (barbiturates, cocaine), urine substitution (when urines are analyzed for drug content), selling and numerous program memberships are all excused by the addict. After all he is on a methadone program and he is sick, so nothing more should be expected.

The City Island Experience

The City Island Center is a 65-patient private methadone program located in the northeastern section of the Bronx, New York. The drug addict seeking treatment there is usually white, male, single, unemployed, and undereducated. He most often carries with him a lifetime of failures: academic (truancy, numerous failed courses, inability to read, high school drop-out), social (few heterosexual relationships, limited number of "straight" friends), economic (criminal record, unemployed, unskilled, unmotivated, welfare recipient).

A poor concept of self results, and drugs are used to erase the failure and fear. He remains infantile, unmotivated, and hostile. He follows the hedonistic pattern of instantaneous gratification and avoidance of responsibility. He is impatient, demanding, and self-destructive, seeking good feelings at any cost. As Van Kaam has written, "He increasingly craves some situation which will grant him an experience of meaning and fulfillment without effort, pain, or labor; a situation which will redeem him from unbearable boredom and anxiety, a situation no matter the social, moral or personal consequences."[3] Having no faith in his abilities or his environment he continues to remain manipulative and aloof. The threat of violence is used to fulfill his desires and to keep possible friends at a distance. He fears extended social contact and personal vulnerability. This means expectations and demands which he feels inadequate to meet. He is unsatisfied with his lifestyle because securing drugs is more difficult and the quality is poor. Yet, he feels powerless to change. Methadone comes to represent the painless way out. He no longer has to "hustle" for drugs. However, he feels with proper manipulation he can still obtain his "high." The pressures of the police, family, and courts are now reduced, since he is taking a socially sanctioned chemical.

The addict initially comes to us in this unique position; seeking limited help (further drugs) on his own terms with someone else's money (family, welfare).

Treatment

In order to alter this pattern of anti-social and self-destructive behavior the City Island Center has begun implementing a confrontation model stressing accountability and responsible behavior. This treatment draws from the works of Glasser (1965) and Bratter (1972) which consists of four phases: (1) establishing the relationship, (2) inducing a therapeutic crisis, (3) restructuring behavior, (4) drawing up behavioral contracts.

Establishing the Relationship: The addict is initially mistrustful of authority, demanding, and abusive. The therapist, if he is to gain entrance into this world of the addict, must first gain trust and acceptance. A sense of openness, honesty, and sincerity must be established to neutralize the hostility and manipulation. This is best achieved by self disclosure on the part of the therapist. The therapist, by revealing his beliefs, values, goals, and expectations, sets the direction and temper of the theraputic encounter. Self-disclosure further tends to ease the addict/professional barrier. The addict can see that while the therapist never used drugs he still had to grapple with many of the same "bad" feelings (i.e. pain, anxiety, frustration). This serves as a foundation for therapy providing a common experiential base.

Due to the failure of past relationships the therapist is strongly tested for corruptibility and contradictions. The therapist must consistently demonstrate his responsible concern and investment in the addict. The therapist must, as Glasser states, ". . . be a very responsible person—tough, interested, human and sensitive. He must be able to fulfill his own needs and must be willing to discuss some of his own struggles so that the patient can see that acting responsibly is possible though sometimes difficult. Neither aloof, superior nor sacrosanct, he must never imply what he does, what he stands for or what he values is unimportant. . . . Willing to admit that, like the patient, he is far from perfect, the therapist must nevertheless show that a person can act responsibly even if it takes a great effort."[4]

It is imperative, at this juncture, that the therapist act as a firm role model. He is thereby called on to set and enforce limits, giving structure through which the addict can direct himself. At our clinic we make demands such as bi-weekly group attendance, one individual counseling session monthly, a limit of two positive urine specimens per month, and no violence or threat of violence in or near the clinic. Failure to comply with such guidelines could result in immediate dismissal. The message is given that there is no excuse for irresponsibility and that self-destructive behavior will have no accomplice. The therapist by these actions further demonstrates compassion, understanding, and strength. The addict needs the reassurance that his fears and frustrations are human problems and only his chemical solutions are self-defeating and must be changed.

Inducing Therapeutic Crisis: Once the therapist perceives the addict's patterns of behavior he must set about to disrupt them. Addicts in the past have avoided any and all of the anxieties of developing maturity by escaping to chemicals. They often, despite their age, remain childlike, having failed to resolve life's three major problems: social, sexual relationships and occupational relations. By refusing to admit these failures to themselves or those with whom they associate they create an image. This image is an impression that the addict wants others to have of him. This impression represents qualities which he does not possess but wishes he did. The image most often invoked is fearless, aggressive, hostile, cunning, and confident. If he can convince others to believe this impression, it becomes true, real. This in turn works to suppress the addict's own private feelings of inadequacy, passivity, boredom, and despair. This "dope fiend" image is dangerous and constraining. Not only does he prevent others from knowing him, he actively avoids knowing himself. The addict says he did things he did not do. He says he feels things he does not feel. He also says he believes things he does not believe. He becomes dependent on the approval of others. Having no confidence in himself or his abilities he must constantly seek their reassurance and attention. This serves to increase his passivity and confusion because his behavior must always be in response to the dictates of those around him. Soon the image becomes so estranged from the real self that the consequence is self-alienation: he no longer knows who he is, what he believes, or where he is going.

As long as this image or representation of self continues unchallenged, the greater the amount of acting-out, irresponsible patterns of behavior. The image can be altered by an induced crisis created by the therapist. The addict is confronted and ridiculed. His statements are exaggerated. Finally, his behavior is attacked as immature, stupid, and irresponsible in order to emphasize the self-defeating nature of his actions. Through this process "the participant is forced to make decisions. Does he wish to become more responsible or does he want to duplicate his immature, irresponsible behavior? Does he wish to continue his dependency on drugs (including methadone) or does he want to be chemically free? Does he want to justify to others his life?"[5] The expectation is to provoke the same ugly feelings that were previously dealt with in a self-destructive manner. Then, with encouragement and support, to face these feelings and to find a more mature and self-respecting solution.

Throughout, the position is taken that each person has the capacity and freedom necessary to alter his behavior. There are certain undeniable environmental factors influencing a person's actions. A man cannot always control the conditions. He can control, however, his responses and his actions.

Dwight: Dwight had one such image; the tough guy. He was an only child of weak and permissive parents, who protected him at all costs. His only job was in his father's grocery store, where he named his hours. Not surprisingly, he was hostile, aggressive and loud. Dwight took fierce pride in his various arrests, the numerous fights he was involved in and the size of his habit. He was demanding and selfish. When denied a request (such as higher dosage) he would bellow and threaten. He was never without his knife and seldom without "shades." As his parents gave in to his demands and fellow addicts recounted his tales, he escalated his abuse. Dwight continually placed himself in the untenable position of having to out-talk even the toughest while still avoiding physical confrontation. Only when he was confronted with the human cost of his behavior and firm, unyielding limitations did he feel the necessity of reexamining his direction and his goals. It was a long arduous task requiring constant encounter and close supervision.

Restructuring Behavior: In creating the disequilibrium and dissonance necessary in the previous phase, a new set of options emerge for the individual client to assess his behavior. It is a difficult and frightening process for those who have avoided emotional discomfort for so long. The therapist must again intervene, as Glasser states, "when confronted with reality by the therapist . . . he (the client) is forced again and again to decide whether or not he wishes to take the responsible path. Reality may be painful, it may be harsh, it may be dangerous. This process involves assessing with the client his continued growth and development in all areas: social, sexual, educational, vocational and physical."[6]

Two major therapeutic tasks are involved with this component:

1. The therapist is often called upon to clarify, teach, demonstrate, or model various available behavioral patterns open to the client.

2. The therapist must "encourage, persuade, cajole, and occasionally insist that the patient engage in some activity (such as doing something he is afraid of doing) which itself will serve as

a forceful counter-propaganda agency against the nonsense he believes."[7]

The addict assumes an active role in his own treatment for the concern is not with the "why" of his behavior but how and when he will change. He is continually asked to evaluate his behavior and to alter his self-destructiveness. The emphasis is on the present. What is he doing to become a more productive, self-reliant, authentic, and mature adult?

A person's past remains, at this stage of treatment, irrelevant. Neither the addict nor the therapist can alter the past. They can together, however, strive to change current conditions and redirect behavior. The addict changes only when his actions change. The ex-addicts have a saying for this concept: "Act as if." A person obtains good feelings about himself after behavior becomes responsible and self-respecting.

Drawing Up Behavioral Contracts: At this juncture a sense of powerlessness on the part of the addict usually prevails. Previously there was a sense of security, a pattern of behavior which prohibited growth but shielded feelings. Now with his behavior pattern disrupted he is open to experience his own worthlessness. He may experience guilt over past failures, loneliness, anxiety over his future. More frightening to him is a lack of self-recognition and of personal uniqueness. These human and potentially constructive feelings must be channeled or they will erupt in violence or apathy. The addict must begin to formulate a positive concept of self; a personal meaning for his existence if he is to grow and develop. This sense of meaning cannot merely be thought about, it must be asserted through behavior. May has written, "The cry for recognition becomes the central psychological cry: I must be able to say I am, to affirm myself in the world into which, by my capacity to assert myself, I put meaning, I create meaning. And I must do this in the face of nature's magnificent indifference to my struggles."[8] The therapist and the addict begin to formulate goals and create a plan of action whereby the addict begins to establish a sense of power and realize his personal potential.

It is desirable that once a commitment is made and plan (of

action) agreed upon that a contract be written. The contract implies accountability, which is unique to the addict. Previously most parents, doctors, teachers, and therapists had labeled the addict as sick, helpless, not responsible for his behavior. His actions were considered beyond his control. The contractual agreement alters this passivity by placing demands, expectations, and equally important, consequences on behavior as would be the case with any mature and responsible adult. The contractual agreement works best when it is written out and based on concrete sequential, progressive action (behavior). By placing the agreements in writing it guarantees clarity and commitment. Both addict and therapist are clear on what is expected of each and the consequences of failure. This written agreement also solidifies behavior and gives the client a better perspective and grasp of the situation and where he is headed.

It is based on sequential action for two major reasons:

1. By constructing small and manageable components the client is encouraged and challenged about his chances of success. Self-confidence is not at this point fully established and must, therefore, be built firmly on a solid foundation.
2. Establishing sequential contract conditions allows for the therapist to continually raise his demands and expectations furthering growth and development. The therapist, consistently demanding more, conveys a confidence in the addict's capabilities and potential. This is usually accepted by the addict as an ultimate expression of caring and involvement as opposed to the possessive demands of his parents.

Peter: Peter entered into one such behavioral contract to cease using cocaine. He could, until this time, refrain from cocaine for no longer than a six-week period. His initial contract stipulated: (1) daily attendance at the clinic for eight weeks, (2) no association with any known addicts, (3) attendance at all group therapy sessions (three times weekly). Upon fulfillment of these conditions the contract was renegotiated to its current status: (1) clinic attendance three days weekly, (2) secure and maintain full-time employment, (3) continued attendance at all group therapy sessions, (4) termination of friendship with anyone currently using drugs. Since beginning the contract system,

Peter has not used cocaine to our knowledge, is working full-time and has begun seeing a young woman who has never used drugs. He has, in addition, mentioned a desire to find his own apartment and finish high school, which will be included in his next contract. (Peter was given an ultimatum either to conform to the contract or to join another program. While his reasons for remaining may be numerous, this suggests he understood the necessity of such demands.)

Throughout this process the therapist continues to offer encouragement and support by acting in behalf of the addict. As a professional he holds influence, personal contacts, and status which may provide opportunities for his client. The therapist becomes his client's advocate, his supporter, his champion, his representative. In many respects this role is similar to the attorney who protects his client's interests and attempts to negotiate the most favorable deal, even at the expense of an adversary. Manipulation of the environment is believed to justify the means.[9]

Treatment, at this stage, is best described as a therapeutic alliance with addict and therapist working together for continued growth and responsibility. As the addict becomes more autonomous and self-sufficient he is given less direction and structure. The addict by this time should have a firm understanding of his personal needs, as well as his abilities. He must be encouraged to assert his independence by developing his own life goals and plans to obtain them. The therapist for his part offers support and acceptance but limits his intervention to clarification and advocacy. He also remains available and informed, should the addict again begin to engage in self-destructive behavior.

Summary and Results

Addiction may be considered from two distinct perspectives: (1) as a medical problem (metabolic disorder) requiring medication (methadone) on a permanent, scheduled basis to assure social functioning, or (2) as a manifestation of irresponsible, infantile, and self-destructive behavior requiring medication (methadone) on a short-term basis, while behavioral and attitudinal difficulties are outgrown.

The emphasis and position of the program is obvious. One year ago we began implementing a confrontation Reality Therapy model with significant results: twenty successfully detoxified patients (remaining drug free, employed, and no arrests to date), four in final stages of detoxification (below twenty milligrams), nine referrals to therapeutic communities (three subsequently have left, six remain drug free to the best of our information and continue to attend group meetings at the clinic), approximately forty of the current forty-eight members on the basis of urine analysis remain free from drugs other than methadone and possibly marijuana.

Methadone maintenance, as it currently exists in most of this country, remains a myth, a cruel hoax, and a fraud. If we are to treat addiction we must go far beyond merely keeping our addict population dependent, passive, and helpless. A confrontation–Reality Therapy approach offers one option. Reality Therapy, according to Glasser,[10] "is a system of ideas designed to keep those who identify with failure learn to gain a successful identity." By demanding accountability, responsibility, and self-reliance we can foster emotional and cognitive growth, in addition to a drug-free existence. We have a choice. We can either write off a sizable portion of our population (300,000 to 500,000) as hopeless or we can begin to develop this vast reservoir of potential manpower. The more appropriate question may be, can we, as a nation, afford not to meet such a challenge?

ACKNOWLEDGMENT

We wish to express our appreciation to Vernon H. Sharp, M.D., our psychiatric consultant, for his encouragement, wisdom, and constructive criticism.

REFERENCES

1. Dole, V., & Nyswander, M., "A Medical Treatment for Diacetylmorphine (Heroin) Addiction: A Clinical Trial with Methadone Hydrochloride, *Journal of the American Medical Association,* 193 (1965), pp. 646–650.

2. Dole, V., "Research on Methadone Maintenance Treatment," *The International Journal of the Addictions,* 5:4 (1970), pp. 359–363.

3. Van Kaam, A., "Addiction and Existence," *Review of Existential Psychology and Psychiatry,* VIII: 1 (Winter, 1968), p. 60.

4. Glasser, W., *Reality Therapy: A New Approach to Psychiatry.* New York: Harper & Row, 1965, p. 22.

5. Bratter, T., "The Therapist as Advocate: Treating Alienated, Unmotivated, Drug Abusing Adolescents," unpublished paper presented at the Society for Adolescent Psychiatry, Inc., New York. April 19, 1972.

6. Glasser, *op. cit.,* p. 41.

7. Ellis, A., *Reason and Emotion in Psychotherapy.* New York: Lyle Stuart, 1962, p. 94.

8. May, R., *Power and Innocence.* New York: Norton, 1972, p. 20.

9. Bratter, T. E., "Group Therapy with Affluent, Alienated, Adolescent Drug Abusers: A Reality Therapy and Confrontation Approach," *Psychotherapy: Theory, Research and Practice,* 9:4 (Winter, 1973) (in press).

10. Glasser, W. *The Identity Society.* New York: Harper & Row, 1972, p. 103.

WILLIAM A. POPPEN
ROBERT NEIL WELCH

Work with Overweight Adolescent Girls

Many attempts have been made in recent years to provide those people who are overweight with a method of reducing. These attempts have met with varying degrees of success. A significant percentage of those who are overweight are adolescents. Statistics indicate that from 31 to 45 percent of the population of girls tested could be categorized as overweight or obese (Hathaway and Sargent, 1962). Mayer (1968) points out that obesity in adolescence differs from that in adults in that it is more difficult to identify, harder to determine its severity, frequently impossible to correct, and difficult to diagnose using height-weight charts exclusively. Yet adolescence may be the most likely time to introduce weight-reducing programs because, as White (1963) points out, obese adolescents are a major source of obesity in adult life. These young people who are obese are more likely to remain obese and have more difficulty losing weight and maintaining the loss than those people who became obese as adults (United States Department of Health, Education, and Welfare, 1966).

Attempts have been made to work with overweight adolescents. The use of Reality Therapy group counseling could provide some additional help in getting the individuals involved to make some changes in dietary or exercise patterns. In fact, because obese adolescents have strong and unfulfilled needs to be viewed as worthwhile by themselves and others, Reality Therapy should be particularly effective as a weight-loss program for them. Emphasis in the group weight-loss program would be one promoting role before goal as advocated by Glasser (1972).

The counselor, using Reality Therapy in the group, can promote the type of involvement between himself and the group members needed to help the overweight adolescents view themselves as more worthwhile. After the basic ingredient of Reality Therapy, involvement, has been developed the counselor can begin to have the group members evaluate their appearance, diet, and exercise habits.

During the phase of the Reality Therapy the counselor would be extremely interested in knowing and having each group member know what she is doing or not doing to promote obesity. Questions asked of each group member are, "How can this behavior help you?" and "Do you feel that what you are doing is right?" In other words, a value judgment of behavior in terms of helpful or unhelpful was made by each group member.

The group can also be used by the counselor to help each of the overweight members determine specific action plans for her weight reduction. A fourth step in the Reality Therapy would be for the group members to "contract" to do homework to help themselves lose weight. Specific commitments would be encouraged from group members who are interested in weight reduction. At each meeting the group would review the results of the action plans. Consistent with the tenets of Reality Therapy unsuccessful group members would not be excused or punished but rather would be recycled through the steps of making a value judgment, determining a plan, and contracting to enact the plan. As group members report successes to the group about their weight loss they are fulfilling another of the basic needs proposed by Reality Therapy, that is, the need for achievement or self-worth.

Overweight adolescents appear to differ significantly in self-concept from persons of normal weight. Obese girls express feelings of worthlessness and lack of importance within the family. These same girls indicated that they felt society saw them as having emotional problems, while the girls assured each other that they had good, healthy personalities. Overeating by the obese persons can lead to feelings and actions such as self-hatred, guilt, withdrawal, and fantasy (Bruch, 1952). Felker (1966) found that boys with heavier builds had lower self-concepts than boys with either balanced or linear builds. Washburn (1962) studied the relationship between physique, self-concept, and family tension. The findings of this study were that family tension and body build might have an effect on self-concept. Changes in self-concept have been produced over relatively short periods of time. Cole et al. (1969) found that extremely high self-concepts were lowered and extremely low self-concepts were raised in a group of adolescent delinquent girls exposed to a ten-week socialization program. Three measures of self-concept were used in a six-week program involving children referred to a mental health clinic because of emotional disorders (Johnson et al., 1968). Significant changes occurred in self-ideal discrepancy in the four areas measured.

Reality Therapy in groups seems especially well suited for working with adolescents. It provides a high level of involvement with a commitment to a counselor and to a group of peers. It also provides an active approach to a problem that might have originally resulted from inactivity. The peer support so necessary at this age is available to those who participate. For these reasons it seems particularly well suited for obese adolescents who need to learn which behaviors to change, how to make the changes, and that encouragement is available for successfully changing. The study of using Reality Therapy with overweight adolescent girls is designed to answer the following null hypothesis: (a) there is no significant difference in weight loss between the treatment group conditions and the control group conditions, (b) there is no significant difference in self-concept change between the treatment group conditions and the control group conditions.

Procedure

The subjects were sixteen overweight adolescent girls who volunteered to participate in a weight-loss counseling program using Reality Therapy. There were eight subjects from each of two high schools who were categorized as overweight using Falkner's (1962) physical growth standards. Subjects were judged as overweight if they were 10 percent or more over the 50th percentile for girls for that height and age. The eight subjects from school I had an average weight of 185.5 pounds with a range of 126 to 266 pounds, while the eight subjects from school II had an average weight of 155 pounds with a range of 139 to 182 pounds. The average age of the entire group was 16.1 years with a range of 15.5 to 17.9.

The treatment conditions were randomly assigned to the groups. The group from school I (Group I) was selected to be given the treatment first while the group from school II (Group II) was selected to serve as the control during the first treatment period.

The counselor was a doctoral student in the Health, Physical Education, and Recreation School of the University of Tennessee. He was trained in counseling based on Reality Therapy (Glasser, 1965). Each counselee was interviewed to give the counselor an opportunity to know the girls and to find out what they were doing at that time to lose weight. The success of their present efforts was evaluated. In the group session the girls were asked to make suggestions on possible methods of losing weight. Each suggestion was examined by the group in terms of its effectiveness in helping the girls lose weight. Each girl then developed a weight-loss program that she felt she was able to do and was willing to follow through. Each program was examined by the counselor to assure that it was not too stringent and yet had the potential to produce the desired goal. Such an approach is consistent with Glasser's Reality Therapy in that small but consistent successes are suggested rather than overly ambitious programs. At the next meeting each girl told what she had done and how well she had managed to carry through on her commitment. Praise was given to those who had been able to do what they said they would do and new plans were developed for those who were unsuccessful. Each counselee would then examine her program for the next week to determine if she wished to make any changes. The girls were encouraged to help each other to clarify their ideas or to state their goals in such a way that they could know when they had achieved what they had set out to accomplish. The experimenter, also trained in Reality

Therapy, sat in on each session to verify that this method of counseling was actually being used.

All subjects were weighed to the nearest pound on a set of standard bathroom scales which was checked for reliability before each measurement. A modification of Bills Index of Adjustment and Values (Bills et al., 1951; Comeaux, 1969) was used as a measure of self-concept. In addition, a sentence completion self-concept instrument by Irvine (1967) was used to measure the same attribute.

Group I met with the counselor and the program was explained to them. The purpose was given to the subjects as helping them to lose weight by developing "action plans" that would cause weight reduction. Each subject was asked what she was presently doing to lose weight and to what degree she had been successful with that approach. The counselor then went through the procedure described earlier in this paper. While the girls were developing their programs, the counselor was trying to help them by discouraging crash diets or elimination of foods from their diets that are necessary for good health. A combination of caloric reduction through diet control and caloric expenditure through exercise were the most frequently used "action plans." The girls worked together in both types of efforts whenever possible. The next five sessions proceeded with much the same format. At the end of six weeks the subjects in Group I were weighed and given the self-concept measures.

On the same day Group II was also weighed and given the self-concept measures. The six-week counseling program was administered to this group in the same manner that it had been given to Group I. At the end of this six-week period the subjects from both groups were again weighed and the self-concept measures were administered.

Analysis of Data

The difference in the first weights (pretest) and the second weights (retest) for each group was analyzed using analysis of covariance. During the first treatment period Group I served as the treatment group and Group II served as the control. The main difference between the groups from pretest to retest was significant at the .01 level of confidence.

A Wilcoxon Sign Test was used to determine the significance of weight loss in Group II from retest to posttest. The results showed that the weight loss at posttest was significant at the .05 level of confidence. The overall results indicate that counseling was effective in producing significant weight loss in Group I in the first treatment period and in Group II in the second treatment period. Both groups gained weight during the phases of the study in which they were not in counseling.

The second variable was examined using the two self-concept measures previously mentioned. The differences between the pretest and retest scores of Group I and the difference between the retest and posttest scores of Group II were separately analyzed. There were no significant differences in self-concept scores in either group from pretest to posttest on either of the instruments used.

Discussions and Conclusions

The results indicate that a group counseling approach based on Reality Therapy (Glasser, 1965) can be effective in producing weight loss in overweight girls. While weight loss was obtained, no changes in self-concept were detected. Perhaps self-concept change among obese adolescent females requires a longer time period than that used for this study. The results do suggest an interesting pattern of changes among weight-reducing adolescent females. It appears that behavioral changes and weight loss precede attitudinal or self-concept changes. This result does not support the argument of so many therapies for the overweight which suggest attitudes must be changed before weight loss can occur. Those who serve as counselors in weight-loss programs must do additional research into weight loss and how to lose weight safely. More specifically, research might be done to clarify the relationship between behavioral change, weight loss, and self-concept changes. The Reality

Therapy process would appear to be a viable means of helping persons with an overweight problem learn how to deal more efficiently with that problem. Of course, all persons who participate in a weight-loss program should first be examined by a physician and some determination made by him as to the person's ability to lose weight safely.

The implications of this study seem to be that a school counselor can use Reality Therapy to deal with a broad range of student problems. When the counselor shows an interest in a student who does not see himself as worthwhile, and helps the student learn how to achieve self-worth, positive results are obtained. When looked at in this manner, counseling the overweight appears to be similar to counseling many other students who might come to the school counselor for different kinds of problems.

REFERENCES

Bills, R. E., Vance, E. L. & McLean, O. W. An index of adjustment and values, *Journal of Consulting Psychology,* 1951, *15,* 250–261.

Bruch, H. Psychological aspects of reducing. *Psychosomatic Medicine,* 1952, *14,* 337–346.

Cole, C. W., Oetting, E. R. & Miskimins, R. W. Self-concept therapy for adolescent females. *Journal of Abnormal Psychology,* 1969, *74,* 642, 645.

Comeaux, C. R. Intensity of group interaction as a factor in change in self-concept and dogmatism. Unpublished doctoral dissertation, University of Arizona, 1969.

Falkner, F. Some physical growth standards for white North American children. *Pediatrics,* 1962, *29,* 470–474.

Felker, D. W. Relationship between self-concept, body build, and perception of father's interest in sports in boys, *The Research Quarterly,* 1968, *39,* 513–517.

Glasser, W. *Reality Therapy.* New York: Harper & Row, 1965.

Glasser, W. *The Identity Society.* New York: Harper & Row, 1972.

Hathaway, M. D. & Sargent, D. W. Overweight in children. *Journal of the American Dietetic Association,* 1962, *40,* 511–515.

Irvine, R. S. Sentence-completion responses and scholastic success or failure. *Journal of Counseling Psychology,* 1967, *14,* 269, 271.

Johnson, W. R., Fretz, B. R. & Johnson, J. A. Changes in self-concepts during a physical development program. *The Research Quarterly,* 1968, *39,* 560–565.

Mayer, J. *Overweight: Causes, Cost and Control.* Englewood Cliffs, N.J.: Prentice-Hall, Inc., 1968.

United States Department of Health, Education, and Welfare, Public

Health Service, Division of Chronic Diseases, Heart Disease Control Program. *Obesity and Health: A Source Book of Current Information for Professional Health Personnel*. Washington, D.C.: Government Printing Office, 1966.

Washburn, W. C. The effects of physique and intrafamily tension on self-concept in adolescent males. *Journal of Consulting Psychology*, 1962, *26*, 460–466.

White, P. L. The nutritionist. *Journal of American Medical Association*. 1963, *186* (6), 34, 37.

Practical Psychotherapy G.P.s Can Use

Reality Therapy began for me during my last year of psychiatric residency with a small, unhappy boy named Aaron.

Aaron was an intelligent 11-year-old who lived with his divorced, emotionally remote mother. He was my first child outpatient and the most obnoxious child I ever met. I used to dread the days that started with Aaron. He ran pell-mell from game to game and from toy to toy; he cried and whined for attention but turned nasty and withdrawn when it was offered; he pictured his mother as a rejecting ogre and boasted about the destructive things he did and was planning to do at home. He would run away, hide, and try to make me look for him all over the clinic. He made a point of never telling me anything of what he was thinking and feeling. If he did tell me something inadvertently, he would stop talking and run, scream, or talk gibberish.

Aaron had been treated before by two therapists with play therapy and general permissiveness. No matter how he behaved, no one had placed a value judgment on his behavior, lest that hamper rapport. Everything he did was interpreted in psychiatric terms and attempts at "understanding" his "anal retention and oral aggression." I set out, at first, to give him more of the same. But after some time, I noticed that Aaron was well aware of his behavior, even to the extent of purposely devising new tests for my patience; it must have been exhausting for him to keep up his misconduct as long as he did. With this, I dimly realized that I was contributing

Former title "Reality Therapy—Practical Psychotherapy G.P.s Can Use." From *Consultant,* October, 1967. © 1967, Cliggott Publishing Co.

to Aaron's present desperation rather than relieving it. Against all my training and reading, and without telling anyone what I planned to do, I made up my mind to change my approach. From that day on, I was through explaining Aaron's behavior in terms of the past; instead, I was going to concentrate on somehow improving his behavior. When Aaron arrived the next time, I led him past the playroom to my office where I informed him that we were finished playing games: we would sit, talk, or walk in adult fashion . . . I would not tolerate any further rudeness or running away . . . he would be cooperative when we talked together . . . he was to tell me everything he did and I would help him decide whether it was right or wrong.

Predictably, Aaron tried to run away right after this speech. I forcibly restrained him. He tried to hit me and I told him that if he did I would hit him back. I then told him that he was the most miserable and obnoxious child I ever met. He seemed greatly surprised. Apparently, he had come to believe that all therapists automatically love their patients. I said that if he were going to stay in therapy he would have to change, because neither I nor anyone else could possibly care for him the way he was now.

Apparently, the suddenness of my new approach shocked him out of further resistance. What happened in the next few visits was astonishing. He became courteous and likable, and I even began to look forward to seeing him. In six weeks, his schoolwork rose to straight A's and his behavior there improved so much that it puzzled his teachers. He got along better with his mother and began to play well with other children; for the first time in his life, children sought his company. About three months later he was discharged from the clinic. Six months after that, at his last follow-up, he was still doing well.

Aaron benefited greatly from therapy and so did I. For I learned that it sometimes pays to break with traditional methods, and I decided to develop a new approach for psychotherapy. Since then I have used this new approach on many hundreds of patients and still find it highly effective. It is called Reality Therapy. I believe it can be used successfully against many forms of emotional or mental illness.

What Is Reality Therapy?

This kind of therapy differs radically from that generally practiced today. It tries to teach patients how to fulfill their basic psychological needs: the needs for love and self-respect. Reality Therapy does this by helping patients to do what is realistic, what is responsible, and what is right.

What Is Realistic?

Most patients with psychiatric problems have one common characteristic: they deny some aspect of the reality of the world around them. Some break the law, denying the likelihood of capture and punishment; some claim their neighbors plot against them, denying the improbability of such behavior and denying lack of evidence. Whether a patient's denial is partial (as in neurotics) or total (as in the chronic "back ward" patient in a mental hospital), some denial of reality lurks in all. Such denial, I hold, seeds and feeds the disorder; therapy, if it is to succeed, must make the patient give up denying reality. It must help him behave responsibly.

Who Is Responsible?

The responsible person fulfills his needs in a way that does not deprive others of theirs. An irresponsible person does what he feels like, what is most convenient, and what is most profitable to himself. He gains no one's respect and in time brings down suffering on himself and others.

I believe that not all emotionally ill people act irresponsibly because they are ill; many are ill because they are acting irresponsibly. This is especially true of patients suffering from psychopathic disorders. It is not true of patients suffering from organic brain disease. Reality Therapy differs greatly from conventional therapy, which claims that mental illness is due not to irresponsibility but to lack of insight. I have found that years of analytic rumination often improve the patient's daily life less (and, after all, it is this improvement the patient seeks when he comes to a physician) than a few weeks' work on personal responsibility.

Why Do Right?

To be and feel worthwhile, every person needs to maintain a satisfactory standard of behavior. To do this, he must learn to evaluate his own behavior realistically and to correct it when it falls below standard. Here, too, the basis of Reality Therapy differs from the basis of conventional psychiatry and psychology—which tend to assume that neurosis arises because the patient's moral standards have been *too high* and he has been *too good*. Conventional psychiatry usually aims to soften a too severe conscience (superego) and *free* the person from inhibitions that impede self-gratification. Reality Therapy assumes something different: *that humans get into emotional binds not because their standards are too high, but because their performance is too low.* Reality Therapy aims not to lower the standards but to increase accomplishments. Freudian theory holds that emotional illness is caused by cultural blocking of biological needs. I believe that emotional illness, in many cases, results from failure or incapacity at the interpersonal or social level. This seems to me an optimistic, hopeful belief, for Reality Therapy implies that the patient himself—not his murky past—controls and can improve his behavior.

How to Practice Reality Therapy

Although the principles of Reality Therapy are essentially simple, they are not always easy to apply. They generally work fastest on patients who are confined in hospitals and other institutions—where the therapist can, by withholding privileges, force the patient to improve his behavior. In dealing with private patients, the therapist can only persuade and this always takes longer. Nonetheless, Reality Therapy can be used successfully for most kinds of mental, emotional, and psychosomatic disorders. If you ever use psychotherapy or counseling on your patients with psychosomatic illness or obvious emotional problems, you may wish to try it this way to see if you can be more helpful.

Take a Personal Approach

Patients with emotional problems need someone who will be warm and personal with them . . . someone who takes the time to talk and who is not afraid of using the pronouns *I* and *me* . . . someone who says "It is important to me that you tell me what is on your mind because *I* wish to help you" . . . someone who perhaps can reveal a little of himself . . . someone not professionally aloof who is willing to get emotionally involved with the patient. To help a person with emotional problems, the doctor should not be cold and professional; he should be humanly warm and close.

Deal Only with the Present

When dealing with a patient you have known for years, you may know very precisely the historical roots of his problem. Nevertheless, ignore them. And do not probe the past. No matter how much the past may have contributed to his problems, the past will never solve them. He must learn to make better choices *now*. He must examine his behavior honestly and think how he can improve it. This approach clearly implies that the patient *can* solve his problems and automatically builds confidence and self-respect. Raking up the past, I believe, often serves to undermine the patient and overwhelm the doctor because the past combined with current problems may be just too much to handle. The main question should be "What are you doing?", not "Why are you doing that?" All the reasons in the world, for example, why an alcoholic drinks will not lead him to stop.

Concentrate on Behavior, Not Feelings

This is very important and, again, is quite different from the conventional approach. When we downplay the patient's feelings, he begins to realize that his behavior is the major problem—*that his feelings stem from his behavior.* If he is going to feel better (and this is what he wants most), he must learn to change his behavior. Actually, we have no way to change a patient's feelings anyhow. If we ask him too often how he feels, he either lies and says he feels fine or admits he feels badly which, in turn, allows him only a sense of helplessness, and eventually disappoints us. When the patient with emotional problems comes in complaining, do not ask him, "How do you feel?" Ask, "What did you do today?" Asking about behavior can lead to progress; asking about feelings leads to a dead end.

Next, Help the Patient to Evaluate His Own Behavior

Once the patient can discuss his behavior with you honestly, ask him to evaluate it. If he believes his behavior is unsatisfactory, he needs to admit it to you. *Avoid making this evaluation for him.* Unless the behavior is clearly dangerous or illegal, never tell him he is doing something bad; let him decide this for himself. If you usurp his decision, the patient loses responsibility for his behavior and therapy stops. But if he accepts responsibility for his behavior, he can move toward correcting it.

If the patient admits that something is wrong with his behavior, get a commitment toward improving it. For example, if your patient is a man who finally admits that he drinks too much and ought to stop, get him to do something constructive about it. That should be specific, carefully planned, and realistic. For example, he can say that for two days he will not drink and will go to work. Make sure the patient commits himself at first to a small action— one that he can accept easily and likely can succeed at. Success at small commitments builds confidence and helps him to make and succeed at larger ones.

Then, don't be disappointed if the patient fails. Perhaps he committed himself excessively, perhaps he didn't understand and perhaps he was not ready. Just get another commitment again—perhaps an even smaller one—but keep getting it until the patient begins to succeed.

Never Excuse Failure

Do not scold, punish, threaten or reject but ask him whether he did what he promised. Remind the patient, for example, that he was going to work for two days, that he wasn't going to drink, that he was going to pay more attention at home, or whatever. Did he do it or didn't he do it? If he didn't do it, then you ask for another commitment, perhaps for only a few hours. If he did do it, increase the commitment. But *never* let the patient feel that you excuse him for not keeping his promise to himself. Don't reject, don't punish, don't scold . . . just don't excuse. This is the kind of discipline that forces patients to change.

I have seen this realistic approach to therapy bring improvement in all kinds of disturbed patients—fat girls who needed to eat less rather than understand why they overate . . . delinquent adolescent girls who were in trouble because they had been acting irresponsibly . . . psychotic men who were immobilized by their disregard for reality. I know, it's true that psychiatric disorders are extremely complex and have no one simple cure such as Reality Therapy. I am convinced, though, after applying this kind of therapy, and after hearing of other doctors' results with it, that it holds great promise. I highly recommend it as a practical approach for treating mental and emotional illness.

Education

Education: Introduction

Reality Therapy was born at the West Los Angeles Veterans Administration Psychiatric Hospital where Dr. Glasser developed the theory and practice in collaboration with Dr. G. L. Harrington, the psychiatrist in charge of Building 206. Reality Therapy then moved into work with delinquents at the Ventura School. After several years of work with delinquent girls and offenders of all varieties, Dr. Glasser came to the conclusion that the cutting edge for preventive work was within the school system. In 1969 he published the result of his deliberations in *Schools Without Failure,* in which he applied the concepts of Reality Therapy to contemporary education. He described the inadequacies of current educational procedures and proposed a program aimed to reduce school failure and thereby help children find involvement, a sense of self-esteem, and a positive identity.

Dr. Glasser has not been content to compose a text and wash his hands of any further responsibility. He has been a tireless lecturer displaying an uncanny ability to hold an audience enthralled by the force of his argument, his stories and anecdotes, his wit and wisdom. He has assisted in the preparation of about fifty films and videotapes which are distributed to all parts of the United States. His Educator Training Center, which is affiliated with La Verne College, has had over 100,000 teachers actively involved in studying and working to make their schools a better educational experience for students. The theses of *Schools Without Failure* are favored topics of discussion in colleges of education throughout the country.

Why is it, Glasser asks, that so many children who have had obvious advantages—good homes, economic security, and doting parents and grandparents—are responding to these benefits with failure in school, the use of drugs, general unhappiness, an unwillingness to work for reasonable goals? His explanation revolves around the concept of *role* versus *goal*. Until 1952 or so, he argues, we lived in what most people perceived as a survival society in which people were prepared to sacrifice immediate pleasure and gratification for the sake of long-range goals. We were prepared to suffer discomfort and even personal indignity for the sake of the future. The basic postulates of the Protestant Ethic, i.e., that people should work hard, be honest and responsible, were accepted without question except, perhaps, by a handful of philosophers and eccentrics.

But, after the termination of World War II at least the people of one-third of the world, on the crest of a wave of affluence, engaged in a basic revision of their philosophy. Those reared in the sunshine of security began to demand a role, a positive identity, as a basic birthright.

Schools, however, have traditionally been slow-moving agencies, invariably years behind in their thinking, and have failed to respond adequately to the new American student.

"It is a paradox that parents who have taken great pains in raising children born since 1940, with a hope that they would be the best-adjusted and most motivated generation ever, often have so little to show for their efforts. The main reason that this hope has not been realized is that the parents do not understand the shift of needs from goal to role. Many of them did an excellent job raising their children for a society that no longer exists. About half our children are having difficulties either in finding a successful role or if they find one, then in finding a goal to work for that supports their role. Unable to find success and handicapped by parents who push him toward goals, the child fails. He fails in school and turns to drugs and sex." Thus does Glasser summarize an important concept for clarification of the current school dilemma.

Mark Twain was once asked the burning question of the day: "What can be done about the submarine menace?"

Twain thought for a moment, scratched his head, and responded, "I have the solution. Boil the ocean!"

"But how do we boil the ocean?" the reporters demanded.

"Gentlemen," Twain responded, "you wanted a solution for a difficult problem. I gave you a solution. Now it's up to you to work out the details."

Glasser goes farther than Twain. He goes beyond a mere theoretical formulation of a solution to the educational problems of America. He presents a specific blueprint and then goes into the battleground to demonstrate how the job should be done.

Glasser suggests that education today is failure oriented to an unconscionable degree. He notes that in seeking identity, a personal role, many students find this recognition by withdrawal or delinquency. As an antidote, Dr. Glasser provides a catalogue of specific ideas for reaching these negatively oriented children. Among his most important innovations is the use of class meetings to develop thinking, social responsibility and a sense of self-worth. The effective use of class meetings makes it possible to solve most problems within the class, so that outside help is rarely needed.

Although Glasser's *Schools Without Failure* stresses elementary education, the thrust of his thinking is toward education as a whole, and his ideas are applicable from kindergarten to graduate school.

In "A New Look at Discipline" Glasser helps teachers cope with the most difficult classroom problem, discipline. He proposes ten steps to dispose of most situations involving unruly pupils. He does not shrink from recommending that in some cases it may be necessary to remove the most difficult kids from the school, and in extreme cases sent to juvenile hall. While he does not ignore feelings, he emphasizes behavior through a series of responses designed to incorporate success experiences.

My paper "The Therapeutic Community Teaching Concept" describes a procedure employed in a college classroom as part of a design to make the university a relevant, interesting, and meaningful experience. The curriculum of this particular course requires that students become acquainted with a variety of treatment methodologies (with emphasis on Reality Therapy, of course!). The class is designed to provide both a didactic and experiential engagement. A token economy is introduced so that students may learn first hand how it feels to be under the pressure of a favored behavior-modification ploy. Reality Therapy is learned by having the students engage in role-playing sessions invariably more interesting than listening to even the most scintillating lecturer. Many students emerge from this class with a comment that it was one of their best educational experiences at the university.

Glasser's paper "Roles, Goals and Failure" summarizes in his usual clear fashion many of the ideas that are explained in greater detail in *Schools Without Failure* and *The Identity Society.*

The paper by Bernice Grunwald is another example of good ideas springing independently out of a number of sources. Her suggestions for achieving positive behavioral change in the school system are a valuable supplement to basic Reality Therapy principles.

Two highly creative and dedicated educators, Donald J. O'Donnell and Keith Maxwell, are the authors of an exciting paper which originally appeared in *The Instructor,* a mass-circulation teacher's magazine. The authors tackle the problem of introducing the principles of Reality Therapy, based on helping students meet their psychological needs for love and self-esteem, without detracting from a school's academic responsibilities. They come to the remarkable conclusion that there is no choice. Today we cannot obtain a reasonable level of academic accomplishment without "treating children right"—recognizing each child as a significant person and acting kindly toward him. Of particular interest are the case histories and application of the idea of cross-grade tutoring. It might be noted that the Ventura School in Palo Alto, the subject of the O'Donnell-Maxwell paper, has been recorded in action by means of a sensitively photographed film titled "School Without Failure."

Sometimes a journalist captures the essence of a concept with more acuity than the best academician. The article by John Pennington describes the application of Reality Therapy principles to the O'Keefe High School in Atlanta. One might be critical in that there appears to be an overemphasis on discussions of highly personal material and Dr. Glasser would probably suggest the exercise of extreme caution before moving into these areas, as a general rule. (Parents have an understandable reluctance about having their kids discuss and describe their intimate home behavior before a classroom of other children.) On the other hand, it may be argued that the children profit from an open discussion of such emotionally laden material. Common sense will dictate, however, that the overall Reality Therapy program in schools does not center about a public discussion of the child's home situation.

Dr. Bratter's revised version of the basic "Three R's" is a well-rounded summation, supported by numerous references, of the concept that educational reform should emphasize responsibility, respect, and appreciation of reality. Bratter's paper is particularly useful in the area of discipline. His specific suggestions for dealing with the disruptive student are particularly valuable in these days of turmoil in the classroom.

Dr. Gary Faltico, who moved from the Counseling Center and Psychology Department of the Florida State University where he first met the editors of this volume, to the SUNY College at Purchase, describes his experience in establishing a therapeutic community based on Reality Therapy principles at a dormitory of his new school. The unexpected problems, difficulties, and solutions constitute the bulk of his paper.

The final paper in this section is an exact transcript based on a tape recording of Dr. Glasser speaking at a symposium sponsored by the Department of Human Ecology, Pediatrics and Postgraduate Medicine of the University of Kansas Medical Center. The paper is unique in that no attempt was made to correct for grammar or clarify any misunderstandings, but it manages to capture the relaxed speaking style and good humor of the originator of Reality Therapy.

A New Look at Discipline

Tommy is your discipline problem. It's now December, and despite frequent conferences with the principal, the school psychologist and Tommy's parents, nothing seems to work.

Perhaps Tommy comes from a broken home or has a physical handicap; perhaps he is an only child or the last of a large family. Likely he has barely learned to read. He may never have had a consistently good school experience. But whatever his problems, you have him in your class for a school year, and if you can't get him to cooperate, he will suffer and your life will be miserable.

Here are ten steps to follow in dealing with your behind-in-his-work, disruptive, doesn't-listen, never-on-time, always-picking-fights Tommy (or Susan). I believe if you doggedly follow them, you may help him change into someone who, though far from perfect, is enough improved to reward your efforts. No miracles will occur; this is hard, slow work. A month is probably your minimum time commitment; certainly you're not likely to see progress before that. But if the slow progress tempts you to give up, consider this question: What do you have that is better?

1. List Your No-No's

What you are doing with him now isn't working. This isn't criticism; your techniques may have worked with others. But if they haven't worked with Tommy by now, they probably aren't

From *Learning, The Magazine for Creative Teaching,* December, 1974, © 1974 by Education Today Co., Inc.

going to, so it seems only logical to change your approach. To start, sit down tonight in a quiet place and jot down the essence of what you do when Tommy upsets you. Forget the things you might have done or wanted to do. Do you talk to him? Yell at him? Threaten him? Ignore him? Have you asked him what's bothering him or how he feels? Be honest and list the pattern of the efforts you are making to help him right now.

For the next four weeks, try to refrain from doing anything you have put on tonight's list—unless it coincides with one or more of these ten steps. When you are tempted (and you will be) to return to old patterns, pull out the no-no list and ask yourself: "If they didn't work in the past, what chance do they have now?"

2. Start Fresh

Now promise yourself that tomorrow, no matter how disruptive Tommy is, you will try to act as if this is the first time he has behaved badly. Don't say, "OK, you're doing it again" or "I have had enough of that." Don't do anything that reminds him that this is repetitive behavior. On the other hand, if he does do something good, whether he's done it before or not, reinforce him: "Tommy, it's great when you sit still" or "I appreciate that." Tell him he was good, pat him on the head, give him some verbal and even physical recognition for good behavior. If you'll start fresh with him tomorrow and each day for the next month, you may be pleasantly surprised.

3. A Better Day Tomorrow

This gets harder. I want you to figure out at least one thing you can do for Tommy, to Tommy, about Tommy that can help him have a better day tomorrow. It doesn't have to be much, a little goes a long way. One thing I have seen and done that fills the prescription is to pat him on the back as soon as he comes in and say, "Good to see you, Tommy." This brief greeting can be amazingly effective. Twenty seconds of unexpected recognition can mean a lot to him. Yes, he may wonder if you've suddenly gone crazy, but he'll still appreciate the simple, warm gesture. (And it will probably make you feel better, too.)

Or maybe a note has to be run to the office. Though you never in a million years would have asked Tommy, how about trying it tomorrow? "Hey, Tommy, would you do me a favor and take this down to the office and then come right back?" Say it calmly and matter-of-factly as if he has done it many times before. He may astonish you.

Commit yourself to do this or something like it each day for the next four weeks. You are trying to give Tommy a new idea: that he has some value in your class. His only recourse for recognition for far too long has been to disrupt. You are trying to break that cycle, and these first three steps are the way to start. Continue to implement them as often as possible in the next month; they are prerequisites for the steps that follow.

The first three steps suggested changing your attitude and resolving to start fresh. The next set of steps suggests nonpunitive responses to Tommy when he breaks the rules—at least nonpunitive in the sense that they eliminate emotion-laden blaming and threatening. Keep the tone cool and crisp until Tommy gives some recognition of the rules and makes some effort to comply; at the same time, continue the effort of the earlier steps to inject some warmth and recognition into his day.

4. Quiet Correction

All too soon, you are almost certain to have a disruption. Despite some success with the first three steps, at some point, Tommy's going to mess up. I am sure that just mentioning this has you apprehensively nodding your head. Perhaps when you ask the class to line up he continues sitting at his desk, or for the hundredth time he messes with the paints and spills some on the floor. Let's say this time he busts the line to find the place he wants and starts a fight in the process. Try to act as if it is the first time he has ever done this (step two) and ask him to stop fighting and go to his place in line. If this doesn't work, then try the scenario that follows, no matter what he replies or doesn't reply.

YOU: What did you do, Tom?
TOM: What?

YOU: What did you do, Tom?

TOM: Nothing.

YOU: Please, Tom, I just asked you what you did. Tell me.

TOM: Well, this is my place in line and they won't let me in.

YOU: What did *you* do, Tom?

TOM: It's my place so I pushed my way in.

Then, with no further discussion, you take him by the hand and walk him to his correct place, and stay with him, maybe still holding his hand.

YOU: Can you walk quietly now?

TOM: What are you going to do?

YOU: I just asked if you can walk quietly now; we'd all like lunch.

TOM: OK, I'll try.

If he doesn't agree to try, don't give up; you still have six more steps.

You are trying to establish that while he must take responsibility for doing something wrong, you are willing to correct him and that, if he accepts the correction, that ends it. Also, your calm demeanor suggests confidence in him. You are not blaming, not threatening or yelling, not doing any of the things you used to do. If step four works and he goes quietly, say nothing more about the incident except to give him a little reinforcement like a pat or "I was sure you could do it."

5. Make a Plan

Unfortunately, we must anticipate that before long there may be a situation for which step four won't work. Try it first, but if it doesn't, here is the scenario for step five. Let's continue with the scuffle in line, but as you walk toward him, Tommy dashes to the playground. He was supposed to go with the class to the cafeteria and he knows he's breaking the rules. But his need for attention is so great that he cares nothing about the rules. Your job is to get him to care, so get someone to take your class—perhaps appoint a monitor—and follow him, saying quietly, "Come here Tommy, I want to talk with you." Don't chase, just walk quietly after him. When eventually you get to him:

YOU: Tom, what did you do?

TOM: I'm just swinging, I'm not hurting anybody.

YOU: Tom, where are you supposed to be?

TOM: Here; I'm not hungry anyway.

YOU: What's the rule?

TOM: I don't like that rule. Why should you have to eat if you're not hungry? Why can't I swing? There's no one here. Who'm I hurting?

YOU: Tom, was it against the rules? (Keep plugging away.)

You have to be very insistent. You are telling Tommy he broke the rules, and he is evading this issue in every possible way. Through all his evasions, you have to stick to a focus on rules. Ultimately, he will say, "Well, so what?" or he'll say nothing, which is a tacit admission that he is beginning to face the issue. Continue then:

YOU: Well, Tom, can you make a plan to follow the rules?

TOM: What do you mean? You mean go to lunch? Jeez, look how long the line is.

YOU: Are you willing to go to lunch? (Doggedly.)

TOM: What happens if I won't?

YOU: You'll have to leave the swings and take a rest. (To be explained.)

TOM: Do I have to go to the end of the whole line?

YOU: Not the whole line, just at the end of our class. After lunch, you can swing all you want.

I'm afraid I'll lose some of you here, because this takes time and, of course, it may not work. Or you'll worry that Tommy may think it's weak and silly. This early in the game, you may be right. But remember, you've admitted that what you usually do doesn't work. Besides, you're only at step five. It *may* work, and anytime something works, Tommy has experienced a success—and so have you. This is how he, how everyone, learns discipline.

6. Conference Time

In steps four and five you were warm and supportive but did not talk much. Here, you bring Tommy to the point of a conference.

Suppose you have trouble on the swings again; he won't take turns and kicks others away.

YOU: You want to use the swings, but we have rules. Can you make a plan with me so that you can get a fair turn on the swings and still give others their chance? You can't kick the others away.

TOM: Well, none of them like me; they never give me a turn. If I don't push, I never get a chance. You going to send me to the office?

YOU: No, Tom, I just want to make a plan with you. Let's try to work it out.

TOM: Heck, I don't like the swings much anyway. I like kickball but those rats never let me play.

YOU: That's funny; you used to play.

TOM: Yeah, but now they won't let me. They don't like me.

YOU: When you used to play, I heard them all yell at you to follow the rules.

TOM: Big deal. I got mad once, and now they won't let me play.

YOU: I tell you what, Tom; why don't we take some time and maybe talk this all over. You're not having too much fun and I think I can help.

Tommy may be leery at first, believing that a conference just delays his ultimate punishment. All you can do is tell him he won't be punished and that you'd like to help him work it out. You listen to his complaints, talk, joke a little, get to know him better and then try to work out a plan for him to follow the rules. Don't rehash old faults but stress that rules are important and that you have faith he can follow them. Finally you'll work out a plan either for the swings or to get him back at kickball. You may want to put it in writing; sometimes a contract helps the commitment. You are saying to Tom that *he has the power to make a good plan*. It takes time, sure, but it takes a lot out of you to yell and get excited, too.

The last four steps are a graduated series of "benching" techniques. In effect, Tommy is interfering so seriously that he has to be taken out of the game to cool off. Once again, these steps come into play only if the earlier ones have failed; rather than acting out of instinct, the teacher by now should have a rather clear idea that it's time to move to the next level of response.

7. Off to the Castle

Now you need to create a place in your room where you can separate Tommy from the class. Not a dunce's seat or a punishment corner, this is an enrichment spot whose occupants can sit comfortably but separately from the class. Get together some books, coloring materials, puzzles and quiet games, so that normally a child wouldn't mind being here for a while. Maybe you could discuss the idea in a class meeting and make a project out of it. This retreat is not only for disruptive children but is a place for others who on occasion want a quiet, separate place. However, the disrupters have priority in the "Castle" or whatever you decide to call it.

If Tommy disrupts, and you are by now sure none of the earlier steps are going to work, then say, "Look, Tom, go sit in the Castle." Don't do or say anything else. Take only a moment and send him firmly there, with no discussion. In the Castle, he can see and hear what's going on, but he is separated. Casually observe him, but pay no obvious attention to him. Don't worry if he spends several hours or most of the day there. The isolation has a way of making the normal class routines look more attractive. More important, *he has to learn that he can be nondisruptive,* and the way to learn is through experience.

Eventually, as nice as the Castle is, he'll want to rejoin the class. He may indicate his readiness by being a little restless. Don't take this necessarily as more disruption. Be ready to work out a plan.

When you believe he has settled down, ask him if he is ready to return to his regular seat and take part. If he answers yes, then in your next break go over the class rules briefly and ask him to make a plan to follow them. The plan may be as simple as "OK, I'll try" or "If you seat me over there away from Johnny, we won't hassle so much." But he has to have some sort of plan.

Try to keep these mini-confrontations as light as possible. Laughter is a magic aid to this whole procedure. If you can keep your sense of humor, he'll have much less tendency to resist. When trouble arises, try to start with a step that will work at that time, but don't be too concerned at this stage if you think it right to start with the Castle. Don't be anxious to get him back to class. Count on the fact that he probably knows best what he can and can't handle. Again, be patient. You're trying to teach him something in a month that he hasn't yet learned in five years.

8. Off to the Office

If Tommy still disrupts, despite steps one through seven, then he must be removed from class. You've put up with a lot, you've bent over backwards, but now you have had it. You can't continue to teach with a constantly disruptive child; it's not fair to you or to the other children. When that point is reached, say, "Tom, go down to the office and take a rest." You take a rest, too. You've earned it.

Your principal must help you now in setting up the office rest place. Here again, it's a comfortable spot: perhaps an old donated couch the kids can scrunch down into. Have some books around, comic magazines, perhaps some peanuts or raisins for Tom and his confreres to munch on. In short, make him comfortable in an atmosphere that shows you care and that you don't want to hurt him.

This nonpunitive atmosphere may be hard for you and your principal to accept, but look again at that list from step one; you can see he's been in the "old" office plenty, with no results. Our task is to get him to change, and new surroundings as well as new methods are necessary. So get together with your principal and perhaps the rest of the faculty to establish this new office rest place. As with the Castle, it should be open to nondisruptive children as well, though Tommy has priority.

Here is sample dialogue from the office (almost repeating step seven):

PRINCIPAL: What did you do, Tom?

TOM: Well, old Miss Green, she kicked me out of the room. She's mean! I wasn't doin' nothing.

PRINCIPAL: Well, this is what she said you did, here on this note.

TOM: Then what did you ask me for?

PRINCIPAL: Because what you say is important. Look, let's work out a plan.

TOM: Oh, God, a plan. Is that all you do around here?

PRINCIPAL: We always do it when you're here in the office.

Again, don't be punitive in act or demeanor. You, as principal, let him sit there comfortably while you get the facts. When he sees you're not about to paddle him or call his mother, he'll settle down. Once you have his story, move into the make-a-plan phase to get him back to class. If he complains about Miss Green and won't make a plan, tell him that it's his class and that, while you'll help him get along there, that's where he has to go. Let him sit there comfortably until he's ready to make a plan. Don't be concerned if he sits there a while. This whole scheme is aimed at reducing the alternatives, at getting him to realize that he really only has two choices: to be in class and behave, or to be outside and sit. Pretty soon, class will begin to look better, but he'll need some help with the plan. Help him. You're trying to convey to him that he has to follow reasonable rules, or he's out. But while he's out, you're not going to hurt him or reject him, which would let him rationalize his misconduct on the basis of his dislike for you.

9. A Tolerance Day

If he is totally out of control and can't be contained in the office rest-spot, then a parent will have to be called in to take him home. This is the first time in this trial month you've contacted his parents (and if you follow steps one through eight, it shouldn't happen too often). Now is the time to put him on a "tolerance day," if possible. This means that he comes to school in the morning and stays until you've reached step nine. You don't have to start at one, but start as far back as you can. If he's quiet in the office, hold at step eight. Perhaps you or the principal could make a graph to show him his daily progress in tolerating more of school. But if he can't be helped in school at all, then he'll have to stay home, which means either a home tutor or, if no parents are at home, going on to step ten.

10. Where There's Life There's Hope

If school can't contain him, either he stays home or some other agency in the community will have to take him. Even juvenile hall is a possibility as a last resort. Though it sounds harsh, you must remember that sometimes this will finally jolt him awake, and he'll then be ready to plan. If he is in the hall, perhaps the judge can be persuaded to try letting him come back to school on a tolerance day from there. He can return from home, hall or from any other agency if he seems ready, reentering at the lowest step possible depending on his behavior. Remember that step ten is for a very rare child, but when a child can no longer make it in school, this step must be used.

We all agree that discipline must be learned. I believe these steps outline an effective way to teach it early. The child who learns it very likely learns it for the rest of his life. As far as I'm concerned, there is no learning more valuable; steps like these should be built into every curriculum.

The Therapeutic Community Teaching Concept

The therapeutic community concept, born out of Alcoholics Anonymous, Synanon, Daytop Village, and their dozens of off-spring now operating in every major city in the USA, has been hailed, despite the absence of hardnosed evaluative data, by the internationally renowned scientist and former president of the American Psychological Association, O. Hobart Mowrer, as the outstanding development known to man for achieving positive change in people.[1] And from a less exalted source, we garner this exchange:

PLAYBOY: Is there any religion you consider superior to any other?

KURT VONNEGUT, JR.: Alcoholics Anonymous. Alcoholics Anonymous gives you an extended family that's very close to a blood brother-hood, because everyone has endured the same catastrophe. And one of the enchanting aspects of Alcoholics Anonymous is that many people join who *aren't* drunks, who pretended to be drunks because the social and spiritual benefits are so large. But they talk about real troubles, which aren't spoken about in church, as a rule. The half-way houses for people out of prisons, or for people recovering from drug habits, have the same problem: people hanging around who just want the companionship, the brotherhood or the sisterhood, who want the extended family.

PLAYBOY: Why?

VONNEGUT: It's a longing for community. This is a lonesome society that has been fragmented by the factory system. . . . People don't

Former title "The Therapeutic Community Teaching Concept in Behavioral Science Education." From *Teaching of Psychology*, Vol. 1, No. 2, Dec. 1974, © 1974, Division Two of the American Psychological Association.

live in communities permanently anymore. But they should. Communities are very comforting to human beings.[2]

The number of authorities ready to vouch that our society, and our educational system in particular, is beset by problems of failure, alienation, anomie, loneliness, is legion. Glasser explores this theme in his *Schools Without Failure*,[3] and in his more recent *The Identity Society*, he observes that we tell students: "Work hard for goals and then we will regard you," rather than, "We will get to know you first and then encourage you to work for goals."[4]

So it appears we have this situation: loneliness and anomie not only in society at large but particularly in the school system, and a possible solution—the simulated extended family, the therapeutic community. What happens when we bring the problem and solution together?

For almost a decade, since our involvement in the founding of Daytop Village, the writer has been experimenting with moving the principles and technology of the therapeutic community into the college classroom in behavioral science education. Over the years, different elements of Daytop have been added, withdrawn, revised to fit the university bed. About 1,200 students have been exposed to various styles of the marriage of the Therapeutic Community Teaching Concept (TCTC for short) to the college classroom, and the version described in brief in this paper is the 1973 model as employed in a class of fifty students enrolled in an elective five-credit course meeting two hours on Tuesday, one on Wednesday, two hours on Thursday, for a quarter session of about ten weeks. The course is numbered CRM 407: *Methods of Treatment in Corrections* at the Florida State University School of Criminology.

Method

Getting to Know You

At precisely the scheduled starting time of the class, the instructor greets the students with a cheerful "Good morning!" and waits for a response. If none is forthcoming, he repeats it until the majority of the class gets the idea that a hearty echo is the desired reaction. He speaks about sociological concepts and findings about anomie and the desperate loneliness that appears to pervade all levels of our civilization. He wonders: Would it be advisable to attempt to overcome this disorder at least in the microcosm of our classroom? If so, how can we possibly do it? A spirited discussion develops leading to a pair of icebreaker experiences: (a) the mutual interviewing procedure, and (b) the first-name group discussion.

For the *mutual interviews,* the class numbers itself aloud from 1 to 50. The odd numbers line up against one wall, and the evens face them against another. The instructor explains that to the skillful interviewer, every human being can emerge as a unique and fascinating identity. The newspaper correspondent, the writer of profiles for *The New Yorker*—these people have developed the technique of extracting elements of history and background that make their subjects interesting. Let the odd-numbered people in this class attempt to do the same with the even-numbered students as their subjects. The interviewers ought to take notes because a few of them, perhaps five in all, will be called upon to introduce their "beautiful" subjects to the class as a whole. We have fifteen minutes for this experiment. Get ready. Start! At the end of the interview period, a student is asked to call out an odd number from 1 to 49, and the student holding that number introduces his partner. The instructor writes both the name of the interviewer and the subject in large letters with colored chalk on the blackboard. The class is invited to question the interviewer and his subject for more data. After five students have been introduced, the procedure is reversed; interviewers become subjects, and more introductions are made to the entire assembled class. If there is an odd number of students in the class, the professor fills in.

The first-name group experience follows comments by the instructor along these lines: A person's first name is frequently an interesting part of his identity. What is your first name? How did you get it? Do you like it? Have you changed it? We form into groups of five students sitting in circles in all parts of the classroom, and each person in turn tells his first-name story. At the end of thirty minutes, we reassemble.

The Graduate Assistant

The graduate assistant plays a key role in the successful operation of the TCTC, and he is ceremoniously introduced at some point during the first class hour. The students are advised that the GA has been trained for his assignment, and he is prepared to counsel and advise students about any phase of this educational experience.

Goal Setting and Contract Negotiation

The class is asked: What do you want from me? What can I do for you? What do you wish to get out of this course? What do you want to learn? Go ahead, ask for what you want. It may actually be possible to provide it in this class. But you'll never know unless you assert yourself. Don't be bashful; speak your heart's desire. Etc. etc. After a long silence, some student mutters an ambiguous goal. The professor pounces on the reply with enthusiasm, rephrases the comment into a four- or five-word statement with the student's approval, and writes it on the blackboard as goal #1. Great! We surely can meet that goal—"Learn history of correctional treatment in USA." What else? Soon anywhere from ten to fifteen goals have been listed on the board. Usually, the students have not dared to venture out of the purely cognitive, intellectual frame of reference. The professor engages in a dialogue with the GA: "Do you think it's possible to reach these goals, John?"

"It won't be very difficult. They're rather conventional statements of educational aspirations. It's stuff you can get in almost any class. The students haven't really challenged the capabilities of the therapeutic community teaching approach. I believe we can do much more in this class than anybody has had the nerve to ask for thus far."

A deep hush falls on the classroom.

"What do you mean, John? Why don't you explain yourself."

John, who has been prepared for this exchange, tells about his own isolation and loneliness as an undergraduate, and his conviction at this point in the presentation of CRM 407 two years ago that he had no right to expect an exciting, joyful, relevant learning experience. But TCTC makes it possible for students to stimulate their billions of moribund brain cells into action by thinking, solving problems, getting involved with one another. He knows that most undergraduates become increasingly cynical with each school quarter, but here in CRM 407 it can be different. We can act like a big family of brothers and sisters, really interested in learning and helping one another. "You can learn and actually enjoy it!" he concludes.

At this point, a number of students who have taken a TCTC course before usually raise their hands and offer testimonials of their experience. They speak of having acquired a better self-concept, more confidence in their intellectual ability and their capacity to deal with the problems of the world of work.

As soon as a lull occurs in the dialogue between students, the professor asks: "Please tell me, is this kind of terminal behavior to be accomplished solely on the basis of some mysterious and esoteric powers possessed by John and myself? Are you expecting some kind of strange miracle to be performed here in class? What is needed to get this delicious stew boiling? Speaking bluntly, what do you imagine *you* have to do to make this class an outstandingly productive and worthwhile educational experience? Let me list on this part of the blackboard (alongside the list of goals) what you have to say."

With the help of the GA and the graduates of other TCTC classes, the provisions of a *contract* emerge:

The student must to the best of his ability:

1. *Attend classes regularly,* absenting himself only for urgent reasons.
2. *Read the prescribed assignments* in accord with curriculum schedule.
3. *Write, write, write,* at least a page a day.
4. Practice being *enthusiastic, friendly, responsibly concerned.* Practice the concept of "Act as if" even when he does not actually feel these emotions.

5. *Volunteer* for oral reports and other class activity.
6. *Cooperate* with Group Coordinator (tutor-coach) outside class-room.
7. *Participate* in group and class discussions. Ask questions.
8. *Challenge and confront* sliding brothers and sisters of this class.
9. *Wear nameplate* at all class sessions.

A formal-sounding contract has been prepared in advance with the above and other provisions organized into separately numbered paragraphs and the students are advised they can agree to any one commitment or all of them by initialing the statement. Or if they believe this contract is an infringement on their civil rights, they need not sign it at all. The assignment for the next session is to purchase texts for the course and to bring back the signed or unsigned contract. File cards are distributed for the student's name, nickname, campus address, telephone number, hometown, social security number, marital status, hobbies, special interests, professional goals. He is also asked if he wishes to volunteer to be one of the class group leaders we call *coordinators,* using Daytop terminology.

Groups: Basic Matrix of the TCTC

Prior to the next session, the instructor meets with the GA, and six volunteers are selected to act as Group Coordinators. Their names are emblazoned across the length of the blackboard before class starts, and two chairs facing each other for interviewing purposes are positioned in front of the class under the name of each coordinator.

The instructor greets the class and waits for a response. He delivers a short lecture about the importance of groups in the operation of therapeutic communities like Daytop and Synanon and explains that group composition may be determined in various ways. In this class, the instructor and GA have selected six volunteers for the Group Coordinator position, and these people will now introduce themselves in alphabetical order. They will tell who they are and the kind of group they would like to form. Listen carefully to what they have to say because each student will soon apply for admission to one of the groups. Each coordinator will be able to select no more than eight or nine students for his group.

After the group leaders have introduced themselves, students line up to be interviewed for admission. The Group Coordinator usually uses the student's signed contract and file card as the basis for admission. Students who have been reluctant to sign many provisions of the contract usually find out at this point that readiness for commitment is a prized characteristic for team membership.

The Group Coordinators usually call a meeting of their members that evening at somebody's home or in the student lounge or cafeteria. Thereafter, they meet every Thursday during the second part of the two-hour session and at least once a week on the outside for periods of one to four hours.

Nameplate

All students receive a nameplate consisting of a folded 5 × 8 card. The student's first name is printed large enough so that a professor with fading eyesight can read it across a crowded classroom without strain. The card also contains the student's second name, his hometown, and his group affiliation, A to F. The nameplate not only identifies the student but is the visible respository of the symbolic expression of the extent of his involvement in class business, as will be explained later. The inside of the folded nameplate contains a schedule of workpoints awarded for various types of class activity. The student keeps the nameplate attached to his clothes by a paperclip, and turns in the nameplate when he has earned some workpoints. He picks up his nameplate on the instructor's desk the next session. Monitoring nameplates is one of the GA's important responsibilities.

Token Economy and Grade Determination

Anxious students will be asking the instructor and badgering the GA with questions about "requirements" and grades. They are blandly assured that the grading system is as fair and objective as human ingenuity can devise, but will be explained to the class as a whole. For the time being, it is important to study the curriculum and keep up with the modest reading requirement of fifteen or so pages of text per hourly session.

The token economy, the students are told, is a fancy term for what factory workers call piece-work wages. In this class, most of the educational activity of the student is promptly rewarded with a set number of workpoints. For example, every time the student sits in class for an hourly session, he earns a workpoint. If he appears for all the weekly sessions, he obtains 5 workpoints plus one bonus point. If he maintains a 100 percent attendance record for the quarter, he is granted an extra five workpoint bonus. Whatever score he obtains in the midterm and final exam is part of his total number of workpoints. (Oh, yes, we tell the class, we are going to administer midterms, finals, group quizzes, take-home exams because research in educational methodology clearly establishes that classes with feedback opportunities achieve a higher learning level. We challenge the "humanist" student to review the literature and we promise him a five to ten point award for his oral report on his findings.)

The student in CRM 407 can earn workpoints by a wide variety of work: presenting an oral or written report on a relevant TV program or movie, listening and reporting on a campus visiting lecturer, reporting on a popular or scholarly article, reporting on a visit to AA, a therapeutic community, prison, halfway house, research center, listening to our collection of reel-to-reel tapes in the university library, attending group sessions, working up an individual or group project. Students can realize large amounts of workpoints by becoming a Group Coordinator or an assistant called an Expeditor or a Ramrod. Roleplay demonstrations pay off, too. Volunteers are reinforced with workpoints.

In short, the university grade system is employed in the TCTC as a feature of reality, not choice. It is exploited creatively to teach a basic behavior-modification technique, to intensify involvement in educational endeavors immediately, rather than waiting until intrinsic motivation takes hold. It is used as a reinforcement tool to reflect small but certain gradients of success.

Grading Schedule

The professor proposes that final grades will be determined according to the following schedule:

A—400 workpoints including a minimum grade of 80 in the final examination. (To preclude any slackening off on the part of students who may reach this total with several weeks of the course remaining. It is hard to believe the amount of student work the token economy system can generate.)

B—350 to 399 workpoints.

C—275 to 349 workpoints.

D—225 to 274 workpoints.

Workpoint Code

Visitors to the TCTC classroom are intrigued by the colorful appearance of the students' nameplates. "They look like an assembly of generals decked out in all their medals and service awards," a military observer once remarked. The effect is obtained by affixing a ¼-inch self-sticking dot to the nameplate by the GA every time the student earns workpoints, or marking the card with a different color magic marker.

Staff Meetings

The instructor, GA, Group Coordinators, and, with the passage of time, other class officers, meet for weekly one-hour sessions to discuss class problems and progress. Strategies and procedures are devised to bolster lagging students, the level of class morale is judged. Suggestions are entertained to achieve our mutually agreed upon goals.

Ombudsman

At the end of the second week, candidates for the position of Ombudsman (30 automatic workpoints) are solicited and a democratic election is held. The Ombudsman is the student representative at staff meetings and is available to hear and act on all student grievances.

Seminar

Every class session (after the first few organizational ones) starts with a ten- to fifteen-minute period called the seminar devoted to an extemporaneous reaction to some slogan, proverb, poem, philosophical item. "No man is an island . . . John Donne, 1640." is the legend placed on the blackboard at an early meeting. "What does this statement mean to you? Who was John Donne? Do you agree with it? Do you have a personal anecdote you can relate to the seminar topic?" the volunteer seminar chairman asks, makes his own contribution, and then turns the podium over to a string of student volunteers who have one to three minutes each to express their ideas.

Quiz Packets for Examinations

A highly popular workpoint activity is constructing five-item objective-type questions based on each day's reading assignment. The best of the questions are selected for the midterm and final examination. Each envelope of five questions is awarded a workpoint. If a question appears in the midterm or final exam, a bonus workpoint is granted.

Projects

Groups are encouraged to present class projects based on the curriculum reading and course content. Workpoints are liberally awarded for creative and imaginative endeavors. Puppet shows, 8-

mm color movies, roleplay demonstrations, slide-illustrated presentations have been made by group members working as a team
in TCTC classes.

Brothers and Sisters Learning Together

The seminar topics, the group sessions, "haircuts/pullups"
(verbal reminders and reprimands), staff sessions, the cheerful,
informal attitude, the Ombudsman, group attendance at plays,
movies, guest lectures, the token economy system—all these elements of the TCTC are consciously designed to create a subculture
that values mutual care and concern as a vital component of the
educational process. The instructor and GA act as role models by
repeatedly and unabashedly expressing ideas favorable to brother-
hood, the greater prospects for self-fulfillment in an atmosphere of
human regard and loving kindness within the college classroom,
*without sacrificing any worthwhile cognitive and intellectual edu-
cational standards.*

Refining and Improving the TCTC

This paper presents in the barest skeletal form some ideological
and technological suggestions for introducing the concepts of AA,
Synanon, Daytop Village into the college classroom. Much room
exists for refinement and improvement on the part of instructors
who may wish to experiment with the TCTC notion of meeting the
demands of students for a role, not a goal, for personal identity
and recognition, as central elements of their university experience.

Fortunately, almost every town in the nation now boasts an
ongoing therapeutic community which can be studied for ideas and
suggestions to improve our teaching model. Most of them welcome
visitors from the academic community, whether students or faculty, and enthusiastically share their experiences, techniques, inspi-
rations. A brainstorming session with TC residents and staff may
yield an educational bonanza. Furthermore, the literature dealing
with therapeutic community applications is growing, providing

another repository of ideas and suggestions for the creative and pioneering university educator.[5]

Feedback and Evaluation

The instructor in a TCTC class can obtain useful data (and demonstrate involvement and concern) by the regular administration of anonymous questionnaires asking the student to grade and comment on aspects of the program. It will be noted that a minuscule minority will respond to all efforts in the direction of concern and involvement with scorn and suspicion. But the great majority, our experience suggests, welcome the friendliness and warmth of the TCTC class with pleasure and gratitude. The writer's SIRS (Student Instructional Rating System) report, derived from a comprehensive instrument which is analyzed by computer to obtain measures of percent of student agreement with "1" indicating strong agreement and "5" strong disagreement, yielded the following favorable reaction to our spring quarter 1973 CRM 407 class:

Category	Items	Mean	Standard Deviation
Instructor Involvement	1–4	1.5	.71
Student Interest	5–8	1.8	.92
Student-Instructor Interaction	9–12	1.7	.85
Course Demands	13–16	3.4	1.24
Course Organization	17–20	2.0	.89

And one student scribbled (Bless his generous heart!): "This was my most valuable experience in four years of college education."

REFERENCES

1. O. Hobart Mowrer of the University of Illinois has been the leading exponent of AA, Synanon, Daytop Village and its derivatives in the academic community. The comment noted in the parapraph was made in the course of a review of Skinner's *Beyond Freedom and Dignity* in the September 1972 issue of *Contemporary Psychology,* p. 904. Mowrer's books and articles relating to the origins and value of the therapeutic community going back

more than twenty years are worthy of serious study. Here is a representative sampling:

O. Hobart Mowrer:*The Crisis in Psychology and Religion.* Princeton, N.J.: Van Nostrand, 1961.

O. Hobart Mowrer: *The New Group Therapy.* Princeton, N.J.: Van Nostrand, 1964.

O. Hobart Mowrer: "Integrity Groups: Principles and Procedures," *The Counseling Psychologist,* 1972, 3:7–33.

O. Hobart Mowrer: "Group Counseling in the Elementary School—The Professional versus Peer-Group Model," in Merle M. Ohlsen (ed.), *Counseling Children in Groups: A Forum.* New York: Holt, Rinehart & Winston, 1973.

2. "Playboy Interview: Kurt Vonnegut, Jr." *Playboy,* July, 1973 (Vol. 20, no. 7), p. 59.

3. William Glasser: *Schools Without Failure.* New York: Harper & Row, 1969.

4. William Glasser: *The Identity Society.* New York: Harper & Row, 1972.

5. Reading William Glasser's *Reality Therapy: A New Approach to Psychiatry* (New York: Haper & Row, 1965) is a good introduction to a number of the ideas and procedures described in this paper. Other items for a bibliography on the subject of AA, Synanon, Daytop Village should include:

Anonymous: *Alcoholics Anonymous.* New York: Cornwall Press, 1969.

Bassin, A.: "Daytop Village—Cure or Stopover," *Psychology Today,* December, 1968, pp. 64–70.

Cartwright, D.: "Achieving Change in People," in L. Mazelrigg: *Prison Within Society.* Garden City, N.Y.: Doubleday & Co., 1971.

Casriel, D.: *So Fair a House.* Englewood Cliffs, N.J.: Prentice-Hall, 1964.

Casriel, D.: *Daytop.* New York: Wong and Co., 1972.

Cressey, D. R.: "Changing Criminals: The Application of the Theory of Differential Association," *American Journal of Sociology,* September, 1955, pp. 116–120.

Drakeford, J. W.: *Farewell to the Lonely Crowd.* Waco, Texas: Word, 1969.

Dreikurs, R.: *Psychology in the Classroom.* New York: Harper & Row, 1957.

Hurvitz, N.: "Peer Self-Help Psychotherapy Groups and Their Implications for Psychotherapy," *Psychotherapy: Theory, Research and Practice,* 1970, 7:41–49.

Keller, O. J. and Aper, B. S.: *Halfway Houses: Community-Centered Correction and Treatment.* Lexington, Mass.: Heath, 1970.

Sugarman, B.: "The Therapeutic Community and the School," *Interchange,* 1970, 1:77–95.

Yablonsky, L.: *Synanon: The Tunnel Back.* New York: Macmillan, 1965.

Roles, Goals and Failure

Quite a few years have passed since I, as consulting psychiatrist at the Ventura School for older delinquent girls in California, first began putting together my ideas about schools and kids and education. I've set forth these ideas in some of my books, and a surprising number of teachers who have tried them out find they work. Only recently, however, did I discover the theory which explains why these methods are effective.

An interview with Marshall McLuhan in the March 1969 issue of *Playboy* seemed to suggest the answer. When asked why there is so much turmoil in high schools and colleges, McLuhan replied that today's students are searching for a *role not a goal*. By role I mean an identity, a belief in who they are which is not directly tied to what they do.

I'd like to make a small alteration in what McLuhan said and put it this way: Students are searching for an identity or a role *before* a goal. By contrast, I looked back at my own pre-World War II school days and asked myself what I was searching for in school, and I can tell you it wasn't my identity. I was looking for a way to make it through school! I was searching for answers that would give me security in the form of good grades, a diploma, and a job—not for ways to satisfy my human or role needs. That was my goal, and that's the way it was for most people then.

The schools said, "You do what we tell you to do when we tell

From *Today's Education,* October, 1971. Reprinted by permission of *Today's Education* and Dr. William Glasser © 1971.

you to do it, and if you don't, you fail." The serious, hard-working student did, of course, get his diploma (the goal) and also some recognition (his role), but *the goal came first*. That is the way it was then and generally is now. Schools still say that the goal, the task, and what we teach must take precedence; the student must subordinate himself and what he feels—his role and identity—to the job we say has to be done.

Today, in an era of affluence and the promised easy life of the fantasy world of television, young people no longer accept this traditional sequence. Students want their roles to precede—if only briefly—what they believe they should or must do. They say, "We want a little pat on the head, a little recognition as a person before we start the job and we want this to continue as we work." But after kindergarten, schools continue to demand that the work come first: "We'll recognize you as a person only *after* you do our job."

It's this idea which I believe causes the trouble and the lack of motivation plaguing so many of today's young people. Kindergarten is the only place where we accept kids as people, and they succeed in kindergarten. If they don't learn everything we had planned, we still value them and we don't get too upset.

First grade? Well, that's different. After all, we've got to teach them to read. The teacher says to the little kid, "Read!" His parents say, "Read!" The community says, "Read!" And if the child doesn't, we fail him.

Usually he takes the failure personally because he is role-oriented. He thinks we not only failed him in reading but as a human being. When this happens, he starts behaving totally as a failure. He stops almost all schoolwork and often becomes a discipline problem in order to gain some recognition, if only as a failure.

We figure out lots of excuses for why he's not reading—his eyes don't track, he reads backwards or sideways. But the real reason is that he sees himself as a failure and he sees no sense in reading. Yet we keep telling him, "Read! Write! Do arithmetic! Sit still! Keep quiet! Shut up! Learn!" and when he doesn't we say he's lazy or educationally handicapped.

We find all kinds of sophisticated explanations for why he isn't learning. We buy all kinds of complicated equipment and establish special classes to help him learn—*but nothing much happens because he believes he is a failure, and failures get attention and recognition only by failing and misbehaving.*

The conditions which produce so many failures in our schools appear to be related to changes which came abruptly after World War II. The reasons for these changes include the possibility that, for the first time, the world can be fused into a meaningless blob by the bomb.

The television industry has known about the new focus on role or identity from at least 1951 (although I didn't find out about it until 1969) and through their recognition of McLuhan's "role not goal" they've been able to sell items of no utility as well as items of negative utility, such as cigarettes. If television can do that, surely we ought to be able to get kids to learn something with as much utility as reading.

But, unlike the world about them, schools say: "Achieve the goal we set for you or we will give no consideration to you and your role." To be sure, some kids will work for goals in school but they have enough role reinforcement in their homes to compensate for not having it at school. They *know* who they are.

In our previous goal-oriented society, success and failure were mostly tied to economic success or failure, economic security or insecurity, and in most cases, this actually meant survival or non-survival. These were the basics of the depression years when people were actually starving. We accepted this state of affairs by saying, "It's too bad, but that's the way things have always been and always will be." We were forced to be so concerned about our own security that we couldn't concern ourselves with others.

All that has changed at every level of society. Business *must* be concerned or it will find profits dropping. Politicians who do not reinforce the role of their constitutents (assuming the latter are economically secure) will lose votes. Our changed society demands that we care for other people as people. Lonely people or those who have no one to care for them think of themselves as failures and become a burden on society.

To follow that thought today everyone wants a role first, but there are two possible kinds of roles. Individuals can believe they're successful and competent human beings or they can believe they're failures. From countless discussions with groups of students, I have determined that even in relatively good high schools only half the kids feel successful; the rest consider themselves failures. In high schools in depressed areas, I have found that as few as 5 percent of the students believe they are successful. I don't think those who now consider themselves failures came to school feeling that way. They learned they were failures as they moved through school. Once they feel they're failures, they reinforce this belief by doing nothing or by resorting to delinquency. Then we threaten or punish, which reinforces their failure.

I believe we have two ways of stopping this destructive process: first, by not failing kids and, second, by making friends with them. Being friendly with a person reinforces his role as a successful human being. When a person feels he's accepted and worthwhile in another's eyes, effective communication begins to take place and constructive things begin to happen.

Industry has known that ever since it found out people were changing about the end of World War II. To make more money industry replaced the hard sell with the soft sell. It began to tell a prospective customer, "We care about you. We think you're a good person and we want to help you become a better one."

Schools haven't yet learned this lesson. That's what they have to work toward; that's what I'm trying to help teachers do.

Teachers can become effectively involved with kids in a number of ways. A structured, well-planned class meeting each day is a good starter. I'm not talking about the ordinary class discussion. I'm talking about a meeting which involves everyone in the room—one in which kids learn to care for and respect each other and where meaningful participation takes precedence over the teacher's "right answer."

I'm concerned about bringing relevance, thinking, and involvement into the school by helping teachers learn to care for and become friends with the kids with whom they work. Our society needs successful, achieving people. We can develop such people only if we concern ourselves with the children with whom we work, letting them know that we like them, as individuals—as people—that we do feel their humanity is of primary importance, that we want to know them as friends, and that we want to work with them to help all of us grow toward our maximum potential as human beings.

If we make this change, learning can become a joyful and exciting experience, both for the children and those of us responsible for working with them.

BERNICE GRUNWALD

Behavior Change in Schools

Our school problems are increasing in magnitude and intensity. They become worse from one day to the next. Teachers tell me that they can't teach because the children won't let them: the children don't listen, they don't follow rules and regulations, they are destructive, and they don't learn. Children fail so consistently that we might say that our schools are failure-oriented today.

At one time, rebellion and destructiveness were mainly associated with older students, but they have now reached the elementary level. In 1970, elementary school children burned down a school in a suburb of Chicago. Fourth grade students walked out of a class in protest against a teacher they did not like and refused to return to class until the principal promised to replace this teacher. These nine and ten year old children did not just walk out spontaneously, without directions; they must have discussed it beforehand. We can see here a group united for a common purpose —namely, to defeat the authority of the administration. A group, if united, is a terrific force at any age. It stands to reason that children who can be thus united in anti-social endeavors could be equally united in socially-acceptable behavior, provided we know how to win the group over to our side. What is required is a knowledge of group techniques. If we lack this knowledge, or if we just don't believe in it—as some teachers do not—we run the risk that leaders within the class will snatch the group away from us,

Former title "Strategies for Behavior Change in Schools." From *The Counseling Psychologist,* Vol. 3, No. 1, 1971. Reprinted by permission.

right from under our very noses. Suddenly you don't know what hit you: nobody listens to you, nobody finishes his work, and you feel that you are losing control, never realizing to whom you have lost.

Administrators have another headache: that of low teacher morale. Teachers who at one time loved their profession and felt they were doing a good job, now feel discouraged; some feel that they are personal failures, others feel that they are in the wrong profession, and still others feel that the fault lies only with the children. Senior teachers take the first opportunity to retire—long before their retirement is due. Young teachers, straight out of college, eager to have a class of their own, become so discouraged that they leave after one year of teaching. These are very serious problems.

Many experts in the field of education, people like Rudolf Dreikurs, William Glasser and others, have warned us for some time that if we don't make drastic changes in our schools we are bound to meet with failure, and that our school system will collapse. Regrettably, evidence of this is already visible. Our schools are outdated. The curriculum, the method of teaching, and our general attitude toward children, all belong to another era. True, for many centuries we were more or less successful with this approach, but it doesn't work any more. For one thing, our children are more sophisticated than children at any time in history; they know more. Yet we evaluate their knowledge primarily on the basis of what they produce in class and how they score on standardized tests, disregarding the fact that children gather a great deal of knowledge outside of school—knowledge and interests which remain untapped by us. What is more, children grow up in a home atmosphere different from that in which most of us grew up. In addition, the roles of the sexes have changed; the mother's role, especially, has been drastically altered with the newly acquired freedom women now have. All of this has significant influence on the child's personality development.

Our children have been caught in the general democratic evolution which is now embracing the entire world, where minority groups as well as minority nations are fighting for equal rights.

Nobody wants to accept the role of being socially inferior to anyone else, including the children. They have declared themselves our equals and are fighting for their rights, whether we like it or not. You will seldom find children, even very young ones, who will accept the role of being seen but not heard; they make themselves heard.

Bringing up children was always based on traditions. Today, in non-western cultures where traditions still exist, society has few difficulties with children. Even the very young, five and six year olds, already assume responsibility for caring for younger siblings, cleaning the house, etc., and they do it because this is how they were brought up; they have definite roles assigned to them. In non-western cultures there is no such thing as a "teen-ager" or "adolescent" as we understand it. People are either children or adults. At a definite age, when a person ceases to be a child, he automatically, overnight, becomes an adult with all the responsibilities as well as all the rights which go with this status.

We have to establish new traditions in regard to raising and teaching children, traditions based on democratic principles. Such principles advocate not only equal rights but also sharing in responsibilities and in decision-making. We accept this as progress or as inevitable in regard to all people except when it concerns the younger generation. Here we stop because we have so little confidence in the ability of children and in their innate goodness and need to contribute and to be useful. Many adults believe that children are basically self-centered and incapable of assuming responsibility unless "made" to do what is "good for them." Many believe that the only way to control children is through autocratic means, based primarily on reward and punishment, so they use this approach in spite of the fact that they experience failure, hoping that what did not work yesterday and today will, by some miracle, work tomorrow. We can no longer control children through reward and punishment as we once did. Children regard a reward as something coming to them anyway, if they have been rewarded for everything all their lives. And as for punishment, they may briefly refrain from doing what they were punished for, but it lasts only a day or two and then they resume their previous behavior. We do not change their values, their outlook on life, or their self-concept through punishment. Mostly we impress them with what "power" can do, and lead them to want such power for themselves. Indeed, they punish us right back. True, they can not send us to the principal or stand us in the corner or paddle us, but they find dozens of ways to get even. Children are much more imaginative in that way than adults; furthermore, they are not restricted by conscience as we are.

We can no longer run schools for children; we must learn how to run schools *with* children. We must take them in as partners in the educative process. For one thing, teachers cannot and should not be held responsible for everything that happens in class. This is a very unrealistic demand: how can a teacher be responsible for every child that whistles, taps, talks, runs to the washroom every few minutes and stays there for half an hour, for children who fight, steal, don't work, etc.? Everyone in class is responsible for what happens in the classroom; each with his unique personality, his individual goals, and his behavior pattern colors the atmosphere in the class. It may be a climate which is conducive to good teaching or it may be an atmosphere where teaching is impossible. Just knowing how to present the subject matter is not enough today. The best teachers in the world will fail if students don't let them teach. It is no longer enough just to know how to teach; today teachers must, by necessity, also be counselors and take the time to help children understand why many of the school's problems exist, to help them find solutions to these problems and to assume responsibility toward themselves as well as toward others. But teachers cannot achieve this by telling students what is wrong and what they must do. It is a mistake for the teacher either to let children take over entirely without giving them any direction, which results in anarchy, in a free-for-all and disruptive atmosphere, or to hold long monologues telling children what they must do. This is preaching, and nothing turns children off as quickly as when someone starts preaching to them. They become teacher-deaf. Nor is it a democratic approach because again, the teacher assumes all the responsibility. The children themselves must be led to come to solutions, to understand cause and effect of behavior, to see which of their demands are logical and possible and which are not. They must themselves come to the conclusion that a society cannot function unless limits are set, unless we have rules and regulations for all people. This does not mean that all rules are good, but it is within our power to re-examine and to change those that are not.

The most effective technique for such training is through group discussions. Today especially, when the peer group is replacing the authority of the adult, we must concentrate on uniting the peer group. Every child must be helped to feel that he has a place in the group, that he is wanted and respected for what he is although we may not like his behavior. Through group discussions the children are united with a sense of dignity, a feeling of belonging. Children learn that they are not alone in their predicaments, whatever they are, that others have the same problems, that everyone is concerned and willing to help. They learn that problems can be solved either entirely or partially, either individually or collectively. As the child begins to feel surer of himself and of his position in the group, his academic interest and achievement automatically goes up. A high correlation has been found between the child's self-evaluation and achievement. In addition, the child is helped to meet life with greater self-assurance. The world does not seem such a dangerous place when we know how to deal with problems.

I am sure that if children were systematically trained by all teachers from the moment they enter school that each class is a working-problem-solving unit, where everyone is responsible not only for his own behavior but also carries responsibility toward others, many of the problems which we now have in the upper grades would not exist. But this is possible only if, in the first place, the teacher herself believes in this philosophy, and secondly, if she is willing to learn group dynamics and group techniques. In addition, teachers must understand the role that they, unwittingly, play in the dilemma in which they find themselves. Their own ambitions, goals, need for prestige or power are a great factor in this. In the first place, they themselves would have to change before they can help children to change. Lastly, they have to learn to understand the child psychologically. Each child has his own private point of view, his own personal goals toward which he is moving. It is necessary for teachers to grasp this process, to help the child know his goals and to engage in the process of encouragement. Without such knowledge and skill, the teacher faces an almost impossible and dreadfully frustrating task.

DONALD J. O'DONNELL

KEITH F. MAXWELL

Reality Therapy Works Here

We call Ventura "A School Without Failure." It is not a coincidence that this echoes the title of William Glasser's book, *Schools Without Failure* (Harper, 1969). Our school program is solidly based on the principles of Reality Therapy as applied to education which are expounded in his book.

Our adaptation of the Glasser principles as the basis of our program followed a search for ways to improve the educational enterprise for both students and staff. What drew us was the realization that Reality Therapy, developed to help people in trouble in our society, was actually a way to help them achieve enough maturity to take charge of their own lives. To give children the tools to achieve such maturity must also be the goal of education, not only for the children in our failure-oriented schools but for all children.

Under our system, there's no purpose in grouping children according to type of problem or to name (diagnose) their condition. The teacher works with the child and the child works with himself as an individual. The emphasis is different from that of schools that have individualized instruction. Our school is concerned primarily with the feelings the child has about himself and school. This affective education not only has personal and social value, which is such a vital necessity in these days wherein the school is accepting responsibility for promoting these values among children; it is also a prime contributor to more effective cognitive learning.

Principles of Reality Therapy

According to Reality Therapy, the two basic psychological needs of all humans are (1) to be able to love and be loved; and (2) to feel we are worthwhile to ourselves and others. This is accomplished through involvement with a responsible person. This person supports his protégé with his involvement, enabling him to face the reality that he is responsible for his own behavior and progress. He then insists that the child make and honor a commitment to change his behavior in such a way as to make progress toward his goal.

Can a program like this be adopted without distracting from a school's academic responsibilities? As we have discovered, how we *treat* children is just as important as how or what we try to *teach* them. Indeed, if we do not treat children right, we are not able to teach them anything at all.

"Treating children right" means recognizing each child as a person and acting toward him accordingly. It means encouraging children to make choices, taking into consideration the consequences to themselves and others. It means furnishing children with a choice of activities under the guidance of a teacher sensitive to their needs. It means children doing work which interests them because it forwards *their* purposes, not ours. All of these steps are with the intention of enabling children to learn to run their lives on a responsible basis through day-to-day experiences in doing it.

School Organization

Although there are many ways to organize a school, we felt that self-contained classrooms with heterogeneously grouped children would do most to facilitate our program. The cultural diversity of our community and school population—almost half of our students belong to minority groups—helped weigh the factors in that direction. The self-contained class facilitates the integration and continuity of the educational process. It recognizes children's urgent need to belong to a group in which they can develop close human relationships. Furnishing a solid base to start from, it encourages experimentation. Self-contained classes give teachers both the opportunity and the authority to assume full responsibility for students, both academic and behavioral. Thus they find it easier to achieve the necessary involvement on which Reality Therapy is based.

The staff of Ventura is balanced as to diversity of ethnic background and cultural heritage, professional training, and career expectation. Each teacher must believe in the integrity of the individual—of himself and other staff members as well as the children. The basic human needs of relatedness and respect are accepted and understood by our teachers. We try to make sure that everyone at Ventura—not only the teaching staff—understands the philosophical foundations of our program.

Believing in his own individuality, a teacher can be the kind of person with whom others, children and teachers, can relate. Believing in the integrity of the individuality of others, he can share his strengths without detracting from his own status; he can also become successfully involved with children. Involvement requires people who can fulfill their own needs. Thus they can be responsible in their relationships with children, as well as have the energy to maintain the relationship when students test the strength of the involvement.

Goals and Process

Ventura School's three primary goals, arising out of the Glasser principles, are to develop (1) the child's sense of self-worth, (2) his sense of responsibility for his own actions, and (3) his ability to think critically and solve relevant problems. These are interrelated. For instance, the child's feelings of self-worth are supported by responsible actions; his sense of responsibility is bolstered by his confidence that he can solve problems because he knows how to do it.

The specific process in affecting a child's behavior is this: The teacher achieves involvement. He then insists that the student face his present behavior and make a value judgment about it. He asks the key questions, "What are you doing? Is it helping you?" Then he helps the child make a commitment and plan to attempt to change his behavior. The teacher follows up the carrying out of the plan, accepting no excuses for failure. He works with the child through the process as many times as necessary, rejecting the unrealistic behavior but maintaining his involvement.

Here's an example of the way it works. In groups or in line, Tom constantly pushed the other children. The teacher felt he had enough involvement with Tom to help him to change. After the next pushing incident, he got Tom to admit that pushing wasn't really solving his problem. They sat down to work out alternate solutions. Although Tom forgot his new solutions at the next opportunity, the teacher immediately got another commitment. When the next chance to push passed without incident, the teacher recognized the accomplishment, maintaining involvement. A few days later, it was necessary to go through the steps again. Tom eventually solved his problem by making sure he always led the line and kept clear of traffic jams. When he had accepted responsibility, the disruptive behavior stopped.

Another problem involved a third-grade child who would not follow directions, would not finish her work, and was generally at odds with authority. When firmness was tried, she screamed and yelled in a tantrum.

The teacher achieved involvement by not pushing Susan. Gradually she showed her that school could be an enjoyable and satisfying place by praising any accomplishment. She also talked to Susan about responsibility.

To help both Susan and the whole class grow in responsibility, the teacher then set up a bulletin board arranging the students' names in three groups. Privileges depended upon completing assignments each day, and other acts of good citizenship. Susan began to realize that her standing depended upon her own actions. She made it to Group 1 about three times in three weeks. When she dropped to a lower group, she accepted it.

However, Susan slipped back. After a particularly bad slip, the teacher proceeded to strip Susan of desk, chair, books, and supplies, saying that since Susan was not acting within school limits, she evidently would prefer to be a visitor. The teacher loaned

Susan a chair, and she watched the class. Finally, Susan asked when she could come back. "When you show you can act as a responsible person," the teacher said, giving her a plant to care for. If Susan could tend the plant successfully, the teacher said, she could choose one subject to start with. If she did her work in that subject, she could choose another, and so on.

It took Susan a week and a half to become a "full-time student" again. A week later, she slipped again, and again became a "visitor." This time she returned to class much more quickly. Now she can accept criticism without tantrums, and she has faced the reality that she must act as a responsible citizen to become an accepted member of society.

Class Meetings

A technique suggested by Dr. Glasser, actually the backbone of a "school without failure," is holding class meetings. The meetings answer several purposes. They help teachers achieve involvement with the group as well as to check on the learnings and attitudes of the various members of the group. They help students learn to think about problems, theirs and society's, and to work out solutions.

Meetings are problem-solving (concerned with students' social behavior or educational problems in school), open-ended (concerned with intellectually important subjects), or educational-diagnostic (concerned with how well students understand curriculum concepts). The same meeting techniques can be used by the staff to find solutions to individual and group problems of any class or of the entire school.

Meetings are held with members sitting in a circle. The teacher-leader either introduces the problem or subject, or probes to find one of current concern. No attacks are allowed. Dealing must be with present behavior in an attempt to solve the problem. Blame or punishment are never acceptable as a solution. They only hide the fact that nothing constructive is being done.

It is not easy to learn to lead a successful class meeting. Questions must be stimulating and open-ended. The leader must try not to let children answer merely as they think they should. He also must try to keep perspective and avoid dead-end absolutes. All replies must be treated with respect and reacted to. If the answer seems off the track, the leader must decide whether to bring the discussion back (and how to do it), or whether the new direction is important enough to follow. Difficulties arise because neither children nor teacher has had practice in the use of meetings as a method of solving relevant problems.

Meetings should end with a commitment to a solution, although it should be made clear that many problems have no single right answer. Their best solution might not be a not-so-bad alternative, or a tentative trial answer. If facts become necessary to a successful solution, children learn why it is worthwhile to learn facts. These meetings are one of the best ways to make education relevant to students' lives, and to keep it relevant to their growing and changing interests. They give children confidence that, individually and in groups, people can analyze, understand, and solve problems.

In school, the extent to which a pupil feels he has control over his own destiny is strongly related to achievement. Children given little help tend to evade problems, lie their way out of situations, depend on others to solve their problems, or just give up. None of these courses of action is good preparation for life. Problem-solving class meetings can help children learn better ways, and, at the same time, gain in scholastic achievement.

Dr. Glasser recommends that class meetings be held every day, especially in elementary school. Our teachers, even in kindergarten, hold them several times a week for an average of about thirty minutes a day. We've found that children gain warm, positive involvement with each other more quickly through meetings in which they discuss ideas relative to their lives than through direct disciplinary meetings. A class successfully involved in thinking will have few disciplinary problems. While it may be useful at times to tie the discussion in with the curriculum, it is better to have a thoughtful, relevant discussion on any subject than to force such a connection.

For educational-diagnostic meetings, in which teachers check up on the depth and correctness of understanding the class has gained from a subject presentation, we've found it best for teachers to team. The teacher who originally presented the material often finds it hard to recognize missed points because he is too close. Our teachers are encouraged to work together, exchanging critiques, experiences, and ideas. It is probably this interaction that makes it most beneficial for class meetings to be used by a majority of teachers in a school.

Other Program Features

Another technique we've found useful is cross-grade tutoring. This is consistent with Reality Therapy principles because these "learning by teaching" experiences help children become involved with each other as well as with the teachers they help. The experiences are carefully planned to be actively problem solving, sometimes for the tutor and sometimes for the tutee. Respectful involvement between students and teachers develops as they define tutor roles, achieve an understanding of task increments, practice positive feedback, stress positive attitudes toward change, and engage in evaluation and replanning.

It is not uncommon to see a whole class moving to another grade level for a session. One activity sees the older class acting as secretaries for twenty minutes, taking dictation from lower-grade students. The tutors later return with a corrected copy of the dictated material. During the last school year, after discussing it with students, the Ventura staff decided to change room assignments so upper grades alternate with lower grades. This move facilitates the tutorial program by shortening the physical distance the upper grades have to travel, and adds to children's involvement with each other across age and grade levels.

There are no grades and no report cards at Ventura. Instead, we provide meetings between students, parents, and teachers. These are designed to help parents understand what is going on at the school, and to keep them up to date on their child's progress and educational plans. The conferences, preplanned by teacher and student, often include a demonstration of new proficiencies, as well as a clear expression of the directions and plans that students have decided upon. The number of conferences is directly related to need and value, with a minimum of two each year. Overwhelmingly, parents have been impressed with the professional, adult, and respectful attitude between teacher and student demonstrated in these conferences.

A final point in our Reality-Therapy-based school program is that children who need special help of any kind are kept in their regular class as far as possible. The special teacher may prepare supportive materials for such students to use in the regular classroom. Sometimes he sets up special work centers. Again, he may work with an individual or small group in the room, or even swap roles with the regular teacher who then teaches the special group. Generally, the assistance teacher is responsible to the homeroom teacher to develop conditions in which the handicapped child can be successful. Interestingly, such children are usually able to participate successfully in the give-and-take of class meetings.

In Summary

The "school without failure" approach to education is in its third year at Ventura School. Like any new school program, it has been developing and changing as we learn more about applying the principles on which it is based. As we have already pointed out, neither children nor teachers have had practice in the techniques we are attempting; and, obviously, in the normal course of events, a certain part of both the school population and staff keeps changing.

Some few of us started learning how to apply Reality Therapy principles at Pershing School in the San Juan School District before coming to Palo Alto to work in Ventura. The staff therefore varies considerably both in training and experience in the Glasser technique. Some have taken the six-week training session, others have just read relevant material. We do not insist on teachers' taking the formal training.

Even with training, however, experience has been found to be the most effective way to learn to run class meetings, as well as to use effectively the involvement-commitment process. In the experience with Tom described previously, for example, the teacher reported several realizations: that one experience with the definition of a problem, involvement, and the satisfaction of the child's human needs does not guarantee responsible behavior in the next experience of a similar nature; that responsible behavior is not necessarily generalized by the student and applied in a cognitive way; that the teacher's demands for behavioral standards may not be realistic to the level of behavior sought by the child; and that the child may find ways of satisfying his psychological needs without using responsible behavior. Each teacher must find his own way to achieve involvement and carry out the other steps in applying Reality Therapy principles in each different situation.

The school district's Research and Development section has been keeping close tabs on our project. The report published last year shows that Ventura School pupils have not so far forged ahead in testable qualities. There are many possible factors for this, as the report points out. One of these is that our students are not used to taking tests, and in fact consider the standardized tests more of an unwelcome interruption of their real schoolwork than a part of it. Another is the limitation of the tests used. Often there were none applicable.

Encouraging signs are the enthusiasm of many of the teachers for the program. Boys especially seem to have benefited by the emphasis on personal adjustment and problem solving. In spite of the de-emphasis on fact finding and direct learning, Ventura pupils have not lagged behind on fact-oriented tests.

In conclusion, then, the Ventura program is offering a viable alternative to the traditional school. Most of the anecdotal evidence attests to its success. One of our regular teachers commented that her students ask questions not to make her happy, as they had in other schools, but because they are interested in the answers. Some of the special-services teachers have noticed marked changes in the Ventura children since the beginning of the program. Others have noted that Ventura students are more ready to challenge statements and to question what others have said than in other schools.

Though we have come far in applying Reality Therapy concepts at Ventura, we still have much to learn. We need information on what kinds of children receive the most benefit from the program, the kinds of cognitive development which occur, the long-term effects of the program, how teachers can best be taught the methods, and how flexibility can be built into the system so it can change and develop with additional experience and assessment. But it is a task well worth attempting in our effort to humanize education for children.

Learning to Face Reality

Two days a week it happens. Room 27. Ground floor. O'Keefe High School at 151 Sixth St. NW. Students file into the classroom for each of five classes, sit at their desks as though a regular study session were about to begin. A few minutes later, following introductory preliminaries, they move their chairs into a circle to pursue a unique experiment in relating school to the outside world. They talk. Back and forth. Not about a textbook, but about problems of life as encountered by young teens. For each discussion period there is a chosen topic. But the talk is not restrained and it ranges far beyond each limited beginning.

What the young people talk about in this unusual classroom of eighth and ninth graders points up a blunt truth. With youthful candor they make it clear that for some of them, life can be pretty raw.

One day recently the topic for discussion was simply, "What makes a friend?"

Each of five classes started on that theme, began on it and went in five different directions. They talked about overprotective parents, drunk parents, living in a family split by divorce, crime and punishment, why people ran away from home and, finally, about the problem of a school girl who wanted to kill herself because she thought she was pregnant by her own father.

A team of teachers, Mrs. Martha Church and Mrs. Marta J.

From John Pennington, "Learning to Face Reality," January 18, 1970. Reprinted by permission of *The Atlanta Journal and Constitution Magazine.* Copyright © 1970 by Atlanta Newspapers, Inc.

Kuckleburg, conduct the class together. They are assisted by Richard Orem, a member of the Peace Corps who will go to Tunisia to teach after the school term is over, and by Jim Frazier, a 20-year-old Georgia Tech student who volunteers his time for several class periods two to four days a week.

The classroom is called a Communication Skills Laboratory, and the purpose is to help young people who are reading two to four years below their grade level. The discussion periods—Mrs. Church got the idea from author William Glasser's books, *Reality Therapy* and *Schools Without Failure*—take up two days each week. During other school days the young people study English as though it were a foreign language. They practice handwriting to music. They are taught to read better and faster.

Communication Skills Laboratories are operating in several Atlanta schools, but as far as Mrs. Church knows, her classroom is the only one using the "reality" discussions as a means of relating school to community problems. She and Mrs. Kuckleburg began the sessions in September.

The laboratory idea itself was begun several years ago when the Atlanta school system recognized that many pupils read well below their grade level, and planned a program to do something about it. It is a simple fact that if one can't read, one doesn't learn. It also is known that poor reading and problem behavior often travel together. Thus the program evolved to teach a select group of teachers to operate the Communication Skills Laboratories in schools located in communities with socioeconomic problems.

"I was teaching American History at Dykes High [on Atlanta's privileged north side]," Mrs. Church says. "When the time came for me to decide whether to go in this lab, I talked to several people about it. I liked it at Dykes, but they said, 'This is real teaching; you're teaching dead stuff when you're teaching history, but you're really working with the kids here.' And it's true."

Mrs. Church began her work at O'Keefe, which is near the Techwood public housing area, in September, 1965. She soon recognized that many of her young pupils have problems they don't know how to solve, and many of the problems are related to their home life. So she started the reality discussions to help them.

" 'Reality Therapy' is the name that William Glasser gave it in his book," she says. "He says we have so much going on in the schools that is not applicable to their life when they get out of school. There is no correlation between school and the outside world in which they live, and that we need to do this kind of thing so they will know how to meet problems."

Reality?

"If you were to wake up tomorrow morning and find that you were the opposite color than you are now, how would that affect your life?"

Ask this of kids in an integrated school in a low economic area, then throw the answers back and forth for an hour.

Mrs. Church opened the school year with this question. O'Keefe had known some strained race relations, so she showed a list of questions to O'Keefe principal Frank Jernigan. The idea was approved.

"There was a lot of soul searching in that classroom," Mrs. Church says. "A lot of depth, a lot of thinking. It was very effective. We stimulated the discussion by giving examples of some racial attitudes. One of my good colored friends, a boy who is now a junior, got mad at the whole school system and went up to the office one day and said, 'I'm tired of you white bastards telling me what to do.' And then there was this white girl who wrote in her journal that she was tired of the niggers getting their way about everything.

"So we brought these things out, let the Negro kids see how the white folks felt, and let the white folks see how the Negroes felt. And it was a very effective discussion with the groups."

The discussions are uninhibited and most of the young people in each class participate. An observer dropped in at the midpoint of one class period recently and found that the original topic—what makes a friend?—had been expanded to dating and parental control. The young people unanimously opposed overprotection of girls by their parents.

"It's not good to keep someone smothered in the house," one girl said. "I know this girl, her father bragged about her a lot. He would keep her in the house, and wouldn't let her go on dates, and when she got out, she got pregnant. You can keep somebody in the house, but when they get out, they don't know how to act."

When Mrs. Church asked how many lived in a home with one parent because of divorce, six out of 22 raised their hands.

"Why do parents get a divorce?" the teacher asked.

"Sometimes the husband is too rough," one pupil said. "Like something happens bad at work, he'll come home and take it out on you."

"I'll tell you why my mama and daddy got a divorce," said another. "My daddy drinks too much."

"Some people do drink too much," the teacher pointed out. "What do you do if you have to live with someone who drinks too much?"

The answers came in an outpouring.

"I lock myself in the bathroom."

"You can leave home and go live somewhere else, if you're old enough."

"You can't do nothing but be ready for him, if you've got to live with him."

"My stepdaddy comes in drunk every Friday night. One night he came in, I was supposed to be asleep, I pretended like I was sleeping when he came in. He grabbed my mama by her nightgown, like that [illustrating]. She told me to go in the kitchen. I got a knife and told him to leave my mama alone or I was going to kill 'im."

"Did he listen to you? Did he leave her alone?"

"Yeah. He left."

Teacher: "Should there be a law against drinking?"

A chorus from the young people: "No."

As that session neared an end, the discussion returned to the original topic. One girl said you make new friends by being introduced to somebody. It was pointed out to her that a person newly acquainted would be an acquaintance, not a friend.

"Some of you have friends from the first grade," the teacher said. "Why would you still be good friends after eight years?"

A tall, quiet boy who had talked little gave an answer. "Because they're a little bit like you," he said.

The bell jangled and terminated that discussion and a new group of youngsters flooded into Room 27.

"Have you all written in your journals?" Mrs. Kuckleburg asked them.

Mrs. Church explained to a visitor that each pupil in the Communication Skills Laboratory is required to write a paragraph each day in a personal journal. This is to help them learn written words, to learn better communication.

"We tell them books are nothing but words written down," Mrs. Church said. "That they already have the vocabulary because they speak it. All they have to do is recognize it." She explained that many of the students, but for the requirements to keep a daily journal, would go for days without writing anything down. What they write is not corrected for grammar: "We just want them to put an idea down." From these ideas the teachers sometimes get new insights into the children.

One boy wrote: "My father said that if I got my hair cut I could go to Texas this summer and that he would take me to town and he would buy me anything I wanted. So we got in an argument about it and he won."

Two days later the journal said: "Today I got my hair cut."

Another student wrote:

The Snow

The snow is soft,
The snow is white,
The snow is cold.
The snow is a very
pretty sight to see.

The same child wrote:

Birds
Blue.
Red
Sing.
Fly
Eat.
I love to watch them.

After the journals were turned in and homework was discussed, the next group took their chairs into a circle and tackled the question: What makes a friend?

"Somebody who will tell you the truth."

"But suppose your friend tells you something you don't want to hear? Suppose she tells you you're too fat?"

"What do you think about this?" Mrs. Church asked a tall boy with a morose expression.

He shrugged.

"You've tuned me out," she said.

He shrugged again.

"How do you make friends?"

"First you buy 'em a soft drink," one boy said.

"You can't buy friends."

"You can, too. When you got money, you got a friend anywhere. If I had some money, I'll bet the whole school would be chasing me . . ." The boy thought this over, then added: "And the next day, when the money was gone, they'd be gone the other way."

"Do poor people ever have friends?"

Chorus: "Yeah. Yeah."

Then on to another subject. Mrs. Church said she heard on the radio about a 35-year-old man attempting to rape a 5-year-old girl. "What should they do about something like this? Suppose they give the man the chair. Do you think that would be right?"

"It wouldn't help the girl to give him the chair."

"Yeah. But this was a grown man and a little bitty baby," another boy said. "Think about that."

"Yeah, but there's no need killing the man."

"He must be mentally ill. He should be treated . . ."

"If he's smart, he'll plead insanity."

"I think he should be electrocuted."

"If it was my sister, I'd kill him myself."

"Give him a second chance. Everybody has his first time to do something. Then when he finds out he can't get away with it, most of the time he won't try it again."

"But," a teacher interposes. "What about those kids down there in Juvenile? Some of them are down there a dozen times, then they graduate to the adult jail. They're always stealing, stealing. How many chances would you give?"

A Negro boy answered, very seriously. "Some people don't know they got no business doing some things, like stealing. Some people are brought up stealing. Like you been brought up not to steal; they could've been brought up to steal."

After some further discussion of punishment as a detriment to crime, two boys whispered to each other and giggled. "Tell the rest of us," Mrs. Church admonished.

"He said some people run red lights every once in a while," one of the boys said. "I told him my mama didn't; she runs 'em every day."

Another group talked about why people run away from home, and parental disfavor or mistreatment figured high in the alleged causes.

One boy said, "I left home. Why? My mother makes me clean the house. Almost every day. Last night when she came in [from work], she said, 'Look, your brother and sister have been working all day, why don't you take out that garbage?' I said, 'Look what I've done, I cleaned up Saturday, stayed in the house all day cleaning up.' She said, 'Don't give me no back talk.' I said, 'I ain't back-talking you.' She said, 'Take out that garbage.' I said, ' You make one of them do something, I ain't doing everything.' And I left. That was last night. I left and come back about midnight."

Another boy said, "Yeah, and your old man was standing by the door, and when you come in, pow."

"I ain't got no father."

"What about your mother?"

"Aw, I can sweet-talk her."

"Where did you go till midnight?" a teacher asked.

"Oh, down on Techwood. Go down there and see what's going on."

"What goes on till midnight?"

"Oh, we all get down there and play football and everything."

Another boy, laughing: "Get down there and break in stores . . ."

The one who left home continued: "There are some boys that have cars, they get out there and drag race."

"What happens when you get picked up for race driving?"

"They don't pick you up. The police down there are real nice. They're Techwood punks, too. They're okay unless you do something they don't like."

"Like what?"

"Oh, run a red light. Something like that. Breaking bottles on the street so they get flat tires. But the cops, they play around with you. They have fun with us. You don't bother them, they don't bother you."

Suddenly the discussion turned very serious. Mrs. Kuckleburg said, of a boy sitting next to her in the circle: "A girl he knows tried to kill herself yesterday morning. And the reason is, she thinks she's pregnant by her father. She held a gun up to her head but she didn't have the nerve to pull the trigger. And the reason I brought this up is to ask, what do you think she should do?"

"Should she tell her mother?" one asks.

"Her mother knows."

"Well, she could have an abortion."

"Where could she get one?" the teacher asks. "In most situations an abortion is illegal. Would you know where to go to find an abortion?"

"She could go to a specialist," one student said.

"I've heard about one doctor who does it," a girl said. "A horse doctor."

"Suppose she decides to just go on and have the baby?"

"She'll just go on and have it," one boy said with resignation.

"What difference would that make in her life?" the teacher asked.

"She'd probably hate her father."

"She probably hates him anyway."

"She might not want the baby."

"How about turning it over to the police?"

Finally, Mrs. Church intervened. "All right, What can this girl do? We have three counselors upstairs. We have Mrs. [Judy] Russell next door, who is a professional social worker. This girl needs to get some advice from somebody who can help her." To the boy who brought it up: "She can tell you all about it, but you're in no position to help her. I'm not either. But one of the counselors or the social worker can talk it over with her and give her some real help. Tell her to go to one of them. It won't do any good to wait. In three months from now, it's going to start showing and she'll have to quit school. If she doesn't want to go to one of these people, tell her to go to her preacher, or to a doctor. Tell her any of these people will talk to her confidentially. She needs good, expert advice. You tell her that . . ."

The bell rang and that class broke up. And another group formed in Room 27 on the ground floor at O'Keefe High School to talk about friendship and other things.

THOMAS E. BRATTER

The Three R's of Educational Reform

Traditional Education

Tragically, many adolescents lose the enthusiasm, spontaneity, and respect for learning which they had as youngsters when the educational process becomes sterile, rigid, redundant, irrelevant, and unrewarding. Secondary education, in fact, may be discouraging students from exploring, creating, expanding, and developing their independent interests. Silberman (1970) contends that academic success is predicated upon students' subordinating their interests and feelings to conform to those of the teacher. In so doing, secondary education robs students of their individuality, creativity, and self-respect. Education is experienced by many as dehumanized and mechanical. Most alarming, perhaps, is that education appears to have adopted many of the principles of mass production. Today's students symbolize automobiles on the General Motors assembly line which move at a consistent speed on a conveyor belt to the various workers who perform a specialized task of putting on a bolt or tightening a screw. At the end of this process, before paint is applied, each car appears to be identical. Each student, in contrast, moves through the system at an identical rate—measured in nine-month segments—and is "worked on" by various specialists who are English, History, Science, Mathematics teachers.

Revised version of paper delivered at the State of Florida Governor's Task Force Conference on Disruptive Youth in the School. Orlando, Florida, June 27, 1974.

Students are encouraged mechanically to memorize the state capitals, the order of presidents, and other academic trivia. In order to control academic conformity, students periodically are given multiple answer examinations. Ironically, spelling tests rarely reinforce the various rules but instead inevitably contain all the exceptions to confuse and frustrate students further. Teachers, in addition, arm themselves with some necessary weapons to ensure sameness and conformity to the norm. They have the awesome power to label a person as an A, B, C, D, or F. Sometimes to be more scientific, a specific numerical grade is assigned—98, 87, 76, 65. . . . Teachers have the power to demand conformity to this often restrictive and oppressive system or they can send the student to the person-in-charge-of-discipline, who either can reprimand the offender or can contact the parents to apprise them that their offspring is being troublesome to the "law and order" of the school. A conference can be arranged in which the parents are informed explicitly as to the nature of the problem. A referral can be arranged to the school psychologist, who is armed with a mystical battery of diagnostic tests. More recently, the penalty for active and curious elementary students who "disrupt" the serenity of the classroom by wandering around or talking to their friends is to be labeled "hyperkinetic," which is the term used to describe overactive, easily distractable, excitable children. Once this syndrome has been identified, which cannot be diagnosed by any standard neurological or psychological test, a referral is made either to a pediatrician or a child psychiatrist who has a more potent armamentarium—medication. This insidious treatment involves the prescription of amphetamines whose long-range safety has never been documented and whose efficacy has never been proven. Fish (1971) concludes that "the usefulness of amphetamines in children with behavior disorders is limited, not by the presence or absence of overt anxiety or hyperactivity, nor by the presence or absence of minimal brain dysfunctions, but it is limited by the intensity of psychomotor excitement. The critical controlled study to test this hypothesis, however, has yet to be done." The rationale for this treatment is to help the child adjust to the classroom routine. Ladd (1970) has discussed the prospect of the drugged classroom which is antithetical to education. Today's patient easily can become tomorrow's drug addict.

Most manage to survive in this academic milieu which frighteningly resembles the "newspeak" of Orwell (1949) and the closed caste system of Huxley (1946). Many who have compiled laudable academic and extracurricular records, however, complain that they feel raped of their self-esteem, of feelings of self-worth, and individuality. The attitude of many has been described by Jacobs (1973), who quotes an anonymous daughter of a prominent physician:

Adolescents are pressured. I, myself, living in my adolescence am faced with some of these pressures. I would say the main pressure is competition to do better in school, in order to compete for a better school, in order to get a better education, in order to get a better job, in order to make more money, in order to buy better clothes, in order to find a better spouse and live in a better neighborhood, and bring up better children, who will get better marks to get into a better school. In short the rat race rut of competition.

The Educational Revolution: Redefining Learning and Restructuring Learning Priorities

There are reactionary and innovative alternatives to the repressive academic tradition. Stretch (1970) describes an educational revolt which is directed toward "the institution itself, against the implicit assumption that learning must be imposed on children by adults, that learning is not something one does by and for oneself but something designated by a teacher. Schools operating on this assumption tend to hold children in a prolonged state of dependency, to keep them from discovering their own capabilities for learning, and to encourage a sense of impotence and a lack of worth. The search is for alternatives to this kind of institution."

Rather than to measure learning on the basis of performance on a standardized, often obsolete and culturally biased test, Holt (1964) offers, in contrast, a more pragmatic and humanistic definition of intelligence:

By intelligence we mean a style of life, a way of behaving in various situations, and particularly in new, strange, and perplexing situations.

The true test of intelligence is not how much we know how to do, but how we behave when we don't know what to do.

The intelligent person, young or old, meeting a new situation or problem, opens himself up to it; he tries to take in with mind and senses everything he can about it; he thinks about it, instead of about himself or what it might cause to happen to him; he grapples with it boldly, imaginatively, resourcefully, and if not confidently at least hopefully; if he fails to master it, he looks without shame or fear at his mistakes and learns what he can from them. This is intelligence.

Holt's definition of learning suggests that the goals of education must be expanded beyond the mastery of the three "R's" to include the uniqueness of the individual, his creativity, his capacity for freedom, and his growth and development. Glasser (1969, p. 228) describes these idealized goals of education as assisting the individual to be a:

. . . thoughtful, creative, emotionally alive, unafraid man, a man willing to try to solve the problems he faces in his world. Although he may not solve all of them, he will solve some of them. Confident that he can build on his success, he may fail for a while, but he will know that some success is possible. And when success does not come easily, he will not give up. If he can think, if he can relate to his fellow man, if he can appreciate the beauty created by man and nature, he has a chance for happiness and a chance to feel worthwhile. Education can do no more for a man. The rest is up to him.

Education can become more flexible to permit the student to learn not only what he wants but also at his own rate. Goodman (1968) has affirmed respect for the student and academic freedom when he writes "every part of the curriculum should be open to need, desire, choice, and trying out." The learning environment will be enlarged to include in addition to the cognitive, the psychological and emotional growth and development of the process as well as his synergenic relationship with society. The optimal concern of education, therefore, becomes the growth and development of the student. The objective of education is to provide conditions whereby innate endowments and talents can be nurtured. Individual learning, thus, is emphasized. Teaching becomes subordinated to learning so that the student has both the freedom and responsibility for much of his formalized learning experiences

within academia. It is assumed that academic freedom will help
people become more intelligent, creative, spontaneous than those
who are directed, manipulated, and ordered. Childs (1950) advised that educational pursuit must concern the moral and ethical
fundamentals of human existence and that:

> . . . basic democratic principles carry significant implications for the
> education of the young. They mean . . . that the growth of the child
> constitutes the controlling moral aim of a democratic program of edu-
> cation, and this process of growth is so conceived that primary empha-
> sis is given to the cultivation of the intellectual capacities of the
> individual. In a democratic society, neither concern for the perpetua-
> tion of an established set of institutions, nor concern for the achieve-
> ment of a projected program of social reconstruction, can justify a
> scheme of training indoctrination which curbs the opportunity of the
> child to learn to think for himself—to develop a mind of his own.

More recently, furthermore, Grunwald (1971) contends that "we
can no longer run schools for children; we must learn how to run
schools with children. We must take them in as partners in the
educational process. For one thing, teachers cannot and should not
be held responsible for everything that happens in class . . .
(Everyone) is responsible for what happens in the classroom;
each with his unique personality, his individualized goals, and his
behavior patterns colors the atmosphere in the class."

Education, if it is to be meaningful, must become a way of life
which stimulates and inspires learning. The conditions for this type
of relevant education have been described by Drews (1968). "It is
assumed that the creative, intellectual and ethical growth of the
individual will be greater if the educational program is individualized to meet his needs, where he can see learning as relevant to his
purposes and development. The student will learn what is real and
important to himself." The individual must learn how to think for
himself rather than to accept dogma no matter how important
those views.

The Role of the Teacher

Concurrent with the Education Revolution, the traditional role
of the teacher who lectures from a State-approved, predetermined

curriculum is being challenged. The Committee for a Comprehensive Education (1970), a part of the New York City Board of Education, proposes that "education will occur if students and teachers have—and share—real responsibility for it." The educator must re-conceptualize his role so that learning can become individualized and relevant. Shoben (1962) describes two roles when he refers to a "teacher-counselor-consultant." Harman (1966) sees the educator as a "philosopher, guide, friend." If viewed from this perspective, the teacher's primary task would be to help students move not only toward discovery of themselves but also toward constructing a coherent world review. The instructor must abandon the traditional roles of lecturer-leader. He can become an advisor, resource person, a friend, who will share with students his own intellectual and emotional experiences. The educator will accompany students on their learning odysseys as a companion and not a judge. In a posthumous essay Dewey (1966) conceptualized the educative process as the interaction of "an immature, undeveloped being . . . (with) certain social aims, meanings, values incarnate in the matured experience of the adult."

An effective teacher attempts to establish a cordial, supportive, personal relationship with his students. The effective teacher will encourage students to become involved with him, to become involved with themselves, and to become involved with the curricula. When adolescents are convinced that an educator genuinely cares for them in a responsible manner, they acquire a more positive sense of self, become more vulnerable to learn, and begin to care for others. Glasser (1972) contends that "in Reality Therapy, as in school, people need to become involved, to eliminate their loneliness and through this involvement, to develop motivation to work toward something worthwhile. . . . People need involvement as a prerequisite to change. . . . Almost everyone is personally engaged in a search for acceptance as a person rather than as a performer of a task." Glasser, moreover, continually pleads with educators and psychotherapists to become personally involved with their students and patients.

As a former chairman of a high school English Department, I

discovered that commensurately with personal involvement class morale increases and discipline problems decrease. When a student attempts to be disruptive, his classmates will urge him to adopt more responsible and productive behavior. This type of positive peer pressure permits the educator to abandon the authoritarian role of disciplinarian and to devote his total energy to teaching. Teachers should attempt to create an open and productive classroom environment where students can learn to respect themselves and others, where students are encouraged to discuss important personal matters, where students are provided with the opportunity to evaluate themselves and make decisions, and where students can show concern for others. Each student searches for a unique, stable, and productive identity. Maslow (1971) believes that "part of learning who you are, part of being able to hear your inner voices, is discovering what it is that you want to do with your life. Finding one's identity is almost synonymous with finding one's career, revealing the altar on which one will sacrifice oneself." In this accepting and nonjudgmental situation where there is involvement and mutual respect for all opinions, learning can occur.

Failure: Antithetical to Learning

Henry (1969), an anthropologist, has observed that "the function of education has never been to free the mind and spirit of man but to bind them. Homo sapiens have employed praise, ridicule, admonition, accusation, mutilation, and even torture to chain them to the cultural pattern." Henry excoriates educational institutions for utilizing competition to achieve spurious learning results. He decries the school for demanding that students deny their individuality and interests and substitute the teacher's criteria for their own. Postman and Weingartner (1971) concur. They have defined teaching as "enabling another to learn." The authors, however, mention that the tests which teachers give reflect a specific definition of what they want students to learn. When students fail the test, the failure must be attributed to instructors who have been unsuccessful in teaching the material in such a way that the students could learn.

Using Glasser's educational methodology, Irwin (1973) concludes that rather than providing ways for students to fail, the school must find alternative ways to help students succeed and learn. If a student encounters difficulty understanding mathematical concepts, for example, he can be encouraged to excel in English or social studies. It is possible for any student to experience some success in at least one subject. By improving his concept of self-worth, the school equips him with the ability to get a job because he believes in himself. If, in contrast, the school causes the student to doubt himself and believe he is a failure, the chance of success is diminished greatly. Glasser (1969, p. 96) urges the elimination of failure from school:

> Because failure is never motivating, when we eliminate failure we cannot harm a child who is failing under the present grading system. Although he may not suddenly start learning when we stop labeling him a failure, at least we leave the door open for a change of heart later on when he may wish to start working and learning. If we label him a failure, often even once, there is less chance that he will ever start to learn. To keep a child working in school, we must let him know, beginning in kindergarten, that from the standpoint of grades or labels, it is not possible to fail. Whether or not any individual student wants to study, he is in a school where he sees many others who do work and enjoy learning. Kept in close contact with successful students in the heterogeneous class, he is stimulated to think during relevant class discussion. In this situation, it is easier to succeed than to fail.

To grant a failing grade which becomes a permanent part of the student's transcript accomplishes nothing productive. It is recommended that no grade or comment be recorded. There should be no obligation to inform either colleges or prospective employers whether the course was passed the first time or not. The student would be given the option to repeat the course with no stigma being recorded. In this way, the quality of education could be improved by removing some of the negative aspects of the fear of failure. It would help to alter a prevailing educational attitude to identify failure and replace it with achievement. This practice could prevent some students from expecting, accepting, and labeling themselves as failures. By eliminating the concept of failure, teachers would have only one option which would be to expect success from their students. The power of positive teaching has been documented by Rosenthal (1973, 1968) and Yuncker (1970) whereby students attempt to conform to the high expectations for progress of their teachers. I (Bratter 1973 and 1974a) have discussed the impact of the high expectations of the psychotherapist on his clients.

Discipline: Its Dynamics

Discipline remains the most unpleasant perpetual professional dilemma for educators. All types of discipline have been relatively ineffective to restore a positive and productive learning environment in the classroom. Dynamically, discipline is the corrective action of a teacher to a disruptive incident or student. Generally, the educator has become frustrated, angry, and/or threatened by students who are interfering with the routine of the class. The instructor feels compelled to make a spontaneous decision, which often appears to be influenced more by emotion than by reason. Consequently, discipline is experienced as punishment and, at times, can be vindictive and unjust, which provides an additional negative payoff to the perpetrators—i.e., "Look how important I am because I really got the teacher angry." If a conspiracy exists to destroy the credibility of the teacher, he unwittingly fuels it by overreacting to disturbances and disruptions. The act of discipline becomes an unpleasant phenomenon because it thrusts the educator into a punitive and authoritarian role, it alienates the perpetrators from the learning process, and it adversely affects the gestalt of classroom reaction. The use of discipline undermines the objectives of learning because it tends to polarize the students from the teacher.

Historically, revolution has occurred when people have believed there is something to revolt against. The tyranny of the classroom has been a rallying cry for students for many years. The instructor who rigidly insists there is only one correct answer thus encourages destructive student dissent. When, however, the educational philosophy emphasizes an appreciation of the worth and dignity of the person, a recognition of individual differences, and a realization of the student's inherent rights regarding self-determination and free-dom of choice, potential discipline problems are neutralized. It is contended that discipline can be minimized when the learner's personal characteristics such as his potential, his interests, and his ambitions are understood. When these conditions are fulfilled and there is genuine teacher involvement, discipline ceases to be a problem.

The teacher can avoid many potential discipline problems by recognizing the conflicts between generations regarding freedom versus responsibility, achievement versus pleasure, innovation versus tradition, etc. Friedenberg (1969) and Miller (1971) de-scribe many of these conflicts. Disagreement and diversity can become scintillating educational experiences where everyone learns.

Discipline: The Process (What to Do When the Disruption Continues)

There will be times when a student or a group will require discipline. Glasser (1974) advises the teacher to try to anticipate this problem and plan the following corrective action which could be condensed into a matter of a few days or prolonged for several months:

First: If a student elects to disturb the class, the teacher should assume that previous educational approaches have not been effec-tive to help the adolescent find meaningful and gratifying activities. The educator must identify the strengths and interests of the stu-dent and then attempt to plan innovative projects. The instructor should consult with the student in a nonjudgmental manner to inquire if the youth has any ideas how he could more productively utilize his time in class. Disruption, at this juncture, is viewed as symptomatic of the student's dissatisfaction with the curriculum. Devising positive alternatives to disruptive behavior is seen as avoiding a discipline conflict. To discuss punishment is premature. If possible, the teacher should attempt to make at least one posi-tive or complimentary comment to the student daily: "You look nice." "I enjoyed your comment." "Hello" can suffice.

Second: At a time when things are progressing harmoniously, if possible, the instructor should request another informal conference at a mutually convenient time. The student, in all probability, will feel defensive and could be antagonistic. The conference should remain task-oriented to help the student formulate some intermediate and longer-range educational and vocational goals. This can be accomplished relatively quickly by asking the adolescent "What would you like to do one year from today?" and "What would you like to do five or ten years from today?" Once the student has volunteered this information, the teacher can offer to assist the student to draw up a plan to achieve these goals.

Third: Should the student continue to present discipline problems, after class the instructor should attempt to help the student evaluate his behavior. The educator can inquire, "Is your behavior helping or hurting you to achieve your goals?"

Fourth: If this fails to prevent disturbances, the educator might wish to involve the class to help the disruptive student. The student should be notified in advance. A low-keyed five- or ten-minute discussion could focus on ways the class believes it can help the student to adopt more responsible and productive behavior. The teacher could begin by saying "I would like to spend a few minutes to try to help our friend to achieve the following goals which he has. Does anyone have any suggestions?"

Fifth: The next step requires a referral to be made to someone whom the student likes and trusts. The referral source should be notified in advance that such action is contemplated and that the objective is to help the student to achieve his stated goals. This conference can be cordial and should remain behavior-oriented. The student should be helped to recognize that his behavior is disruptive and prevents others from learning. This situation can no longer be tolerated. The student can be asked how he would be willing to change so as not to disturb others.

Sixth: Another referral is made to the person-in-charge-of-discipline where formal behavioral limits are defined for the student. These limits should be in writing and the student should acknowledge his agreement by signing his name. Copies are given to the student and the teacher. The student is notified that if there are continued disruptions his parents will be notified and might be called in for a conference.

Seventh: After the parents have been consulted, the next step is to suspend the disruptive student for a few days. It is important that the parents understand he will be expected to return home where he will be assigned work to complete.

Eighth: The student is requested to attend a conference with the person-in-charge-of-discipline and his teacher. He is now given the option to return to class. Assuming he wishes to resume his studies, he is explicitly asked what he is prepared to do to be readmitted. Again, a behavioral contract is written and the student is informed that any further infraction will result in his expulsion. The choice is his and not the school's.

Ninth: The student finally is referred to an alternative institution. If geographically feasible the student once again is given the option to return to school on a part-time basis with the understanding that when his behavior improves he can be readmitted.

Discipline, when it becomes a well-conceived process, can be a profound learning experience for the disruptive student. The disruptive student learns acceptable behavioral limits, and if he elects to violate them he anticipates the consequences of his behavior. Throughout this sequentially escalating process, the strengths of the student are recognized. He is treated as if he were a responsible person and the expectation is that he can function in any class situation if he so chooses.

While being annoyed, generally, the other students appreciate the fact that the perpetrator was given many opportunities to rectify his behavior and elected not to do so. They realize, in the final analysis, it is the student himself and not the system which caused his expulsion.

Class Meetings

If students are to feel part of the school, they must share responsibility for the instructional and managerial processes. Most public schools subscribe to the proposition that students should be involved but generally do not provide the necessary structures to permit meaningful and active participation. Glasser has suggested that class meetings be conducted daily which provide students and teachers with the opportunity to communicate about vital mutual issues. These class meetings of Glasser's, O'Donnell and Maxwell (1971) report, serve several purposes:

They help teachers achieve involvement with the group as well as to check on the learning and attitudes of the various members of the group. They help students learn to think about problems, theirs and society's, and to work out solutions. Meetings are problem-solving (concerned with students' social behavior or educational problems in school), open-ended (concerned with intellectually important subjects), or educational-diagnostic (concerned with how well students understand curriculum concepts). The same meeting techniques can be used by the staff to find solutions to individual and group problems of any class or of the entire school.

Students are encouraged to contribute to these open-ended discussions where every answer is correct. Class meetings become a pragmatic discussion about anything. Glasser (1969, pp. 162–185) lists approximately seventy-five suggested topics. It is appropriate for the class to try to resolve a behavior problem by describing it, by evaluating it, and by presenting several options to prevent the situation from recurring. (Punishment and discipline are believed to fall outside the purview of these class discussions.)

Hawes (1973) provides three basic guidelines which he has found helpful in conducting class meetings:

The first guideline is that pupils should be encouraged to define something. Once again, questions leading off with what, where, when, who, and how are helpful. The second guideline is that questions pertaining to the subject of the discussion should encourage a personal opinion or choice. . . . The teacher is interested in stimulating the child to think reasonably and to relate his response in a personal manner. This makes the discussion relevant. The third guideline is that children should be encouraged to challenge one another.

The class meeting becomes an innovative technique to help students think for themselves. It helps to include them in the educational process which stresses personal decision-making and self-evaluation. It, furthermore, enables the teacher to learn more about the student as an individual and permits the instructor to become involved with him in a meaningful way.

Alternatives to Detention: A Case Study

The New York City Department of Probation in 1973 implemented an innovative educational program for approximately twenty-five adolescents, whose behavior had been so threatening and disruptive that they were expelled from their respective high schools. There are, of course, divergent perceptions of this educational program. The Department of Probation views it as a creative effort to provide positive educational habilitative and rehabilitative services for the adolescent who has created behavior problems within the traditional school. Courts view it as an opportunity to give the probationer "one last chance" to remain in the community before being incarcerated. The students view it as a form of punishment and ostracism but are grateful that they still are permitted to remain in the community. The local schools view it as "a dumping ground" for the uneducable, the untreatable, the uncooperative, the unpredictable, and the undesirable. The politicians view it as a relatively inexpensive way to maintain a "care, custody, and control" authoritarian relationship with twenty-five troublesome adolescents. The families of these students remain ambivalent depending on whether or not they prefer to have their offspring remain at home or be sent away. The local merchants view the program with suspicion and fear because they recognize the bright colors of the neighborhood gangs and they see the locked doors and barred windows. If the community were privy to the exotic varieties of schizophrenic and psychotic labels graciously provided by the pejorative Psychiatric Establishment, they would demand that the program be closed immediately. In addition, more terrifying, perhaps, are some of the behavior performances of these students: a boy who knifed a teacher, a girl who defeated a policeman by knocking him unconscious, a boy who destroyed thousands of dollars' worth of high school property, a girl who consistently fights with her parents, a boy who assaulted a principal, a girl who is the elected leader of an all-male fighting gang, a boy who likes to set fires.

Glasser suggests, whenever possible, there should be heterogeneous grouping. Several are unwed mothers, others are unwed fathers. Some are maintained on high dosages of medication, others elect to prescribe illicit drugs for themselves, and a few are drug-free. Some drink, others do not. Some are sadistic, others are masochistic. They are black, brown, yellow, and white. Some are intelligent, others are dull. They are simultaneously homogeneous: All are members of rival, warring gangs. All have convinced many that they cannot conform to the routine of the classroom. All are angry, alienated, aggressive, and anti-authoritarian. All view the classroom as a battleground and the teacher as the enemy. All are unwanted, unloved, untamed. There are no productive, responsible, "well adjusted" adolescents who love school. None have optimistic personal, educational, and vocational prognoses. Collectively, these adolescents constitute a teacher's nightmare. The interracial, inter-gang, inter-sexual, and inter-personal dynamics make the environment potentially explosive. Behaviorally, they are failures. Psychologically, they are failures. Educationally, they are failures. Clinically, they are failures.

The staff consists of a probation officer in charge, two New York City Board of Education certified teachers, two community workers, several volunteers, and a part-time group dynamics consultant. I am the consultant.

I was assigned to the Alternatives to Detention Program six months after it had been inaugurated. As could be anticipated, when I arrived the classroom was a battlefield. While it was a relatively easy task to determine the "good guys," who are the professionals, I was unable to determine who were the officers, or "the bad guys." In the band of twenty-four there appeared to be as many chiefs, generals, and warriors. Fortunately, they were disorganized because, while agreeing that the staff was the enemy, they could agree on nothing else. There was perpetual motion. It was as if everyone was playing musical chairs without any music. The noise was deafening. Yet the place remained intact and clean.

While there was overt hostility punctuated with scatological language, no one ever fought. Perhaps that was the only ground rule. No fighting!

Somehow I survived that first day—the longest day of my professional career. I had been asked "Who the fuck are you?" "How much money do you make?" "Are you going to label all of us crazy?" "How come you are here?" "Do you want to fight?" I was confused because the staff was united and their morale was high. When the kids became abusive, the staff smiled and tolerated it. Never did they lose their composure.

A most curious event occurred. When the school day finally ended and the kids had the option to leave, they elected to stay. In fact, it took the staff more than half an hour to physically evict all the kids who remained outside and hammered on the windows. The staff assembled silently and obediently. They were most anxious to obtain my reaction. The first question which broke the silence was "Well, what do you think?" Think! I did not have to think . . . I knew what to think. But as I started to talk I was startled to hear what I said. First, I congratulated everyone for not overreacting and killing a kid. I said I saw and experienced a lot of love by the staff to those . . . I paused because I did not know what to call them. They defied traditional labels. They certainly were not students. They were not adults. They were not sick. I was tempted to call them monsters but I know the damage caused by labeling and, besides, "monsters" did not sound clinical. For lack of a better word, I called them kids. Fortunately no one asked me to define kids. I pointed out the confusion about the kind of love these kids need. They do not need forgiveness. They do not need the unconditional positive regard which Rogers (1961) describes. They do not need people to lend them five dollars when it will be used to purchase drugs. They do not need people who will commiserate and tell them that it is a miserable "fucked-up" world and they are the casualties and victims. What they need is people who will confront them with the malignant, self-destructive, and sadistic aspects of their behavior and who will tell them that often it is damned difficult to love them when they are abusive and behave irresponsibly. They need people who will define and enforce limits.

Elsewhere I have discussed the therapeutic aspects of forced behavioral change (Bratter, 1974c). They need people who will
expect and demand the best from them. They need, as Glasser
(1969, p. 24) has written, "teachers who will not excuse them
when they fail their commitments, but who will work with them
again and again as they commit and recommit until they finally
learn to fulfill a commitment. When they learn to do so, they are
no longer lonely; they gain maturity, respect, love, and a successful
identity." Abruptly stopping, I asked the staff why they thought the
kids were reluctant to leave. No one had thought about it. No one
had an explanation. I told the staff that the kids genuinely were
fond of them and the place but for the wrong reasons. No one in
their lives ever had tolerated so much abuse. No one had ever
accepted them. And they had nowhere else to go without getting
into trouble. But we must rechannel their energy and transform it
from being self-destructive to self-enhancing.

We needed a basic, uncomplicated code of deportment. We
could tolerate no threat or any fighting. We would insist upon
respect when a person would be given the opportunity to talk and
others would not interrupt. If a student wanted to study, he could
do so without being disturbed. No property could be stolen or
destroyed. These rules were non-negotiable and any infraction
would mean immediate dismissal with a report being sent to the
court. Each student would be expected to agree to these terms and
if they believed they could not, they would be referred to the court
without prejudice.

Educational Goals

All the energy of the staff could be redirected from attempting
to maintain order to teaching. We decided to formulate some educational goals. Rather than to strive for academic excellence, we
decided to focus on the cognitive and emotional factors in learning. We wanted our students to accept the consequences of their
behavior and to become more responsible and productive to themselves, others, and to society. Each student would accept the responsibility for his own education. We wanted to make education

relevant. Education is, as Bell (1969) argues, "a confrontation with a discipline, a confrontation with a teacher." But we decided to expand education to become a confrontation with oneself. Grene (1966) contends "in fact, there is only one process, that is, ourselves trying to make sense of things, trying to find significance in what would else be chaos. . . . Learning is a transformation of the whole person." The teacher's primary responsibility was to help each student to think for himself. We wanted to help our students learn to listen, to think, and then to respond. We wanted to create an atmosphere where our students would feel free to discuss any concern related to themselves, the curriculum, and society.

Manipulating the Manipulators: The Game for Respect

We knew first we would be forced to gain the respect of the class. We knew we had to assert ourselves but we were not sure how. We could not accept the challenges to fight. We could not acknowledge the seductions. We decided to gamble. We would defend our "honor" on the basketball court! Two of us had previous basketball experience and were 6'2" and weighed more than 220. We knew our prime had passed us quietly almost a decade ago but believed we could control the backboards if we could coordinate our efforts. If we lost, we reasoned, we would have demonstrated our courage and that is the "code of their street." We issued the invitation and were greeted with the longest silence I had witnessed since starting two months before. The kids became excited because they were confident they clearly would establish their superiority and humiliate us. Jimmy the Greek would offer no odds. They found it hilarious that I was playing basketball before they were born. (My reaction, I admit, was depression, recognizing that age was winning its battle against me.) Being the senior member, I asked for a three-week period to try to get into shape. They agreed immediately. I had the brilliant idea that we now would look for legitimate reasons to deprive anyone from playing against us. We invited infractions of the most insignificant rules. For the next three weeks we had "law and order" which would have made any school look bad by comparison. Inexorably as the days passed, our inner confidence began to ebb. Outwardly, however, I threatened them all to a confrontation on the court. Any bluff, I imagined, is better than no bluff at all.

The game was decided in the first minute of play. With God and Glasser on our side, I miraculously blocked a jump shot of the tallest player on the court, which intimidated the kids the way Jabbar and Walton do. They refused to come near me. In their efforts to become individual stars, the kids' game deteriorated to a street display. The kid who rebounded would dribble the length of the court and shoot. In comparison, we passed and even managed a few fast breaks. The score wasn't even close. We won. Even if we had lost, we would have established the respect and rapport we needed.

Toward a Definition of Education

Our first class meeting after the game was a task, which the kids did not know was fictitious, for the writing of a two-hundred-word description of our educational program for the Probation Department. I doubt that any task—even the drafting of the United States Constitution—was ever taken so seriously. We wanted simple sentences but our kids insisted on formal language. After all, they reasoned, the Department of Probation could refuse to fund this program unless every "t" was crossed and every "i" dotted. The kids sincerely believed that the entire fate of the program hinged on this effort:

Undoubtedly the most singular aspect in the spectra of Man is his capacity for growth: to be alive, a person must grow and when he ceases to grow, he ceases to live. Life is essentially growth and development, and conversely, to develop is to live. The optimal concern of education is with growth—the growth of the individual who has the capacity to develop. The major aim of education is to provide the conditions under which native endowments and capacities can be properly developed. Without this inherent capacity for growth in human beings, education would be impossible but when properly utilized it can provide a vitality to the total process of learning. The task of education is not to provide students with an abundance of information because the possession of knowledge must not be viewed as an end in itself. Education, if it is to be successful, must become a way of living which stimulates and inspires learning by active effort as naturally as does education outside the formal confines of the classroom. Otherwise growth of the right sort, which involves the total development of the individual, will not take place.

Cooperative versus Competitive Learning

We still are trying to create an atmosphere where one student will help another. We would like to implement the "helper principle" where helpers often gain more from the helping process than the person who ostensibly is being helped. A student who has expertise in one area will attempt to help a peer who may not be so proficient. One of the first to describe this principle, Reissman (1965) concludes that "it is probably no accident that it is often said that one of the best ways to learn is to teach."

We would like to stimulate a cooperative climate of learning rather than a competitive one. We agree with Rothenberg, Johnson, and Slatkin (1969–1970) who discovered that the most effective teaching method was to increase cooperation among peers. "Grades and tests would be de-emphasized. Most important of all, teachers would avoid making derogatory comparisons between students."

Since it is possible to motivate unmotivated, angry, alienated adolescents who collectively initially intensified the worst in each other, we believe Leonard (1968) is correct when he contends that the pursuit of education can result in the achievement of ecstasy. This becomes possible when consistent limits are set and enforced and when students are given the opportunity to participate in class discussions. The necessary ingredient is for educators to become involved with their students and their students' struggles. Education should emphasize what Maslow (1971) called the "human goal, the humanistic goal . . . (of education) . . . is ultimately the self-actualization of a person, the becoming fully human, the development of the fullest height that the human species can stand up to or that the particular individual can come to. In a less technical way, it is helping the person to become the best that he is able to become."

To Sir With Love: The Teacher as a Philosopher-Human Relations Specialist

Wherever we turn today, we find the yearning for something which will give the individual direction, purpose, and dignity. There is a feeling of need, of insecurity and frustration, which leads people to seek an external source of wisdom and direction. Wolfe (1936) poetically has written "and this central idea was this: the deepest search in life, it seemed to me, the thing that in one way or another was central to all living was man's search to find a father, not merely the father of his flesh, not merely the lost father of his youth, but the image of a strength and wisdom external to his need and superior to his hunger, to which the belief and power of his own life could be united." To meet the demands by which modern life challenges the individual, one must discover the way for himself. At best, he can find in the experience and ideas of others those suggestions and instruction, but the ultimate decision remains that of the individual. Every person needs a set of guiding principles by which he can govern his existence. It is in this realm that the gifted and dedicated teacher must carry through his obligations. His first obligation is similar to that of a human relations specialist because the teacher should stimulate the individual to think for himself rather than to accept dogma and the philosophical views of any other, no matter how important those views may be.

Perhaps the teacher-philosopher-human relations specialist must be the overseer of the student's intellectual and emotional growth and development, a conglomerate growth which has as its end result a working philosophy of life which derives from an inner calmness of spirit and which originates from knowing what the individual believes and why—and that outer strength of purpose which comes with a sense of inner peace and security. This is what teaching means: no more, no less.

REFERENCES

Bell, Daniel. "Social Change in Education and the Change in Educational Concepts," in Clarence H. Faust and Jessica Feingold (eds.), *Approaches to Education for Character*. New York: Columbia University Press, 1969.

Bratter, Thomas Edward. "Treating Alienated, Unmotivated, Drug Abusing Adolescents," *American Journal of Psychotherapy*, XXVII: 4 (October, 1973), pp. 593–594.

Bratter, Thomas Edward. "Reality Therapy: A Group Psychotherapeutic Approach with Adolescent Alcoholics," *Annals of the New York Academy of Sciences*, 233 (April 15, 1974), pp. 104–114. New York: The New York Academy of Sciences, 1974.

Bratter, Thomas Edward. "Guardian, Behavioral Engineer, Advocate, Friend: Humanistic Roles for Probation Officers," *Corrective and Social Psychiatry*, 20:3 (1974), pp. 1–9.

Childs, John L. *Education and Morals*. New York: John Wiley & Sons, Inc., 1950, pp. 178–179.

Committee for a Comprehensive Education Center, "Proposal for an Experimental Secondary School Research Project to be Conducted Jointly by the New York City Board of Education and the Committee for a Comprehensive Education Center," September 1, 1970, p. 7. (Mimeographed.)

Dewey, John. *Lectures in the Philosophy of Education*. New York: Random House, 1966, p. 49.

Drews, Elizabeth Monroe. "Beyond Curriculum," *Journal of Humanistic Psychology*, VIII:2 (Fall, 1968), p. 101.

Fish, Barbara. "The 'One Child, One Drug' Myth of Stimulants in Hyperkinesis: Importance of Diagnostic Categories in Evaluating Treatment," *Archives of General Psychiatry*, 25:10 (September, 1971), p. 197.

Friedenberg, Edgar Z. "Current Patterns of Generational Conflict," *Journal of Social Issues*, XXV:2 (1969), pp. 21–38.

Glasser, William. "Creating a School Without Failure," presented to the Staff-Parent Association of L. W. Beecher and S. S. Sherida Schools. New Haven, Connecticut. April 2, 1974.

Glasser, William. *The Identity Society*. New York: Harper & Row, 1972, p. 9.

Glasser, William. *Schools Without Failure*. New York: Harper & Row, 1969.

Glasser, William. *Reality Therapy: A New Approach to Psychiatry*. New York: Harper & Row, 1965.

Goodman, Paul. "Freedom and Learning: The Need for Choice," *Saturday Review* (May 18, 1968), p. 16.

Grene, Marjorie. *The Knower and the Known*. New York: Basic Books, 1966.

Grunwald, Bernice. "Strategies for Behavior Change in Schools," *Counseling Psychologist*, 3:1 (1971), p. 56.

Harman, W. W. "Explorations in Human Potentialities," in H. A. Otto (ed.), *Explorations in Human Potentialities*. Springfield, Ill.: Charles C. Thomas, 1966.

Hawes, Richard M. "Getting Along in the Classroom," in Merle M. Ohlsen (ed.), *Counseling Children in Groups: A Forum*. New York: Holt, Rinehart & Winston, Publishers, 1973, p. 196.

Henry, Jules. "The Suburban Nightmare," in R. Gross (ed.), *Radical School Reform*. New York: Simon & Schuster, 1969, p. 85.

Holt, John. *How Children Fail*. New York: Dell Publishing Company, Inc., 1964, p. 165.

Huxley, Aldous. *Brave New World*. New York: Modern Library, 1946.

Irwin, Theodore. "Schools Where No One Fails," *Parade* (October 21, 1973), pp. 1–2.

Jacobs, Ruth Harriet. "School, Identity, and Success: Adolescents in Gloom," *Youth and Society: A Quarterly Journal*, 4:3 (March, 1973), p. 282.

Ladd, Edward T. "Pills for Classroom Peace?" *Saturday Review* (November 21, 1970), pp. 66–68, 81–83.

Leonard, George B. *Education and Ecstasy*. New York: Delacorte Press, 1968, p. 16.

Maslow, Abraham H. "Education and Peak Experiences," in Abraham H. Maslow (ed.), *The Farther Reaches of Human Nature*. New York: The Viking Press, 1971, pp. 168–169.

Miller, Henry. "On Hanging Loose and Loving: The Dilemma of Present Youth," *Journal of Social Issues*, 27:3 (1971), pp. 35–46.

O'Donnell, Donald J. and Keith F. Maxwell. "Reality Therapy Works Here," *Instructor* (March, 1971), p. 71.

Orwell, George. *1984*. New York: Harcourt Brace, 1949.

Postman, Neil and Charles Weingartner. *The Soft Revolution*. New York: Dell Publishing Co., 1971, p. 118.

Riessman, Frank. "The 'Helper' Therapy Principle," *Social Work*, 10:2 (April, 1965), p. 32.

Rogers, Carl R. "The Characteristics of a Helping Relationship," in Carl A. Rogers (ed.), *On Becoming a Person*. Cambridge, Mass.: Riverside Press, 1961, pp. 39–58.

Rosenthal, Robert. "The Pygmalion Effect Lives," *Psychology Today*, 7:4 (September, 1973), pp. 56–62.

Rosenthal, Robert. "Teacher Expectations and Pupil Learning," in Robert D. Stromm (ed.), *Teachers and the Learning Process*. Englewood Cliffs, N.J.: Prentice-Hall, 1971.

Rothenberg, Albert, Julia C. Johnson, and Stephen Slatkin. "A School in a Therapeutic Community," *The International Journal of Social Psychiatry*, XVI:1 (Winter, 1969–1970), p. 28.

Shoben, Jr., Edward J. "Guidance: Remedial Function or Social Reconstruction?" *Harvard Educational Review*, 33 (1962), pp. 430–433.

Silberman, Charles E. *Crisis in the Classroom: The Remaking of American Education*. New York: Random House, 1970, p. 151.

Stretch, Bonnie Barret. "The Rise of the 'Free School,'" *The Saturday Review* (June 20, 1970), p. 76.

Wolfe, Thomas. *The Story of a Novel*. New York: Charles Scribner's Sons, 1935, p. 39.

Yuncker, Barbara. "The Power of Positive Teaching," *Family Circle* (May, 1970), pp. 34, 95, 96, 98.

The Caring Community

Part I: Introduction

HARRY: Life in this dormitory is really a hassle—for me and a lot of others. I know twenty people who are thinking of moving out, many of them might drop out of school, too.

GARY: Why do you think so many people are giving up so soon on this place?

HARRY: The school may be new but the problems are old: it's a big rip-off. I feel alienated from the faculty, the other students, and even myself living in this crazy place. People aren't really interested in helping one another or getting to know one another. My Resident Assistant is drunk or stoned all the time and plays his stereo so loud that no one on his hall can study or sleep. There are a lot of lonely and timid people who hardly ever come out of their rooms. The Black Student Association isn't even able to interest the majority of the kids who are black. They really seem paranoid. My roommate won't go to B.S.A. meetings and he won't open up to me or anyone. This is just a lonely campus.

GARY: Do you think people would work together to change the situation?

HARRY: I think some would, but others are already so bitter that they just want to escape.

Presented at a symposium for Divisions 29 and 32 at the 81st Annual Meeting of the American Psychological Association in Montreal, Quebec, 1973.

GARY: I wonder how the idea of encounter groups and a communal structure within the dormitory might go over? I'd like to see the students and faculty really get involved in building a community spirit and take advantage of the fact that we are new and small.

HARRY: It sounds exciting to me. What do you have in mind, specifically?

This fragment of a late-evening conversation I had with one of my counseling clients illustrates the discontent that was so widespread among students on a college campus that was barely a semester old. As a resident Counseling Director and faculty member, I became personally and deeply involved in the many issues which surrounded the feelings Harry and many others expressed to me during their first year on campus.

It became clear to me that the "ivory tower" has not insulated its inhabitants from the pressures and threats of the larger society. The college campus shares the political, economic, religious, and racial conflicts which threaten the security and existence of many other social institutions. In addition, the college environment, with a preponderance of youthful members, provides a temporary and fragmented involvement for its students. The pressures toward achievement, competition, and specialization which often are identified with business or marketing contexts, also pervade the ivory tower, separating students from one another and catalyzing the confusion in their interpersonal relationships.

For many students, the campus is experienced as a first station along the path toward independence and freedom from family and traditional lifestyles. They find the campus environment both a source of inspiration and a source of frustration in their search for a meaningful lifestyle. The opportunity for exploration of self is enhanced by contact with new subjects and new relationships. The risk of identity diffusion develops as the student explores a variety of possible definitions of self in the sequence of choices which college requires. Alienation and apathy infect the process of self-discovery when students encounter barriers to their growth such as their own limitations and the inhibiting influences of others. Altruism can fade to apathy when they discover that their choices are no more effective in the "ivory tower" than they were in the "real world" of work and family relations.

Students seeking solutions to these problems have become involved with everything from drugs to radical politics and religion (Keniston, 1965; De Ropp, 1968; Nowlis, 1968; Roszak, 1969; Nahal, 1971; Hunter, 1972). Increasing numbers have rejected traditional models and methods in favor of more experimental approaches to personal, social, and vocational identity. These developments have not been easily integrated within the structures, practices, and policies of the academic institutions (Hutchins, 1953; Leonard, 1968; Farber, 1969; Rogers, 1969). Diminishing membership in fraternities and sororities, diminishing participation in student government, and declining levels of school spirit in general, have alarmed student personnel administrators who view alternatives with fear and confusion.

During the Spring semester of 1973, I implemented and directed a program known as the Caring Community at a new branch of the State University of New York at Purchase. The residential program was located in the college dormitory building. Its membership consisted of selected students whose participation in encounter groups indicated strong motivation for more intensive involvement. The specific elements of this program, sponsored by the counseling services of the college, will be described in Part II. It should be noted that the origins for such a project were three models of personal and interpersonal growth which have been developed elsewhere: the communal movement, the therapeutic community model of treatment, and Glasser's concept of the Community Involvement Center (Glasser, 1972).

The Communal Movement

Several of the original members of the Caring Community had communal living experiences prior to attending the College at Purchase. They were motivated primarily by their desire to continue what they had learned previously at communes. For a few, the notion of a commune had become a negative one. They found in the unstructured lifestyles of some communal settings the kind of confusion and identity diffusion which limited rather than enhanced their personal growth. Houriet (1971) has noted a general trend in the communal movements of recent years away from unstructured anarchistic communes to more structured ones. They joined the Caring Community when they discovered there would be more structure. Others, who had participated in more structured communes with political or religious themes, welcomed this opportunity to build their own commune on a college campus. Probably curiosity and confusion about the meaning and nature of communal living inspired a few of the students to explore this as a possible living alternative within the college dormitory setting. The program has also served as an example of communal social structures for a number of students conducting studies of communes. The historical antecedents of the communal aspects of this program have been described by Fairchild (1972), Melville (1972), and Veysey (1973) and will not be reviewed here.

The Therapeutic Community

The therapeutic community is a concept of treatment and rehabilitation which has been described by Bassin (1968), Casriel (1971, 1972), and Yablonsky (1965). Therapeutic communities such as Daytop Village, Synanon, and DISC Village, as well as the prototype for such programs, Alcoholics Anonymous, share a common goal of responsible concern. They utilize the unique insights and motivations of the ex-addict or ex-alcoholic to help an addict or alcoholic overcome his own destructive and irresponsible patterns of behavior.

I had the opportunity to live with a Daytop Village facility at Millbrook, New York, six months before the Caring Community was opened. The fact that alienated, self-destructive individuals, who had long histories of drug abuse and criminal behavior, could change their attitudes and behavior in constructive ways, impressed me greatly as I shared in confrontation sessions, work assignments, and a general atmosphere of love and concern in the Daytop Village program. This experience and the belief that the therapeutic community could be modified to provide college students with a productive learning experience prompted me to create the Caring Community. Indeed, I saw how this program could play a self-actualizing role in the lives of individuals who are already productive and responsible.

The implications of a therapeutic community model for individuals who do not perceive themselves as having a drug or alcohol problem can be very complicated. Some students, fearful that the program would include treatment and rehabilitation, did not join. The connotations of confrontation sessions, encounter groups, and the hostile "Synanon games" discouraged some prospective members. My own efforts to borrow techniques and terminology from the Daytop Village concepts also alienated some individuals whose backgrounds were atypical of Daytop members and for whom drug abuse was not a personal concern. There was some recognition by students, however, that selfish and irresponsible "junkie attitudes" are not exclusive to drug addicts.

Staff and residents of Daytop Village programs were enthusiastic about the possibility of developing a therapeutic community for nonaddicted students. They were generous in their efforts to assist us in the initial training and screening of the members of the Caring Community. One drug abuse program utilized the Caring Community as a kind of halfway house experience for a graduate of its facility who had enrolled in the College at Purchase. We did not, however, emphasize the link to Daytop Village in our general formulation of the Caring Community because the program was not primarily oriented toward drug abuse treatment.

The Community Involvement Center

William Glasser's concepts of Reality Therapy have been extended from the psychiatric hospital to the educational system and, in a recent work, to society as a whole (Glasser, 1965, 1969, 1972). In his most recent work, *The Identity Society,* Dr. Glasser proposed a new model for replacing many traditional and ineffective mental health and community agencies with a positive and preventive alternative. His concept of a Community Involvement

Center is based upon the assumption that cooperating individuals, pooling their diverse talents and resources, can provide a host of services for one another which will reduce the need for a variety of existing social agencies. His recommendations are based upon assumptions concerning the cooperative and affiliative needs of people. Glasser also emphasizes a positive growth model for human learning and mental health rather than the dynamics of failure and anxiety-oriented models of other schools of therapy.

Glasser suggests that contemporary society, with its relative advantages of economic security, technological achievement, and mass communication, has become an *identity society*—a culture in which its members seek "a pleasurable belief in themselves and their own humanity and the companionship of others in ways not necessarily related to work" (Glasser, 1972, p. 28). The primary needs which emerge from this social context are involvement and independence. This special orientation of a member of the identity society causes the person to seek pleasure and meaning in the communication with others and roles of intrinsic value whose activities do not necessarily lead to specific vocational goals. In the classroom, the home, and the job situation we find increasing demand for nontraditional structures and goals which *"immediately* and *directly* reinforce our basic human role" (Glasser, 1972, p. 41).

The Caring Community is an attempt to explore this concept of a Community Involvement Center within a college campus environment. It was designed to provide peer counseling as well as social services for both its membership and other students. We sponsored a campus gardening project in which students cultivated and harvested some of their own food. The notion of shared participation and traded resources was, perhaps, the hallmark of the Caring Community. Glasser's concept of a Community Involvement Center has not yet been implemented and tested. I, therefore, regard the Caring Community as a pilot study of the viability of Glasser's assumptions in a college environment.

The Caring Community opened on a new campus of about one thousand students, half of whom live in a college dormitory. The small size and relatively brief history of the college presented some obstacles. Delays in the construction of buildings and decreased funding disappointed and frustrated those who hoped to pioneer many programs on the college campus. Confusion concerning campus priorities and policies inhibited the communication between students and faculty and among faculty members. Departmental commitments limited student access to elective courses of other divisions and the availability of students for extracurricular involvements.

Part II: Structure and Functions of the Caring Community

CAROL: What do you think about Gary's choosing you to be a coordinator?

HARRY: I felt that a lot had to be done to improve my relations with people. I was really interested in psychology and a Daytop experiment being conducted on campus. I was really into Daytop when I visited there and was impressed by how real and sensitive people were there. They believed that people had to be worked on in terms of people working together.

In order to be a coordinator you have to be able to test people—help them get to their feelings. In Daytop there is also a person called an Expeditor—he speeds up the process. These are very important and responsible positions. You have to be someone who can handle your emotions and when you get other people's emotions out in the open you have to keep your head together. Having the job made me keep my head together and be very serious about this experiment. I had to be very responsible. I became part of the organizational structure.

CAROL: What do you think about Harry as a coordinator?

DON: He changed under the pressure of the responsibility. The way he was acting wasn't like him at all. It's amazing what an authority position can do to some people. A couple of us who knew Harry before the community started confronted him about it.

CAROL: What happened to you and the community as a result of the Daytop structure?

HARRY: I was really upset when people—even my close friends—

got down on the idea of having coordinators. I still believe in the Daytop model but people didn't really give it a chance before changing it.

CAROL: Why did this happen?

HARRY: I think that this college tends to attract the sort of student who is looking for an alternative to highly structured and supervised school situations. Gary and I were both very sincere but it was necessary to bring other people in on the planning as well. When this happened, the structure lossened up a bit and people seemed happier and more involved.

Organizational Structure

The Caring Community's activities and structures evolved in response to the needs of its members and their relationship to the growth of the campus in which the Caring Community is located. At its inception, the Caring Community had a formal and rigid organizational structure borrowed in the large part from Daytop Village. The need for a more flexible and democratic organizational model emerged as members could not relate to many of the techniques used by Daytop Village. The debates concerning the advantages and disadvantages of each structure became important forums for the ideas of Caring Community members who truly shaped the program and enabled it to survive the many threats to its early existence. Growth and communication were enhanced by efforts to revise the initial model to fulfill the needs of productive and responsible college students. The organizational structure which emerged is described in Figure 4. The form and atmosphere of the organization continues to evolve and existing models and structures are phased out as new needs and new members emerge.

The structure of the Caring Community included indirect relationships (shown in Figure 4 with dotted lines) to the Dean of the Division of Student Affairs and the Residence Hall staff administration. As the Project Director, I also served as Director of Counseling Services for the college, and was directly responsible to the Dean of Student Affairs.

I was accountable not only to the Caring Community, but also represented the program's interests on the campus. I provided both counseling and administrative services to the program in addition to working with other students. My daily involvement in the program included an average of two to three hours initially and decreased to an average of five hours per week. My goal as director was to develop the resources of the group for operating independently of faculty and staff direction. I was, in essence, attempting

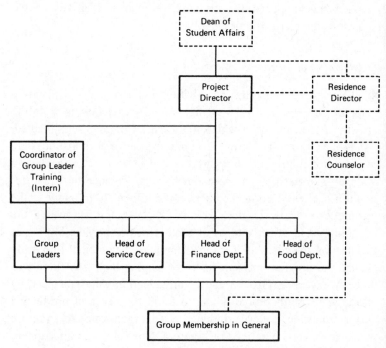

Figure 4. Organizational Structure for the Caring Community.

to put myself out of work by facilitating the development of the group's own resources for organizing and administering the Caring Community's programs.

I was assisted by a graduate student counseling intern who served as the Coordinator of Group Leader Training for this program. The Coordinator of Group Leader Training also provided some public relations and liaison services for the project. Because of her professional role as an intern in the Counseling Services of the Division of Student Affairs for the college, her program participation had to be limited to approximately five hours per week. She conducted experiential and didactic training sessions for peer group counselors and co-led a number of "human potential" groups with Caring Community members. The functions of the Caring Community were organized into departmental units. The heads of departments in this program were responsible not only to the director of the project but also to the membership for organizing and evaluating the activities in their particular areas of responsibility. The extent of their involvement in the program and the quality of their concern about its progress made them vital members of the Caring Community. Their rotating assignments were voluntary. The chairmanship of the Service Crew, for example, was rotated four times in one year.

Four specialized departments or areas of responsibility emerged. The Group Leaders functioned as a vital department, offering peer counseling in a human potential group format which will be described later. The Head of the Food Department was responsible for purchasing food and assigning duties in order to prepare potluck Sunday suppers and other events which the Caring Community occasionally sponsored. The Head of the Finance Department functioned as a treasurer who maintained the Caring Community checking account and disbursed petty cash for incidental costs of the program.

The Head of the Service Crew assigned house work duties on a weekly basis to all members and checked up on the performance of those duties. This self-maintaining Service Crew produced a cleaner and more attractively decorated environment than all the other areas of the dormitory where a paid housekeeping staff maintained the building. The students were expected to spend approximately 45 minutes per week in shared cleaning of public areas of the community. The activities of the Service Crew were not only designed to keep the community neat and clean, but they provided many opportunities for the members to evaluate attitudes and relationships. The program exemplifies to some extent Bion's (1961) notion of a work-oriented group, where patterns that interfere with the group's productivity are the basis of process discussion and personal self-assessment. Rotations in some of these positions provided more meaningful and diverse learning experiences even though it would have been more efficient to assign one person to a given role for the academic year.

The group membership was effective in evaluating the work of the various departments. At group meetings, department heads occasionally were criticized for arbitrary use of their authority or negligence of their responsibility to challenge those individuals who failed to do their part.

Initially we attempted to resolve problems with group consensus. As the program expanded and its locations multiplied, however, it became impossible to find times when all members could attend. Decision making became a voting process generally conducted by using sign-up sheets and memoranda on a central bulletin board, on which opinions were polled concerning various topics of importance to the entire membership.

Physical Setting

The Caring Community began as one wing of a four-floor U-shaped dormitory building. The building was designed to include suites for eight individuals who shared a bathroom and a small study as well as corridors containing double-rooms for twelve, two single rooms, a bathroom plus a television lounge to be shared by the fourteen. The Caring Community contained one suite for eight and one corridor for fourteen in its first semester of operation. The Project Director's apartment was located on the same wing of the dormitory adjacent to the lounge of the Caring Community corridor. The following semester, the Caring Community required more space in order to accommodate approximately twenty additional members who were housed in two suites and one corridor on other floors of the same building. Communication among the members of Caring Community became more difficult as the result of the fact that they were widely separated spatially.

The design of the building facilitated the kinds of group programs that the Caring Community sponsored. The suites and study areas were adapted easily to small group meetings and permitted establishment of a kitchenette for preparation of occasional pot-luck meals. The first semester of operation, the adjacent suite and faculty apartment permitted immediate and convenient access among all members of the program. As a result an open-door atmosphere of closeness developed in that section of the building.

The building presented some problems for its occupants. It was a new residence hall, whose rooms were smaller than the average college dormitory rooms. Its equipment and heating systems required many repairs during most of the first semester. Delays in the delivery of essential furnishings and temporary interruptions in lighting, heating, and water created inconvenience and annoyance for all. Some damage to other areas of the building was the result of students' anger and frustration for these discomforts. In comparison to other students, the Caring Community responded more constructively. Instead of complaining and defacing the building, they shared service crew responsibilities.

Selection of Members

"What do you want from the Caring Community?"

"A supportive, but confronting environment where we are actively committed to breaking patterns/defenses/boundaries, and exploring new interpersonal spaces, in trust and honesty . . . while respecting each other's privacy . . ."

"I would like very much to be able to meet and get to know people easily and be a little less introverted and self-conscious. Also to be a little more patient with others when I am working with them . . ."

"Something that can give me a solid start in meeting people and forming relationships . . ."

"New friends . . ."

"Emotional growth and increased understanding of myself and others . . ."

"I would like to be a part of a caring community. As a transfer student, my experience of dorm life has been one of status seeking and isolation. I would like to be part of an ongoing encounter group . . ."

"I came to college for emotional and intellectual growth. I can grow intellectually from the academic program at Purchase. I feel that to facilitate my emotional growth and understanding the Caring Community would be the closest to an ideal situation . . ."

The initial screening and selection of members for the Caring Community was done by using a questionnaire and interview format. The questionnaire requested background data and asked specific questions concerning the individual's reasons for wanting to join the Caring Community. In addition, a group of sentence-completion items were included to survey the strengths and limitations and general outlook of the person applying for membership. Half-hour individual interviews were used in addition to the questionnaire to orient the applicant to what the Caring Community would be doing and to ask questions concerning the individual's preparation for becoming a member.

In the questionnaire, it was learned that the reasons for joining the Caring Community were varied. They are summarized in Table I, which provides a listing and ranking of the reasons given by students who applied to join the Caring Community.

Reasons for Joining	%
Opportunity to meet people	66
Opportunity to become open and honest	55
Opportunity to help others	44
Opportunity to humanize the college	33

TABLE 1: Percentage of applicants to the Caring Community who indicated specific reasons for joining the program.

After extensive contact with the original group of members, I concluded membership in the Caring Community should be both an individual and group decision and that questionnaires and interviews should not be employed as rigid selection procedures but should function as opportunities for orientation. Every student who applied to join the Caring Community was accepted. For some students it was clear that residential participation would exceed the time limits they had for such programs and they were encouraged to live at their home or in other sections of the dormitory and attend only certain functions which the Caring Community sponsored.

The general policy of the Caring Community concerning selection is that anyone can contribute and gain something in the Caring Community. This open (and revolving) door policy creates some advantages and disadvantages for the group organization. Some members contribute more than others and the length of membership tends to be highly variable.

Orientation of New Members

New members of the Caring Community received an orientation to the program which used sensitivity training and encounter group marathons. Early in each semester, the group went on extended sensitivity training weekend retreats. Additional on-campus marathons, which utilized some of the micro-lab techniques of encounter group leaders in the human potential movement, served to introduce new members to the Caring Community (Otto and Mann, 1963; Rogers, 1970; Schutz, 1967, 1971; Stevens, 1973).

This type of intensive orientation to group involvement and self-expression facilitated the formation of the Caring Community. An enthusiastic and positive feeling emerged from these early marathon experiences which provided new members with the feeling of closeness to a relatively large number of people from the very first week of their involvement on campus. For many, the seeds of friendship were sown in these early groups which matured with the passage of time and the sharing of experiences.

During the second year the orientation for new members emphasized the role that returning members could play in acquainting the new members with the program and helping them feel welcome and at home in it. This role has been described as the "twelfth step work" by Bratter (1974), in his interpretation of the sponsorship principle of the Alcoholics Anonymous program. The senior member of the program reinforces his own growth and responsibility in the process of helping the neophyte member achieve similar goals. One general meeting at the beginning of each semester was also utilized for presenting the practical, business, and scheduling aspects of the program to the membership as a whole.

On-Going Group Activities

On-going group activity within the Caring Community took four different forms. All groups were voluntary and involved as few as five and as many as all members. The Caring Community emphasized group involvement and all were encouraged to participate in a minimum of one group a week. However, for some members scheduling permitted only an occasional group.

1. Morning Meeting

GARY: Who is going to read the pull-ups and push-ups?

DON: I am. The first pull-up is: "Who left the attitude in the women's bathtub yesterday?" OK, who wrote this?

ELLEN: I did.

DON: What do you mean?

ELLEN: I have been on Service Crew doing the women's bathroom for two weeks now. Yesterday I spent half an hour scrubbing out the tubs and sinks. I came back about two hours later and found the tub with a really grimy ring around it and somebody's blond hair all around the drain. I'm getting tired of knocking myself out around here when no one else gives a damn!

DON: Well—who's going to cop to this?

CAROL: I did it, but I was in a hurry.

DON: Carol, you're always in a hurry when there's work to be done around here. What's your attitude, anyway?

CAROL: Attitude?! I'm working like hell here *and* in classes and I just can't get up in time some mornings. Why are people on my back again?

ELLEN: It's no harder for you than it is for me. Why don't you show a little consideration—and why not ask someone to wake you if you have an early class?

DON: I think you know what we're talking about and you could start showing some of the same concern for the rest of us that you expect for yourself.

CAROL: I guess you're right. My roommate pointed out the same thing. I seem to get selfish when I get uptight about getting all my work done.

The morning meeting was held each weekday for approximately 40 minutes before classes. The morning meeting had three recognizable segments. The initial segment included announcements. During the announcements period any projects for the specific day were described. Volunteers were invited and plans for accomplishing the day's goals were discussed. In the pull-ups and push-ups segment of the morning meeting, individuals confronted the group with their positive and negative reactions to events of the day before. The pull-up is illustrated by the line of questioning in the sample of dialogue above. The answers to such questions prompted further exploration of the attitudes underlying these behaviors. The "push-up" is illustrated by the statement of gratitude by a member who thanked the group for looking after her when she was ill and unable to sleep most of the night before. The push-up provides the opposite kind of opportunity that is presented by the pull-up. It is a time of recognition and acceptance that expresses the positive feelings of the member and the group. This function of the Caring Community was emphasized and was a unique aspect of the program, in contrast with the emphasis on pull-ups and confrontation in a therapeutic community. The pull-ups and the push-ups provided daily channels of expression of feelings that might build to the point of grudges in other living situations on a college campus. The third segment of the morning meeting involved some form of theater games, singing, yoga, or sensory awakening experiences for waking people up and starting the day with a positive outlook.

The responsibility for leading the morning meeting was shared among the members. A member could volunteer to conduct a morning meeting for a day or for a week. This person not only would discuss the plans with the group but also invited candid reactions afterwards. In this way the morning meeting served as an informal group leadership training experience.

2. *Human Potential Encounter Group*

"I want to be in an encounter group with Harry to work on my anger about his criticism. Carol" (a slip)

The human potential encounter group was composed of individuals who "dropped slips" on one another as well as other members who requested to be in an encounter group each week. Dropping a slip consisted of naming the complainant and the two parties of an unresolved conflict on a piece of paper and noting the feeling or attitude which a person experienced. These reminders of interpersonal conflict were deposited in an encounter box at a central location which was used by the group leaders each week to determine who should be assigned to which group. Members who had dropped slips were encouraged to verbalize these feelings at the outset of each group. Other members participated in on-going encounter groups.

The groups emphasized here-and-now feelings and feedback. Those groups which I conducted also attempted to train leaders in Reality Therapy. These were the predecessors of a more formalized group leaders' training group which evolved. My encounter groups were an eclectic combination of principles and procedures drawn from Glasser's (1965) Reality Therapy, Mowrer's (1972) concept of the Integrity Group, the Peer Self-Help Psychotherapy Group described by Hurvitz (1970), and the Microcounseling techniques of Ivey (1971, 1973).

Currently, the Human Potential Groups are co-led by the counseling intern who also is responsible for training and supervising peer group leaders.

3. *The Seminar*

Brief discussions of general themes were conducted for the purpose of exploring all the members' reactions and interpretations. Often the seminar was included with other types of meetings and was usually limited to 15 or 20 minutes. The discussion was conducted "round robin" fashion, which offered each member a chance to either pass or make an interpretation of the seminar statement. The leadership of seminars was shared and voluntary. The leader usually began the seminar by stating the topic or quoting a passage from a source of interest to him. He initiated the discussion by giving a personal reaction to the seminar topic and inviting others to do so. Excerpts from poems and other literature were often selected for these group interpretations (e.g., "To thine own self be true"). The unwritten philosophy of Daytop Village also provided many seminar statements for the group. The unwritten philosophy of Daytop Village, a collection of phrases and epigrams, offers a wide range of interpretations which also captures the essence of the Daytop concept. Some examples which Caring Community members chose during our seminars included:

What goes around comes around.	Growth before status.
You can't keep it unless you give it away.	Be careful what you ask for—you just might get it.
When you're looking bad you're looking good.	It's better to understand than to be understood.

4. *General Meeting*

The general meeting was the fourth variety of group held on a regular basis in the Caring Community. General meetings, which were topical in nature, were called when a significant number of participants believed that an issue required the community's consideration. General meeting topics varied from interpersonal relationships to the formulation of policy. Their atmosphere simulated that of a town meeting in which all members were encouraged to express their opinions and democratic decisions were attained. As the program expanded, general meetings became more difficult to schedule for the membership who had conflicting appointments. It was decided that the general meetings should be shortened and increased in number to permit involvement by individuals in activities other than those of the Caring Community.

Outreach Activities

The outreach activities of the Caring Community included four types of programs. These programs were attempts to extend the values and opportunities of the Caring Community experience to the campus. This became a high priority for the group. It was felt that the goals of the Caring Community could not be fully achieved until it had a positive role to play in the life of the campus. The Caring Community, furthermore, should not content itself with providing a comfortable meaningful living situation for a limited number of students who considered themselves exclusive members of the project. It was felt that an exclusive or ingroup attitude within or about the program would limit severely its functioning and that outreach contact with the campus would be a viable way to prevent this from taking place. All outreach programs were voluntary in nature.

1. *Orienters*

At the beginning of the 1974 academic year, a group of Caring Community members and other students on the campus volunteered as "Orienters" to assist the freshmen and transfer students during their first week on the campus. They provided services ranging from assistance with baggage and room location to advice and companionship during the advisement and registration process. The orienters were trained not only to provide information but also to serve as friendly big brothers and big sisters to the new students on campus. Orienters were assigned to small groups of new students and were encouraged to meet with them both formally and informally.

Their presence in the orientation week program enhanced the

atmosphere and efficiency of the week. This success has prompted consideration of using orienters at an even earlier phase in the admissions process of the college. Orienters might be used during the interview and audition period to provide tours of the campus for prospective students and feedback about the students to the Admission Office. It has been suggested that orienters also could assist the dormitory counseling staff in decisions related to room assignment and activities for new students within the residence hall in general.

2. *Group Leadership Training*

A second outreach activity of the Caring Community was the group leaders training program, which has already been mentioned. This program, conducted by the Counseling Services Intern, included a combination of experiential and didactic work in the areas of group dynamics and peer counseling. The program involved five members of the Caring Community in weekly meetings in which readings in the literature on Reality Therapy, group dynamics, and encounter group techniques were discussed. Ethics and responsibility of group leaders were explored and plans for developing student-run human potential groups were also developed. The trainees role-played a number of group issues and interactions, and were expected to function as both members and leaders of this specialized group. Concurrently, the group leaders offered human potential groups in which they served as co-leaders. They utilized the training group as a supervisory session in which feedback from both the Counseling Services intern and from one another helped the leaders evaluate and plan their groups.

3. *Off-Campus Training and Demonstrations*

The Caring Community participated in two training programs for peer counseling projects in other school settings. A group from the Caring Community participated in a series of high school peer counseling training sessions in neighboring areas. The Caring Community provided role playing and seminar discussion of the responsibilities of a peer counselor and the techniques that a peer counselor might use in one-to-one crisis counseling. Small-group counseling techniques were also demonstrated and a Reality Therapy model of peer interaction was proposed.

Two members of the Caring Community submitted a proposal to the Psychology Department and to the Division of Student Affairs for opening a peer counseling training program that would eventually sponsor a hot line and crisis center for the campus. Their proposal, based upon experiences within the Caring Community as well as visits to a number of peer counseling programs in other colleges and communities, is currently being considered as a basis for a credit course in peer counseling techniques.

The Caring Community made presentations at a number of professional meetings including symposia and demonstration workshops for the American Psychological Association, the Association for Humanistic Psychology, and the American Personnel and Guidance Association meetings.

4. *Campus Clean-Up*

A fourth outreach program of the Caring Community was a clean-up campaign sponsored during the Spring semester of 1973. At that time, the construction of the campus was responsible for a very cluttered and littered environment which students frequently complained about and occasionally contributed to. At least one day a week during that semester, Caring Community members distributed garbage bags to students as they left the lunchroom and shared in a litter campaign to pick up the trash that was accumulating in various sections of the campus. Not only did the campus appearance improve, but also the shared participation in this activity seemed to enhance many attitudes toward the Caring Community and the campus in general.

Among the on-going activities of the Caring Community were social and recreational events which were essentially nonstructured and spontaneous but which were very characteristic of the atmosphere of this program. Potluck meals, musical happenings, and car pool trips to nearby New York City for galleries or other entertainment involved the members of this program and other individuals from the campus.

The mood in the area of the Caring Community was a friendly

one. Many visitors to the Caring Community remarked about its open-door atmosphere in contrast with other sections of the dormitory. It is perhaps this atmosphere of open friendship that forms the essence of the Caring Community and is its primary contribution to the lives of those within and around it.

Evaluation

The Caring Community has been in existence for one year and a preliminary evaluation has been completed. The program has emerged from an initial position of confusion and dependency on me for day-to-day leadership to a more autonomous, self-governing one. Departmental and interpersonal conflicts are resolved among the members themselves rather than at general meetings or in private discussions with me. Peer-sponsored human potential groups are meeting and have become important for many. New models, methods, and language have emerged to replace the essentially borrowed model of the therapeutic community. Perhaps, more importantly and positively, the Caring Community serves an outreach function on the campus.

There are some areas where improvements are needed. As my direct involvement with the program decreased, there has not been a corresponding increase in the involvement of every member. For some, the Caring Community was incompatible with other interests, priorities, and requirements, and the extent of their involvement decreased. Attendance at peer-sponsored encounter groups fell off during the middle period of the second semester and group participation in general appeared to suffer with the advent of the examination and term project due dates. Efforts to shorten the meetings have been made and will need to be improved in the future.

A few faculty believe that the Caring Community may inhibit rather than enhance the growth and development of its members. Their concerns seemed to center on two issues. They feared that the intense group involvement might distract some students from their academic and other social involvements and that the Caring Community might become an excuse for not functioning in other spheres of the student's life. The voluntary nature of all Caring Community programs should reduce the probability of this happening. However, in those instances where students have neglected contact with nonmembers or appeared to be sliding in their academic work responsibilities, the group's concern was expressed and the individual has been encouraged to evaluate and correct his own behavior. The intensity of group pressure and the impact of peer approval seemed to vary with the person. For some, participation in encounter and other group sessions seemed overly dependent. However, these problems surfaced early in the orientation to the Caring Community and the combination of self-selection and peer support helped each one to make appropriate adjustments.

Another concern of some staff members had to do with the organized aspects of the Caring Community as a group. Fearing the "political" use of the Caring Community's influence, some staff have expressed attitudes relating this program to some of the more radical student protest activities on the campus. The membership of the Caring Community, however, has not participated in student activist programs. The Caring Community has not had a united attitude or policy related to the dominant political issues on or off the campus. Diversity of interests, attitudes, and backgrounds precluded doing so in this community. The Caring Community could sponsor more effective public relations and encourage greater faculty involvement to acquaint the staff with its actual goals and functions to dispel these fears.

Student opinion was divided concerning the value of the Caring Community experience. Members found that their involvement was of great personal significance but it had to be limited to those activities which were compatible with other priorities in their programs and their lifestyles. Nonmembers have pointed out a tendency toward in-group cliquishness which caused suspicions about the Caring Community. Other nonmembers, however, have sought involvement in some of the program's activities and there have been increasing requests for information about the project. The extent of alienation in other areas of the dormitory has become so great in some sections that a number of students have recently reversed their original attitudes about the Caring Community from hostility and suspicion to acceptance and support.

Many have expressed the view that the Caring Community should not be an isolated area within the dormitory but an attitude which characterizes the entire campus. The progress with which the initial membership of this pilot program developed such attitudes can be taken as a sign of hope for such a model in the campus environment in the future.

Part III: Critical Issues Confronting the Caring Community

In-Group versus Out-Group

The Caring Community began in an isolated corner of a new college dormitory on a campus where few standards or models of lifestyles had been established. It was viewed by its members and some nonmembers as an exclusive and unique living situation. Its membership was perceived by some as a privileged and superior minority. Others viewed the Caring Community in negative terms. Images of the membership varied from superleaders and intellectuals to a disturbed ward of the lunatic fringe. The fact that its membership was scattered among the various divisions of the college which were relatively isolated and autonomous made a concerted effort to break down such stereotypes difficult. The tendency of some members to associate almost exclusively with other members of the groups added fuel to the fire of in-group versus out-group and stereotyped thinking. The strongest criticism of the program was in relationship to such attitudes and images.

Both the communal and the therapeutic community models have endured out-group status in the early stages of their implementation. Those communes which were unable to relate to the larger social context in which they existed have had very short histories, rife with conflict and alienation. Therapeutic communities in the field of drug rehabilitation have also been in conflict with society because there were fears about the influence of addicts. The methods of treatment which emphasize self-help, peer counseling still have not gained evidence within the professional establishment. The absence of professionals in these programs justifies for many the assumption of the added risk if the therapeutic community were to be located in their neighborhood. The presence of such programs also serves to remind a neighborhood that unacknowledged problems and conflicts exist.

The Caring Community was in many ways a more difficult program to implement because it chose to locate itself within a college dormitory structure. Its successes, its struggles, and its problems were subject to direct and indirect evaluation by many nonmembers. It was perceived as different and, therefore, superior or inferior to other options of college lifestyle. The choice of a name was perhaps unfortunate because some surmised that we believed that only in the Caring Community was there concern and understanding. The program required considerable investment of time and energy by its initial group members. Some were unavailable for other college activities and were perceived by themselves and some of the college administration as having special status.

These attitudes were detrimental to the spirit and functioning of the Caring Community. Early efforts were made to overcome what appeared to be mounting prejudice concerning the activities of this program. Members put a "partial ban" on one another, insisting at mealtimes in the dormitory dining room that Caring Community members would eat together only when nonmembers were invited. Open social functions and morning meetings were conducted in which nonmembers were invited to participate. Detailed releases and interviews in the school newspaper were used to acquaint the campus with the activities of this project. Insufficient effort was made, however, to invite the participation of faculty, student leaders, and other influential individuals in the operation of the program. At one point, the program was sufficiently controversial that an open meeting in which student and faculty complaints and criticisms of the programs were discussed.

During this turbulent period, an analogy was suggested between the existence of the Caring Community on the campus and the heart transplant operation, in which the greatest risk to the patient and the new heart results from the body's resistance to its new but alien life-supporting organ. Reconciliation concerning differences of opinion about the program still remains an unfinished task for this program and its campus. In the future, open-house meetings probably will be utilized in the same manner that therapeutic communities such as Daytop Village have made their programs accessible to the public. Members could provide orientation to interested individuals and could encourage their ideas and involvement in various aspects of the project. Questions and criticisms concerning its activities could be dealt with on an individual basis rather than in a network of rumors and grapevine gossip. In addition, the extension of the Caring Community through its outreach activities and through recruitment of nonresidential participation should assist the program in achieving fuller credibility and acceptance on campus.

Involvement versus (?) Individuality

Many programs on the college campus are infected by apathy, alienation, and confusion. The college climate has been described as "turned off" and indifferent by those commentators who watched the protest movement rise and fade just prior to the period in which the Caring Community was created. Student apathy, isolation, and involvement in drugs seemed to provide substitutes for the kind of involvement militant protest movements demanded (Hunter, 1972; Keniston, 1965; Nowlis, 1968; Roszak, 1969). Pessimism and frustration with the outcome of student government and student activist programs also permeated the mood on most campuses (Farber, 1969; Kanter, 1972; Roszak, 1969).

The Caring Community appeared to attract individuals whose enthusiasm for these options had burned out and who were searching for more constructive alternatives. Most who joined were high achievers who expected more from themselves in college than just getting by and who demanded more recognition than a mechanical grade-oriented college system could provide. Many of them arrived at the college expecting an open classroom atmosphere which would facilitate learning and personal growth (Glasser, 1969).

Most perceived their involvement in the group as access to greater intimacy as well as individuality. However, the nature of the involvement required by the Caring Community could also threaten the student's notion of individual identity. Not only time, but feelings, ideas, energies, and attitudes were contributed by the members of the Caring Community. These contributions were made in a group context with much peer support and influence. Just as in a therapeutic community, the Caring Community offered a series of role models to the members for their growth and development. Concepts of responsibility became fused with the priorities of the group. Feedback concerning one's behavior from other group members exerted powerful influences upon the members' choices and self-evaluations.

Glasser's concept of Reality Therapy emphasizes the importance of involvement in all therapeutic and growth processes. Mutual investments of attitudes, ideas, energies, and feelings have been identified as a raw material for successful educational and personal change (Glasser, 1965, 1969, 1972). An environment of human involvement and confrontation would appear to offer the ideal atmosphere for such growth. Encounter groups, which emphasize responsibility in peer relationships and self-assessment of one's behavior, can contribute significantly to growth and development. This occurs in situations where success rather than failure, where reward rather than punishment, and where achievement rather than frustration are options available to the participant. These principles have been demonstrated in Glasser's work with elementary and secondary schools. It would appear from a preliminary evaluation of the Caring Community that similar principles apply to the college experience as well. It is important to recognize, furthermore, that the diversity of individual backgrounds, talents, interests and lifestyles must be respected in the development of collegiate programs of this sort. Glasser's notion of a community involvement center in which multiple talents and goals are achieved through the shared participation and involvement of diverse individuals and groups seems an appropriate and valuable model for the development of such programs in the future.

REFERENCES

Bassin, Alexander. Daytop Village—Stopover or Cure? *Psychology Today*, Dec., 1969.

Bion, W. R. *Experiences in Groups*. New York: Basic Books, 1961.

Bratter, Thomas E. "Reality Therapy: A Group Psychotherapeutic Approach with Adolescent Alcoholics." (unpublished manuscript)

Casriel, D. H. and Amen, Grover. *Daytop: Three Addicts and Their Cure*. New York: Hill & Wang, 1971.

Casriel, D. H. *A Scream Away From Happiness*. New York: Grosset & Dunlap, 1972.

DeRopp, R. S. *The Master Game*. New York: Dell, 1963.

Fairfield, Richard. *Communes, U.S.A.: A Personal Tour*. Baltimore: Penguin Books, 1972.

Farber, Jerry. *The Student as Nigger*. New York: Pocket Books, 1969.

Glasser, William. *Reality Therapy: A New Approach to Psychiatry*. New York: Harper & Row, 1965.

Glasser, William. *Schools Without Failure*. New York: Harper & Row, 1969.

Glasser, William. *The Identity Society*. New York: Harper & Row, 1972.

Houriet, Robert. *Getting Back Together*. New York: Coward, McCann & Geoghegan, 1971.

Hunter, Robert. *The Storming of the Mind*. Garden City: Doubleday, 1972.

Hurvitz, Nathan. Peer Self-Help Psychotherapy Groups and Their Implications for Psychotherapy. *Psychotherapy: Theory, Research and Practice*, 7 (1), 1970, 41–49.

Hutchins, Robert M. *The University of Utopia*. Chicago: University of Chicago Press, 1953.

Ivey, A. E. *Microcounseling: Innovations in Interviewing Training*. Springfield: Charles Thomas, 1971.

Ivey, A. E. Demystifying the Group Process: Adapting Microcounseling Procedures to Counseling in Groups. *Educational Technology*, Feb., 1973, 27–31.

Kanter, Rosabeth M. *Commitment and Community*. Cambridge, Mass.: Harvard University Press, 1972.

Keniston, Kenneth. *The Uncommitted*. New York: Harcourt, Brace & World, 1965.

Leonard, George B. *Education and Ecstasy*. New York: Delta, 1968.

Melville, Keith. *Communes in the Counter Culture*. New York: William Morrow & Co., 1972.

Mowrer, O. Hobart. Integrity Groups: Principles and Procedures. *The Counseling Psychologist*, 3 (2), 1972, 7–33.

Nahal, Chaman. *Drugs and the Other Self*. New York: Harper & Row, 1971.

Nowlis, Helen H. *Drugs on the College Campus*. Garden City: Doubleday, 1968.

Otto, Herbert and Mann, John (eds.). *Ways of Growth*. New York: Viking, 1968.

Rogers, Carl R. *Freedom to Learn*. Columbus, Ohio: Charles E. Merrill, 1969.

Rogers, Carl R. *Carl Rogers on Encounter Groups*. New York: Harper & Row, 1970.

Roszak, Theodore. *The Making of a Counter Culture*. Garden City: Doubleday, 1969.

Schutz, William C. *Joy: Expanding Human Awareness*. New York: Grove, 1967.

Schutz, William C. *Here Comes Everybody*. New York: Harper & Row, 1971.

Stevens, John O. *Awareness*. New York: Bantam, 1973.

Veysey, Laurence. *The Communal Experience*. New York: Harper & Row, 1973.

Yablonsky, Lewis. *The Tunnel Back: Synanon*. New York: Macmillan, 1965.

What Children Need

It has been my experience that when people talk about mental health, they're not really talking about mental health. They are talking about helping people who have some kind of problem get better. There is certainly a large place for that in our community because a lot of people have problems and need help. But the real concept of mental health or mental hygiene (another term almost synonymous with mental health) is helping people so they can solve their own problems. In other words, develop some kind of broad-based program that will help people to the point that they don't have to depend upon agencies, clinics and doctors to help them solve problems which could be solvable if they were more effective themselves.

Most of my training as a psychiatrist and my work in dealing with people who were functioning ineffectively took place at a correctional school. This obviously wasn't mental hygiene or mental health. It was a way to try to help them get over whatever it is that was causing them to upset the community and get locked up. We developed programs at this girls' school which evolved into the concepts of Reality Therapy.

The concepts were, as far as I could see, moderately useful. If

From Wynona S. Hartley, ed., *The Roots of Responsibility: A Solution to Community Intervention for the Health of Children and Youth III.* Proceedings of a Workshop of the University of Kansas Medical Center, September 1973. Reprinted by permission of the editor.

Note: Tape transcript. No attempt has been made to correct for grammar or clear up misunderstandings where perhaps a blackboard or hand gestures were used.

they were applied the way we had figured them out, they seemed to work. As I thought through these ideas, I was increasingly convinced that they could be applied in a mental health way, not to patch people up, but to help people from getting to the point where they needed patching up.

As I thought about this more and more and worked with the girls at the school, a problem arose: Where do you go to apply the ideas that we are talking about? In a sense true mental health. The only place I could figure out where you could reach young people was in the schools. I didn't approach the schools; the schools approached me. They didn't, however, approach me from a mental health standpoint. They approached me from this standpoint: "We in the schools have a lot of problems and could use some kind of expertise to help us. We have a lot of nasty kids and we don't know what to do with them. You have a reputation for dealing effectively with nasty kids, so come and help us."

I went into the schools and made up my mind that I wasn't going to do what they said I should do for several reasons. If I wanted to patch people up, there were lots of better places to work than the schools, in terms of pay and everything else. The second thing was that I probably couldn't do it. What they were asking people to do was more or less fantasy. There are lots of schools with lots of kids in trouble. Everybody is looking for something to come along (some kind of work process technique, something magic) or some kind of expert, a specialist who'll come to take that little kid who is upset and do something with him so he's functioning more effectively as a student. What they want you to do with him is ordinarily fairly simple. If they have you as an expert and they've got an upset kid, they want you to sit in the room with him. In there they want something to go on so when he leaves the room, he's no longer upset, either after one session or 100 sessions—but hopefully after one because they've got lots of kids.

That was what they wanted of me, even though when I negotiated to work at a public school I hadn't really told them what I was going to do. I just said, "I'll come and help." I had not committed myself to sit in a room with nasty little kids. I don't enjoy it and neither do the kids.

The first time I walked into the schools to start my so-called "school career"—which was back in 1965 and now I spend almost all my time working with school people—they didn't have any particular opening amenities at all. They just ushered me into a room, pushed a little kid in and closed the door. I had suspected this was going to happen and I was prepared for it. After we sat there a moment or two I said to the kid, "Kid, do you know where you came from?" He said, "Yeah, I came from room 23." So I opened the door and said, "Well go on back there." The kid left with a smile because kids don't like to sit in rooms with people like me.

The school people were overjoyed because I had done this job in no time at all. Whatever it was I was supposed to do in that room, I seemed to be highly effective at it. They immediately beckoned around the corner. I hadn't noticed there were a bunch of other kids sitting there. They ushered another kid in and said, "Go on in with him." I said, "Wait a second. Let's stop here." They said, "What do you mean?" I said, "I'm not going to do this!" They said, "Well, why not?" I said, "Lots of reasons. I don't like to, and I don't think it's going to do any good and I'm just not going to do it—that's all. However, if that's what you want me to do, I won't charge you anything for the moment or two I've spent. It's on me. If we're going to quit here, then whatever you've gotten from me this morning is free. I quit." They said, "Gee, don't quit." I said, "All right, I won't quit." They said, "Well, what *can* you do? If you can't do that, can you do anything?" I said, "Oh, I might be able to. What I'll start with is giving you some advice."

They sat down and relaxed and said, "What advice do you have?" I said, "Start trying mental hygiene. I was really thinking seriously about this, and still am, because I am convinced that programs we run in the schools here and there around the United States is true mental hygiene, even though it has nothing to do with psychiatry, mental health or anything like that. It helps more children to be more effective in school. We could say it's a good student program, if you don't want to use the term mental hygiene. You have a lot of upset kids in this system, like that little kid who sat with me for a moment or two." And they said, "Yeah, we've got plenty of them. More than you believe." I said, "Well, I'll give you my first bit of advice. Stop irritating the kids."

That suggestion didn't fall on receptive ears. I was trying to make a point. "You've got upset kids and they're in school. You might be doing something that is upsetting them." And they protested (as normal people would), "We're just running school." I implied there might be a correlation and they didn't deny it. They said, "But what, specifically, are we doing?" I said, "Well, are all these kids failing?" They said, "Yeah, most of them are failing. Practically all of them." I said, "Well, then don't fail them. That probably upsets them."

I'm not going to get into all the details of *Schools Without Failure,* but generally it starts with the fact that we don't fail kids. Most places in the world failure isn't used. It's mainly used in schools. Most places where you don't do a satisfactory job somebody says to you, "You don't do a satisfactory job." That's sufficient. In school we say, "You don't do a satisfactory job and you fail." We add that little extra. And it's that little extra that breaks the back of many a child, who says, "Well, I guess I am a failure." He gives up in school, which is bad, but even worse, he gives up on himself, then he is going to be a problem to himself and possibly a problem to others, too, until he picks up on himself, which he may never do if he has enough failure.

I felt that if we could develop an adequate program within the school, students wouldn't get in the condition where they gave up on themselves. In other words, they would function more effectively in school. My claim is that they don't come to school to give up on themselves.

We've had lots of training to say that kids come from bad homes and all that. These bad homes have caused them to do badly in school. Let's look at the kindergarten class. Are these kids really in rough shape? Are they antagonistic? Are they anxious to destroy the school? Are they behavior problems? No. Kindergarten kids are not too bad. Do they come from a different home when they're in the eighth grade than they did in kindergarten? They generally come from the same communities and homes. And yet as you go through the country, you don't hear too many people wailing and weeping about the condition of kindergarten. The kids aren't in that bad a shape. There are some differences between inner-city kids and outer-city kids, but the kids are much more similar than if you look at the students in the sixth or eighth or twelfth grade where the differences between inner-city and outer-city kids are pronounced. Therefore, you can come to the conclusion that if this difference is a major difference as time goes on, the variable which is most effectively producing the difference is probably the school. And I think it is.

We're doing something right in kindergarten because in most places you don't fail kindergarten. However, in the United States right now about ten percent of the first graders actually fail and are labelled failures. I think lots of them never recover from that. Many of the problems that you'll be dealing with in any agency will be kids who have failed in school. A program which will cause more kids to succeed in school is probably a mental hygiene program.

What I wanted to do with children in school was to create something that would get rid of failure. In essence, I began to think that the concepts of Reality Therapy probably would be applicable. The concepts of Reality Therapy are not specifically psychiatric concepts. They are (this is, of course, my belief) a way of life. They are a way of living your life or working with people or large groups of people. If you work this way, whatever you do can become more effective.

The concepts of Reality Therapy are based upon the idea that people, all people—children and adults—have certain needs. We are born with certain built-in, neurological needs which, I think, are a part of our very nervous system. If these needs are not fulfilled, we feel pain. Whenever we feel pain, things are obviously not going right.

One thing you need is to believe all the time—from the time you're born until the time you die—that somebody in the world cares about you and that there's someone in the world you care about. You have to give and receive love all your life or it starts to hurt. You feel this pain in a variety of ways. You may not recognize the cause of the pain. The problem with pain is that when you have it, it doesn't always tell you what the trouble is. Pain is sometimes very specific. If you have a stone in your shoe, you feel the pain, take off your shoe and shake out the stone. But if you feel kind of badly about yourself—inadequate, nervous, depressed, upset, tense, antagonistic or a little hostile you may not always know exactly where that comes from. When we hurt we try to do something about it. Some of the things we try are not effective, but that doesn't mean we don't try.

The second thing people need is survival. Man survived originally because he cared for his young. We were born helpless and if we weren't cared for, we would die. We also survived because we were smarter than some of the more powerful animals around. We learned something that animals in many cases didn't learn: how to intelligently cooperate with each other.

We are, then, by nature an intelligent and cooperative animal. We generally get together when we have a big problem. Survival problems are usually not solved individually. We're obviously coming up with some big problems in terms of our ecology. They won't be solved by each individual trying to figure out his little bit. If you drive less, it won't do one bit for the oil shortage. A lot of people have to get together and figure out a way to drive less, for that's an intelligent, cooperative approach. We are geared to do this under the proper conditions. We need this.

Even when our life isn't threatened, we are still left with the neurological need to do something which we believe is worthwhile. For instance, if you take a child and you just love him—don't do anything else but love him—the child will eventually rebel against this and say, "O.K., O.K., you love me, but I want to do something."

This need for worth first exhibits itself in an infant five, six, seven or eight months of age, maybe a year. Up until that time you have plopped him in highchair, taken a little can of food and jammed it down his throat. He's opened his mouth like a little bird and sucked it down. Then one day, you shove the food in his mouth and he goes "Pooph!" and spits it out all over you. Well, you don't want to hit a little kid. He spits out a couple more spoonsful and you finally say, "The hell with it, kid. Feed yourself." Which is exactly what he wants. He picks up the spoon in his own miserable way and feeds himself. He shoves it in his eye, his ear, his nose, but he'll get enough in his mouth to survive.

If we frustrate a person to the extent that he can't do anything worthwhile, then he'll suffer even if he has social involvements and love.

If these are the two things we need, we have to get them. We have to be raised in a social milieu where they are available: a good family who takes care of us and gives us a chance to grow. Most people who are raised in that kind of family will get along moderately well in the world. They'll eventually develop the strength to socialize and do things worthwhile on their own. If they're unable to do these things, they suffer.

Therefore, whatever we call mental hygiene should create the opportunity for children to have love and a chance to develop some worthwhile means of behavior as they grow. Homes should provide that. And schools should provide it. But all of our social agencies, like medicine, are concerned with people who in most cases aren't able to find love and a sense of worth.

If a person is able to find love and worth, however, he does this through involvement with other people. You can do worthwhile things on your own quite a bit, but most people eventually like to go and say to somebody, "Look, look what I'm doing. Isn't it good?" This is a very normal, human characteristic. You may practice the piano for fifty years in a cave and become the world's greatest pianist, but eventually you want to come out of the cave and hold a concert and have some people clap. We need others. We need to feel the warmth and the recognition of others. If you don't feel this, you hurt.

When we feel the warmth and recognition of others, we develop what I call the "successful identity." If you are successful it doesn't mean you don't have problems, upsets, pains, aches, disillusionments, rejections. But if you develop the strengths, you believe: "I am a successful person. Even if I am rejected, I can find someone else. If this path to worthwhileness is closed, maybe I can figure out another path to worthwhileness. I think I can try." If you're that kind of person, when you run into stress and strain, you somehow or other manage to go through it and again find success. As you do this, you feel good because the payoff for fulfilling your needs is to feel good. The penalty for not fulfilling your needs is to feel bad. Our feelings tell us how we're doing. They're the gauges.

All people have two gauges. You have a short-term feeling gauge and a long-term feeling gauge. If you are successful, your long-term feeling gauge says, "Most of the time I'll feel pretty good." If your short-term gauge pops over to feeling bad, you rely upon the fact that you'll feel good eventually and you do feel basically strong most of the time. You'll work intelligently, logically and systematically to get over the problem and solve it. This is how most people solve problems. Most people don't go to an agency for help.

People who aren't this way have a basic failure identity which, of course, produces pain. They have a basic identity that says, "I am a failure. I am not making it in this world. Why am I not making it?" The answer: "I don't think anybody loves me. I don't believe I'm very worthwhile." They spend their time trying desperately to get rid of the pain that they feel because they hurt. They aren't able to take the long-term, rational, hard-work methods to get rid of pain that successful people take.

A successful man and an unsuccessful man both may run into a great deal of stress. The successful man says, "I can do it." He goes about correcting his life, even if it takes a while and a lot of effort. A man who's not successful says, "I can't do it. That's too much for me. I'm overwhelmed and, oh, but God, I hurt so much. What can I do? Well, I better get drunk." We have nine million people who choose that route in the United States. It's probably the single biggest problem we have. As Mark Twain used to say, "I'll take two drinks before bedtime to prevent toothache." And he said, "I never had a toothache." These people take 32 drinks before bedtime and 23 in the morning and 45 in between to prevent any kind of ache at all. An alcoholic is one who spends his life drinking, not always because he has so much pain in his life, but because he feels so inadequate and he knows when something happens, he won't be able to handle it anyway.

If we have a person like this who is lonely and feels failure, who does he have? The one person that everybody has is himself. They say, "Well, I'm the one guy nobody can take away from me." When you turn toward yourself in moments of stress, it does diminish the pain to some extent.

Unfortunately, when you turn toward yourself, it's not successful for any period of time, because the need is for love and worth from others. As you stay more and more by yourself, the pain starts in again. You only reduce the pain when you leave others because you say, "They reject me and it's better by myself."

People have discovered the capacity to suffer in at least four major ways in an attempt to reduce the pain of this general suffering. One is: "Let's face it. All I've got is myself." When you get to that point, it is so painful and overwhelming that some people even commit suicide. That's the most serious pain a person can feel.

In order to avoid this pain, we've discovered involvement with our own emotions. The common emotion in civilized society is depression. We become wrapped up in our depression. It becomes our friend, our companion, our constant ally. Whatever else happens, we're depressed.

People come to me and say, "Doctor, I'm depressed." I say, "Well, why don't you cheer up?" "What do you mean, Doctor?" I say, "Well, if you're depressed, cheer up. Hell, it's a pretty good world. Live in it." "You don't seem to understand. I'm very seriously depressed, Doctor. I'm sick." "Are you sick? What do you mean, 'You're sick.' Got a sore throat, bad feet, or what?" "Oh, no, no, I don't mean that way. But I'm sick, Doctor. I'm depressed." "No. All you're telling me is you're depressed. You know that's a state of mind. Cheer up." By that time they think they're in the room with a mad man. They either leave or they start doing something. Usually they're no longer depressed because they're so interested in my particular mental problems that they've given up their depression temporarily.

The point is that if you were wise, the next time you became depressed you would cheer up. It's much better than being depressed. But it's easier to be depressed, so we hang on to our depression, not because it hurts so much, but because it hurts less than it would without it. Otherwise people would all give up their symptoms immediately. You've got a stone in your shoe; you don't walk for three days with it. You take it out because you know that reality without the stone is better. But if you're depressed, you're fairly well convinced that reality without the depression isn't as good as it is with the depression.

We can also become involved with our own behavior. Take a kid who's roaring down the highway. He may run from a policeman and they chase him at 100 miles an hour. The policemen are just as crazy as the kid. They chase him and he kills nine citizens when he crashes into a building. Leave him go. He'll soon be stopped without the car getting damaged or anything else. We see these people getting involved in their own behavior and the behavior in itself becomes an end.

The third choice that we have to get rid of the pain is to be crazy. This route used to be a very common choice for a bad reality. It isn't so common today. People choose the emotional or behavioral routes much more. But if we have a very, very bad reality, then we can change the reality within our own minds. In several hospitals I worked at I ran into a Jesus. In Ypsilanti, Michigan there were three. The point is that if you have to be crazy, that's a nice way to be crazy. How could you have more love and involvement than to take on the role of the deity?

We see people in the hospital who don't seem to be terribly sick, although they're crazy. Their craziness has supplanted the pain. They're remarkably healthy. They don't need to be sick. The craziness is enough. They sometimes don't have any emotional problems. They sometimes behave very correctly. Just being crazy is usually sufficient. It's a choice.

When you work with a person who's crazy, what you are trying to do is tell him to give up this choice. And he'll give it up if he believes he's cared for and can do something worthwhile. By providing love and a feeling of worth you help him give it up. When he gives it up, you say to him, "Why did you decide to stop being crazy?" He'll say, "Well, you know, I thought it over, Doc. This hospital is pretty good and you treated me pretty well. We had a great nurse and I had something to do here, but I kinda just, you know, I just gave it up." It's a conscious decision when you give up being crazy. It's probably a conscious decision when you start becoming crazy, but it usually happens very slowly and you get into it sometimes not aware of how it's coming to you. When you give it up, however, it's usually quite abrupt and quite conscious. I've had patients who become crazy on and off. They say, "Well, if things keep going like this, I'm going to be crazy again." And they will be. They recognize that they're becoming lonely and worthless and they get back their old symptom or companion, just like an alcoholic will say, "If things continue like this, I'm really gonna get drunk." And he's not kidding. He will.

The last choice is to become sick. We learn about sickness and it's available. Sickness is a very acceptable choice in our society. More and more people are choosing it, which is over-burdening the medical profession who are generally trained to deal with people who have something wrong with them and are not trained to deal with people who are making the choice of illness because they don't know what else to do. These people feel, "I can get some care. I may get some love. I may get some attention. But I have to be sick to get it." It's unfortunate, but that's what may have to happen. Ultimately, these people become involved in the medical system, which is: You're sick and you get care. Sick, care; sick, care. And sickness becomes a way of life.

Ordinarily, people who are sick, are sick. And they are sick on and on for long periods. Huge groups of people are rarely sick, because they don't make that choice. Every once in a while someone gets tuberculosis or a strep throat or polio or a broken leg or something like that and they really are sick and need care. They get very good care. But fairly soon we're going to have to face the reality that we can't afford the medical delivery system we've developed in this country. Too much of our money is being spent in an attempt to deliver medical care to people who really aren't medically ill. We could easily afford to deal with only the people who have true disease. What we have to do is develop some kind of a program through which people who get the kinds of illness that we can't deal with effectively don't get them.

Most of the choices people make still involve pain. To be sick hurts. To be depressed hurts. To act out doesn't hurt, but usually you are caught and then it starts to hurt. To be psychotic may or may not hurt, depending upon your ability to change reality. These, then, are the four major pain relievers of our society.

Then there are the ordinary tensions and stresses and strains of ordinary living which we'd like to reduce. When you're feeling the pain of loneliness and worthlessness both, we have opium, the super pain reliever. Anyone who has ever taken it for this kind of pain relief, will take it the rest of his life for all practical purposes. One of the most harmful myths that has been perpetrated has been the myth that one can get rid of the morphine or the heroin habit.

Close on heroin's heels is alcohol. When you've got pain and misery, alcohol does to some degree reduce it. One can get addicted or habituated to alcohol as well as heroin and it's hard to kick that habit, although certainly easier than heroin. Still it's not too successful unless you're involved in some kind of massive socialization program. You can rarely kick it all by yourself. You've got to get involved with people to do it.

Caffeine and nicotine are the common tension relievers that people who live pretty successful lives still use but find hard to get rid of once they get started with them.

Obviously, mental hygiene could be used to create a world in which people can grow up not needing these drugs because they can get along without the pain relief that drugs produce.

The best way to help people is to affect agencies like schools that work with people. Affect families. Start some kind of program where families can learn how to live more effective lives. I don't know yet how to get families together, but there are community health programs that I believe families would become involved in.

Once the agencies are affected, they then affect people. The principles that you use, whether you affect the agencies or the people, are essentially the same. Let's apply the principles to an individual with some kind of difficulty and then extrapolate how they might also be applied to agencies.

He comes in and complains of this difficulty because he's involved with the system. Let's say that he's a juvenile delinquent kid who's been out rattling around in the community and everybody is upset by him. They send him in to a probation officer and say, "You talk to this guy or you're gonna end up in the pen." So the kid does it. You still have to do something to help him feel better. Just threatening to send him to jail won't help because if it worked, there would be nobody in jail.

We should do something to help him get rid of the pain. We know he's lonely. We know he feels failure. You can't solve loneliness except through a human being spending time in a caring way with another human being. If you're dealing with this kid, you have to somehow become to some degree his friend, so that he believes (even though he knows you have other things to do) you could devote some time to him and you are his friend.

The first step of Reality Therapy is the same, whether you are applying it to an individual or an institution, whether you're applying it preventively in your own life or to help someone: You must try to become involved and stay involved so you have a chance to begin to find the love and worth you can't find when you're lonely. The second step, if you're trying to help an individual or trying to correct an agency, is to say, "What are you doing?" You must develop the behavior of the individual or the agency and get it out on the table where it can be examined. The kid says, "Well, I just hang around the house. I smoke a little marijuana and we just bop around a little bit. Don't go to school." That's what he's doing. If you're involved with him and you're his friend, he'll tell you what he's doing. He knows you're not going to push him around. Still you ask him, "What are you doing? Let's look at what we're doing. Let's examine really what we're doing." That's the first step. Nobody will examine effectively what they're doing because they'll be frightened to unless they feel they're examining it in the presence of friends. That's the key.

If you're consulting with an agency, they have to believe that you're someone who really wants to help them, otherwise they won't tell you what they're doing. Unless they do, they can't correct it if they're doing something inadequate. If they're doing something adequate, examine it and say it's adequate. That's all right.

This kid is doing badly. You say to him, "Well look, kid. This is what you're doing." You don't ask him how he's feeling. He's in trouble for what he's doing. When you ask him how he's feeling, you give him the implication that you can change his feelings from bad to good. You can't. What we want to do is help him to change, so asking people how they feel is a trap. Accepting the fact that they feel bad is fine, but don't get involved deeply in their feelings. Don't get involved deeply in their history. We are dealing with a problem of loneliness and effectiveness. We are dealing with a "right now" problem and it can only be helped in the "right now."

So you say, "What are you doing?" And the guy says, "Well, this is what I'm doing." The third step is: "If this is what you are doing, are you satisfied with it?" Ordinarily you'd expect, "Well, yeah, I like it," which he would say defensively. But if he believes you're his friend and are involved with him and you care and want to help him and there might be a possibility to get his life more effective and get rid of this pain, then he's not going to say that. He's going to say, "What I'm doing is no good. Nah, it's bad. No, ya know it's no good." He's then made a value judgment of his behavior.

He is looking toward you. Really, he is saying, "O.K. I say it's no good. Now what are you going to do?" This is where you have to be actively a part of the therapeutic process. You have to say, "Well, if you say what you are doing is no good, then can you and I together figure something out." This is where you have to help most people.

If this is an agency, it's the same way. You've looked at their program and said, "This program isn't too effective." (If an agency has a highly effective program they won't be calling you in to help them anyway.) They've looked at their program now and said, "No. It's not too effective." You say, "Well, maybe we can figure something out. Let's see if we can arrive at some kind of plan through which you can do a little bit better."

In the case of the kid the plan ultimately has to direct him toward love and worth. The kid says, "You know, I oughta go back to school, but, God, they hate me at that school. I mean, I really loused them up and they really hate me. And when I walk by the school, the principal would like to kick me in the pants, you know." I say, "Yeah, O.K., but how are we gonna get back in? Maybe if you'd clean yourself up and look better." "Yeah," the kid says, "he'd like that."

The plan is he cleans himself up a little bit. "Maybe if you drop him a note or call up and say you'd like to come in and talk about it so he'll be prepared for you. And you tell him, 'Look, I really want to get back in school, and I know I've given you a hard time.'" The kid says, "That'd be hard to do." "Well, sure it'll be hard to do. There's nothing easy about changing this identity from failure to success. It's tough. It's easy to stay a failure. It's easier to walk past the school and throw a rock through one of the windows. But that doesn't do any good and both of us know it." The kid says, "All right. O.K. Well, will you come with me?" "Well, I can't come with you. I can drop a note to the principal saying I've been seeing you, but I can't come with you. I don't have time."

The fourth step of Reality Therapy, once the kid says, "I'm not doing well," is, then, to make a plan to help him. The plan has to be a possible plan, something that can be done, not an impossible plan. It has to be a plan of small increments.

The next thing is to try and get a commitment to the plan. Say, "All right, will you do it?" "Well, uh. . . ." "Let's shake hands on it. Let's write it down or something." Commitment is impor- tant. It gives the person the solidity that someone is really behind them. It also gives a little more power because when you make a commitment, it's stronger.

The kid goes in to school and comes back to you and says, "Aw, that school's no good. I went to that principal and he said I gotta take English again. You know I can't stand English, so the hell with it." "All right. That's what you did. What's your plan now?" "Well, I gotta go back to school, but I can't take English." "Well, how are we going to work this out?" What he's trying to say is,

"I'd like to go back but my excuse is I don't like English." So you say, "Look, if you wanna go back to school, don't tell me how you can't go back to school."

If you want to practice Reality Therapy, you've got to be tough enough to reject excuses. Don't spend half an hour talking about how he can't go back. Say to him, "How are you gonna figure out a way to go back. Do you need English?" "I need it." "Well, then, what's the plan? If you need it and you won't take it then let's not talk about going back to school. That's no plan." "Well, you think I could take it?" "I don't know. All I know is if you want to go back to school and you gotta take English, that's the way it is. If you want to cross the street, you gotta cross the street." "Well, maybe I need some help in English." Make a plan to get him some help. Maybe a tutor is possible; maybe another kid will help him. Schools work out lots of things for people who want help.

He goes back to school and spends a couple days there and says, "I don't feel like it anymore." At this point, you have to resist being punitive because in Reality Therapy there is no punishment. You have to resist saying, "Ah, hell, kid, why did I waste my time on you." We like to use punishment. We have the illusion that it works. It doesn't.

When the kid says, "What are you going to do to me? Are you really going to throw me out?" You say, "No, I'm not gonna throw you out. I just want to ask: Do you want to go back to school or not? Did you mean what you said?" "I did." "Well, then, what's the plan?"

In other words, you continue to doggedly hammer home to him that it's his life and he's responsible for it: "I'm not going to punish you. I'm not here to accept excuses from you. I'm here to help you fulfill the things you say you want to do. And I'll help you in every possible way, but it's your life and if you don't want to do it, then it's up to you." If you're friendly and involved with him, he can't leave. He's stuck. He's trapped. He needs you. And you're working and continue to say, "You've gotta do more for yourself."

If you've got enough patience, step eight of Reality Therapy is: You never give up. He has to give up; you never give up. I worked for two years in Watts before I really felt that I was getting any place at all in those schools. I used to come home and my head was bursting. I would get up in the morning and everything in me said, "Don't go down there today. There's got to be something better than this." I went down there because I had made a commitment to myself and to the people I work with: There's got to be some way we can help kids in a tough school situation. It's hard, but there is. I became involved with the situation and I couldn't leave it even though I suffered.

These are the steps of Reality Therapy as they can be applied to individuals and agencies. They are simple to talk about. In application they're tough—the never giving up, the sticking to it, the hanging in there, the no punishing, the no accepting excuses, the working desperately to become involved with people who really don't want you. Things don't happen quickly. You have to hang in there. That's what it's all about.

PART FIVE

Corrections

ALEXANDER BASSIN

Reality Therapy and Corrections: Introduction

The policeman's lot is not a happy one, sang Gilbert and Sullivan, and the plight of the conscientious worker in corrections, be it probation, parole, halfway house, or prison, is no euphoric Garden of Eden either. He is assigned the stigmatized flotsam and jetsam of society, almost all 18-karat certified failures, with the mandate Rehabilitate! At the same time, he is denied adequate facilities and the sweet reinforcement of social recognition and money. He is criticized by ivory-tower academicians and well-meaning federal commissions for failing to rehabilitate inmates when statistics on recidivism hit the press. If he attempts to introduce educational programs and social interactional measures he is called a "bleeding heart" and accused of running a country club for felons. Nothing he tries to do in prison appears to be very effective in transforming it into a center for the character development and personal growth of its residents.

The situation of the probation, parole, or halfway house worker is not much better. These functionaries of the criminal justice system are frequently taken for granted by the street-wise youngster who views them as "soft" and subject to flagrant manipulation.

The training of officers in corrections at the college level has tended to concentrate on a search for illusive "causes" of delinquent behavior and their academic mentors most frequently theorize that society, the family, the school, the ghetto are at fault— sometimes the chromosomes and genes are the culprits—and the

484

offender is a mere victim, not to be held responsible for his misdeeds.

The officer's college education, if it touched on the theory and practice of altering attitude and behavior at all, was concerned with teaching him an orthodox treatment approach derived from the theories of Sigmund Freud. He was taught that it is of great importance that he delve very deeply into the history of the client to locate the possible early childhood trauma that most directly relates to his current behavior. Was he breast-fed or bottle-fed, the officer tries to establish. What accidents and deprivations did he suffer as a child? Did he get along with his siblings? Asking these and dozens of other probing questions, the probation officer was taught, is the best way to begin a therapeutic relationship.

At the same time, in accord with orthodox theory, the officer is warned against involvement, particularly *emotional* involvement (as though there was any other kind).

"But how can I be helpful if I am not deeply involved with my client?" the idealistic young officer, fresh on the job, might respond to the directive of his more experienced casework-oriented supervisor.

"You're thinking of a Lady Bountiful approach. That went out the window with high-buttoned shoes. Here we strive to be objective, scientific, detached."

"But why?"

"Because, my dear fellow, you must remember *transference*. It's dangerous and could get out of hand. You've got to watch out for transference. All sorts of terrible things can happen if you permit the unchecked growth of transference."

"Sounds bad, all right. I'll be careful," the new officer responds at this display of erudition and he continues by accepting the medical-model explanation of the origin and treatment of deviant behavior. He begins to believe that the basis for criminal activity is somehow akin to the operation of a physical disorder like chicken pox.

The new correctional officer is likely to be further cautioned about the need to maintain an attitude of moral neutrality and permissiveness. He begins to accept the concept immortalized by Officer Krupke of *West Side Story* that criminality is a disease and the offender deserves all the special considerations and privileges accorded to an individual who has broken his leg.

Finally, the novitiate in correctional practices is taught a generally gloomy and pessimistic philosophy about his capacity to change his wards in any positive direction. Since personality changes are the result of immersion in the psychoanalytic process resulting in insight, and the officer is patently not competent to practice psychoanalysis, all his efforts can be of little avail, he learns.

The point is that the correctional officer receives very little in the way of college education or on-the-job training to prepare him for the difficult task of influencing deviant persons to follow a more promising path to achieve a law-abiding, self-fulfilling personal goal.

It was Dr. Glasser's unique fate to enter the correctional treatment morass as a result of a combination of circumstances. He had encountered Dr. G. L. Harrington in the now well known Building 206 of the Los Angeles VA Hospital and had been introduced by him to a philosophy and treatment approach that Glasser polished, developed, and presented to the world as Reality Therapy. However, his heretical views became known to the UCLA authorities who promptly withdrew an offer of professorship at the university. Simultaneously, Glasser received an invitation from the California correctional authorities to become Psychiatric Director of the Ventura School for Girls, probably the largest female reformatory in the world. Glasser effectively transferred the basic procedures employed in Building 206 to the education of the seven hundred hardcore delinquent girls of Ventura—and the rest is history.

The literature dealing with correctional treatment is a wasteland with regard to reasonable advice and suggestions for the practitioner. The two most recent volumes (Fox, *Corrections,* 1973, and Smith and Berlin, *Treatment of the Offender,* 1974) describe the intricacies of psychoanalytic (casework) theory and principles with the appropriate note that obviously such treatment is neither available nor suitable for the mass of offenders. Reality Therapy is dismissed with a few paragraphs in one book and several sentences in the other.

A review of the literature in criminology and corrections provides only a handful of papers that reflect and expand on the principles of Reality Therapy. The papers selected for this section represent the most relevant we could locate.

The first two articles by Glasser and Iverson were extracted from an out-of-print manual to guide group leaders at the Ventura School. They are notable for their clarity, freedom from jargon and abstraction, and attention to practical details. The discussion about the organization of groups in an institution for offenders, the problems one encounters in the operation of groups, the illustrative material, all provide a good basis for a reply to the student of Reality Therapy who asks, "Where can I find information on starting and working with groups in a correctional setting?"

The third paper represents Glasser's first significant foray into the correctional publication field. It is adapted from a speech delivered to the British Columbia Correctional Association in 1962 and has been widely quoted and reprinted.

Bratter follows with the argument that the probation officer adopt a humanistic role by being guardian, advocate, friend and "behavioral engineer" on behalf of his clientele.

Dr. Schmidhofer's article "Acting Out or Acting Up?" is a good example of material composed independent of formal contact with Reality Therapy, yet echoing and confirming sentiments in agreement with concepts and principles associated with Dr. Glasser. The author complains about psychoanalytically oriented therapists who attempt to apply the theories of "depth" treatment to the corrections field and "are quite content to sit unmoved and implacable while their patients engage in all manner and variety of dysocial antics."

Daytop Village, a therapeutic community for the treatment of hardcore drug addicts, was begun in 1963 and appears to be a setting where the basic principles of Reality Therapy relating to emphasis on personal responsibility for behavior, denial of the mental illness excuse for acting out behavior, involvement, creative problem solving, love and the growth of self-worth, are accepted and practiced. Dr. Glasser has mentioned Daytop Village (along with Alcoholics Anonymous, Gamblers Anonymous and Synanon) as examples of relevant Reality Therapy applications. Dr. Bassin, a co-founder of Daytop Village and a champion of Reality Therapy, traces the history and describes the treatment format that has become the model for dozens of therapeutic communities operated primarily by former addicts in the United States and Europe.

"Reality Therapy with Offenders" is a succinct statement presented at a convention of the American Psychological Association by an acknowledged leader in the field of corrections, currently dean of the School of Criminology at Florida State University, Dr. Eugene H. Czajkoski.

The man frequently identified as the dean of American criminologists, Dr. Donald R. Cressey, formulates a basic tenet of AA—that one cannot retain the benefits of personal rehabilitation unless one becomes involved in helping fellow sufferers—as the foundation for work with offenders. He suggests that criminal A will reform to the extent that he starts to attempt the reformation of criminal B.

Dr. Bratter describes his practice over a seven-year period with a unique clientele of seventy-five alienated, unmotivated, drug-abusing adolescents from an affluent community of Westchester County in New York. His direct, uncompromising, utterly open and transparent technique may not be everybody's cup of tea, but what else, he asks, can work with this population? In scholarly fashion, he musters a host of authorities to lend support to his contention that this group of clients requires measures that differ in many respects from a conventional approach. Bratter concludes that his Reality Therapy confrontation style, with the therapist assuming an advocate role in many life situations, has yielded dramatic results—and he provides the statistics to prove it.

Stephen Chinlund's paper "You Still Make Choices!" is based on his experience as director of an institution for female offenders. He reiterates a favorite theme of Reality Therapy: those people we can convince that despite handicaps, hardships, poverty and misfortune, still have a considerable degree of control over their destinies, are most likely to cope successfully with the strains and pressures of living in a free community.

"We rely wearily on elaborate psychiatric and psychological testing rituals to give us direction when most offenders must be lumped together in the institution anyway. After diagnosis and classification, few institutions either can afford or are geared to provide the kinds of ameliorative services which the clinician recommends. Psychiatric and psychological protocols help dress up case records . . . but provide little assistance in planning treatment strategies." So notes Richard L. Rachin, who writes from years of direct experience and observation as an administrator of the Florida Division of Youth Services, which officially and formally has adopted Reality Therapy as the treatment of choice in working with the delinquents who are referred to that agency. Florida may well be serving as a field laboratory testing a specific treatment approach to help establish its effectiveness. At long last, Florida has substituted a scientific posture for the heat of rhetoric, to determine the relative worth of contending treatment modalities in corrections!

WILLIAM GLASSER
NORMAN IVERSON

The Role of the Leader in Counseling

Experience with the fifty-girl group has shown the leader to be a major factor in group success or failure. While small groups of five to ten girls function often with little to moderate leadership, this does not seem to be possible with large groups. For example, in the area of group control and discipline, the leader of the large group has to develop ways to maintain order and flow of discussion, a task not ordinarily necessary or pressing in small groups.

Philosophy of Leading the Large Group

To lead a large group successfully the leader must master a variety of approaches, and often use these approaches almost simultaneously during the meeting. First, the leader must maintain order and regulate the flow of discussion. To do this he must be in control of the group at all times. He may vary widely in doing so, according to his judgment, ranging from rigid control to letting the group approach almost free interruption of speakers. But the control must be there, and the group must recognize that the control is there.

The question which naturally arises is, how does the leader maintain control and yet vary his approach? Probably he does this best by leading the group for a relatively long time—perhaps two to three months. One cannot develop this aspect of leadership

Former title "The Role of the Leader." From *Reality Therapy in Large Group Counseling: A Manual of Procedure and Practice*. Los Angeles, Calif., the Reality Press (no date). Reprinted by permission.

overnight; even if one has the skill to do this rather well, it is hard to apply this skill with a new group. Therefore, this maintenance of control is partly dependent upon the length of time the leader is with the group and the skill which he develops in leading. A variety of inexperienced leaders is confusing to a group, and also places the group in a position where they may challenge a transient leader to get rid of him. Only when all staff are experienced in leading may this role be shifted frequently. All staff members who participate should prepare themselves for leading; but in the beginning, one of the staff whom the group recognizes and trusts should lead. When he becomes proficient, the leadership may be transferred to another regular participant and in that way everyone has a chance to learn.

A good leader will learn that first he has to be able to display strength by virtue of his voice and demeanor. When the group becomes loud and unruly he has to be able to raise his voice and be heard. When the group is speaking out of turn he has to be able to stop discussion in the middle, or the beginning, and give the designated person time to speak. He must protect that time and give the speaker who has been recognized a chance to finish her thought, relevant or not. But if she continues to be irrelevant to the discussion at hand, the leader should be able politely to stop her. He must recognize people in the order he chooses, not necessarily in the order they have raised their hands to speak. He should take people out of turn for two reasons: (1) they have not spoken previously, and the leader's job is to spread the discussion as evenly as possible; (2) he feels through previous experience with this particular group that a certain girl will speak in a constructive, problem-solving fashion and will keep the meeting going toward solving the problem, where another will tend to be disruptive, change the subject, or raise issues which make the problem more difficult for the group to solve. It is the leader's responsibility to keep discussion flowing positively and he must, therefore, exercise his authority where at times he arbitrarily chooses someone to speak. He should, however, develop the ability to make this seem as spontaneous and unpremeditated as possible.

The leader should feel free to call upon the girls who do not volunteer but who he feels will contribute if called upon. To do this, however, one must develop certain techniques, among which is to remark: "You seem to be giving this discussion a great deal of thought. Could you give us your opinion?"; or, "I am very interested in what you think," a comment which leads the girl into the discussion and recognizes her as being a thoughtful participant, even though she did not volunteer to speak.

The leader should also enforce strictly the rule that *one topic be discussed at a time.* Any deviation from this rule will lead to loss of control of the group. Besides these rather parliamentary but still judgmental aspects of the leader's job, there are other important aspects of his role.

The leader must take the brunt of group resistance and not allow the group to push him aside. He should at times take an unpopular stand and hold the line against group pressure. No leader should suffer from the need to be a "good guy." For example, in trying to implement the concept of caring for others and being responsible for others, the leader should feel free to offer unpopular disciplinary solutions, such as sending all girls to their rooms for the action of a few girls who break the rules. This doesn't mean the leader sets the rules, but the leader stands by the rules and won't back away from them because of group pressure. Suggestion of such drastic measures will arouse much antagonism against the leader, because he is the one making the stand. It will also produce constructive discussion when the leader points out that he is quite willing to listen to alternate solutions. A leader who does not take stands presupposes that the group will have individuals mature enough within it to take a stand against the group. It is possible that girls like this may be present and certainly, if the kind of group therapy described in this manual is implemented, girls like this will arise. But when they are not there, the leader must make the stand.

In order that the girls can see his side of the question, he should pose questions such as: "What other suggestions do you have to solve the problem? This is the only way I see it, and if I were you I might not like the suggested solution either; but this does solve the problem. However, I am very interested in any other solutions you may have."

If the leader uses this flexible kind of approach to the group, he will find that he can hold his position much more easily. There is no inconsistency between taking a stand and at the same time being reasonable.

The leader should be flexible enough to bend if the group discovers a solution which did not occur to him, and rigid enough to hold the group in discussion if there is an obvious solution that the members seem to be avoiding. The leader is not trying to be popular and get the group to agree with him, nor is he trying to be purposely unpopular and always disagree with the group's solution. *His job is to hold the group to a problem-solving discussion,* because some of the problems raised have very difficult solutions, especially in terms of the group members taking much responsibility.

Group discussion often bogs down. The leader must be able to think of techniques, as these difficulties occur, to get the group meeting rolling again. To do this takes experience; but the group, especially a new group, must be able to have the security that the leader does have some methods of helping the group out of situations where it seems completely stuck. The leader must eventually give some direction to a group that is floundering; although again, the judgment of how long to let it flounder before direction is attempted is something the leader can learn only by experience. The leader must be able to gauge the anxiety level of the group and not let the level get so high that problem solving will be impossible. At the same time, anxiety should be maintained at sufficient levels so that problem solving by the group, not by the leader, is the function of the meeting. When anxiety rises too high, the leader should be able to inject humor into the meeting, especially in very tense moments, because humor breaks the tension in a positive way. Humor should never be a substitute for firmness, but it can be an aid to firmness during tense situations.

The leader must not pussyfoot. He should not be afraid to bring up emotionally-charged subjects. He must encourage the group to name names and must be honest in naming names himself without discouraging the group. He must not demand anything of the group that he is unwilling to do himself. If the leader evades the truth, his leadership will be set back, sometimes almost indefinitely. There are times when telling the truth will admit poor leadership or irresponsible behavior on the part of other staff members who are assisting in the meeting, but there is no substitute for the truth even when the truth hurts. The staff must be willing to accept the decision of the group when their bad judgment is exposed; but if the truth is adhered to strictly, this will rarely occur. Mistakes should be admitted quickly and matter-of-factly, and these instances can stand positively as an example of leadership honesty. The leader shows the group by example that they too should be honest in exposing their poor judgment and irresponsibility.

Therefore, the leader must gain the reputation of being able to lead actively when necessary, and to play a passive role when the group is handling itself well and solving problems. Any group which is secure and confident that the leader will be able to do most of what has been described in the previous paragraphs will move further and faster toward solving problems and accepting responsibility. Of course, all staff participating in the meeting should follow the leader's example in the processes stated here.

Examples of Leadership Techniques

Example No. 1: The group is out of order, won't quiet down, and there is much side talk while a girl is talking. The subject at hand is unpopular because it is either too anxiety-provoking or too boring. Here the leader must be clear and firm. A gavel may be used or he may use his voice. He should not threaten, but rather firmly remind the girls of the basic rules. Only as an absolute last resort should he threaten to remove girls from the group or actually remove them if they are disruptive, but he should stop the discussion and discuss the problem of the disruption. He may say that further outbursts only emphasize the need to discuss the outburst. The leader may also probe the outburst to find out whether or not the subject was too sensitive, or if the outburst was more an example of general disrespect for the whole group process. Perhaps the original subject should be dropped for a period of time while the whole group discusses order. The leader should point out that nothing can come from a group that does not maintain enough discipline to discuss a subject properly. The subject (group order) may need to be continued for several meetings, sometimes even for weeks, until the group understands that nothing constructive can happen until the members respect each other enough to carry on a discussion. If a leader cannot discuss this basic point and gain order, there can be no group meetings.

Example No. 2: It is evident that a popular girl is causing much difficulty and disruption in the cottage, but the girls are afraid to bring the matter up since they fear the pressure of other girls because of this girl's popularity. Here the leader must take a firm stand and perhaps bring up the subject himself. This will take the burden away from the girls, who might otherwise be afraid to mention it. He uses the technique of asking the popular girl if she thinks she would like to be discussed and whether she thinks she could aid her progress in the cottage by discussing herself before the group. If the girl can introduce the discussion at the leader's suggestion, this will provide an opening for others to contribute. Sometimes it is impossible for other girls to discuss her truthfully and constructively. For example, all girls might say she is doing well, that there is no sense in discussing her, and immediately want to discuss someone else. Here the leader might hold firm for a while, but eventually go on to another subject, keeping the unfinished business in mind for future discussions.

Example No. 3: When the girls cannot discuss a cottage problem, the leader should relate the problem to their outside world, and use this as an example of the cottage problem. When a girl can't face her cottage behavior, she might discuss trouble she had in school or home, which could then be related. The girls *can* sometimes discuss very clearly something outside their present living situation which is very similar to that which is now going on in the cottage. The leader can show the cottage how this material *is* parallel to what is going on in the cottage and say, "Since we discussed *that* so well, can we now discuss this?" Some of the girls may say it isn't parallel, and this could also be grounds for discussion in order to switch the group from the easy parallel to the more difficult problem at hand.

Some problems can't be faced directly. The group doesn't have enough strength, enough responsibility, or enough confidence in the leader or in the cottage staff. Discussing a less threatening parallel is a step toward gaining strength and confidence. Again, it's not the best way, and might not work, but the leader will experience times when it is worthwhile to try anything to motivate the group.

Example No. 4: The leader notices that certain girls tend to dominate the conversation and want to talk about unsolvable subjects, such as "noise in the cottage" or some problem girl, over and over as a "scapegoat." This is one way for girls to avoid responsibility for the whole group meeting. It is up to the leader at this point to introduce basic issues in a way that will arouse others in the group. The leader should try to divert them from the particular unproductive subject. This takes ingenuity on the part of the leader but it *can* be done in the following way: say that noise is *not important;* that the leader and the house staff are in the cottage only a certain number of hours a day and they can stand noise; the girls are there all the time, and they should do something about the disturbing noise themselves. This minimizes the minor problem that the girls were trying to make too important.

Initially girls feel that basic, but minor, disciplinary issues such as cottage noise are more important to the staff than solving interpersonal problems, and they are likely to stall the group on disciplinary problems. The leader, along with other staff members, should minimize some of the disciplinary issues in order to get to the cause of the disciplinary problems. This allows the topic to shift from "noise in the cottage" to something more basic, such as poor relationships between the girls which are causing cliques and bickering.

These are general examples of leadership. While examples help to give some flavor to the material, they should not be taken literally as ways that must be used in these situations. They merely reflect the fact that leadership takes the understanding that the leader must keep the group to its basic problem-solving purpose. It takes experience to gain the strength to do this when the group rebels, but this skill has been learned by many leaders at Ventura, and is best learned by leading a meeting which is followed by a good critique.

WILLIAM GLASSER

NORMAN IVERSON

Discipline as a Function of Large Group Meetings

Discipline

Discipline is best defined as the treatment of an individual in such a way that she can better utilize the program of the institution while there, and the opportunities of society when she leaves. Inherent in this concept is the idea that discipline is a *positive force*, a way to motivate a girl to do better, and to get her to understand that staff cares very much that she change her behavior in a positive direction. Discipline is not to be confused with punishment, which is an attempt to inflict pain for wrongdoing in the hope that the pain will be strongly associated with wrongdoing to prevent it in the future. In contrast, discipline, while it may have included within it an element of pain, should be an attempt from the start to set the individual upon the right track—nor merely a hope that pain will keep him off the wrong track. Correct discipline has within it the discomfort that is felt when a person tries to change his ways of behaving for the better, rather than the pain of punishment which is primarily retribution for doing wrong. In order to make this important point clear, several examples will be cited.

(1) In a cottage, a girl gets upset and breaks several windows in her room. When questioned, she says, "I blew it" and, usually because of her emotional upset at the time, no clearer statement

Former title "Discipline as a Function of the Large Group Meetings." From *Reality Therapy in Large Group Counseling: A Manual of Procedure and Practice*. Los Angeles, Calif., the Reality Press (no date).

can be elicited as to what made her upset. Prior to the onset of Large Group Counseling (L.G.C.) at Ventura, she would be removed to our discipline cottage, Rio Vista (R.V.), and placed in a room where she is restricted for approximately a week before being returned to the cottage. At this point, without further explanation, the necessary discipline could be interpreted either as discipline or punishment. For this staff decision to be considered punishment, the following steps would be necessary: as soon as she broke the windows, she would be told that she would be in R.V. for an arbitrary period of time, and if she were not good, there would be further arbitrary periods; when the arbitrary period was up, she would be transferred back to the cottage, with the threat that if she broke windows again, a longer period of arbitrary time would be imposed; the only counseling would be individual; the group would be uninvolved. For the same staff behavior to be considered disciplinary, it is important that when she was taken to R.V. she would be told that she would stay in R.V. until she could offer a good plan for returning to the open cottage and be willing to discuss her plan in L.G.C. Some discussion would be held with her when she met with the Disciplinary Committee on R.V. regarding what plan she was making, but the major discussion would be transferred to the cottage group so that her behavior could be discussed as a group problem. If her plan seemed reasonable, as soon as possible she would be placed back in the cottage and her plan discussed in L.G.C. No further threat of confinement would be in order. In this manner, the girl would gain the impression that she and the group were primarily responsible for discovering new answers to her problem.[1]

(2) A girl is loud, profane, and abusive of another girl and also of a staff member when the staff member tries to intervene to mediate the dispute. The girl is placed in her room. For this to be punishment, she is told to stay eight hours. No further attention is paid to her and after eight hours she is released with the admonition that she will be returned to meditation if she has any further difficulty with this girl. For discipline for this same offense, the girl would be asked to go to her room and a staff member would walk her to her room, explaining that this kind of language cannot be

tolerated in the cottage. She would be told that she will be placed in her room until she can explain to the supervisor in charge how she could prevent herself from further trouble of this nature. She would also be told that she would be given approximately eight hours to work out her explanation, during which time the cottage supervisor would have some free period available to talk over her explanation with her. If her explanation seemed reasonable, and if it seemed to the supervisor in charge that her behavior would be acceptable to the group, this would be carried out with the understanding that she make an effort to resolve the issue with the other girl in the large group meeting. Disciplinary measures would not succeed unless the issue was resolved and an attempt was made for the girls to get along better together.

(3) A girl refuses to do her classwork and is noisy and inattentive in class. She is given a work report and assigned to pull weeds for two hours. For this measure to be considered punishment, little attention would be paid to her work, the time carefully checked, and when she is finished she would be sent back to school. For this to be discipline, she would be told clearly the job to be done, the standards expected, and under guidance and supervision, the progress of her work would be checked. Her work would be discussed briefly and objectively, and praise would be given if warranted for good work. If the work was not satisfactory, the assignment would be stopped for the day, but the girl would have to bring her failure and the background for it to the large group for discussion. Naturally, some effort would have to be made to judge the girl's capabilities and emotional status at the time, because what would be considered good work for one girl perhaps would not be good work for another girl. Some girls would be able to produce more acceptable work than others. In each case, however, the group has a responsibility, albeit a far greater one when the work was poorly done. Work reports and other chore-type discipline can still be used, but it must be discussed and related to the basic problem; therefore it is a L.G.C. responsibility.

These three examples should help to clarify the difference between discipline and punishment. The philosophy of discipline is to use a work report or restricted environment as a *tool* to help a girl to gain better feelings of worthwhileness and to give her time to plan to do better in the future.

The Large Group

The purpose of involving the large group in disciplinary measures is to increase involvement, and to widen the scope of possible solutions to individual and cottage problems. Under no circumstances should the large group implement punishments, but it *can* suggest discipline and enable other girls of the cottage to become involved in thinking toward disciplinary solutions or, as previously noted, problem-solving solutions. It should be noted, however, that discipline need not and, except in unusual cases, should not wait for large group meetings. Nor should all rule infractions be a part of the large group discussion. The purpose of the large group discussion is to inspire the girls to think in terms of disciplinary or problem-solving measures. One problem is as good as another for discussion, but obviously, for reasons of time, all problems cannot be discussed. Measures worked out for solving one problem, however, can be implemented by the group supervisors for similar problems, which also would be products of the large group meeting.

The supervisor, teacher, principal, or assistant head should almost always institute discipline immediately. The cottage, in the large group meeting, should be responsible wherever feasible for helping the girl arrive at the necessary plan which should become part of her disciplinary procedure. The large group should also serve as a focus point for a girl to report back her progress, or for the large group to criticize the progress of a girl when a previous plan was made. This criticism, however, should include a constructive solution toward making a new plan when the old plan was not working out successfully.

Examples of Cottage Involvement in Disciplinary Procedures

Example No. 1: Two girls were discovered in the same room and were placed in individual rooms and kept there until the next meeting. This might be for as long as three days, but usually will be 24 to 36 hours. At the meeting, the girls are invited to explain their behavior. This is done in preference to reading the incident report. Ordinarily, the girls will explain their behavior fairly accurately, and their explanation should be accepted if it is accurate and the report need not be read immediately. If the whole meeting is taken up with the girls' refusing to tell an accurate story, or the group criticizing the staff excessively while excusing the girls' behavior, the girls should be kept in their rooms until the next meeting. Ordinarily this procedure will not be necessary or, if necessary, will have to be used only once. Staff should not fall into the trap of excessively defending their incident report. If the girls explain themselves fairly accurately, as they usually will, there is little need for staff criticism and the problem can be approached with a minimum of diversion.

Once the girls make their explanation, and this may take a considerable period of time, the group is requested to assist the girls with a solution to the problem. In their explanation for this example, the girls state they are "very close," and find it impossible to converse privately and quietly in the cottage. The group suggests that there is more to it than merely this "closeness," and that the girls are "going together" and want privacy for behavior other than conversational purposes. The girls deny this, and there is an impasse at the meeting. Then the group suggests that maybe these girls feel rejected by other girls in the cottage, or by a group of girls. The group also suggests to the staff that girls who wish to talk quietly and privately be allowed to do so under supervision in the dining room while other activities are taking place in the day room. The girls agree to try to make more friends and to ask the supervisors when they want time to talk privately. The cottage team agrees that, under proper supervision, girls be allowed to use the dining room for quiet or serious talk as well as for quiet activities, such as cards. There is good group and staff cooperation in this disciplinary solution.

Example No. 2: A girl refuses to get up in the morning. Staff places her in her room until the group meeting. The group is confronted with the problem and the girl refuses to add anything to the discussion. She is sullen and uncommunicative. She says that "all she has to do is die," but she doesn't want staff or girls on her back, or "messing into her business." The group finds this problem difficult to approach and the leader encourages the group not to give up, but to talk about the girl and toward a solution, whether or not she cooperates.

After a bit of discussion the group suggests that perhaps the girl is antagonistic toward the morning supervisor, who the group feels perhaps wakes the girl in a way that is unpleasant to her. The girl continues to say nothing except the fact that she doesn't want her problem discussed. The group asks if the girl has any close friends in the cottage who might shed more light on the problem. One girl volunteers that she feels the same way, but she is afraid to stay in her bed in the morning because of the chance that she will be diciplined. This reinforces the girl's not getting up in the morning and is in a negative direction, but these kinds of comments must be accepted and no attempt should be made by the leader to refute them. Rather, it should be accepted and a brief statement made to the effect that this is not *solving* the problem, and the discussion may then continue in the right direction.

One girl asks if the disciplined girl has visitors or letters. She answers in an angry way, stating she doesn't care, but doesn't have any visitors or any letters. The group suggests that perhaps an effort should be made to get her a volunteer visitor.[2] In the group meeting, it becomes readily apparent how lonely and isolated this girl is and that the group is now getting down to the roots of her problem. The group also suggests that the leader appoint a committee to talk to the girl privately and find out if there is any other way they can help. If this is done, the committee will report back to the large group, and in this way the girl can be more favorably integrated into the group. The big step from her isolation to group participation was too much for her in her present condition.

After this discussion and perhaps toward the end of the meeting, the girl opens up and says she is sorry, and that she will make an effort to get up in the morning. This may take place in the meeting, it may take place several meetings later, or it may never be stated; she may just start getting up on time. The group suggests also that the girl talk to the housemother or the supervisor in charge in order to better understand cottage rules, especially about getting up in the morning. It isn't that the girl doesn't know the rules. She does. What she needs is contact with the supervisor on the pretext that it is necessary to re-explain the rules. These girls are lonely and need this contact and the kind, warm explanations necessary to provide the contact, even though they know the rules. If the group can continue in a disciplinary mood, and no support is given to punishment procedures, the girl will feel more accepted. The girl will sense the non-hostile attitude and be more accepting of cottage rules and regulations.

After a visitor is obtained, the girl may still have an occasional late morning, because she needs to prove the point that she can't get over her irresponsible behavior too quickly. No threats should be made. The whole problem should be discussed with the group and, even though she may spend periods of time in her room, this should not be done in a threatening way. The girl should not be accused of not appreciating what the cottage has done, or of not appreciating the obtaining of a volunteer visitor for her. These negative "preaching" practices don't work. When she finds they are not used, she will move more quickly in a positive direction.

Example No. 3: Cottage discipline has slackened, the girls are angry, out of order, using excessive profanity and pressuring excessively. Large group meetings seem unable to cope with the problem because girls spend their time in the meetings attacking staff rather than examining and trying to remedy their own shortcomings, both individually and as a group. Solution: this problem is especially difficult, because staff and girls have become antagonistic and the girls are not willing to use the large group to solve the problem. To remedy this, the girls must become distracted from their antagonism. A good procedure is for the leader to focus on an important but essentially neutral problem, and use this gradually to direct the group into a positive, cooperative mood. To implement his approach, the leader should use the "round robin" technique.

At the beginning of the next meeting he should state that each girl will be asked to speak in turn, going around the complete circle, and to express herself on a question posed by the leader. The question can be variously phrased, but in a very antagonistic group it is usually best if the question is neutral rather than the direct query, "what do you believe we should do to help the cottage?" This direct approach works best where there is minimal group deterioration, and where the question is posed more by the girls than by the leader. When cottage discipline has deteriorated considerably, a better question would be, "what are your plans for the future?" or, "what do you plan to do after you leave the school?" This is neutral, yet positive. In the round robin technique the leader can encourage, through a friendly dialogue with each girl, a positive expression toward the girl's future.

If it is not possible to poll the entire group in one meeting, another meeting can be used. Conversation should be friendly and kept going at all times. Inasmuch as possible, a little friendly humor should be injected into the dialogue between the leader and each girl. Controversial and very personal material should be avoided generally, but a certain amount of moderately personal material, such as "how did the girl get along in school previously?" and, "are there going to be problems at home with her mother?" may certainly be in order. The girls will be very interested in this procedure and, during this round robin technique for one or two meetings, antagonism (at least at the meeting) will be reduced, and the group will be ready for the next stage.

If positive discussion proceeds, and there is a good chance that it will, the discussion in this and the next several meetings can gradually be directed toward the cottage problem and things the girls could do to help make the cottage program better. When the discussion becomes positive, the leader can rather *subtly* abandon the round robin technique and return to usual procedures.

One technique which needs to be used more frequently is to call on girls who don't have their hands up to answer a question. If the girl refuses to comment, no effort should be made to force a comment. Quite often a direct, friendly question toward a girl who is not volunteering will elicit an excellent answer. Very often when the cottage attitude is negative, the girls who are positively motivated don't volunteer to speak, but will speak when called upon.

Example No. 4: Problem: a girl loses her key. Solution: the leader presents the problem and asks the girl to make a statement. The girl gives her excuse, and the key is indeed gone. The excuse is relatively unimportant. At this point, the group necessarily flounders for a solution, because it is hard to replace a lost key. The group does protest that one girl's loss of a key is not due to the *group's* carelessness. The leader insists that the group solve the problem and suggests further that unless they can produce a solution, the whole cottage will be restricted to their rooms because of the lost key. The leader explains that if too many keys are lost, keys will have to be taken away from all of the girls because they lack the responsibility to handle keys. They *have* to work out a plan for lost keys.

The girls tend to resent this bitterly and are very frustrated. They suggest that maybe they should look for the key. The leader insists that they search systematically. The girls are given an opportunity later to look for the key, but it is not found. (Keys are rarely found, and if staff expects that the key will be found to solve the problem, they will be disappointed.) Girls are asked to continue to search for a solution. The major purpose here, and this will not be accomplished quickly or in one meeting, is to enable the girls to see that an individual problem is a *cottage responsibility*. Experience has proven that the cottage rarely finds the key, but when the girls are thoroughly frustrated, the leader may suggest a solution. This problem is usually too difficult for the girls to solve without the help of a leader.

One solution which the girls may offer, or which can be suggested, is that the girl involved go to her room and while in her room, work out a plan to care for her key more carefully in the future. A better solution the leader may suggest is that the cottage have a massive clean-up rather than a recreational program that evening. All girls should work and a thorough search for the key is made during this clean-up process. The cottage clean-up aids the solution, because all girls are involved in a cooperative effort, something has been accomplished positively, and there is also a chance that the key *may* be found. This solution depends upon a cooperative effort. The subject should be dropped once the cooperative effort has been exerted. Clinging to this problem, which is essentially unsolvable, will only create frustration and antagonism, so it is up to the judgment of the leader to find the proper closing time.

Example No. 5: Problem: a girl runs away while on off-grounds privileges, or from furlough. Solution: the cottage understands that the Superintendent can restrict the entire cottage for a month or longer, for abusing both off-grounds privileges and furlough privileges. Restriction may not be lifted for a month, unless the Superintendent is satisfied that the cottage can solve this problem. The girl may or may not be returned, but the cottage responsibility is the same. Let us assume the girl has not come back. The leader turns the problem over to the cottage for solution. Ordinarily the girls will avoid the subject and say, (1) it's her fault alone; or (2) staff has no right to restrict them; they did not want her to run. The leader now has to be firm and withstand much abuse from the girls, because they do not want to face this issue, and they do not want to be restricted. The leader must point out that escapees can lose off-grounds privileges and furloughs for the whole school, and that the cottage must work out an acceptable solution. Pressure is continued by the leader until the girls admit that they knew about the intended escape, or until the whole cottage team is convinced that the girls knew nothing.

Assuming some of them did know, they must understand through discussion that it is the cottage's responsibility to tell a staff member that a girl has escape intentions, and their responsibility privately to dissuade her from her plan to leave. This is a difficult concept for the girls to understand, because it is against their code. But if responsibility is understood and genuinely observed, it can provide a major break-through in terms of their understanding *the value to a group of personal discipline, and the value to the individual wrongdoer of group discipline.* The leader should persist until this becomes part of the group concept, because it is gaining responsibility which should have positive carryover to their future. It is not that the problem will necessarily be solved, but it is the growth that occurs in the groping for a solution. Out of this groping for a solution comes the understanding that each girl has a responsibility to the group. Solutions are therefore suggested for the prevention of future problems, not solely for solving this one.

Summary

These examples are not meant to be used as prescriptions for group leaders to follow. They represent ways which have been used and which have worked in some cottages during the past year. They adhere to the basic problem-solving group methods which we believe are important. They deal with behavior and are aimed toward solving upsets in feelings by directly working toward better behavior. Everything in the meeting should be aimed at the group's responsibility and the individual's responsibility to the group. The ultimate goal is for the group to be self-motivated toward this goal of acceptance of responsibility. Because the group continually changes, staff must accept the fact that when a number of positive girls are discharged, the group will usually regress. This happens over and over and is discouraging to staff; but constantly changing group structure is natural and is really the goal, because if the group continues to be responsible for a long period, staff has been lax in discharging responsible girls who should leave.

While the previous material was written about a group and one leader, actually in practice it is encouraged that group discussions have more staff participation. All staff should feel free to contribute their observations, opinions or criticism to the group. Staff contributions should be made in a warm, interested way. *Hostile provocation should not be answered with sarcasm or ridicule,* as this is what many girls *want* staff to do, and these girls will try to provoke staff. Honest anger, however, is acceptable, and shows the girls that staff have feelings and are genuinely interested in the success of the meetings. As much as possible, however, hostility should not be returned in kind, because girls then can blame the staff member for provoking them. They don't wish to see their own provocatory behavior and it is hard to point this out to them, except through the example of not becoming provoked. This demonstration by staff of control and acceptance of their hostile attitude teaches girls more than any lecture could possibly achieve.

It is the purpose of the critique to examine staff participation in the meeting and to try to better our own ability to direct the group. If we expect openness from the girls, we have to be able to be open ourselves, and the critique is the place to do so. If a staff member was doing or saying things in the meeting which were distracting the meeting, provoking hostile behavior, or not leading toward problem solving, it is up to other staff to make the staff member aware of his behavior. Critique is not a time to prove who is the best therapist. Critique is a time to realize that we all have much to learn and that one of the superior ways for us to learn is by helping each other. Since it is impossible for any one person to see exactly what he does, his behavior, which is often clear to others, should be made known to him.

NOTES

1. A procedure which would certainly apply to many situations outside of corrections. For example, in counseling in a college dormitory, rule infractions could be handled very well in this same way.

2. This is a program where interested mature women volunteer to come to the school at least once a week to visit with the girls who have no regular visitors.

A Realistic Approach to the Young Offender

The first important step in correcting a young offender's behavior is to find out what it is you are trying to correct. Most of the theories contained in the literature on juvenile delinquency are psychoanalytic in nature (emphasizing unconscious intrapersonal conflict), sociological (stressing environmental difficulties), or some combination of both. To illustrate, let me present the case of a sixteen-year-old girl who has run away from home, indulged in heterosexual and homosexual activity, prostituted, experimented with narcotics, tattooed herself and, in final custody, attempted suicide by slashing her wrists. If I stopped now and asked you the cause of her behavior I'm sure no one would venture an opinion. Rather, you would ask me to give more information than this brief description. From your training and experience, you would feel uncomfortable about committing yourself without some history, psychological tests, and background investigation of the girl. Very likely you would call on someone to make a psychiatric evaluation. Even with this information, many of you would still disagree, according to the way you have been taught, your experience, and the amount of introspection you have done.

One value of our theory (which is explained below), and the therapy based upon it, is that it circumvents any disagreement over what caused the girl's behavior and it sharply reduces the need for

Former title "Reality Therapy: A Realistic Approach to the Young Offender." Adapted from a speech presented to the British Columbia Correctional Association, Vancouver, Canada, Nov. 3, 1962. Reprinted by permission of the author.

the usual diagnostic procedures. Further, this theory, if clearly understood, can be used not only by trained psychotherapists but by everyone who comes in contact with the young offender, from the arresting officer to the parole officer. Only a consistent method of treatment, an approach that can be used to some extent by everyone in correction, will help young people in trouble.

The Theory

Personal Responsibility

The theory of Reality Therapy has been developed in the past seven years in consultation with a colleague, Dr. G. L. Harrington, who uses it exclusively with mental patients at the Los Angeles Veterans Administration Center Neuropsychiatric Hospital and in his private practice. It is based on our belief that regardless of what he has done, how he feels, where he comes from, his size, shape, mental ability, physical condition or heredity, the young offender suffers from a universal malady: he is unwilling to take responsibility for his behavior. We further believe that correctional problems are only a more dramatic expression of the lack of responsibility, which is really a basic problem in all psychiatric work. The children and adults we deal with in correction express this irresponsibility directly by the act of breaking the law. Patients in mental hospitals express it by partially or completely withdrawing into a world of their own creation. The depressed patient is unable responsibly to express the intense anger he feels, so he turns it inward and becomes depressed. The obsessive-compulsive neurotic tries desperately to compensate for his basic lack of responsibility by becoming superresponsible—so much so that he can accomplish little because of his compulsive symptoms. Thus, all people who function badly in our society suffer from this difficulty, but none of them expresses it as clearly and as directly as the lawbreaker.

All the effort in the world to discover why a child is irresponsible and breaks the law won't change the fact that he *is* irresponsible. Neither will all the treatment we can muster, unless this treatment is from the start concerned with guiding the patient toward becoming a more responsible person right now. This is why we claim that diagnosis based on detailed studies is meaningless; however superficial or deep the explanation may be, the ultimate fact remains that the person involved is not acting or thinking in a responsible manner.

In the traditional process of looking for explanations and diagnoses, a reason for deviant behavior will often seem clear. For example, the psychotherapist may find out that a homosexual girl is afraid of men because her father was both brutal and seductive, so she turns toward women for gratification. When he understands this, and even when she understands this, he is in a poor position to help her because he has advanced a reasonable cause for her behavior. Dr. Harrington and I do not believe, as the traditional therapist does, that this understanding will allow her to relate to a man who is not her father. We believe that all she will understand is that the situation is just as she feared—men can be brutal and so it is much safer to remain homosexual. The psychotherapist's initial efforts have, in a sense, only made the girl's trouble more reasonable. She now has an excuse to stay the way she is. In fact, everyone is looking for an excuse for her behavior.

But our job is to make her behavior less reasonable, to help her take the responsibility she must take as a woman in order for her to turn away from this deviant approach to sex. Our job is not to discuss her father (who may or may not have been brutal) but to relate to her now so that she can feel that men are human beings with whom she can make emotional contact.

Therefore, if we want to face reality, we must admit that we can never rewrite a person's history. No matter how much we can understand about the cruel and unusual circumstances which led to his behavior, his neurosis, his ulcer, his depression, or his drug addiction, there is nothing this information can do for us or for him except reinforce the concept that indeed he has a reason to break the law and excuse this transgression on the ground that he is "sick." Therefore we emphasize what traditional therapy tries to ignore: no matter what happened to him, he still has the responsibility for what he does.

If we continue to accept the offender's irresponsibility because of his traumatic history, we become trapped from a therapeutic standpoint. With noncriminal psychiatric problems, we often avoid facing this trap directly. A man with a neurosis can come for traditional treatment indefinitely or a psychotic patient can be locked up for years in a mental hospital; neither exerts great pressure on anyone because his irresponsibility primarily hurts himself.

When a man breaks the law, however, we have to help him because, unless he becomes more responsible, he endangers us. Either we must help him to become more responsible or we must lock him up indefinitely. It is unrealistic to keep him locked up once he has demonstrated that he has gained responsibility. It is not up to us in corrections to advance explanations for irresponsibility, but to recognize that individual responsibility must be the goal of our treatment.

Treatment, Not Punishment

At this point many will think that I just want to return to the old Mosaic concept of "an eye for an eye" to punish the wrongdoer severely. Nothing could be further from my intention. What I advocate is treatment, not punishment. Until an offender can accept the fact that he is responsible for what he did, there can be no treatment in our field. If, as in the first example, the girl prostituted, both she and those who treat her must understand that she did it voluntarily and that better possibilities were open to her than prostitution. Until this is established, there is no treatment. I do not consider it punishment to confront her with her wrongdoing. She has to face both her lack of responsibility and the implication that this is not the way she has to be. She must see that we think she can do better.

From a treatment standpoint, exactly what a person did is of little importance. What matters is in how many areas of his present life he is responsible. The more we find, the easier he is to treat and the better his prognosis. (This is why in many cases it is easier to rehabilitate a murderer than any other criminal. Except for the single grossly irresponsible act, many murderers are fairly responsible people.) Thus, the crux of our theory of Reality Therapy is personal responsibility.

Describing the Offender

Under our concept, a helpful description of a young female offender might consist of a phrase such as "chronic runaway with minor sex delinquency but moderately responsible" and a brief outline of the areas in which she is responsible and those in which she is not. This description would give everyone working with her some basis for what to expect from her. It would indicate where we should work and where not too much of our effort is needed. It might further indicate, if she were a fairly responsible older girl, that she would be a good candidate for self-parole. We might, on the other hand, describe a narcotics addict as a young man who takes no responsibility for his behavior and lives only for the feeling that narcotics bring him. He can then be periodically reevaluated and treated until he can take more responsibility in important areas of his life.

The theory can be used by the judge, the probation or parole officer, and the psychiatrist, as well as by nonprofessional correctional personnel because it can be easily understood without the use of such nebulous jargon as "insight," "conflict resolution," or "transference workthrough."

Happiness a Stumbling Block

In addition to coming to grips with his irresponsible behavior, the offender must also face the question of that ill-defined term, happiness. From a treatment standpoint, happiness can be a huge stumbling block. Most children who get into trouble do so in the pursuit of what they conceive to be happiness—"kicks" to escape boredom, to "feel high." The big obstacle in treatment is that upon inquiry into the life of the young offender, we generally find a wealth of material to indicate that he was unhappy. We then wrongly conclude that unhappiness leads to delinquency. When we find the mountains of misery that these children carry on their shoulders, our first human reaction is to do something to make them happy. So we try to change their environment, find them a good foster home, feed, clothe, and provide for their recreation. Then we wonder why they are not happier after we have done so much. After our good treatment why do they return to their old habits? We are puzzled because we haven't been taught that we can't make people happy, that unhappiness is the result, not the cause, of irresponsibility.

Therefore, in Reality Therapy, we ignore the unhappy past, but provide the offender with an opportunity to benefit himself in a responsible way. When a girl at Ventura comes to me and says she is unhappy, I won't sympathize. I'll listen, and then I'll suggest that she herself could do something about her problems. I'll further suggest what she might do. I'm a compassionate human being who wants to teach her better ways, but I'm not a crying towel. I don't promise to produce happiness or alleviate misery; it's not my job as a psychiatrist. That is up to her. In the same vein, I'll never do anything to keep her from taking responsibility, no matter how initially upsetting this may be. I'll never change the rules, no matter how much she begs, and I won't give her tranquilizers which promise her happiness without responsibility. Only when she becomes more responsible will she be in a position to find some lasting happiness.

Past Nonessential to Treatment

A final part of the theory is our belief that what happens to a person now is more important than anything which happened in the near or remote past. One has to assume that everything a person thinks and does in the present is a sum total of his past, that each present action carries with it roots from his whole existence. Although few psychiatrists will argue against this statement, most will nevertheless draw conclusions far different from the ones Dr. Harrington and I propose. The precept traditionally accepted and taught as essential to therapy is that a person cannot understand or change his present behavior unless he is able to tie it clearly to roots in the past. Logically, however, this view becomes redundant if one accepts the previous statement that the present is already a summation of the past. This redundancy, the crux of traditional therapy, is what causes the fruitless historical journeys, diagnostic studies, and unending psychotherapy which lead to excusing the offender's present actions as an unfortunate culmination of his history.

Our view of this assumption is much different. The present as the sum of the past is all that's really important. If a delinquent boy can understand that what he has been doing is irresponsible and can modify his present behavior, then his pathological past is effectively nullified. The object of our treatment is to replace his past experiences with what goes on between him and his various Reality Therapists. The boy will be willing and ready to accept Reality Therapy because he realizes it was his present behavior that resulted in his being locked up, and the indirect cause—his father's rejection of him, let us say—is forever beyond his or our control. In attempting to relate to the Reality Therapist, he must overcome the obstacles of reality, not run from them. Although this course is harder for both, he will readily accept it if it is presented in a firm but compassionate way. Reality Therapy treats the youngster as a potentially responsible adult rather than as an unfortunate child. On the other hand, traditional psychiatry, by dragging him back into his forgotten past, blocks his progress and excuses his behavior, thereby leaving him exactly where he was before—or worse.

The Therapist

All psychiatric theory is meaningless unless there is a therapist who knows how to use it to help the young offender. One therapist may know theory from A to Z and still be unable to provide the warmth and strength needed to make contact, while another who has these essential qualities may have no knowledge of theory whatever and still do some good. No one, delinquent or not, can become responsible without some warm human involvement with a strong mature person who cares about him. It takes human contact alone to initiate treatment. Books, movies, records, music, poetry, or lectures all will help make a responsible person more responsible, but he will be powerless to use these cultural advantages unless he has had good human relationships to start with.

The Reality Therapist has to *assume that in the life of the young offender no one was close enough to enable him to feel worthwhile enough to take responsibility for himself.* Unless we can provide this person, we will fail. The more people we can provide, the greater chance we have in succeeding. One caution, however: the delinquent youngster must be seen in a situation where his behavior can be controlled before a therapist can make progress. Merely sending the young offender to a psychiatrist while placing no control over the rest of his life is rarely successful. Without some external control, few therapists can provide enough firm contact in the brief time allotted to have a practical effect on their patient.

Abiding by the Rules

Expensive, well-designed, fully staffed institutions will have little effect unless each staff member takes a personal interest in the inmates. But "personal interest" does not mean condoning poor behavior. It means rigorous enforcement of the rules and realistic praise. No matter how bad his offense, we must show belief that the offender can become more responsible.

Never missing an opportunity to praise present responsible behavior, we must become as involved as possible with his strong points, his interests, his hopes, his fears—anything not tied up with his irresponsible past. If he wants to talk about his escapades, we should show little interest because he is testing us. If we are real friends, we should not be interested in his wrongdoing. If we are interested in it, then he has gained our attention through harming himself, and when he leaves will do so again. Our interest must emphasize the positive, never reinforce the negative aspect.

Just what do we, the Reality Therapists, do in an actual situation? Suppose, for example, the youngster runs away. What should be done with him once he's found? If the institution rules say he must be locked up securely for a few weeks, then the rules must be followed. This does not mean, however, that we reject him personally because of it. We're both sorry for the act but we go on from there. We do not ask him *why* he ran away, but we show him how his doing so has caused him to suffer.

Although this sort of treatment may sound rigid, we have so very little time that what we might overlook in more responsible people we have to be on guard for with the young people in our charge. Ventura School is one of the strictest institutions in California, yet most of the girls are happy and anyone is free to come in and talk with any girl at any time. No matter how strict we get, the girls always tell us we are too lenient, that we ought to tighten up.

Each person in an institution must function in his own framework. The cook is not a psychiatrist, the psychiatrist is not a cook. All persons in contact with the young offender must stick to their own skills and help in their areas of competence. The mechanics instructor should expect high standards of work performance from the young men assigned to him; he should not become their counselor because that would be false. The boys and girls have met many phonies in the world who feign deep interest in their problems but who, by their excessive willingness to listen to their tales of wrongdoing, are—at best—unwillingly evading their responsibility of guiding them toward a better life or—at worst—living vicariously through the children's misdeeds.

Too much listening to problems is one of the best ways of remaining detached and uninvolved because the young person knows that you can do nothing about his troubles. Listen for a short time, then offer him your skills. Accept him at your level, not his.

Reality Therapy in Practice

I would like to describe an ideal Reality Therapy situation— something we try very hard to approximate at Ventura School. But even what I describe as ideal for this institution has inherent shortcomings because when the young offender is apprehended it is usually late in his career. In many cases the school authorities, his parents, and others were aware of his delinquent potential well before he was arrested. With this in mind, let us look at realistic treatment of the young offender.

Let us suppose that tonight at 11 P.M. a police officer apprehended a sixteen-year-old boy who has just wrecked a stolen car in his effort to escape pursuit. In custody, he should first be given a careful physical examination and be checked to see whether he is under the influence of narcotics or alcohol. Police questions should be fair but brief. His parents should be notified and asked to cooperate, and he should be informed about his legal rights. The police should let him know the charge and ask him, in an unthreatening manner, whether he wants to make a statement. No attempt should be made to obtain a long statement that night. When questions are mandatory, they should concern the circumstances of, not the reasons for, his offenses. Open-end questions, such as "Why did you do it?" should be avoided. If he wishes, his story should be recorded without comment and he should be locked up, preferably alone, for the night. From a treatment standpoint, it's best, at first, to engage him in little conversation or questioning but to allow him time to think over his behavior.

Even if he is to be released in the morning, he should spend one night by himself in custody because now, more than at any other time, he may begin to think that he has done something wrong and that he has some responsibility for it. Too much questioning, too much initial conversation, gives him the opportunity to make excuses, to feel antagonistic toward authority, to justify in his mind that what he did was not very wrong or, if wrong, not really his fault. As soon as possible and throughout Reality Therapy, we must give him a chance to compare his values to his behavior, because ultimately the strength of this comparison will determine his future.

In the morning, assuming that he is to be kept, he should be taken to the detention home, where the rules should be carefully explained to him, whether or not he has been there before. We can never assume that the youngster already knows the rules, for, if he

⋮

breaks one of them, this assumption allows him to blame us for not carefully explaining them.

An experienced staff member—a counselor, caseworker, or psychologist—should work with him until his case is decided in court. This counselor should see him as soon as possible and at regular intervals during his detention. In the interviews, he should put the boy at ease (allowing him to smoke if necessary), reread the charge along with the boy's statement, and ask him whether he wants to add or subtract anything. This should be done in a friendly, unaccusing way, but the situation should be reviewed so that the boy knows definitely what he is charged with.

Discussion should continue until the boy understands that he is being locked up because he broke the law. When this point has been reached (hopefully, during the first interview), the counselor should tell the boy that he would like to help him keep out of further trouble. If the boy is hostile or uncooperative, the counselor should tell him to think about it. The counselor should never return his hostility and never pressure him with "help." He should continue to see the boy regularly, but make no further issue over treatment.

The remainder of the counseling situation should be a discussion of the following three points:

1. Has the boy done anything else illegal or wrong? This is a short, factual discussion, not a case history. Here the question of right and wrong will probably arise, as will the question of the boy's own values and standards. The counselor should ask the boy what his parents or relatives think of his offense. How do their values compare to his? Is he ashamed of what he has done? Does he feel guilty? If he does, this is good; he should. (The counselor should never lighten the guilt; it is the most powerful weapon we have. This does not mean he should add to it, but he should not attempt to reduce it.) The therapist should also ask the boy what he has done that he considers responsible, something he can be proud of.
2. How is he getting along in the detention home right now? Does he feel that anything is unfair? If he has any complaints or he

⋮

feels unjustly treated, the realities of life in a detention home should again be clarified.

3. Subsequent interviews should dwell more and more on his future plans. The counselor should review the various possibilities that will be decided in court—release to parents, probation, or training school. The therapist should be open with the boy, keep nothing secret from him. Both have to face the reality of the disposition. Does the boy have a home to go to? Does he want to go home? What does he think is the best place for him? Does he want to go to school, to work, to be trained for a vocation? A long discussion of his future will help him begin to feel responsibility for himself, the goal of Reality Therapy.

The counselor must never discuss causes—just or unjust—for the boy's actions or imply that he was emotionally disturbed. Our job is to help him, not convince him he's deeply maladjusted.

Further conversations can inquire about his friends. Whom would he like to visit him? The counselor should encourage the boy to write to the people he likes. The boy should not be made to feel that he would be better off without anyone he considers near or dear to him—even if the counselor feels these people are not a good influence. Attempts to sever close attachments will usually produce more trouble than benefits. Above all, the counselor should never imply that the boy's family or anyone else is in any way responsible for his predicament. The boy's responsibility is to be a better person, and doing so may cause his parents and society to improve their attitudes toward him.

The counselor's report to the court should sum up the degree of responsibility and maturity found in the boy. Does he have a workable set of standards or values which he can use when not closely supervised? How much of what he says is just talk and how much does he really mean? Is he somewhat overwilling to admit irresponsibility (which is another way of saying, "I'm so mixed up I don't know what I'm doing")? Will someone enjoy working with him? What kind of person would work best with him? What is the best treatment for him in view of the material gathered?

When the report is completed and the recommendation made, it should be read and discussed with the boy so he knows where he stands and what will be brought up in court.

In court, the judge should again review the charges and the report. This repetition, though monotonous, is extremely important to the boy. It means we care. The boy's parents should be present and be given a chance to make a statement. If the judge, on the counselor's recommendation, decides to send the boy to a training school, he should state exactly where the boy will go, the approximate length of his stay, and what he can expect to do there. This means that the judge himself should have an accurate idea of the program at that school. The judge will also want to discuss how often the parents may visit and what responsibility they will take for their son while he is away. The judge then should take the boy aside, wish him luck, and perhaps tell him of other boys who have succeeded after going through training school. This extra personal touch from an authoritative power can often make a great impression on young people in trouble who, despite appearances, are as impressionable about good things as they are about the bad.

The boy leaves the court with the idea that a better future is up to him, not us, but that we'll help as much as we can. He arrives at the training school understanding that what was done has been done for him, not to him. Once there, he should be assigned a primary counselor trained in Reality Therapy who can continue what has been started, usually in group therapy. Here again, the charge is reviewed and the rules carefully explained. As soon as possible, he should participate in a training program conducted by staff who do not "counsel" but who point out what he is doing wrong and show him better ways.

What constitutes a good training program is, of course, another subject in itself. Briefly, I think it should be a program that teaches a youngster something useful for at least eight hours a day. Idleness and make-work are deadly.

A youngster's progress should be praised, but if he breaks the rules he should suffer reasonable consequences. Discipline for serious breaches should be complete isolation from the main program, followed by isolation from the recreational aspects of the program, and finally return to full program. This will be adequate punishment, however, only if the program is attractive enough to be missed. Corporal punishment is never justified.

Gradually, the youngster should be given more responsibility. He should be permitted weekend visits home in order to become acclimated to the place where he will live when he leaves the school. This is preferable to a sudden shift from school to parole.

The therapist who becomes involved with a boy's life cannot help feeling a little hurt and angry when the boy breaks the rules or gets into trouble in the school. If there is real feeling between them, the boy will always have the ability, in a sense, to hurt the therapist; but the therapist should always point out that when he is hurt, the boy is the real loser. The counselor who shows no emotion really isn't involved in treating this particular boy.

When the boy is discharged, treatment should be continued by the parole officer until a responsible adjustment is made at work, at school, or at home.

Reality Therapy is much more than this brief introductory article can possibly explain. It is, in our opinion, the only kind of psychiatric treatment which works for behavior problems. When employed by everyone in the institution it works extremely well, and the positive results can be easily seen.

Young delinquents want the mature, responsible treatment that we offer and they are young and flexible enough to be helped quickly. Where this therapy is employed, there is no schism between treatment and custody.

Because Reality Therapy works so well in both large and small group therapy situations, it is especially suited for institutional practice. It does away with the need for expensive testing, record keeping, and numerous time-consuming speculative conferences. The only records needed are occasional notes about what has occurred that shows increased responsibility. If the boy fails, the reason is that we were not able to help him become responsible enough to live in society. We need no detailed record of this failure to explain why. The fact that the boy failed speaks for itself. We are human enough to admit that extenuating circumstances are of solace to us as therapists, but they are meaningless to the child whose parole is revoked. If all the time spent in keeping records and conferring about why we or our patients failed were devoted to doing Reality Therapy, there would be far fewer failures in correctional psychiatry.

THOMAS E. BRATTER

Guardian, Behavioral Engineer, Advocate, Friend

The Adolescent Delinquent: A Behavioral Analysis

The adolescent on probation in the 1970's engages in more potent forms of life or death behavior than his generational predecessors. He, in addition, has access to the awesome and annihilative armamentaria of the "Age of Aquarius": deadly precision weapons, toxic drugs, lethal cars, etc. The mass media contain daily descriptions of violent deaths due to narcotism, suicide, and homicide.

The delinquent engages in impulsive, illicit, self-destructive, and irresponsible behavior. This behavior has caused others to label him as being uneducable, untreatable, unemployable, unreliable, helpless and hopeless. He begins to see himself as an abject failure and becomes resigned to the numerous inevitable failures which result as a consequence of a negative self-fulfilling prophecy. Glasser (1972: 161–162) portrays this type of individual, who has adopted a failure identity, as lacking "a concept of self as a loved and worthwhile individual, (who) will not work for any long-term goals. . . . His life is full of pain, and he lives in a haphazard, erratic struggle to get rid of the pain." The probationer, who has a failure identity, becomes angry with the environment which, he feels, punishes and persecutes him. Bernstein (1969:

Adapted from "Guardian, Behavioral Engineer, Advocate, Friend: Humanistic Roles for Probation Officers." From *Corrective and Social Psychiatry,* July, 1974. Copyright © 1974.

4), in addition, believes that many alienated youth "especially those in low status minority groups, faced serious difficulties with their identities and with their sense of their own worth. . . . Their reactions seem to take the form of needing to fight for a feeling of self-worth." Frequently, the offender's thinking process is more emotional than logical. He feels, in addition, he possesses magical powers which will enable him to escape detection.

Generally, the adolescent has a distrust of adults. Aichhorn (1964: 158) suggests that "such suspiciousness is not in any way pathological; we (adults) are strangers, and he is convinced we will harm him. In keeping with the unpleasant experiences he has had so far with adults, he is entitled to expect something distasteful." With an offender, in contrast, the realistic fear of detection regarding his illicit behavior and the threat of incarceration combine to intensify the suspicion, hostility, and hatred of adults, especially those connected with law enforcement.

The Goal of Probation: Responsible and Productive Behavior

The counseling literature is replete with diverse goals of therapy: insight, adjustment, maturity, problem-solving, increased self-confidence, elimination of specific behavior, self-actualization, etc. The primary goal when working with a delinquent is to assist him to be aware of the impact of his behavior, to understand the consequences of his acts, and to become more responsible to himself, others, and society. Utilizing an existential psychotherapeutic orientation, Frankl (1962: 111) attempts to help the individual become "fully aware of his own responsibleness; and therefore it must leave to him the option for what, to what or to whom, he understands himself to be responsible." It is important for the probationer to accept total responsibility for his irresponsible, illicit, stupid, impulsive, self-destructive behavior and not to blame societal conditions. The narcotic addict, for example, must accept responsibility for "sticking a needle in his arm." The probation officer can stress to the delinquent that he, indeed, can control his behavior, that he retains freedom of choice, and that he has the capacity to learn and to grow. It becomes possible to transcend a person's irresponsible and sadistic past by changing his behavior. The offender possesses the capacity to profit from previous mistakes. The probationer must realize realistically that, at times, he cannot control external conditions by which he is challenged but he can regulate his responses to them.

The probation officer communicates a positive expectation for improved behavior performance. A positive expectation of improvement, it is assumed, will be most likely to produce more responsible behavior. Krasner (1962: 4–5) reports that "most therapists are uncomfortable in a role labeled as a 'controller' or 'manipulator' of behavior. The evidence, however, is that this is an accurate description of what the therapist role actually is. . . . The therapist . . . has the power to influence and control the behavior and values of other human beings. For the therapist not to accept this situation and to be continually unaware of influencing effects of his behavior on his patients would in itself be 'unethical.' "

This writer has cooperated with various Country and City Departments of Probation while servicing a similar client subpopulation of alienated, unmotivated, hostile, acting-out adolescent drug abusers and addicts—many of whom currently were on probation or parole. I have directed five drug abuse and addiction control programs in various community settings. The roles of guardian, behavioral engineer, advocate, and friend which are sequential role changes in the probation relationship are believed to expedite positive and responsible behavioral change. These four roles that the probation officer plays will be the primary focus of this paper.

(I) Guardian:
Forced Behavioral Change

After not only hearing testimony but also studying a comprehensive case report, the Court determines that the adolescent's behavior needs to be modified by an external resource—i.e., the Probation Department. Concurrently, the Court issues a non-negotiable ultimatum to the probationer and responsible adults that, unless the offender can adopt more appropriate behavior, further infractions will culminate with removal from society—i.e., incarceration. The Probation Department, thus, legally becomes the guardian of the offender. The probation officer, by legal mandate, must reconstruct the parent-child relationship, must establish and enforce limits. According to Samorajczyk (1971: 115) alienated and acting-out adolescents "want to know where the limits are— and that someone 'gives a damn' enough to guide (them) in (their) search of what's expected of (them)." This control and guided intervention by the probation officer reassures the offender that his illicit and self-destructive behavior can be controlled temporarily by an external source. The probation officer should be prepared to use the pressure of incarceration provided him by the Court to force the offender to cease and desist. This position has been described by Redl and Wineman (1957: 463) as the "technique of authoritative Verbot. . . . We simply say No, and we say it in such a way that it is clear we mean it and don't soften it up by arguing, explaining." The probation officer must believe that responsible behavior is, indeed, desirable. He must see himself initially as an enforcer of responsible behavior. He must recognize that when left to his own devices, the offender has a propensity to engage in a life or death struggle. Initially, there is a battle between the probation officer and the offender. In brief, it is a battle between the health and strength of the probation officer against the pathology and self-annihilative tendencies of the offender. The delinquent will test limits. He might argue convincingly that, he feels, he is being victimized either to behavioral control or to thought control. The probation officer can state that realistically in any democracy there is a need for a social contract—i.e., law and order. The philosophical basis for such laws are to protect not only the individual from harming himself but also society from being harmed by the same individual. The offender does retain, however, a fundamental choice: Does he wish to conform to basic laws and remain in society or does he prefer to violate laws and be incarcerated? The probation officer must not appear apologetic or ambivalent because he is performing a vital therapeutic function. The probation officer can share his displeasure at being forced to respond to the offender in such an authoritarian manner but affirm that he cares enough for the individual to continue to enforce limits. If the delinquent demonstrates he cannot remain in society, the probation officer must be prepared to violate his probation. Such action will be prompted by a resignation that (1) the probation officer was not able to provide the necessary treatment at the time and/or (2) the probationer was unable to profit from a relationship with the probation officer. The probation officer must be in control of the situation at all times, must be alert to the potential dangers, and must be ready to intervene directly to avoid them. It is appropriate for the probation officer to mention that he would prefer to respect the offender and permit him to accept responsibility for his life. Too much freedom, when premature, can result in an escalation of self-destructive behavior which might culminate with death. Any probation officer who would permit the destruction of a human being, indeed, must be considered sadistic and professionally irresponsible.

The judicious and therapeutic application of rational authority can curtail the probationer's illicit, irresponsible, and self-destructive behavior by imposing a series of coercions and controls. Brill and Lieberman (1969: 75) suggest the treatment rationale when they write "in the sense of providing a firm structuring of the treatment relationship, setting limits, and providing controls through the use of a graduated series of sanctions, it was conjectured that rational authority might minimize the (offender's) acting-out behavior, help him grow within the structure and internalize the controls he lacks, and, hopefully, help give up his destructive way of life."

When the offender is forced to remain on probation, usually despite his protestations, he begins to tolerate frustration, he learns to delay instantaneous gratification and to assume responsibility for his life. He understands that he is expected to conform to certain behaviors and to be more responsible to himself, others, and society. Once the offender has internalized these lessons, the probation officer can begin to decrease his authority in direct proportion to the degree the adolescent can regulate his life.

(II) Behavioral Engineer:
Problem-Solving

The fundamental task in psychotherapy, Marmor (1966: 364) writes, is "how best to enable or cause a patient to give up certain acquired patterns of thought, feeling, or behavior in favor of others which are considered more 'mature,' 'adaptive,' 'productive,' or 'self-realizing.' " This process can be viewed as strengthening the positive aspects of the adolescent's behavior rather than as a radical reconstruction of his personality. Solomon (1971: 37) contends "it is easier to build on a deprived child's strengths—of which he has many—than to try to eradicate his weaknesses. While working on his strengths we automatically bypass many of his negative patterns of behavior. . . . We must understand that many of these youngsters possess a high degree of intelligence and given the opportunity, will reach creditable heights."

It is assumed that by teaching the offender appropriate behaviors to cope with reality and responsibility would eliminate self-defeating and dysfunctional behavior. If viewed from this perspective, the role of the therapist changes from the more traditional image. Bijou (1966: 44) writes "instead of conceiving the counselor as a reflector of feelings, or an explorer of resources, or a habit changer, or a remediator of self-concepts and values, or as a releaser of repressions, we might come to think of him as a behavioral engineer." This parallels the function of a probation officer. The probation officer encourages the offender to test new behavior and ways of thinking. This aspect of treatment becomes problem-solving. Bergin and Strupp (1972: 39) believe that "if psychotherapy is viewed as a learning process, then principles of learning at all levels apply." Glasser (1965: 60) views treatment as educating the adolescent how to behave so that the probability of attaining success is maximized. The psychiatrist suggests "we take every opportunity to teach patients better ways to fulfill their needs. We spend much time painstakingly examining the patient's daily activity and suggesting better ways for him to behave. We answer many questions that patients ask and suggest ways to solve problems and approach people. Patients who have not been able to fulfill their needs must learn both how to approach people so that they can become more involved and how to accomplish enough so that they can gain an increased feeling of self-worth."

The probationer is helped to identify how he believes he should behave. He is encouraged to formulate intermediate and longer-range goals. Once this has been completed the adolescent develops a plan for action. The probation officer has become an ally, a resource, and a consultant. The probation officer continually questions the probationer's current behavior and whether or not it is productive. The most effective technique to enable the probationer to view himself realistically is confrontation. Carkhuff and Berenson (1967: 171) define confrontation as an act "initiated by the therapist, based on his understanding of the client. It brings the client into more direct contact with himself, his strengths and resources, as well as his self-destructive behavior. The purpose of confrontation is . . . a challenge to the client to become integrated. . . . It is directed at discrepancies within the client . . . between what the client says and does . . . and between illusion and reality. . . . It implies a constructive attack upon the healthy. . . . The strength and intensity of a confrontation may correspond with how dominant and central the emotional pattern is to the client's life style."

(III) Advocate:
The Probation Officer's Commitment to Action

Most offenders have many similar characteristics which complicate their assimilation into our technologic and industrial society. They have failed in school. They have inconsistent work records. They have acquired a police record. They lack the credentials which are necessary in a competitive economic system. It is important to recall Reed and Nance's (1972: 27) observation that "probation and parole are rehabilitatively thought of as more desirable for the convicted offender than the completion of a sentence in prison. Yet both visibly display the offender in the community under a disability—his conditions of probation or parole. In some jurisdictions, he must register as a criminal, supposedly for the protection of the community." Offenders, no matter how well motivated, if left to their own personal resources, will be unable to secure appropriate employment, admissions to college, etc. There are long waiting lists, subtle discriminations, and blatant prejudices which will preclude placement. A need exists for an advocate who will aggressively attempt to expedite a preferential referral even at the expense of an adversary. If the probation officer is to facilitate educational and vocational mobility and encourage economic autonomy, he must be prepared to function as an advocate.

The advocate becomes the offender's representative, negotiator, intervener, expeditor, broker, supporter, consultant, champion, etc. In many respects this role is similar to the attorney who protects his client's interest and attempts to negotiate the most favorable deal. This pressure might enable the client to secure what he needs to continue his growth and development—i.e., a college placement, an adjournment, etc. Interestingly, the French term for attorney is "l'avocat." The attorney retains the prerogative to determine whom he will represent. The probation officer cannot afford to endorse his entire case load. He must determine selectively those whose behavior indicates they are motivated and will profit from additional services. As a representative of the judicial system, the probation officer must endeavor to maintain his credibility with all community agencies and organizations. It is to the advantage of the probation officer and the offender, if the professional can familiarize himself with all community resources.

Grosser (1965: 17) has described the advocate as "a partisan in a social conflict and his expertise is available to serve client interests." Often, the probation officer might accompany the offender to an interview, write letters, and/or make phone calls. Periodically, the advocate must be prepared to challenge the system when he believes there has been an injustice or discrimination. The Ad Hoc Committee on Advocacy (1969: 18) stresses that "it is implicit, but clear, in this prescript that the obligation to the client takes primacy over the obligation to the employer when the two interests compete with one another." The advocate is obligated to protect the individual against the system, and, therefore, cannot remain silent. It is suggested that the probation officer discuss with his supervisor what specific strategy to pursue.

The probation officer must remember he is both a representative and extension of the judicial system. He must be candid. Any referral source recognizes that, as a result of his relationship with the Court, the offender has been in trouble. Since there are numerous statutes protecting the confidentiality of the offender, the probation officer is advised to secure written permission to divulge records. In addition, since the basis of any recommendation is due to growth and development, it seems unnecessary to dwell in detail about the past.

The following example concerns an offender who was on probation in two different states for drug-related offenses. I sent a candid five page appraisal of this nineteen year old's past, present, and future prognosis to the Director of Admissions with a xerox copy to the College President. On the basis of my recommendation, he was admitted to one of the ten most prestigious and competitive colleges in the country. (In order to protect the identity of the youngster, I have altered several details.)

Based on an intimate relationship with Putney Jones and all the members of his family, I would like to suggest and support enthusiastically the proposal that he be admitted to Z college. In all candor, I believe I would be totally irresponsible and, indeed, somewhat sadistic if I deliberately were to advocate placing an individual, who already has inflicted great pain on himself and his family, in a situation where there would be no possibility of success. I would be less than realistic if I were to suggest that statistically Putney's chances of completing Z college were guaranteed by a proven record of achievement.

For the duration of his junior and senior high school experience, Putney never applied himself academically. The net result was the abysmal rank 488 in a class of 493. The highest grade achieved was a "B-" during his sophomore year. Certainly the Dean was warranted in writing that "to say the least, Putney has a spotty academic career, and the prognosis for his success in the future in the more traditional college curricula is highly questionable."

Putney apparently reached the nadir of his existence when recently he was apprehended for alleged possession of marihuana. . . . If convicted, outrageous and obsolete state laws require a jail sentence of not less than ten years or more than fifty. . . .

In retrospect, Putney's adolescence—academically, emotionally, intellectually, and legally—was almost a disaster. Miraculously, this young man's self-preservation instinct enabled him to fly close to the flames of destruction—to be burned—but to emerge from those flames, as did the phoenix, and continue to grow and develop. . . .

I recognize that Z college academically is one of the most elite and demanding educational institutions in the country. . . . What is the basis for the inordinate amount of faith I have placed in Putney? Having worked in various capacities with troubled youth and their families for more than a decade, occasionally the agency professional is "rewarded" by having a stimulating and mutually gratifying relationship. . . . I entered Putney's life when he clearly was out of control—i.e., he was in danger of jeopardizing his future. I entered his life at the request of the Police who were alarmed at this young man's propensity for punishing himself and others. I have seen him "win" battles with himself, with his family, with college. I have seen him achieve a major victory with heroin (three years ago). His resilience has intrigued me. Most people who experienced the degradation and defeats would have been destroyed. But not Putney who is anxiously awaiting a decision from Z college so that he can continue to grow and to develop.

I know he has the creative capacity and the energy to make a contribution to society—although, I must confess I do not know in what specific area it will be in. Now that he is no longer at war with himself, his family, society, he will be able to establish a stable identity. He will be able to justify to himself, his parents, and others his existence. He will prove to himself his intrinsic worth as a human being. He will be able to extricate himself from the "damning prognosis" of not being worth a damn. And I am confident that he will make the world a better place in which to live. I have sufficient faith that Z college has not only the personnel but also the enlightened academic philosophy to move Putney further along on the all-important continuum of growth and development. . . .

I believe Putney will be a better man, a more sensitive human being for all of his struggles. I believe he will enrich his fellow students at Z college because, while he is one of them, he certainly has deviated radically from the paths that they have pursued. It won't be easy for Putney to succeed at Z college. But, then again, nothing worthwhile ever came without a struggle. I do believe firmly, however, that Putney now is ready to dedicate himself totally to success. . . .

In conclusion, obviously Putney Jones has deviated from the path of productivity, achievement, and has been on the verge of disaster during his rather turbulent and nihilistic adolescence. I feel it would be a tragedy, indeed, if Putney should be denied the chance to secure an education—to erase some of the bitter failures which characterized his first nineteen years. While admittedly premature, I believe firmly that in view of the above Putney's prognosis can be revised from negative to very guardedly optimistic. I favor his admission to Z college at this juncture because I am confident that, if given the opportunity, Putney will justify my optimism and faith. . . .

ONE MORE CHANCE to salvage his life by attending college—is that really too much to request for him?

Playing the role of advocate for the offender enables the probation officer to make more demands on the adolescent to continue to actualize his potential. The probation officer now becomes a partner with the adolescent.

As an added incentive to the perspective employer and/or college, the probation officer can volunteer to be an active on-the-job supervisor who can ensure that the offender will be a productive, honest, and loyal employee. Such assurances can be a persuasive point in convincing someone to give a probationer a chance.

(IV) Friend:
The Final Phase of the Probation Relationship

The initial phase of the probation relationship was authoritarian because the offender demonstrated an inability to regulate his own life. This phase often involved intense and unpleasant confrontations concerning the number of required sessions, the forced regulation of behavior, etc. As the probation relationship progressed, gradually the offender assumed more responsibility for the direction and control of his life. The newly evidenced growth and development necessitated a renegotiation of the relationship since the probationer no longer needed an active and authoritarian approach to guide him.

During the latter phase of the relationship the probation officer can begin to resemble Strupp and Fox's (1969: 117) composite of the "good therapist . . . (who is) a keenly attentive, interested, benign, and concerned listener—a friend who is warm and natural, is not adverse to giving direct advice, who speaks one's language."

If the probation process has been effective, furthermore, in helping the offender to function at his optimal capacity, a feeling of mutuality begins to develop. Schofield (1970: 214–215) reports:

It has been suggested that friendship evolves out of functional interdependencies. They represent a secondary but nonetheless vital order of relationship. They are the means whereby the human personality exercises his need for a sense of "togetherness," his need for a feeling of mutuality, his need to share his successes and his sorrows. Without friends with whom to share them our achievements are diminished and our torments are augmented. In this is the simplest meaning of friend—the person we know to whom it matters if we are victorious or defeated, the person who will be truly happy *with* us in our gain, sad *with* us in our loss. Our friend *cares* about us and *feels* with us.

This is a relationship of unequals because the probation officer is older and more established than the offender. Obviously before this type of relationship can be consummated, both must decide independently whether the other is the type of person he would want as a friend.

Friendship has been conceptualized to include responsible concern, trust, affection, and equality. This relationship requires that both partners must prove themselves worthy of friendship. Aristotle (1962: 228) suggested thousands of years ago that "one cannot extend friendship to or be a friend of another person until each partner has impressed the other that he is worthy of affection, and until each has won the other's confidence." These conditions probably could not exist until the termination of the formal probation relationship. Perhaps, then, it might be possible to reconstruct a relationship of equals—i.e., a friendship. Easson (1971: 641) discusses the evolution from a psychotherapeutic relationship to a friendship:

Obviously the psychotherapist cannot and should not become a personal friend to all his patients. In those situations where the personality of the former patient and the former psychotherapist make continuing friendship a natural and appropriate development, the psychotherapist can use the increasing self-understanding that he will achieve with this new kind of relationship to make his continuing psychotherapy even richer and more meaningful. He will become more sensitive to his own treatment processes and more alert to the technique he uses. A continued friendship with a former psychotherapist may strengthen the gains made by the patient in the previous psychotherapy and may lead to very rapid emotional growth. For the former patient, the psychotherapy process may have been a preparation for the friendship and the friendship is the realization and the proof—a proof that the patient can see and a proof that encourages him to develop his relationship ability with many other people. For both the patient and the psychotherapist, this friendship can give them an opportunity to grow as friends and as individuals in the years ahead but, at the same time, it allows them to look back into their earlier treatment relationship, to the psychotherapy, and to strengthen, stabilize, and rebuild what went on then.

Conclusion

Being a probation officer has its rewards and its painful defeats. If we can continue to keep our idealism and commitment to helping individuals to help themselves, there is no reason why we cannot become more effective. Failure is an occupational hazard. We can learn from our failures. We must not become embittered. We must struggle, at times, to continue to keep the faith that our charges can rebound from a momentary defeat and become better, more beautiful, people as a result of their mistakes. Our continued challenge is to find the key which can unlock their closed doors. Some respond to kindness and gentleness. Others need brutal confrontation. We must keep trying because the future of society rests with their generation and not ours! We are the "end of the line" for many youngsters. Rehabilitation or habilitation must start with us or it may never materialize.

REFERENCES

Aichhorn, A., On the Technique of Child Guidance: The Process of Transference, in Aichhorn, A. (ed.) *Delinquency and Child Guidance Selected Papers.* New York: International Universities Press, Inc., 1964.

Ad Hoc Committee on Advocacy National Association of Social Workers, The Social Worker as Advocate: Champion of Social Victims. *Social Work,* 14:2 (April, 1969).

Aristotle, *Nichomachean Ethics.* Ostwald, M. (translator). Indianapolis: Bobbs-Merrill Company, 1962.

Bergin, A. E. and H. H. Strupp, *Changing Frontiers in the Science of Psychotherapy.* Chicago: Aldine & Atherton, 1972.

Bernstein, S., Alienated Youth. *Federal Probation,* XXXIII:2 (June, 1969).

Bijou, S. W., Implications of Behavioral Science for Counseling and Guidance, in Krumboltz, J. D. (ed.) *Revolution in Counseling.* Boston: Houghton Mifflin Company, 1966.

Bratter, T. E., Group Therapy with Affluent, Alienated, Adolescent Drug Abusers: A Reality Therapy and Confrontation Approach. *Psychotherapy: Theory, Research, and Practice,* 9:4 (Winter, 1972).

Brill, L., and L. Lieberman, *Authority and Addiction.* Boston: Little, Brown and Company, 1969.

Carkhuff, R. R., and B. G. Berenson, *Beyond Counseling and Therapy.* Holt, Rinehart and Winston, Inc., 1967.

Easson, W. M., Patient and Therapist After Termination of Psychotherapy. *American Journal of Psychotherapy,* XXV:4 (October, 1971).

Frankl, V., *Man's Search for Meaning.* Boston: Beacon Press, 1962.

Glasser, W., *The Identity Society.* New York: Harper & Row, Publishers, 1972.

Glasser, W., *Reality Therapy: A New Approach to Psychiatry.* New York: Harper & Row, Publishers, 1965.

Grosser, C. F., Community Development Programs for Serving the Urban Poor. *Social Work,* 10:3 (July, 1965).

Krasner, L., The Therapist as a Social Reinforcement Machine, in Strupp, H. H., and L. Luborsky (eds.), *Research in Psychotherapy Volume II.* Washington, D.C.: American Psychological Association, Inc., 1962.

Marmor, J., Theories of Learning and the Psychotherapeutic Process. *British Journal of Psychiatry,* 112 (1966).

Redl, F., and D. Wineman, *The Aggressive Child.* Chicago: The Free Press of Glencoe, 1957.

Reed, J. P., and D. Nance, Society Perpetuates the Stigma of a Conviction. *Federal Probation,* XXXVI: 2 (June, 1972).

Samorajczyk, J., The Psychotherapist as a Meaningful Parental Figure with Alienated Adolescents. *American Journal of Psychotherapy,* XXV:1 (January, 1971).

Schofield, W., The Psychotherapist as Friend. *Humanitas Journal of the Institute of Man,* VI:2 (Fall, 1970).

Solomon, B., Helping the Deprived Child. *Federal Probation,* XXXV:4 (December, 1971).

Strupp, H. H., and R. E. Fox, *Patients View Their Psychotherapy.* Baltimore: Johns Hopkins Press, 1969.

ERNST SCHMIDHOFER

Acting Out or Acting Up?

Practitioners of certain schools of psychotherapy condone reckless, ruthless, inconsiderate, and wild behavior in their patients. Presumably, the patient is under so much stress that his uncontrolled impulses are bursting forth with ungovernable intensity.

Such therapists are quite content to sit unmoved and implacable while their patients engage in all manner and variety of dyssocial antics. The healer frequently believes sincerely that such unseemly conduct represents psychotherapeutic progress.

It appears the phrase "acting out" originated with the psychoanalysts. It is used by them in a highly sophisticated fashion, evocations of which are expressed both verbally and in writing.

The phrase "acting out" is also used by much less sophisticated and much less experienced psychotherapists as a convenience which is available readily to account for behavior which is otherwise unaccountable to them.

I question seriously the validity of the indiscriminate notion that "acting out" is determined unconsciously and that the motor expressions are beyond the control of the patient.

I do not question that certain aspects of the psychotherapeutic relationship can bring about improvement or recovery. However, I do question very much that the phenomenon of "acting out" is one of them.

Happily not every analyst is in full agreement with the concept of "acting out" in its rawest form. If I interpret correctly from his

From *Journal of Offender Therapy*, Vol. 8, No. 1, 1964. Reprinted by permission of the publisher.

writings, Dr. Jack Ewalt is one of these [*Community Mental Health Centers: Plans and Progress,* Unpublished].

Dr. Ewalt is renowned for many things. Among them are the facts that he was a past president of the American Psychiatric Association and Commissioner of Mental Health for the Commonwealth of Massachusetts. He is now Superintendent of the Massachusetts Mental Health Center as well as Bullard Professor of Psychiatry at Harvard Medical School.

Dr. Ewalt speaks of the Massachusetts Mental Health Center as a place where patients are encouraged to talk about impulses instead of acting on them. They are also expected to be responsible for their own behavior.

I was once in charge of a therapy section which was working with delinquent children. I was caught in an administrative mesh between a boss who was vigorously oriented in orthodox psychoanalytic techniques, and inexperienced therapists who were eager to learn and to apply those very practices. In a matter of a few short weeks the institution was in an uproar. My boss wrote me a letter which read in part:

". . . are manifesting excessive acting out as a result of anxieties from experiential reliving their libido traumas. It created too many disciplinary problems. . . . Would suggest the 'Indirective Technique' with a 'Freudian Attitude' for a period of time until our patients settle down. . . . The Mental Health Team is congratulated by me on their effective therapy to arouse anxieties and 'thinking' towards insight by their patients, as far as treatment is concerned. However, let up on it and give the disciplinarians a rest for a while. Later on, cautiously, resume same."

This is only one of the situations wherein even unskilled psychotherapists are commended and applauded for provoking and allowing social indiscretions of varying magnitude and duration.

One of the junior therapists on the Mental Health Team said to me with a blandness which is more than startling unless it has been encountered before: "This child was very angry. He was just acting out." The therapist was referring to a 17 year old youth who wrecked a stolen car after driving it 95 miles per hour. He then assaulted with an eight-inch pipe an elderly night watchman who was sent to the hospital because of a subdural hemotoma resulting from the vicious attack.

The junior therapist knew very well from her theoretic teachings and from its esoteric usage that the phrase "acting out" confers upon the one who uses it a rather special form of almost God-like immunity from criticism, censure, or judgment.

The assumption runs rampant among a certain type of professional that only those therapists who have been blessed with a sufficient degree of length and breadth of experience and intelligence are capable of understanding and condoning the dynamics involved in and implied by the magic phrase "acting out." It constitutes a mark of distinction as well as one of sophistication.

It gives powerful backing to the user because the concept is championed so fiercely by certain vested interests. It gives the institutional therapist license to continue with his stereotype style over and above the remonstrations of the administrator.

Additionally, it means that the therapist really knows what he is doing. It is also descriptive of a form of reaction which is highly desirable or at least allowable, according to psychoanalytic theory.

Finally, to allow a patient to go on an "acting out" spree is some sort of boon to mankind. Otherwise, his unleashed tensions would have caused within him an explosion of such magnitude as to endanger the lives of all who were within a radius of several city blocks.

But in my judgment, this is not so. Nor is acting out necessary. My clinical experience indicates that the phrase "acting up" is much more applicable. I say the phrase "acting up" is also much more accurate for several reasons.

In the first place, there are certain forms of stress of considerable intensity which, in the sociopathic personality, bring about no manifestations of acting out. In matter of fact, I have known occasions when such periods brought to an abrupt halt a bout of acting up.

It has been possible under certain special conditions of coercion to bring to a rapid close various manifestations of acting up.

On other occasions, it has been possible to win over those who are acting up and through reasoning or other forms of rational appeal to stop them. However, this is only rarely true in the instance of sociopaths.

Finally, I have for many years made it a practice to conduct a terminal, over-all evaluative interview. During the terminal interview, I have been told repeatedly by the delinquent person that if he had but chosen to do so, there would have been no necessity whatsoever for him to carry on his acting up.

Now how can one explain the discrepancy between those workers who feel that the "acting out" experience is an inevitable accompaniment of successful therapy? If you believe that a patient can't help himself when he is "acting out," you won't ask him about it or question him intensively regarding it.

If you don't question him about it, you think he can't help it. If you do question him about it, you'll find he can. To contend that "acting out" which responded to disciplinary measures couldn't have been the real thing and that it was probably just acting up, is probably no more accurate than the assertion of those who actually believe that psychotherapy can be used to distinguish functional disorders from organic diseases. If the process yields to psychotherapy, it is functional. If it does not, it is organic.

There is a very practical consideration to this whole business of "acting out" versus acting up. If the therapist believes that "acting out" is an essential part of the process, there is justification in his eyes for allowing it to repeat itself. This not only protracts the convalescence of the patient but also does damage to the persons and the proprieties of society.

Conversely, if the therapist interprets the process as acting up and as constituting an unnecessary artifact in the reeducative process, he cannot so easily justify with unctuous assurances the continuation of the phenomenon. Accordingly, there will be a commensurate diminution in the time needed for the rehabilitative process plus a sparing of injuries and damages to society.

ALEXANDER BASSIN

Reality Therapy at Daytop Village

"Man, what a joint!"

A New York City heroin addict catching his first glimpse of the original Daytop Lodge or Daytop Village in Staten Island, Swan Lake, Millbrook, New York, or the new magnificent quarters across the street from Bryant Park and the Fifth Avenue library might well emit this remark with a low whistle of astonishment. "Wow!"

For the original Daytop Lodge on Staten Island was, indeed, a reflection of the gracious living standards of an earlier age. It consisted of a tile-roofed, 3-story, stucco, 20-room mansion with a handsome porch, an attached hothouse within 7½ acres of wooded and cultivated landscape overlooking the sparkling waters of Raritan Bay with a distant view of the Verrazano-Narrows Bridge.

Daytop Village was born against the depressing backdrop of failure and frustration known to every probation and parole officer who has attempted to work with addicts. No matter how warm the relationship or close the surveillance, it appeared to be almost inevitable that sooner or later the user would lapse and build up a new habit, a condition the correction officer discovers only after the client has been involved in a new whirlwind of crimes.

Nalline Testing

Joseph A. Shelly, the former chief probation officer for the Supreme Court of the State of New York, Second Judicial Dis-

From *Journal of Drug Issues,* Fall, 1974, Volume 4, Number 4. Copyright © 1974 Journal of Drug Issues, Inc.

trict, where the writer was director of research and education, came across an article in that most unusual of scientific journals, *The Reader's Digest,* describing the nalline testing program of California which was supposed to be accomplishing wonders in controlling drug abuse on the West coast. Nalline was a substance, the article said, which could invariably detect whether a person was under the influence of heroin.

As a desperate measure Mr. Shelly and I talked about experimenting with nalline as a possible medium for the early detection and possible subsequent control of addiction. We reasoned along these lines: if the probation or parole officer had an instrument at hand that enabled him to establish whether his client was using drugs, he would be able to take preventive action at a critical point before the addiction reached proportions that made treatment in the community out of the question. Furthermore, we argued, if the addict were aware at all times that he was subject to detection and subsequent violation on the part of the supervising agency, it would help marshal his ego forces to check the temptation to start "fooling around."

We submitted a formal research proposal to the National Institutes of Mental Health and in response received an invitation from Dr. Carl L. Anderson, NIMH consultant on alcoholism and drug addiction (now retired and living in Denver, Colorado), for an informal discussion.

Dr. Anderson pointed out some faults of nalline as a research detection instrument. In the first place, it was not reliable. An alarming number of false negatives and false positives would be generated. Secondly, nalline required a skilled licensed physician to administer the dosage. A special lifeguarding apparatus would have to be kept at hand because sometimes the reaction of an addicted individual to nalline brings on symptoms of lethal proportions. Furthermore, the use of a hypodermic needle to inject the nalline almost inevitably stimulated a latent "yen" on the part of the addict. Finally, Dr. Anderson asked, had we heard of an exciting new chemical procedure for the detection of narcotics—thin-layer chromatography?

The NIMH Team

Dr. Anderson explained that NIMH was underwriting basic research in this area and perhaps we ought to attempt to apply some of their findings. He suggested we give thought to the establishment of a halfway house for treatment of the narcotic offender on probation. He invited us to organize a research team to explore TLC (thin-layer chromatography) and halfway house treatment procedures in various parts of the United States in order to provide an experiential background for an up-to-date and sophisticated research proposal.

A team was organized consisting of the outstanding criminologist from Brooklyn College, the late Herbert A. Bloch, psychiatrist Dr. Daniel Casriel, who had been engaged for many years in the treatment of drug addicts at the Metropolitan Hospital in New York City, Joseph A. Shelly and the writer. The team visited the laboratories of the National Institutes of Health at Bethesda, Maryland, to confer with Dr. Joseph Cochin, a physician and biochemist who had engaged in basic research on the potential of TLC for the detection of narcotic usage. He convinced us, without too much difficulty, of the patent superiority of the urine analysis procedure of TLC over nalline.

The mission also visited narcotic treatment and detection centers in Illinois, Wisconsin, and California. We spoke to the directors of treatment facilities using nalline and, whenever possible, we conferred with addicts. We were impressed by the simple confession of several drug users who told us that a detection procedure gave the addict the "strength" to say no when confronted by a fellow junkie who proposed injecting together. "I got to take a test tomorrow and can't afford to shoot up." Usually this statement, we were told, was sufficient to send the associate on his way.

Synanon at Santa Monica

However, our most astonishing experience was Synanon, which had only recently been organized at Santa Monica, California.

Here we met Dr. Lewis Yablonsky, an old NYU classmate who suggested we be prepared for the surprise of our lives. Dr. Casriel soon confirmed Yablonsky's warning. Within a few minutes after entering Synanon, Dr. Casriel encountered a patient he had known at Metropolitan Hospital and had diagnosed as being utterly beyond hope. Soon afterwards he met a number of other of his previous patients, all with hopeless prognoses. However, within the environment of Synanon, they were physically healthy, mentally alert and, most important—free of drugs.

We met with the founder of Synanon, Chuck Dederich, a former alcoholic business executive who had been exposed to the self-help principles of Alcoholics Anonymous and quite by accident had discovered that his own version of these principles seemed uniquely potent in working with drug addicts. He immodestly assured us that what was taking place at Synanon was one of the wonders of the world.

"If somewhere in the middle of the African Congo, someone were to discover a cure for cancer, the scientific world would beat a path to the door of the genius. But here in California we are the subject of all kinds of suspicion and abuse. The facts are all around you. We have almost a hundred junkies who are clean of heroin. We have several dozen who have not used heroin for almost a year. This is the first time in medical history that a phenomenon of that kind has occurred!"

In his gravel-toned voice, our bull-necked host explained: "We attempt to create an extended family of the type found in preliterate tribes with a strong, perhaps autocratic, father-figure who dispenses firm justice combined with warm concern, who is a model extolling inner-directed convictions about the old-fashioned virtues of honesty, sobriety, learning, and hard work."

Dr. Casriel promptly decided to give up a planned expedition to last several months in Okinawa, where he was to engage in an anthropological study of the natives' changes since he had last seen them during World War II, and instead move into Synanon for a participant-observer period of residence.

The Daytop NIMH Proposal

Based on the observations and experience gained as a result of our mission, a new proposal was forwarded to the National Institutes of Mental Health with the following aims:

—to establish a halfway house for the treatment of drug addicts on probation.

—to evaluate the rehabilitative effects of such a facility in comparison with the results of supervising drug addicts on probation on a small specialized caseload and in a large general caseload.

—to formulate and operate a program of activity designed to provide the addict in the halfway house with a value system and status organization leading to his eventual successful integration into normal society.

—to employ a testing procedure (TLC) to quantify the progress of the drug abstinence program and to determine if such a chemical testing procedure may of itself be an inhibitory mechanism in keeping the addict from returning to the use of narcotics.

—to apply and evaluate a series of specific treatment procedures such as role training, intensive small group therapy sessions, field trips, cultural activity, Reality Therapy with a group of drug addicts in a halfway house.

It was felt that positive returns from such a project would provide an important breakthrough in the treatment of an otherwise nearly insoluble problem. In simple dollars-and-cents terms the savings to the community might well amount to hundreds of thousands of dollars. But more important than these material considerations, we argued, was the prospect of salvaging human beings from a nearly bestial level of existence, full of horror, suffering and deterioration—the usual fate of the junkie in the ghetto.

The successful outcome of such a proposal, our argument continued, would provide important empirical support for a number of theoretical formulations about the influence of role training, the positive use of status striving, the theory of self-concepts, small group dynamics, the therapeutic community and the potential of self-help groups and Reality Therapy in correcting deviant behavior.

Research Plans

We pictured the proposed halfway house as a comfortable residential building of the "white elephant" type located in a suburban area within the geographic confines of New York City but far removed from "Junkville" in order to minimize the temptations of contact with the drug addict.

We proposed to have the research study extend over a 5-year period and involve a minimum of about 100 addicts between the ages of 16 and 45 who had been using heroin for extended periods. The halfway house would be filled with addicts in rotation until the full complement of 25 had been amassed and thereafter a small "special caseload" of 25 comparable addicts would be accumulated for regular probation supervision. Each person, both in the halfway house and in the control group, would be involved in periodic testing by thin-layer chromatography. It was proposed that thereafter "overflow" persons who met the same basic criteria as the original groupings would be continued on probation but not subjected to periodic urinalysis testing.

Since the research proposal had been designed to influence the value system and self-identification of the drug addict, an instrument which would be valid to generate data within these boundaries was employed. The attitude inventory promulgated by Dr. Jack Monroe and his colleague, Dr. Harris Hill of the U.S. Public Health Service Hospital at Lexington, Kentucky, answered our needs. The Hill-Monroe Inventory poses such questions, on a true or false check-off basis, as follows:

"I take drugs to avoid boredom."
"I am most happy when I have no responsibilities."
"When I am not on drugs, I often feel sad and depressed."
"I am sure I got a raw deal from life."

Each defendant with a history of drug addiction would have this test administered in the course of the presentence investigation. The resulting score would provide a pretreatment item of data which could be compared with the results of a reexamination at the conclusion of treatment.

NIMH Grant Received

On April 15, 1963, we were informed by the National Institutes of Mental Health that a grant of $390,000 had been awarded for our research project. The proposal had been accepted!

With this news came the heart-chilling prospect of putting the proposal into operation, translating the fine words of theoretical formulations into the brick and mortar of a halfway house, the flesh and blood of human beings, orienting judges and our staff, preparing the community, signing leases and contracts, locating personnel, and selecting residents. Frequently, at this stage, we asked ourselves: What did we need this headache for!

As the first task in making rabbit stew is to catch a rabbit, we decided that in research with a halfway house our initial problem was to locate the building. After weeks of canvassing real estate brokers and chasing clues, we obtained a lease on a millionaire's mansion that, years before, had been a showplace of Staten Island. It was located within landscaped grounds and a forest-like preserve, within walking distance of a bathing beach, far removed from the haunts of pushers and users.

A contest was organized among staff to pick a name for our establishment. The winner was "Daytop," standing for Drug-Addicts-Treated-On-Probation, and suggesting, we thought, a hopeful, optimistic outlook for the basic problem. We selected the designation "Lodge" as the second part of the title in order to avoid the usual unfortunate semantic institutional associations of an orthodox treatment facility.

Our original proposal involved the appointment of a graduate of the Synanon Foundation to help our institution. But for reasons which that organization deemed sufficient, it backed off from the agreement and we were left in a difficult quandary of finding a qualified person who could understand the theory and tactics for establishing a therapeutic community completely unlike the traditional house of detention, hospital, prison.

Our first appointee was a member of Alcoholics Anonymous who was desperately anxious to make a success of the program. The first resident manager resigned because of the strain and anguish of the developing program on his spouse; the second resident manager, a social worker, lasted only a month before throwing in the towel. The third manager, a retired military educator, quickly left the job for a higher paying assignment in private industry. Finally, we located Dave Deitch, a 32-year-old former drug addict who had been expelled from Synanon because of differences with Dederich and his staff. Under his charismatic control Daytop Lodge became Daytop Village and was soon soaring into a long period of exciting discoveries, innovations, and revelations in the treatment of the drug addict.

John Morgan at Daytop Village

The operation of Daytop Village and its application of Reality Therapy might best be understood by following the fortunes of a specific resident we might call John Morgan.

Morgan is a mythical figure, a composite of several men now at the facility. He is approximately 22 years of age and had been convicted of grand larceny for the theft of merchandise to support his habit. Almost all of his half dozen previous arrests involved crimes related to the use of drugs. He had never been involved in a crime of violence, was never committed to a state hospital for a serious mental disorder, and has no history of homosexual activity. He completed elementary school and was a high school dropout usually in his sophomore year. He reads on the 7th grade level and has an IQ of 101.

Morgan kicked his habit, which involved the use of about five bags of heroin daily, while awaiting sentence in prison. He had been using drugs for about five years by his own admission. When interviewed by the investigating probation officer he spoke of his interest in entering some program that would help him give up the drug habit. "I'm getting tired of chasing the bag," he told the probation officer preparing the presentence investigation.

The recommendation of the Probation Department to the sentencing judge was that he be given a 30-day period to prove to the management at Daytop Village that he was sincerely interested in his rehabilitation. It was pointed out to the judge that admission to the Village is not automatic. It is necessary for the defendant to pass muster with the people in charge. It was therefore respectfully suggested: (a) that sentence be deferred for a month; (b) that the defendant be paroled in custody of counsel; (c) that he be instructed to gain admission to the halfway house; (d) that he be ordered to report to the Probation Department for further directions; (e) that, if he is not successful in gaining admission to the Village, he is to return to the Probation Department and thence to the Court for sentencing; and (f) that the Probation Department, if he is successful, notify the Court and place him on the next sentence calendar so that he might be formally put on probation with the court order that he remain at Daytop Village for as long as is deemed necessary by the management and that he cooperate with the program.

Morgan's First Day at Daytop

In the case of our defendant, Morgan, the judge was most cooperative. He praised the Daytop Village program and urged Morgan to take full advantage of this singular opportunity to save his life. Morgan nodded agreement in a frozen panic. He was given a slip to cross the street and enter the Probation Department about 100 yards distant from the walnut-paneled halls of the Supreme Court. At the Probation Department he was interviewed by a special officer assigned to the project who explained the nature of Daytop, gave him some literature to read on the way, wrote detailed instructions for reaching the facility, provided $1 carfare, and sent him on his way to the ferry to Staten Island. When he arrived at the hamlet of Tottenville in some 90 minutes he was to telephone Daytop.

Within a few minutes of his telephone call, the Daytop microbus picked Morgan up and brought him to our mansion. He was directed into the premises and asked to wait in the veranda facing an open, unlocked door. All about him was the hustle and bustle of laughing youths, many of whom he recognized from the street. He enthusiastically greeted one of them, a fellow junkie with whom he had shot up many times in cellars, roofs, and public toilets, with whom he had boosted many items from local department stores. He anticipated a kind of open welcome from a buddy he would have obtained had he been sent to even the strictest of prisons. But to Morgan's astonishment, the junkie friend seemed not to recognize him, to disregard his greeting as if it had not been heard, to look at him with icy silence as if he were some kind of contemptible worm life. "Man, this really shook me," Morgan later confessed. "What kind of brainwashing have they got going here?"

After an agonizing wait of almost an hour, during which he repeatedly told the cute receptionist that he was in a hurry only to be told that everybody was busy and he could leave if he didn't like it, Morgan was ushered into a neat office and confronted by three young men and a young woman who he assumed were some variety of social workers.

"Do you want to give up your habit? Are you tired of being a junkie?" he was asked gently.

At last Morgan felt he was on familiar ground. These were obviously the same square social worker types he could con out of their gold fillings without raising a sweat. He started to tell them about the extent of his habit (exaggerating generously), how tired he was of the drug addict life, how much he detested taking a shot, how much he wanted to turn over a new leaf and become a decent citizen.

His auditors listened in apparent sympathetic silence.

Suddenly Morgan was jolted by a curt command from one of the men: "Hold it! Cut out the crap. Who the hell do you think you're talking to? When're you going to stop trying to con everybody?"

Morgan listened with his jaw slack while his interrogators identified themselves as fellow junkies who understood his thinking processes because they had tried the same stunt on entering Daytop a short time before.

But this 's not just another joint, another prison or a detention center.

"Here it's like a home and we are like all members of the same big family. We care for each other. We help each other," they said.

The first concept they attempted to explain was that at Daytop for the first time in their lives, everybody tries to be open and honest with one another. No more con games or manipulations. Here we work on staying away from dope and learning how to handle the problems of living a straight life. We know this program is helping us and we're not going to let anybody screw it up. They continued explaining the house administration culminating with two basic rules:

1. Total, complete, undeviating abstinence from all drugs of any kind whatsoever.
2. No physical violence or the threat of physical violence.

The indoctrination of the new arrival also involved an explanation by the program director and his coordinators to the effect that the halfway house was a voluntary institution he may leave at his discretion. See, there are no bars over the windows, there is no guard at the door. However, splits lower the morale and treatment effectiveness of the facility. Therefore, great care must be taken to evaluate the sincerity of any applicant before making a decision to admit him as a new member. The committee wants the applicant to grasp this message: the reputation and destiny of Daytop depend on the behavior of the newcomer. All the current residents are determined to make a success of the treatment procedure because if it fails they, too, will be dragged through the hells of addiction again. They have managed to remain clean for periods up to 10 months and they like it! They don't want to be tortured anymore. Did the newcomer understand what they are talking about?

Morgan nods and walking as though he had been hit over the head by a mallet, he is taken upstairs to the bathroom, stripped and shaken down for any concealed narcotics by another addict who seems to know all the hiding places where an emergency shot or pill might be secreted.

Having thus passed the intitial intake procedure, Morgan is promptly assigned to a chore, one of the lowest status possible:

swabbing the toilet, washing the floors, scrubbing the kitchen pots, taking out the garbage.

Group Therapy at Daytop

Within a day or two Morgan is admitted to his first group session. These take place three times a week from approximately 7:30 to 9:00 P.M. Instead of the polite, inconsequential Gaston and Alphonse type of therapy procedures characteristic of most clinics and prisons, where the rule of "Don't pull the covers off me and I won't pull them off you" prevails, the therapy sessions at Daytop are based on Reality Therapy principles. For the confirmed dope fiend to change, the therapeutic approach must be a "gut" experience, free of phony attempts at self-defense, self-deception, self-pity, or extended biographical self-study. The speaker is forced to accept responsibility for his immediate behavior, not to pass it off on society, poverty, an unloving mother, or a punitive father. Honesty, even of the most painful kind, integrity, concentration on the "here and now" are the marks of the group therapy experience at Daytop. Reality Therapy[1] rather than orthodox psychoanalytic concepts and procedures prevail during the resident's stay at the halfway house.

Morgan is told that attendance at the group therapy sessions is compulsory so long as he remains at the facility. Does he wish to withdraw? The door is open back to the Probation Department and an opportunity to convince the judge about another sentence. The decision is up to him. Morgan thinks to himself, "What have I got to lose," and promptly contracts to remain and attend sessions faithfully in the future.

Group Therapy Session

It is difficult to describe the content and flavor of a Daytop group counseling session. Guy Endore's rendering[2] suggests that we imagine a group with no particular person in charge, where all are alike and everyone is permitted to question anyone else, to probe into his deepest motives, expose him, praise him, use any language that comes to mind. Morgan might hear this type of exchange between two group members and others chiming in:

"I hear you're getting yourself a job on the outside?"

"That's right. But first I go to school for a couple of weeks. Learn how to work it."

"You feel you're ready for a job on the outside?"

"I've been clean for a long time now."

"Yes. I know. I hear your legal problem is all squared away too."

"All tied up with a ribbon."

"Feel good to be divorced?"

"Wonderful."

"I suppose you're looking over the girls already. Made your choice yet?"

"Give me a chance, brother."

"Say, what about your kid?"

"Oh, she stays with the mother."

"So that gives you real freedom, eh?"

"You said it."

"Tell me, Joe. How is it you suddenly decided to divorce your wife?"

"It wasn't sudden. I've been thinking about it for a long time."

"You have? You been married for about 10 years, haven't you?"

"Just about."

"Say, Joe, I remember you telling me once about that woman that used to visit you when you were in the pen. Was that your wife?"

"Yes."

"The one you're divorcing?"

"Yes, the same one."

"And she'd come to visit you?"

"Yes."

"And bring you little things you wanted?"

"That's right."

"Anyone else visit you while you were in prison?"

"No."

"You had the baby already, didn't you? Who was taking care of it?"

"Why, she was. My wife."

"And she met you when you were released?"

"Yes."

"And you went home with her?"

"Sure, where would I go? I was broke."

"I get the picture, Joe . . . I'm just asking. Then when she found out you were going back on drugs . . ."

With the incisive skill of expert cross-examiners, one member of the group after another questions Joe until he is backed into a corner and is screaming responses.

"Well, let me explain . . ."

"That's exactly what I want you to do, Joe. And I'm going to give you a chance right now. You said that you didn't suddenly decide to divorce your wife, that you'd been thinking about it for a long time. So what I want to get straight first is when was this?"

"You mean when I first thought of getting a divorce?"

"Yes, when?"

"Well, I don't exactly know . . ."

"Well, was it when you were in jail and your wife was staying home with the kid and paying the rent and visiting you? Was it then you decided to get rid of her? Or was it when she was the only one to meet you when you came out of the pen? Or was it when you couldn't find a job and kept living off her earnings . . . ?"

"Well, skip it. Just tell me this. Whenever it was that you decided, did you tell her right away? Did you say: 'We're through.' Or did you wait? Letting her visit you, take care of your kid, meet you when you came out of prison, give you a place to sleep, wash your clothes . . . Stringing her along until you had got yourself straightened out and had yourself a good job."

"Gee, I don't know why you ask me all kinds of questions. I didn't do nothing wrong. If I want to get a divorce, I got a right. Besides, it's all legal now."

"You always do the legal thing, Joe? Answer me. Do you?"

"Well, I make some mistakes. Plenty, I guess. But I'm clean now."

"And you figure on staying clean?"

"I sure do."

"Good. And so now you're looking over the girls for another marriage."

"Why not? I'm free. I got a right."

"Course you got a right, Joe. But do you think you got character?"

"How about this job of yours? How about your employers? You going to treat them like your wife? Taking everything, giving nothing? With that kind of attitude how long before you won't have a job? How long before you'll be pushing dope again? How soon before you're back in the pen? And are you sure your next wife will visit you there? And if she does, do you think you'll deserve it?"

It is a bruising, straight-armed tackling of values and personality defects that Morgan will hear three times a week. At the beginning he will remain quiet and abashed but before long, he is brought directly into the interaction. His diligence on assigned jobs is evaluated. His loyalty to the "rat pack" is castigated. Again and again he is reminded that as a dope fiend he is a child in a man's body, an adult with the maturity of a 3-year-old. Soon his inhibitions about verbal encounters will leave him. Frequently voices will be raised so loud that neighbors may believe that a homicide is in progress. At times members of the group will be standing nose to nose, fists clenched, lips pale with anger, spitting insults at one another. Morgan will be challenged over and over. Was he ready to grow up, to become a man in spirit as well as in physique?

New Roles

Once Morgan is accepted as a full-fledged member of the Daytop family, the senior residents start preparing him for various roles. He is told he would be acquiring "clean-man days" and as soon as he has 60 to his credit he may invite his family to visit him on a Sunday. Up to this point, no communication with the family is permitted in order to avoid any outside disturbing influences. Residents are not allowed to communicate with their parents for a period of about two months. If a resident should appear at his family household they are advised that to save his life they should order him back to Daytop and slam the door in his face.

Morgan is encouraged to take an increasingly vigorous role in the group counseling sessions. He is initiated into the rites of "welcoming" a new member—by ignoring the applicant completely although they may have been blood brothers on the street. He is reminded he is eligible to strive for any position in the hierarchal structure of the facility from director down. "Seek and assume responsibility!" he is reminded over and over.

Seminar Meeting and Open House

Every weekday, Morgan observes, all residents gather immediately after lunch at 1:00 P.M. for a seminar meeting. On the blackboard is a proverb, a slogan, or an excerpt from the writings of a philosopher. One day it is: "A rolling stone gathers no moss." Another day: "Pride goeth before a fall." The third day: "Emerson said: 'Nothing good in this world was ever accomplished without enthusiasm.' "

The meeting leader asks the assembled house members: "What does this mean to you? What do you make of this saying? Who will start?" Almost before the words are out of his mouth, a forest of hands are vigorously shaking in the air. A member comes forward and at first haltingly, hesitatingly, groping for words, reacts to the statement. For the first time in their lives, many of the members will begin struggling with abstract concepts based on the accumulated wisdom of the ages. In a surprisingly short time, Morgan discovers that he, too, can get up on his feet and make a statement. His participation in the seminar meeting, as well as the manner in which he performs his daily chores, provides grist for the group therapy mill on Monday, Wednesday, and Friday.

The Daytop procedure is predicated on the proposition that the confirmed drug addict has been alienated from the larger society, is suspicious of normal people, and exists in a special subculture which effectively inhibits his rehabilitation. To help free him from this encapsulation, the addict is provided with a regular opportunity to mingle with middle-class people in order to begin taking effective steps toward the formation of a new identity. In the process of "rapping with squares," the addict gradually learns that not every member of the larger society is crooked, selfish, or suspicious.

The mechanism employed to help obtain this degree of socializing experience is the *Saturday Night Open House*. Daytop circulates invitations to professionals and lay circles to "Come on down and see Daytop Village!" A person need merely telephone the Village to make a reservation, giving the number of persons in his party and he is welcome.

In preparation for the Saturday night company, the residents scrub the premises from attic to basement, wash up, dress in their best clothes to make a good appearance. A program planned and conducted by the residents is then presented to acquaint visitors with the work of the Village. One Saturday may involve a series of testimonial speeches by the residents. Another week will be set aside for a question box session. A third week will have a panel format with members of Daytop acting as a board of experts. And happiest of all will be the anniversary of a resident's admission to the family.

Many residents confess that prior to coming to the Village, they found it difficult to speak to anyone outside their immediate circle of dope fiends, but within a few months at Daytop many appear able to hold an audience of Saturday night visitors spellbound. Others confess that besides their chemical addiction they were also prone to manufacture excuses for all their acts of deception and dishonesty. They invariably blamed society, schools, their parents. They trusted no one and wondered why no one had any confidence in them. They provided the ingredients for a guaranteed self-fulfilling prophecy.

By the application of principles derived from the pioneering operation of Synanon but refined and humanized through Reality Therapy, the Daytop Village facilities have developed both a theory and modality of treatment that is effective with the most difficult of all clients: the confirmed drug addict. Many graduates of Daytop are engaged in other facilities working as missionaries to pass the message of brotherly concern and love as the medium for saving one's life and achieving self-fulfillment.

REFERENCES

1. William Glasser, "Reality Therapy: A Realistic Approach to the Young Offender," *Crime and Delinquency,* April 1964, pp. 135–144, was used as a guide during the early days of the Daytop treatment plan.

2. Guy Endore, "Synanon, A Meaningful New Word," *Los Angeles Mirror-News,* September 19, 1961, p. 14.

EUGENE CZAJKOSKI

Reality Therapy with Offenders

The deployment of Reality Therapy in the field of offender treatment is now significant. All indications are that Reality Therapy's impact on corrections is rapidly growing both in scope and intensity. The future seems certain to see Reality Therapy in wide use throughout the effective range of psychotherapy as well as within the particular sphere of correctional treatment.

This paper examines Reality Therapy from four angles: its special applicability to corrections; its timeliness; its substance; and its heritage.

Applicability to Offender Treatment

The corrective treatment of a person who has committed a crime raises unique problems, many of which are philosophical in nature.

Despite the involvement of the correctional therapist in the multiple adjustments of an offender's life—family, educational, vocational, cultural, etc.—the treatment goal which emerges as a distillate of these several involvements is the adoption of more responsible and productive behavior—i.e., the elimination of criminal acts. From a philosophical point, this must be the goal of the therapist in corrections. Otherwise, there is no justification for his working under the aegis of corrections, which is an extension of the irresistible power of the state, rather than working under the

From paper presented at the 77th Annual Convention of the American Psychological Association, Sept. 1, 1969, Washington, D.C.

cover of some other institution, sect, or systematized belief. This
narrow goal may not always be consonant with the goal of psychotherapy in individual treatment circumstances where, for example,
the client is seeking some highly personal readjustment in less
explicitly fettered areas.

There is no intention here to delve into such thorny philosophical issues in corrections such as relate to: the tendency to assume
that every offender needs treatment simply because he has violated
something as transient as the criminal law; the tendency to equate
the "wrongness" of behavior with the "sickness" of behavior; the
difficulty of exercising the value of self-determination; and the
searching for the psychological roots of criminal behavior, which
behavior is originally and essentially defined in nonpsychological
terms. It is sufficient here to state that in treating the offender, one
is inevitably bound up with morality, values, and the acts of an
offender. Such emphasis begins to limit or alter the kinds of psychotherapy which may be easily used in corrections.

Further limitation stems from the fact that the bulk of the
offender population is unintellectual, unsophisticated, and inarticu-
late. There are really not many in the offender group who can
respond to psychotherapies which depend on a high level of verbal
ability and a capacity to deal with abstractions or symbolic behavior.

Another limiting factor, less intrinsic than either the correctional goal or the correctional population, is the lack of professionally trained personnel in corrections. If a significant number of
clients are to be effectively reached by some form of psychotherapy, it will have to be a form which can be easily learned and
economically applied by subprofessional or nonprofessional staff.
Although surely not for economic reasons alone, corrections is
firmly establishing the group and indigenous leadership as media
for therapy. The kind of psychotherapy which can be employed by
indigenous leaders within groups has to be one that is straightforward, contemporarily oriented, and free of expert jargon. In short,
the kind of psychotherapy that is likely to be most useful in the
general correctional setting is one which is prepared to come to
grips with moral questions; one which will focus on the present

and future acts of the offender (or on altering behavior rather than self-attitude); and one which is adaptable to both unintellectual clients and subprofessional therapists.

Timeliness

Reality Therapy is strongly manifesting itself at a time when the great psychic problem of our society can be expressed in terms of alienation. Our youth struggle to find identity and in the process they fiercely probe our values. Perhaps the only straight line that can be detected in the turmoil is a quest for humanity and individuality. The Reality Therapist, by his willingness to discuss morality, by exposing his own values without imposing them, and by his always being himself rather than some sort of transference figure or coolly detached clinician, comes forth with the humanity being desperately sought.

Reality Therapy also shows itself at a time when the crisis in psychoanalysis has become well known beyond esoteric professional circles. The disenchantment with psychoanalysis has filtered down to the general public as a result of what has appeared in the popular press. The venerable *New York Times* published a front page story in its Sunday edition of August 4, 1968 which was headlined, "Psychoanalysis, After Fifty Years of Strong Influence in Many Fields, Reaches Crossroads." The lengthy article quotes a number of prominent psychiatrists, psychoanalysts, and psychologists, who report that psychoanalysis is well on its way out.

Another unit of the popular press, *Esquire* magazine, published a similar story in its issue of October 1968. The story was succinctly headlined, "Psychoanalysis Must Go." *Time* published an article in its March 7, 1969 issue which was entitled, "Psychoanalysis: In Search of Its Soul." The *Time* article quotes H. J. Eysenck as saying about psychoanalysis, ". . . there is nothing we can do for it except ensure it a decent burial." The same article also reports that even Anna Freud acknowledges that psychoanalysis seems to be going out of style.

Apparently, the decline of psychoanalysis represents recent news to the general public. However, the public has also seen challenges to psychoanalysis made outside of news stories. The reviews of such books as *Thomas Woodrow Wilson* by William C. Bullitt and Sigmund Freud (himself) and *Friendship and Fratricide: An Analysis of Whittaker Chambers and Alger Hiss* by Meyer Zeligs have been critical of the bizarre psychoanalytic interpretations of great or notorious men and events offered retroactively by analyst-authors who never had their subjects as patients. Freud's co-authored biography of Wilson pictures Wilson as a somewhat mentally ill individual playing out his psychic hangups on a world stage. In the book, Wilson is excluded from any ethical or political perspective and his failure is made to seem unaffected by ideological forces.

In Zeligs' book on the Hiss-Chambers relationship, the famous pumpkin episode is described in terms of the insemination of a vegetable womb from which Chambers was able to deliver himself of a brainchild after a ten-year period of gestation. The *Time* magazine book reviewer wryly commented that "The House Committee on Un-American Activities has been called many things but it has never before been mistaken for a panel of gynecologists."

Irreverence for the psychoanalytic approach to therapy or for the psychoanalytic interpretation of art and literature was unheard of from the lay public a few years ago. Few people in any of the fields influenced by psychoanalysis had the temerity to challenge its precepts. This was particularly true in corrections, where the gaudy and dramatic behavioral symptoms lend themselves to rich symbolic interpretations.

As the psychoanalytic grip on offender treatment relaxes, workers in corrections are set to consider new theory formulations and try new models of therapy. This release from the yoke of psychoanalysis is better demonstrated by fundamental changes which have been occurring in the field of social work, but corrections has been less well defined than social work and the future changes in corrections promise to be more varied. It should be noted parenthetically that there is, perhaps, the danger of everyone jumping on the bandwagon in the attack on psychoanalysis. Much more of it may be swept away than is warranted. Freudian strawmen are being erected and there are signs of a failure to distinguish between psychoanalysis as a direct tool of treatment (never quite intended by Freud) and psychoanalysis as a scheme for understanding psychosocial development. Psychoanalysis in the latter sense seems considerably less vulnerable.

As a final comment on the timeliness of Reality Therapy, it can be pointed out that it fits in with the community mental health movement where there is a need to mobilize nonprofessionals and to provide consultation in explicit terms.

The Principles and Technique of Reality Therapy

In synthesizing the treatment approach he named Reality Therapy, Dr. William Glasser, a conventionally trained psychiatrist, did not proclaim the creation of entirely new ideas nor did he regard his synthesis as something so perfect as to be beyond modification. He has outlined Reality Therapy in simple terms and he freely demonstrates its technique. The openness and simplicity of Reality Therapy will facilitate research into its validity.

In stating six principles of Reality Therapy, Glasser puts them in direct opposition to major beliefs of conventional or psychoanalytically oriented psychotherapy.

1. Glasser, like Dr. Thomas Szasz and a growing number of other psychiatrists today, does not accept the concept of mental illness and rejects the idea that anyone who behaves in a way unacceptable to the majority of society is somehow mentally sick. He rejects the faith that the so-called mentally ill person can be cured in the same way a physician most often cures a physically ill person—that is, by removing a cause. Glasser believes that this idea misleads both the doctor and the patient by setting up the false belief that the doctor's job is to treat some definite condition after which the patient will get well. Glasser believes that the medical analogy appropriate to psychiatric problems is not illness but weakness. While illness can be cured only by strengthening the existing body to cope with the stress of the world, Reality Therapy dispenses with the idea of mental illness and instead calls the individual irresponsible.

2. Reality Therapy aims at strengthening the patient to take responsibility to fulfill his needs satisfactorily, regardless of his past circumstances. Reality Therapy emphasizes working in the present and toward the future. It does not get deeply involved with the patient's history because what has happened to the patient in the past cannot be changed and there is no acceptance of the belief that the patient is limited by his past. Reality Therapy emphasizes immediate behavior. Once the patient is taught new ways of behavior, his attitude will change regardless of whether or not he understands his old ways. What starts the process is a small, initial change in behavior and it is toward this end that the Reality Therapist works.

3. Reality Therapy ignores conventional transference, emphasizing that the therapist must relate to the patient as himself, not as a transference figure. Glasser points out the difficulty of becoming involved with the therapist who instead of establishing a close personal relationship with the patient in his own capacity sometimes plays the role of someone else and sometimes acts as himself. The Reality Therapist does not hesitate to become personally involved with the patient.

4. Contrary to the conventional, psychoanalytically oriented psychotherapist, the Reality Therapist does not look for unconscious conflicts or the reasons for them. Glasser believes that the patient cannot become involved with the therapist by excusing his behavior on the basis of infantile conflicts or unconscious motivations. The Reality Therapist insists that the patient must accept responsibility for his present behavior and not attribute irresponsibility to factors beyond his control.

5. While conventional psychotherapy tends to avoid the problem of morality, Reality Therapy emphasizes the morality of behavior. The Reality Therapist confronts the issue of right and wrong and thus solidifies the therapeutic involvement. Disregard for morality is unrealistic inasmuch as all of society is based on morality and if the important people in the patient's life, especially his therapist, do not discuss whether behavior is right or wrong, reality is not being brought home to the patient.

6. Reality Therapy does not ignore teaching the patient better

ways of behaving in favor of teaching him the unconscious sources of his problem. Reality Therapy seeks to teach patients better ways to fulfill their needs. The emphasis is on the therapist's role as a teacher—not for the teaching insight into the causes of behavior, but for a teaching based on a painstaking examination of the patient's daily activity.

The key to Reality Therapy is involvement aimed at providing the patient with a series of success experiences of gradually increasing proportions. The student of psychology is often struck by the vast number of different psychotherapies, many of which are antithetical to one another and all of which can boast some degree of success. The common denominator for nearly all of them would be human involvement.

The technique of Reality Therapy is directed toward obtaining involvement. The involvement is obtained by the therapist being personal and subjective, by his using first person pronouns "I" and "me," by his revealing a little of himself, and by concentrating on the present rather than on case history. The Reality Therapist focuses on behavior rather than feeling. He asks "what" questions rather than "why" questions. Patient behavior is evaluated by the patient and once the evaluation occurs, the Reality Therapist helps the patient formulate a plan of action for improved future behavior which will displace negatively evaluated present behavior. Developing a commitment to the plan is an important and perhaps unique feature of Reality Therapy.

Antecedents of Reality Therapy

Examiners of Reality Therapy are quick to perceive that it is indeed made up of many old ideas, some of which relate to the Judeo-Christian ethic, and, at the risk of damning the scheme in the eyes of a few professionals, it might be said that Reality Therapy is a common-sense approach.

Various aspects of Reality Therapy can be identified with concepts already well established elsewhere. The concentration on the present can be traced to Adlerian psychotherapy. The educative aspect is also Adlerian. The fostering of a success experience follows the Skinnerian model of operant conditioning. The focus on behavior rather than feeling goes back to Watson, among others, and reflects the long-standing issue between description and insight. Involvement is like the "Quality of the Relationship" notion of Rogers. Self-responsibility is exactly what the existential psychologists have been talking about for some time.

What, then, has Glasser contributed with his Reality Therapy? If nothing else, he has systematically drawn together the aforementioned concepts and translated them into technique terminology. He has responded to the contemporary call for greater humanity in our institutionalized relationships. And, for offender treatment, he has provided an understandable and economical model suited to meet the special needs of the correctional field.

DONALD R. CRESSEY

Theoretical Foundations for Using Criminals in the Rehabilitation of Criminals

It is time to put to use in correctional work some of the sound social psychology we have developed both inside and outside the field of criminology. The implications of social psychological theories of criminal conduct should be explicitly spelled out and explicitly utilized in the attempts to change criminals into noncriminals. The idea, simply stated, is that if we know something about the process by which men move from the status of "noncriminal" to the status of "criminal," we ought to be able to use that knowledge to move men from the status of "criminal" to the status of "non-criminal."

Both sociologists and correctional workers have been grossly negligent, it seems to me, in matters of rehabilitation theory. We have not been able to develop, or publicize, an explicit rehabilitation procedure based on solid theory. Further, we have let ourselves fall into a trap inadvertently set by the psychiatrists and social workers, whose psychiatric theory of rehabilitation has been given great publicity and has, accordingly, gained widespread acceptance. So far as rehabilitation procedures are concerned, this kind of theory implies, by and large, that until one has had about ten years of college training he is not qualified to try to rehabilitate a criminal. Moreover, we are sometimes warned, on theoretical

From Hans W. Mattick, ed., *The Future of Imprisonment in a Free Society,* volume II. Chicago: St. Leonard's House, 1965. *Key Issues,* II (1965). Reprinted by permission of the publisher.

grounds, that a person who does not have about ten years of college—a non-psychiatrist—may do irreparable damage to the psyches of delinquents and criminals if he tries to rehabilitate them. The theoretical position, then, has led to the conclusion that rehabilitation work by persons other than "professionals" is both ineffective and potentially dangerous. Of course some exceptions are made—in certain situations it is all right for persons with only about *six* years of college (social workers) to talk to criminals, and sometimes it is all right for "uneducated" people with only an A.B. degree to talk with criminals, providing the talking is done under the watchful eye of a "professional."

The trap is this: We subscribe to a psychiatric theory of rehabilitation that can be implemented only by highly educated, "professionally trained" persons, while at the same time we recognize that there are not now, and never will be enough psychiatrists around to man our correctional agencies. According to the last count (for the Spring of 1954), there were only twenty-nine psychiatrists working full-time in all the state and federal prisons in the United States. Twelve of these men were located in California, seven in New York. Eighteen states had no psychiatric services at all, and only nine had the services of a full-time psychiatrist.[1] If we retain the psychiatric notion about rehabilitation, the "correctional industry" will be able to use every psychiatrist and every social worker produced in the United States in the remainder of this century. We will not get these "professional personnel" in the future for the same reason we are not getting them now—they really don't want to talk to criminals, at least not at our prices.

To get through the mountain of inconsistencies we have so nicely constructed, I propose that we start tunnelling from the other side of the hill. Rather than trying to bore through by means of vain pleas for greater and greater numbers of highly trained psychiatrists or psychiatrically oriented personnel, I propose that we start digging a tunnel that will enable us to make maximum use of the personnel actually available to act as rehabilitation agents. There is no shortage of mature, moral, average, fine, run-of-the-mill men and women of the kind making up the majority of the personnel manning our factories, our businesses, and our prisons

—men and women who have a high school education at most. With increasing automation, in fact, more and more personnel of this kind will be leaving "production" occupations and will be available for "service" occupations, including the occupation of rehabilitating criminals. Our first task, a simple one, is to recognize the tremendous force of manpower that is available to us. Our second task, and in my opinion the most difficult and most important task that criminologists face during the remainder of this century, is development of sound rehabilitation theory and procedures which will enable us to utilize this vast reservoir of manpower.

The task is not impossible. We already have made some feeble beginnings which I will discuss later. If we can put a man on the moon, we can develop sound rehabilitation theory and sound systems for changing criminals, systems that are "practical" in the sense that they are based on theory which acknowledges that highly educated personnel are not needed to change criminals into non-criminals, any more than highly educated personnel are needed to change non-criminals into criminals. I expect that we are going to get to the moon; if we do, it will be because we have constructed a highly efficient organization for doing so, an organization that includes at least four types of personnel: Policy Makers, Theoreticians, Engineers, and Technicians. It is this kind of division of labor, plus a lot of money, that has increased the rate of technological change in the years since World War II. But in correctional work the rate of technological change has been slow because we have been insisting, by analogy, that the psychiatric Policy Maker and Theoretician also be the Engineer or Technician that actually turns the loose screws, cracks the nuts, and straightens out the kinks and crooks. I do not imply that the Technician cannot make a contribution to theory; neither do I imply that he should have no voice in policy-making decisions. I do say that in corrections we should decide as a matter of policy that theoreticians must develop a theory of rehabilitation which wardens and other agency administrators can implement by creating an organization made up principally of men trained on the trade school level to be skilled correctional technicians.

Moreover, already sitting under our noses is a manpower pool that could easily supply many of the skilled correctional technicians we need, providing Policy Makers will decide that the source is to be used, and providing Theoreticians will provide a foundation for utilization of this source. I refer to the copious supply of ex-convicts being discharged from probation, prison, and parole every year, and to the copious supply of persons who actually are *ex*-convicts even if they are still under supervision by a correctional agency. Even if we develop skilled technicians—"people changers"—by training non-criminals to do correctional work, we can no longer ignore the ex-criminals. There are general theoretical grounds for believing that ex-criminals can be highly effective *agents* of change and, further, that as they act as agents of change they themselves become the *targets* of change, thus insuring their own rehabilitation. Still to be done is the difficult task of showing how general social psychological theory and criminal theory can be transformed into a theory of correction, and the difficult task of transforming the new theory of correction into a program of action.

"Symbolic Interaction" Theory and Crime Causation

In his statement of the theory of differential association, the late Edwin H. Sutherland placed great emphasis upon the kinds of variables that must be considered as fundamental if one is to explain delinquent and criminal behavior.[2] One can best appreciate the "individual conduct" part of this theory, in contrast to the "epidemiological" part, if it is viewed as a set of directives about the kinds of things that ought to be included in a theory of criminality, rather than as an actual statement of theory.[3] The variables Sutherland pointed to are the same variables considered in social psychology's general "symbolic interaction" theory as the basic elements in any kind of social behavior—verbalizations ("symbolizations") in the form of norms, values, definitions, attitudes, rationalizations, rules, etc. Moreover, Sutherland also shared the theory of the "symbolic interactionists" when he told us that we must be concerned with the fact that the process of receiving a behavior pattern is greatly affected by the nature of the relationship between donor and receiver. In short, Sutherland told us to stop looking for emotional disturbances and personality traits, which are secondary, and to start looking at the verbalizations of groups in which individuals participate, which are primary.

In telling us to look at people's words ("symbols") when we try to explain why most people are non-criminals and only a small proportion are criminals, Sutherland early aligned himself with a group of social scientists whose ideas are quite different from the psychiatric view that "personality" is an outgrowth of the effect that the "restrictions" necessary to social order have on the individual's expressions of his own pristine needs. These social scientists (called, for convenience, "symbolic interactionists") view "social organization" and "personality" as two facets of the same thing.[4] The person is seen as a part of the kinds of social relationships and values in which he participates; he obtains his essence from participation in rituals, values, norms, rules, schedules, customs, and regulations of various kinds which surround him. The person (personality) is not separable from the social relationships in which he lives. He behaves according to the rules (which are sometimes contradictory) of the social organizations in which he participates; he cannot behave any other way. This is to say that criminal behavior is, like other behaviors, attitudes, beliefs, and values which a person exhibits, the *property of groups,* not of individuals. Criminal and delinquent behavior are not just *products* of an individual's contacts with certain kinds of groups; they are in a very real sense "owned" by groups rather than by individuals, just as the French language or the English language is owned by a collectivity rather than by any individual.

"Participation" in "social relationships" and in "social organization" is, of course, the subject matter of all of anthropology, sociology, and social psychology. Nevertheless, "participation" in "social organization" is rather meaningless as an explanatory principle when it stands alone, for it "serves only to indicate in a general way, to oversimplify, and to dramatize social interactions which are so confused, entangled, complicated, and subtle that even the participants are unable to describe clearly their own involvements."[5] Sutherland's criminological principle, like more general symbolic interactionist theory, tells us what to look for after we have moved toward consideration of the specific effects that "participation in social relationships" has on individual conduct. What Sutherland says we should study if we are going to establish a theory for explaining criminal conduct is, in a word, *words*. Values, attitudes, norms, rationalizations, and rules all are composed of symbols ("verbalizations") and these verbalizations, of course, are learned from others, as symbolic interaction theorists like Mead, Dewey, Cooley, Baldwin, Whorf, Langer and others pointed out years ago.

In simplified form, symbolic interactionist theory tells us that cultures and subcultures consist of collections of behaviors contained in the use of *words* in prescribed ways. These words make it "proper" to behave in a certain way toward an object designated by the word "cat," and "improper" to behave in this same way toward an object designated by the word "hammer." They also make it "wrong" or "illegal" to behave in certain ways, and "right" or "legal" to behave in other ways. It is highly relevant to a theory of criminal behavior and to a theory of corrections that words also make it "all right" to behave in some situations in a manner which also is "wrong" or "illegal."

Words exist as *group definitions* of what is appropriate; they necessarily are learned from persons who have had prior experience with them. In our culture, for example, there are many ideologies, contained in words, which sanction crime. To give some easy examples: "Honesty is the best policy, *but* business is business." "It is all right to steal a loaf of bread when you are starving." "All people steal when they get into a tight spot." "Some of our most respectable citizens got their start in life by using other people's money temporarily."

An anthropologist has given us an excellent example from another culture of the highly significant effect that words have in the production of individual conduct of the kind likely to be labelled "deviant," if not "criminal":

The Burmese are Buddhist, hence must not take the life of animals. Fishermen are threatened with dire punishment for their murderous occupation, but they find a loophole by not literally killing the fish.

"These are merely put on the bank to dry, after their long soaking in the river, and if they are foolish and ill-judged enough to die while undergoing the process, it is their own fault." . . . When so convenient a theory had once been expounded, it naturally became an apology of the whole guild of fishermen.[6]

Other examples of the significant influence words have on individual conduct can be found in my study of criminal violators of financial trust.[7] In that study, we were able to observe that each embezzler defines the relationship between an unshareable financial problem and an illegal solution to that problem (embezzlement) in words which enable him to look upon his embezzlement as something other than embezzlement. Most commonly, they use words, supplied by their culture, which enable them to look upon dishonesty as something other than dishonesty. To illustrate the significance of words, suppose that a bank clerk with no significant history of criminality finds himself with an unshareable financial problem and an opportunity to solve that problem by stealing from his company. Suppose, further, that you walked up to him and used the following words: "Jack, steal the money from your boss." The chances are that in response to these words he would simply look at you in horror, just as he would look at you in horror if you suggested that he solve his problem by sticking a pistol into the face of an attendant at the corner gasoline station. Try some other words now. "Jack, steal the money from your *company*," would probably bring about less of a horror reaction,[8] but still honest and trusted men "just don't do such things." However, honest and trusted men do "borrow," and if you were to suggest that he surreptitiously "borrow" some money from the bank, you would have helped him over a tremendous hurdle. As a matter of fact, the idea of "borrowing" is used by some embezzlers as a verbalization that adjusts the two contradictory roles involved: the role of an honest man and the role of a crook. This verbalization, then, is one of a number of verbalizations that make embezzlement possible.

Verbalizations such as "borrowing," it should be emphasized, are not invented by embezzlers, or anyone else, on the spur of the moment. On the contrary, they necessarily are learned from persons who have had prior experience with them. They must exist as group definitions of what is "proper." Symbolic interaction theory suggested to Sutherland that all criminals, not just embezzlers, become dishonest because of the words available to them. Accordingly, his theory of differential association stresses the importance of verbalizations in criminal conduct. The theory is important to those who would try to understand criminal conduct before trying to change it. One implication of the theory is, as we shall see later, that ex-criminals or criminals themselves can be most effective in changing the words—motives, rationalizations, attitudes, etc.— used by other criminals.

A great deal of evidence supporting the importance of verbalizations in both criminal and non-criminal conduct is found in the literature, but it has not been systematically collected and published. Here we can give just a few examples, drawn from the criminological literature. Stated in oversimplified form, Lindesmith in 1947 reported that if a person habituated to drugs talks to himself in certain ways he will become an addict, while if he talks to himself in other ways, he will avoid addiction entirely.[9] Lindesmith's most general conclusion was that persons can become addicts only if certain kinds of verbalizations are available to them. Consistently, Becker's studies of marijuana addicts showed that perception of the effect of marijuana is determined by the kinds of words given to smokers by users.[10] Lane found that differences in the white-collar crime rate among New England shoe manufacturing firms was determined by the verbalizations available in local communities.[11] For example, seven per cent of the firms in one town violated the laws, while in another town forty-four per cent violated. Lane concluded that at least one of the reasons for the difference is "the difference in attitude toward the law, the government, and the morality of illegality." Similarly, Clinard analyzed violations of O.P.A. regulations during World War II and concluded that businessmen violated the regulations because they did not "believe in" them—they possessed verbalizations which made the criminal law seem irrelevant.[12] In a study of delinquents, Sykes and Matza followed up the idea suggested in *Other People's Money,* concluding that since all youths accept conventional values to some degree they must "neutralize" these conventional values before they can commit delinquencies.[13] As illustrations of the "techniques of neutralization" used by delinquents, they cite use of verbalizations which blame parents or misfortune for one's theft, define the victim as worthless, justify offenses as a duty toward one's friends, and note the faults of those who condemn delinquency.

On a more general level, in a recent discussion of the research on social class and childhood personality, Sewell, who might be called a general "symbolic interaction" theorist, stressed the importance of attitudes and values (verbalizations), in contrast to emotional traits:

It now seems clear that scientific concern with the relations between social class and personality has perhaps been too much focussed on global aspects of personality and possibly too much on early socialization. Therefore, it is suggested that the more promising direction for future research will come from a shift in emphasis, toward greater concern with those particular aspects of personality which are most likely to be directly influenced by the positions of the child's family in the social stratification system, such as attitudes, values, and aspirations, rather than with deeper personality characteristics.[14]

The trend which Sewell has noted in general social psychological research has been noted by Glaser in criminological research and thinking. Since criminology must get at least the general direction of its theory from the behavioral sciences, it is not surprising to find it following the general trends in theory. Glaser summarized the theoretical position in criminology as follows:

The process of rationalization reconciles crime or delinquency with conventionality; it permits a person to maintain a favorable conception of himself, while acting in ways which others see as inconsistent with a favorable self-conception. In this analysis of motivation by the verbal representation of the world with which a person justifies his behavior, sociologists are converging with many psychologists. This seems to be an individualistic analysis of behavior, but the so-called "symbolic interactionists" viewpoint is gaining acceptance, and it sees individual human thought as essentially a social interaction process: the individual "talks to himself" in thinking and reacts to his own words and gestures in "working himself" into an emotional state in much the same manner as he does in discussion or in emotional interaction with others.[15]

"Symbolic Interaction" Theory and the Problem of Changing Criminals

If social conduct is a function of attitudes embodied in words learned from membership groups and reference groups, attempts to change that conduct should concentrate on processes for avoiding verbalizations and acquiring others. Theory indicates that men conceive of themselves as a type (*e.g.*, "criminal") when they have intimate associates who conceive of themselves as that type and when they are officially handled as if they were members of that type. Both processes have verbalizations as their content. This observation has enabled us to start working on a consistent set of "rehabilitation theory" which holds that a person can be stopped from conceiving of himself as one type (*e.g.*, "criminal") and stimulated to conceive of himself as another type (*e.g.*, "square John") by isolating him from persons who conceive of themselves as the first type, and refraining from handling him as if he were a member of that type, while at the same time surrounding him with intimate associates who think of themselves as the second type. The basic idea here is that one set of attitudes, values, rationalizations, definitions, etc., must be substituted for the set that he has been using in performing the social conduct said to be undesirable, illegal, or immoral. The concern must be for the fact that criminal conduct is *wrong*.

The infrequency of crime in our society cannot be accounted for by proposing that the population lacks opportunities for learning illegitimate skills. Neither can it be accounted for by proposing that the population fears that the risk of committing criminal acts is too great. The opportunity to acquire the skills of the criminal is great, and the probability of being arrested for a crime committed is low. Why, then, don't more people commit crime? Toby, who asked this question, has answered it by saying, essentially, that people have learned that criminal conduct is wrong, indecent, immoral. He points out that the tremendous amount of conforming behavior in any society can be understood only if we can see that individuals possess self-conceptions which make it impossible for them to engage in criminal or delinquent conduct without arousing guilt reactions and feelings of guilt and shame that are incompatible with the self-conceptions.[16] "Guilt" and "shame" are contained in the verbalizations that make up a culture, and in changing criminals the basic problem is one of insuring that these criminals become active members of intimate groups whose verbalizations produce "guilt" and "shame" when criminal acts are performed, or even contemplated. Stated negatively, the problem is one of insuring that persons do not learn to behave according to verbalizations which make crime psychologically possible.[17]

Implementation of this basic idea is not, however, as simple as it seems. First of all, our attempts to change a criminal's conduct might merely reinforce his use of the myriads of verbalizations that have made and are making the actor what he is. Next, the procedures invented to change criminals might change them into different kinds of criminals. At a minimum, then, we must learn more about the processes of social interaction in correctional settings, where the criminal whose change is being attempted is sometimes given words that make his criminality worse, or which substitute one form of criminality for another.

Using Criminals to Reform Criminals

"Symbolic interaction" theory supports the idea that criminals can be used effectively to introduce "guilt" and "shame" into the psychological make-up of those who would commit crime. It also supports the idea that criminals can be used effectively to avoid production of further criminality, or a different form of criminality, among the population whose change is sought. In the first place, criminals who have committed crimes and delinquencies by means of certain verbalizations, and who have rejected these verbalizations in favor of verbalizations making crime psychologically difficult or even impossible, should be more effective in changing criminals' self-conceptions than would men who have never had close familiarity with the pro-criminal verbalizations. In the second place, when criminals are used as agents of change they should be more efficient than non-criminals in avoiding the presentation of the verbalizations appropriate to a new kind of criminality or deviancy.

There are two different approaches to the first problem, that of expecting criminals to present anti-criminal verbalizations to other criminals. In the first approach, the criminal-turned-reformer is viewed as the agent of change, and in the second he is viewed as the *target* of change.

The literature on group therapy reports many examples of therapy groups in which the subjects served as effective agents of change. Opinion is almost unanimous that group therapy is a remarkably effective technique for treating mental patients, and that the principal contribution of group therapy for mental patients has been the reduction of social isolation and egocentricity among the subjects.[18] Arguments in favor of group therapy for criminals are less frequent, and they tend to be organized around "emotional disturbances" theory of criminality, rather than around symbolic interaction theory. One principal argument centers on the criminal's ability to establish rapport with other criminals.[19] Another argument centers on the function of therapy in reducing isolation and egocentricity among criminals.[20] Neither of these is actually an argument for the effectiveness of group therapy in changing criminals, as we pointed out some ten years ago.[21]

From the standpoint of the theory sketched out above, group therapy for criminals ought to be effective to the degree that the criminal-as-an-agent-of-change prevents criminals from using the "techniques of neutralization"—the verbalizations—which he himself used in perpetrating offenses, and to the degree that new anti-criminal verbalizations are substituted. In one experiment with group therapy for female offenders, the old verbalizations were not prevented, so in the words of the therapist, "the participants would not accept the propositon that the source of their predicament was not 'bad luck' or a 'bad judge'."[22] In another report, it was said that delinquents "were convinced that everyone is dishonest, even the police, the government and the judges took bribes. Thus, they sought to convince themselves that they were not different from anyone else."[23] This author goes on to say,

"They needed persons with socially acceptable standards and conduct with whom they could identify." Theoretically, at least, the degree of rapport is increased if these "persons with socially acceptable standards and conduct" are themselves criminals-turned-reformers, rather than professional reformers such as social workers and prison guards. Just as men are relatively unaffected by radio and television dramatizations, they are unaffected by verbalizations presented by men they cannot understand and do not respect. On a general level, Festinger and his co-workers have provided extensive documentation of the principle that the persons who are to be changed and the persons doing the changing must have a strong sense of belonging to one group.[24]

The implications of the social psychological ideas discussed above seem even clearer in connection with making the criminal "rehabilitator" the *target* of change. The basic notion here is that as a person tries to change others, he necessarily must use the verbalizations appropriate to the behavior he is trying to create in those others. In an earlier article, we named this process "retro-flexive reformation," for in attempting to change others, the criminal almost automatically identifies himself with other persons engaging in reformation and, accordingly, with persons whose behavior is controlled by non-criminal and anti-criminal verbalizations.[25] He then must assign status to others and to himself on the basis of non-criminal and anti-criminal conduct or, at least, on the basis of exhibition of non-criminal and anti-criminal verbalizations. When this is the case, he is by definition a member of law-abiding groups, the objective of reformation programs. At the same time, he is alienated from his previous pro-criminal groups, in the sense that he loses the verbalizations which enable him to assign high status to men whose conduct has been considered "all right," even if "illegal" and "criminal."

It is my hypothesis that such success as has been experienced by Alcoholics Anonymous, Synanon, and even "official" programs like institutional group therapy and group counseling programs, is attributable to the fact that such programs require the reformee to perform the role of the reformer, thus enabling him to gain experience in the role which the group has identified as desirable. As I said eight years ago, "The most effective mechanism for exerting group pressure on members will be found in groups so organized that criminals are induced to join with non-criminals for the purpose of changing other criminals. A group in which criminal A joins with some non-criminals to change criminal B is probably most effective in changing criminal A, not B; in order to change criminal B, criminal A must necessarily share the values of the anti-criminal members."[26]

This notion proposes that the same mechanisms which produce criminality be utilized in attempts to change criminals into non-criminals. The criminal has learned that he can gain desired status in one or more groups by participation in the use of verbalizations that enable him to perform in a manner our law defines as "criminal." Now he must learn that he can "make out" in a group by participating in verbalizations conducive to non-criminality. Further, this learning must be reinforced by arranging for him to be an "elite," one who not only knows the proper verbalizations and, therefore, the modes of conduct, but who attempts to enforce his conceptions of right conduct among those beneath him in the status system. When these two things occur, he becomes more than a passive non-criminal; he becomes an active reformer of criminals, a true "square."

We now turn to the problem of avoiding the presentation, in the rehabilitation process, of verbalizations that inadvertently make criminals worse. In recent years, sociologists and social psychologists have displayed increasing concern for this problem, as reflected in the large numbers of studies of the detailed operations of rehabilitation organizations like mental hospitals and prisons. So far as criminology is concerned, the problem seems to have been first identified in 1938 by Tannenbaum, whose book, *Crime and the Community,* was written with the help of two famous "symbolic interactionists," John Dewey and Thorsten Veblen. Tannenbaum's basic idea was that officially separating the delinquent child from his group for special handling amounts to a "dramatization of evil" that plays a greater role in making him a criminal than any other experience: "The process of making the criminal is a process of tagging, defining, identifying, segregating, describing, emphasizing, making conscious and self-conscious; it becomes a way of stimulating, suggesting, emphasizing, and evoking the very traits that are complained of."[27] In more recent years, this notion has been discussed by Merton as "the self-fulfilling prophecy,"[28] and in 1951 Lemert gave the name "secondary deviation" to the outcome of the process.[29] The important point is that in attempting to correct what Lemert calls "primary deviation" we sometimes give the deviants words which make their problems worse.

It is possible to carry this notion of "dramatization of evil" and "secondary deviation" so far that it can be erroneously deduced that the police and other official instrumentalities of the state are more important in producing criminality and other forms of deviancy than is informal interaction. There seems to be a current tendency among social scientists to view police, prison workers and parole officers as the "bad guys" that are producing criminality, while the crooks and other carriers of crooked values are the "good guys." This is absurd. Nevertheless, the current focus on both secondary deviation and primary deviation places our scientific concern exactly where, according to symbolic interaction theory, it needs to be placed—on the subcultures made up of verbalizations which inadvertently, but nevertheless inexorably, are presented to persons who adopt them and who, in adopting them, become criminals. To take a simple example from outside the field of criminology, speech experts have found that stutterers often are people whose parents have dealt with them severely in order to get them to speak correctly.[30] Similarly, others have shown that the male homosexual is often a person who has been stigmatized for effeminacy or who applies a verbalization like "queer" to himself when he recognizes in himself different responses from other males.[31]

Recent studies have indicated that even in physical illness the physician's attention plays a considerable part in bringing on the very symptoms which it is designed to diagnose. For example, Scheff points out that false diagnoses of illness (made because the physician is obligated to suspect illness even when the evidence is not clear) often incapacitate the person being diagnosed:

Perhaps the combination of a physician determined to find disease signs, if they are to be found, and the suggestible patient, searching for subjective *symptoms* among the many amorphous and usually unattended bodily impulses, is often sufficient to unearth a disease which changes the patient's status from well to sick, and may also have effects on his familial and occupational status. . . . It can be argued that when a person is in a confused and suggestible state, when he organizes his feelings, and behavior by using the sick role, and when his choice of roles is validated by a physician and/or others, that he is "hooked" and will proceed on a career of chronic illness.[32]

Consistently, a physician reports the case of a woman who began to suffer the symptoms of heart trouble only after she was informed that a routine chest x-ray revealed that she had an enlarged heart.[33]

From these observations in areas other than criminology, it may safely be concluded that official action by rehabilitators of criminals is important in producing a "vicious circle" of the kind described by Toby:

When an individual commits one crime, forces are set in motion which increase the probability of his committing others. When he uses alcohol to help himself cope with an unpleasant social situation, the reactions of his friends, employers and relatives may be such as to give him additional reason to drink.[34]

While the problem of "secondary deviation" is by no means solved when criminals are used as agents for changing other criminals, or themselves, symbolic interaction theory hints that there might be an essential difference between situations in which "secondary deviation verbalizations" are provided by professional agents of change, and situations in which such verbalizations are presented by ex-criminals. When the former criminal presents verbalizations making secondary deviation appropriate, he is at the same time presenting verbalizations making it possible to move out of the secondary deviant's role. This is not true when the noncriminal, and especially a "professional" rehabilitator, presents the verbalizations. For example, I might easily be able to show a man signs that will lead him to a conception of himself as a homosexual, with resultant secondary deviation; but an ex-homosexual can show the same man the same signs, together with other signs (exemplified in his own case) that mark the road to abandoning both the primary deviation and the secondary deviation. Or, to take an easier example, in presenting anti-criminal verbalizations to a criminal, I might inadvertently convince him that the life of a square is undesirable because there is no way for a square John to get his kicks; a criminal, however, could show the subject that there is a kick in just being square.

Volkman and Cressey have observed, in this connection, that addicts who go through withdrawal distress at Synanon, a self-help organization made up of ex-addicts, universally report that the withdrawal sickness is not as severe as it is in involuntary organizations such as jails and mental hospitals.[35] The suggestion from theory is that much of the sickness ordinarily accompanying withdrawal distress is brought about by close familiarity with verbalizations making it appropriate to become sick when opiates are withdrawn. At Synanon, these verbalizations are not available—a newcomer learns that sickness is not important to men and women who have themselves gone through withdrawal distress; he "kicks" on a davenport in the center of the large living room, not in a special isolation room or other quarantine room where, in effect, someone would tell him that he is "supposed to get sick." In one sense, however, Synanon members do force newcomers into a "sick role," for a large part of the reception process is devoted to convincing newcomers that only crazy, sick people would go around sticking needles in their arms. The important point, however, is that this "sick role" is not the one that addicts experience when drugs are withdrawn in a jail or hospital. It is a role that is learned at the same time a new "non-sick role" is being learned; the learning process is facilitated by the fact that the teachers are themselves persons who have learned the new "non-sick role." We have heard the following verbalizations, and many similar ones, made to new addicts at Synanon.[36] It should be noted that none of the comments could reasonably have been made by a rehabilitation official or a "professional" therapist, and that each of them provides a route out of both addiction and the special sick role expected of newcomers to the organization:

"It's OK, boy, we've all been through it before."

"For once you're with people like us. You've got everything to gain here, and nothing to lose."

"You think you're tough. Listen, we've got guys in here who could run circles around you, so quit your bull shit."

"You're one of us now, so keep your eyes open, your mouth shut, and try to listen for a while. Maybe you'll learn a few things."

"Hang tough, baby. We won't let you die."

Summary and Conclusions

The theory of differential association and more general "symbolic interaction theory" suggest that whether criminals are viewed as agents of change or the targets of change when they are used as rehabilitators of other criminals, the concern must be for the fact that criminal conduct is *wrong*. "Guilt" and "shame" are contained in the verbalizations that make up a culture, and the problem of changing criminals is a problem of insuring that criminals become active members of intimate groups whose verbalizations make all criminality as guilt-producing, shameful, repulsive, and impossible as, say, cannibalism. Stated negatively, the problem is one of insuring that persons do not behave according to verbalizations which make criminality psychologically possible. Since reformed ex-criminals have learned both to feel guilty and not to feel not guilty when they participate in crimes, they are elite carriers of anti-criminal verbalizations and they can be used effectively in the effort to prevent crime and reform criminals.

REFERENCES

1. United Prison Association of Massachusetts, "What's new in Prison Psychiatry and Psychology?" *Correctional Research,* Bulletin No. 5, June, 1954, pp. 6–7.

2. Sutherland, Edwin H., and Cressey, Donald R. *Principles of Criminology,* Sixth Edition, New York: Lippincott, 1960, pp. 74–80. See also Cohen,

Albert K., Lindesmith, Alfred R., and Schuessler, Karl F. *The Sutherland Papers,* Bloomington: Indiana University Press, 1956.

3. Cressey, Donald R. "Epidemiology and Individual Conduct: A Case From Criminology," *Pacific Sociological Review,* 3:47–58, 1960.

4. Stanton, A. H., and Schwartz, M. S. *The Mental Hospital: A Study of Institutional Participation in Psychiatric Illness and Treatment,* New York: Basic Books, 1954, pp. 37–38.

5. Cressey, Donald R., Editor, *The Prison,* New York: Holt, Rinehart, and Winston, 1961, pp. 2–4.

6. Lowie, Robert H. *An Introduction to Cultural Anthropology,* Enlarged Edition, New York: Rinehart, 1940, p. 379.

7. Cressey, Donald R. *Other People's Money: A Study in the Social Psychology of Embezzlement,* Glencoe: The Free Press, 1953.

8. Smigel, Edwin O. "Public Attitudes Toward Stealing as Related to the Size of the Victim Organization," *American Sociological Review,* 21: 320–327, 1956.

9. Lindesmith, Alfred R. *Opiate Addiction,* Bloomington: Principia Press, 1947.

10. Becker, Howard S. "Becoming a Marijuana User," *American Journal of Sociology,* 59:235–242, 1953; "Marijuana Use and Social Control," *Social Problems,* 3:35–44, 1955.

11. Lane, R. E. "Why Businessmen Violate the Law," *Journal of Criminal Law and Criminology,* 44:151–165, 1953.

12. Clinard, Marshall B. "Criminological Theories of Violations of Wartime Regulations," *American Journal of Sociology,* 11:258–270, 1946; *The Black Market,* New York: Rinehart, 1952.

13. Sykes, Gresham, and Matza, D. "Techniques of Neutralization: A Theory of Delinquency," *American Sociological Review,* 22:664–670, 1957.

14. Sewell, William H. "Social Class and Childhood Personality," *Sociometry,* 24:340–356, 1961.

15. Glaser, Daniel. "The Sociological Approach to Crime and Correction," *Law and Contemporary Problems,* 23:683–702, 1958.

16. Toby, Jackson. "Criminal Motivation," *British Journal of Criminology,* 1962, pp. 317–336.

17. Reckless, W. C., Dinitz, S., and Murray, Ellen. "Self Concept as An Insulator Against Delinquency," *American Sociological Review,* 21:744–746, 1956; Reckless, W. C., Dinitz, S., and Kay, Barabara. "The Self Concept in Potential Delinquency and Potential Non-delinquency," *American Sociological Review,* 22:566–570, 1957; Lively, E. L., Dinitz, S., and Reckless, W. C. "Self Concept As a Predictor of Juvenile Delinquency," *American Journal of Orthopsychiatry,* 32:159–168, 1962; and Dinitz, S., Scarpitti, F. R., and Reckless, W. C. "Delinquency Vulnerability: A Cross-Group and Longitudinal Analysis," *American Sociological Review,* 27:515–517, 1962.

18. Clinard, Marshall B. "The Group Approach to Social Reintegration," *American Sociological Review,* 14:257–262, 1949.

19. Bixby, F. L., and McCorkle, L. W. "Applying the Principles of Group Therapy in Correctional Institutions," *Federal Probation,* 14:36–40, 1950.

20. McCorkle, L. W. "Group Therapy in the Treatment of Offenders," *Federal Probation,* 16:22–27, 1952.

21. Cressey, Donald R. "Contradictory Theories in Correctional Group Therapy Programs," *Federal Probation,* 18:20–26, 1954.

22. Fidler, J. W. "Possibility of Group Therapy With Female Offenders," *International Journal of Group Psychotherapy,* 1:330–336, 1951.

23. Gersten, C. "An Experimental Evaluation of Group Therapy with Juvenile Delinquents," *International Journal of Group Psychotherapy,* 1:311–318, 1951.

24. Festinger, L. et. al., *Theory and Experiment in Social Communication: Collected Papers,* Ann Arbor: Institute for Social Research, 1951.

25. Cressey, Donald R. "Changing Criminals: The Application of the Theory of Differential Association," *American Journal of Sociology,* 61:116–120, 1955.

26. *Ibid.*

27. Tannenbaum, Frank. *Crime and the Community,* Boston: Ginn, 1938, p. 21.

28. Merton, Robert K. *Social Theory and Social Structure,* Revised Edition, Glencoe: The Free Press, 1957, pp. 421–436.

29. Lemert, Edwin M. *Social Pathology,* New York: McGraw-Hill, 1951, pp. 75–76.

30. Johnson, W. "The Indians Have No Word For It: Stuttering in Children," *Quarterly Journal of Speech,* 30:330–337, 1944.

31. Fry, C. C. *Mental Health in College,* New York: Commonwealth Fund, 1942, pp. 139–140, 146–148; Leshan, L. "A Case of Schizophrenia, Paranoid Type," *Etc.,* 5:169–173, 1949.

32. Scheff, Thomas J. "Decision Rules, Types of Error, and Their Consequence In Medical Diagnosis," *Behavioral Science,* 8:97–107, 1963.

33. Gardiner-Hill, H. *Clinical Involvements,* London: Butterworth, 1958, p. 158.

34. Toby, *op. cit.*

35. Volkman, Rita, and Cressey, Donald R. "Differential Association and the Rehabilitation of Drug Addicts," *American Journal of Sociology,* 69:129–142, 1963.

36. *Ibid.*

Group Reality Therapy with Drug Abusers

Description of Group Setting

Sponsored by the Village of Scarsdale, a group therapy program has been designed to provide affluent, alienated, adolescent drug abusers an opportunity to convene with an academically trained group therapist in a casual atmosphere. Groups meet at different times in different locales four times a week. More than 325 youngsters have attended at least five sessions during the project's two-and-a-half years. There currently is a nucleus of 20 youngsters who attend the majority of sessions. Group membership, where participation is voluntary, changes with each session. The average attendance has been 16 with the range being 71 to six. Participants' ages have varied from a great-grandmother to preadolescent with the proponderance being 14 to 18.

Any community resident can attend. Adult presence does not seem to inhibit the character of the sessions and it appears as if adolescents enjoy their company. Significantly, when parents attend at the invitation of either a participant or the group therapist, their youngster becomes more active than he is at other times. These adolescents apparently want communication with their parents but also want their independence.

Each session format remains flexible. Youngsters arrive and depart at various times. Usually there is no predetermined agenda

---

Former title "Group Therapy with Affluent, Alienated, Adolescent Drug Abusers: A Reality Therapy and Confrontation Approach." From *Psychotherapy: Theory, Research and Practice*, Volume 9, #4, Winter, 1972.

since group membership changes. The group is committed to convene while working with an individual. The longest session has been seven hours; the shortest one hour, with the average being three hours. The length of the session pressures the individual to make a commitment to change his behavior.

The Target Population and Families:
Their Social-Psychological Characteristics

The target population serviced currently attends the same high school, lives in a middle to upper middle class suburban community within convenient commuting distance to a large urban center. Collectively, the adolescents have described a disillusionment—indeed, an absolute rejection—of their parents' values. Having been labelled as failures and viewing themselves in this fashion, these adolescents have decided to withdraw from a system which appears inimical and dehumanized. While failure is painful, it represents an abdication from commitment, involvement, and responsibility. Failure is tolerated because youngsters frequently rationalize that had they made the effort, they probably would have succeeded. By using this self-destructive adaptive mechanism, the drug abuser avoids learning that he might not be as intelligent or powerful as he previously believed. Their drug involvement spans the spectrum: occasional marihuana use to heroin addiction.

The families of these adolescents are cultured and well-educated, successful in their professions, affluent, and some are socially prominent. Many of the families became so involved either in pursuing affluence or social prominence that their youngsters earlier in their lives felt neglected and rejected. Many are exposed to extreme permissiveness, inconsistent or inadequate limit setting. While the family constellation remains intact, there seems to be little genuine love and concern. There is a rage when the parents feel embarrassed by the behavior of their children, and conversely, the children feel rejected because no one cares about them.

Group Dynamics: Coping with Reality and Accepting Responsibility

A primary short-term goal is to diminish current drug abuse by encouraging abstinence without enforcing it. Anyone who attends a group while under the influence of drugs incurs the wrath and disapproval of the members. Consequently, few attend in an intoxicated state.

Utilizing a confrontation-teaching-interpretative-reasoning approach, the group demonstrates to the drug abuser the irresponsible and self-defeating aspects of his behavior. The individual becomes aware of the impact of his behavior, begins to understand the consequences of his acts, and attempts to become more responsible to himself, others, and society. Emphasis is placed on the "eigenwelt" (the relation to one's self)—i.e., the immediate experience. The individual must acknowledge his perceptions of the conflict, the problem, his irresponsibility, etc. He must focus on the "here and now" in the group setting and cannot delay, evade, and/or hide. One person generally becomes the focal point. He begins to relate to his conflicts amidst much hostility from his peers. Self-appointed advocates, protectors of the weak, are discouraged. This becomes an odyssey which the person must take alone (Yablonsky, 1965). The ritual requires that the individual risk being ostracized by self-exposure which involves putting aside his defenses. Any sort of protective support denies the individual the adult experience of both defending and relying on his own resources as he must do in everyday activities. While there is a dialogue between the adolescent on the hot seat and the therapist, peer involvement is preferred. The individual, gaining the candid opinions and admonishments of his peers regarding the more destructive elements of his behavior, considers a new orientation and behavior.

After each appraisal, the individual is confronted about whether or not he wishes to change—i.e., to act more responsibly—or does he wish to continue his "madness"? During this therapeutic inquisition, which forces the person to recognize the "stupidity," "immaturity," "irresponsibility," "self-defeating" aspects of his behavior, he begins to experience discomfort, humiliation, and rejection. For perhaps the first time in his life, the adolescent is forced to accept total responsibility for his behavior and cannot rationalize the causes. Behavior is stressed. The goal of treatment is directed toward the termination of irresponsible and self-destructive behavior.

Once the individual has accepted responsibility for his actions, he is encouraged to make a commitment to change his behavior. Of tantamount importance is the knowledge that the group will not accept any excuse for a violation of the commitment. In extreme cases, a formal, written contract has been drafted which has been signed by the person on the hot seat. Refusing to accept any excuse reinforces the notion that people can control their behavior. If, however, the participant cannot determine positive behavioral alternatives, the group will make specific suggestions regarding improved functioning. This might involve teaching the individual how to behave so as to ensure a maximum probability of success. In addition, two or three members either will volunteer or be asked to serve as quasi-consultants who will advise the individual and report any contractual infractions. When the person begins to discard his failure identity and actively experiences some success, he begins to feel much better about himself. He experiences a sense of gratification because he can assert himself as autonomous without being self-destructive. The adolescent learns that he possesses the elements of freedom of choice as well as the capacity to grow and develop. While he cannot control external conditions, any person can control his responses to these conditions. (This is an affluent, powerful, and atypical group who has access to many opportunities the general population does not.)

The Group Therapist: His Role

Adolescents have a distrust of their parents, their teachers, and their government. With drug abusers, furthermore, the twin fears of detection and subsequent incarceration combine to produce much suspicion and hostility which must be neutralized before any meaningful relationship can be established. It is imperative for the group leader to prove himself worthy of their confidence.

Since there exists an age differential and a social distance between the therapist and the adolescent, the professional is thrust into various father roles for the group constituency—i.e., the good, the bad, the accepting, the rejecting, the strong, the weak, the understanding, the punitive (Samorajczyk, 1971). In this situation, the group therapist becomes the parent whose tolerance must be tested—i.e., to determine behavioral and therapeutic limits, to absorb personal insults, etc. The therapist should attempt to avoid becoming the inconsistent father. In this group situation, the leader often assumes a charismatic role. Some adolescents seek parental approbation, encouragement, understanding, acceptance, and/or reinforcement. Many project their hostility, anger, mistrust, and/or rejection. There are those who remain ambivalent. The most important question which must be answered before the therapist can gain entry is: DOES HE REALLY CARE ABOUT ME AS A HUMAN BEING?

By answering questions about himself with candor when it seems appropriate, the therapist both allays distrust and simultaneously becomes a responsible role model (Glasser, 1965).

Questions will be asked about the group therapist's personal views regarding drugs. Has he used any? Which ones? What does he believe? Assuming the therapist believes that any chemical depending on the quantity and quality consumed may become compulsive when utilized either to avoid or to deny the uncertainties and anxieties of life, he should affirm his commitment to a drug-free life style. The professional, by adopting a chemically-free life style, proves it is possible to function productively and be happy without any dependency on drugs.

The Therapeutic Relationship: The Therapist's Commitment

While reviewing 20 years of research concerning the therapeutic working alliance, Swensen (1971) concludes that "the successful psychotherapist is the one who genuinely cares about, and is committed to his client. . . . The really crucial element in the therapist's contribution to therapeutic success is the therapist's commitment to the client." There are two ways which the therapist can demonstrate this commitment:

First: To maintain high expectations of improvement and performance. Demanding the best of any person emphatically implies that someone cares enough about him not to accept a mediocre record. It is important to note that the drug abusing adolescent feels worthless because few people, if any, continue to believe he has any potential. Clinically, the high expectation of the therapist differs from parental pressures because there is neither a possessive demand nor any reflection on the group leader personally if goals are not attained. The therapist must be willing to risk by becoming involved with the youngster. To some degree, the group leader should be affected by progress and/or failure. As soon as a goal is attained, a more ambitious one should be set. While momentarily frustrating, the explicit message communicated to the adolescent is that he has more ability than he currently dared to believe. Conversely, if the adolescent fails to attain or maintain high standards, the therapist can share candidly his disappointment. The quality of disappointment is not pejorative but connotes concern with high expectations. These adolescents equate caring commensurately with the amount of energy expended. The louder the yell, therefore, the more the adolescent feels reassured. According to Glasser (1969, p. 24) these adolescents need·adults "who will work with them again and again as they commit and recommit until they finally learn to fulfill a commitment. When they learn to do so, they are no longer lonely; they gain maturity, respect, love, and a successful identity."

Second: To function in the role of advocate. An attendant integral part of the helping relationship would be the therapist's commitment to action on behalf of his client. The group therapist becomes an advocate where he may be required to pressure aggressively—i.e., to confront agencies—for special consideration on behalf of a youngster. In his effort to secure direct services, the therapist becomes his client's advocate, his supporter, his champion, his representative. In many respects this role is similar to the attorney who protects his client's interests and attempts to negotiate the most favorable deal—even at the expense of an adversary. The professional must be willing to jeopardize his reputation and challenge directly the public agency, the bureaucracy (Bratter, 1972). This pressure might enable the client to secure what he needs to continue his growth and development—i.e., a college placement, an adjournment in court, etc.

Before agreeing to assume the advocate role for any participant, the group leader traditionally shares the decision-making responsibility with the group. Mobilizing the collective resources of the group enables the therapist to appraise accurately any growth and development. In order to ensure candor, the group is notified that the leader's reputation is their asset, because if he were to lose his credibility, he would no longer be in a position to elicit favors and preferred services. The group, as an entity, has a vested interest in the performance of the individual whom the therapist endorses. The group reinforces any growth and development and exerts pressure for continued commitment and responsibility. If, however, an individual is informed by the group that he does not deserve the leader's support, he is informed specifically what he must do to receive the endorsement. Becoming joint partners in the adolescent's battle enables both the group and the therapist to make more ambitious demands on the youngster to continue to actualize his potential.

Case Study: A Behavioral Analysis

As a successful business executive, Craig Kantor's father, 47, was rarely home during his son's childhood and adolescence because his work day started at 7:00 and ended twelve hours later. Mr. Kantor has been described by each of his three sons as being emotionally remote, overly demanding, judgmental, and punitive. As a child, Craig feared his father's authority. He was a compliant child who would repress his anger until he became exhausted. Consequently, his father has remained omnipotent. Socially sophisticated, Mr. Kantor appears extroverted and pleasant. His intelligence facilitates pleasant and scintillating conversation. He seems self-assured.

Mrs. Kantor, 46, never wanted boys. She has devoted much of her life to pampering herself, and thereby, has neglected her family. She cannot relate to her sons and feels threatened by them. When they disappoint her, she becomes vindictive. Their frequent disappointments and failures tend to confirm to her that she is a failure. Mrs. Kantor constantly berates herself.

The three sons feel abandoned by their parents who frequently dine at restaurants or spend time at their country club. The family rarely eats together and has no common interests. Each of the sons, at different times, has described his parents as being "emotionally dead." There seems to be a marital conflict which has been seething for several years. This is compounded because Mrs. Kantor has bestowed her affection on Craig who becomes the target of his brothers' and father's rage.

Since his mother perpetually diets and has numerous prescriptions for amphetamines and tranquilizers to enable her to sleep, there has been a well-stocked medicine cabinet. Mr. Kantor nightly has several cocktails before and after dinner. At fourteen, the adolescent started using marihuana. Shortly thereafter, he began experimentation with his mother's barbiturates and amphetamines. Craig nurtured the image of a drug abuser to the point where his knowledge of medication—the generic names, the pharmacology, the appropriate dosage, etc.—was extensive even if judged by medical standards.

Craig's earliest recollection of failure was in the fourth grade when he was not promoted. Eight years later he was suspended from the high school because of truancy. (He was suspected of being a major illicit seller of drugs by both the high school and police.) A few days after his suspension, Craig returned to the school not only to challenge authority but also to test limits imposed by the authorities. When he refused to leave the premises and became belligerent, the police were summoned. With less than two months remaining in his junior year, Craig was expelled indefinitely. He had jeopardized his turbulent and unproductive school career. Since they could neither understand nor help their

18 year old son, Mr. and Mrs. Kantor insisted that Craig begin analysis. The use and abuse of amphetamines, barbiturates, and the hallucinogens reached their zenith during the period when Craig was being seen by a psychiatrist. In order to help Craig control his impulsive behavior, librium was prescribed. When his patient did not respond to thorazine (which Craig admitted he sold), the physician suggested placement in a psychiatric residence. Mr. and Mrs. Kantor felt relieved because this placement would remove Craig from the household. In addition, a psychiatric diagnosis confirmed mental illness which would exonerate Mr. and Mrs. Kantor from any responsibility. Their guilt would be ameliorated because they were purchasing expensive medical treatment.

Two months after he started his analysis, Craig attended group therapy because several of his friends did. He was hostile and abusive to the group leader. The adolescent group, Craig felt, would protect him against the adult-father-therapist. Simultaneously he could impress everyone with his ability to be the bad boy. Craig was put on the hot seat in the second session he attended. During this session, Craig exhibited much defensive grandiosity while he tried to convince the group of his emotional illness. One of his favorite activities was to drive his sports car at excessive speeds while under the influence of LSD. Whenever asked a question, Craig would offer an elaborate autobiographical explanation to justify his self-defeating behavior. He seemed to enjoy the fact that he was manipulating the group to believe he was unable to control his impulses. In an effort to discourage this dynamic, the group leader either interrupted or attacked the adolescent's answers. Behavior became the primary consideration. Craig was unable to defend his irresponsible and self-destructive acts when questioned: "What kind of a person drives his car at high speeds when tripping?" "What kind of a person deliberately gets himself expelled and then provokes the police?" Within an hour-and-a-half, Craig had been forced to evaluate his behavior. He had received some candid feedback from his peers regarding his self-destructive behavior. The adolescent concluded that he had been motivated by stupidity rather than illness and was, in fact, able to control his behavior. He exhibited insight because after the group he verbalized a feeling of relief that he no longer felt compelled to play the game of deception—i.e., of being sick.

During the next session, his disastrous academic performance was examined. Craig admitted deliberately failing examinations because he feared any success would establish a precedent. He did not wish to be subjected to any pressures to achieve or attain success. Most adults, at this juncture, had decided he was "too disturbed to be helped" and avoided him. He acknowledged having fundamental doubts as to whether he was capable of sustaining any type of success. Despite this fear of success, Craig decided he wanted another chance to learn even if he would risk failing. (Several months later, Craig admitted he had felt pressured by the group. He had been confident that his parents would not finance private school nor would the local high school re-admit him.) The group leader convinced the high school to consider granting the adolescent credit for his attendance at a graduate psychology course which the therapist was scheduled to teach at a university. Before Kantor would be permitted to take the graduate course, a contract was negotiated which included no drugs for the duration of the course, perfect attendance, and completing all assignments on time. Craig agreed to regulate his behavior and to conform to the provisions. Toward the end of the course, Craig violated his contract and smoked marihuana. An entire graduate class focused on his need to test authority which jeopardized his position, his self-destructive and irresponsible behavior. The repetition pattern was discussed. The class decided that since Craig had violated his contractual agreement with the group leader, he must petition the school on his own and explain why the therapist no longer would support him. As a condition for continuing the graduate course, another contract was negotiated which had more stringent stipulations such as lengthening the drug-free period to three months, more responsible behavior at home, and an additional assignment. By continually raising his behavioral expectations of Craig, the group therapist communicated a faith and optimism few still maintained. Craig was awarded two points of academic credit and was readmitted to high school. He was two years behind his graduating class. As an additional incentive, the group leader mentioned he would attempt to secure a college placement at the end of his first semester of his junior year. The college placement was contingent on a "B—" average. The adolescent returned to school feeling much better about himself. He entered into a mutually gratifying relationship with a girl who was considered to be one of the brightest and most talented in the junior class. This relationship further reinforced his recently improved concept of self. Craig questioned his ability to sustain an intimate interpersonal relationship, and consequently sabotaged it. Consumed with depression and despair, his academic average fell to a "C" for the term. Because he had contained his self-destructive behavior, the high school and college agreed to permit Craig to enroll and receive credit.

Prior to leaving for college, Craig gave assurance he would achieve a "B" average and remain drug-free. Toward the end of the semester, the adolescent duplicated his pattern of self-destructive behavior and was notified by the college not to return after finishing the term. Significantly, however, after receiving his suspension, Craig completed the semester with a "B—" average. His drug involvement had been confined to four episodes.

Craig, who is in the unique position of having completed one semester at college, still needs a year of high school for his diploma. In one year, however, much of his self-destructive behavior has been eliminated. In an effort to continue to whet Craig's desire to actualize his potential, the group therapist located another incentive. He recognized Craig's fantasy wish to become a psychologist, and contacted a program where the youngster could be trained as a paraprofessional and receive a group leader's certificate. The program required 500 hours of classroom participation. An agreement was reached whereby Craig would abstain from drugs for one year, to pursue his education until he completes his college degree, and eliminate all self-destructive behavior. Nine months ago, Craig received his group leader's certificate. One month ago, he passed the high school equivalency examination. Currently, he moved out of his house and secured full-time employment. He has been accepted to a prestigious and competitive

New York State college and plans to matriculate on a full-time basis starting January 1973.

Placed on a behavioral continuum, there is considerable evidence to suggest that he has begun to limit his self-destructive behavior while actualizing some of his potential. His prognosis currently is guardedly optimistic. Perhaps one day Craig Kantor will become a psychologist.

Results

The behavioral results of this Reality Therapy-Confrontation approach where the therapist becomes an advocate have been dramatic. In almost three years, twenty adolescents who had terminated or been expelled from school have returned. Ten are attending college without having a high school diploma. Six have received their high school equivalency. Twenty, who were addicted to the opiates, are drug-free. Nine are employed in meaningful work.

REFERENCES

Bratter, T. E. Treating adolescent drug abusers in a community-based interaction group program: Some philosophical considerations. *Journal of Drug Issues,* 1(3), 237–252, 1971.

Bratter, T. E. The therapist as advocate: treating alienated, unmotivated, drug abusing adolescents, paper presented at the Society for Adolescent Psychiatry, Inc. (New York Medical College) April 19, 1972.

Glasser, W. *Reality therapy: a new approach to psychiatry.* New York: Harper & Row, 1965.

Glasser, W. *Schools without failure.* New York: Harper & Row, 1969.

Samorajczyk, J. The psychotherapist as a meaningful parental figure with alienated adolescents. *American Journal of Psychotherapy,* XXV:1, 115, 1971.

Swensen, C. H. Commitment and the personality of the successful therapist. *Psychotherapy: Theory, Research, and Practice,* 8(1), 34, 1971.

STEPHEN CHINLUND

You Still Make Choices!

Introduction

The various correctional disciplines are in their greatest development since the creation of the parole system in the middle of the nineteenth century. These exciting changes are long overdue. The sufferings of the inmates, their families, and the victims of crimes have combined to make a clearly intolerable burden on society.

The traditional pattern of work for correctional services emphasized care, custody, and control. The purpose was a combination of punishment and the temporary removal of the offender from the society which was angry with him for the crimes he committed.

More recently, however, the general public has become aware that the offender *returns* to society. He cannot, and should not, be incarcerated forever. When he re-enters society, his inclination to resort to crimes again is influenced, in part, by the way he has been treated while incarcerated and the opportunities which were made available to him while he was confined. If he has been able to learn marketable skills, get involved with responsible people, discover ways to satisfy his needs and to formulate some realistic and attainable plans, then he will be less likely to commit further crimes. The ex-offender will be happier and more fulfilled. Society not only will be protected, but also will benefit from his productivity. The long-term cost to society, therefore, will be diminished commensu-

---

Former title "Even When You Are Locked Up—You Still Make Choices! Reality Therapy in Correctional Disciplines." Unpublished, 1974.

rately because the offender can work and thereby pay taxes rather than go on public assistance.

The typical population of a New York State correctional facility comprises individuals who have committed felonies, the more serious category of crimes such as grand larceny, fraud, burglary, armed robbery, aggravated assault, and homicide.

Those who have committed "paper crimes" such as fraud, embezzlement, certain types of grand larceny and bribery may be quite frightened people, little inclined to violence. Others, who were convicted of a crime of violence, may be individuals who elected to engage in irresponsible, physically violent, and illicit behavior to support themselves. Finally there are those who seem chronically addicted to crimes of violence (like felonious assault) or implied violence (like armed robbery).

It is extremely difficult to categorize or classify offenders accurately, just as it is difficult to classify any other large group of people. Warden Duffy, formerly warden at San Quentin and a progressive penologist, has said that murderers are the best security risks. He employed them himself to work in and around his house. On the other hand, some of those who have not yet committed any crimes except paper crimes may be experiencing a rising frustration which will finally explode in physical violence.

Generally speaking, however, those convicted of felonies and incarcerated have less education than the average of the total population. They also are vocationally less skilled and have fewer social resources. If they were more integrated socially, many would have been able to secure better counsel or even avoid the crime in the first place.

All of these offenders have dramatically acted out their unwillingness to satisfy their needs within the law. They were not aware of making choices; many believed themselves to be "out of control." They lacked the opportunity to meet in a setting in which they could learn to make choices responsibly. It is a basic assumption of my work that all of them would prefer to feel their true strengths, make their choices consciously, and satisfy their needs without resorting to crime.

The principles and techniques of Reality Therapy have made an enormous contribution both inside institutions and outside in parole discipline. When William Glasser wrote *Reality Therapy: A New Approach to Psychiatry,* many correctional services personnel felt: "That's what I've been doing for years!" In retrospect, it appeared that many were practicing fragmented parts, but had neither integrated nor implemented them as a whole. The logical approach of Reality Therapy is one of its major strengths.

There are three primary contributions:

One: Viewing human behavior through the lens provided by Dr. Glasser, it is possible to be realistically *hopeful* about human beings who previously have been seen as helpless and hopeless. Now instead of dismissing anyone as "psychotic," or "chronic offender," or "hopeless sociopath," we can try to help him to learn ways of behaving which are more responsible and satisfying.

Two: Help is not limited to the old medical model which stresses sickness, etiology, and external "cure." Offenders, officers, counselors, parole officers can all help each other. It is possible to proceed in an open, honest, common-sense way with a minimum of training. Yet there are important safeguards. The dynamic pattern of working, which Dr. Glasser outlines, prevents workers from stagnating (with the rest of the group) in an endless exploration of emotions.

Three: Offenders do not have to wait to get out into the "real world." They can begin right in prison, the real world they *presently* inhabit, with all the limitations, frustrations, and *opportunities* which distinguish it from unsupervised life in the streets. They do not need to await release to get into the "real world." They can begin *now*.

In spite of all this, the great *potential* of these principles and techniques continues to be largely unrealized. The inertia of old ways continues to be a powerful force. The feelings of revenge, outlined by Dr. Karl Menninger in his book *The Crime of Punishment,* prevent some from being involved in Reality Therapy work. Even more important is the understandable anxiety, on the part of many workers, that this sort of work has reciprocal consequences.

That is, helping others to plan and choose more effectively will in turn stimulate the group leaders to do the same. I can think of two correction officers in particular, one of whom is now a teacher, the other an official in the central office, who feel that their group leadership played an important role in their own career development. Even those who have continued as correction officers feel significantly different about their relationships to their work, their wives, and their children. Though this is not the case with all, it is a common enough occurrence that those who are not yet involved remain cautious. Change is always a risk. It is the intention of this article to describe several possibilities in the hope that those involved in correctional work not only will adopt them, but will also develop them further.

Principles

Dr. Glasser has outlined the principles of Reality Therapy with admirable clarity. It is important to highlight four of these as they apply to the correction disciplines:

One: There must be *involvement* if Reality Therapy is the goal. Involvement is a combination of qualities. It is the capacity to share relevant dimensions of one's own life, avoiding the twin dangers of overexposure (telling more about oneself than is helpful) and being closed (adopting the attitude that "I am well; you are sick, I listen; you talk, I will heal you.").

It is also the demonstration of responsible concern: "I care about you. What you do and the level of satisfaction in your life are important to me. However, only you can live your life. Only you can make your choices. If you do well, I cannot claim your success as my victory. If you fail, I will not blame myself. The responsibility is yours."

Involvement also indicates that I will be a responsible role model, not a "tin saint" or an enigma, but one who shares with others the need to make decisions, succeed and fail, begin again.

There is, therefore, no such thing as "overinvolvement." There can be *distorted* involvement. One cannot be "too human," one can only distort one aspect of humanity at the expense of another.

This quality of true involvement is the cornerstone of professionally led Reality Therapy. A true professional is someone who knows what he is doing and does it well. A person leading Reality Therapy groups professionally must know about such groups and conduct them effectively. He may be a correction officer, inmate, community volunteer, counselor, parole officer, a psychologist or psychiatrist. Whatever else he may have learned in life only adds to his effectiveness if he will let it be so.

Anyone, including ex-cons and psychiatrists, may let his other training and experience get in the way. He then will not be sufficiently involved to manage Reality Therapy well. He may be a cartoon of a professional, aloof and sneering, or a "professional" ex-con, supercool; in each case he is too uninvolved to be helpful.

Two: Every person is responsible for his behavior. In order to practice Reality Therapy in a prison or with parolees, it is necessary to emphasize this principle with more vigor than with those who have no criminal background. Many offenders feel that they have been victimized as the result of being framed or from some misunderstanding. Incentive to change is predicated on the fact that offenders must not only acknowledge but also accept their responsibility for their actions.

In prison groups I have conducted, inmates frequently will maintain their technical innocence of a particular charge. Pressure from their peers, however, will help them concede that they committed other crimes which were undetected. They furthermore may admit that their innocence is only technical. This admission is a significant step toward accepting responsibility.

Three: Current behavior (rather than childhood experiences) is the special focus of working in group. Many offenders have traumatic backgrounds. An exploration of these problems would provide the offender with a rationalization to excuse his behavior. In emphasizing present reality, there are also the benefits of avoiding fabrication about the past. Offenders, as much as or more than the rest of us, have a tendency to exaggerate details about their pasts.

Four: Making decisions about values is a crucial part of therapy. This principle, like the others, has its antecedents in the counseling literature. It is, however, a matter of major emphasis in Reality Therapy and should certainly continue to be so in correctional work. Many offenders believe that their powerlessness is abysmal. They believe that events control them rather than believing that they can control some events. Some use this conviction as a justification for avoiding responsibility. A significant number have adopted an irresponsible and illicit lifestyle to the extent that they need help to consider a different orientation. Reality Therapy is unique in that together the counselor/therapist and the offender plan specific ways to behave to insure a maximum probability of success.

An emotionally brutalized youngster who grows up to provoke others to make him an emotionally brutalized adult requires much assistance before he has a personal understanding of the word "choice." But he can learn it.

There are five sequential phases to making a choice: (1) identify goals, (2) discuss alternatives, (3) make a choice, (4) make a commitment to follow through, and then (5) report to the group regarding success and/or failure.

In the first phase, identifying needs or goals, the offender faces the most deceptive challenge. He may suggest generalities which seem meaningful to him—"I need to get it together; get my head straight; square up; stop messing around; etc." However, he may find it difficult to be more precise about work, family, and social life. The challenge usually consists of making the need "small" enough. For example, if an offender wants to do a particular type of work, he must examine the education and training required to do it. He then must consider his talents and resources to determine the *very next step* if he is to go in *that* direction.

In the second phase, he considers the alternatives. What are the several possibilities for a *next step?* It is important in doing this to consider both the long-range good and the immediate next step. Too often offenders (like Johnny Tomorrow in *The Iceman Cometh* by Eugene O'Neill) only dream of the destination on the horizon, never writing for the information or filling out the application, or telephoning for an appointment.

Making a choice is a separate step. It is not enough to "incline" one way or another. "Preferring" this over that is not a choice. Rather, a conscious selection is necessary.

Making a commitment to the group is also a step distinct from choosing. Offenders have lied to themselves so much that they have a special need for this commitment. Without it, they can too easily pretend to themselves that they never made a choice. The commitment also gives a sense of support. The individual knows that the group is behind him, that they expect the best he can manage. For many offenders, this is their first such experience, the first time they feel that they have people on *their* side.

Finally, the report to the group on the success or failure of the commitment is crucially important. It is the occasion for the new beginning of identifying needs, finding alternatives, and going through the cycle again.

This process is rarely neat. It tends to wind through many sessions, but it is important for the group leader to keep in mind so that his own choices, within the group process, may be more sound.

Techniques

One of the most important aspects of Reality Therapy work in correctional discipline is the need for teaming an authoritative staff person with an ex-offender. In work which I did at Green Haven Correctional Facility in Stormville, N.Y.; Great Meadow Correctional Facility in Comstock, N.Y.; Riker's Island City Prison in New York City and six treatment centers of the New York State Drug Addiction Control Commission, this dynamic treatment structure proved critically important.

One poor alternative is to have all groups run only by the correction staff. During the initial phases of the group, inmates are understandably suspicious and anti-authoritarian. They tend to disbelieve staff people, who are perceived as threats due to the inmate's illicit behavior. Inmates feel that "squares" and "hacks" are unable either to identify with or relate to the offender. Norman

Fenton, nevertheless, has championed this type of work in California and has demonstrated its effectiveness.[1]

Another alternative, which is equally untenable, is to have all groups led by only ex-offenders. The latent anti-authoritarian attitudes which may still be present in an ex-offender may surface at particular times, creating great difficulties for both inmates and staff.

For example, there is a constant need for disciplinary decisions within a correctional facility. Some staff members are fair and helpful; others are capricious, given to outbursts of temper and vindictiveness. The increased development of various inmate liaison groups is intended to minimize the poisonous effects of the latter type of staff person. Correction policy generally, the increased interest of law students, various advocacy groups, and growing members of outside volunteers help improve fair conditions for inmates.

If an inmate wishes to discuss a discipline question in a Reality Therapy group, the leader should try to focus on the "here and now." The group leader should attempt to discourage discussion about an absent staff member. An ex-inmate, conducting his own group, would find this to be a temptation. This could cause increased inmate unrest, the sabotaging of the effective channels of communication (inmate liaison committee), even retribution against the staff person, and in extreme cases, a riot.

An inmate once started a session by saying "I was keep-locked"[2] because "some goddamn officer said I was talking in line. He slapped me around on the way back to my cell, too. What are you [looking at me] going to do about him?"

I mentioned we had discussed this previously, that everyone knew that group was not the place to bring such complaints. I refused to jeopardize the program by complaining to the warden. At that time in the development of the Department of Correctional Service, it would have been unthinkable to bring even an informal complaint on inmate "hearsay."

One of the other inmates asked the first which officer it was and his name was stated. There were murmurs and growls from others in the group of twelve. The long silence was broken when one inmate said, "Frank, why the hell did you talk in line with *him* watching? Everyone knows he's got a quick temper so we stay out of his way." The conversation then examined Frank's tendency to "get his head busted" whether he was in the street or in prison. The innumerable scars on his face and scalp were eloquent testimony to the long-standing problem.

In retrospect, this episode became a turning point for Frank, who made great subsequent progress. The lover of justice in me struggled to control my desire to get the volatile officer on the carpet. Choosing to adhere to the principles of Reality Therapy and concentrate on the behavior over which *Frank* exercised choice, the group helped Frank understand the consequences of his behavior. An ex-inmate *alone* probably would have been more tempted than I was to collect data and make a case against the officer. It is more important to help the person to understand the impact and consequences of his behavior.

In an effort to be liked by the inmates, the ex-offender might succumb to group pressures and adopt an anti-therapeutic/anti-authoritarian posture ("You're an Uncle Tom," etc.). Often when the ex-offender group leader remains unsupervised, many of his own unresolved conflicts can surface to disrupt the group.

Considerable initial resistance was encountered when the idea was presented creating teams of correction officers and ex-offenders. Each half of the team started out resenting the other half. The officers thought that the ex-offenders were beyond such elaborate rehabilitation; the ex-offenders tended to think that there was no such thing as an officer who was capable of responsible concern. Many separate steps were required to bridge this gap. Separate central office permission was required for *each* of the following:

1. Having *any* sort of group meeting with inmates (prior to 1964 I could not even *visit* two inmates simultaneously).
2. Having an ex-addict with no criminal record co-lead a group.
3. Having an ex-con, off parole, co-lead a group.

4. Having an ex-con, off parole but formerly an inmate of Green Haven (where the program was), co-lead a group.
5. Having an ex-con, still on parole, co-lead a group.

This was a two-year process. The program consistently showed itself to be effective, so Commissioner Paul D. McGinnis allowed these changes in a Department of Correction which was then very security conscious and conservative. The officers stress the Reality Therapy principle of responsibility. The ex-offenders generally emphasize Reality Therapy by involvement. They also provide a focus for the identification of inmates. This happens even when the ex-offender urges increased responsible behavior. A staff person from Reality House was taken aside repeatedly by former crime partners still in prison, who would ask, "Come on, man, what's the hustle?" The inmates refused to believe that he had straightened out at last; even running groups in prison had to be a hustle, so strongly did they identify with him.

The ex-con co-leader, therefore, also becomes a responsible role model. He is living proof that positive and responsible change is possible.

The we/they chasm is bridged by the presence of the ex-con co-leader. Once that bridge is built, everyone can use it and the resulting unity even survives a loss in credibility of the ex-con. For example, when one group began, the ex-con co-leader dressed sloppily and wore funny hats. After several groups, he adopted a more conservative and traditional dress style. It seemed as if his behavior and attitudes reflected the three-piece suit he elected to wear.

The ex-con co-leader was intrigued by an unsolved inmate death. This topic was inappropriate because it fell outside the purview of the group, but he nevertheless persisted. Sensing this, the officer intervened to focus on a more relevant subject. The ex-con, however, persisted. One inmate interrupted and supported the officer by saying, "He's right. He understands; we can't get into all that here. You're no ex-con anymore. The yard is like it used to be, man. But you've forgotten."

While the ex-con perceived this rejection from his "peers," he understood that this was inevitable if he wanted to adopt a more responsible lifestyle. He had made his choice to leave the "street" and try to succeed in society. For perhaps the first time the group accepted the officer more than they did the ex-con co-leader. The ex-con, however, was instrumental initially in establishing involvement; now he impeded it.

Subsequently the ex-con revealed to me that he had *tried* to "forget what it's like in the yard." He wanted so much to start in a new life that he denied himself the benefits of integrating the reality of his past into his new way of life. It continued to be a problem for him, but he was conscious of it and managed to avoid the sort of misunderstanding described above.

This rejection of a former lifestyle of crime and irresponsibility can create problems in a group. Inmates who have had a history of criminal behavior, who feel committed to an illicit lifestyle, who subsequently "square up," often experience a reversal in lifestyle. In a group, for example, one inmate was discussing his anger toward another inmate (in another group) who was still receiving contraband inside the prison. With tears in his eyes, his well-muscled body trembling, the inmate said, "If he doesn't stop, I'll kill him." This amalagmation of street ethics and responsible behavior to solve a problem is common. A group leader working with convicts must attempt to resolve this ambivalence. The group confronted the co-leader with the reality that he was planning to *behave* more irresponsibly than the program member for whom he was taking "responsibility." Finally, the co-leader could understand that *behavior* was the important thing. Violence and intimidation could not be justified by his *feelings* of idealism and loyalty to the program.

The Stratification Principle

The techniques of establishing graduated levels as students, employees, inmates, and other individuals in a large institution setting is as old as the institutions themselves. Efren Ramirez, in his work in the mid-1960s in Puerto Rico, developed this idea in ways which are important for the new patterns of correctional work. Ramirez established the three-level drug treatment program, moving from Intake to Treatment to Re-Entry, which has been duplicated in numerous ex-addict-administered therapeutic communities such as Daytop Village, Marathon House, Reality House, etc. The concept meshes with the principle of Reality Therapy because it offers status and privileges when a person accepts more responsibility. It differs from Behavior Modification models in that there is no token economy; the economy is real, as in community life— more responsibility produces more privilege.

For example, in a live-in therapeutic community, there normally is a demand that a resident demonstrate the capacity to be responsible for his assigned household chores before he advances to a higher therapy level. On a higher level, if a group co-leader is late for group or misses it entirely, unless he has a dramatically persuasive excuse, he will be dropped to a lower level and have to demonstrate his responsibility anew in order to be promoted.

This same principle has been adapted to correctional work. Inmates exhibiting responsible behavior are being placed in settings where they can benefit to the greatest extent from their choice to be responsible. Present plans in many states call for a four-level system in correction work.

One: Maximum Security

This is a system which presently confines 98 percent of all state inmates who are incarcerated behind thick walls in individual tile and steel cells. These installations are located mostly in rural settings. It is believed by many penal experts that a major number of those persons confined do not need such stringent security.

Many whose previous illicit behavior suggests marginal irresponsibility leave prison with newly acquired sophistication regarding criminal lifestyles. As a direct result of their imprisonment, they may learn more deviant, irresponsible behavior. Care, custody, and control are emphasized because there are problems of security which preclude much movement. Often, the expectation is that, upon release, the inmates will fail, and this becomes a negative, self-fulfilling prophecy. Training, education, counseling, and productive utilization of leisure time are minimized.

It is possible, nevertheless, to run group sessions with Reality Therapy in maximum security. Some critical questions for the inmate are:

1. Do I want to live or die?

Many inmates are, to a significant degree, suicidal. Some of them are more committed to a suicidal course than others. Any one of us sometimes has a desire to pull the covers over his head, go to sleep, and never wake up. Those who are confined need to be held still long enough to consider this basic question seriously. If they have a fundamental desire to sleep and never wake up, it would be the first treatment goal simply to have them prefer life over death.

2. Do I need help?

Having made a basic choice in preferring life over death, the inmate may then consider whether he has sufficient equipment to manage in this world. Due to the lack of reality in his perspective, he may not feel he needs any help. It would then be an appropriate goal of treatment simply to recognize the need for help with emotional, school, family, or work problems.

3. Do I want help?

Most inmates, having recognized that they *need* help, find it extremely difficult to take the additional step of actually admitting to themselves that they *want* that which, in fact, they need. Again, the rest of us have had the experience of acknowledging that we need to go to the dentist, to the doctor, to a counselor or some other helping person, and yet find that we do not want to go enough actually to get there. This is, once again, an exaggerated condition in many offenders. Taking this step from need to want may be the most important of all for any given individual.

4. Am I willing to make any sacrifices or take any risks getting the help that I want?

This, too, may seem to be a small and overwhelmingly logical step to take. Again, for many inmates, it is an extremely difficult one. Risking embarrassment, the loss of an image of themselves, the discovery of new strengths with their added responsibilities, all may be prohibitively alarming. Once again, we can see reflections of the problem in our own lives. The reluctance to open conversations which may be painful, the difficulties in speaking honestly with friends, making decisions about careers, raising families, and all the other important decisions of life, all of these expose to us our own reluctance to take appropriate, positive risks. For an inmate to be able to make this sort of decision and act upon it may be the most important step in rehabilitation.

The problem of getting affirmative answers to all these questions is the problem of therapy itself. It involves building trust between the leader and the group, being clear about the level of development of a particular inmate at a particular time, having the imagination to help him see his choices clearly and the skill to guide the group to be effectively supportive.

Two: Medium Security

This type of institution generally has been a forest conservation camp, a prison farm or prison industry. It now includes work and study release opportunities. Inmates go out to work, sometimes traveling great distances, and return to the facility in the evening. They do the same on study release, going to local community colleges to take post-high-school courses. The structuring of life which is achieved by returning to the facility is of great emotional importance. Inmates tend not to like it, of course, but it is a valuable brace for their developing self-control.

This activity may be used in a section of a maximum security institution or in a completely separate facility. Since these inmates are showing themselves every day to be capable of managing themselves sensibly in the community, they do not need massive security. There is no need for high, thick walls, or the tile and steel, three-tiered security of a typical large prison.

The medium security setting needs to be greatly expanded in most states. They could soon become the major type of felony-convicted confinement. Inmates would not only feel but enjoy the fact of participation in their own process of rehabilitation. They would be more actively learning and testing new ways of behaving which would resemble the conditions of the community.

There is increasing acceptance of this way of proceeding around the nation and, at the moment, specifically in New York State. It is clearly a great improvement over the old ways. "Good program *is* security." This maxim is becoming the operative word. Where inmates are functioning in productive ways, there is a minimization of security risks.

There is idealistic talk about tearing down prison walls. Inmates themselves are sometimes the first to agree that if the prison walls come down, something significant must take their place. Those who have been convicted of major felonies are individuals who behaved in an irresponsible, self-destructive, and impulsive manner. Many of them need to learn some self-control, i.e., how to become more responsible and productive. This quasi-therapeutic, quasi-educational process may require a prolonged structured setting for some.

The increase in the number of medium security settings is the necessary ingredient to this process. There must be more places where individuals can have the benefit of contact with the community without too drastically reducing the structured quality of living.

Three: Minimum Security

Halfway houses with a structured life would constitute the minimum security setting. Such a setting would involve living, usually in an urban setting, with groups of between 20 and 100 other inmates. The only security is the requirement that inmates must check in before a certain time and continue verifiably in their work assignments. Correction officer staff would be present to monitor the life of the house. They would verify the fact that inmates were not checking in on the first floor and leaving by the fire escape. They would also monitor coercive activity in the living areas. This affords more opportunity to remain in the community, more opportunity to test new levels of responsibility and positive risk taking (looking for jobs, trying to reconstitute family life, and the like). It involves living in the halfway house all the time for a short period (2 weeks). The next phase involves leaving the half-way house during the day to work, for family visits, and so on. These visits increase and decrease commensurately with demon-strated ability to accept them.

Reality Therapy is a process affirming the desirability of having a person focus clearly on his problems and then seek solutions *step by step*.

For those who have been confined for many years, the abrupt return to the street without much prior preparation and counseling can be a cruel gift. The gift is forfeited easily but often works hardship. A man who has been instructed when to awake, when to eat, when to work, what training to take, and when to go to bed will be confused and encounter problems becoming self-reliant and autonomous. The released inmate both treasures and anticipates freedom but, if left to his own resources, may abuse it.

In a minimum security setting, inmates should be given the opportunity to have groups. They can test their behavior and share their feelings when they are challenged by the whirlwind of the street, wives who have new boyfriends, employers who do not want to hire, families who are unsympathetic, children who are unrecognizable. For someone who has uncertain stability these pressures can be devastating. Therefore, the need for group ses-sions utilitizing Reality Therapy techniques continues even into minimum security. Reality Therapy can help anticipate failures and educate in how to avoid them.

Reality Therapy is valuable for resolving these problems since it stresses increased responsibility. Some operative questions are:

1. What are your goals?
2. Are you willing to make an investment?
3. Do you want to make a plan?
4. Will you complete all steps in the plan?

The pressures of the street move in on a newly released inmate in a way which he experiences as negative. He had not thought home life would be so upsetting. He had not expected that jobs would be so hard to find. He had not realized how much he would miss certain friends back in the correctional facility from which he has come. These negative experiences can be turned to advantage if he responds by moving more assuredly toward the life of the group.

Four: Full Parole

The need for support and constructive advice from peers and the discipline of getting help with the problem areas of life continue. On full parole, of course, the former inmate no longer checks in anywhere but home in the evening. He sees his parole officer for counseling on a weekly, then bi-weekly, and finally monthly basis. This may seem to be very light supervision, but for an inmate, who knows he may be returned to his previous place of confinement, it is a serious matter. He feels the continuation of control and structure. Those of us who have done correctional work see this in the failure of individuals who have been successful in the community for years, but then collapse in some way when they are released from parole because they have not learned how to accept responsibility. They have remained dependent on external controls. This may reflect on the rigidity of the system, but more often, I believe, it is the result of a need for more help in internalizing controls.

The most effective model for group leadership is a team of co-leaders comprised of a parole officer and an ex-offender who still may be on parole. The ex-offender should be honest about his conflicts, willing to discuss, and to resolve these problems. The ex-offender can anticipate and articulate potential problem areas. He can prepare the inmate to avoid failure. The ex-offender can spot "psychopathic manipulations" and confront the self-destructive piece of behavior effectively.

Conclusion

In the years to come this budding discipline will come to full flower and fruition. Some inmates presently confined will either commit new crimes or will rehabilitate themselves depending on our resourcefulness in making Reality Therapy skills a possibility for them. Some of us walking the streets today will either be the victims of future crimes or continue to enjoy our freedom depending on that same resourcefulness. The basic tools are available; they only need to be widely offered and further elaborated for us to enjoy their benefits.

Reality Therapy, while still in its infancy, appears to offer promise for helping to rehabilitate a disruptive segment of society which has a high rate of recidivism. By focusing on behavior and reality, this approach can assist the ex-offender to actualize his positive potential.

NOTES

1. See Norman Fenton, Ph.D., An Introduction to Group Counseling in Correctional Service, the American Correctional Association, Shoreham Building, 15th and H Streets, N.W., Washington, D.C. 20005.

2. Locked in his cell (as distinct from segregation) as disciplinary measure.

The Message Corrections Must Get Across

The bulk of our offender population benefits little from exposure to traditional behavior change processes. With some important exceptions, much of what is done today to correct antisocial behavior is not much different from that practiced years ago. For one thing, we continue to rely heavily on isolated, congregate, institutional warehousing operations.

Corrections has a fragile and frequently distorted public image. As long as things go well—that is, as long as everything looks placid and under control—public interest is not often aroused by what is happening behind (and in some cases, outside) the walls. Rarely are correctional accomplishments front page news. Such is not the case, as we know, when problems occur.

If there is anything fortunate about the cost of crime, it lies in preventing the focus of the taxpayer's concern from straying too far from the administration of justice and its repository of so many of society's rejects. Although many might hope that institutionalization may yet save the day, few could persuasively contend that the days of yesteryear can provide answers to the problems which corrections faces today.

Corrections Is Failing—and There Are Reasons

It is no longer sufficient to contain and control. Nor is it satisfactory to provide the best of care and concern and excuse appall-

Revised from "The Message Corrections Must Get Across," *Federal Probation Quarterly,* June, 1970. Reprinted by permission.

ing recidivism rates on the basis of our having done as much as we could. We are neither changing the behavior of most offenders nor are we girding ourselves to make the most efficient and effective use of the resources we have.

No one can quarrel with the need for a massive infusion of funds to permit the correctional system—long since slowed by inertia—to step into the twentieth century; but until and unless we can change our emphasis from hiding or ignoring our problems, and wistfully hoping for spontaneous change, we should not expect much, no matter what.

An important ameliorative step would be to face facts and determine where our strengths and weaknesses lie. This should require no elaborate extended research design. It is not as if we had never thought about our problems or lack knowledge regarding what must be done to improve the situation. What must be different, however, is that this list needs to be translated into known or expected results. We are aware, for example, that corporal punishment not only fails to rehabilitate anyone, but it also lessens whatever potential for change the offender may possess. On the other hand, we have found that when offenders are given responsible decision-making authority they usually exercise it maturely and constructively. That is, when we expect, encourage, and provide opportunities for people to behave in a positive (or for that matter negative) manner, the probability of their doing so is usually significantly enhanced.

We must spell out exactly what results we have had with our mammoth correctional institutions which traditionally have been the dumping grounds for the most diverse agglomeration of society's rejects. We must translate the cost effectiveness of such programs, as contrasted with a progressive correctional system, for people to comprehend. It is not that the institution cannot be made to work. The trouble is, in its publicly popular function, it has not really failed.

We must begin to build upon the potential value of institutionalization (as part of a correctional spectrum of services) and work toward eliminating or avoiding its failings. Those who have attempted this know it is not a simple process. Social malignancies are not easy to remove. The ogre of the stereotyped offender and his custodial needs are hard to erase from the public eye. As difficult as this may be to do, the alternative is continuing to play blindman's buff with the lives of offenders, to say nothing of the cost of the continued recycling of the correctional merry-go-round.

Among our liabilities, the traditional institution hangs around our necks like the proverbial albatross. Poorly equipped, removed and separated from the benefits and amenities of normal social living, far too large in size, packed with all forms and varieties of personalities and problems, it offers little expectation that its inmates will develop socially acceptable attitudes and behavior.

Among our assets, even in some of our worst institutions, there are many skillful and dedicated staff. While people are usually made uneasy by changes in program and goals, efforts which are well planned and organized to redirect emphasis from control and custody to treatment and concern frequently resolve some long-festering problems which "can win the votes" of some of the most hardened old-liners. The point is that the most important ingredients in any organized behavior-change experience—the people who will be changing people—are in good supply and of good quality.

While certainly there is much lacking to begin with—the inherent handicaps of institutionalization, per se—all is far from being lost. That is, provided the institution is redesigned in its architecture, location, program, and goals and made part of a treatment system in which positive expectations and opportunities for personal and social development exist.

The institution, then, is anything but an anachronism. No one knowledgeable about helping people can be opposed to its proper and important place in the correctional spectrum. It would be as naive as it would be foolhardy to pretend that the time will ever come when a small percentage of offenders will not need the security and structure which institutionalization provides best. For this small group no effort or expense should be spared. That is, unless we expect to cage them for the remainder of their lives. Quite the opposite of what we have today! Corrections has too long limped along with all kinds of hand-me-downs. Remarkable when you consider the concern so often expressed about crime and recidivism.

It is important to understand that traditional correctional institutions do not change or redirect the behavior of many of their wards. Few of these establishments are equippped with adequate resources to avoid even nurturing the development of additional social and psychological handicaps. Too often, so far removed ideologically from the world to which its charges must return, the institution often compounds the problems its corrective mechanisms are intended to cure. Training school academic programs, for example, range from poor to totally inadequate and usually reinforce (and for good reason) negative feelings toward future learning experiences. Vocational programs are frequently designed to benefit the institution without regard to the inmate, and the usual low-keyed, common-denominator "treatment" program (when one exists) scarcely begins to meet the needs of many offenders.

While exceptions exist, correctional institutions must mobilize their limited resources in time and talent over the omnipresent concern about runaways or escapes. This intimidating sword of Damocles which hangs precariously over the heads of correctional administrators (this is especially true for the innovative and truly treatment-oriented breed) not only retards progress but often results in programs in which considerable energy is sapped from changing human behavior. No one could quarrel rationally with the need to safeguard the community and control the behavior of people who are dangerous. It is ridiculous and counter-productive, however, for secure programming to be required for the bulk of our correctional population. Interestingly, and a fact of which many people are ignorant, runaways from training schools are usually the younger, immature, and less dangerous children whose offenses are usually of a noncriminal nature (truancy, previous runs, etc.). These children form a sizable percentage of training school populations. Certainly, other noninstitutional kinds of programs could better meet their needs.

Improved Institutional Programs Only Part of the Answer

What can we do to change our largely useless and outmoded correctional programs? As an important first step, small (100-bed) institutions, with truly decentralized cottage programs, and well-trained, treatment-oriented, adequately compensated staffs would be helpful. Unquestionably there is a need for modern, functionally designed physical plants with meaningful treatment services and realistic academic and vocational programs. Top this off with access to and involvement in the world outside these institutions and this would help perhaps 20 to 30 percent of our present institutional populations.

As for the 70 to 80 percent of the commitments whose being institutionalized is destructive if only because it removes them unnecessarily from normal living experiences, small wonder they become worse under our care. It is not likely that institutionalization ever helped anyone who did not require it in the first place. By the same token, it is equally unlikely that it has not harmed anyone sent there unnecessarily.

It seems improbable that the correctional institution will change soon from being a dehumanizing, damaging, and destructive experience. It should also cause no surprise that many will continue to be sent, only to be released later with greater potential for pursuing antisocial careers than was true at the time of their commitment. That a few who can benefit from institutionalization will only polish and further develop their delinquent skills should make us uneasy. That some may come out "rehabilitated" is miraculous.

While institutionalization unquestionably is necessary for a small percentage of offenders whose removal from the free community is required, its place in the correctional spectrum, rather than its utilization as a correctional seine, needs immediate reexamination and restructuring.

Corrections makes absolutely no sense unless it can provide different kinds of programs and services to match the diversity of human needs. While it will always be necessary to keep some people in correctional intensive-care units—prisons and training schools

—lengths of stay certainly can be reduced. There should also be no question about providing the most intensive and best care for this small percentage of offenders to permit their transfer to non-institutional services when developmental signs warrant such a move. Each succeeding move—ideally there should be several—should take the offender one step closer toward the correctional outpatient world of aftercare supervision and eventual discharge. We may be delighted to learn that this process could not only shorten the time involved to change offender behavior, but it holds every promise of being both less costly and more effective.

Meaningful improvement of correctional resources requires that we not sacrifice the future for the sanctity or politics of the past. Nor will it help to ignore the diversity of offender needs—which includes both secure and open programs of all kinds.

Correctional administrators must be willing to take a position which is clear and unequivocal. The rehabilitative tools which most have available are inadequate and unsuited to the times. The old unimodal machine (and myths) must be discarded. A vastly different kind of correctional system must be designed and implemented. And our knowledge about people and prisons must be translated into personnel and programs to make this system work.

Dependence on the institution must give way to viable, innovative, and experimentally researched alternatives to this single-shot approach. Diversified services, however, would be as useless as our traditional monolithic treatment system unless each is interwoven and interrelated. Movement between programs, both to and away from the community, must be made simple, encouraged, and expeditiously pursued.

Corrections requires a host of residential and nonresidential services, which may precede, take the place of, and follow institutionalization. Institutions must become involved with and not isolated from the free community. In both design and program they should be suited to the needs of a very select group of people whose only reason for being institutionalized should be that community living presents a clear danger to themselves or others. There is no other sensible reason to institutionalize people.

A New Approach Is in Order

The failure of corrections to do the job expected of it may be attributed in large part to our not having paid heed to the more obvious needs of offenders. We rely wearily on elaborate psychiatric and psychological rituals to give us direction when most offenders must be lumped together in the institution anyway. After diagnosis and classification, few institutions can either afford or are geared to provide the kinds of ameliorative services which the clinician recommends. Psychiatric and psychological protocols help dress up case records and give some understanding of offender behavior, but provide little assistance in planning treatment strategies.

Treatment requires much more than an hour every other week facing a desk and a diploma on the wall. In addition, our "treaters" are too often absorbed in the bowels of past experiences, oftentimes ignoring the more relevant and treatable aspects of human behavior. It is also questionable how helpful and valid the medical model has been for understanding and treating offender behavior. Research has yet to confirm that highly trained, highly compensated, well qualified professionals succeed with any greater efficiency than placebos. Spontaneous remission rates where behavior change occurs without any planned intervention should certainly require us to look hard and long at traditional "people-changing processes."

One such innovation resulting from this has been the growing use of Reality Therapy. It is not esoteric or difficult to understand, nor is it available only to the properly diplomaed practioner. Much to the dismay of the more orthodox and traditional therapists, it is even a means by which prisoners can become treators, teachers can do more than teach, and help can be easily and economically provided. It is really nothing more than a few common-sense assumptions about human behavior and a prescription for doing something about it. Aptly called Reality Therapy by Dr. William Glasser, a California psychiatrist who developed it, its appeal is severalfold: it can be practiced by almost anyone with reasonable intelligence who cares about people; it is inexpensive, and treatment goals can be accomplished in a relatively short period of time. What makes it particularly attractive to corrections is that it can be made available widely and regularly and is clearly affordable. In fact, if properly used, it not only can help people live more responsibly and in a law-abiding manner, but its utilization has a dramatic and salutary effect on reducing the divergence and conflict between official and inmate social systems. This in itself makes its utilization worthwhile.

However, no new treatment approach by itself is likely to change the system. Nor for that matter will corrections find its salvation only in building no more institutions. Changing offender behavior is related to a whole host of factors of which treatment, setting, personnel, architecture, program, economics, politics, and so forth are all interrelated. No amount of money, talent, or perseverance appears likely to overcome the problems created by denying people access to and involvement in the free society to which they must be expected to return.

We will doubtless move toward an era where the bulk of our correctional resources will be put to work in the free community. Existing institutional programs will become specialized parts of the correctional spectrum dealing with probably no more than 20 percent of our committed offender population. We will probably also witness a much greater use of self-help treatment groups and revisions of sentencing practices which will curtail commitments to minimal periods of time in which release will be a graduated process wherein the offender will be given access to conventional community living as quickly as he seems prepared. Most important, decision-making will become a responsibility in which offenders will share.

Of course, legislators, the courts, correctional administrators, and parole boards must always return to the readiness of the free community to tolerate practices which on the surface seem contrary to public concern that law violators be required to "pay their due." That so many recidivate, however, may prove to be more a factor of where and how we now try to rehabilitate people than it is to any inherent difficulty in changing human behavior. There is no more important message that corrections must get across.

PART SIX

Role Playing

RICHARD RACHIN

Role-Playing Sessions: Introduction

The Reality Therapist, whether he is a physician seeing patients in an office, a guidance counselor or teacher working with students, a parole or probation officer supervising offenders—regardless what—utilizes the same principles and techniques. He conveys to his clients that he is personally caring and concerned about them. In a warm and open manner, the Reality Therapist demonstrates these feelings. He realizes that unless he can establish a relationship based upon mutual trust and esteem not much will be accomplished. He is honest and never promises more than he can deliver. He also does not pretend to know things about which he is ignorant.

The Reality Therapist is concerned with present behavior—the "here and now"—and not the past. The problems upon which he focuses his attention are immediate and relevant. He does not waste time leading his clients down a historical primrose path. Rather, he makes efforts to help his clients talk about and evaluate what is taking place now. If someone is to change his behavior, he must be helped to consider its personal utility and evaluate its benefits. Given reason to believe that a happier and more rewarding life is possible, the client is helped to develop a plan for accomplishing goals which are compatible with an improved and more satisfying life.

People do not ordinarily change their way of doing things for anyone but themselves. Usually they do this only when they decide it serves their interest and is to their benefit. This is a lesson many change agents have yet to learn. Neither moralizing, imploring, entreating, nor punishing can accomplish what simple and honest self-examination can bring about. The Reality Therapist strives to help a client take an honest look at his behavior and what is being accomplished. Appearances aside, few people genuinely enjoy failure. Many cling to behavior which appears to insure their misery or discomfort if only for the simple reason that they do not know or have had little incentive to explore alternatives. As people rarely escape the consequences of their own irresponsible and self-defeating behavior, they also have no one to blame for not doing something to make their lives more rewarding and worthwhile. The Reality Therapist does not do things for people; rather he helps them do things for themselves.

The principles we have discussed are illustrated by Dr. Glasser in the three role plays that follow. The techniques of the Reality Therapist are applicable in almost any context in which one person is attempting to help another. For those of us who have used Reality Therapy, we can only tell our readers—it really works.

In "Dr. Glasser Plays Two Roles: Patient and Therapist," Glasser and Arthur LeBlanc alternately take the parts of a parent and a Reality Therapist. In the first instance, Glasser is a distraught father troubled about his eighteen-year-old son. Although the boy's activities and involvements are fairly typical of most well-adjusted eighteen-year-olds growing up today, the father's reactions to his son's behavior—also typical of most fathers of eighteen-year-olds—range from embarrassment to incomprehension.

In the second section of the same role play, Glasser is the Reality Therapist and LeBlanc plays the son. In a summary, Glasser explains how this role play demonstrates what the Reality Therapist attempts to accomplish with his clients.

In "Dr. Glasser and Shirley" Glasser plays the part of a vocational education and training counselor. A young mother and ghetto resident applying for a job is interviewed. Here Glasser illustrates how Reality Therapy can be helpful in working with suspicious and seemingly low-motivated clients.

A final role play, "Dr. Glasser and Joan," illustrates Glasser's efforts to help a young runaway ponder the possible consequences of her behavior and the possibility of exploring some ameliorative steps. In a brief summary Glasser explains the difficulties of "hanging in there" when it appears little progress is being made.

Dr. Glasser Plays Two Roles: Patient and Therapist

ROLE ONE: LeBlanc playing therapist and Glasser playing
              father of teenage boy.

THERAPIST: Welcome, Mr. Glasser.
  FATHER: Well, it took me a long time to kind of get up the
              feeling that I ought to come in here but I have heard
              a lot about these kinds of problems and I got a prob-
              lem and I want to talk to you about it.
     T: Would you tell me a little about the problem?
     F: Well, it's my kid. You know I got this eighteen-year-
              old kid and when he was small we seemed to get
              along okay, but as soon as he got into the eighth
              grade I guess he started running with a bad group
              of kids. He seemed to be a nice kid and the next
              thing I knew he was wearing these odd clothes and
              his hair was getting longer and longer and I was
              getting calls from the school. You know we live in a
              pretty conservative neighborhood. I'm not quite as
              conservative as the other people but it was bothering
              me a little bit too, you know. I was talking to the kid
              and we had quite a few hassles about it. His mother
              is upset and the next thing you know he started to
              use drugs. I mean I never caught him with drugs, but
              I got a feeling he is using them and his school grades
              went bad. He used to be interested in sports and

————————
    Transcribed from taped recording made at meeting in Los Angeles during
1973.

now he thinks that is fascist activity. Anyway, I think he is up in San Francisco now and I don't know what to do. I think I can get ahold of him and I think the kid won't pass completely out of sight. Well, this is the problem to work with. What do you think I ought to do?

T: You're coming to me because your boy has left home?

F: Yeah, he's left home but it isn't only that. If he comes back home it is no bargain either with the way things have been going. What I really want him to do is . . . well, I would like him . . . well, he is not my idea of a kid, you know?

T: So it is really your child, Mr. Glasser, that we are concerned with, not so much you?

F: Well, I don't know, I never had any serious problems. I got a fairly good job. I get along with the neighbors. My wife and I only hassle a reasonable amount of time. I got a little kid and we seem to get along. I won't say I am a pillar in the community but I pay my bills and I have got friends. I might have a problem. God knows it might be my fault this kid has gone down the drain; but I am not convinced of it.

T: But basically you are here because you want me to help your boy?

F: Yeah, I want help on this problem, right.

T: But the problem is your boy?

F: Yeah.

T: Do you and your wife get along reasonably well?

F: Reasonably well.

T: You and your other children get along?

F: Reasonably. This is the oldest kid. I got one eight and one twelve and we get along pretty well. We go on these trips. We have a camper, the kids like it. On weekends I take my vacation that way and they enjoy it.

T: I hear that you are a man who is working, paying your bills, fairly happy, and we got one little problem in the family, one big problem.

F: Yeah, I don't come to see someone like you with little problems; this is a pretty big problem.

T: Now you say you can get this boy back home?

F: I think so. He just said he was going up to San Francisco for a little bit. I don't think I will have to get him back. He will be back in a week or two. You know, just a bunch of kids in one of those Volkswagens with all the paint on the outside. They all look alike. I don't know if they were boys or girls in the wagon but they always come back.

T: Well, I suggest when your boy gets back home that you bring him in to see me.

F: Weeelll, I don't know. He doesn't have a high opinion of therapists. You know, he used to talk to school counselors a lot and he thinks they are square and creepy. He might, he might. I might put it to him that it is a different kind of a trip. Try a different kind of a trip, go see Dr. LeBlanc, and the kid might do it.

T: Well, we are only guessing whether or not he will come in. What day do you think he will be back?

F: I would say usually when he leaves, and he has left several times this summer, he is gone about six or seven days. He comes back kind of hungry.

T: So we can expect him back next Wednesday?

F: Yeah, maybe even Monday; but I am certain he will be back by Wednesday.

T: Then why don't I have my girl make an appointment to bring this boy in on Thursday? Could you bring him on your lunch hour?

F: I can take off. You know, everyone these days knows about problems with kids and when you tell your boss you got a problem with your kid they understand and then they let you have a few hours off.

T: Well, then we will make an appointment for 11:00 next Thursday for you and your boy.

F: How do you think I ought to behave when he comes back? I mean, I am a logical man and it seems to me that what I have been doing up to now hasn't been working too well. You don't know the kid, but do you have any suggestions?

T: I think you ought to be honest with the boy. Tell him you are befuddled and you don't know how to behave with him and . . .

F: Well, I haven't tried that tactic, I have always been right and told him, well look, kid, if you will just do these things everything is going to be okay. You know, I worked in these aerospace industries and I am supposed to be one of the thinkers of this country and my thinkin' hasn't been working too well along these lines.

T: Well, I think, Mr. Glasser, if you tell him that he has you confused, so confused that you came to see me . . .

F: Yeah, that will impress him all right. I have never expressed much confusion to him anyway. To my wife I have expressed a lot of confusion.

T: Well, this boy really has you confused and there are many people who are confused.

F: Yeah, I talked to my minister a little bit about it and he kind of suggested that it wouldn't be a bad idea to talk to you, he knows you.

T: Well, I see many people, Mr. Glasser, and we have no idea how this boy will respond to coming next week.

F: No, no, I just have a feeling that he will come in, I think he will.

T: And if we kept sitting here and guessing how he will respond, he could say the hell with you, pop.

F: He is not a mean kid and he is not one of these kids that is really antagonistic. He is kind of cool in his vernacular and whenever I reach for him he is not there. You know, he listens to his music all the time. The plaster is cracking in the whole back part of the house but we get used to it because the neighbors don't complain. Their kids listen to the same music.

T: You say you reach for him and he is not there?

F: Well, you try to talk to him and he listens to you and everything, but I have a feeling that he hasn't heard what I am saying. I talk to my eight-year-old and he listens to me a little bit and the twelve-year-old a little bit and the wife . . .

T: You know, I have a feeling that physically he is not even there. You reach out for this boy and I bet he runs.

F: Well, we don't snuggle anymore. He is eighteen, but to tell you the truth I don't remember shaking his hand. He is kind of dirty a lot of times and I don't even want to touch him.

T: What do you say we even change this appointment to make sure that he is here. What time can you get him up in the morning?

F: Oh, I think he will come here if you have a free hour next Thursday. Sometime I really prefer to bring him in in the beginning or the end of the day on account of my job because I do work about eighteen miles from here. He kind of rolls out of bed, I don't know what time, but he will get up, that is no problem.

T: Well, let's make it my first appointment, 8:30 Thursday morning.

F: 8:30. Well, I don't know, let's make it 9:00, let's be realistic, 8:30 is a little bit early for the kid. Can you make it 9:00?

T: No, I think we will make it 8:30. It might seem unreasonable to you, but I bet we can make it. If he is coming home from San Francisco he will make the 8:30.

F: Okay, well, I will give you a call if I can't get him in. I will talk this over with him the day before so it won't be any surprise. Ordinarily he is not the kind of kid that won't do something he says he will. If I ask him and he agrees, he will. He will gripe, but be will do it.

T: Remember, tell him that you are quite confused and you don't know how to handle it and you are so confused that you are willing to get up and give up work and get him in here at 8:30. It might mean something to the kid—my pop goes to work every morning on time and he is going to give it up.

F: Yeah, yeah that is true.

T: You are going to give up your work time for him.

F: Am I going to be in here with the kid or will you talk to him by himself?

T: Well, at first you will be in here with the boy and then I will probably talk to him alone.

F: Just for a few minutes I will be in here because I kind of got a feeling, I don't know much about this psychology-psychiatry bit, but I kind of got a feeling that you will get more if he is by himself. I might be wrong, but I think that way.

T: He sounds like a pretty open kid.

F: Yeah, he will be open all right. That is the whole problem, he is open to everything!

T: Well, I am sorry but I will have to quit for today, but Thursday at 8:30 I have great confidence that you will get him in here. In fact, the more you talk about the boy, the more I bet you can get him in here. I am not going to promise you miracles.

F: Is this going to be expensive, this deal, if he has to see you? Is this going to cost a lot of money?

T: Yes, this is.

F: You know the company where I work has an insurance policy. I think it covers about 50 percent up to about $500.00 a year. You will handle it through that, okay?

T: Yes. I would like to help you immediately because it will get worse before it gets better.

F: Okay, I will bring him in. Bye.

ROLE TWO: Arthur LeBlanc playing the boy, Dr. Glasser the therapist.

BOY: Pretty early in the morning to be around here.

THERAPIST: Yeah, do you get up early often?

B: No.

T: You know, your dad came in last week and talked to me.

B: He is always talking to someone about me.

T: Who else has he gone to?

B: Ahh, to the principal, the minister . . . He has been going since I was a kid. He went to the Boy Scout leader when I was fourteen.

T: Do you think your dad gets shaken up pretty easily? Is he that kind of a guy?

B: He ain't got no cool.

T: You think it was a reasonable request to come in and see me?

B: I'm used to it by now. I will see you this one time.

T: Just this one time?

B: I go to everybody once.

T: I can see why your dad gets kind of puzzled. Because if you are just going to see me one time there isn't an awful lot we can do. Why do you say just one time? What is one time to you?

B: I got things to do, man. I can't play.

T: Are you coming in here because you are doing your dad a favor? You don't want to hassle him, in other words?

B: Yeah.

T: What are some of the things you *got* to do? It kind of interests me. I realize your time is busy and I just want an hour a week of it for a few weeks, but what else do you have to do?

B: Well, today I got to go to the beach.

T: Yeah, yeah, what time do you usually get to the beach?

B: 1:00 P.M.

T: So this talk today is not going to interfere with your trip to the beach?

B: No, I will make it, I can thumb down. I will miss my ride, but I can get there.

T: It is not too hard thumbing, there are always guys to pick you up. What do you do at the beach? What's the thing at the beach?

B: Well, we run the board a little, get a little tan, talk to the chicks, smoke a little.

T: What time do you usually leave the beach, about dark?

B: No, I don't like it when it is cold. I leave early, 5:30 P.M.

T: Where do you usually head for then?

B: Go shoot pool for an hour or an hour and a half.

T: Do you come home for dinner usually?

B: I'm usually late.

T: Late for dinner. Is your mom the kind that gives you your dinner anyway even if you are late?

B: Yeah, she puts it in the refrigerator.

T: And you take it for yourself, okay?

B: Then I go out to the drive-in.

T: After dinner, what do you do out there?

B: Watch the show.

T: Oh, the drive-in movie, not the drive-in restaurant. Do you like movies? What show did you like that you have seen recently?

B: *Easy Rider.*

T: How many times did you see *Easy Rider?*

B: Four times.

T: Four times?

B: I don't have a cycle. My old man won't let me have a cycle, I am eighteen and he won't let me have a cycle.

T: At eighteen you can't get it on your own?

B: I will need money.

T: You mean your old man won't buy you a cycle. I see. Would he be mad if you went to work and earned a cycle?

B: No, he would be delighted.

T: Even if you rode a cycle, do you think it is more the money than the idea of the cycle?

B: Yeah, I think it is the money. I ride on the back of other bikes.

T: Yeah, your old man has seen that?

B: Yeah, but he makes a lot of dough, though.

T: But you want your own cycle?

B: Yeah.

T: What would you do on a cycle, just get around or would you do something special with it?

B: I could ride up front rather than on the back. I could take people for a ride.

T: There are certain kinds of guys that hang around on cycles. Are these the kinds of guys you like?

B: Yeah, they are cool guys. They don't work.

T: How do they get their cycles, their dads buy them?

B: Yeah, or somebody.

T: Somebody buys them for them? How do they get the money to keep the cycle in repairs and all that?

B: Oh, we get dough, little money.

T: It's the big money that is the problem?

B: I can always get gasoline money from my mother.

T: Your mom gives you money. How much does your mom give you during the week?

B: I never counted it, maybe $10.00 or $15.00.

T: One of the things your dad was worried about was school. What do you think about school?

B: I'm in my last year and I'm bored.

T: Are you going back to school this year?

B: Yeah, I am a senior.

T: Do you want to graduate or maybe just not hassle the family or what?

B: I don't want to hassle the family.

T: Are you thinking about college?

B: I might go to junior college. It is not that hard and I could handle that with ease.

T: Yeah, it is probably not any harder than high school. How 'bout work? Do you think you will work a little bit or just take it easy?

B: My dad has a lot of money, I told you.

T: How much do you think your dad has?

B: Well, he goes to work every day and he is a big engineer.

T: How much do you think your dad ought to give you? Just whatever you want or a certain amount? What do you think?

B: Well, he is always saying I am his kid and I am not on my own until I am twenty-one and he ought to give me some dough. What is he going to do with it, put it in the bank?

T: I don't know. We would have to talk to him about what he does with his money.

B: He has got lots of dough.

T: You are pretty convinced of that? How much do you think you ought to get, about $20.00 a week?

B: Yeah, then I could get some out of mother, yeah.

T: You think you could make it okay? What if your dad put a condition that you were to go to college. Would that be a rough condition, the junior college?

B: No, I would handle that; in fact I am planning to go to junior college. I think all the guys are planning to go there.

T: Do you think that is going to be the place to be? Do you have any particular aim in mind in college? Anything you want to take up there, anything interesting? You know there is a lot of stuff from auto mechanics to premedicine.

B: No, I will just . . . if they require four courses I will take four courses.

T: Do you care about what teacher you have or anything like that?

B: No, I hear there is one good teacher in mathematics.

T: What do you hear about him?

B: I hear he is real cool. He knows what he is doing.

T: Do you think you will try to get him?

B: Yeah, I am pretty good at that, even though I flunked.

T: You flunked it because you didn't go very often, huh?

B: I was bored.

T: In other words you have confidence you can do math but you didn't take the tests, was that it?

B: I never showed up for the exam. I did that problem once, why should I do it again?

T: Tests are kind of a hassle anyway. Now is there anyone at your school now that you think is okay?

B: Yeah, the English teacher is okay. He lets us read anything.

T: What have you been reading?

B: Oh, *Portnoy's Complaint?*

T: I read it; what did you like about it?

B: A riot, a big hassle in their house, nobody in control.

T: What do you think of his mother? Is she like your mother?

B: Naw, not at all.

T: What about the boy's father, the one with the stomach trouble, is he like your dad?

B: Naw, naw, my dad is strict, real strict.

T: This guy was kind of a nothing kind of a guy.

B: He might have yelled a lot but he wasn't strict; he just thought about himself. My dad is thinking about the whole family.

T: This guy Portnoy, after he got out of the house and stopped masturbating, he started making out with the girls pretty good. What do you think about that, in other words, screwing a lot of girls, is that a good deal?

B: Oh, I haven't done that yet.

T: Do you have a girl or girlfriends, or do you just hang around with the guys?

B: We hang in our group, there are girls in the group. I am kind of frightened of the girls truthfully. I shouldn't be telling you this stuff, I am only going to see you one time, you know.

T: Yeah, that's right, but I am interested in this being frightened of the girls because I thought all the girls were real cool nowadays and everybody just grooved.

B: Well, no, I am sort of scared of them really. My folks don't know this. Nobody knows.

T: Are you concerned that if you talk to me I will tell your folks what we talk about, or should I or shouldn't I? What are your feelings, it is up to you?

B: If it is on this girl issue I don't want you to talk about it. I don't care if you talk about school, they know I hate it and I am bored.

T: How about drugs, do they know that you use drugs or don't you use drugs?

B: I didn't say I used drugs.

T: I didn't say that either. Do you smoke a little weed? Hard drugs?

B: Yeah, once in a while. What do you mean hard drugs? You mean hash?

T: No, I am talking more like Speed or something like that.

B: No! No, you have to be a kook to take that stuff. No, no.

T: Do you think drugs are kind of important in your life or kind of unimportant?

B: No, I could take them or leave them.

T: In other words, is it worthwhile for us to talk about drugs?

B: Well, my old man thought I smoked.

T: Well, that is his thing. Do you think we ought to spend any time talking about drugs as just a topic of conversation? We have an hour to spend here and that is a long time to be together, even if you are going to come once, an hour is still a long time.

B: It really has got my old man uptight. I keep telling him that marijuana should be licensed, no shooting, or pills or anything else, just marijuana.

T: But a little marijuana is okay as far as you are concerned?

B: Yeah, occasionally I take a pill, somebody's always got it. He gets upset.

T: How does he know, do you tell him?

B: Yeah, I tell him practically everything. What can he do?

T: Well, what he has done? Come to see me?

B: He can afford to see you.

T: Do you think I should see your old man? Maybe I can talk him into getting off your back, do you think that might help you?

B: Yeah, it might.

T: How would that help you? I think I could be able to do it.

B: Well, he wouldn't yell at night when I come home late. He wouldn't come screaming at me; it is lousy when all you get is screamed at.

T: So if we talk your dad into not yelling and keeping quiet this might make things more pleasant around the house. How about your mom, does she do a lot of yelling?

B: No, Mom is on my side.

T: She can talk to you pretty well? She knows about the things you do except about the girls? Have you talked to her a little bit about the girls?

B: No, not much. She doesn't know about the girls and I don't want to tell her.

T: But what about your dad?

B: He knows.

T: So he tells her but she doesn't mention it to you. She plays it cool, about the whole thing?

B: I don't want to hurt her, she is good to me.

T: Do you want to keep living home this coming summer? Do you have any plans to leave home or go out with a bunch of guys?

B: I would like to go and live in the Valley with a bunch of guys but we had a big hassle about that. He won't give me the money to live in an apartment.

T: It takes money, you have to pay rent, huh?

B: Yeah, I got a ride and he will pay for that.

T: But it is the rent that has you stopped? Have you ever worked? Any kind of a job?

B: I took care of a tennis court when I was sixteen.

T: Did you have any interest in tennis at that time?

B: Yeah, I was pretty good. I played in high school teams.

T: Have you given up tennis now?

B: Oh, yeah, that is for squares.

T: Did you get paid for taking care of the tennis courts?

B: Yeah, eighteen bucks a week.

T: Did you do anything with the money? Save it, spend it, what did you do?

B: Yeah, saved it for clothes. Second of high school I bought all my clothes.

T: Were you concerned about your clothes then?

B: Yeah.

T: How about clothes now?

B: No, no, I like these levis.

T: Do you dress like this most of the time, bare feet?

B: Yeah, Dad doesn't like it. He doesn't like anything. Mom doesn't care.

T: Is there anything about you that you think your dad likes?

B: No. Well, I helped him with his trailer. He is bugs on this crazy trailer.

T: You don't go with them when they go away for the weekend, do you?

B: No, I wash it and polish it and clean it out every time they come home. He thinks that is great. He goes to work on Monday and I have to do that.

T: Do you help on the wiring and things like that?

B: Yeah.

T: Does he give you something for it? Does that maybe make your gas money?

B: No.

T: How about your little brother and sister, what do you think about them? Do you talk to them much?

B: No, they are too small. They are thirteen and twelve.

T: Well, the little one is only eight.

T: Oh, he really gets around.

B: The twelve-year-old, the brother, you think he would get your dad's goat the same way you get it?

B: Oh, no, he will be okay.

T: What do you mean okay, are you not okay?

B: I'm okay, but he will be different, I should say.

T: Because older kids sometimes are different. But how do you think he will be when he is, let's say, when he is eighteen, do you think he is one of these kids that will buckle down in school?

B: Yeah, he will do real well. He is square. He will even go to college, maybe UCLA.

T: He is interested in tennis too?

B: Yeah, he is going to be a champ.

T: Do you ever bat a ball around with him anymore?

B: He is just a kid. I meant a champ for his age. I could beat him.

T: Does he ever ask you to hit a ball with him?

B: Yeah, he is a pain in the ass, he keeps asking me. Are we finished?

T: No, we got a lot of time. You said you would just come here this one time.

B: Yeah, one time.

T: Well, that is what you said. I am going to try and talk you into coming more. I am just getting to know you. Actually guys like you come and see me and I got to admit they usually just come one time. But I always hope that some guy will maybe come more than one time so that I could kind of get to know him. Sometimes if people like me get to know them more it is just good.

B: Why do you want to know me? You don't know me from a hole in the wall.

T: Because I want to know you.

B: What for?

T: Well, I kind of feel that the more people I know and understand it is just better for me. I don't know if you have ever felt that way.

B: Better for you? I am giving you therapy?

T: I think so. I think you might be able to in a certain sense. Maybe not call it therapy. I will give you therapy but I think I would like to get to know you. So far you have told me that you take a little drugs, you hassle your parents, but you do clean out the trailer, you are going to finish school, you are good at certain subjects but the tests hassle you. This is kind of interesting but it is pretty standard stuff. Nine guys could come in here and tell me about the same thing, but I am interested in other things that are on your mind. The things that you don't like and things that you do like. Is there anything that you like to do that you think is important? Maybe that is a touchy question, but what do you think about that?

B: Not now. Well, wait a minute. I like to surf and I

would like to have my own cycle or car, I don't care, I haven't ruled out going to college.

T: I am not worried about college because that is a year away. I am kind of worried about now. You say you would like to have your own cycle or car.

B: I don't like to depend on people, it is lousy. I have to wait until a guy gives me a ride.

T: Does the old man let you use the car at all?

B: Once in a while to do an errand for him.

T: How about if you want to go out to the drive-in movie or something like that?

B: Once in a while.

T: Let's say you wanted to have the car tonight to go someplace, how would you go about getting the car from your dad? Is there any way that you would use, so I can get an idea of how you would react when you want something from him?

B: Well, I am pretty good at that. No, I am not too good at that. I would need my mother's help.

T: You mean you would slip the word to your mom this afternoon?

B: I would go home this afternoon, I get home early, and I would change clothes. I got another pair of levis.

T: Your mom keeps a clean pair in your room. doesn't she?

B: Yeah, and I would probably put my moccasins on and I would wear a clean shirt and I would get her to ask Pop. It is a good show, it is rated GP, do you know what that means?

T: Yeah, that means for everybody.

B: I would tell her that I want to go and I haven't seen it and a lot of kids have seen it and I am going to take some kids and their parents said they could go.

T: She knows these kids?

B: Yeah, I am going to take two kids and she will ask Dad.

T: Now under these circumstances does he say that I want you home at such and such a time? What do you think a reasonable time to come home is? Let's say the show is over at 12:00.

B: Oh, 2:30.

T: What do you do after the show ordinarily?

B: Well, ride around and ride down to the beach, see the waves. If we got any money we would get something to eat, maybe smoke up something watching the waves.

T: The thing that throws me a lot—and this is because I am a talker and my business is talking—what I wonder about a lot of times is like if you go to the beach and get down there about 12:30, maybe you got a few cigarettes and you smoke them, what do you talk about? You sit there for maybe an hour or more, do you talk at all?

B: A little. We talk about the movie, like if it was good or bad, like *Easy Rider* we talked for hours on that.

T: What are some of the things you talked about from *Easy Rider?* What was your point of view on the picture?

B: He had freedom, boy, he would just go when he wanted to go and he had power and he had everything.

T: He got his freedom by making a score, didn't he? He sold a bunch of heroin, didn't he, and he has some cash? Then he went around the country and met a lot of people and I hear that he got killed at the end, is that right?

B: Yeah, it was an accident, I guess; you got to get killed anyway.

T: Anyway the killing wasn't important, it was the fact that he had all this freedom?

B: Do you realize that he didn't have to talk to anybody? He could stay out all night if he wanted to. I have never been able to stay out all night. I tried it once and my old man wouldn't let me go out of the house for three days.

T: He really locked you up after that.

B: He is a skunk at times.

T: But back here at the beach you are talking to the kids about this.

B: You talked to my old man, didn't you think that he was a skunk?

T: No, I'm not his son and I am not asking him for anything, he is paying me and it is hard for me to think he is a skunk.

B: He probably put a big front up.

T: No, he was really pretty concerned. You know, he even said, "You know, if I am doing something that is screwing things up I would like to change."

B: My old man change?

T: Well, he just said that, and I said let me talk to you first because if all I do is listen to what he says about you I don't get to know you at all.

B: What did he say about me?

T: Pretty much what you said. If I had a tape recorder and played what he said about you and what you said it would be the same thing. The only difference is that he said what you do really goes against his beliefs, but he described what you said pretty accurately.

B: He is of the old school, you know.

T: Yeah, he is working and everything like that.

B: I can't be like that.

T: Well, that is one of the reasons I would like to get to know you because I think you will not be like him and I don't think he would like you to be. Do you think he was like his old man?

B: Naw, I bet he wasn't.

T: Did you ever know your grandfather, did you see pictures of him or anything?

B: Yeah, he was a square, he was a farmer.

T: Yeah, but I still want to get back to *Easy Rider*. This freedom, what is it all about? Like I am asking you to come in here once a week and in a certain way I am restricting your freedom because what if you wanted to be in San Francisco that day and you had an appointment with me?

B: You may be waiting alone. I may be up there.

T: Are you the kind of fellow that if you made an appointment you wouldn't show up?

B: No, not usually.

T: Like if you make a date with the guys, you show up?

B: Oh yeah, I am very good about things like that. I don't like to be late. When I tell you I am going to be there. Notice I was on time this morning, 8:30.

T: In fact I was a few minutes late myself.

B: That's okay.

T: I still want to talk about this freedom bit because . . .

B: Do you have freedom?

T: A reasonable amount. I got to come here to the office every day. I had to come here at 8:30 this morning and in a sense when you lose your freedom I lose mine, but I want that because if it is voluntary maybe it is not losing freedom.

B: You freely chose to come, I had to come.

T: Right. I freely chose to go to this school and get all those things up on the wall and things like that so I can talk to people that either have problems or claim they have problems or someone claims they have problems. You would be in the last category, right? Somebody claims you have problems, I didn't say you had problems.

B: Right.

T: I want to get to know you and I haven't lived with you for eighteen years like your dad has and yet . . .

B: I ain't got no problems.

T: I didn't say you did, I said I want to get to know you

and that it is going to be hard if I only see you one time. Now there is no reason for you to get to know me maybe, but I got a reason to want to know you.

B: What's that?

T: That is your father came in and he said that he is concerned about you and he said that I ought to see you and my claim is that all I said to him is that I would see you. I didn't promise him I would turn you into this kind of a person or that kind of a person. I just said that I would see you.

B: How much is he paying you?

T: $30.00 an hour. His company will pay half.

B: I knew it, that cheap bastard!

T: No, no, that insurance comes out of his pay. They take a lot out of his pay.

B: He is going to pay $30.00 bucks an hour for me to see you?

T: Only $15.00 out of his pocket to see me, that's right.

B: Every week?

T: Oh yeah, he will pay or I won't see you. I am not the kind of guy that works for nothing.

B: What will we talk about?

T: We will just get to know each other.

B: You know all about me, I am eighteen.

T: No, that isn't important. I don't even know what you think about freedom, for instance, and this is very important to you. I just don't know much. You say you want to go to New Orleans on a bike or to Woodstock or things like that.

B: Yeah, there is a big concert coming up in Big Sur this weekend and I can't go. All the guys are going and I can't go. The old man won't let me go.

T: Oh, the old man won't let you go. It is the old man that is in your way?

B: Yeah, he won't let me go.

T: He would probably call the police if you were gone.

B: Oh, yeah, he would have the whole National Guard.

T: Have you ever been in trouble with the police?

B: Yeah, I took a car once.

T: You mean a joyriding kind of thing and the police picked you up? What happened and who stood behind you? How did you get out?

B: My mother came down and they got a lawyer and got me out. I was in there one day. They paid the fine.

T: Are you on probation now?

B: No, first offense.

T: They put you in the custody of your parents, right?

B: Yeah.

T: You are not going to take cars anymore, that was kid stuff, I gather. Well, the time has gone by and we are getting toward the end of this interview.

B: Can we talk a little longer?

T: I would like to really, but could we make an appointment for next week? Let's make it one week at a time; can you come in next week?

B: What day?

T: To tell you the truth I got some free time on Thursday. I could make it in the morning or toward the end of the day. In the middle of the day I have to go over to Camarillo Hospital to work, and I can't do it then.

B: You go to see kooks?

T: Yeah, yeah I do.

B: In the morning?

T: Yeah, you go surfing in the afternoon.

B: What time?

T: 9:00?

B: That is kind of early but I will make it, though.

T: You will make it here.

B: When I say I will make it I will make it, one more time, right?

T: Yeah, just one more time.

B: What will we talk about?

T: I don't know. That is something to think about. I got to know you now and I will think during the week.

B: Do you want me to do anything?

T: Come in next week.

B: Nothing else?

T: Anything you can think of, but I've got no orders for you, just come here and we will talk. Good to meet you. Bye.

This has been typed directly from the tape. There is no doubt that spoken conversation like this is not entirely grammatical but to edit or punctuate too much would not be truthful. We understood each other, that's what counts. A lot of my talk has unsaid words which he understands are there. This tape is available and can be purchased at cost so you can hear the inflections, the pauses, the warmth, all difficult to detect in a verbatim transcript. What I was doing was step one of Reality Therapy, getting involved step two, getting what he is doing on the table, and a little of step three, getting him to evaluate his behavior. Finally we came up with a plan for him to come to see me, step four. That's all you can do in one interview. I was always open and honest. I stuck to his present behavior. I did not probe into his past or moralize. I did not talk much about his feelings, I accepted them and moved the conversation to his present behavior. I take one session at a time. If he comes in several times and he begins to behave better, he'll continue. That's all you can do. If you study this carefully you'll see that I follow faithfully what I advocate. It seems simple, but try it, it's much more difficult than it looks.

WILLIAM GLASSER, M.D.

Dr. Glasser and Shirley

SITUATION: Dr. Glasser interviews a seventeen-year-old girl who has walked into a federal agency which is supposed to provide education and training for ghetto citizens to help them get jobs. This is a first interview and goes as follows:

DR. GLASSER: Sit down and make yourself comfortable. What have you heard about our programs? I'd like to know what you have heard of it so I can . . . have you heard anything about it?

SHIRLEY: I don't want to tell you because I can't.

DR. G.: Who sent you here . . . can you tell me that?

SHIRLEY: My girlfriend told me about it.

DR. G.: Is your girlfriend someone that's come here to our office? Do I know her? Could you give me her name?

SHIRLEY: Her name's June.

DR. G.: You don't know her last name?

SHIRLEY: Jones.

DR. G.: O.K. Fine, and is she in the program now?

SHIRLEY: Yes.

DR. G.: What school does she go to?

SHIRLEY: She goes to Adult Education.

DR. G.: All right, and . . . uh . . . uh . . . what school is closest to your house? Have you gone to that school in the past?

SHIRLEY: No.

Transcription of tape of role-play demonstration before large audience in New Jersey, 1973.

DR. G.: What school did you last go to?

SHIRLEY: Myron K. Herrick Junior High School.

DR. G.: O.K., and . . . what did you do yesterday? Tell me what
you did yesterday . . . could you tell me a little bit about what
you did yesterday before you came here?

SHIRLEY: I stayed at home and took care of my baby.

DR. G.: Where is your home? Where is it located?

SHIRLEY: I live in the projects over on Fear.

DR. G.: O.K. Now, if you would come into our program that
would mean going to school. Who would take care of your
baby . . . could you tell me that?

SHIRLEY: My mother.

DR. G.: Has she agreed to do this?

SHIRLEY: No, but she would.

DR. G.: Do you want to go to school? Would you like to go a
little bit more to school?

SHIRLEY: No.

DR. G.: All right . . . and what was on your mind when you
came in here because this is a place where we arrange for people
to go to school. Is there anything else I can do for you if you
don't want to go to school?

SHIRLEY: I want to work in a department store.

DR. G.: I see . . . well, it's been so far that the department
stores where we send girls to work . . . they won't take them
until they finish school or they have some kind of a test that
shows they've finished school. Now, they *will* take girls who
have finished school.

SHIRLEY: Why?

DR. G.: I don't know. I think maybe they believe that girls who
have finished school are better workers . . . that's maybe what
they think . . . yet, I don't know.

SHIRLEY: I'm not going to school.

DR. G.: Yet you do want to work in a department store? Well, if
department stores will only take girls who have finished school
. . . and you don't want to go to school . . . well, maybe you
could suggest how I could help you because I would be willing
to but I'm kind of . . .

SHIRLEY: Why do I have to go to school and learn how to dress a dummy?

DR. G.: Is that what you'd like to do . . . is to put clothes . . . pretty clothes on these dummies in department stores?

SHIRLEY: Yes.

DR. G.: I see. Have you been interested in things like art and things like that . . . is that what would interest you if you were going to school? Were those some courses you liked?

SHIRLEY: We didn't have art in my school.

DR. G.: Well, tell me a little bit more about this interest in dressing dummies . . . lots of girls want to sell or work behind the counter as cashier . . . but for the first time in a long time I've heard someone who wants to dress the dummies.

SHIRLEY: I just like to put clothes together . . . that's all.

DR. G.: When you were a little kid did you enjoy playing with paper dolls . . . dressing dollies and things like that?

SHIRLEY: Dolls?

DR. G.: You don't remember that time? All right . . . but if you want to put clothes on these things you have to go to school. Well, I don't know what to do . . . I'm puzzled . . . I really am because I could call up and ask . . . I'll call up the department stores and I'll ask the people if they take people that haven't graduated school and you can listen on the other phone. And I will ask . . .

SHIRLEY: No, I believe you . . . but I don't want to go to school . . . you don't have to call the department store . . . but I don't want to go to school . . . I just want to go work in a store and put clothes together because I do that good.

DR. G.: O.K. Well, like I say . . . It's kind of puzzling but I'll see if I can figure something out. Suppose . . . let's say that you would change your mind and you would go to school . . . maybe you'd go to school not a whole day . . . at night or something like that. Have you ever thought about that?

SHIRLEY: No . . . but where could I go to school like that? That would take a long time . . . I've only finished the seventh grade . . . and . . . they would laugh at me if I go to school because I'm seventeen . . . I'm almost eighteen years old.

DR. G.: Well . . . are you worried that I'll put you back in the seventh grade? Is that what worries you?

SHIRLEY: They wouldn't want me.

DR. G.:Well, I don't think so either. If you went to school you'd want to go with kids your own age . . . that would be okay, wouldn't it? You wouldn't want to go with thirteen-year-olds?

SHIRLEY: No, they're babies.

DR. G.: Well, we have classes where there are girls your own age attending and going and earning credit . . . you don't have to go with babies . . .

SHIRLEY: How long would it take me before I could work in a department store and dress dummies?

DR. G.: I think until you graduated.

SHIRLEY: How long would that take?

DR. G.: Well, our program here is only two years so we have to arrange it so you make it in two years . . . so I can say offhand we'd try and do it within the next two years although a couple years is a long time.

SHIRLEY: Well, if I spend all my time while I'm on my seat going to school, how am I going to learn how to get a job in a department store and dress dummies?

DR. G.: Well, we have to kind of work something out to that effect . . . I'm not sure I can tell you about it today but all I know is that I could tell you that girls have come here and have worked with us . . . lots of them have gotten what they wanted . . . they really have . . . we've worked it out . . . I can't guarantee it for you but I could bring you in here on a day when we had some other girls and you could talk to them and see that what I'm telling is the truth. I'd be willing to have you meet with a few of them and see . . . girls like you who didn't want to go to school but now went. That's all I can say . . . but I'd be willing to do it.

SHIRLEY: And would I have to go to school all the time?

DR. G.: What do you mean, all the time? All day long or just part of the day . . . you mean you would like to go part of the day? Listen, how much would you be willing to go if we could work something out that you said was O.K. How many hours a day would you be willing to go? Let's say you started in the morning at 9:00 . . . how long would you go?

SHIRLEY: I'd go until noon.

DR. G.: You would go three hours a day . . . well . . . I can say that it's probably not impossible . . . we could start it and then if you liked it maybe you'd go more and if you didn't like it you could always quit. It's worth a try, isn't it?

SHIRLEY: If I didn't like it and I quit, then what could I do?

DR. G.: We'd have to talk about that then. I don't know. Probably not very much . . . I mean the truth is . . . not very much. How do you know? . . . we don't know if you're going to like it or not until you try it.

SHIRLEY: Then . . . I have to go to school . . .

DR. G.: Well . . . that doesn't mean you have to go to school . . . that means if you want to get a job in a department store and be in the program you have to go to school. I'm not holding you here . . . you could leave . . . but I'm only telling honestly what we have here. You wouldn't want me to lie to you . . . that wouldn't be any good . . . would it?

SHIRLEY: No. I can't leave because if I leave I won't have any money.

DR. G.: Well, all I can say is that all the time that I see you . . . all right . . . anyone that works here and sees you will always tell you the truth. Whether that's worth anything or not we are never going to lie to you and the fact is if you get in our program I think you do get a small amount of money.

SHIRLEY: Yes.

DR. G.: And you'll have to go to school for the money. And you'll have to do a reasonable amount of work in school and if you have trouble we'll try and help you.

SHIRLEY: If I go to school and I pass all my subjects, then can I learn how to dress dummies?

DR. G.: Well, let me say this because I'm always going to be honest with you. The honest answer is that right this moment I don't know but I could find out and you wouldn't have to sign up until I find out. I could make an appointment say in two . . . three days and then I'd be able to tell you whether that would be possible or not. Honestly, you are the first girl that's asked that so I really don't know. If you had told me you want to be a cashier or you want to sell cosmetics or something like that I could say yes to that.

SHIRLEY: Well, I don't understand why you don't know because they told me when I came in here that you were in charge of education and you knew all about education and you knew all about jobs and I don't understand why you don't know why I can't get a job in a department store dressing dummies. I thought you were supposed to know those things.

DR. G.: Well, I don't know.

SHIRLEY: So you say you can find out in two days.

DR. G.: I can definitely find out. That's one of the things I say when I don't know something. Instead of giving you a lot of bullshit, I say I'll find out.

SHIRLEY: How soon would I have to start school?

DR. G.: Well, when are you ready? I don't want you to start before you are ready but I think that probably within a week or so . . . yeah, we would be starting.

SHIRLEY: I guess I'll be ready to start school after you tell me about working in a department store dressing dummies.

DR. G.: Well, we've got one thing here that we ought to clarify. Which is what if I find out that you have to finish school before you can take the training . . . that it happens in the department store. It might be . . . I mean I don't know . . . but that might be the way it is . . . that the department that would hire you . . . that they'd say they want to train you and you would have to show that you could do it and in school all you'd learn is enough to get the job in the department store. I mean that's a possibility and I don't want you to leave here thinking that it's all fixed up. We're talking about this honesty business and I'm trying to be honest.

SHIRLEY: Well, when you talk to the department store find out all about getting a job dressing dummies, do you think you could really fix it up so I could do both things at the same time . . . maybe I could go to school part time and while I'm doing that I could learn how to dress dummies?

DR. G.: Well, to tell you the truth, it may be that there is a school you could learn how to do it in. It's possible . . . I'm going to call the department store and I'm also going to call the schools and see if they have any of that training going on there . . . I don't know . . . I can't tell you . . . I'll make a lot of calls and when you come back I'll let you know.

SHIRLEY: You mean I have to go to school to do that too?

DR. G.: Well, it would probably be more fun than doing something else in school.

SHIRLEY: Mmmmm.

DR. G.: Have you got any other questions? Well, what we've got to do now is to make another appointment. How did you get here today?

SHIRLEY: My boyfriend brought me. (Giggles)

DR. G.: He has a car? Do you think your boyfriend could bring you on Thursday? Today is Monday . . . could he bring you in on Thursday?

SHIRLEY: Not on Thursday. (More giggles)

DR. G.: What day do you think he could bring you?

SHIRLEY: If today is Monday and you said you would know in two days, he can bring me on Wednesday.

DR. G.: Okay, fine. I just want to make sure that if I am to go to all the effort of making these calls and checking into all these things, that I know when you are coming and if you can get here. And if you can be here Wednesday, I think I won't know until Wednesday after lunch, I think you would have to come about 1:15. Will that be all right?

SHIRLEY: Oh, that will be fine, because my boyfriend really wants me to get a job.

DR. G.: Well, that's good. Is your boyfriend out there in the waiting room? Do you think I could meet him?

SHIRLEY: He's in the car. He won't come in.

DR. G.: Well, maybe on Wednesday you could invite him in . . . I would just like to say hello to him.

SHIRLEY: I don't think so . . . he doesn't like to talk to you people too much.

DR. G.: I know, but just ask him and tell him I would like to say hello to him, I appreciate him bringing you here and I'd like to thank him and say hello. And if he doesn't want to come in I'll understand.

SHIRLEY: I'll ask him.

DR. G.: Okay, good. Be sure you do because you never know. Sometimes you never know. He might come on right in. Has he finished school?

SHIRLEY: No.

DR. G.: Maybe he'd like to hear about this program too.

SHIRLEY: Are you kidding?

DR. G.: You never know.

SHIRLEY: He knows about it . . . he's the one who told me to come down here, so I could get a job.

DR. G.: Okay, fine, fine. Well then, he does know about it. That much we've ascertained, okay. Then I'll see you Wednesday at 1:00, but first there's a few forms I'd like you to fill in with, you know, your name and address and everything else . . . and if you have trouble I'd like to help you, 'cause sometimes these forms get a little complicated. See, the more we do right, the quicker things happen.

SHIRLEY: Okay, thank you.

DR. G.: Okay, you're welcome.

Dr. Glasser and Joan

SITUATION: A fifteen-year-old girl, who has run away from home several times, has come to see Dr. Glasser on the urging of a mutual friend.

DR. GLASSER: How did you get here?

JOAN: I ran away from home and a friend of mine who says he knew you brought me down to see you.

DR. G.: You're not referred through the court or anything like that . . . you're here on your own. Okay, and there's no coercion or compulsion in this thing. Tell me, Joan, you were sent here by our mutual friend, is that right?

JOAN: Yeah, Roger sent me.

DR. G.: And did he . . . feel that you needed some help, is that it?

JOAN: Yeah.

DR. G.: Well, what is your belief; do you think that you need some help?

JOAN: . . .

DR. G.: Did you come just 'cause Roger sent you?

JOAN: Yeah, I guess so.

DR. G.: Okay. Well, how long have you known him? Have you known him for a while?

JOAN: Yeah, I babysit for him.

From taped recording of roleplay session of Dr. Glasser and volunteer from audience at meeting held in New Jersey in 1973.

Dr. G.: For Roger?

Joan: Yeah.

Dr. G.: Okay, and do you live here in this neighborhood?

Joan: No, I live in another town.

Dr. G.: I see. Roger suggested that you come over here . . .
how'd you get here today?

Joan: Roger drove me.

Dr. G.: Okay. Do you go to school?

Joan: Not right now.

Dr. G.: When did you last go to school?

Joan: Last week.

Dr. G.: What did you do then between last week and now? I'd
like to know so I can understand a little more about how I
might help you.

Joan: Well, I took off. I just couldn't take it anymore.

Dr. G.: Couldn't take it at school or at home?

Joan: Both.

Dr. G.: I see. Well, let's talk about home first. What couldn't you
take at home?

Joan: They're always hassling me; they're always looking at my
mail. I can't do anything. They're always after me, always
hassling me. My mother she's sick, she's crazy. The old guy he's
always picking on me and . . .

Dr. G.: What made you come home then? What did you do, come
home on your own or were you picked up by the police, or
what?

Joan: My old man found me.

Dr. G.: He found you and brought you home. Well, where were
you? Where did you go?

Joan: Ohio.

Dr. G.: What did you do in Ohio?

Joan: Well, I don't know.

Dr. G.: Maybe you were in a situation you don't want to talk
about. Is that it? All right, I guess that's it then. Was it in your
mind to stick around for a little bit and then run away? What is
your plan right now? I don't mean to hold you to it, but what
would be your plan?

JOAN: I don't know, whatever will happen, will happen.

DR. G.: Did you run away because of something? You sound like something happened and you ran away. Didn't you plan to run away? Didn't you do it because you figured out to do it?

JOAN: Yeah.

DR. G.: In other words, you made it happen.

JOAN: Yeah.

DR. G.: What you are saying is it could happen again.

JOAN: You better believe it.

DR.. G.: How about school, tell me about it. You say they hassle you there too?

JOAN: Yeah.

DR. G.: Do you have any friends in school? People you really like . . .

JOAN: No.

DR. G.: No girlfriends, boyfriends, no one?

JOAN: No, 'cause they just moved.

DR. G.: Your folks just moved? Are you in a new school?

JOAN: Yeah.

DR. G.: What grade are you in?

JOAN: I'm in tenth grade.

DR. G.: How about schoolwork? Let's say that you like school. Could you do tenth-grade schoolwork if you wanted to, or are you smart enough to do it?

JOAN: No.

DR. G.: What's the subject that's kind of got you flipped?

JOAN: Everything.

DR. G.: Can you read all right? Can you read books and magazines and newspapers and stuff like that?

JOAN: Yeah, I can read.

DR. G.: But you just don't do well on school subjects, huh?

JOAN: That doesn't interest me. I don't want to go to school . . . I just want to go out and get a job, but I'm not old enough. And if I run away the old man is just going to hassle me. I don't want to go to school and I'm not going back there.

DR. G.: Well, you kind of got me puzzled, 'cause in this state I think you must go to school until you are sixteen, and you say you don't want to go, huh? Do you want to drop out before sixteen?

JOAN: Yeah, many of my friends have done that.

DR. G.: Well, then you know some kids under sixteen who aren't going to school, right? What do they do?

JOAN: Just hang around and get high.

DR. G.: Do you do drugs?

JOAN: Yeah.

DR. G.: The old man hassles you about that too, I imagine, huh?

JOAN: Yup, sure, he's a cop.

DR. G.: Has he threatened to turn you in to the authorities and put you in the hall?

JOAN: He turned in my sister.

DR. G.: How old is she? Is she older than you?

JOAN: She's ninteen; she's a junkie.

DR. G.: Is she locked up now, or is she out?

JOAN: I don't know.

DR. G.: You don't know where she is, huh? Is it just you and your sister in the family?

JOAN: I'm the only one left at home.

DR. G.: Are you the youngest?

JOAN: Yeah.

DR. G.: Well, this is kind of a difficult problem. I've talked to a lot of kids with similar problems and I really don't know what to tell you. It's a hard problem. Do you have any suggestions at all that I might get a hold of to help you?

JOAN: Why don't you talk to my old man and tell him to get off my back, 'cause I want to go out to Ohio and get a job.

DR. G.: You want to work in Ohio? What kind of a job do you have in mind?

JOAN: I'll do anything . . . I'll scrub floors, I'll work in a restaurant, I'll do anything . . . just to get out of that house.

DR. G.: Your idea is to take off to Ohio? Where do you live now?

JOAN: I live in Bridgeport.

DR. G.: Is that New Jersey?

JOAN: No.

DR. G.: Is that New York?

JOAN: No.

DR. G.: Connecticut? Well, why do you want to go to Ohio? I've been in Ohio myself quite a bit and I wonder why Ohio?

JOAN: I've got some friends there who live in a commune.

DR. G.: Oh I see. It's a place where you know some people . . . and those people said you could live with them?

JOAN: I don't know.

DR. G.: But you're pretty sure your old man wouldn't go for that?

JOAN: Yup.

DR. G.: Well, I think I would talk to your old man, but I'm afraid I might screw things up. He sounds like he's got his mind made up that you are going to stay home. I'm just wondering if you can give me any hint on how I might talk to him, assuming that you want me to. Have you got any ideas?

JOAN: I'll just run away again. He can't make me stay home . . . what's he going to do, put the whole state police after me?

DR. G.: He might if he's a state trooper.

JOAN: Fuck him.

DR. G.: I think I see enough kids who run away from home to know that no one can really stop them if they want to run. I'll go along with that. But you are not home now and you are coming here. Where are you living?

JOAN: I'm staying with Roger.

DR. G.: Oh, you're over at Roger's? Is that okay with your old man?

JOAN: No, he's hassling me. He wants me to come home, but I ain't going there.

DR. G.: At Roger's house you're helping out with the babysitting and stuff?

JOAN: Yeah.

DR. G.: You say you're not going home. Does your old man know that you're seeing me by any chance?

JOAN: Yeah, he knows. He's going to pay for it.

DR. G.: I'll bill him then, huh? Well, if he's going to pay for it, then probably he'd be willing to come in and talk to me. I'd say that's ordinarily the case if people pay for something.

JOAN: Yeah, he'll come and talk with you, but he's going to tell you that he wants me home and I ain't going home. Also, I can't stay with Roger any longer either . . . 'cause the old lady is beginning to bother me, the lady's on my ass now.

DR. G.: All right. Tell me if it was up to you and you had something you could do now, is there anything that you would particularly like to do?

JOAN: I just want to get out of the house, that's what I want to do. I'll do anything to get out of that house.

DR. G.: Well, one thing that's available sometimes is some kind of foster home arrangement that maybe your old man would go for. You've heard of those?

JOAN: I'm not going.

DR. G.: All right, so what you say about doing anything to get out of the house . . . that's not really true . . . you'll do anything that you want to do to get out of that house.

JOAN: That's right. I'm not going to any foster home.

DR. G.: You've heard about foster homes?

JOAN: My sister, the junkie, went to a foster home.

DR. G.: Okay.

JOAN: I just want to go out and get a job and live on my own and get out of that house and I'm not old enough in this state . . .

DR. G.: Nor in Ohio either. As a matter of fact, I don't know any other state where you're old enough. Maybe some of the southern states.

JOAN: Well, then I'll go to the southern states.

DR. G.: All right, that's something to think about. You seem so sure of everything. You know, you kind of got me. I'm trying to figure things out and I don't know you too well and you say to me, "This is the way it is, buddy." Do you just want me to get your old man off your back, and you go ahead and do what you want. Is that the story?

JOAN: Right.

DR. G.: Well, what if I can't do that? I mean it's not as if I wouldn't want to. You know your old man is a pretty tough nut. He may come in here and say, "Look, I want that goddamned kid home." So . . . what if it doesn't work out that way?

JOAN: Good-bye.

DR. G.: Is that it?

JOAN: I ain't going home.

DR. G.: Suppose that I had your dad in here and we all talked together, would that be all right?

JOAN: No, because my old lady she's crazy, she's got this Parkinson's Disease, and she's crazy. She drives me crazy. I can't do nothing right at home. She hassles me all the time. She makes me clean the house. I don't even get a thank-you for it. She's constantly on my back and I want to do what I want to do. I want to come home when I want to come home. I want to get high. They've got a different value system. They're not going to convince me and I'm not going to convince them, so that's it.

DR. G.: Well, that sounds pretty much like it. I'm puzzled, I really am. The only thing that concerns me is that . . . I've worked with quite a few girls that have talked to me like you've talked to me and they've also said that's it and in a short period of time they're sent to juvenile hall. I don't want to lie to you . . . that's what happens. I feel it would be wrong if I didn't point this possibility out to you, I'm sure you thought of it.

JOAN: If that's what the old bastard wants to do, let him do it.

DR. G.: In other words, if you go in the hall, you go in the hall, right? You will be away from home.

JOAN: The only way I'm going to get there is if he puts me there, like he did to my sister.

DR. G.: Well, he could put you there, but if you're on the run and you're picked up and under sixteen, anybody will put you there . . . that's just the way it is in most places.

JOAN: Yeah, but I'm going to be sixteen in two months, and I've got a lot of friends in Ohio.

DR. G.: Well, the truth is that it's really up to eighteen in terms of going to the hall. Sixteen is okay to be outside of the house with your parents' permission . . . eighteen without your parents' permission. So in terms of the two months that doesn't mean too much.

JOAN: They can't get me in Ohio if I'm sixteen. Besides, I have a lot of friends there.

DR. G.: Well, maybe you'll end up in juvenile hall and maybe you won't. Anyway, it seems to me we're missing the point. It seems something's missing, 'cause I do help people . . . but, I'm puzzled.

JOAN: Well, Roger said I should come and see you, so I came.

DR. G.: Suppose I ask you to hold off on running away and ask to see you a couple of more times. Would you come in again before you took off? 'Cause I want to think about this a little bit. I just can't come up with anything now. Maybe I need to talk to your dad, then talk to you again. You seem to like Roger and Roger's also a friend of mine. Would that be okay, to come in a few more times?

JOAN: Yeah, I'll come in, but I ain't going home.

DR. G.: You'll stay at Roger's house, till you come in, huh? How much longer can you stay at Roger's? You say the old lady's starting to hassle you over there too? What is she hassling you about? The same things as your mother?

JOAN: She went through my mail the other day. She's checking up on me 'cause she's afraid I'm going to run away.

DR. G.: Do you do drugs inside Roger's house, or do you stay clean there?

JOAN: I don't do drugs in Roger's house.

DR. G.: Does Roger ask you to stay clean?

JOAN: No, we haven't talked about it.

DR. G.: Okay, then let's forget that. Well, I guess I have to talk to your father. There's no doubt about that and you don't want to talk to him together with me, huh?

JOAN: No way.

DR. G.: Well, it's okay if I talk to Roger and have you come back here?

JOAN: I ain't going home.

DR. G.: Well, all right, why don't we do that? I'll see you again . . . today is Thursday, I'll see you again on Monday.

JOAN: Are you going to try and make me go home?

DR. G.: All I want to do now is talk to your dad, that's all I want to do. I'm not going to try and make you do anything. What I'm going to try and do, although I don't know if it'll work, is try and figure out some way for you and your dad to get together on things. Now if going home won't work for you, then that wouldn't be it. If staying out wouldn't work for your dad, then that wouldn't be it. I don't know now what's in between, but I'm going to try and figure it out. I can't do that just talking to you, 'cause you tell me the way you stand and now I got to talk to him. Maybe he'll say the hell with her, let her go, I don't know, so I have to talk to him.

JOAN: He ain't going to say that.

DR. G.: All right, we'll find out if you're right. Why don't you come back on Monday and send your dad in tomorrow, okay?

JOAN: All right. (*Exit*)

SUMMARY (Comments by Dr Glasser): We might talk a little longer, but this girl is putting it to me like many fifteen-year-olds will. I had one myself and she finally reached nineteen without us killing her. But this is pretty much the way it is. I mean she didn't run away or anything like that, but she did see things pretty much one way, and that was it. It causes a little bit of friction sometimes, here and there. All I'm trying to do in this role play is hang in there a little bit with her. Mostly I'll do what she wants me to do. I'll talk to her dad. I also believe her when she says she'll run away from home. I doubt if she's kidding. I also want to see her again, so I'll make an appointment to do that. I'm not sure she'll be back in, but if she stays at Roger's she might.

CONTRIBUTORS

THOMAS W. ALLEN, PH.D.: Professor, Washington University, St. Louis, Missouri; editor, *The Counseling Psychologist.*

ALEXANDER BASSIN, PH.D.: Professor of criminology, Florida State University, Tallahassee; regional consultant, Reality Therapy Institute; co-founder, Daytop Village.

MARSHALL BERGES: Journalist, staff writer for the Los Angeles *Times.*

THOMAS E. BRATTER, ED.D.: Faculty, Teachers College, Columbia University, New Rochelle College, New York; consultant to New York City Probation Division; private practice.

PHILLIP Z. COLE: Clinical psychologist, former California state parole officer; associated with Parlour Medical Group of Claremont, California.

DONALD R. CRESSEY, PH.D.: Professor of sociology, University of California; co-author of best-selling text, *Principles of Criminology.*

EUGENE H. CZAJKOSKI, D.P.A.: Dean, School of Criminology, Florida State University, Tallahassee; senior assistant editor, *Journal of Drug Issues.*

WILLIAM M. EASSON, M.D.: Professor and chairman, Department of Psychiatry, Medical College of Ohio, Toledo.

GARY J. FALTICO, PH.D.: Faculty, New Rochelle College, New York; consultant to New York City Police Department.

WILLIAM GLASSER, M.D.: Los Angeles psychiatrist, founder of Reality Therapy; author of *Reality Therapy* (1965), *Schools Without Failure* (1969), *The Identity Society* (1972), *Positive Addiction* (1976), all published by Harper & Row.

671

IRA A. GREENBERG, PH.D.: Psychodramatist and clinical psychologist, Camarillo State Hospital, California.

BERNICE GRUNWALD: Teacher, Gary, Indiana, public schools; faculty member of the Alfred Adler Institute of Chicago.

GLEN A. HOLLAND, PH.D.: Clinical psychologist in private practice, Los Angeles.

NATHAN HURVITZ, PH.D.: Faculty, San Francisco Valley State College, California; private practice, Los Angeles.

NORMAN IVERSON, PH.D.: Associate of Dr. Glasser in the direction of the group counseling program of the Ventura State School, California.

ARTHUR F. LeBLANC, PH.D.: Psychotherapist in private practice, Sherman Oaks, California.

WILLARD A. MAINORD, PH.D.: Professor of psychology, University of Louisville, Kentucky.

KEITH F. MAXWELL: Teacher, special instructor at the Ventura School, Palo Alto, California.

O. HOBART MOWRER, PH.D.: Research professor of psychology (retired), University of Illinois, Urbana; author; former president of the American Psychological Association.

DONALD J. O'DONNELL: Principal, Ventura School, Palo Alto, California.

RICHARD PARLOUR, M.D.: Psychiatrist, director of the Parlour Medical Group of Claremont, California.

C. H. PATTERSON, PH.D.: Professor, College of Education, University of Illinois, Urbana.

JOHN PENNINGTON: Journalist, staff writer for the *Atlanta Journal*.

WILLIAM A. POPPEN, PH.D.: Associate professor of psychology, University of Tennessee, Knoxville.

RICHARD L. RACHIN: Chief, Bureau of Group Treatment, Division of Youth Services, Florida; editor, *Journal of Drug Issues*.

RICHARD R. RAUBOLT: Psychologist, drug addiction treatment clinics, Westchester County, New York.

SUE REILLY: Freelance journalist residing in Los Angeles.

ERNEST SCHMIDHOFER, M.D.: Psychiatrist with longstanding interest in work with the offender.

CLIFFORD H. SWENSEN, PH.D.: Professor of psychology, Purdue University, Lafayette, Indiana.

ROBERT V. VAN VORST: Former psychologist at a California women's prison, associate of Dr. Richard Parlour, Claremont, California.

ROBERT NEIL WELCH: Counselor, Caesar Rodney Senior High School, Camden–Wyoming, Delaware.

Index

Index

677